Contents

II Travel information

II **European driving:** cut through the confusion
IV **Driving regulations**
VII **Ski resorts**

1 Route planning maps

1 **Key map · Distance table**

17 Road maps

17 **Key map**

121 City plans and urban area maps

121 **Legends to city plans and urban area maps**

Alicante [C]	121	Luxembourg [C]	135
Amsterdam [C][U]	122	Lyon [C][U]	135
Antwerpen Antwerp [C]	121	Madrid [U]	135
Athina Athens [U]	122	Madrid [C]	136
Athina Athens [C]	123	Málaga [C]	136
Barcelona [C][U]	123	Marseille Marseilles [C]	136
Basel [C]	123	Milano Milan [C][U]	137
Beograd Belgrade [C]	125	Moskva Moscow [C][U]	138
Berlin [C][U]	124	München Munich [C][U]	138
Bordeaux [C][U]	125	Nápoli Naples [C][U]	139
Bruxelles Brussels [U]	125	Oslo [U]	139
Bruxelles Brussels [C]	126	Oslo [C]	140
Budapest [C][U]	126	Paris [C]	140
Dublin [C][U]	127	Paris [U]	141
Düsseldorf [C]	127	Praha Prague [C][U]	142
Düsseldorf (Ruhrgebiet)[U]	128	Roma Rome [C][U]	143
		Rotterdam [C]	142
Edinburgh [C]	127	Sankt Peterburg	
Firenze Florence [C]	129	St Petersburg [U]	142
Frankfurt [C]	129	Sevilla Seville [C]	144
Genève Geneva [C]	129	Stockholm [C][U]	145
Génova Genoa [C]	129	Strasbourg [C][U]	144
Göteborg Gothenburg [C]	130	Stuttgart [C]	144
Granada [C]	130	Torino Turin [U]	146
Hamburg [C][U]	130	Torino Turin [C]	147
Helsinki [C][U]	131	Venézia Venice [C]	146
İstanbul [U]	131	Warszawa Warsaw [C][U]	147
København Copenhagen [C][U]	132	Wien Vienna [U]	147
Köln Cologne [C]	132	Wien Vienna [C]	148
Lisboa Lisbon [C][U]	133	Zagreb [C]	148
London [C]	133	Zürich [C]	148
London [U]	134	[C] City street plan	
		[U] Urban area map	

149 Index to road maps

www.philips-maps.co.uk

First published in 1998 as **Philip's Multiscale Europe** by Philip's, a division of Octopus Publishing Group Ltd
www.octopusbooks.co.uk
Carmelite House,
50 Victoria Embankment
London EC4Y 0DZ
An Hachette UK Company
www.hachette.co.uk

Twenty-first edition 2019
First impression 2019
ISBN 978-1-84907-500-8

Map data

This product includes mapping data licensed from Ordnance Survey®, with the permission of the Controller of Her Majesty's Stationery Office © Crown copyright 2019. All rights reserved. Licence number 100011710

is a registered Trade Mark of the Northern Ireland Department of Finance and Personnel. This product includes mapping data licensed from Ordnance Survey of Northern Ireland®, reproduced with the permission of Land and Property Services under delegated authority from the Controller of Her Majesty's Stationery Office, © Crown Copyright 2019.

All rights reserved. Apart from any fair dealing for the purpose of private study, research, criticism or review, as permitted under the Copyright Designs and Patents Act, 1988, no part of this publication may be reproduced, stored in a retrieval system, or transmitted in any form or by any means, electronic, electrical, chemical, mechanical, optical, photocopying, recording, or otherwise, without prior written permission. All enquiries should be addressed to the Publisher.

While every reasonable effort has been made to ensure that the information compiled in this atlas is accurate, complete and up-to-date at the time of publication, some of this information is subject to change and the Publisher cannot guarantee its correctness or completeness.

The information in this atlas is provided without any representation or warranty, express or implied and the Publisher cannot be held liable for any loss or damage due to any use or reliance on the information in this atlas, nor for any errors, omissions or subsequent changes in such information.

The representation in this atlas of any road, drive or track is not evidence of the existence of a right of way.

The maps of Ireland on pages 18 to 21 and the urban area map and town plan of Dublin are based upon the Crown Copyright and are reproduced with the permission of Land & Property Services under delegated authority from the Controller of Her Majesty's Stationery Office, © Crown Copyright and database right 2019, PMLPA No 100503, and on Ordnance Survey Ireland by permission of the Government © Ordnance Survey Ireland / Government of Ireland Permit number 9181.

Cartography by Philip's
Copyright © Philip's 2019

Printed in Malaysia

*Independent research survey, from research carried out by Outlook Research Limited, 2005/06.

Photographic acknowledgements:
Page II: top *Agencja Fotograficzna Caro / Alamy* • right *James Hughes* • bottom *Mode Images / Alamy*.
Page III: centre *Pete Titmuss / Alamy* • bottom right *Mim Friday / Alamy*.

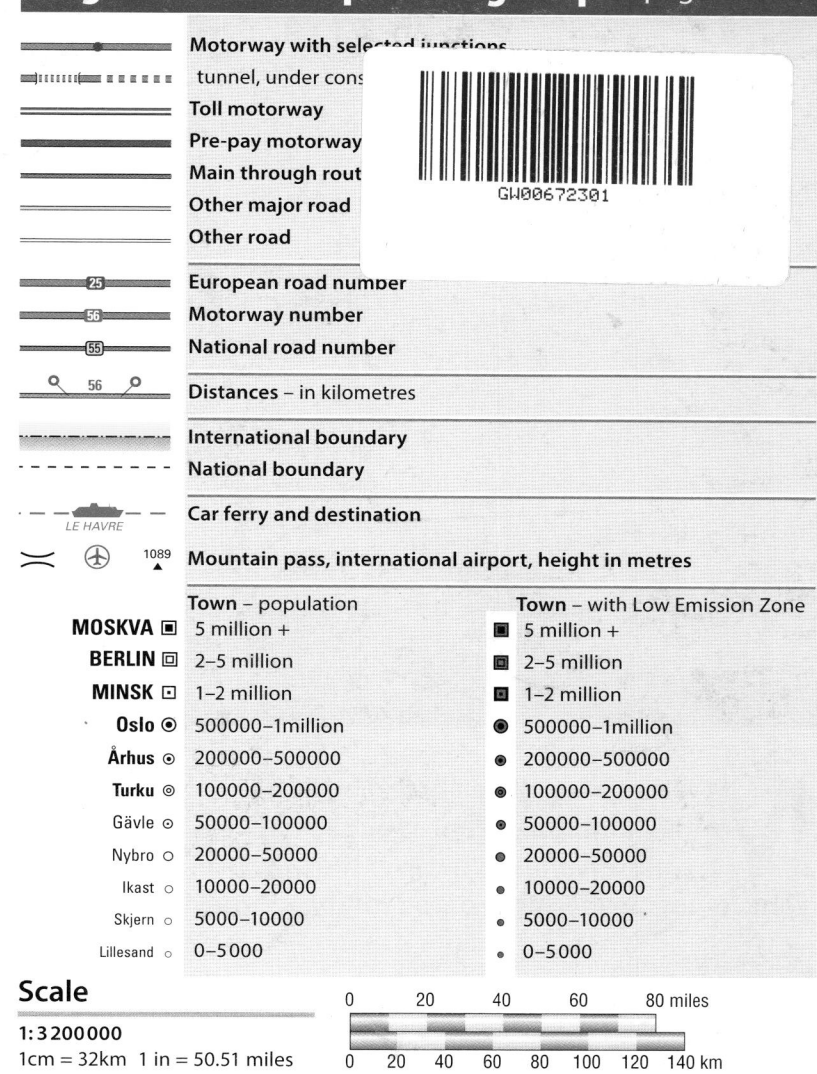

Legend to route planning maps pages 2–16

- Motorway with selected junctions
- tunnel, under construction
- Toll motorway
- Pre-pay motorway
- Main through route
- Other major road
- Other road
- **25** European road number
- **56** Motorway number
- **55** National road number
- Distances – in kilometres
- International boundary
- National boundary
- LE HAVRE Car ferry and destination
- Mountain pass, international airport, height in metres

Town – population		Town – with Low Emission Zone	
MOSKVA	5 million +		5 million +
BERLIN	2–5 million		2–5 million
MINSK	1–2 million		1–2 million
Oslo	500000–1million		500000–1million
Århus	200000–500000		200000–500000
Turku	100000–200000		100000–200000
Gävle	50000–100000		50000–100000
Nybro	20000–50000		20000–50000
Ikast	10000–20000		10000–20000
Skjern	5000–10000		5000–10000
Lillesand	0–5000		0–5000

Scale
1:3 200 000
1cm = 32km   1 in = 50.51 miles

0 20 40 60 80 miles
0 20 40 60 80 100 120 140 km

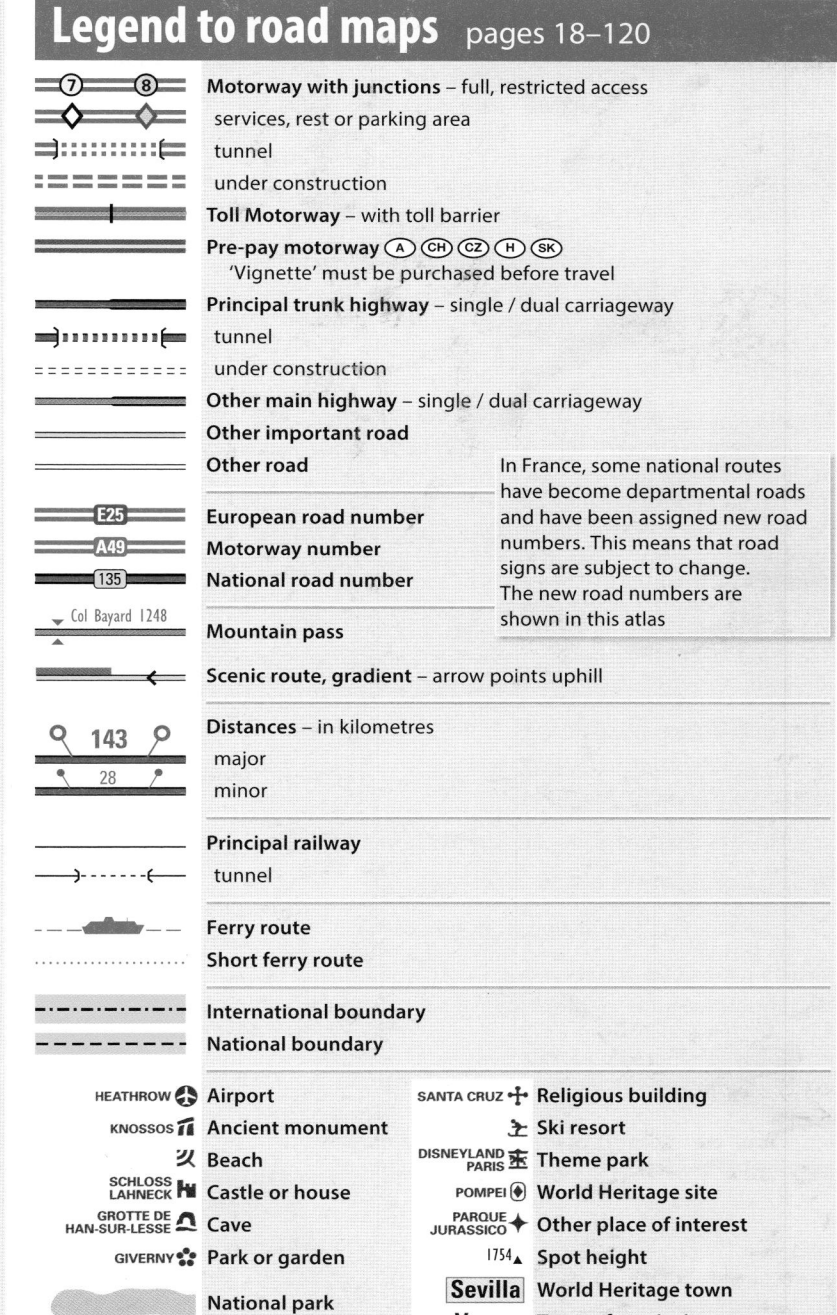

Legend to road maps pages 18–120

- **7 8** Motorway with junctions – full, restricted access
- services, rest or parking area
- tunnel
- under construction
- Toll Motorway – with toll barrier
- Pre-pay motorway (A) (CH) (CZ) (H) (SK) 'Vignette' must be purchased before travel
- Principal trunk highway – single / dual carriageway
- tunnel
- under construction
- Other main highway – single / dual carriageway
- Other important road
- Other road
- **E25** European road number
- **A49** Motorway number
- **135** National road number
- Col Bayard 1248 Mountain pass
- Scenic route, gradient – arrow points uphill
- **143** Distances – in kilometres
- **28** major / minor
- Principal railway
- tunnel
- Ferry route
- Short ferry route
- International boundary
- National boundary

In France, some national routes have become departmental roads and have been assigned new road numbers. This means that road signs are subject to change. The new road numbers are shown in this atlas

HEATHROW	Airport	SANTA CRUZ	Religious building
KNOSSOS	Ancient monument		Ski resort
	Beach	DISNEYLAND PARIS	Theme park
SCHLOSS LAHNECK	Castle or house	POMPEI	World Heritage site
GROTTE DE HAN-SUR-LESSE	Cave	PARQUE JURASSICO	Other place of interest
GIVERNY	Park or garden	1754	Spot height
	National park	**Sevilla**	World Heritage town
	Natural park	**Verona**	Town of tourist interest
			Town with Low Emission Zone

Scales

1:753 800 • Pages 18–110 and 120
1cm = 7.5km   1 inch = 12 miles

0 5 10 15 20 miles
0 5 10 15 20 25 30 35 km

1:1 507 600 • Pages 111–119
1cm = 15km, 1 inch = 24 miles

0 10 20 30 40 miles
0 10 20 30 40 50 60 70 km

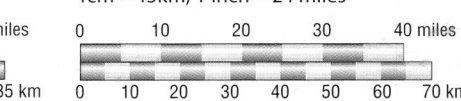
GW00672301

European driving:
cut through the confusion
Stay safe with GEM Motoring Assist

- Do you need advice about equipment requirements and which documents to take?
- Are you confused about European driving laws?
- How will you know what speed limits apply?
- Are you new to driving on the right hand side?
- Who do you call if you have an accident or break down?

Since its foundation in 1932, GEM Motoring Assist has been at the forefront of road safety in the UK. Now one of the largest member-led road safety organisations, GEM provides a wide range of discounts and benefits for its 75,000+ members, including the UK's best-value range of breakdown recovery insurance products for motorists, motorcyclists and caravanners. GEM members also benefit from discounts on European breakdown cover and travel insurance, as well as enjoying free access to GEM's Accident Management Service, which provides free-of-charge legal help following any road traffic collision. Members receive Good Motoring, a free quarterly magazine and access to an excellent line-up of road safety leaflets and web-based advice. Why not make GEM Motoring Assist your one-stop shop for trouble-free motoring! Visit www.motoringassist.com/philipsmaps today.

Millions of us drive abroad on holiday each year. Perhaps it's a long motorway trip to the Mediterranean, a selection of historic cities and sites or a gentle tour along quiet country lanes. Whatever the purpose, it makes sense to ensure that both we and our vehicles are properly prepared for the journey.

It's not easy getting to grips with the finer points of driving in other countries, however experienced you may be as a motorist. Whether you have notched up thousands of miles of European driving or are preparing to make your first journey, the chances are you will always manage to find some road sign or legal requirement that will cause confusion.

What's more, 'driving in Europe' covers such a huge area. There are currently 28 countries in the European Union alone, each with its own set of road traffic laws and motoring customs. Driving in Europe can mean a spectacular and sunny coastal road that's within sight of Africa, or a snowy track amid the biting cold of the Arctic Circle, where the only others on the road are reindeer. Add to this some of the world's most congested cities, dense clusters of motorways (many with confusing numbers) and a big variation in safety standards and attitudes to risk. No wonder we often risk getting lost, taking wrong turnings or perhaps stopping where we shouldn't.

Depending on the country we're in, our errors at the wheel or our lack of familiarity with the rules of the road can sometimes bring unwelcome consequences. In any country, foreign drivers are subject to the same traffic rules as residents, enforceable in many situations by hefty on-the-spot fines and other sanctions. The situation across Europe is complex, simply because of the number of different sets of rules. For example, failure to carry a specific piece of breakdown equipment may be an offence in one country, but not in another. It's easy to see why the fun and excitement of a road trip in Europe could be spoilt by a minefield of regulations.

But we want to ensure that doesn't happen. Preparation and planning are key to a great holiday. It certainly pays to do a bit of research before you go, just to ensure you and your vehicle are up to the journey, your documents are in order and you're carrying the correct levels of equipment to keep the law enforcers happy.

Before you go

Some sensible planning will help make sure your European journey is enjoyable and – we hope – stress-free. So take some time before departure to ensure everything is in good shape: and that includes you, your travelling companions and your vehicle.

For you:

Try to become familiar with the driving laws of your holiday destination, including the local speed limits and which side of the road to drive on. You will be subject to these laws when driving abroad and if you are stopped by the police, it is not an excuse to say that you were unaware of them. Police officers in many countries have the power to impose (and collect) substantial on-the-spot fines for motoring offences, whether you are a resident or a visitor.

The European Commission's 'Driving Abroad' website **http://ec.europa.eu/transport/road_safety/going_abroad** gives detailed information on different road traffic rules in different European countries.

The Foreign and Commonwealth Office also gives country-specific travel advice **www.gov.uk/driving-abroad** with information on driving.

Passports

Check everyone's passport to make sure they are all valid.

Don't wait for your passport to expire. Unused time, rounded up to whole months (minimum one month, maximum nine months), will usually be added to your new passport.

New passports usually take two weeks to arrive. The Passport Office (0300 222 0000, **www.gov.uk/renew-adult-passport**) offers a faster service if you need a replacement passport urgently, but you'll have to pay a lot more.

Driving Licence

The new style photocard driving licence is currently valid in all European Union countries. Some non-EU countries may also require an International Driving Permit (£5.50, available from Post Offices). The previously used pink EU format UK paper licence is no longer a valid document. If you're planning to hire a car, the company may ask for a check code (**www.gov.uk/view-driving-licence**) so they can view your driving record, entitlement and any penalty points you may have. So if you haven't already done so, now is the time to update your old licence. For more information, contact the DVLA (0300 790 6802, **www.gov.uk/government/organisations/driver-and-vehicle-licensing-agency**)

Travel Insurance

Travel insurance is vital as it covers you against medical emergencies, accidents, thefts and cancellations, and repatriation. Ask for details before buying any travel insurance policy. Find out what it covers you for, and to what value. More important, check what's not covered. One of the key benefits of GEM membership is the excellent discount you can get on travel insurance. For more details, please visit: **www.motoringassist.com/philipsmaps**

European Breakdown Cover

Don't risk letting a breakdown ruin your European trip. Ensure you purchase a policy that will cover you for roadside assistance, emergency repair and recovery of your vehicle to the UK, wherever in Europe you may be heading. Once again, GEM members enjoy a specially discounted rate. You'll find the details at **www.motoringassist.com/philipsmaps**

EHIC

You wil need an EHIC card for everyone travelling. These are free and cover you for any medical treatment you may need during a trip to another EU or EEA country or Switzerland. However, do check at the time of requiring assistance that your EHIC will be accepted. Apply online (**www.gov.uk/european-health-insurance-card**), by telephone (0300 3301350) or complete an application form, available from a [ ] Post office. Allow up to 14 days for the cards [ ] to arrive.

For your vehicle:

Service
It makes sense to get your car serviced before you travel. At the very least, ensure the tyres have plenty of tread left and that coolant and oil levels are checked and topped up if required. Check them regularly during your time away.

Vehicle Registration Document
Police in many countries can demand that you prove you have the right to be driving your car. That means you need to show the registration document, or a suitable letter of authorisation if the registration document is not in your name. Remember you should never leave the registration document in the car.

Nationality plate
Your vehicle must display a nationality plate of an approved pattern, design and size.

MOT
If your car is more than three years old, make sure you take its current MOT test certificate with you.

Insurance
If you are planning a trip to Europe, you should find that your car insurance policy provides you with the minimum amount of cover you need. But it's important to contact your insurer before you go, to confirm exactly what level of cover you have and for how many days it will be valid.

Mechanical adjustments
Check the adjustments required for your headlights before you go. Beam deflectors are a legal requirement if you drive in Europe. They are generally sold at the ports, on ferries and in the Folkestone Eurotunnel terminal, but be warned – the instructions can be a little confusing! The alternative is to ask a local garage to do the job for you before you go. If you choose this, then make sure you shop around as prices for undertaking this very simple task vary enormously.

Equipment check-list
This checklist represents GEM's suggestions for what you should take with you in the car. Different countries have different rules about what's compulsory and these rules change from time to time. So it's important to check carefully before you set out. For country-by-country guidance, visit **www.motoringassist.com/europe** or see page IV of this atlas.

- Fire extinguisher
- First aid kit
- High-visibility jacket – one for each occupant
- Two warning triangles
- Replacement bulbs and fuses
- Spare spectacles (if worn) for each driver
- Snow chains for winter journeys into the mountains
- Camera and notebook. Keep in your glove compartment and record any collisions or damage for insurance purposes (if it is safe).

Contact details
Make sure you have all relevant emergency helpline numbers with you, including emergency services, breakdown assistance, the local British consulate and your insurance company. There are links to embassies and consulates around the world from the Foreign Office website. (**www.fco.gov.uk**) For information, the European emergency telephone number (our equivalent of 999) is 112.

II

STOP AND GIVE WAY

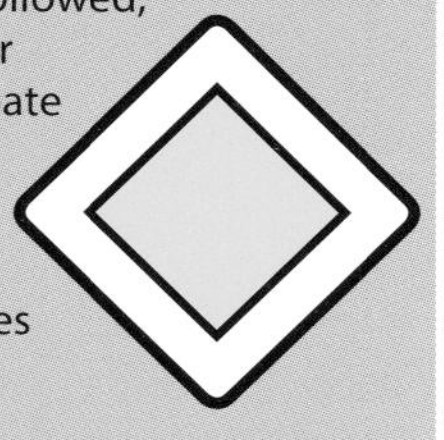

Who has priority?

Make sure you keep a watchful eye on signs telling you who has priority on the road. Look for a yellow diamond sign, which tells you that traffic already on the road has priority. If you see the yellow diamond sign crossed out, then you must give way to traffic joining the road.

Priorité a droite

Despite the use of the yellow diamond signs, be aware that on some French roads (especially roundabouts in Paris), the traditional 'priorité a droite' practice is followed, even though it may no longer be legal. In theory these days, the rule no longer applies unless it is clearly signed. In practice, though, it makes sense to anticipate a driver pulling out in front of you, even though the priority may be yours.

Headlight flash

Bear in mind that the practice of flashing headlights at a junction in France does not mean the same thing as it might in the UK. If another motorists flashes his headlights at you, he's telling you that he has priority and will be coming through in front of you.

Stop means stop!

If you come to a solid white line with an octagonal 'STOP' sign, then you must come to a complete stop. In other words your wheels must stop turning. Adherence to the 'STOP' sign is generally much more rigorously enforced in European countries than you may be used to here.

HELP ME, PLEASE!

If you're in a difficult situation and need local help, then the following words and phrases might prove useful if language is a problem:

Do you speak English?	Parlez-vous anglais?	¿Habla usted inglés?	Parla inglese?	Sprechen Sie Englisch?
Thank you (very much)	Merci (beaucoup)	(Muchas) Gracias	Grazie (mille)	Danke (sehr)
Is there a police station near here?	Est-ce qu'il y a un commissariat de police près d'ici?	¿Hay una comisaría cerca?	C'e' un commissariato qui vicino?	Gibt es ein Polizeirevier hier in der Nähe?
I have lost my passport.	J'ai perdu mon passeport.	He perdido mi pasaporte	Ho perso il mio passaporto.	Ich have meinen Reisepass verloren.
I have broken down.	Je suis tombé en panne	Mi coche se ha averiado.	Ho un guasto.	Ich habe eine Panne.
I have run out of fuel.	Je suis tombé en panne d'essence.	Me he quedado sin gasolina.	Ho terminato la benzina.	Ich habe kein Benzin mehr.

WORTH KNOWING

You will need a separate GB sticker in EU countries if your car doesn't have a registration plate containing the GB euro-symbol.

Fuel is generally most expensive at motorway service areas and cheapest at supermarkets. However, these are usually shut on Sundays and Bank Holidays. So-called '24 hour' regional fuel stations in France generally accept payment by UK credit card these days, but some drivers still occasionally report difficulties. It would be better not to rely on them if your tank is running low during a night-time journey.

If you see several fuel stations in short succession before a national border, it's likely that fuel on the other side will be more expensive, so take the opportunity to fill up.

Radar speed camera detectors are illegal in most European countries.

The insurance 'green card' is no longer required for journeys in Europe, but it is important to make sure you have contact details for your insurer in case of an accident or claim.

Speed limits in France are enforced rigorously. Radar controls are frequent, and any driver (including non-residents) detected at more than 25km/h above the speed limit can have their licence confiscated on the spot. If you are caught exceeding the limit by 50km/h, even on a first offence, your car may be confiscated.

In Spain you must carry two warning triangles, plus a spare pair of glasses for every driver who needs to use them.

In Luxembourg, there are specific rules relating to how you fix a satnav device to your windscreen. Get it wrong and you could be fined on the spot.

In Germany it is against the law to run out of fuel on the motorway. If you do run out, then you face an on-the-spot fine.

Norway and Sweden have particularly low limits for drink-driving: just 20mg per 100ml of blood (compared to 80 in the UK). In Slovakia, the limit is zero.

In Hungary, the limit is also zero. If you are found to be drink-driving, your driving licence will be withdrawn by police officers on the spot.

In most countries, maps and signs will have the European road number (shown in white on a green background) alongside the appropriate national road number. However, in Sweden and Belgium only the E-road number will be shown.

Other laws and motoring advice to be aware of across Europe:

Austria Recent rules require the mandatory use of winter tyres between 1 November and 15 April. You should not use your horn when driving near hospitals. There are also restrictions on use of vehicle horns in Vienna.

Belgium You will have to pay to use most public toilets – including those at motorway service stations • You are not permitted to use cruise control on motorways when traffic is heavy • There are also specific penalties for close-following on motorways • Roadside drug-testing of drivers (using oral fluid testing devices) forms a regular part of any police controls • Drivers must carry a reflective vest in case of breakdown

Cyprus There have been important changes in how speeding and drink-driving are sanctioned. Cyprus now has a graduated system of speeding fines, ranging from one euro per km/h over the limit in marginal cases through to fines of up to €5,000 and a term of imprisonment for the most severe infringements. There are also graduated fines for drink-driving, ranging from fixed penalties for being slightly over the limit to terms of imprisonment and fines of up to €5,000 for the most severe. Eating and drinking at the wheel are both prohibited.

Denmark Cars towing caravans and trailers are prohibited from overtaking on motorways at certain times of day.

Finland Speeding fines are worked out according to your income. Access to a national database allows police at the roadside to establish a Finnish resident's income and number of dependants. Officers then impose a fine based on a specific number of days' income. The minimum speeding fine is 115 euros • If you hit an elk or deer, you must report the collision to the police.

France Legislation introduced in France in 2012 requires every driver and motorcyclist to be in possession of a valid breath-alyser (displaying an 'NF' number), either electronic or chemical, to be shown to a police officer in case of control. However, the imposition of an €11 fine for failing to produce a breathalyser when required has been postponed indefinitely. So, in theory, you are required to carry a breathalyser kit, but no fine can be imposed if you don't • Motorcyclists' helmets must have four reflective stickers fitted, and there is an on-the-spot fine of €135 for non-compliance (by foreign riders as well as French). In common with other vehicle users, motorcyclists must also carry high-visibility vests to be worn on the roadside in case of emergency • Radar detectors, are banned with fines of €1500 for anyone using them • There are stiff penalties for driving while using a mobile phone. • The drink-drive limit for those who have held a licence for less than three years has been reduced to 20mg per 100ml of blood. For other drivers, the limit is 50mg. This compares with 80mg in England and Wales.

Germany Check your fuel contents regularly as it's an offence to run out of fuel on a German motorway • It's also an offence to make rude signs to other road users.

Greece Greece has one of Europe's highest accident rates in terms of the number of crashes per vehicle. Pay particular attention at traffic light junctions, as red lights are frequently ignored • Drivers detected with more than 110mg per 100ml of blood will face revocation of their licence, and possibly up to two years imprisonment • Carrying a petrol can in a vehicle is forbidden.

Ireland The drink-drive limit was reduced in 2011 from 80mg per 100ml of blood to 50mg • Beware of rural three-lane roads, where the middle overtaking lane is used by traffic travelling in both directions. On wider rural roads it's the accepted practice for slower vehicles to pull over to let faster traffic through.

Italy Police can impound your vehicle if you cannot present the relevant ownership documents when requested • You will need a red and white warning sign if you plan to use any rear-mounted luggage rack such as a bike rack • Zero alcohol tolerance is now applied for drivers who have held a driving licence for less than three years, as well as to drivers aged 18 to 21, professional drivers, taxi drivers and truckers.

Norway Under new legislation, police officers can perform roadside drug impairment saliva tests. There are specific limits set for the presence of 20 common non-alcohol drugs • You'll find what amounts to zero tolerance where drinking and driving is concerned. Only 10mg of alcohol per 100ml of blood is permitted (compared to 80mg in the UK) • Speeding fines are high. For example, a driver caught at 25 km/h over the 80 km/h speed limit on a national road could expect a fine of around £600. • No overtaking' signs apply to cars overtaking other cars and motorbikes overtaking cars, but curiously not to cars overtaking motorbikes.

Portugal If you are towing a caravan, you must have a current inventory of the caravan's contents to show a police officer if requested.

Slovakia It is mandatory to use dipped headlights on every road journey, regardless of the time of day, season or weather conditions.

Spain Motorway speed limits in Spain are 120km/h • If you need glasses for driving, then the law requires you to carry a spare pair with you in the car • It's compulsory to carry two spare warning triangles, spare bulbs for your car and reflective jackets.

Turkey Take great caution if you're driving at dusk. Many local drivers put off using their lights until it's properly dark, so you may find oncoming traffic very hard to spot • During the time of Ramadan, many people will not eat or drink between the hours of sunrise and sunset. This can seriously reduce levels of alertness, especially among people driving buses, trucks and taxis.

TOP TIPS FOR STAYING SAFE

Collisions abroad occur not just because of poor driving conditions locally, but also because we do not always take the same safety precautions as we might expect to take at home, for example by not wearing a seatbelt or by drinking and driving.

1. Plan your route before you go. That includes the journey you make to reach your destination (with sufficient breaks built in) and any excursions or local journeys you make while you're there.

2. Remember that, wherever you drive, you will be subject to the same laws as local drivers. Claiming ignorance of these laws will not be accepted as an excuse.

3. Take extra care at junctions when you're driving on the 'right side' of the road. Also, be careful if you are reversing out of a parking space on the street, as things will feel in the wrong place. If driving in a family group, involve every member in a quick 'junction safety check' to help reduce the risk of a collision. Having everybody in the car call out a catchphrase such as "DriLL DriLL DriLL" (Driver Look Left) on the approach to junctions and roundabouts is a small but potentially life-saving habit.

4. Take fatigue seriously. The excellent European motorway network means you can cover big distances with ease. But you must also make time for proper breaks (experts recommend a break of at least 15 minutes after every two hours of driving). If possible, share the driving and set strict daily limits to the number of driving hours. Watch a short video that explains the risks of driver fatigue: **www.motoringassist.com/fatigue**

5. Drink-driving limits across Europe are lower than those in the UK. The only exception is Malta, where the limit is the same. Bear this in mind if you're flying to a holiday or business destination and plan to have a drink on the plane, as the combination of unfamiliar roads and alcohol in your bloodstream is not a safe one. It's also worth remembering that drivers who cause collisions because they were drinking are likely to find their insurance policy will not cover them.

6. Expect the unexpected. Styles of driving in your destination country are likely to be very different from those you know in the UK. Drive defensively and certainly don't get involved in any altercations on the road.

7. Don't overload your car, however tempting the local bargains may appear. Make sure you have good all-round visibility by ensuring you don't pile up items on the parcel shelf or boot, and keep your windscreen clean.

8. Always wear a seatbelt and ensure everyone else on board wears one. Check specific regulations regarding the carriage of children: in some countries children under the age of 12 may not travel in the front of the car.

9. Don't use your mobile phone while driving. Even though laws on phone use while driving differ from country to country, the practice is just as dangerous wherever you are.

10. When you're exploring on foot, be wise to road safety as a pedestrian. You may get into trouble for 'jay-walking' so don't just wander across a road. Use a proper crossing, but remember that drivers may not stop for you! Don't forget that traffic closest to you approaches from the LEFT.

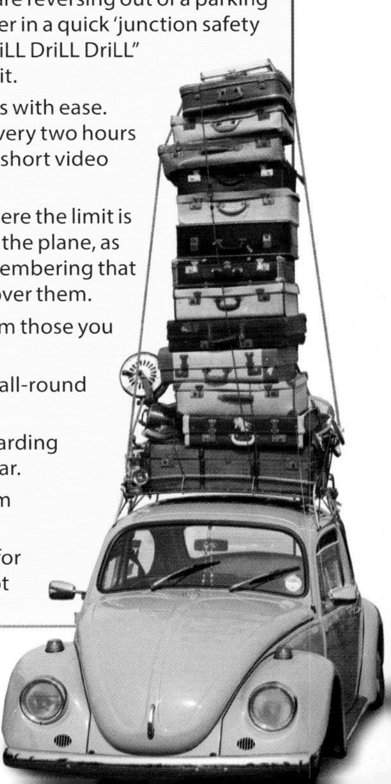

Driving regulations

Vehicle

A national vehicle identification plate is always required when taking a vehicle abroad.

Fitting headlamp converters or beam deflectors when taking a right-hand drive car to a country where driving is on the right (every country in Europe except the UK and Ireland) is compulsory.

Within the EU, if not driving a locally hired car, it is compulsory to have either Europlates or a country of origin (eg GB) sticker. Outside the EU (and in Andorra) a sticker is compulsory, even with Europlates.

Documentation

All countries require that you carry a valid passport, vehicle registration document, hire certificate or letter of authority for the use of someone else's vehicle, full driving licence/International Driving Permit and insurance documentation (and/or green card outside the EU). Some non-EU countries also require a visa. Minimum driving ages are often higher for people holding foreign licences. Exit checks at the Eurotunnel and ferry terminals mean that drivers taking vehicles from the UK should allow extra time. Drivers of vehicles over three years old should ensure that the MOT is up to date and take the certificate with them.

EHIC cards are free and give you entitlement to healthcare in other EU countries and Switzerland. *www.gov/european-health-insurance-card*.

Licence

A photo licence is preferred; with an old-style paper licence, an International Driving Permit (IDP) should also be carried. In some countries, an IDP is compulsory, whatever form of licence is held. Non-EU drivers should always have both a licence and and IDP. UK (except NI) drivers should check in advance whether a hire company will wish to check for endorsements and vehicle categories. If so, visit *https://www.gov.uk/view-driving-licence* to create a digital code (valid for 72 hours) that allows their details to be shared. For more information, contact the DVLA (0300 790 6802, *www.dft.gov.uk/dvla*).

Insurance

Third-party cover is compulsory across Europe. Most insurance policies give only basic cover when driving abroad, so you should check that your policy provides at least third-party cover for the countries in which you will be driving and upgrade it to the level that you require. You may be forced to take out extra cover at the frontier if you cannot produce acceptable proof that you have adequate insurance. Even in countries in which a green card is not required, carrying one is recommended for extra proof of insurance.

Motorcycles

It is compulsory for all motorcyclists and passengers to wear crash helmets. In France it may become compulsory for all motorcyclists and passengers to wear a minimum amount of reflective gear.

Other

In countries in which visibility vests are compulsory one for each person should be carried in the passenger compartment, or panniers on a motorbike, where they can be reached easily.

Warning triangles should also be carried in the passenger compartment.

The penalties for infringements of regulations vary considerably from one country to another. In many countries the police have the right to impose on-the-spot fines (ask for a receipt). Penalties can be severe for serious infringements, particularly for exceeding the blood-alcohol limit; in some countries this can result in immediate imprisonment.

In some countries, vignettes for toll roads are being replaced by electronic tags. See country details.

Please note that driving regulations often change, and that it has not been possible to cover all the information for every type of vehicle. The figures given for capitals' populations are for the whole metropolitan area.

The symbols used are:

- 🛣 Motorway
- ⋀ Dual carriageway
- ▲ Single carriageway
- 🛤 Surfaced road
- ⛐ Unsurfaced or gravel road
- 🏭 Urban area
- ⏲ Speed limit in kilometres per hour (kph). These are the maximum speeds for the types of roads listed. In some places and under certain conditions they may be considerably lower. Always obey local signs.
- 🔗 Seat belts
- 👶 Children
- 🍷 Blood alcohol level
- △ Warning triangle
- ⊞ First aid kit
- 💡 Spare bulb kit
- 🧯 Fire extinguisher
- ⊖ Minimum driving age
- 📄 Additional documents required
- 📱 Mobile phones
- LEZ Low Emission Zone
- 🔦 Dipped headlights
- ❄ Winter driving
- ★ Other information

The publishers have made every effort to ensure that the information given here was correct at the time of going to press. No responsibility can be accepted for any errors or their consequences.

Andorra Principat d'Andorra (AND)

Area 468 sq km (181 sq miles)
Population 85,500
Capital Andorra la Vella (44,000)
Languages Catalan (official), French, Castilian and Portuguese
Currency Euro = 100 cents
Website http://visitandorra.com

	🛣	⋀	▲	🏭
⏲	n/a	90	60/90	50

- 🔗 Compulsory
- 👶 Under 10 and below 150 cm must travel in an EU-approved restraint system adapted to their size in the rear. Airbag must be deactivated if a child is in the front passenger seat.
- 🍷 0.05%
- △ Compulsory
- ⊞ Recommended
- 💡 Compulsory
- 🧯 Recommended
- ⊖ 18
- 📱 Not permitted whilst driving
- 🔦 Compulsory for motorcycles during day and for other vehicles during poor daytime visibility.
- ❄ Winter tyres recommended. Snow chains compulsory in poor conditions or when indicated.
- ★ On-the-spot fines imposed
- ★ Visibility vests compulsory

Austria Österreich (A)

Area 83,859 sq km (32,377 sq miles)
Population 8,823,000
Capital Vienna / Wien (1,890,000)
Languages German (official)
Currency Euro = 100 cents
Website www.austria.org

	🛣	⋀	▲	🏭
⏲	130	100	100	50
If towing trailer under 750kg / over 750 kg				
⏲	100	100	100/80	50

- 🔗 Compulsory
- 👶 Under 14 and under 150cm cannot travel as a front or rear passenger unless they use a suitable child restraint; under 14 over 150cm must wear adult seat belt
- 🍷 0.049% • 0.01% if licence held less than 2 years
- △ Compulsory
- ⊞ Compulsory
- 💡 Recommended
- 🧯 Recommended
- ⊖ 17 (20 for motorbikes over 50cc)
- 📄 Paper driving licences must be accompanied by photographic proof of identity.
- 📱 Only allowed with hands-free kit
- LEZ Several cities and regions have LEZs affecting HGVs that ban non-compliant vehicles, impose speed restrictions and night-time bans.
- 🔦 Must be used during the day by all road users. Headlamp converters compulsory
- ❄ Winter tyres compulsory 1 Nov–15 Apr
- ★ On-the-spot fines imposed
- ★ Radar detectors and dashcams prohibited
- ★ To drive on motorways or expressways, a motorway sticker must be purchased at the border or main petrol station. These are available for 10 days, 2 months or 1 year. Vehicles 3.5 tonnes or over must display an electronic tag.
- ★ Visibility vests compulsory

Belarus (BY)

Area 207,600 sq km (80,154 sq miles)
Population 9,492,000 **Capital** Minsk (1,982,000)
Languages Belarusian, Russian (both official)
Currency Belarusian ruble = 100 kopek
Website www.belarus.by/en/government

	🛣	⋀	▲	🏭
⏲	110	90	90	40*
If towing trailer under 750kg				
⏲	90	70	70	

*In residential areas limit is 20 km/h • Vehicle towing another vehicle 50 kph limit • If full driving licence held for less than two years, must not exceed 70 kph

- 🔗 Compulsory in front seats, and rear seats if fitted
- 👶 Under 12 not allowed in front seat and must use appropriate child restraint
- 🍷 0.00%
- △ Compulsory
- ⊞ Compulsory
- 💡 Recommended
- 🧯 Compulsory
- ⊖ 18
- 📄 Visa, vehicle technical check stamp, international driving permit, green card, local health insurance. Even with a green card, local third-party insurance may be imposed at the border
- 📱 Use prohibited
- 🔦 Compulsory during the day Nov–Mar and at all other times in conditions of poor visibility or when towing or being towed.
- ❄ Winter tyres compulsory; snow chains recommended
- ★ A temporary vehicle import certificate must be purchased on entry and driver must be registered
- ★ It is illegal for vehicles to be dirty
- ★ On-the-spot fines imposed
- ★ Radar-detectors prohibited
- ★ Road tax imposed at the border
- ★ To drive on main motorways an on-board unit must be acquired at the border or a petrol station in order to pay tolls. See **www.beltoll.by/index.php/en**

Belgium Belgique (B)

Area 30,528 sq km (11,786 sq miles)
Population 11,358,000 **Capital** Brussels/Bruxelles (1,175,000) **Languages** Dutch, French, German (all official)
Currency Euro = 100 cents **Website** www.belgium.be/en

	🛣	⋀	▲	🏭
⏲	120[1]	120[1]	90[2]	50[3]
If towing trailer				
⏲	90	90	60	50[3]
Over 3.5 tonnes				
⏲	90	90	60	50

[1]Minimum speed of 70 kph may be applied in certain conditions on motorways and some dual carriageways. [2]70 kph in Flanders. [3]20 kph in residential areas, 30 kph near some schools, hospitals and churches.

- 🔗 Compulsory
- 👶 All under 18s under 135 cm must wear an appropriate child restraint. Airbags must be deactivated if a rear-facing child seat is used in the front
- 🍷 0.049% △ Compulsory ⊞ Recommended
- 💡 Recommended 🧯 Compulsory
- ⛑ Motorcyclists must wear fully protective clothing
- ⊖ 18 📱 Only allowed with a hands-free kit
- LEZ LEZs in operation in Antwerp, Brussels and areas of Flanders. Preregistration necessary and fees payable for most vehicles.
- 🔦 Mandatory at all times for motorcycles and during the day in poor conditions for other vehicles
- ★ Cruise control must be deactivated on motorways where indicated
- ★ On-the-spot fines imposed
- ★ Radar detectors prohibited
- ★ Sticker indicating maximum recommended speed for winter tyres must be displayed on dashboard if using them
- ★ Visibility vest compulsory

Bosnia and Herzegovina Bosna i Hercegovina (BIH)

Area 51,197 km² (19,767 mi²) **Population** 3,872,000 **Capital** Sarajevo (643,000) **Languages** Bosnian/Croatian/ Serbian **Currency** Convertible Marka = 100 convertible pfenniga **Website** www.fbihvlada.gov.ba/english

	🛣	⋀	▲	🏭
⏲	130	100	80	50

- 🔗 Compulsory if fitted
- 👶 Under 12s must sit in rear using an appropriate child restraint. Under-2s may travel in a rear-facing child seat in the front only if the airbags have been deactivated.
- 🍷 0.03% △ Compulsory ⊞ Compulsory
- 💡 Compulsory 🧯 Compulsory for LPG vehicles ⊖ 18
- 📄 Visa, International Driving Permit, green card
- 📱 Prohibited
- 🔦 Compulsory for all vehicles at all times
- ❄ Winter tyres compulsory 15 Nov–15 Apr; snow chains recommended
- ★ GPS must have fixed speed camera function deactivated; radar detectors prohibited.
- ★ On-the-spot fines imposed
- ★ Visibility vest, tow rope or tow bar compulsory
- ★ Spare wheel compulsory, except for two-wheeled vehicles

Bulgaria Bulgariya (BG)

Area 110,912 sq km (42,822 sq miles)
Population 7,050,000 **Capital** Sofia (1,682,000)
Currency Lev=100 stotinki **Languages** Bulgarian (official), Turkish **Website** www.government.bg

	🛣	⋀	▲	🏭
⏲	130	90	90	50
If towing trailer				
⏲	100	70	70	50

- 🔗 Compulsory in front and rear seats
- 👶 Under 3s not permitted in vehicles with no child restraints; 3–10 year olds must sit in rear in an appropriate restraint. Rear-facing child seats may be used in the front only if the airbag has been deactivated
- 🍷 0.049% △ Compulsory ⊞ Compulsory
- 💡 Recommended 🧯 Compulsory ⊖ 18
- 📄 Photo driving licence preferred; a paper licence must be accompanied by an International Driving Permit. Green card or insurance specific to Bulgaria.
- 📱 Only allowed with a hands-free kit
- 🔦 Compulsory
- ❄ Winter tyres compulsory. Snow chains should be carried from 1 Nov–1 Mar. Max speed with chains 50 kph
- ★ Fee at border
- ★ GPS must have fixed speed camera function deactivated; radar detectors prohibited
- ★ On-the-spot fines imposed
- ★ Road tax stickers (annual, monthly or weekly) must be purchased at the border and displayed prominently with the vehicle registration number written on them.
- ★ Visibility vest compulsory

Croatia Hrvatska (HR)

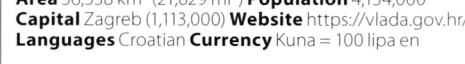

Area 56,538 km² (21,829 mi²) **Population** 4,154,000 **Capital** Zagreb (1,113,000) **Website** https://vlada.gov.hr/ **Languages** Croatian **Currency** Kuna = 100 lipa en

	🛣	⋀	▲	🏭
⏲	130	110	90	50
Under 24				
⏲	120	100	80	50
If towing				
⏲	90	90	80	50

- 🔗 Compulsory if fitted
- 👶 Children under 12 not permitted in front seat and must use appropriate child seat or restraint in rear. Children under 2 may use a rear-facing seat in the front only if the airbag is deactivated
- 🍷 0.05% • 0.00 % for drivers under 24
- △ Compulsory (two if towing) ⊞ Compulsory
- 💡 Compulsory 🧯 Recommended ⊖ 18
- 📄 Green card recommended
- 📱 Only allowed with hands-free kit 🔦 Compulsory
- ❄ Winter tyres, snow chains and shovel compulsory in winter
- ★ On-the-spot fines imposed
- ★ Radar detectors prohibited
- ★ Tow bar and rope compulsory
- ★ Visibility vest compulsory

Czechia Česko (CZ)

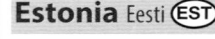

Area 78,864 sq km (30,449 sq miles)
Population 10,611,000 **Capital** Prague/Praha (2,619,000)
Languages Czech (official), Moravian **Currency** Czech Koruna = 100 haler **Website** https://vlada.cz/en/

	🛣	⋀	▲	🏭
⏲	130	90	90	50
If towing				
⏲	80	80	80	50

- 🔗 Compulsory in front seats and, if fitted, in rear
- 👶 Children under 36 kg and 150 cm must use appropriate child restraint. Only front-facing child retraints are permitted in the front in vehicles with airbags fitted. Airbags must be deactivated if a rear-facing child seat is used in the front.
- 🍷 0.00% △ Compulsory ⊞ Compulsory
- 💡 Compulsory 🧯 Compulsory
- ⊖ 18 (17 for motorcycles under 125 cc)
- 📄 Licences with a photo preferred. Paper licences should be accompanied by an International Driving Permit.
- 📱 Only allowed with a hands-free kit
- LEZ Two-stage LEZ in Prague for vehicles over 3.5 and 6 tonnes. Permit system.
- 🔦 Compulsory at all times
- ❄ Winter tyres compulsory Nov-Mar, roads are icy/snow-covered or snow is expected. Max speed 50 kph.
- ★ GPS must have fixed speed camera function deactivated; radar detectors prohibited
- ★ On-the-spot fines imposed
- ★ Replacement fuses must be carried
- ★ Spectacles or contact lens wearers must carry a spare pair in their vehicle at all times
- ★ Vignette needed for motorway driving, available for 1 year, 60 days, 15 days. Lorries over 12 tonnes must buy an electronic tag
- ★ Visibility vest compulsory

Denmark Danmark (DK)

Area 43,094 sq km (16,638 sq miles)
Population 5,786,000 **Capital** Copenhagen / København (1,922,000) **Languages** Danish (official)
Currency Krone = 100 øre **Website** www.denmark.dk/en

	🛣	⋀	▲	🏭
⏲	110-130	80-90	80	50*
If towing				
⏲	80	70	70	50*

*Central Copenhagen 40 kph

- 🔗 Compulsory front and rear
- 👶 Under 135cm must use appropriate child restraint; in front permitted only in an appropriate rear-facing seat with any airbags disabled.
- 🍷 0.05% △ Compulsory ⊞ Recommended
- 💡 Recommended 🧯 Recommended ⊖ 17
- 📱 Only allowed with a hands-free kit
- LEZ Aalborg, Arhus, Copenhagen, Frederiksberg and Odense. Proofs of emissions compliance or compliant filter needed to obtain sticker. Non-compliant vehicles banned.
- 🔦 Must be used at all times
- ❄ Spiked tyres may be fitted 1 Nov–15 April, if used on all wheels
- ★ On-the-spot fines imposed
- ★ Radar detectors prohibited
- ★ Tolls apply on the Storebaeltsbroen and Oresundsbron bridges.
- ★ Visibility vest recommended

Estonia Eesti (EST)

Area 45,100 sq km (17,413 sq miles)
Population 1,319,000 **Capital** Tallinn (610,000)
Languages Estonian (official), Russian
Currency Euro = 100 cents **Website** www.valitsus.ee/en

	🛣	⋀	▲	🏭
⏲	n/a	90*	90	50
If full driving licence held for less than two years				
⏲	90	90	90	50

*In summer, the speed limit on some dual carriageways may be raised to 100/110 kph

- 🔗 Compulsory if fitted
- 👶 Children too small for adult seatbelts must wear a seat restraint appropriate to their size. Rear-facing safety seats must not be used in the front if an air bag is fitted, unless this has been deactivated.
- 🍷 0.00% △ 2 compulsory ⊞ Compulsory
- 💡 Recommended 🧯 Compulsory ⊖ 18
- 📱 Only allowed with a hands-free kit
- 🔦 Compulsory at all times
- ❄ Winter tyres are compulsory from Dec–Mar. Studded winter tyres are allowed from 15 Oct–31 Mar, but this can be extended to start 1 October and/or end 30 April

★ A toll system is in operation in Tallinn
★ On-the-spot fines imposed
★ Two wheel chocks compulsory
★ Visibility vest compulsory

Finland Suomi (FIN)

Area 338,145 sq km (130,557 sq miles) **Languages** Finnish, Swedish (both official) **Population** 5,517,000 **Capital** Helsinki (1,471,000) **Currency** Euro = 100 cents **Website** https://valtioneuvosto.fi/en/frontpage

	120	100	80/100*	20/50
Vans, lorries and if towing				
	80	80	60	20/50

*100 in summer • If towing a vehicle by rope, cable or rod, max speed limit 60 kph • Maximum of 80 kph for vans and lorries • Speed limits are often lowered in winter

- Compulsory in front and rear
- Below 135 cm must use a child restraint or seat
- 0.05% Compulsory Recommended
- Recommended Recommended
- 18 (motorbikes below 125cc 16)
- Only allowed with hands-free kit
- Must be used at all times
- Winter tyres compulsory Dec–Feb
- ★ On-the-spot fines imposed
- ★ Radar-detectors are prohibited
- ★ Visibility vest compulsory

France (F)

Area 551,500 sq km (212,934 sq miles) **Population** 65,058,000 **Capital** Paris (12,405,000) **Languages** French (official), Breton, Occitan **Currency** Euro = 100 cents **Website** www.diplomatie.gouv.fr/en

	130	110	80	50
On wet roads or if full driving licence held for less than 3 years				
	110	100	70	50
If towing below / above 3.5 tonnes gross				
	110/90	100/90	90/80	50

50kph on all roads if fog reduces visibility to less than 50m

- Compulsory in front seats and, if fitted, in rear
- In rear, 4 or under must have a child safety seat (rear facing if up to 9 months); if 5–10 must use an appropriate restraint system. Under 10 permitted in the front only if rear seats are fully occupied by other under 10s or there are no rear safety belts. In front, if child is in rear-facing child seat, any airbag must be deactivated.
- 0.049% • If towing or with less than 2 years with full driving licence, 0.00% • All drivers/motorcyclists must carry an unused breathalyser to French certification standards, showing an NF number.
- Compulsory Recommended
- Recommended 18 (16 for motorbikes up to 80cc)
- Use not permitted whilst driving
- LEZ LEZs operate in the Mont Blanc Tunnel, Paris, Marseille and many other major cities. Crit'air vignettes must be displayed by compliant vehicles in such areas. Non-compliant vehicles are banned. See **https://www.certificat-air.gouv.fr/en**
- Compulsory in poor daytime visibility and at all times for motorcycles
- Winter tyres recommended. Carrying snow chains recommended in winter as these may have to be fitted if driving on snow-covered roads, in accordance with signage. Max speed 50kph.
- ★ GPS must have fixed speed camera function deactivated; radar-detection equipment is prohibited
- ★ Motorcyclists and passengers must have four reflective stickers on their helmets (front, back and both sides) and wear CE-certified gloves.
- ★ On-the-spot fines imposed
- ★ Tolls on motorways. Electronic tag needed if using automatic tolls.
- ★ Visibility vests, to be worn on the roadside in case of emergency or breakdown, must be carried for all vehicle occupants and riders.
- ★ Wearers of contact lenses or spectacles or lenses should carry a spare pair

Germany Deutschland (D)

Area 357,022 sq km (137,846 sq miles) **Population** 82,806,000 **Capital** Berlin (6,005,000) **Languages** German (official) **Currency** Euro = 100 cents **Website** www.bundesregierung.de

	*	*	100	50
If towing				
	80	80	80	50

*no limit, 130 kph recommended

- Compulsory
- Aged 3-12 and under 150cm must use an appropriate child seat or restraint and sit in the rear. In the front, if child under 3 is in a rear-facing seat, airbags must be deactivated
- 0.049% • 0.0% for drivers 21 or under or with less than two years full licence
- Compulsory Compulsory Compulsory
- Recommended 18
- Use permitted only with hands-free kit – also applies to drivers of motorbikes and bicycles
- LEZ More than 60 cities have or are planning LEZs. Proof of compliance needed to acquire sticker. Non-compliant vehicles banned.
- Compulsory during poor daytime visibility and tunnels; recommended at other times. Compulsory at all times for motorcyclists.

- Winter tyres compulsory in all winter weather conditions; snow chains recommended
- ★ GPS must have fixed speed camera function deactivated; radar detectors prohibited
- ★ On-the-spot fines imposed
- ★ Tolls on autobahns for lorries
- ★ Visibility vest compulsory

Greece Ellas (GR)

Area 131,957 sq km (50,948 sq miles) **Population** 10,768,000 **Capital** Athens / Athina (3,781,000) **Languages** Greek (official) **Currency** Euro = 100 cents **Website** https://primeminister.gr/en/home

	130	110	90	50
Motorbikes, and if towing				
	90	70	70	40

- Compulsory in front seats and, if fitted, in rear
- Under 12 or below 135cm must use appropriate child restraint. In front if child is in rear-facing child seat, any airbags must be deactivated.
- 0.05% • 0.00% for drivers with less than 2 years' full licence and motorcyclists
- Compulsory Compulsory Recommended
- Compulsory 17 Not permitted.
- Compulsory during poor daytime visibility and at all times for motorcycles
- Snow chains permitted on ice- or snow-covered roads. Max speed 50 kph.
- ★ On-the-spot fines imposed
- ★ Radar-detection equipment is prohibited
- ★ Tolls on several newer motorways.

Hungary Magyarország (H)

Area 93,032 sq km (35,919 sq miles) **Population** 9,798,000 **Capital** Budapest (3,304,000) **Languages** Hungarian (official) **Currency** Forint = 100 filler **Website** www.kormany.hu/en

	130	110	90	50*
If towing				
	80	70	70	50*

*30 kph zones have been introduced in many cities

- Compulsory
- Under 135cm and over 3 must be seated in rear and use appropriate child restraint. Under 3 allowed in front only in rear-facing child seat with any airbags deactivated.
- 0.00% Compulsory Compulsory
- Compulsory Recommended 17
- Only allowed with a hands-free kit
- LEZ Budapest has vehicle restrictions on days with heavy dust and is planning an LEZ.
- Compulsory during the day outside built-up areas; compulsory at all times for motorcycles
- Snow chains compulsory where conditions dictate. Max speed 50 kph.
- ★ Many motorways are toll and operate electronic vignette system with automatic number plate recognition, tickets are available for 10 days, 1 month, 13 months
- ★ On-the-spot fines issued
- ★ Radar detectors prohibited
- ★ Tow rope recommended
- ★ Visibility vest compulsory

Iceland Ísland (IS)

Area 103,000 sq km (39,768 sq miles) **Population** 351,000 **Capital** Reykjavik (217,000) **Languages** Icelandic **Currency** Krona = 100 aurar **Website** www.government.is

	n/a	90	80	50

- Compulsory in front and rear seats
- Under 12 or below 150cm not allowed in front seat and must use appropriate child restraint.
- 0.05% Compulsory Compulsory
- Compulsory Compulsory
- 17; 21 to drive a hire car; 25 to hire a jeep
- Only allowed with a hands-free kit
- Compulsory at all times
- Winter tyres compulsory c.1 Nov–14 Apr (variable). Snow chains may be used when necessary.
- ★ Driving off marked roads is forbidden
- ★ Highland roads are not suitable for ordinary cars
- ★ On-the-spot fines imposed

Ireland Eire (IRL)

Area 70,273 sq km (27,132 sq miles) **Population** 4,857,200 **Capital** Dublin (1,905,000) **Languages** Irish, English (both official) **Currency** Euro = 100 cents **Website** www.gov.ie/en

	120	60–100	60–100	50*
If towing				
	80	60	60	50*

*Dublin and some other areas have introduced 30 kph zones

- Compulsory where fitted. Driver responsible for ensuring passengers under 17 comply
- Children 3 and under must be in a suitable child restraint system. Airbags must be deactivated if a rear-facing child seat is used in the front. Those under 150 cm and 36 kg must use appropriate child restraint.
- 0.05% • 0.02% for novice and professional drivers
- Compulsory Recommended
- Recommended Recommended
- 17 (16 for motorbikes up to 125cc; 18 for over 125cc)
- Only allowed with a hands-free kit
- Compulsory for motorbikes at all times and in poor visibility for other vehicles
- ★ Driving is on the left
- ★ GPS must have fixed speed camera function deactivated; radar detectors prohibited
- ★ On-the-spot fines imposed
- ★ Tolls are being introduced on some motorways; the M50 Dublin has barrier-free tolling with number-plate recognition.

Italy Italia (I)

Area 301,318 sq km (116,338 sq miles) **Population** 60,500,000 **Capital** Rome / Roma (4,356,000) **Languages** Italian (official) **Currency** Euro = 100 cents **Website** www.italia.it

	130	110	90	50
If towing				
	80	70	70	50
Less than three years with full licence				
	100	90	90	50
When wet				
	110	90	80	50

Some motorways with emergency lanes have speed limit of 150 kph

- Compulsory in front seats and, if fitted, in rear
- Under 12 not allowed in front seats except in child safety seat; children under 3 must have special seat in the back. For foreign-registered cars, the country of origin's legislation applies.
- 0.05% • 0.00% for professional drivers or with less than 3 years full licence
- Compulsory Recommended
- Compulsory Recommended
- 18 (14 for mopeds, 16 up to 125cc, 20 up to 350cc)
- Only allowed with hands-free kit
- LEZ Most northern and several southern regions operate seasonal LEZs and many towns and cities have various schemes that restrict access. There is an LEZ in the Mont Blanc tunnel
- Compulsory outside built-up areas, in tunnels, on motorways and dual carriageways and in poor visibility; compulsory at all times for motorcycles
- Snow chains compulsory where signs indicate 15 Oct–15 Apr. Max speed 50 kph
- ★ On-the-spot fines imposed
- ★ Radar-detection equipment is prohibited
- ★ Tolls on motorways. Blue lanes accept credit cards; yellow lanes restricted to holders of Telepass pay-toll device.
- ★ Visibility vest compulsory

Kosovo Republika e Kosoves / Republika Kosovo (RKS)

Area 10,887 sq km (4203 sq miles) **Population** 1,921,000 **Capital** Pristina (504,000) **Languages** Albanian, Serbian (both official), Bosnian, Turkish, Roma **Currency** Euro (Serbian dinar in Serb enclaves) **Website** http://kryeministri-ks.net/en/

	130	80	80	50

- Compulsory
- Under 12 must sit in rear seats in an appropriate restraint.
- 0.00% Compulsory Compulsory
- Compulsory Compulsory
- 18 (16 for motorbikes less than 125 cc, 14 for mopeds)
- International driving permit, locally purchased third-party insurance (green card is not recognised), documents with proof of ability to cover costs and valid reason for visiting. Visitors from many non-EU countries require a visa.
- Only allowed with a hands-free kit
- Compulsory at all times
- Winter tyres or snow chains compulsory in poor winter weather conditions

Latvia Latvija (LV)

Area 64,589 sq km (24,942 sq miles) **Population** 1,953,000 **Capital** Riga (1,070,000) **Languages** Latvian (official), Russian **Currency** Euro = 100 cents **Website** https://www.mk.gov.lv/en

	n/a	100	90	50
If towing				
	n/a	80	80	50

In residential areas limit is 20kph • If full driving licence held for less than two years, must not exceed 80 kph

- Compulsory in front seats and if fitted in rear
- If under 12 years and 150cm must use child restraint in front and rear seats
- 0.05% • 0.02% with less than 2 years experience
- Compulsory Compulsory
- Recommended Compulsory 18
- Only allowed with hands-free kit
- Must be used at all times all year round
- Winter tyres compulsory for vehicles up to 3.5 tonnes Dec–Feb, but illegal May–Sept
- ★ On-the-spot fines imposed
- ★ Pedestrians have priority
- ★ Radar-detection equipment prohibited
- ★ Visibility vests compulsory

Lithuania Lietuva (LT)

Area 65,200 sq km (25,173 sq miles) **Population** 2,801,000 **Capital** Vilnius (805,000) **Languages** Lithuanian (official), Russian, Polish **Currency** Euro = 100 cents **Website** http://lrvk.lrv.lt/en

	130	110	70–90	50
If towing				
	n/a	70	70	50
If licence held for less than two years				
	90	90	70	50

In winter speed limits are reduced by 10–20 km/h

- Compulsory
- Under 12 or below 135 cm not allowed in front seats unless in suitable restraint; under 3 must use appropriate child seat. A rear-facing child seat may be used in front only if airbags are deactivated.
- 0.04% • 0.00% if full licence held less than 2 years
- Compulsory
- Compulsory
- Recommended
- Compulsory
- 18
- Licences without a photograph must be accompanied by photographic proof of identity, e.g. a passport
- Only allowed with a hands-free kit
- Must be used at all times
- Winter tyres compulsory 10 Nov–1 Apr
- ★ On-the-spot fines imposed
- ★ Visibility vest compulsory

Luxembourg (L)

Area 2,586 sq km (998 sq miles) **Population** 602,000 **Capital** Luxembourg (107,000) **Languages** Luxembourgian / Letzeburgish (official), French, German **Currency** Euro = 100 cents **Website** http://luxembourg.public.lu/en

	130/110	90	90	50*
If towing				
	90	75	75	50*

If full driving licence held for less than two years, must not exceed 75 kph • *30 kph zones are progressively being introduced.

- Compulsory
- Children under 3 must use an appropriate restraint system. Airbags must be disabled if a rear-facing child seat is used in the front. Children 3–18 and/or under 150 cm must use a restraint system appropriate to their size. If over 36kg a seatbelt may be used in rear only
- 0.049%, 0.019 for young drivers, drivers with less than 2 years experience and drivers of taxis and commercial vehicles
- Compulsory
- Compulsory (buses)
- Compulsory
- Compulsory (buses, transport of dangerous goods)
- 18
- Use permitted only with hands-free kit
- Compulsory for motorcyclists and in poor visibility and in tunnels for other vehicles
- Winter tyres compulsory in winter weather
- ★ On-the-spot fines imposed
- ★ Visibility vest compulsory

Macedonia Makedonija (MK)

Area 25,713 sq km (9,927 sq miles) **Population** 2,104,000 **Capital** Skopje (544,000) **Languages** Macedonian (official), Albanian **Currency** Denar = 100 deni

	120	100	80	50
Newly qualified drivers or if towing				
	100	80	60	50

- Compulsory
- Under 12 not allowed in front seats
- 0.05% • 0.00% for business, commercial and professional drivers and with less than 2 years experience
- Compulsory
- Compulsory
- Compulsory
- Recommended; compulsory for LPG vehicles
- 18 (mopeds 16)
- International driving permit; visa
- Use not permitted whilst driving
- Compulsory at all times
- Winter tyres or snow chains compulsory 15 Nov–15 Mar. Max speed 70 kph
- ★ GPS must have fixed speed camera function deactivated; radar detectors prohibited
- ★ Novice drivers may only drive between 11pm and 5am if there is someone over 25 with a valid licence in the vehicle.
- ★ On-the-spot fines imposed
- ★ Tolls apply on many roads
- ★ Tow rope compulsory
- ★ Visibility vest must be kept in the passenger compartment and worn to leave the vehicle in the dark outside built-up areas

Moldova (MD)

Area 33,851 sq km (13,069 sq miles)
Population 2,551,000 **Capital** Chisinau (736,000)
Languages Moldovan / Romanian (official)
Currency Leu = 100 bani **Website** www.moldova.md

	🛣	⩓	▲	🏭
⏲	90	90	90	60
If towing or if licence held under 1 year				
⏲	70	70	70	60

💺 Compulsory in front seats and, if fitted, in rear seats
👶 Under 12 not allowed in front seats
🍷 0.00% △ Compulsory ⊞ Compulsory
💡 Recommended 🧯 Compulsory
⊖ 18 (mopeds and motorbikes, 16; vehicles with more than eight passenger places, taxis or towing heavy vehicles, 21)
🪪 International Driving Permit (preferred), visa
📱 Only allowed with hands-free kit
🔦 Must use dipped headlights at all times
❄ Winter tyres recommended Nov–Feb

Montenegro Crna Gora (MNE)

Area 14,026 sq km, (5,415 sq miles)
Population 643,000 **Capital** Podgorica (187,000)
Languages Serbian (of the Ijekavian dialect)
Currency Euro = 100 cents
Website www.gov.me/en/homepage

	🛣	⩓	▲	🏭
⏲	n/a	100	80	50

80kph speed limit if towing a caravan

💺 Compulsory in front and rear seats
👶 Under 12 not allowed in front seats. Under-5s must use an appropriate child seat.
🍷 0.03 % △ Compulsory ⊞ Compulsory
💡 Compulsory 🧯 Compulsory
⊖ 18 (16 for motorbikes less than 125cc; 14 for mopeds)
🪪 International Driving Permit recommended
📱 Prohibited
🔦 Must be used at all times
❄ From mid-Nov to March, driving wheels must be fitted with winter tyres
★ An 'eco' tax vignette must be obtained when crossing the border and displayed in the upper right-hand corner of the windscreen
★ On-the-spot fines imposed
★ Tolls on some primary roads and in the Sozina tunnel between Lake Skadar and the sea
★ Visibility vest compulsory

Netherlands Nederland (NL)

Area 41,526 sq km (16,033 sq miles)
Population 17,250,000
Capital Amsterdam 2,431,000 • administrative capital 's-Gravenhage (The Hague) 1,055,000
Languages Dutch (official), Frisian
Currency Euro = 100 cents
Website www.government.nl

	🛣	⩓	▲	🏭
⏲	130	80/100	80/100	50

💺 Compulsory
👶 Under 3 must travel in the back, using an appropriate child restraint; 3–18 and under 135cm must use an appropriate child restraint. A rear-facing child seat may be used in front only if airbags are deactivated.
🍷 0.05% • 0.02% with less than 5 years experience or moped riders under 24
△ Compulsory ⊞ Recommended
💡 Recommended 🧯 Recommended ⊖ 18
📱 Only allowed with a hands-free kit
LEZ About 20 cities operate or are planning LEZs.
🔦 Recommended in poor visibility and on open roads. Compulsory for motorcycles.
★ On-the-spot fines imposed
★ Radar-detection equipment is prohibited

Norway Norge (N)

Area 323,877 sq km (125,049 sq miles)
Population 5,303,000 **Capital** Oslo (1,588,000)
Languages Norwegian (official), Lappish, Finnish
Currency Krone = 100 øre
Website www.norway.no/en/uk

	🛣	⩓	▲	🏭
⏲	90–110	80	80	30/50
If towing trailer with brakes				
⏲	80	80	80	50
If towing trailer without brakes				
⏲	60	60	60	50

💺 Compulsory in front seats and, if fitted, in rear
👶 Children less than 150cm tall must use appropriate child restraint. Children under 4 must use child safety seat or safety restraint (cot). A rear-facing child seat may be used in front only if airbags are deactivated.
🍷 0.01% △ Compulsory ⊞ Recommended
💡 Recommended 🧯 Recommended
⊖ 18 (heavy vehicles 18/21)
📱 Only allowed with a hands-free kit
🔦 Must be used at all times
❄ Winter tyres or summer tyres with snow chains compulsory for snow- or ice-covered roads
★ On-the-spot fines imposed
★ Radar-detectors are prohibited
★ Tolls apply on some bridges, tunnels and access roads into Bergen, Haugesund, Kristiensand, Oslo, Stavangar, Tonsberg and Trondheim. Several use electronic fee collection only.
★ Visibility vest compulsory

Poland Polska (PL)

Area 323,250 sq km (124,807 sq miles)
Population 38,434,000 **Capital** Warsaw / Warszawa (3,106,000) **Languages** Polish (official) **Currency** Zloty = 100 groszy **Website** www.premier.gov.pl/en.html

	🛣	⩓	▲	🏭
Motor-vehicle only roads[1], under/over 3.5 tonnes				
⏲	130[2]/80[2]	110/80	100/80	n/a
Motor-vehicle only roads[1] if towing				
⏲	n/a	80	80	n/a
Other roads, under 3.5 tonnes				
⏲	n/a	100	90	50/60[3]
Other roads, 3.5 tonnes or over				
⏲	n/a	80	70	50/60[3]
Other roads, if towing				
⏲	n/a	60	60	30

[1]Indicated by signs with white car on blue background •[2]Minimum speed 40 kph •[3]50 kph 05.00–23.00; 60 kph 23.00–05.00; 20 kph in marked residential areas

💺 Compulsory in front seats and, if fitted, in rear
👶 Under 12 and below 150 cm must use an appropriate child restraint. Rear-facing child seats not permitted in vehicles with airbags.
🍷 0.02% △ Compulsory ⊞ Recommended
💡 Recommended 🧯 Compulsory
⊖ 18 (mopeds and motorbikes under 125cc – 16)
📱 Only allowed with a hands-free kit
🔦 Compulsory for all vehicles
❄ Snow chains permitted only on roads completely covered in snow
★ On-the-spot fines imposed
★ Radar-detection equipment is prohibited
★ Vehicles over 3.5 tonnes (including cars towing caravans) must have a VIAbox for the electronic toll system
★ Visibility vests compulsory

Portugal (P)

Area 88,797 sq km (34,284 sq miles)
Population 10,291,000 **Capital** Lisbon / Lisboa (2,828,000) **Languages** Portuguese (official)
Currency Euro = 100 cents
Website www.portugal.gov.pt/en/gc21

	🛣	⩓	▲	🏭
⏲	120*	90/100	90	50/20
If towing				
⏲	100*	90	80	50

*50kph minimum; 90kph maximum if licence held under 1 year

💺 Compulsory in front seats and, if fitted, in rear
👶 Under 12 and below 135cm must travel in the rear in an appropriate child restraint; rear-facing child seats permitted in front for under 3s only if airbags deactivated
🍷 0.049% • 0.019% if full licence held less than 3 years
△ Compulsory ⊞ Recommended
💡 Recommended 🧯 Recommended ⊖ 17
🪪 MOT certificate for vehicles over 3 years old, photographic proof of identity must be carried at all times.
📱 Only allowed with hands-free kit
LEZ An LEZ prohibits vehicles without catalytic converters from certain parts of Lisbon. There are plans to extend the scheme city-wide
🔦 Compulsory for motorcycles, compulsory for other vehicles in poor visibility and tunnels
★ On-the-spot fines imposed
★ Radar detectors and dash-cams prohibited
★ Tolls on motorways; do not use green lanes, these are reserved for auto-payment users. Some motorways require an automatic toll device.
★ Visibility vest compulsory
★ Wearers of spectacles or contact lenses should carry a spare pair

Romania (RO)

Area 238,391 sq km (92,042 sq miles)
Population 19,638,000 **Capital** Bucharest / Bucuresti (2,413,000) **Languages** Romanian (official), Hungarian
Currency Romanian leu = 100 bani **Website** www.gov.ro

	🛣	⩓	▲	🏭
Cars and motorcycles				
⏲	120/130	100	90	50
Vans				
⏲	110	90	80	40
Motorcycles				
⏲	100	80	80	50

For motor vehicles with trailers or if full driving licence has been held for less than one year, speed limits are 20kph lower than those listed above •Jeep-like vehicles: 70kph outside built-up areas but 60kph in all areas if diesel. For mopeds, the speed limit is 45 kph.

💺 Compulsory
👶 Under 12s not allowed in front and must use an appropriate restraint in the rear
🍷 0.00% △ Compulsory ⊞ Compulsory
💡 Compulsory 🧯 Compulsory ⊖ 18
📱 Only allowed with hands-free kit
🔦 Compulsory outside built-up areas, compulsory everywhere for motorcycles
❄ Winter tyres compulsory Nov–Mar if roads are snow- or ice-covered, especially in mountainous areas
★ Compulsory road tax can be paid for at the border, post offices and some petrol stations. Price depends on emissions category and length of stay
★ It is illegal for vehicles to be dirty
★ On-the-spot fines imposed
★ Visibility vest compulsory

Russia Rossiya (RUS)

Area 17,075,000 sq km (6,592,800 sq miles)
Population 144,427,000 **Capital** Moscow / Moskva (17,100,000) **Languages** Russian (official), and many others
Currency Russian ruble = 100 kopeks
Website government.ru/en/

	🛣	⩓	▲	🏭
⏲	110	90	90	60/20
If licence held for under 2 years				
⏲	70	70	70	60/20

💺 Compulsory if fitted
👶 Under 12s permitted only in an appropriate child restraint
🍷 0.03 % △ Compulsory ⊞ Compulsory
💡 Compulsory 🧯 Compulsory ⊖ 17
🪪 International Driving Permit with Russian translation, visa, green card endorsed for Russia, International Certificate for Motor Vehicles
📱 Only allowed with a hands-free kit
🔦 Compulsory during the day
❄ Winter tyres compulsory 1 Dec–1 Mar
★ On-the-spot fines imposed
★ Picking up hitchhikers is prohibited
★ Radar detectors/blockers prohibited
★ Road tax payable at the border

Serbia Srbija (SRB)

Area 77,474 sq km, 29,913 sq miles **Population** 7,040,000
Capital Belgrade / Beograd (1,167,000)
Languages Serbian **Currency** Dinar = 100 paras
Website www.srbija.gov.rs

	🛣	⩓	▲	🏭
⏲	120	100	80	50
If towing				
⏲	80	80	80	50

Novice drivers limited to 90% of speed limit and not permitted to drive 11pm–5am.

💺 Compulsory in front and rear seats
👶 Age 3–12 must be in rear seats and wear seat belt or appropriate child restraint; under 3 in rear-facing child seat permitted in front only if airbag deactivated
🍷 0.029% • 0.0% for commercial drivers, motorcyclists, or if full licence held less than 1 year
△ Compulsory ⊞ Compulsory
💡 Compulsory 🧯 Compulsory
⊖ 18 (16 for motorbikes less than 125cc; 14 for mopeds)
🪪 International Driving Permit, green card, insurance that is valid for Serbia or locally bought third-party insurance
🔦 Compulsory
❄ Winter tyres compulsory Nov–Apr for vehicles up to 3.5 tonnes. Carrying snow chains recommended in winter as these may have to be fitted if driving on snow-covered roads, in accordance with signage.
★ 3-metre tow bar or rope
★ Spare wheel compulsory
★ On-the-spot fines imposed
★ Radar detectors prohibited
★ Tolls on motorways and some primary roads
★ Visibility vest compulsory

Slovakia Slovenska Republika (SK)

Area 49,012 sq km (18,923 sq miles)
Population 5,435,000 **Capital** Bratislava (656,000)
Languages Slovak (official), Hungarian
Currency Euro = 100 cents
Website www.government.gov.sk

	🛣	⩓	▲	🏭
⏲	130/90	90	90	50

💺 Compulsory
👶 Under 12 or below 150cm must be in rear in appropriate child restraint
🍷 0.0% △ Compulsory ⊞ Compulsory
💡 Compulsory 🧯 Recommended
⊖ 18, 17 for motorbikes over 50cc, 15 for mopeds
🪪 International driving permit, proof of health insurance
📱 Only allowed with a hands-free kit
🔦 Compulsory at all times
❄ Winter tyres compulsory
★ On-the-spot fines imposed
★ Radar-detection equipment is prohibited
★ Tow rope recommended
★ Vignette required for motorways, car valid for 1 year, 30 days, 7 days; lorry vignettes carry a higher charge.
★ Visibility vests compulsory

Slovenia Slovenija (SLO)

Area 20,256 sq km (7,820 sq miles) **Population** 2,067,000
Capital Ljubljana (538,000) **Languages** Slovene
Currency Euro = 100 cents **Website** www.vlada.si/en

	🛣	⩓	▲	🏭
⏲	130	110[1]	90[1]	50[2]
If towing				
⏲	80	80[1]	80[1]	50[2]

[1] 70 kph in urban areas, [2] 30 kph zones are increasingly common in cities. 50 kph in poor visibility or with snow chains

💺 Compulsory
👶 Below 150cm must use appropriate child restraint. A rear-facing baby seat may be used in front only if airbags are deactivated.
🍷 0.05% • 0.0% for commercial drivers, under 21s or with less than one year with a full licence
△ Compulsory ⊞ Compulsory
💡 Compulsory 🧯 Recommended
⊖ 18 (motorbikes up to 125cc – 16, up to 350cc – 18)
🪪 Licences without photographs must be accompanied by an International Driving Permit
📱 Only allowed with hands-free kit
🔦 Must be used at all times
❄ Snow chains or winter tyres compulsory mid-Nov to mid-March, and in wintery conditions at other times. Max speed 50 kph. This limit also applies if visibility is below 50m.
★ On-the-spot fines imposed
★ Radar detectors prohibited
★ Vignettes valid for variety of periods compulsory for vehicles below 3.5 tonnes for toll roads. Write your vehicle registration number on the vignette before displaying it. For heavier vehicles electronic tolling system applies; several routes are cargo-traffic free during high tourist season.
★ Visibility vest compulsory

Spain España (E)

Area 497,548 sq km (192,103 sq miles)
Population 46,700,000 **Capital** Madrid (6,675,000)
Languages Castilian Spanish (official), Catalan, Galician, Basque **Currency** Euro = 100 cents **Website** www.lamoncloa.gob.es/lang/en/Paginas/index.aspx

	🛣	⩓	▲	🏭
⏲	120*	100*	90	50*
If towing				
⏲	80	80	70	50*

*Urban motorways and dual carriageways 80 kph. 20 kph zones are being introduced in many cities

💺 Compulsory
👶 Under 135cm and below 12 must use appropriate child restraint and sit in rear.
🍷 0.049% • 0.029% if less than 2 years full licence or if vehicle is over 3.5 tonnes or carries more than 9 passengers
△ Two compulsory (one for in front, one for behind)
⊞ Recommended
💡 Compulsory 🧯 Recommended
⊖ 18 (21 for heavy vehicles; 16 for motorbikes up to 125cc)
📱 Hands-free only
🔦 Compulsory for motorcycles and in poor daytime visibility and in tunnels for other vehicles.
❄ Snow chains recommended for mountainous areas in winter
★ Drivers who wear spectacles or contact lenses must carry a spare pair.
★ On-the-spot fines imposed
★ Radar-detection equipment is prohibited
★ Spare wheel compulsory
★ Tolls on motorways
★ Visibility vest compulsory

Sweden Sverige (S)

Area 449,964 sq km (173,731 sq miles)
Population 10,162,000 **Capital** Stockholm (2,227,000)
Languages Swedish (official), Finnish **Currency** Swedish krona = 100 ore **Website** www.sweden.gov.se

	🛣	⩓	▲	🏭
⏲	90–120	80	70–100	30–60
If towing trailer with brakes				
⏲	80	80	70	50

💺 Compulsory in front and rear seats
👶 Under 15 or below 135cm must use an appropriate child restraint and may sit in the front only if airbag is deactivated; rear-facing baby seat permitted in front only if airbag deactivated.
🍷 0.019% △ Compulsory ⊞ Recommended
💡 Recommended 🧯 Recommended ⊖ 18
🪪 Licences without a photograph must be accompanied by photographic proof of identity, e.g. a passport
LEZ Gothenberg, Helsingborg, Lund, Malmo, Mölndal and Stockholm have LEZs, progressively prohibiting older vehicles.
🔦 Must be used at all times
❄ 1 Dec–31 Mar winter tyres, anti-freeze, screenwash additive and shovel compulsory
★ On-the-spot fines imposed
★ Radar-detection equipment is prohibited
★ Tow rope recommended
★ Visibility vest recommended

Switzerland Schweiz (CH)

Area 41,284 sq km (15,939 sq miles)
Population 8,401,000 **Capital** Bern (407,000)
Languages French, German, Italian, Romansch (all official) **Currency** Swiss Franc = 100 centimes / rappen
Website www.admin.ch

	🛣	⩓	▲	🏭
⏲	120	80	80	50/30
If towing up to 1 tonne / over 1 tonne				
⏲	80	80	80/60	50/30

💺 Compulsory
👶 Up to 12 years or below 150 cm must use an appropriate child restraint. Children 6 and under must sit in the rear.
🍷 0.05%, but 0.0% for commercial drivers or with less than three years with a full licence
△ Compulsory ⊞ Recommended
💡 Recommended 🧯 Recommended
⊖ 18 (mopeds up to 50cc – 16)
📱 Only allowed with a hands-free kit
🔦 Compulsory
❄ Winter tyres recommended Nov–Mar; snow chains compulsory in designated areas in poor winter weather
★ GPS must have fixed speed camera function deactivated; radar detectors prohibited

- ★ Motorways are all toll and for vehicles below 3.5 tonnes a vignette must be purchased at the border. The vignette is valid for one calendar year. Vehicles over 3.5 tonnes must have an electronic tag for travel on any road.
- ★ On-the-spot fines imposed
- ★ Pedestrians have right of way
- ★ Picking up hitchhikers is prohibited on motorways and main roads
- ★ Spectacles or contact lens wearers must carry a spare pair in their vehicle at all times

Turkey Türkiye (TR)

Area 774,815 sq km (299,156 sq miles)
Population 80,811,000 **Capital** Ankara (5,445,000)
Languages Turkish (official), Kurdish
Currency New Turkish lira = 100 kurus
Website www.mfa.gov.tr/default.en.mfa

	120	90	90	50
If towing				
	80	80	80	40
Motorbikes				
	80	70	70	50

- Compulsory if fitted
- Under 150 cm and below 36kg must use suitable child restraint. Under 3s can only travel in the front in a rear facing seat if the airbag is deactivated. Children 3–12 may not travel in the front seat.
- 0.00%
- Two compulsory (one in front, one behind)
- Compulsory
- Compulsory Compulsory 18
- International driving permit advised, and required for use with licences without photographs; note that Turkey is in both Europe and Asia, green card/UK insurance that covers whole of Turkey or locally bought insurance, e-visa obtained in advance.
- Prohibited
- Compulsory in daylight hours
- ★ Spare wheel compulsory
- ★ On-the-spot fines imposed
- ★ Several motorways, and the Bosphorus bridges are toll roads
- ★ Tow rope and tool kit must be carried

Ukraine Ukraina (UA)

Area 603,700 sq km (233,088 sq miles)
Population 42,418,000 **Capital** Kiev / Kyviv (3,375,000)
Languages Ukrainian (official), Russian
Currency Hryvnia = 100 kopiykas
Website www.kmu.gov.ua/control/en

	130	110	90	20/60
If towing				
	80	80	80	20/60

If driving licence held less than 2 years, must not exceed 70 kph

- Compulsory in front and rear seats
- Under 12 and below 145cm must use an appropriate child restraint and sit in rear
- 0.02% – if use of medication can be proved. Otherwise 0.00%
- Compulsory Compulsory
- Optional Compulsory 18
- International Driving Permit, visa, International Certificate for Motor Vehicles, green card
- No legislation
- Compulsory in poor daytime and from Oct–Apr
- Winter tyres compulsory Nov–Apr in snowy conditions
- ★ A road tax is payable on entry to the country.
- ★ On-the-spot fines imposed
- ★ Tow rope and tool kit recommended

United Kingdom (GB)

Area 241,857 sq km (93,381 sq miles)
Population 66,040,000
Capital London (14,040,000) **Languages** English (official), Welsh (also official in Wales), Gaelic
Currency Sterling (pound) = 100 pence
Website www.direct.gov.uk

	112	112	96	48
If towing				
	96	96	80	48

Several cities have introduced 32 kph (20 mph) zones away from main roads

- Compulsory in front seats and if fitted in rear seats
- Under 3 not allowed in front seats except with appropriate restraint, and in rear must use child restraint if available; in front 3–12 or under 135cm must use appropriate child restraint, in rear must use appropriate child restraint (or seat belt if no child restraint is available, e.g. because two occupied restraints prevent fitting of a third).
- 0.08% (England, Northern Ireland, Wales) • 0.05% (Scotland)
- Recommended Recommended
- Recommended Recommended
- 17 (16 for mopeds)
- Only allowed with hands-free kit
- LEZ London's LEZ operates by number-plate recognition; non-compliant vehicles face hefty daily charges. Foreign-registered vehicles must register.
- ★ Driving is on the left
- ★ On-the-spot fines imposed
- ★ Smoking is banned in all commercial vehicles
- ★ Some toll motorways, bridges and tunnels

Ski resorts

The resorts listed are popular ski centres, therefore road access to most is normally good and supported by road clearing during snow falls. However, mountain driving is never predictable and drivers should make sure they take suitable snow chains as well as emergency provisions and clothing. Listed for each resort are: the atlas page and grid square; the resort/minimum piste altitude (where only one figure is shown, they are at the same height) and maximum altitude of its own lifts; the number of lifts and gondolas (the total for lift-linked resorts); the season start and end dates (snow cover allowing); whether snow is augmented by cannon; the nearest town (with its distance in km) and, where available, the website and/or telephone number of the local tourist information centre or ski centre ('00' prefix required for calls from the UK).

Walking with snow shoes, La Plagne, France blickwinkel / Alamy

The ❄ symbol indicates resorts with snow cannon

Andorra

Pyrenees

Pas de la Casa / Grau Roig 91 A4 ❄ 2050–2640m • 31 lifts • Dec–Apr • Andorra La Vella (30km) www.pasdelacasa.com
• Access via Envalira Pass (2407m), highest in Pyrenees, snow chains essential.

Austria

Alps

Bad Gastein 72 A3 ❄ 1050/1100–2700m • 50 lifts • Dec–Mar • St Johann im Pongau (45km) +43 6432 3393 0 www.gastein.com/en

Bad Hofgastein 72 A3 ❄ 860–2295m • 50 lifts • Dec–Mar • St Johann im Pongau (40km) +43 6432 3393 0 www.gastein.com/en

Bad Kleinkirchheim 72 B3 ❄ 1070–2310m • 27 lifts • Dec–Mar • Villach (35km) +43 4240 8212 www.badkleinkirchheim.at

Ehrwald 71 A5 ❄ 1000–2965m • 24 lifts • Dec–Apr • Imst (30km) +43 5673 2501 0 www.wetterstein-bahnen.at/en

Innsbruck 71 A6 ❄ 574/850–3200m • 59 lifts • Dec–Apr • Innsbruck +43 512 5356 0 www.innsbruck.info/en/
• Motorway normally clear. The motorway through to Italy and through the Arlberg Tunnel are both toll roads.

Ischgl 71 A5 ❄ 1880/1400–2900m • 82 lifts • Dec–May • Landeck (25km) +43 50990 100 www.ischgl.com
• Car entry to resort prohibited between 2200hrs and 0600hrs. Lift linked to Samnaun (Switzerland).

Kaprun 72 A2 ❄ 800/770–3030m, • 25 lifts • Nov–Apr • Zell am See (10km) +43 6542 770 www.zellamsee-kaprun.com

Kirchberg in Tirol 72 A2 ❄ 860–2000m • 197 lifts • Nov–Apr • Kitzbühel (6km) +43 57507 2100 www.kitzbueheler-alpen.com/en
• Easily reached from Munich International Airport (120 km)

Kitzbühel (Brixen im Thale) 72 A2 ❄ 800/790–2000m • 197 lifts • Dec–Apr • Wörgl (40km) +43 57057 2000 www.kitzbueheler-alpen.com/en

Lech/Oberlech 71 A5 ❄ 1450–2810m • 97 lifts • Dec–Apr • Bludenz (50km) +43 5583 2161 0 www.lechzuers.com
• Roads normally cleared but keep chains accessible because of altitude. Linked to the other Arlberg resorts.

Mayrhofen 72 A1 ❄ 630–2500m • 57 lifts • Dec–Apr • Jenbach (35km) +43 5285 6760 www.mayrhofen.at
• Chains rarely required.

Obertauern 72 A3 ❄ 1740/1640–2350m • 26 lifts • Dec–Apr • Radstadt (20km) +43 6456 7252 www.obertauern.com
• Roads normally cleared but chain accessibility recommended. Camper vans and caravans not allowed; park these in Radstadt

Saalbach Hinterglemm 72 A2 ❄ 1000/1030–2100m • 52 lifts • Nov–Apr • Zell am See (19km) +43 6541 6800-68 www.saalbach.com *• Both village centres are pedestrianised and there is a good ski bus service during the daytime*

St Anton am Arlberg 71 A5 ❄ 1300–2810m • 97 lifts • Dec–Apr • Innsbruck (104km) +43 5446 22690 www.stantonamarlberg.com
• Linked to the other Arlberg resorts.

Schladming 72 A3 ❄ 745–1900m • 45 lifts • Dec–Mar • Schladming + 43 36 87 233 10 www.schladming-dachstein.at

Serfaus 71 A5 ❄ 1427/1200–2820m • 68 lifts • Dec–Apr • Landeck (30km) +43 5476 6239 www.serfaus-fiss-ladis.at
• Private vehicles banned from village. Use Dorfbahn Serfaus, an underground funicular that runs on an air cushion.

Sölden 71 B6 ❄ 1380–3250m, • 33 lifts • Oct–Apr • Imst (50km) +43 57200 200 www.soelden.com
• Roads normally cleared but snow chains recommended because of altitude. The route from Italy and the south over the Timmelsjoch via Obergurgl is closed Oct–May and anyone arriving from the south should use the Brenner Pass motorway.

Zell am See 72 A2 ❄ 750–1950m • 28 lifts • Dec–Mar • Zell am See +43 6542 770 www.zellamsee-kaprun.com
• Low altitude, so good access and no mountain passes to cross.

Zell im Zillertal (Zell am Ziller) 72 A1 ❄ 580/930–2410m • 22 lifts • Dec–Apr • Jenbach (25km) +43 5282 7165–226 www.zillertalarena.com

Zürs 71 A5 ❄ 1720/1700–2450m • 87 lifts • Dec–Apr • Bludenz (30km) +43 5583 2161 251 www.lechzuers.com
• Roads normally cleared but keep chains accessible because of altitude. Village has garage with 24-hour self-service gas/petrol, breakdown service and wheel chains supply. Linked to the other Arlberg resorts.

France

Alps

Alpe d'Huez 79 A5 ❄ 1860–3330m • 85 lifts • Dec–Apr • Grenoble (63km) www.alpedhuez.com
• Snow chains may be required on access road to resort.

Avoriaz 70 B1 ❄ 1800/1100–2280m • 35 lifts • Dec–May • Morzine (14km) +33 4 50 74 02 11 www.avoriaz.com/en
• Chains may be required for access road from Morzine. Car-free resort, park on edge of village.

Chamonix-Mont-Blanc 70 C1 ❄ 1035–3840m • 49 lifts • Dec–Apr • Martigny (38km) www.chamonix.com

Chamrousse 79 A4 ❄ 1700/1420–2250m • 26 lifts • Dec–Apr • Grenoble (30km) www.chamrousse.com
• Roads normally cleared, keep chains accessible because of altitude.

Châtel 70 B1 ❄ 1200/1110–2200m • 41 lifts • Dec–Apr • Thonon-Les-Bains (35km) +33 4 50 73 22 44 www.chatel.com

Courchevel 70 C1 ❄ 1300–2470m • 67 lifts • Dec–Apr • Moûtiers (23km) www.courchevel.com
• Roads normally cleared but keep chains accessible. Traffic 'discouraged' within the four resort bases.

Flaine 70 B1 ❄ 1600–2500m • 26 lifts • Dec–Apr • Cluses (25km) +33 4 50 90 80 01 www.flaine.com
• Keep chains accessible for D6 from Cluses to Flaine. Car access for depositing luggage and passengers only. 1500-space car park outside resort. Near Sixt-Fer-á-Cheval.

La Clusaz 69 C6 ❄ 1100–2600m • 55 lifts • Dec–Apr • Annecy (32km) www.laclusaz.com *• Roads normally clear but keep chains accessible for final road from Annecy.*

La Plagne 70 C1 ❄ 2500/1250–3250m • 109 lifts • Dec–Apr Moûtiers (32km) www.la-plagne.com
• Ten different centres up to 2100m altitude. Road access via Bozel, Landry or Aime normally cleared. Linked to Les Arcs by cablecar

Les Arcs 70 C1 ❄ 1600/1200–3230m • 77 lifts • Dec–May • Bourg-St-Maurice (15km) +33 4 79 07 12 57 www.lesarcs.com
• Four base areas up to 2000 metres; keep chains accessible. Pay parking at edge of each base resort. Linked to La Plagne by cablecar

Les Carroz d'Araches 70 B1 ❄ 1140–2500m • 80 lifts • Dec–Apr • Cluses (13km) http://winter.lescarroz.com

Les Deux-Alpes 79 B5 ❄ 1650/1300–3600m • 55 lifts • Dec–Apr • Grenoble (75km) +33 4 76 79 22 00 www.les2alpes.com/en *• Roads normally cleared, however snow chains recommended for D213 up from valley road (D1091).*

Les Gets 70 B1 ❄ 1170/1000–2000m • 52 lifts • Dec–Apr • Cluses (18km) +33 4 50 74 74 74 www.lesgets.com

Les Ménuires 69 C6 ❄ 1815/1850–3200m • 40 lifts • Dec–Apr • Moûtiers (27km) www.lesmenuires.com
• Keep chains accessible for D117 from Moûtiers.

Les Sept Laux Prapoutel 69 C6 ❄ 1350–2400m, • 24 lifts • Dec–Apr • Grenoble (38km) www.les7laux.com (in French only)
• Roads normally cleared, however keep chains accessible for mountain road up from the A41 motorway. Near St Sorlin d'Arves.

Megève 69 C6 ❄ 1100/1050–2350m • 79 lifts • Dec–Apr • Sallanches (12km) www.megeve.com

Méribel 69 C6 ❄ 1400/1100–2950m • 61 lifts • Dec–May • Moûtiers (18km) +33 4 79 08 60 01 www.meribel.net
• Keep chains accessible for 18km to resort on D90 from Moûtiers.

Morzine 70 B1 ❄ 1000–2460m • 67 lifts, • Dec–Apr • Thonon-Les-Bains (30km) +33 4 50 74 72 72 http://en.morzine-avoriaz.com

Pra Loup 79 B5 ❄ 1500–2600m • 53 lifts • Dec–Apr • Barcelonnette (10km) www.praloup.com
• Roads normally cleared but chains accessibility recommended.

Risoul 79 B5 ❄ 1850/1650–2750m • 59 lifts • Dec–Apr • Briançon (40km) +33 4 92 46 02 60 www.risoul.com
• Keep chains accessible. Near Guillestre. Linked with Vars Les Claux

St-Gervais Mont-Blanc 70 C1 ❄ 850/1150–2350m • 27 lifts • Dec–Apr • Sallanches (10km) +33 4 50 47 76 08 www.saintgervais.com/en

Serre Chevalier 79 B5 ❄ 1350/1200–2800m • 77 lifts • Dec–Apr • Briançon (10km) + 33 4 92 24 98 98 www.serre-chevalier.com *• Made up of 13 small villages along the valley road, which is normally cleared.*

Tignes 70 C1 ❄ 2100/1550–3450m • 87 lifts • Jan–Dec • Bourg St Maurice (26km) +33 4 79 40 04 40 www.tignes.net
• Keep chains accessible because of altitude. Linked to Val d'Isère.

Val d'Isère 70 C1 ❄ 1850/1550–3450m • 87 lifts • Dec–Apr • Bourg-St-Maurice (30km) www.valdisere.com
• Roads normally cleared but keep chains accessible.

Val Thorens 69 C6 ❄ 2300/1850–3200m • 29 lifts • Dec–Apr • Moûtiers (37km) +33 4 79 00 08 08 www.les3vallees.com/en/ski-resort/val-thorens
• Chains essential – highest ski resort in Europe. Obligatory paid parking on edge of resort.

Valloire 69 C6 ❄ 1430–2600m • 34 lifts • Dec–Apr • Modane (20km) +33 4 79 59 03 96 www.valloire.net
• Road normally clear up to the Col du Galbier, to the south of the resort, which is closed from 1st November to 1st June. Linked to Valmeinier.

Valmeinier 69 C6 ❄ 1500–2600m • 34 lifts • Dec–Apr • St Michel de Maurienne (47km) www.valmeinier.com
• Access from north on D1006 / D902. Col du Galbier, to the south of the resort closed from 1st November to 1st June. Linked to Valloire.

Valmorel 69 C6 ❄ 1400–2550m • 90 lifts • Dec–Apr • Moûtiers (15km) www.valmorel.com
• Near St Jean-de-Belleville. Linked with ski areas of Doucy-Combelouvière and St François-Longchamp.

Vars Les Claux 79 B5 ❄ 1850/1650–2750m • 59 lifts • Dec–Apr • Briançon (40km) +33 4 92 46 51 31 www.vars.com/en/winter *• Four base resorts up to 1850 metres. Keep chains accessible. Linked with Risoul.*

Villard de Lans 79 A4 ❄ 1050/1160–2170m • 28 lifts • Dec–Apr • Grenoble (32km) +33 4 76 95 10 38 www.villarddelans.com

Pyrenees

Font-Romeu 91 A5 ❄ 1800/1600–2200m • 25 lifts • Nov–Apr • Perpignan (87km) www.font-romeu.fr
• Roads normally cleared but keep chains accessible.

Saint-Lary Soulan 77 D3 ❄ 830/1650/1700–2515m • 31 lifts • Dec–Mar • Tarbes (75km) +33 5 62 39 50 81 www.saintlary.com *• Access roads constantly cleared of snow.*

Vosges

La Bresse-Hohneck 60 B2 ❄ 600–1370m • 33 lifts • Dec–Mar • Cornimont (6km) +33 3 29 25 41 29 www.labresse.net

Germany

Alps

Garmisch-Partenkirchen 71 A6 ❄ 700–2830m · 38 lifts · Dec–Apr · Munich (95km) · ☎+49 8821 180 700 🖵www.gapa.de
· Roads usually clear, chains rarely needed.

Oberaudorf 62 C3 ❄ 480–1850m · 30 lifts · Dec–Apr · Kufstein (15km) 🖵www.oberaudorf.de
· Motorway normally kept clear. Near Bayrischzell.

Oberstdorf 71 A5 820/830–2200m · 26 lifts · Dec–Apr · Sonthofen (15km) ☎+49 8322 7000 🖵www.oberstdorf.de

Rothaargebirge

Winterberg 51 B4 ❄ 700/620–830m · 19 lifts · Dec–Mar · Brilon (30km) ☎+49 2981 925 00
🖵www.winterberg.de (German only)
· Roads usually cleared, chains rarely required.

Greece

Central Greece

Mount Parnassos: Kelaria-Fterolakka 116 D4 1640–2260m · 14 lifts · Dec–Apr · Amfiklia
🖵www.parnassos-ski.gr (Greek only)

Mount Parnassos: Gerondovrahos 116 D4 1800–1900m · 3 lifts · Dec–Apr · Amfiklia ☎+30 29444 70371

Peloponnisos

Mount Helmos: Kalavrita Ski Centre 117 D4 1650–2100m · 7 lifts · Dec–Mar · Kalavrita ☎+30 276920 24451-2
🖵www.kalavrita-ski.gr (in Greek only)

Mount Menalo: Ostrakina 117 E4 1500–1600m · 4 lifts · Dec–Mar · Tripoli ☎+30 27960 22227

Macedonia

Mount Falakro: Agio Pnevma 116 A6 1720/1620–2230m · 7 lifts · Dec–Apr · Drama ☎+ 30 25210 23691

Mount Vermio: Seli 116 B4 1500–1900m · 8 lifts · Dec–Mar · Kozani ☎+30 23310 26237 🖵www.seli-ski.gr (in Greek)

Mount Vermio: Tria-Pente Pigadia 116 B3 ❄ 1420–2005m · 5 lifts · Dec–Mar · Ptolemaida ☎+30 23320 44464

Mount Verno: Vigla 116 B3 1650–1900m · 5 lifts · Dec–Mar · Florina ☎+30 23850 22354
🖵www.vigla-ski.gr (in Greek)

Mount Vrondous: Lailias 116 A5 1600–1850m · 4 lifts · Dec–Mar · Serres ☎+30 23210 53790

Thessalia

Mount Pilio: Agriolefkes 116 C5 1300–1500m · 5 lifts · Dec–Mar · Volos ☎+30 24280 73719

Italy

Alps

Bardonecchia 79 A5 ❄ 1312–2750m · 21 lifts · Dec–Apr · Bardonecchia 🖵www.bardonecchiaski.com · Resort reached through the 11km Frejus tunnel from France, roads normally cleared.

Bórmio 71 B5 ❄ 1200/1230–3020m · 24 lifts · Dec–Apr · Tirano (40km) 🖵www.bormio.com · Tolls payable in Ponte del Gallo Tunnel, open 0800hrs–2000hrs.

Breuil-Cervinia 70 C2 ❄ 2050–3500m · 21 lifts · Jan–Dec · Aosta (54km) ☎+39 166 944311 🖵www.cervinia.it
· Snow chains strongly recommended. Bus from Milan airport.

Courmayeur 70 C1 ❄ 1200–2760m · 21 lifts · Dec–Apr · Aosta (40km) 🖵www.courmayeurmontblanc.it
· Access through the Mont Blanc tunnel from France. Roads constantly cleared.

Limone Piemonte 80 B1 ❄ 1000/1050–2050m · 29 lifts · Dec–Apr · Cuneo (27km) 🖵www.limoneturismo.it
· Roads normally cleared, chains rarely required.

Livigno 71 B5 ❄ 1800–3000m · 31 lifts · Nov–May · Zernez (CH) (27km) 🖵www.livigno.com
· Keep chains accessible. The traffic direction through Munt la Schera Tunnel to/from Zernez is regulated on Saturdays. Check in advance.

Sestrière 79 B5 ❄ 2035/1840–2840m · 92 lifts · Dec–Apr · Oulx (22km) 🖵www.sestriere-online.com
· One of Europe's highest resorts; although roads are normally cleared keep chains accessible.

Appennines

Roccaraso – Aremogna 103 B7 ❄ 1285/1240–2140m · 24 lifts · Dec–Apr · Castel di Sangro (7km)
🖵https://roccaraso.net (Italian only)

Dolomites

Andalo – Fai della Paganella 71 B5 ❄
1042/1050/2125m · 17 lifts · Dec–Apr · Trento (40km)
🖵www.visitdolomitipaganella.it ☎+39 461 585836

Arabba 72 B1 ❄ 1600/1450–2950m · 29 lifts · Dec–Mar · Brunico (45km) ☎+39 436 79130 🖵www.arabba.it
· Roads normally cleared but keep chains accessible.

Cortina d'Ampezzo 72 B2 ❄ 1224/1050–2930m · 37 lifts · Dec–Apr · Belluno (72km) ☎+39 436 869086
🖵www.dolomiti.org/it/cortina · Access from north on route 51 over the Cimabanche Pass may require chains.

Corvara (Alta Badia) 72 B1 ❄ 1568–2500m · 56 lifts · Dec–Apr · Brunico (38km) 🖵www.altabadia.it
· Roads normally clear but keep chains accessible.

Madonna di Campiglio 71 B5 ❄ 1550/1500–2600m · 72 lifts · Dec–Apr · Trento (60km) ☎+39 465 447501
🖵www.campigliodolomiti.it/homepage
· Roads normally cleared but keep chains accessible. Linked to Folgarida and Marilleva.

Moena di Fassa (Sorte/Ronchi) 72 B1 ❄
1184/1450–2520m · 8 lifts · Dec–Apr · Bolzano (40km)
🖵www.fassa.com

Selva di Val Gardena/Wolkenstein Groden 72 B1 ❄ 1563/1570–2450m · 81 lifts · Dec–Apr · Bolzano (40km)
☎+39 471 777777 🖵www.valgardena.it
· Roads normally cleared but keep chains accessible.

Norway

Hemsedal 32 B5 ❄ 700/640–1450m · 24 lifts · Nov–May · Honefoss (150km) ☎+47 32 055030 🖵www.hemsedal.com
· Be prepared for extreme weather conditions.

Slovakia

Chopok (Jasna-Chopok) 65 B5 ❄ 900/950–1840m · 17 lifts · Dec–Apr · Jasna ☎+421 907 886644 🖵www.jasna.sk

Donovaly 65 B5 ❄ 913–1360m · 17 lifts · Nov–Apr · Ruzomberok ☎+421 48 4199900 🖵www.parksnow.sk/zima/en

Martinské Hole 65 A4 1250/1150–1456m · 8 lifts · Nov–May · Zilina ☎+421 43 430 6000 🖵http://leto.martinky.com/sk (Slovak only)

Plejsy 65 B6 470–912m · 9 lifts · Dec–Mar · Krompachy ☎+421 53 429 8015 🖵www.plejsy.sk

Strbske Pleso 65 A6 1380–1825m · 7 lifts · Dec–Mar · Poprad ☎+421 917 682 260 🖵www.vt.sk

Slovenia

Julijske Alpe

Kanin (Bovec) 72 B3 460/1690–2293m · 5 lifts · Dec–Apr · Bovec 🖵www.boveckanin.si

Kranjska Gora 72 B3 ❄ 800–1210m · 19 lifts · Dec–Mar · Kranjska Gora ☎+386 4 5809 440 🖵www.kranjska-gora.si

Vogel 72 B3 570–1800m · 8 lifts · Dec–Apr · Bohinjska Bistrica ☎+386 4 5729 712 🖵www.vogel.si

Kawiniške Savinjske Alpe

Krvavec 73 B4 ❄ 1450–1970m · 10 lifts · Dec–Apr · Kranj ☎ 386 4 25 25 911 🖵http://www.rtc-krvavec.si/en

Pohorje

Rogla 73 B5 1517/1050–1500m · 13 lifts · Dec–Apr · Slovenska Bistrica ☎+386 3 75 77 100 🖵www.rogla.eu/en

Spain

Pyrenees

Baqueira-Beret/Bonaigua 90 A3 ❄ 1500–2500m · 33 lifts · Dec–Apr · Vielha (15km) ☎+34 902 415 415 🖵www.baqueira.es
· Roads normally clear but keep chains accessible. Near Salardú.

Sistema Penibetico

Sierra Nevada 100 B2 ❄ 2100–3300m · 24 lifts · Dec–May · Granada (32km) ☎+34 902 70 80 90 🖵http://sierranevada.es
· Access road designed to be avalanche safe and is snow cleared.

Sweden

Idre Fjäll 115 F9 ❄ 590–890m · 33 lifts · Nov–Apr · Mora (140km) ☎+46 253 41000 🖵www.idrefjall.se
· Be prepared for extreme weather conditions.

Sälen 34 A5 360m · 100 lifts · Nov–Apr · Malung (70km) ☎+46 771 84 00 00 🖵www.skistar.com/salen
· Be prepared for extreme weather conditions.

Switzerland

Alps

Adelboden 70 B2 1353m · 55 lifts · Dec–Apr · Frutigen (15km) ☎+41 33 673 80 80 🖵www.adelboden.ch · Linked with Lenk.

Arosa 71 B4 1800/1740–2650m · 16 lifts · Dec–Apr · Chur (30km) ☎+41 81 378 70 20 🖵www.arosa.ch
· Roads cleared but keep chains accessible due to high altitude.

Crans Montana 70 B2 ❄ 1500–3000m · 34 lifts · Dec–Apr, Jul–Oct · Sierre (15km) ☎+41 848 22 10 12
🖵www.crans-montana.ch · Roads normally cleared but keep chains accessible for ascent from Sierre.

Davos 71 B4 ❄ 1560/1100–2840m · 38 lifts · Nov–Apr · Davos. ☎+41 81 415 21 21 🖵www.davos.ch

Engelberg 70 B3 ❄ 1000/1050–3020m · 26 lifts · Nov–May · Luzern (39km) ☎+41 41 639 77 77 🖵www.engelberg.ch
· Straight access road normally cleared.

Flums (Flumserberg) 71 A4 ❄ 1400/1000–2220m · 17 lifts · Dec–Apr · Buchs (25km) ☎+41 81 720 18 18
🖵www.flumserberg.ch
· Roads normally cleared, but 1000-metre vertical ascent; keep chains accessible.

Grindelwald 70 B3 ❄ 1050–2950m · 39 lifts · Dec–Apr · Interlaken (20km) ☎+41 33 854 12 12
🖵www.jungfraregion.ch · Linked with Wengen.

Gstaad – Saanenland 70 B2 ❄ 1050/950–3000m · 74 lifts · Dec–Apr · Gstaad ☎+41 33 748 81 81 🖵www.gstaad.ch
· Linked to Anzère.

Klosters 71 B4 ❄ 1191/1110–2840m · 52 lifts · Dec–Apr · Davos (10km). ☎+41 81 410 20 20 🖵www.davos.ch/klosters
· Roads normally clear but keep chains accessible.

Leysin 70 B2 ❄ 2260–2330m · 16 lifts · Dec–Apr · Aigle (6km) ☎+41 24 493 33 00 🖵www.aigle-leysin-lesmosses.ch

Mürren 70 B2 ❄ 1650–2970m · 12 lifts · Dec–Apr · Interlaken (18km) ☎+41 33 856 86 86 🖵www.muerren.ch
· No road access. Park in Strechelberg (1500 free places) and take the two-stage cable car.

Nendaz 70 B2 ❄ 1365/1400–3300m · 20 lifts · Nov–Apr · Sion (16km) ☎+41 27 289 55 89 🖵www.nendaz.ch
· Roads normally cleared, however keep chains accessible for ascent from Sion. Near Vex.

Saas-Fee 70 B2 ❄ 1800–3500m · 23 lifts · Jan–Dec · Brig (35km) ☎+41 27 958 18 58 🖵www.saas-fee.ch/en/
· Roads normally cleared but keep chains accessible because of altitude.

St Moritz 71 B4 ❄ 1856/1730–3300m · 24 lifts · Nov–May · Chur (89km) ☎+41 81 837 33 33 🖵www.stmoritz.ch
· Roads normally cleared but keep chains accessible.

Samnaun 71 B5 ❄ 1846/1400–2900m · 82 lifts · Dec–May · Scuol (30km) ☎+41 81 861 88 30 🖵www.engadin.com/en
· Roads normally cleared but keep chains accessible. Lift linked to Ischgl (Austria).

Verbier 70 B2 ❄ 1500–3330m · 17 lifts · Nov–Apr · Martigny (27km) ☎+41 27 775 38 88 🖵www.verbier.ch
· Roads normally cleared.

Villars-Gryon 70 B2 ❄ 1253/1200–2100m · 16 lifts · Dec–Apr, Jun–Jul · Montreux (35km) ☎+41 24 495 32 32
🖵www.villars.ch · Roads normally cleared but keep chains accessible for ascent from N9. Near Bex.

Wengen 70 B2 ❄ 1270–2320m · 39 lifts · Dec–Apr · Interlaken (12km) ☎+41 33 856 85 85 🖵http://wengen.ch
· No road access. Park at Lauterbrunnen and take mountain railway. Linked with Grindelwald.

Zermatt 70 B2 ❄ 1620–3900m · 40 lifts · all year · Brig (42km) ☎+41 27 966 81 00 🖵www.zermatt.ch
· Cars not permitted in resort, park in Täsch (3km) and take shuttle train.

Turkey

North Anatolian Mountains

Uludag 118 B4 1770–2320m · 15 lifts · Dec–Mar · Bursa (36km) 🖵http://skiingturkey.com/resorts/uludag.html

To the best of the Publisher's knowledge the information in this table was correct at the time of going to press. No responsibility can be accepted for any errors or their consequences.

Skiing near Valmorel, France
Jacques Pierre / hemis.fr / Alamy

Distances

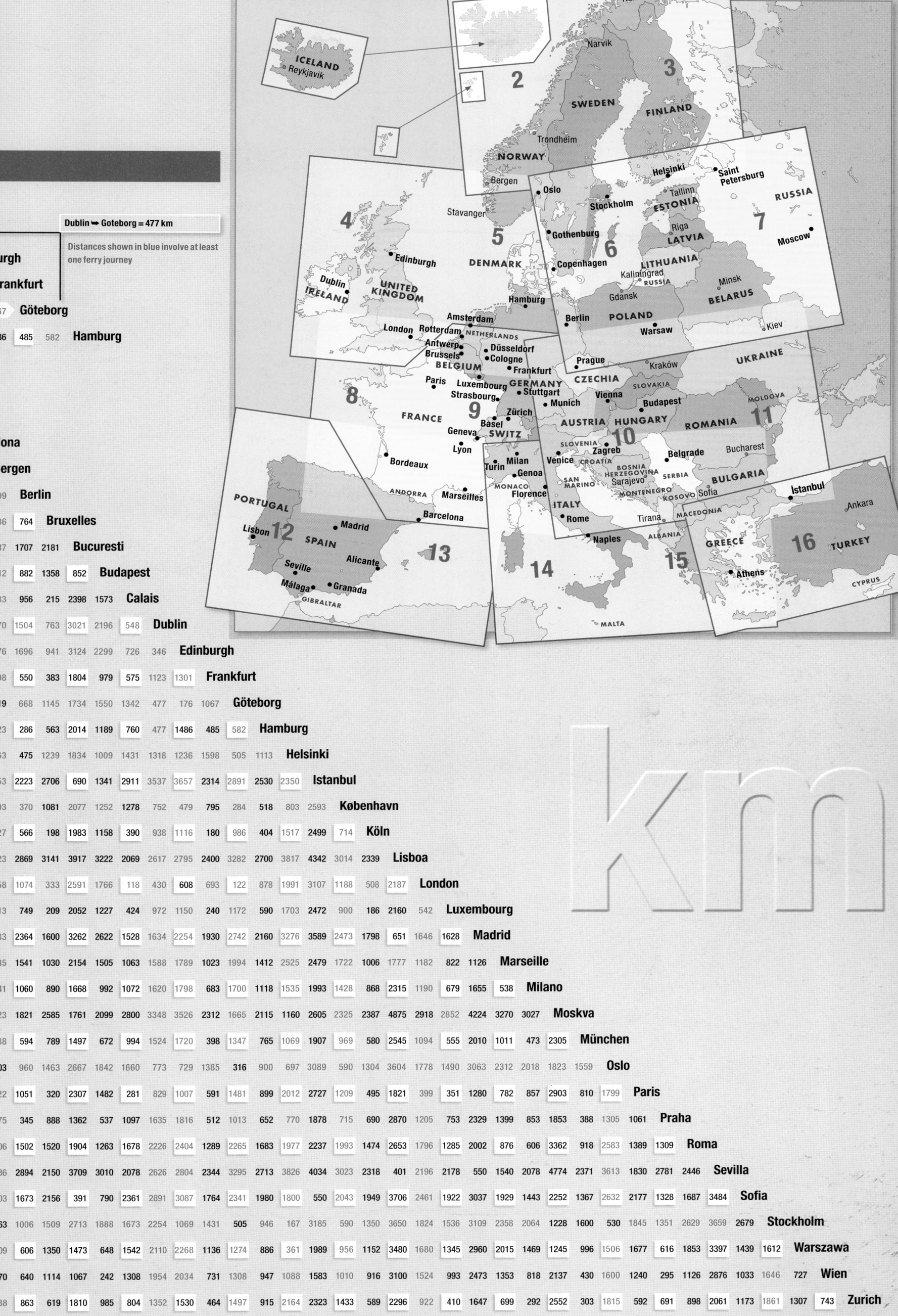

1 : 3 200 000 map pages

Calais

548	**Dublin**				
726	346	**Edinburgh**			
575	1123	1301	**Frankfurt**		
1342	477	176	1067	**Göteborg**	
1189	760	477	1486	485	582	**Hamburg**

Dublin → Goteborg = 477 km

Distances shown in blue involve at least one ferry journey

Amsterdam

2945	**Athina**
1505	3192	**Barcelona**
1484	3742	2803	**Bergen**
650	2412	1863	1309	**Berlin**
197	2895	1308	1586	764	**Bruxelles**
2245	1219	2644	3037	1707	2181	**Bucuresti**
1420	1530	1999	2212	882	1358	852	**Budapest**
367	3100	1269	1783	956	215	2398	1573	**Calais**
533	3630	1817	270	1504	763	3021	2196	548	**Dublin**
1093	3826	1995	176	1696	941	3124	2299	726	346	**Edinburgh**
441	2499	1313	1508	550	383	1804	979	575	1123	1301	**Frankfurt**
1029	3080	2362	819	668	1145	1734	1550	1342	477	176	1067	**Göteborg**
447	2719	1780	1023	286	563	2014	1189	760	477	1486	485	582	**Hamburg**
1560	2539	2338	1063	475	1239	1834	1009	1431	1318	1236	1598	505	1113	**Helsinki**
2756	1145	2990	3653	2223	2706	690	1341	2911	3537	3657	2314	2891	2530	2350	**Istanbul**
965	2782	2090	1103	370	1081	2077	1252	1278	752	479	795	284	518	803	2593	**København**
256	2684	1376	1427	566	198	1983	1158	390	938	1116	180	986	404	1517	2499	714	**Köln**
2331	4460	1268	3723	2869	3141	3917	3222	2069	2617	2795	2400	3282	2700	3817	4342	3014	2339	**Lisboa**
480	3200	1387	458	1074	333	2591	1766	118	430	608	693	122	878	1991	3107	1188	508	2187	**London**
406	2661	1190	1613	749	209	2052	1227	424	972	1150	240	1172	590	1703	2472	900	186	2160	542	**Luxembourg**
1790	3809	617	3183	2364	1600	3262	2622	1528	1634	2254	1930	2742	2160	3276	3589	2473	1798	651	1646	1628	**Madrid**
1210	2683	509	2435	1541	1030	2154	1505	1063	1588	1789	1023	1994	1412	2525	2479	1722	1006	1777	1182	822	1126	**Marseille**
1085	2182	1038	2141	1060	890	1668	992	1072	1620	1798	683	1700	1118	1535	1993	1428	868	2315	1190	679	1655	538	**Milano**
2457	2930	3655	2223	1821	2585	1761	2099	2800	3348	3526	2312	1665	2115	1160	2605	2325	2387	4875	2918	2852	4224	3270	3027	**Moskva**
839	2106	1340	1788	594	789	1497	672	994	1524	1720	398	1347	765	1069	1907	969	580	2545	1094	555	2010	1011	473	2305	**München**
1347	3372	2680	503	960	1463	2667	1842	1660	773	729	1385	316	900	697	3089	590	1304	3604	1778	1490	3063	2312	2018	1823	1559	**Oslo**
510	2917	988	1922	1051	320	2307	1482	281	829	1007	591	1481	899	2012	2727	1209	495	1821	399	351	1280	782	857	2903	810	1799	**Paris**
950	2067	1750	1675	345	888	1362	537	1097	1635	1816	512	1013	652	770	1878	715	690	2870	1205	753	2329	1399	853	1853	388	1305	1061	**Praha**
1691	1140	1385	2706	1502	1520	1904	1263	1678	2226	2404	1289	2265	1683	1977	2237	1993	1474	2653	1796	1285	2002	876	606	3362	918	2583	1389	1309	**Roma**
2347	4223	1031	3736	2894	2150	3709	3010	2078	2626	2804	2344	3295	2713	3826	4034	3023	2318	401	2196	2178	550	1540	2078	4774	2371	3613	1830	2781	2446	**Sevilla**
2206	828	2453	3103	1673	2156	391	790	2361	2891	3087	1764	2341	1980	1800	550	2043	1949	3706	2461	1922	3037	1929	1443	2252	1367	2632	2177	1328	1687	3484	**Sofia**
1393	3418	2726	1063	1006	1509	2713	1888	1673	2254	1069	1431	505	946	167	3185	590	1350	3650	1824	1536	3109	2358	2064	1228	1600	530	1845	1351	2629	3659	2679	**Stockholm**
1256	2128	2366	1909	606	1350	1473	648	1542	2110	2268	1136	1274	886	361	1989	956	1152	3480	1680	1345	2960	2015	1469	1245	996	1506	1677	616	1853	3397	1439	1612	**Warszawa**
1168	1772	1856	1970	640	1114	1067	242	1308	1954	2034	731	1308	947	1088	1583	1010	916	3100	1524	993	2473	1353	818	2137	430	1600	1240	295	1126	2876	1033	1646	727	**Wien**
816	2426	1030	1938	863	619	1810	985	804	1352	1530	464	1497	915	2164	2323	1433	589	2296	922	410	1647	699	292	2552	303	1815	592	691	898	2061	1173	1861	1307	743	**Zurich**

km

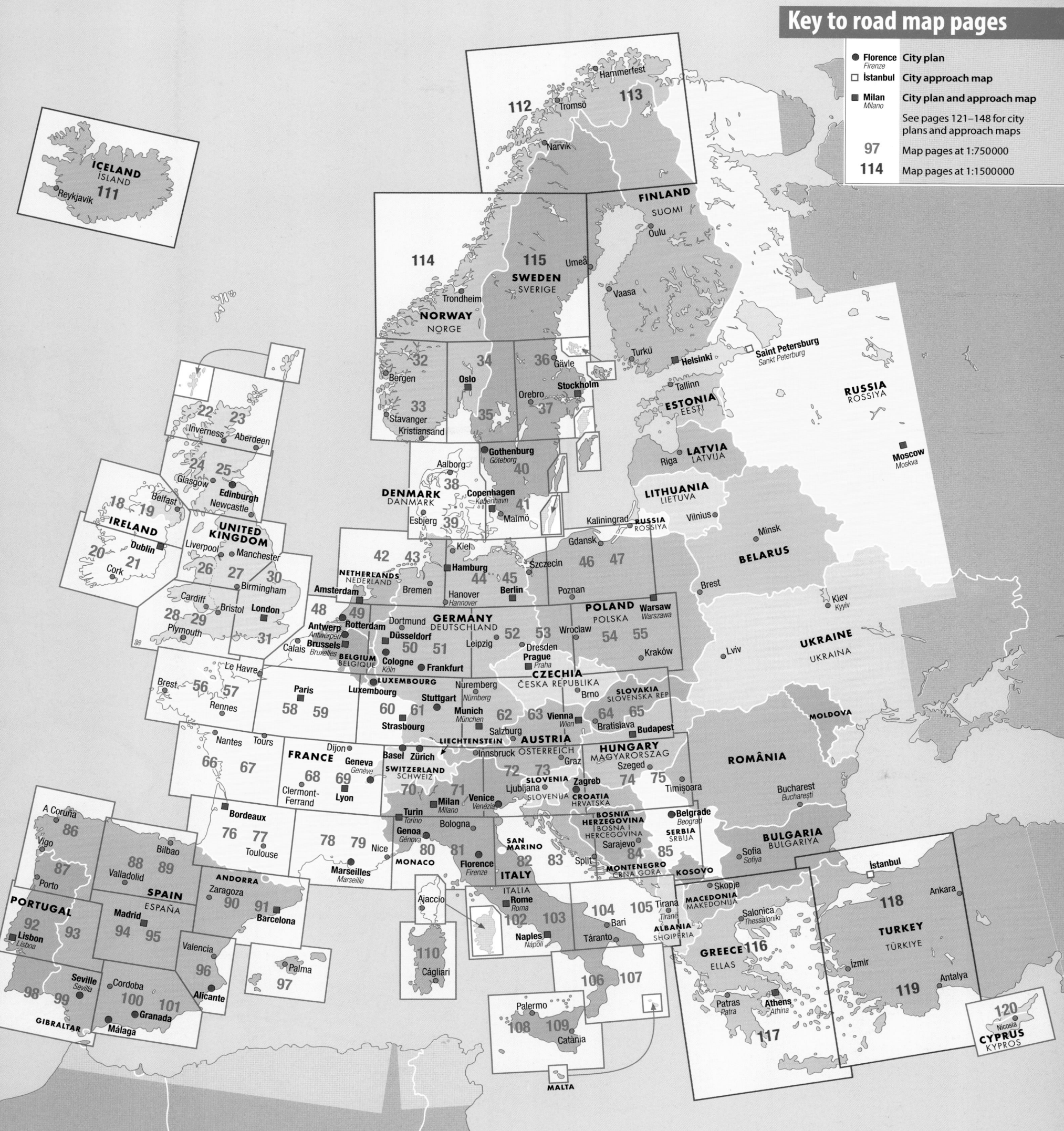

Key to road map pages

- ● Florence *Firenze* — City plan
- ☐ İstanbul — City approach map
- ▪ Milan *Milano* — City plan and approach map

See pages 121–148 for city plans and approach maps

97 — Map pages at 1:750000

114 — Map pages at 1:1500000

Motorway vignettes

Some countries require you to purchase (and in some cases display) a vignette before using motorways.

In Austria you will need to purchase and display a vignette on the inside of your windscreen. Vignettes are available for purchase at border crossings and petrol stations. More details from www.asfinag.at/toll/toll-sticker

In Belarus all vehicles over 3.5 tonnes and cars and vans under 3.5 tonnes registered outside the Eurasion Economic Union are required to have a BelToll unit installed. This device exchanges data with roadside gantries, enabling motorway tolls to be automatically deducted from the driver's account. http://beltoll.by/index.php/en/

In Czechia, you can buy a vignette at the border and also at petrol stations. Make sure you write your vehicle registration number on the vignette before displaying it. The roads without toll are indicated by a traffic sign saying "Bez poplatku". More details from www.motorway.cz

In Hungary a new e-vignette system was introduced in 2008. It is therefore no longer necessary to display the vignette, though you should make doubly sure the information you give on your vehicle is accurate. Vignettes are sold at petrol stations throughout the country. Buy online at http://toll-charge.hu/

In Slovakia, an electronic vignette must purchased before using the motorways. Vignettes may be purchased online, via a mobile app or at Slovak border crossings and petrol stations displaying the 'eznamka' logo. More details from https://eznamka.sk/selfcare/home/

In Switzerland, you will need to purchase and display a vignette before you drive on the motorway. Bear in mind you will need a separate vignette if you are towing a caravan. www.ezv.admin.ch/ezv/en/home/information-individuals/documents-for-travellers-and-road-taxes/motorway-charge-sticker--vignette-.html

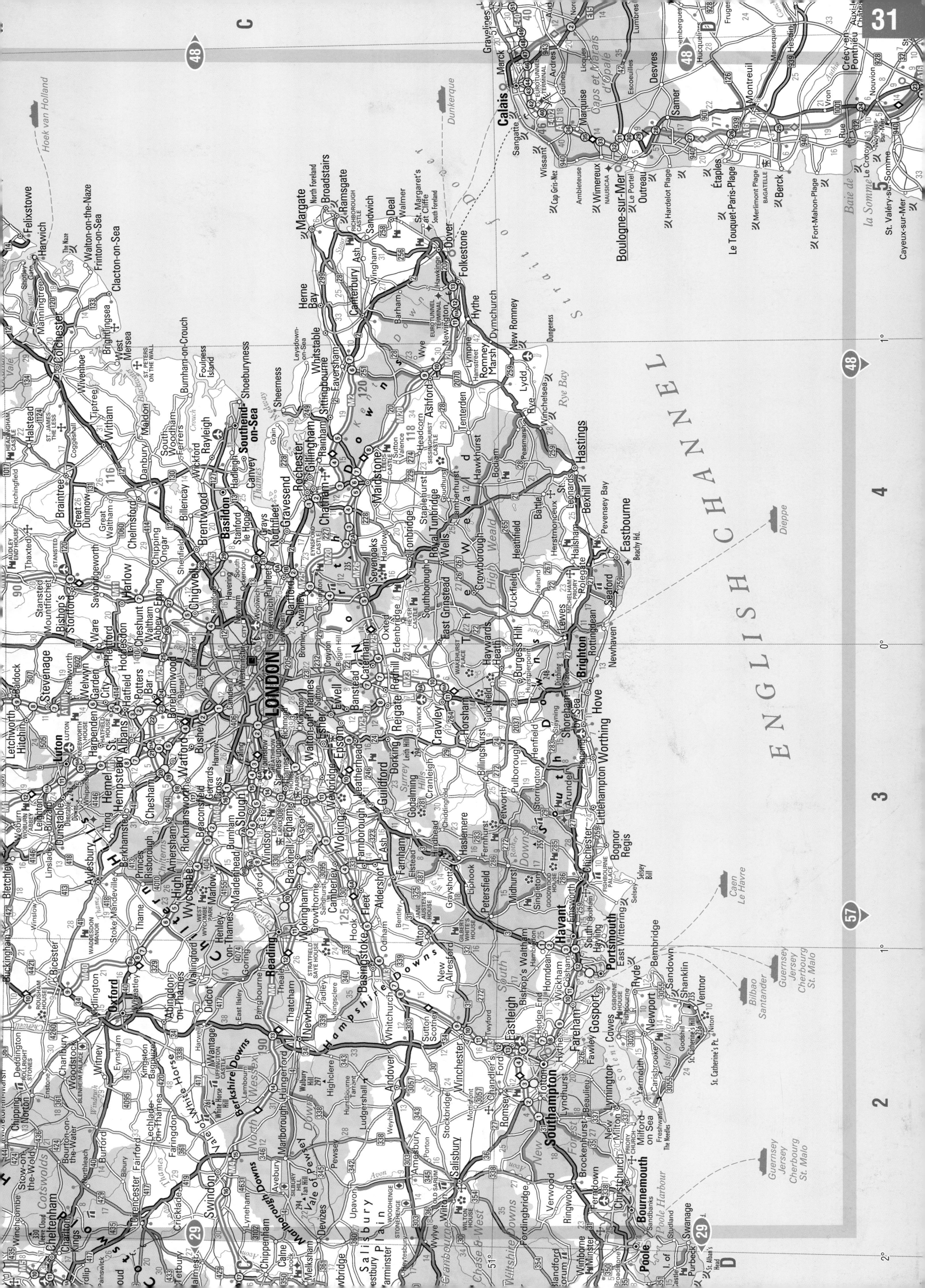

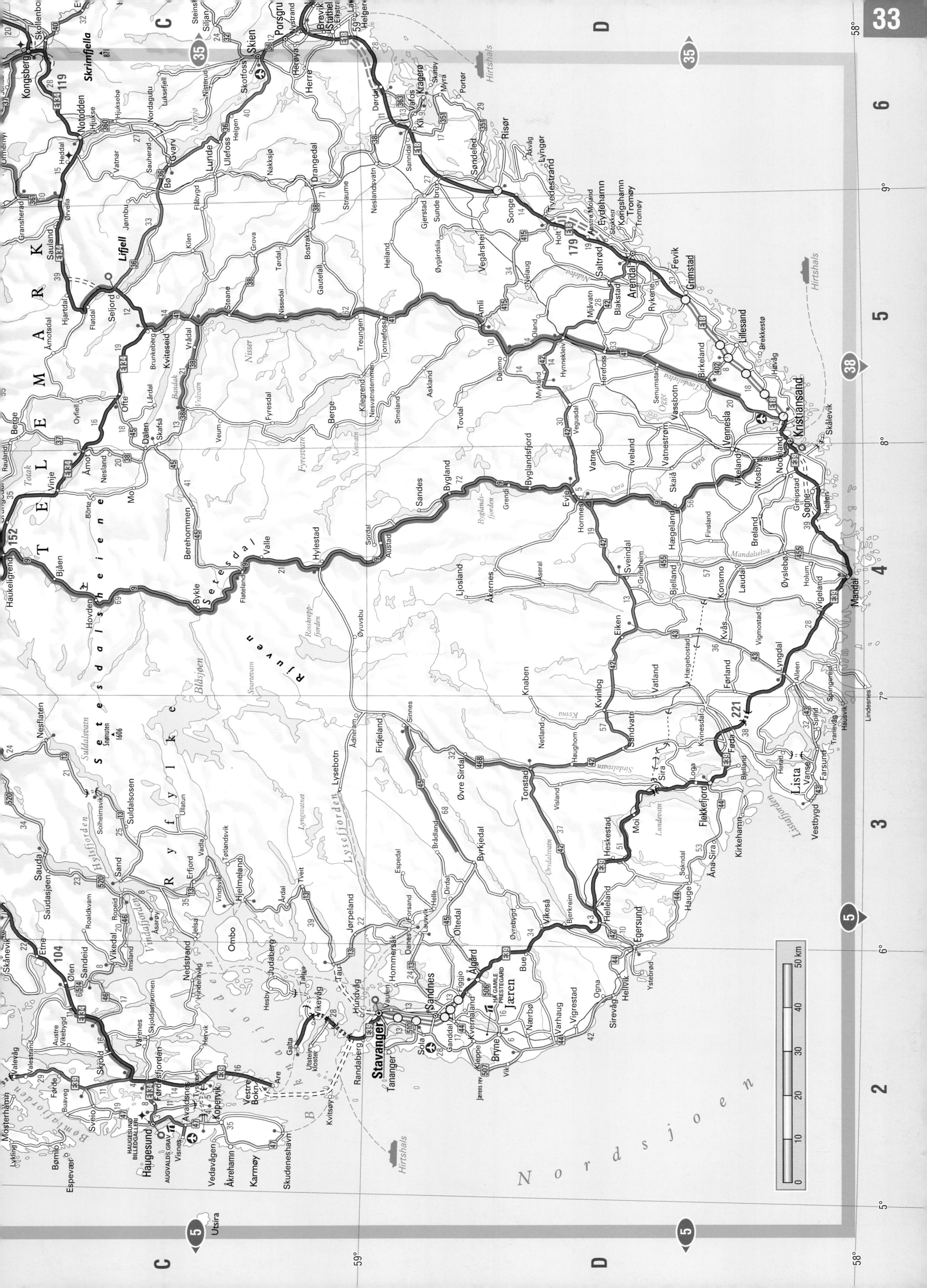

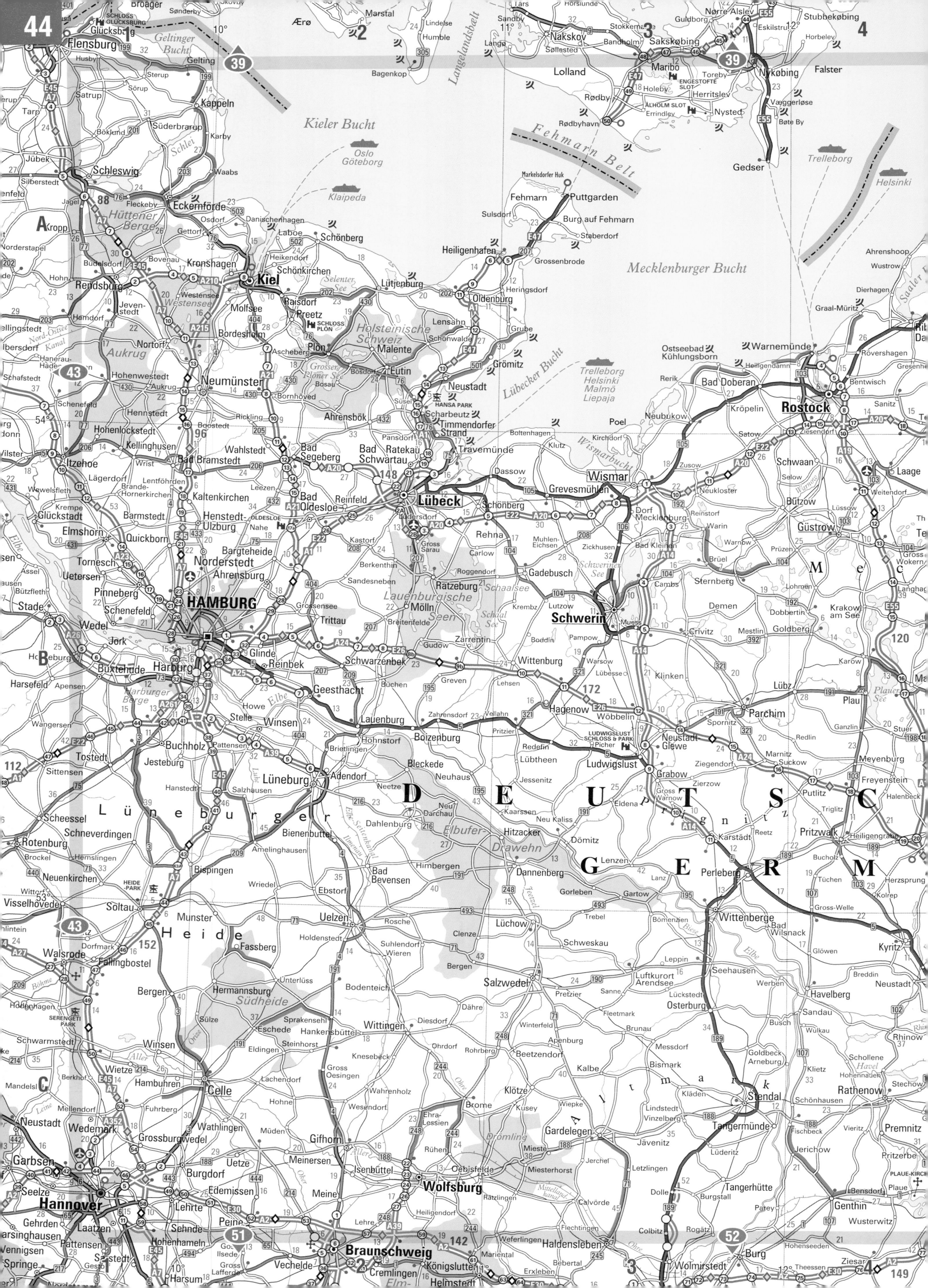

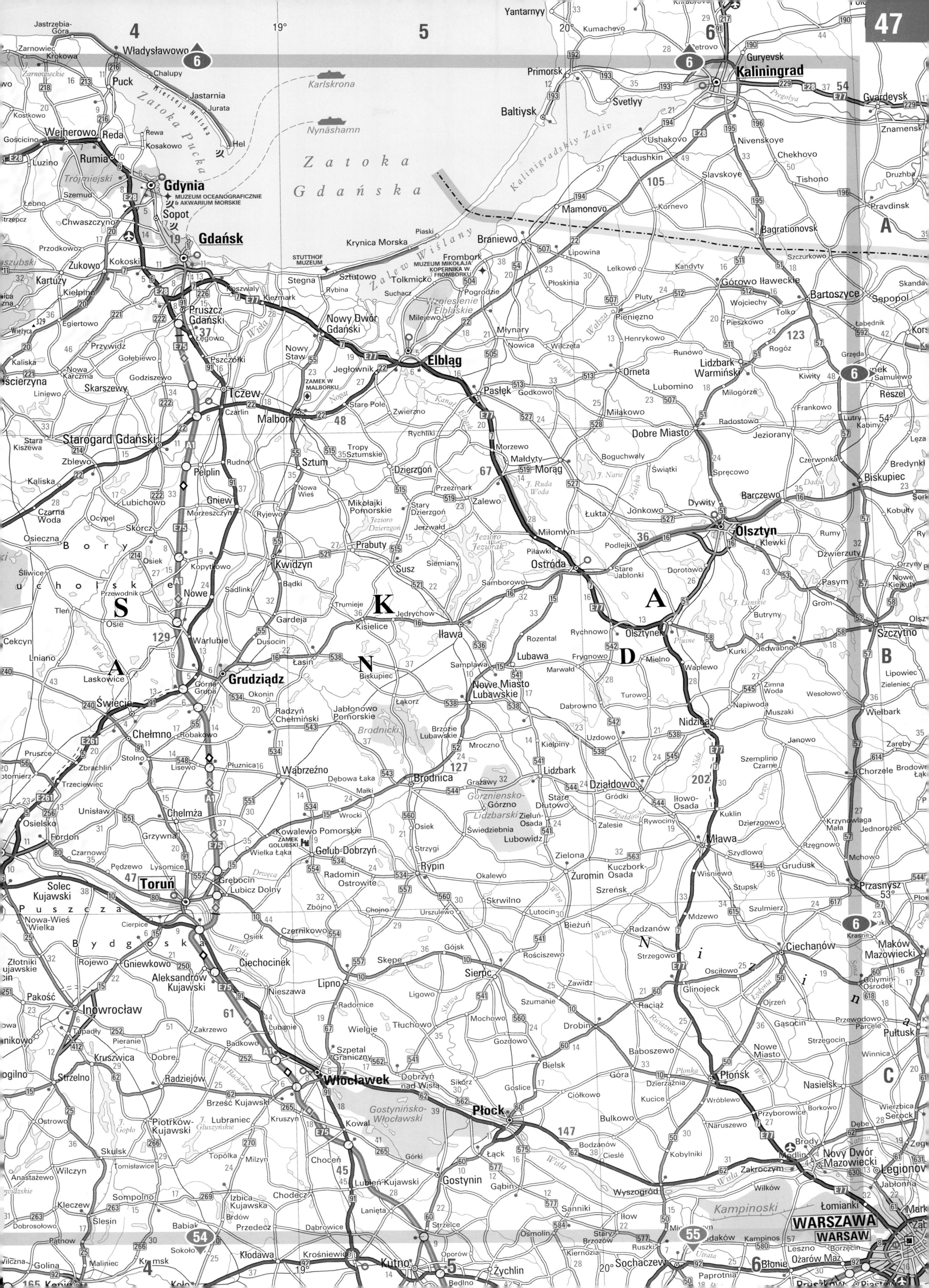

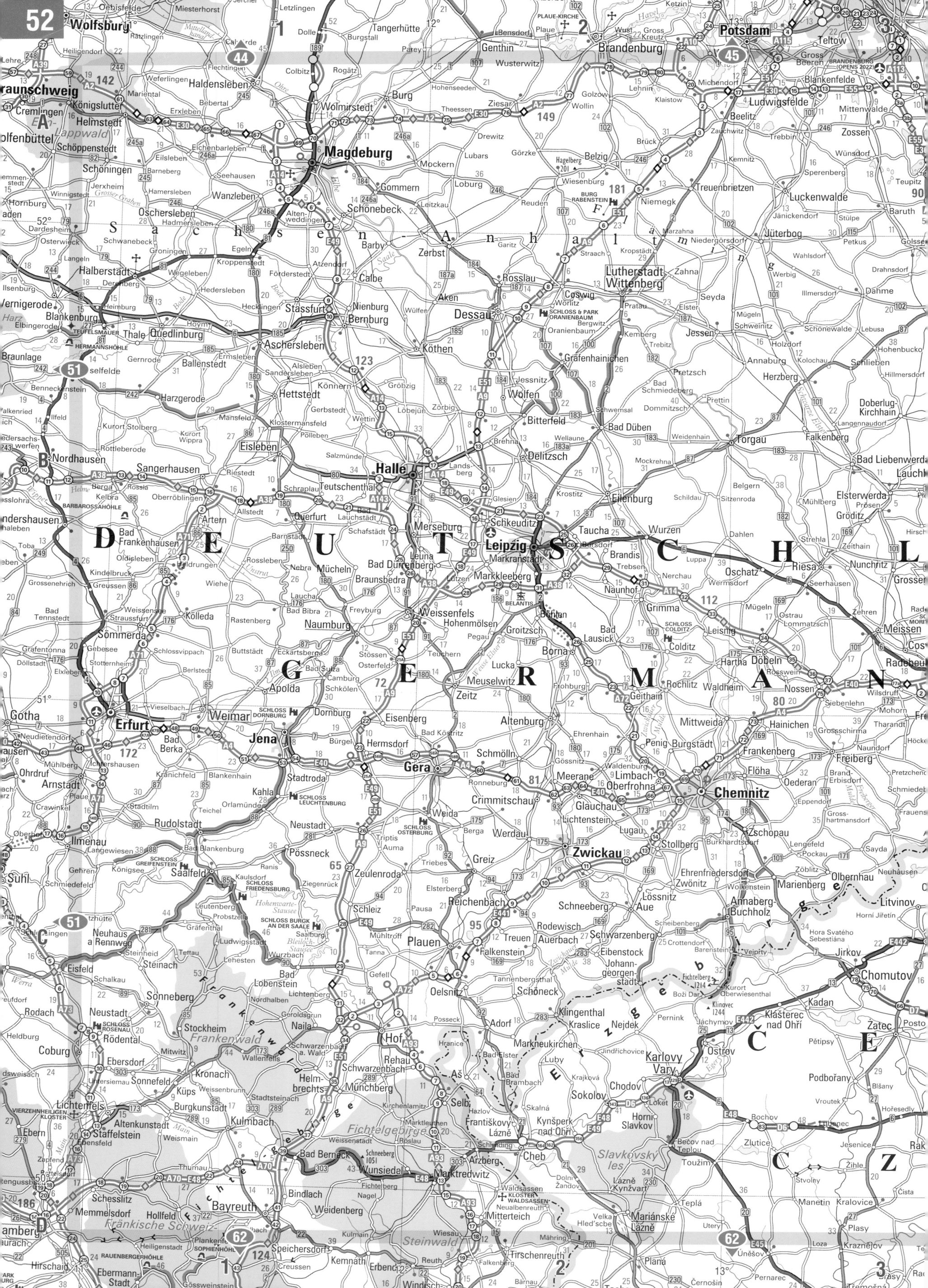

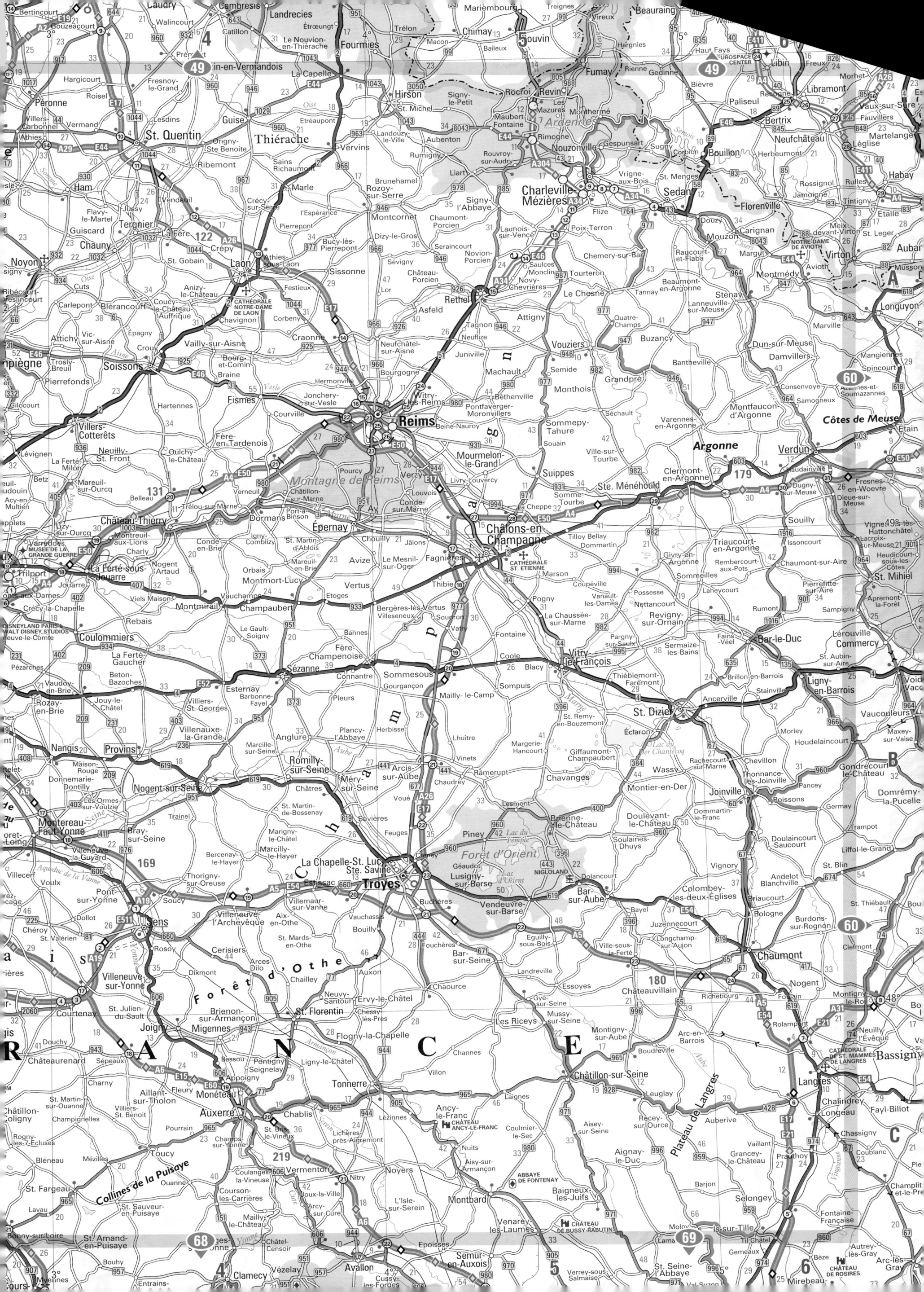

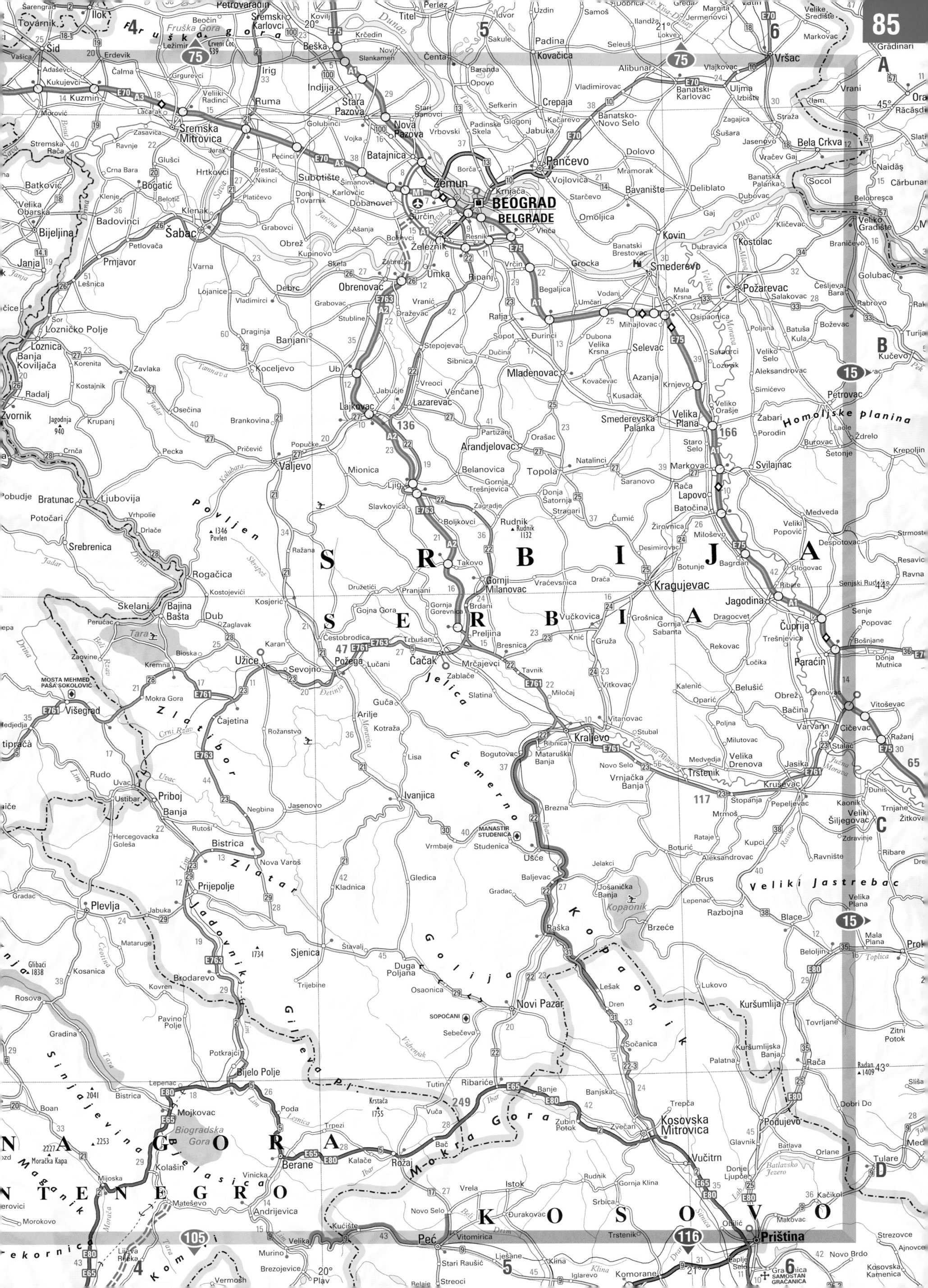

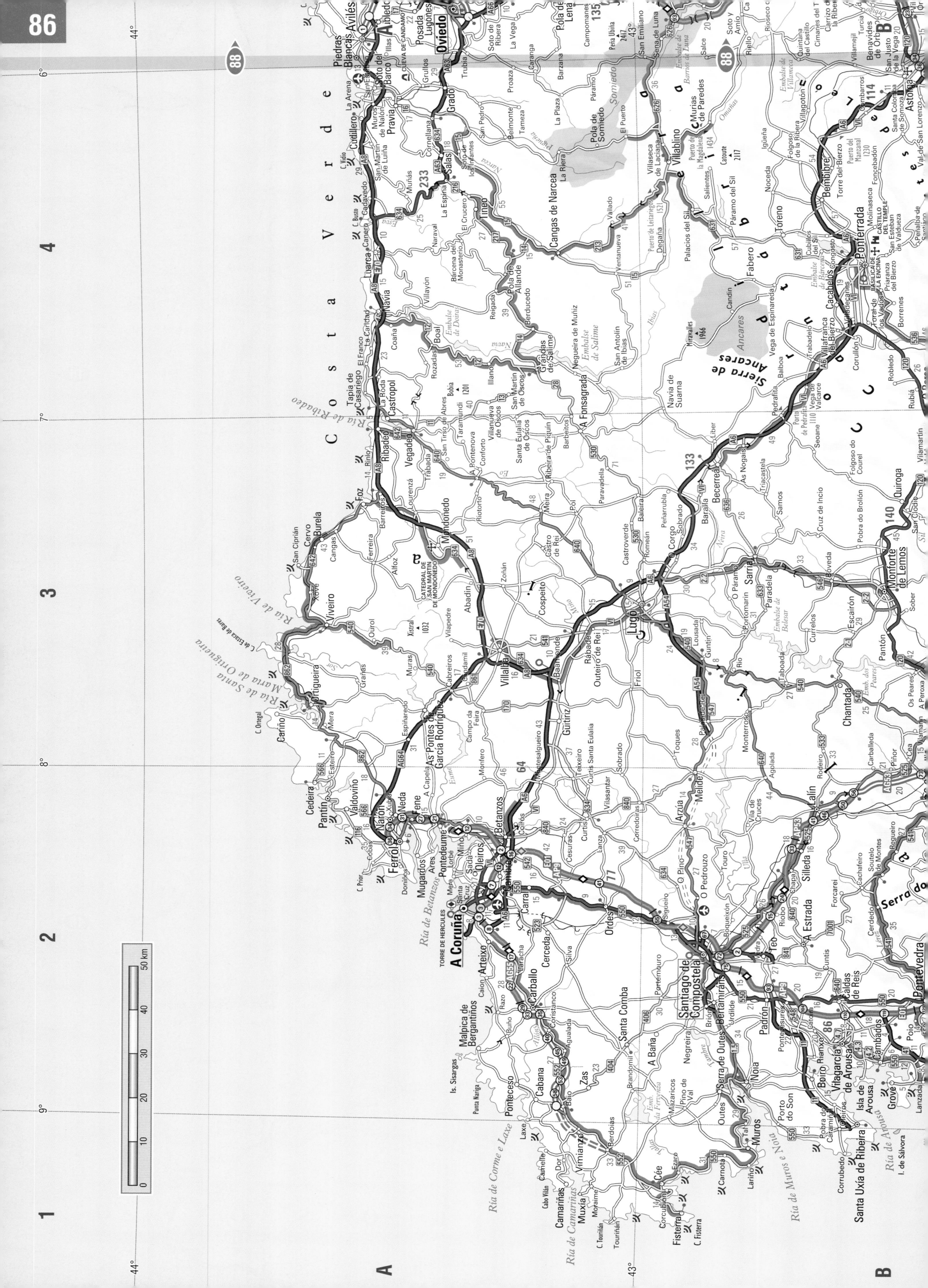

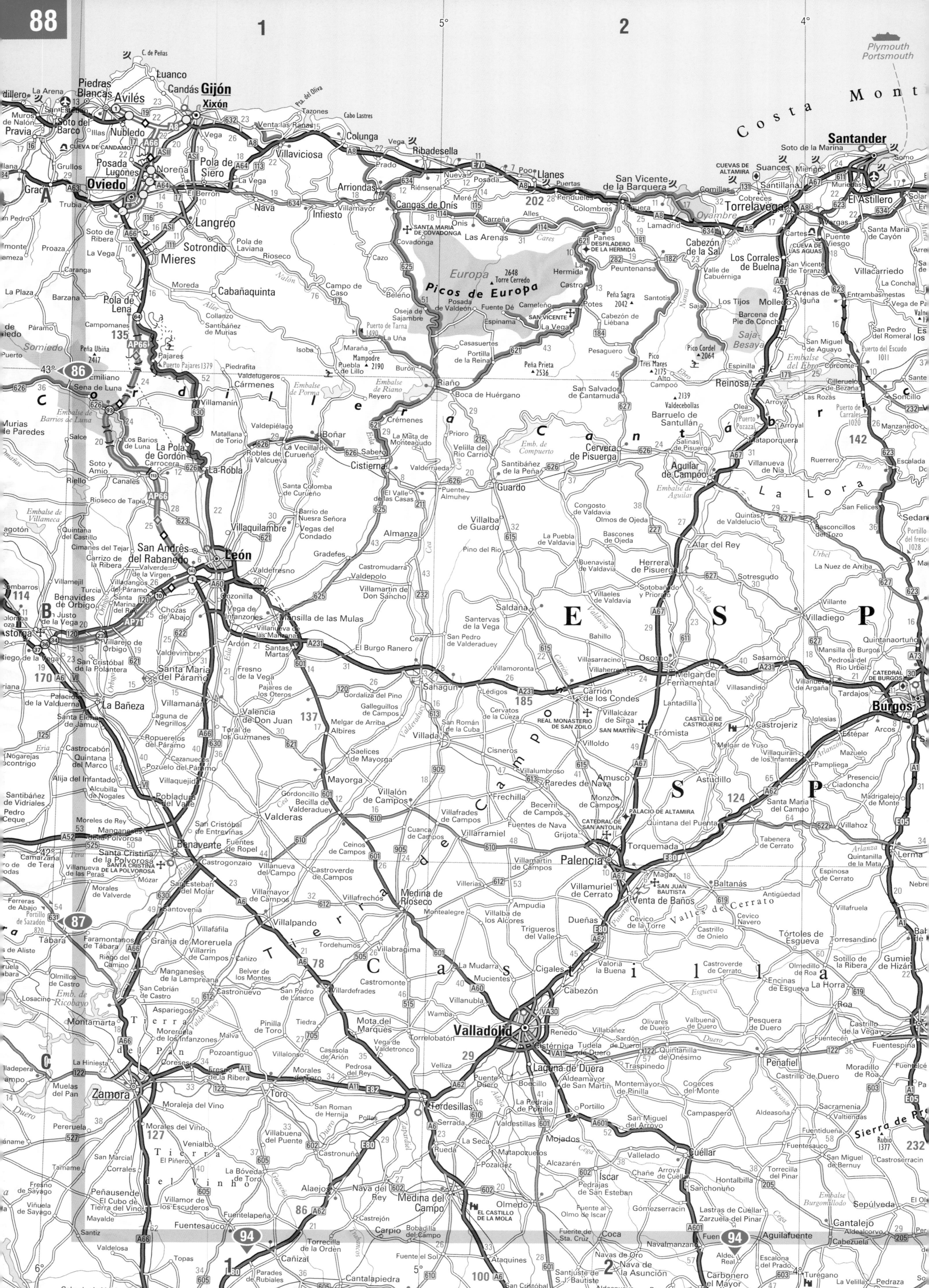

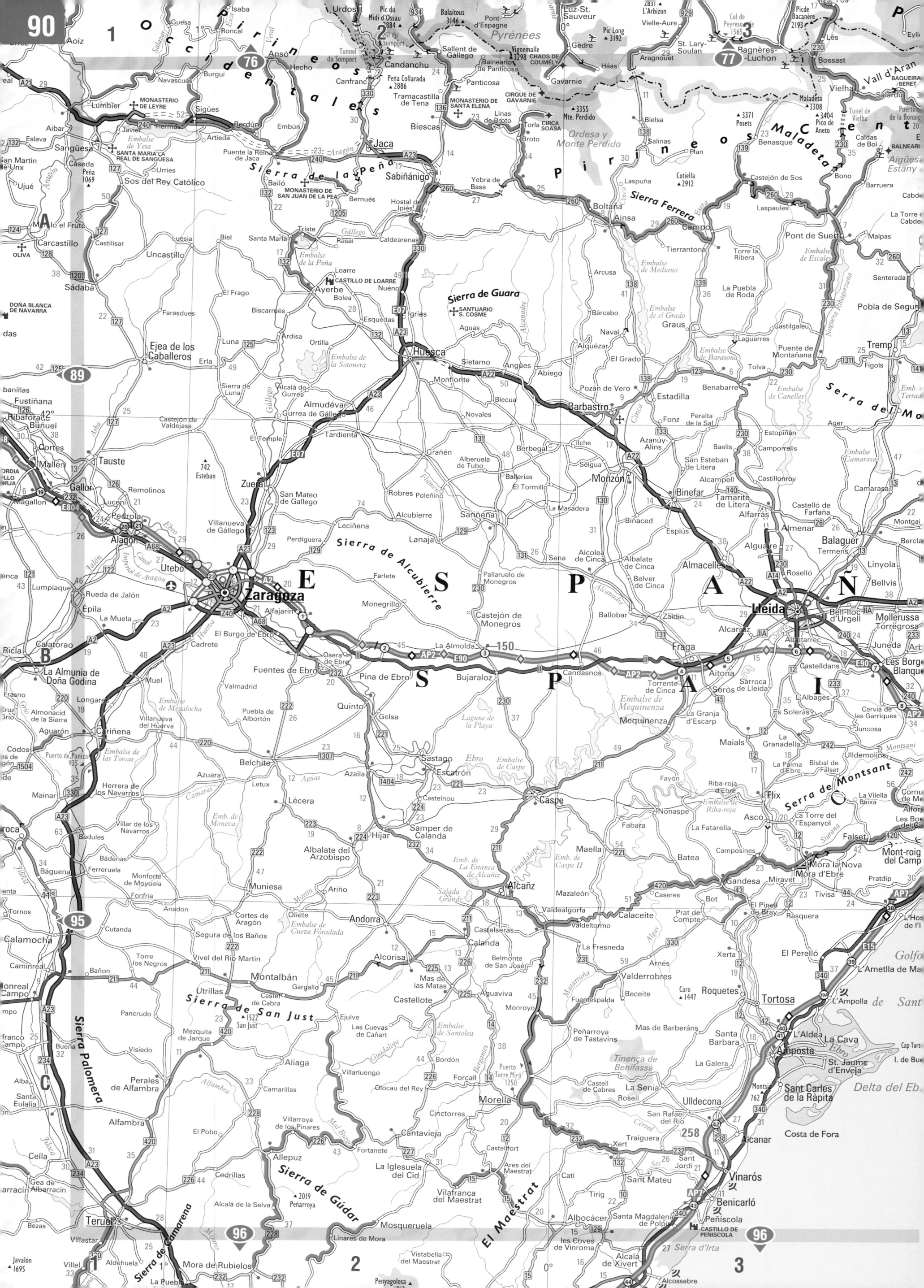

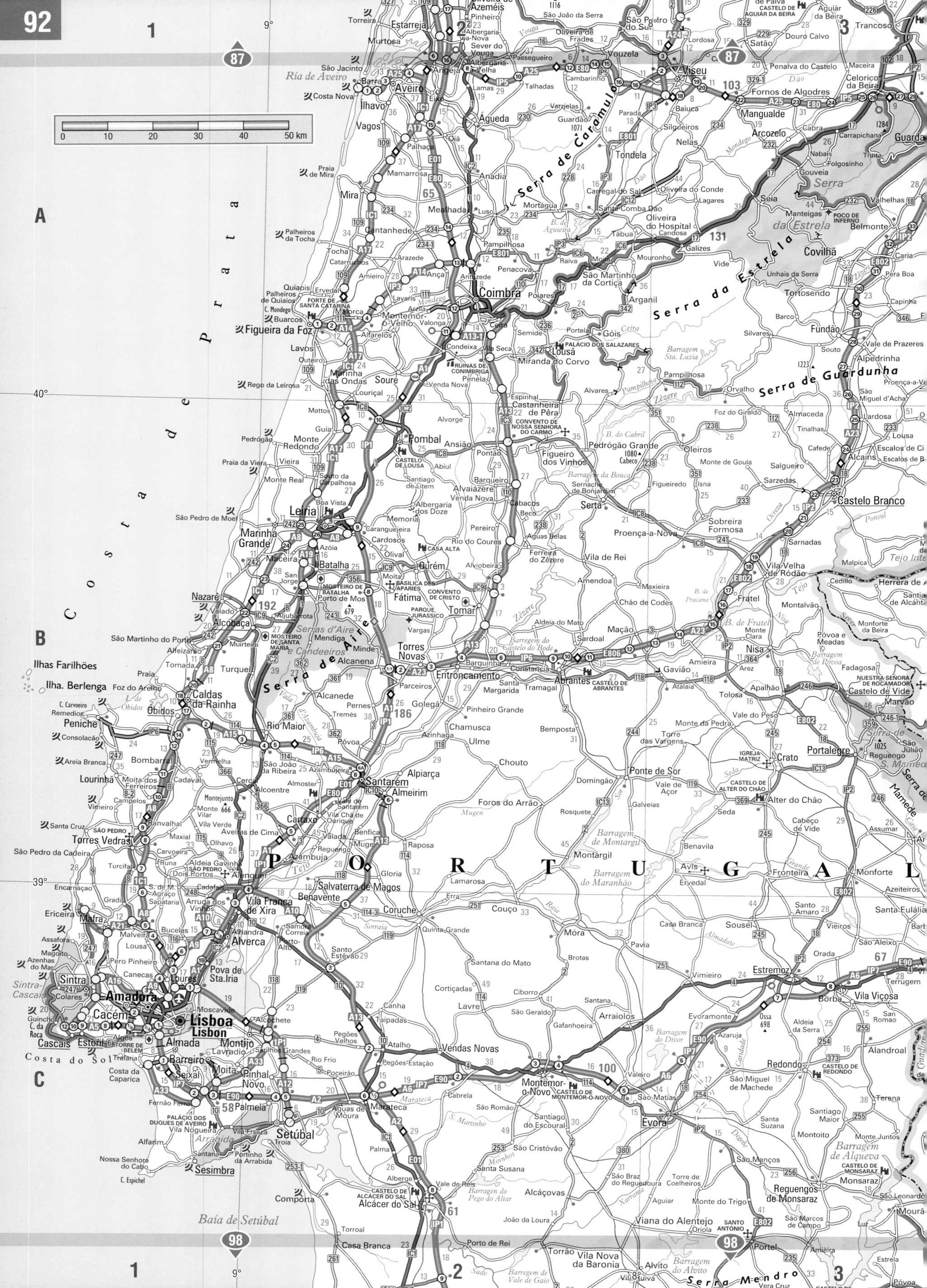

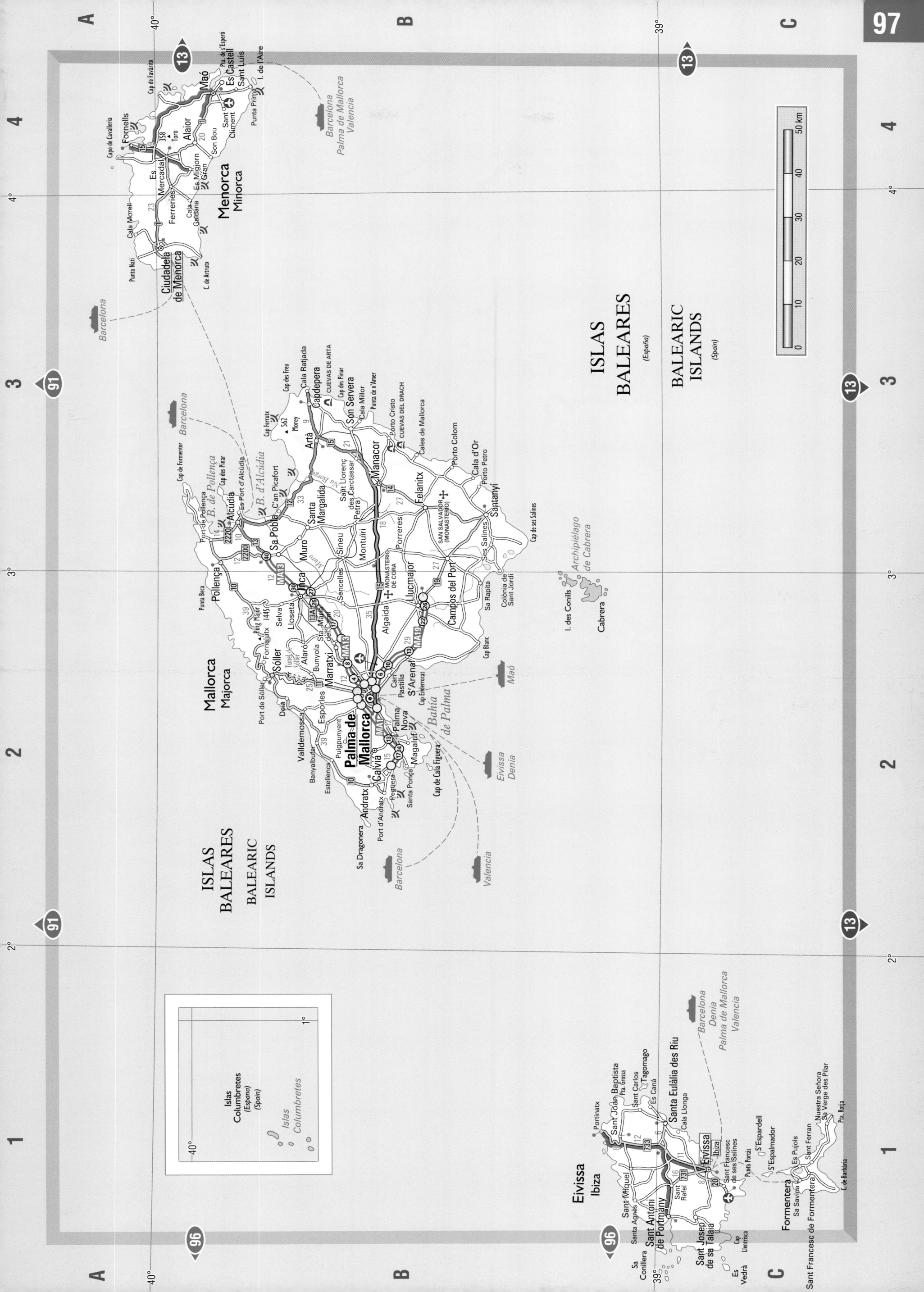

ISLAS
BALEARES
(España)

BALEARIC
ISLANDS
(Spain)

ISLAS
BALEARES

BALEARIC
ISLANDS

Mallorca
Majorca

Menorca
Minorca

Eivissa
Ibiza

Formentera

Islas
Columbretes
(España)

Islas
Columbretes
(Spain)

Marina di Ginosa
Lido di Metaponto
PARCO ARCHEOLOGICO METAPONTO

di Scanzano
Jónico
licoro

Talsano
Pulsano
Lizzano 24
Sava
San Pancrazio
Salentino
Salice
Salentino
Véglie
Lequile
Leverano
Copertino
Porto Cesáreo
Guagnano
Campi
Salentino
San Cesário
di Lecce
Trepuzzi
Surbo
543
Lecce
12
Monteroni di Lecce
Vérnole
San Foca
Melendugno
Torre dell'Orso

G o l f o
d i
T á r a n t o

104

Mandúria
Torricella
Avetrana
Marúggio
Silvana

174
101

105

Nardò
Galátone
Santa Maria al Bagno
Gallípoli
Sant'Andrea
Galatina
Soleto
Cutrofiano
Máglie
Alézio
Collepasso
Parábita
Casarano
Ruffano
Taviano
Rácale
Taurisano
Ugento
Presicce
Alessano
Castrignano del Capo
C. Santa Maria di Léuca

Calimera
Martano
Otranto
C. d'Otranto
Uggiano la Chiesa
Poggiardo
Nociglia
Diso
Castro
Miggiano
Tricase
Marina di Nováglie
Gagliano del Capo
Marina di Léuca

A

40°

Santa Cesárea Terme
GROTTA DI ROMANELLI
& ZINZULUSA

116

rionto
rosia
ccio

Cariati
108
Campana
Crúcoli
Cirò
Umbriático
San Nicola
del'Alto
Stróngoli
vanni in Fiore
Cotronei
Santa Severina
Roccabernarda
Mesoraca
ronà
Cutro
rópani
Botricello

Pta. Fiume Nicá
Pta. Alice
Cirò Marina

E90
106

Crotone
C. Colonna

Ísola di Capo Rizzuto
C. Rizzuto

B

39°

117

M A R E

I O N I O

I O N I A N

S E A

14° 30'

Gozo
San
Dimitri
Pt
Victoria
(Rabat)
Mgarr
Comino

Pozzallo

36°

C

Mellieha
Mosta
Rabat
MALTA
Birzebbugia
Filfla

San Pawl il-Bahar
Sliema
Valletta
Birkirkara
Paola
Benghisa Pt

14° 30'

fo di
llace

0   10   20   30   40   50 km

38°

D

15   4   15   5

17°   18°   19°

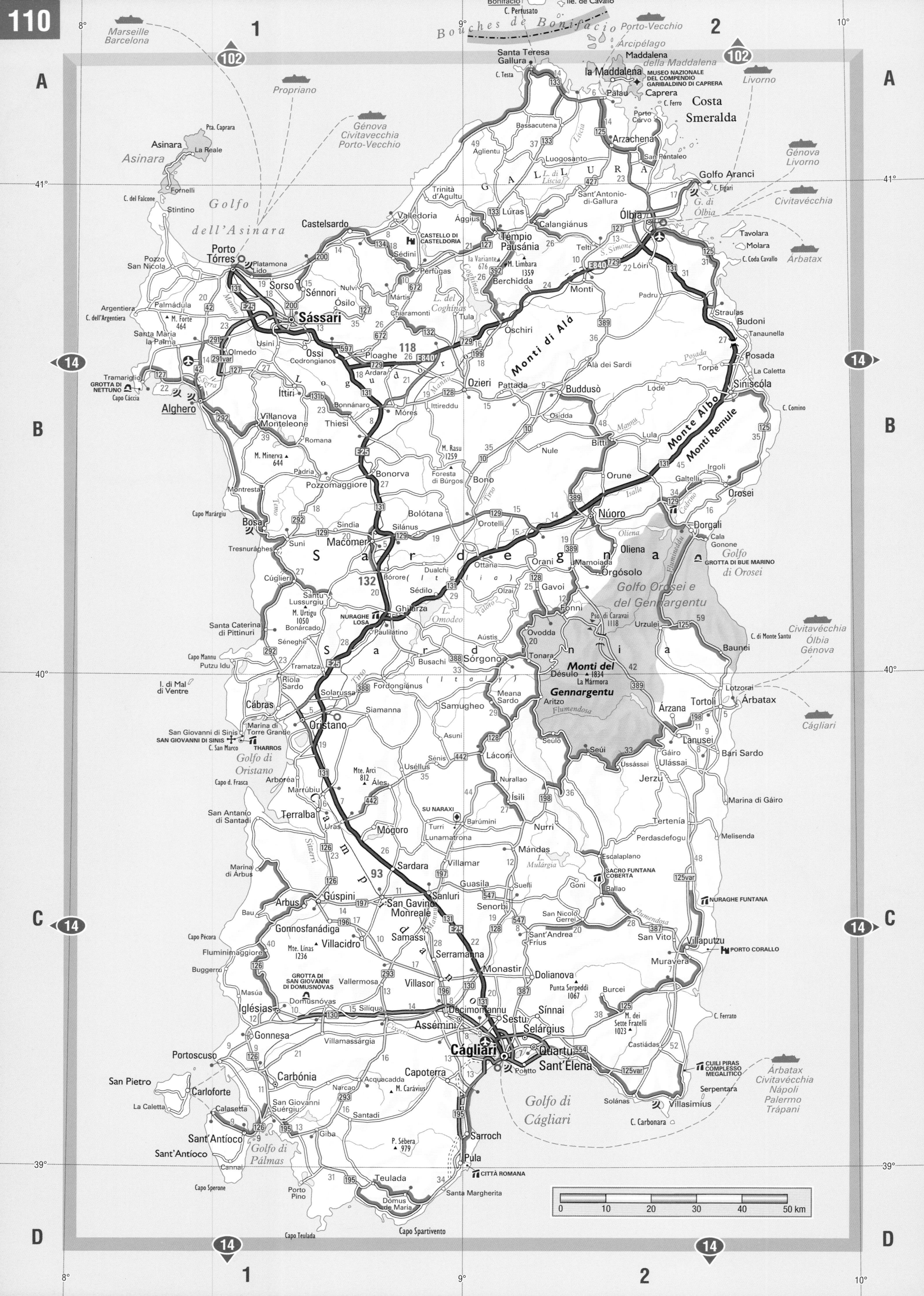

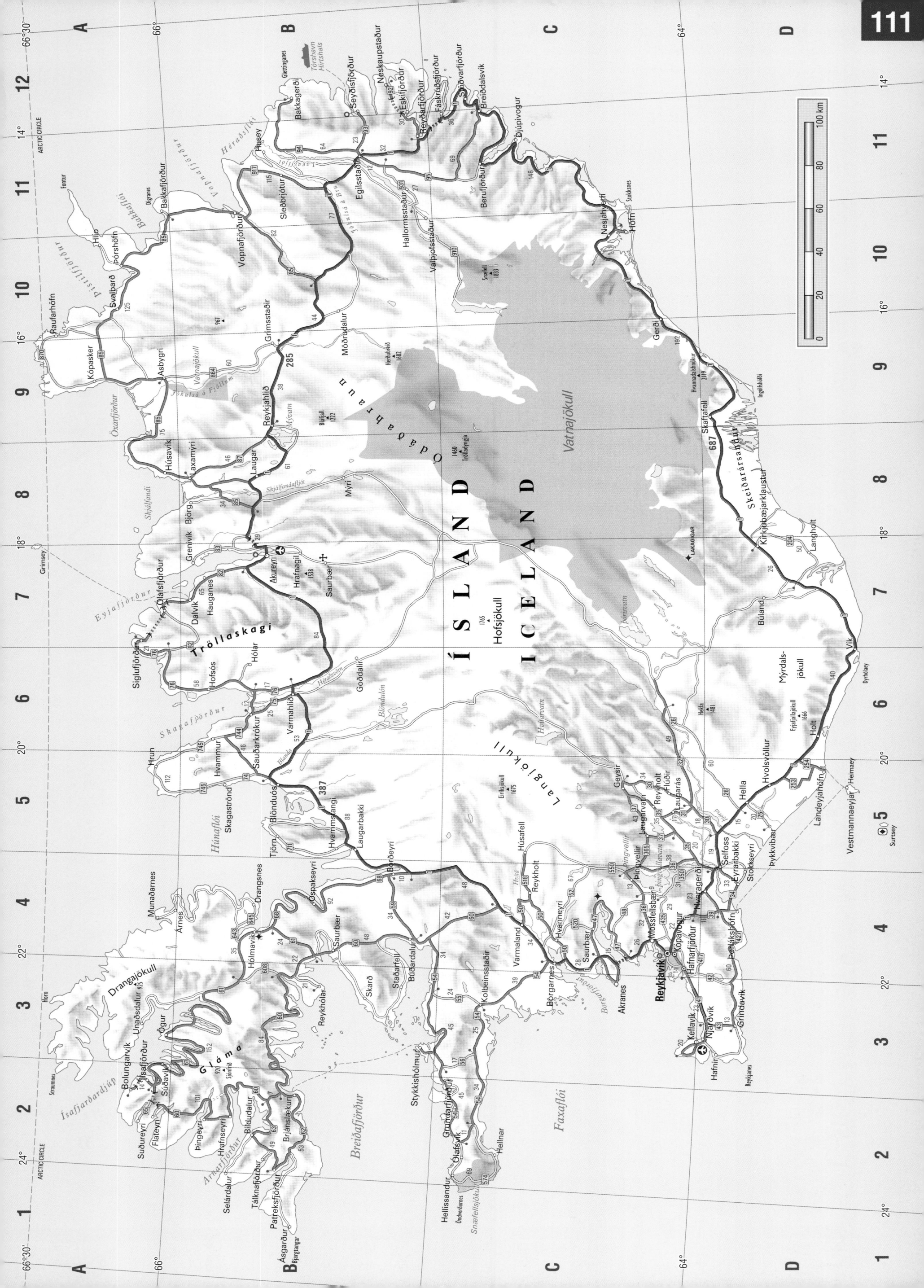

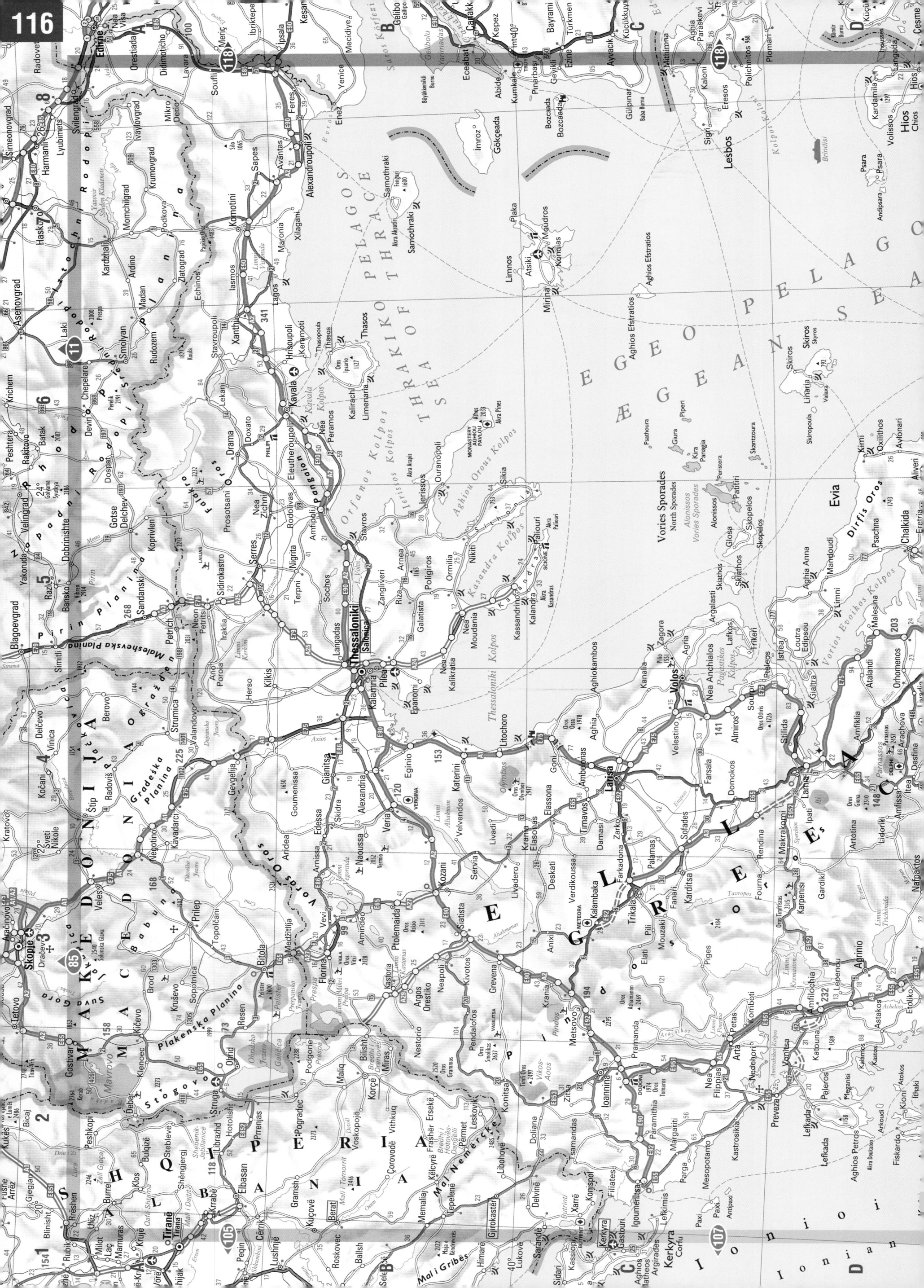

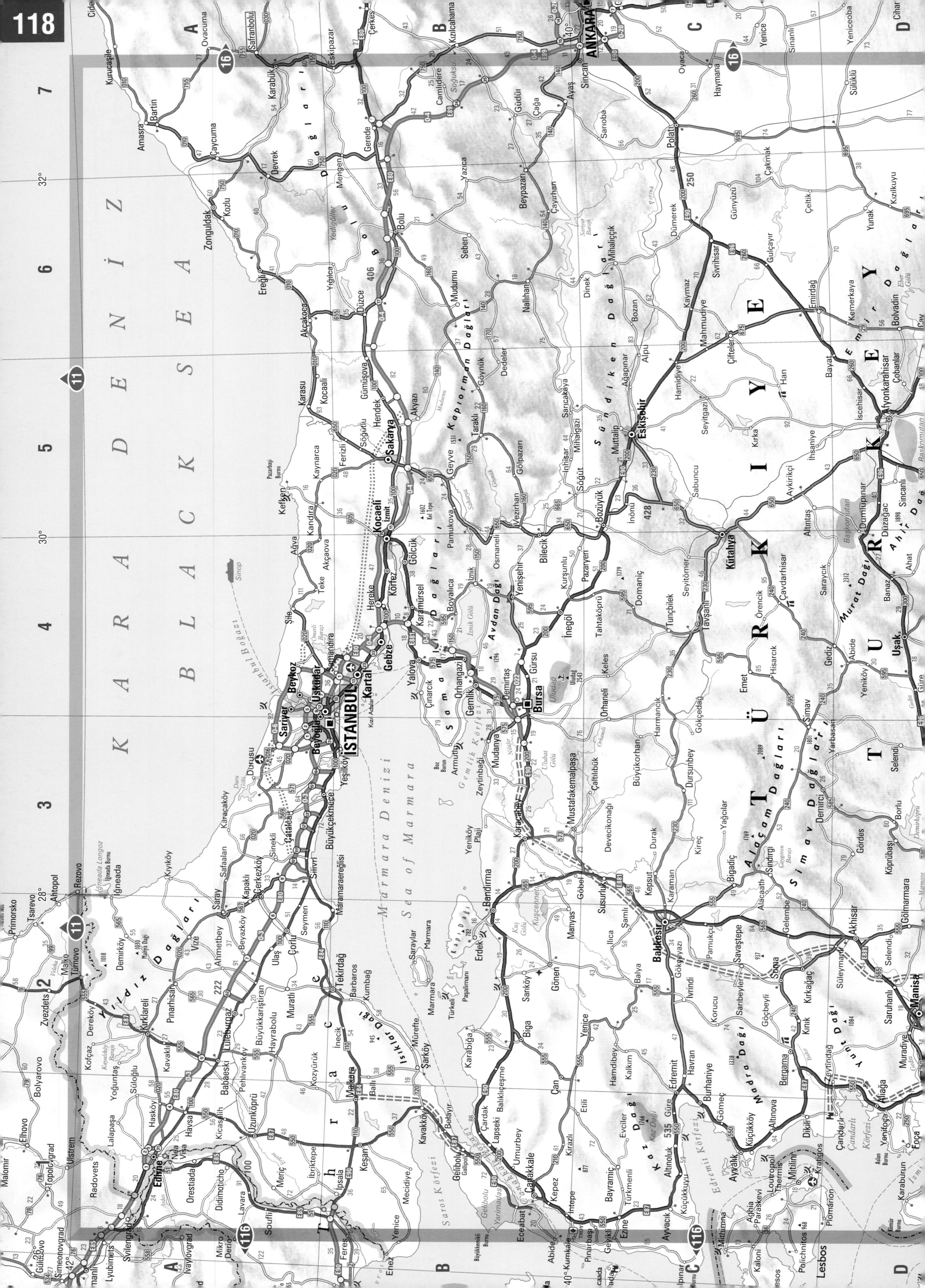

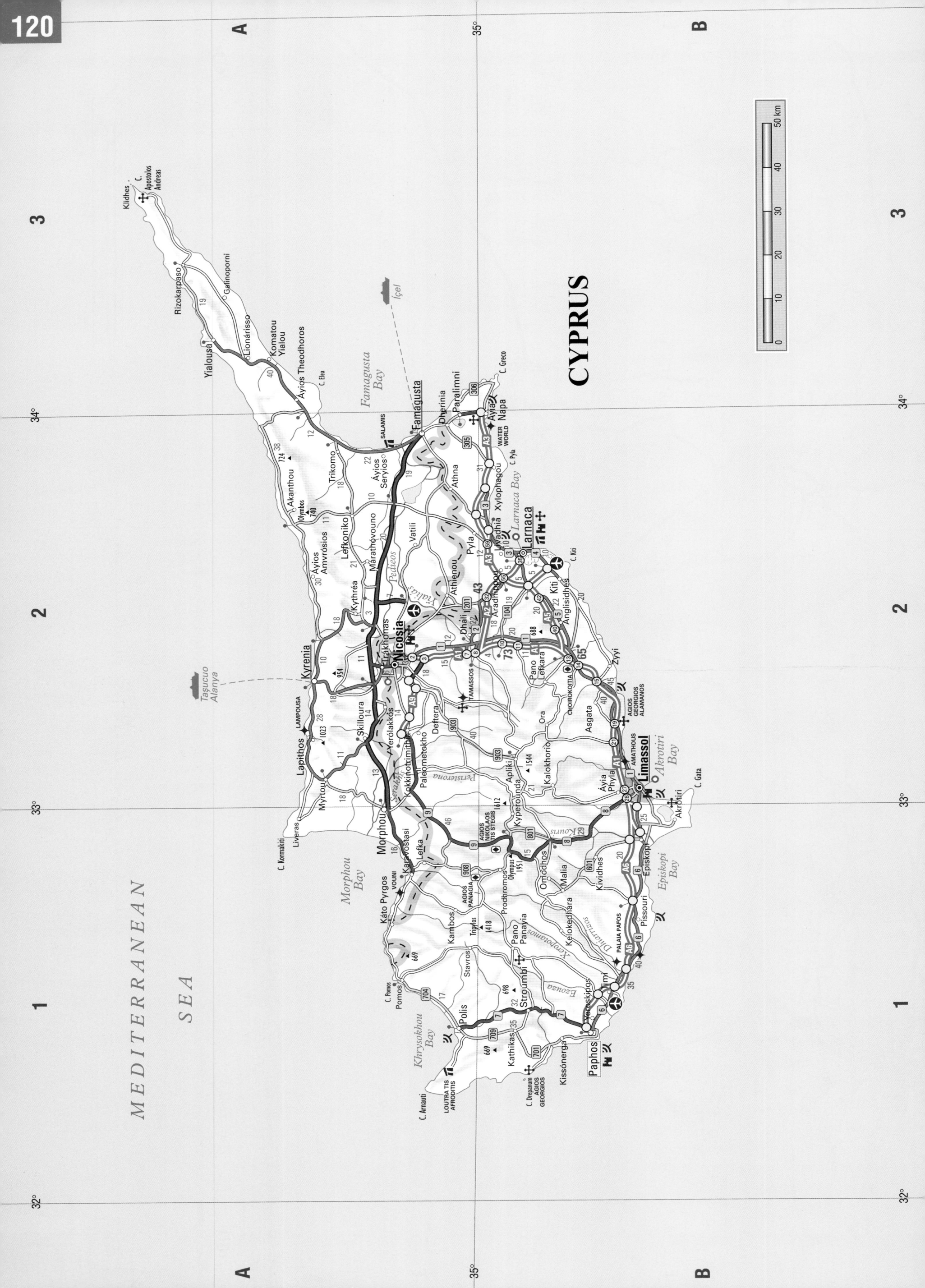

CYPRUS

MEDITERRANEAN

SEA

Khrysokhou Bay

Morphou Bay

Famagusta Bay

Larnaca Bay

Akrotiri Bay

Episkopi Bay

C. Apostolos Andreas
Klidhes
Rizokarpaso
Galinoporni
Yialousa
Lionarisso
Komatou Yialou
Ayios Theodhoros
C. Elea
Akanthou
Olymbos
Trikomo
Ayios Seryios
SALAMIS
Famagusta
Dherinia
Paralimni
C. Greco
Ayia Napa
WATER WORLD
C. Pyla

Kyrenia
LAMPOUSA
Lapithos
Lapithos
Myrtou
Liveras
C. Kormakiti
Skilloura
Verolakkos
Kokkinotrimith
Paleometokho
Deftera
Trakhonas
Nicosia
Ayios Amvrosios
Lefkoniko
Marathovouno
Kythrea
Vatili
Pyla
Athienou
Dhali
Aradhippou
Livadhia
Larnaca
C. Kiti
Kiti
Anglisidhes
Zyyi
Pano Lefkara
Athna
Xylophagou

Tsucuo
Alanya
Tasucu
Ipel
Ipel

C. Kormakiti
Morphou
Kato Pyrgos
C. Pomos
Pomos
VOUNI
Karavostasi
Lefka
AGIOS PANAGIA
Kambos
Stavros
Tripylos
Pano Panayia
Kelokedhara
Kividhes
Pissouri
PALAIA PAFOS
Timi
Yeroskipos
Kissonerga
AGIOS GEORGIOS
C. Drepanum
LOUTRA TIS AFRODITIS
C. Arnauti
Polis
Stroumbi
Kathikas

Paphos

Kokkinotrimith
AGIOS NIKOLAOS TIS STEGIS
Prodhromos
Olympus
Pano
Panayia
Ornidhos
Malia
Asgata
Ora
Kalokhorio
Apliki
Kyperounda
Ayia Phyla
AMATHOUS
Limassol
Akrotiri
C. Gata
AGIOS GEORGIOS ALAMANOS
CHOIROKOITIA
Episkopi

Persterona
Peristerona
Ayios Seryios
Pedieos
Yialias
Yialias
TAMASSOS
Pano Lefkara
Kouris
Dhiarizos
Xeropotamos
Ezousa

Mediterranean
Sea

City plans • Plans de villes
Stadtpläne • Piante di città

Motorway	Autoroute	Autobahn	Autostrada
Major through route	Route principale majeur	Hauptstrecke	Strada di grande communicazione
Through route	Route principale	Schnellstrasse	Strada d'importanza regionale
Secondary road	Route secondaire	Nebenstrasse	Strada d'interesse locale
Dual carriageway	Chaussées séparées	Zweispurig Schnellstrasse	Strada a carreggiate doppie
Other road	Autre route	Nebenstrecke	Altra strada
Tunnel	Tunnel	Tunnel	Galleria stradale
Limited access / pedestrian road	Rue réglementée / rue piétonne	Beschränkter Zugang/ Fussgängerzone	Strada pedonale / a accesso limitato
One-way street	Sens unique	Einbahnstrasse	Senso unico
Parking	Parc de stationnement	Parkplatz	Parcheggio
Motorway number	A7 Numéro d'autoroute	Autobahnnummer A7	Numero di autostrada
National road number	447 Numéro de route nationale	Nationalstrassen-nummer 447	Numero di strada nazionale
European road number	E45 Numéro de route européenne	Europäische Strassennummer E45	Numero di strada europea
Destination	GENT Destination	Ziel GENT	Destinazione
Car ferry	Bac passant les autos	Autofähre	Traghetto automobili
Railway	Chemin de fer	Eisenbahn	Ferrovia
Rail/bus station	Gare / gare routière	Bahnhof / Busstation	Stazione ferrovia / pullman
Underground, metro station	Station de métro	U-Bahnstation	Metropolitano
Cable car	Téléférique	Drahtseilbahn	Funivia
Abbey, cathedral	Abbaye, cathédrale	Abtei, Kloster, Kathedrale	Abbazia, duomo
Church of interest	Église intéressante	Interessante Kirche	Chiesa da vedere
Synagogue	Synagogue	Synagoge	Sinagoga
Hospital	Hôpital	Krankenhaus	Ospedale
Police station	Police	Polizeiwache	Polizia
Post office	Bureau de poste	Postamt	Ufficio postale
Tourist information	Office de tourisme	Informationsbüro	Ufficio informazioni turistiche
Place of interest	Theatre Autre curiosité	Sonstige Sehenswürdigkeit	Theatre Luogo da vedere

Approach maps • Agglomérations
Carte régionale • Regionalkarte

Toll motorway – with motorway number	A10 Autoroute à péage – avec numéro d'autoroute	Gebührenpflichtige Autobahn – mit Autobahnnummer A10	Autostrada a pedaggio – con numero
Toll-free motorway – with European road number	E51 Autoroute – avec numéro de route européenne	Gebührenfreie Autobahn – Europäische Strassennummer E51	Autostrada – con numero di strada europea
Pre-pay motorway – vignette required	Autoroute – 'vignette'	Autobahn – 'vignette'	Autostrada – 'vignette'
Motorway services	Aire de service	Autobahnservice	Area di servizio autostradale
Motorway junction full access, restricted access	Échangeur d'autoroute accès libre, accès reglémenté	Autobahnkreuz – voller/begrenzter Zugang	Raccordi autostradali – completo/parziali
Under construction	En construction	Im Bau	In construzione
Tunnel	Tunnel	Tunnel	Galleria stradale
Major route dual carriageway single carriageway	Route principale chausées séparées chausée sans séparation	Hauptstrecke – zweispurige Schnellstrasse	Strada di grande communicazione carreggiata doppia carreggiata unica
Secondary route dual carriageway single carriageway	Route secondaire chausées séparées chausée sans séparation	Nebenstrasse – zweispurige Schnellstrasse	Strada d'interesse locale carreggiata doppia carreggiata unica
Other road	Autre route	Nebenstrecke	Altra strada
Car ferry	Bac passant les autos	Autofähre	Traghetto automobili
Destination GIRONA	Destination	Ziel GIRONA	Destinazione
Railway	Chemin de fer	Eisenbahn	Ferrovia
Railway station Estación Central	Gare	Hauptbahnhof Estación Central	Stazione ferrovia
Height – in metres 234	Altitude – en mètres	Höhe – über dem Meeresspiegel 234	Altezza in metri
Airport	Aéroport principal	Flughafen	Aeroporto
Airfield	Autre aéroport	Flugplatz	Aerodromo/ campo d'aviazione
City plan coverage area	Région de plan de ville	Vom Stadtplan abgedecktes Gebiet	Area della pianta della città

Alicante

0 — km — 0.5

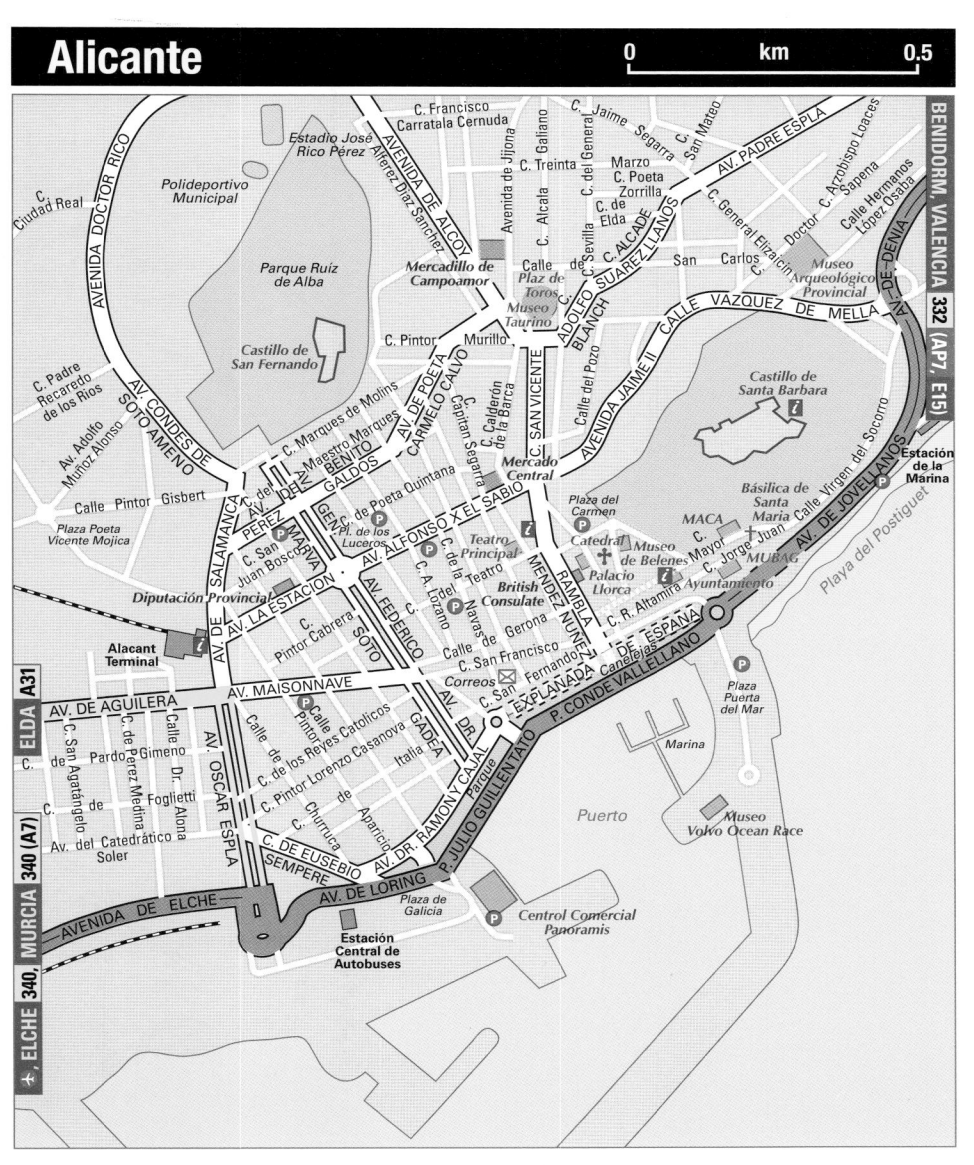

Antwerpen Antwerp

0 — km — 1

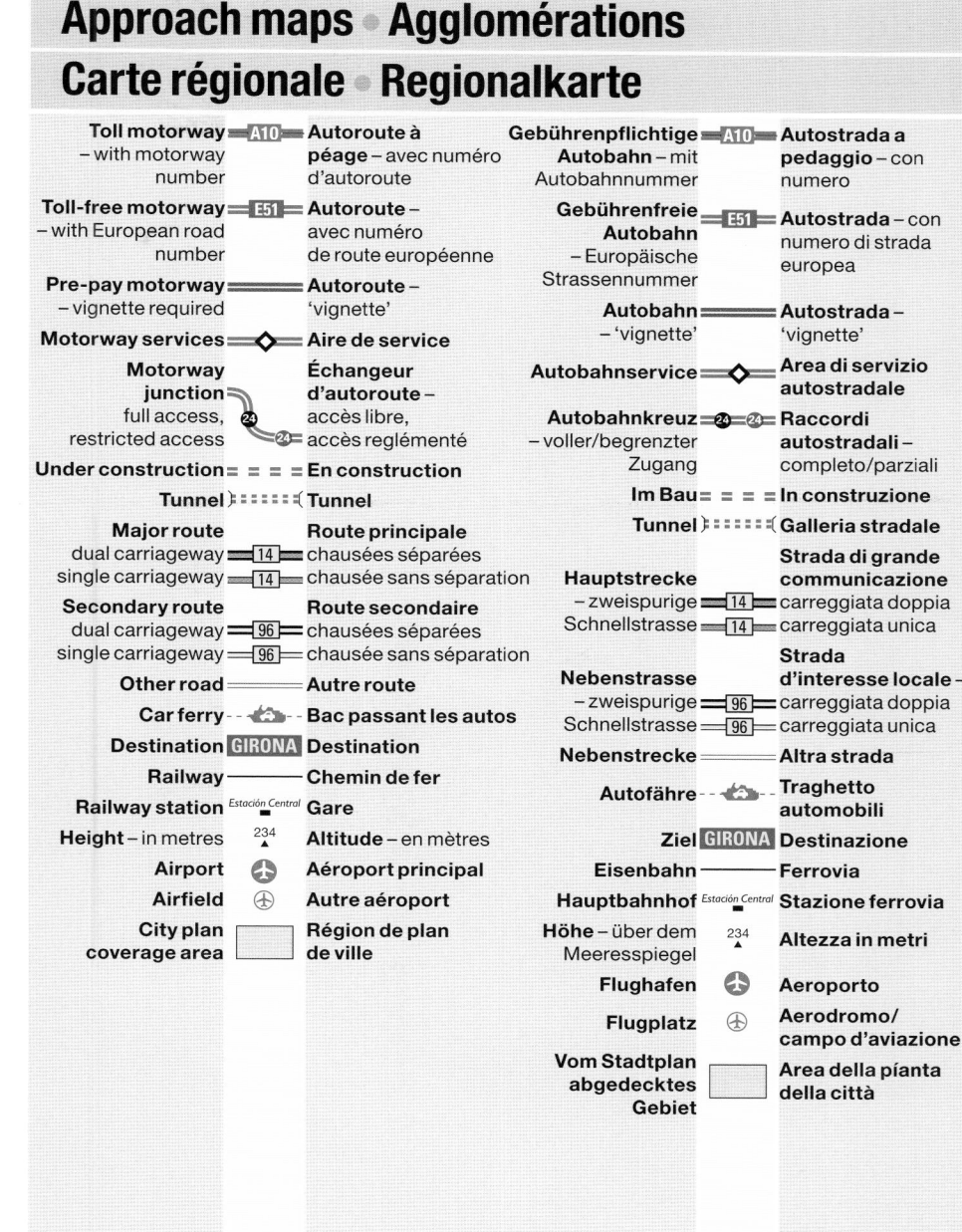
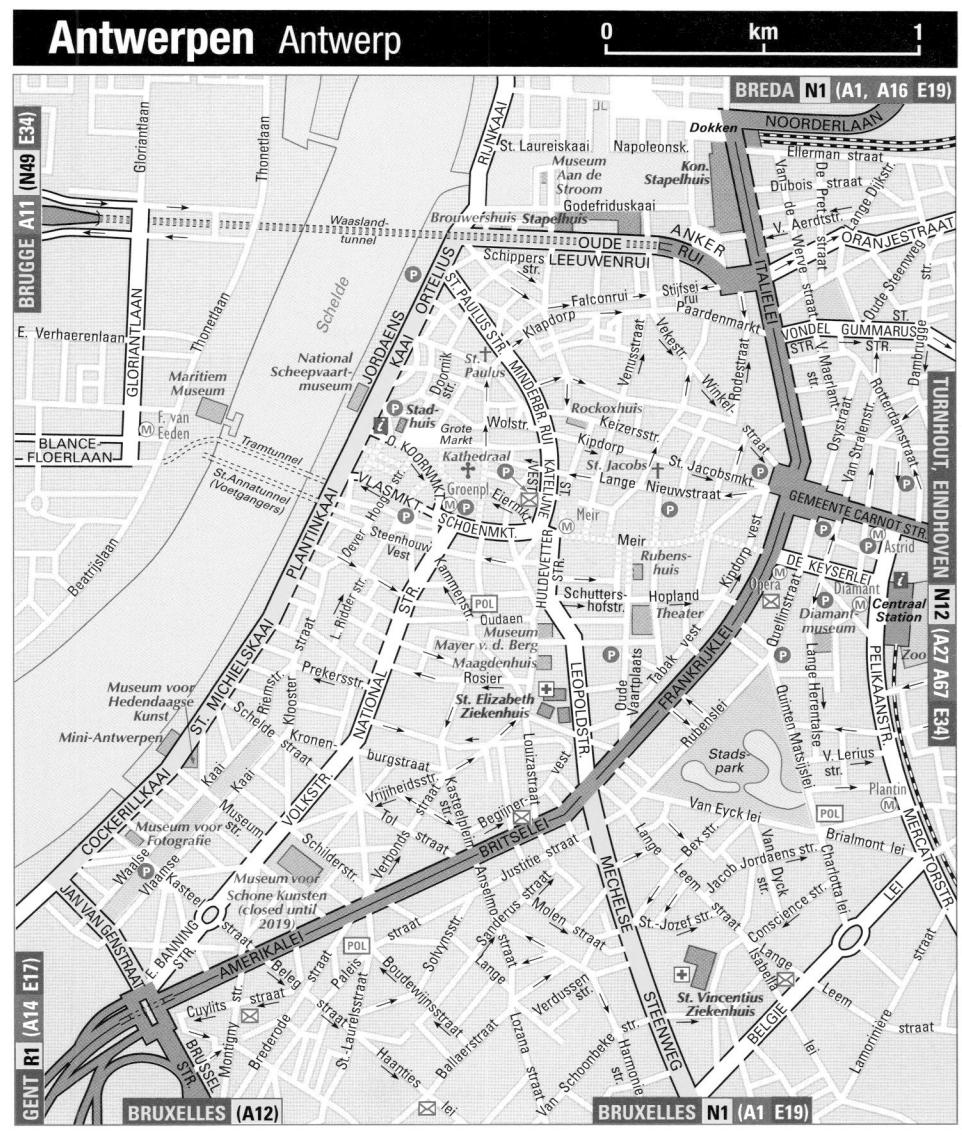

Amsterdam

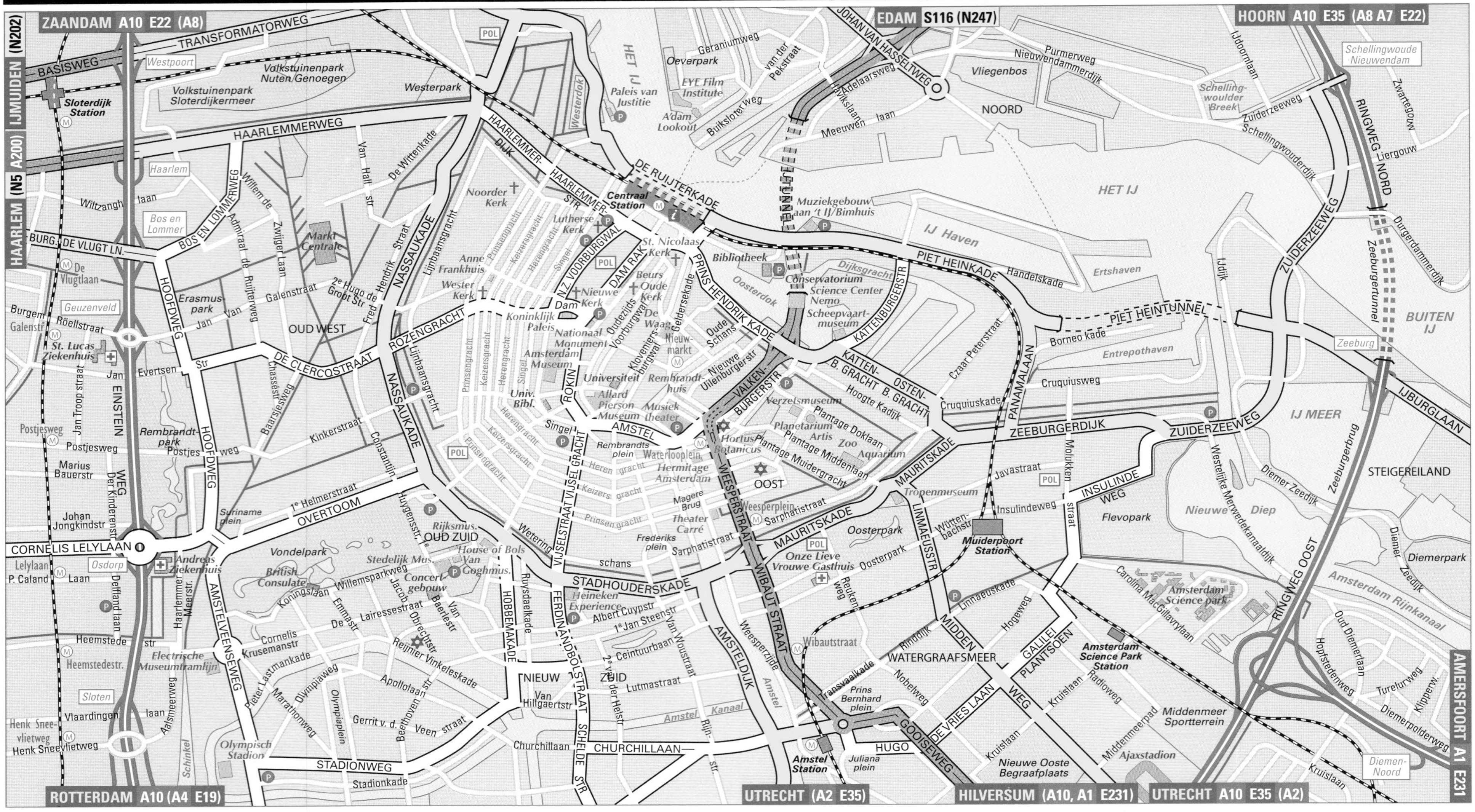

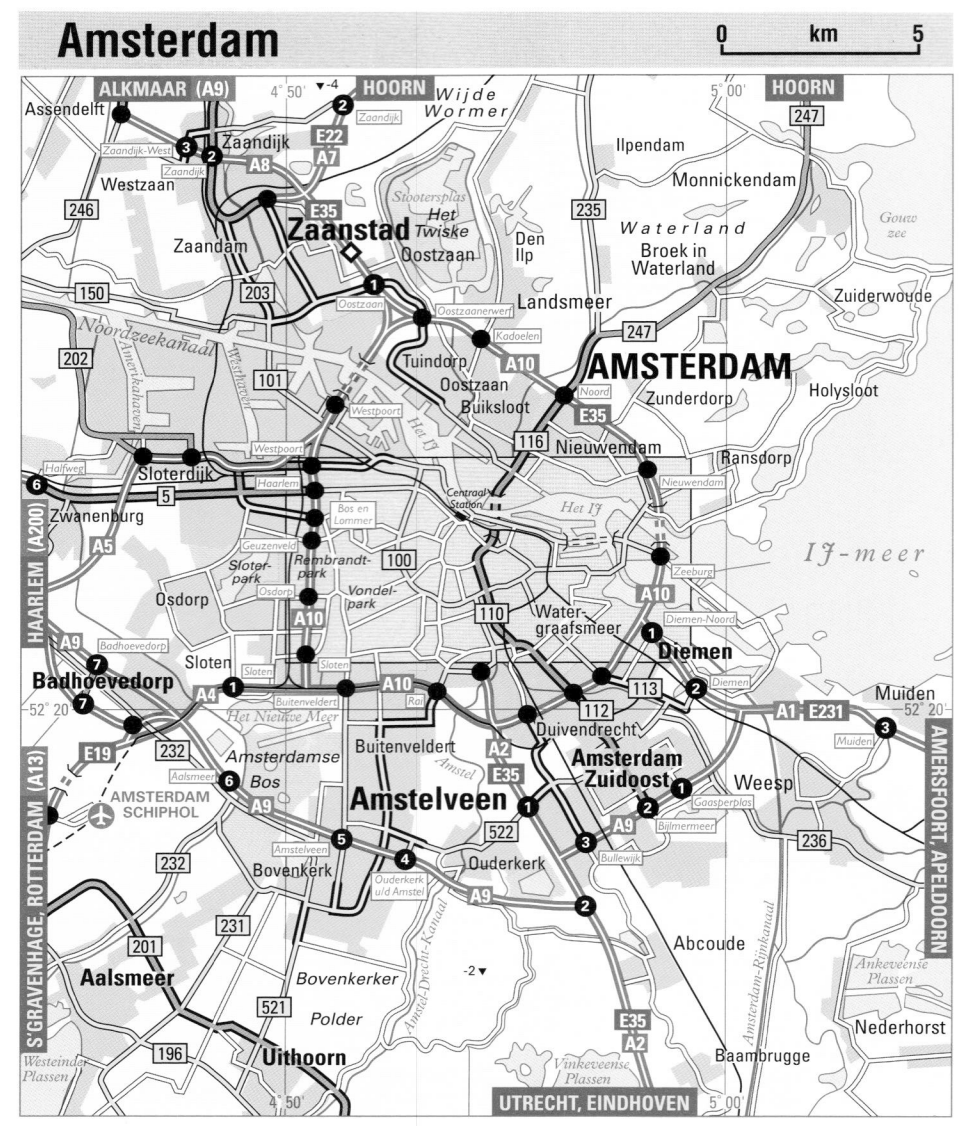

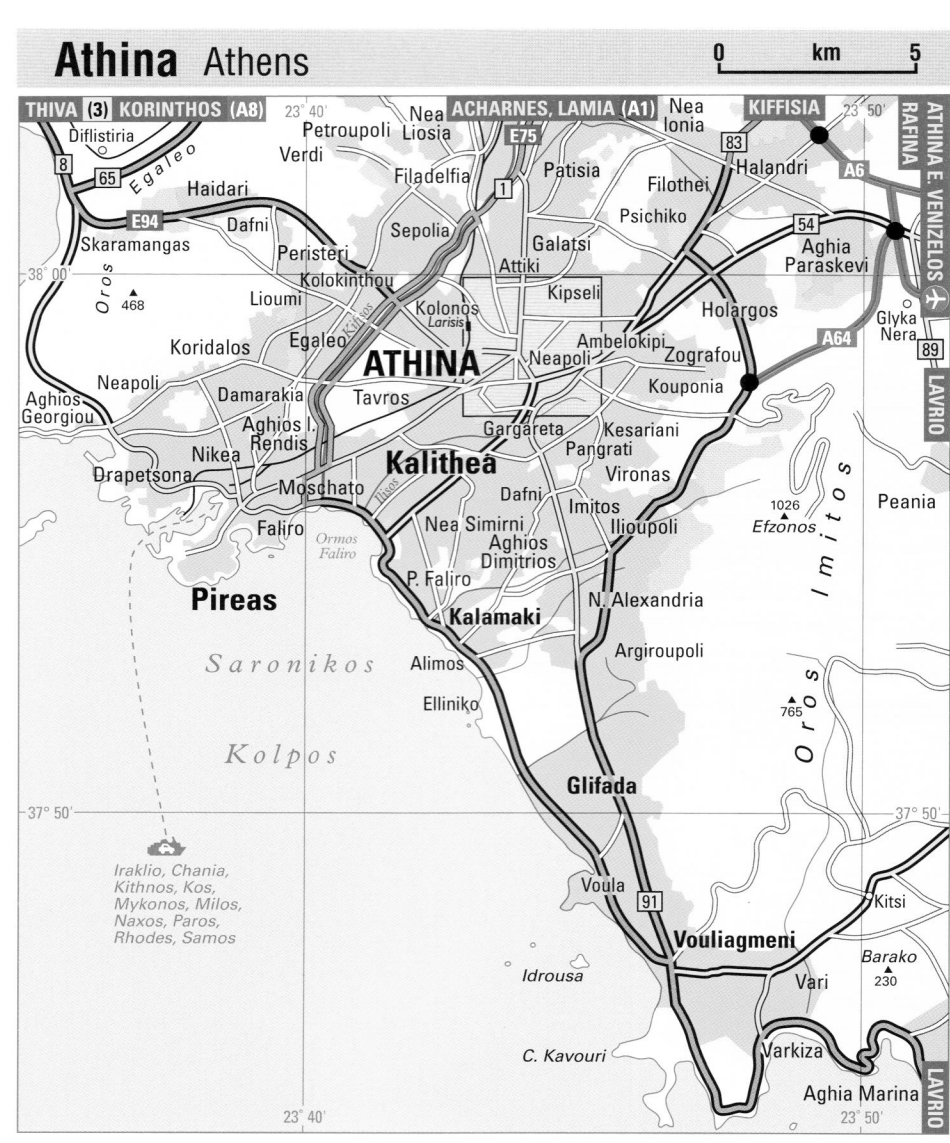

Athina Athens

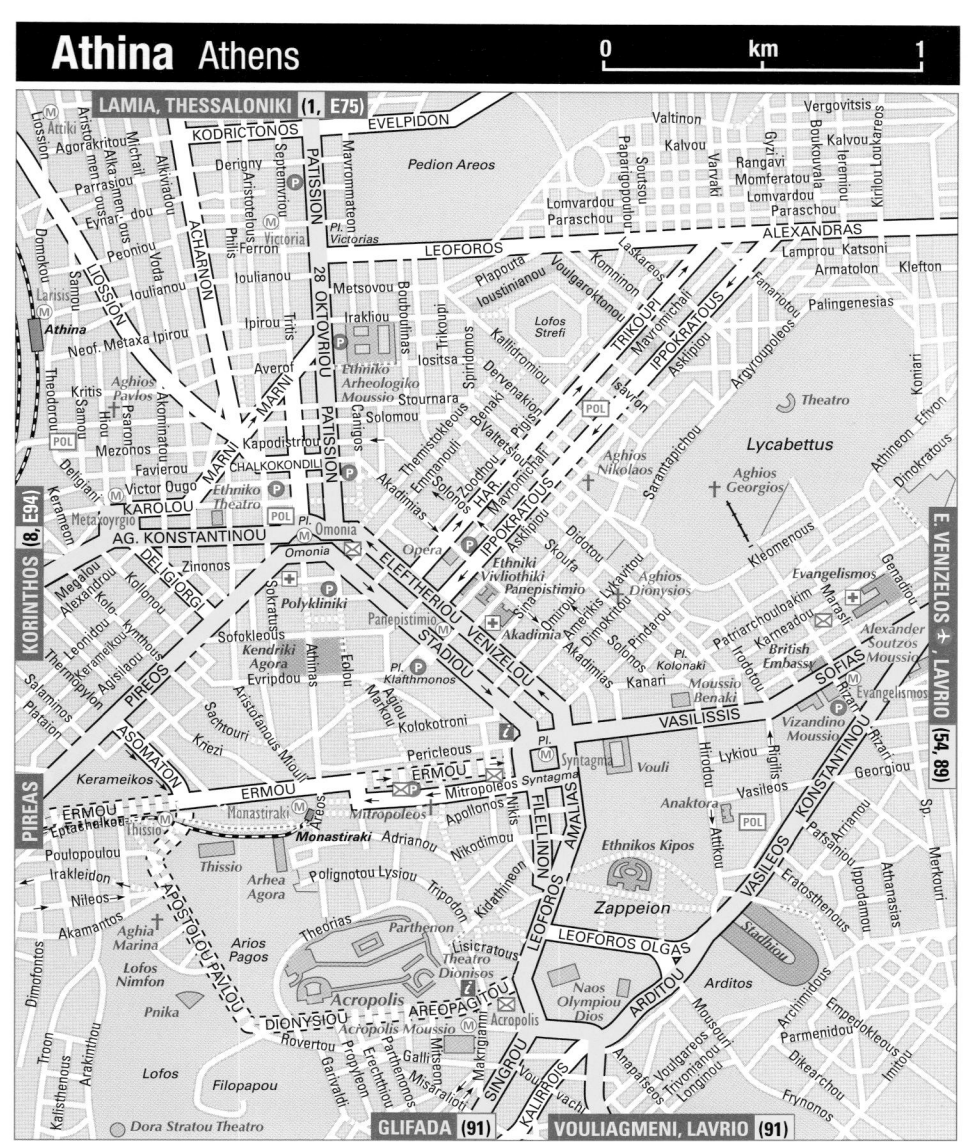

Basel

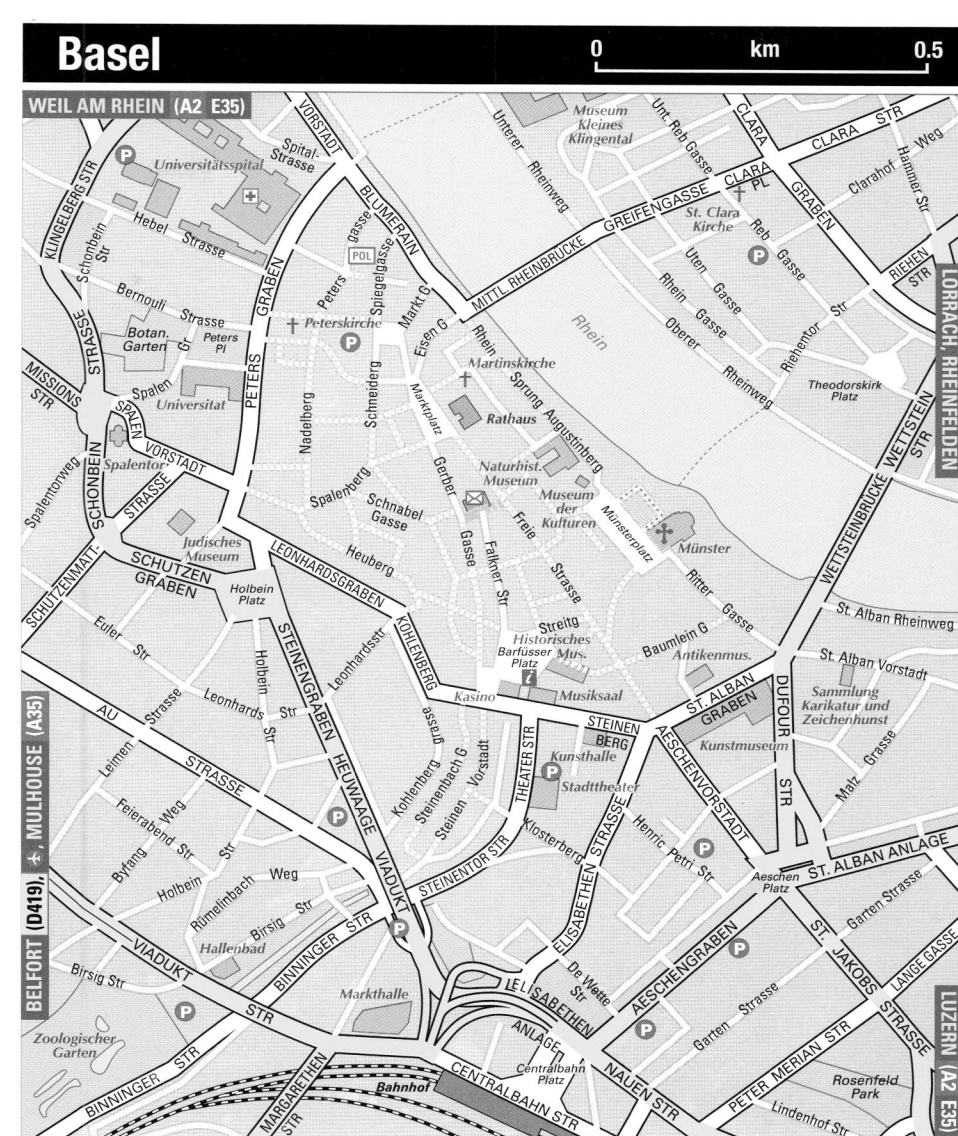

Barcelona

Barcelona

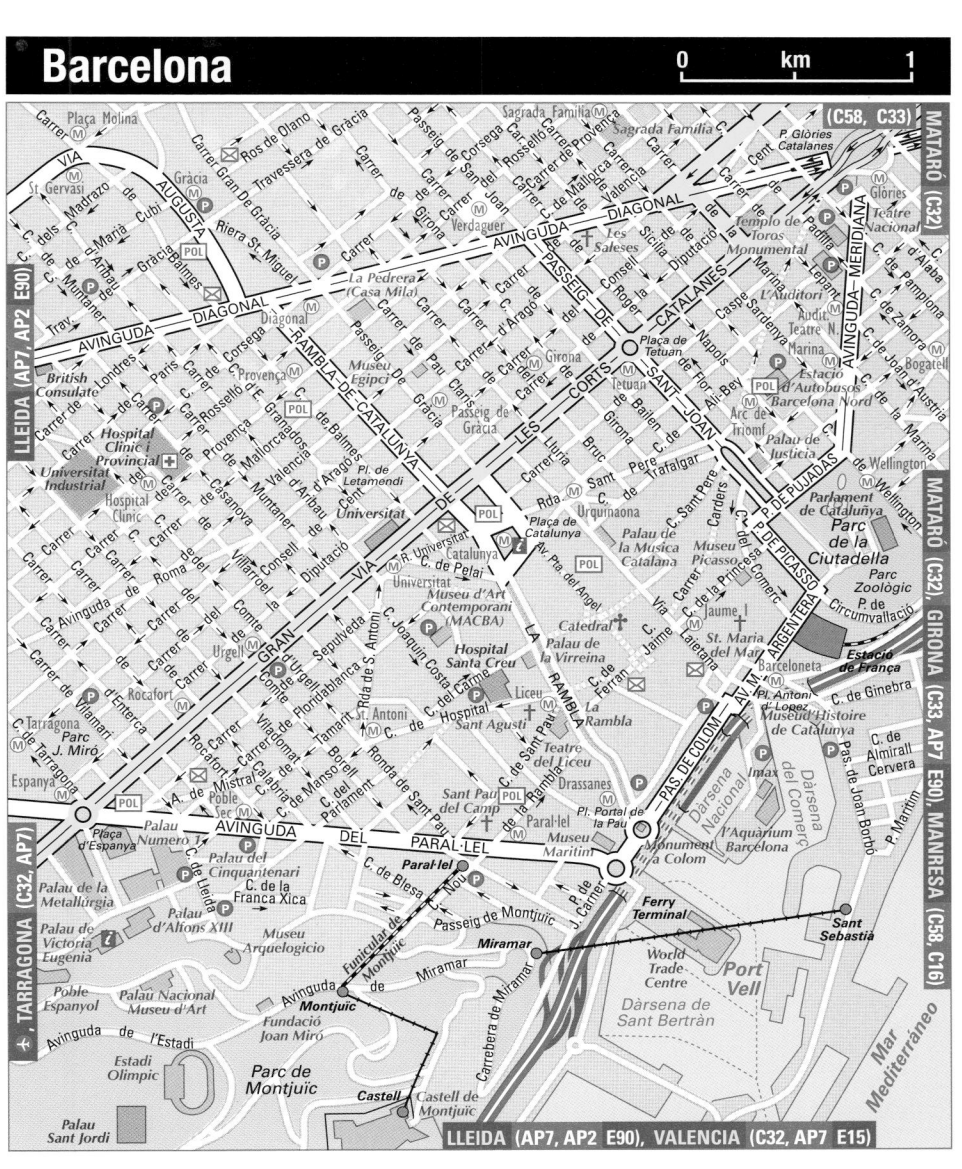

Berlin

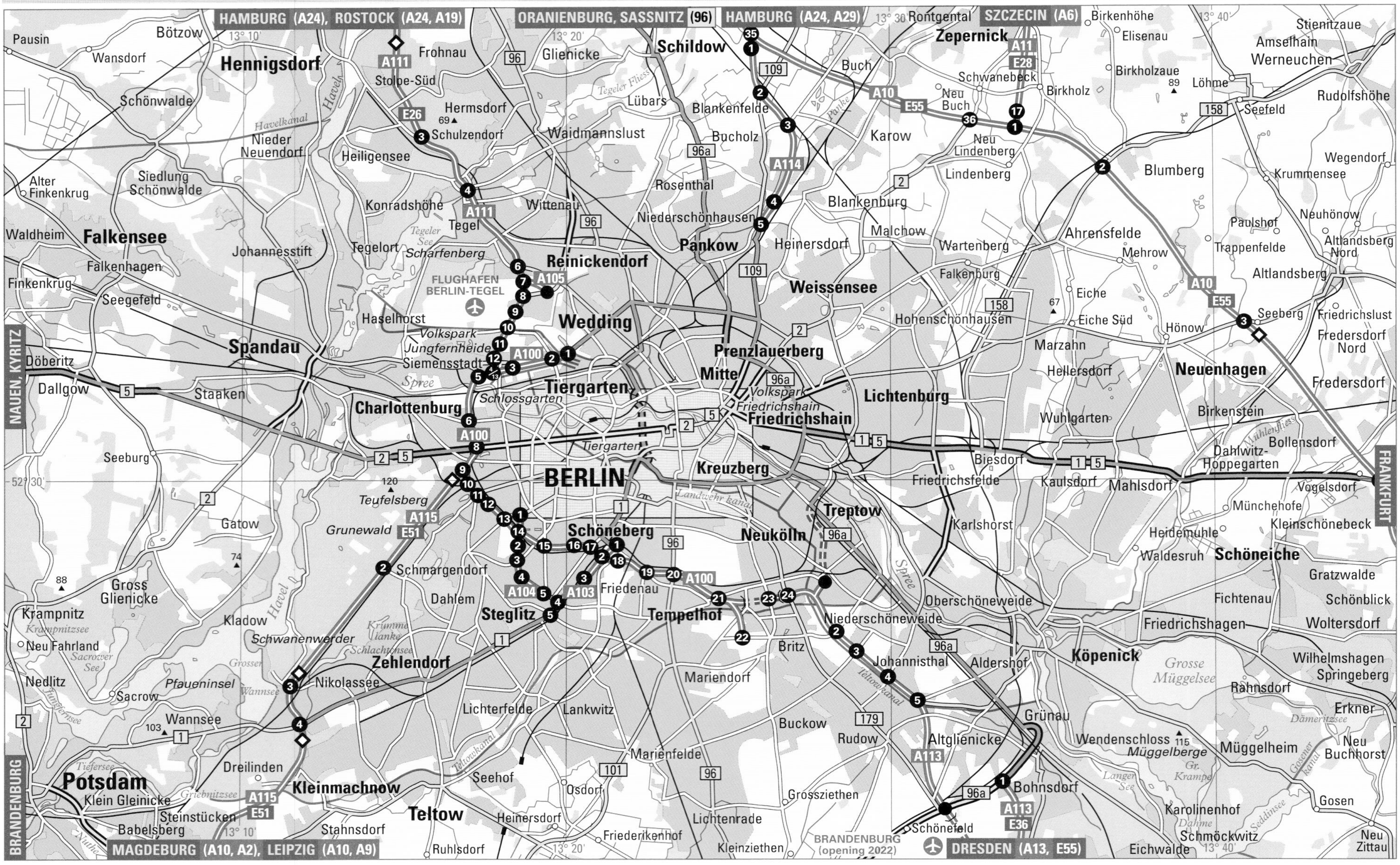

Berlin

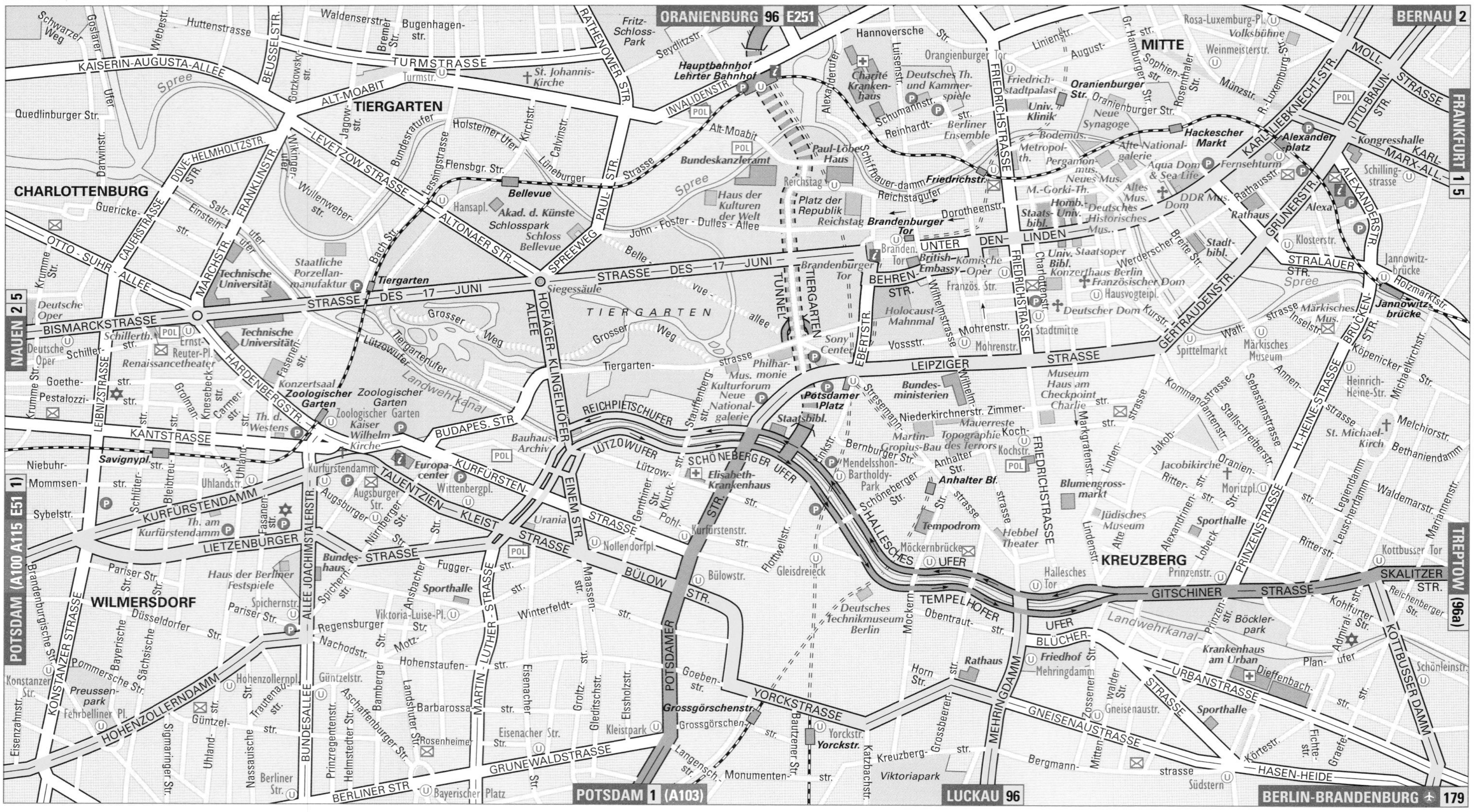

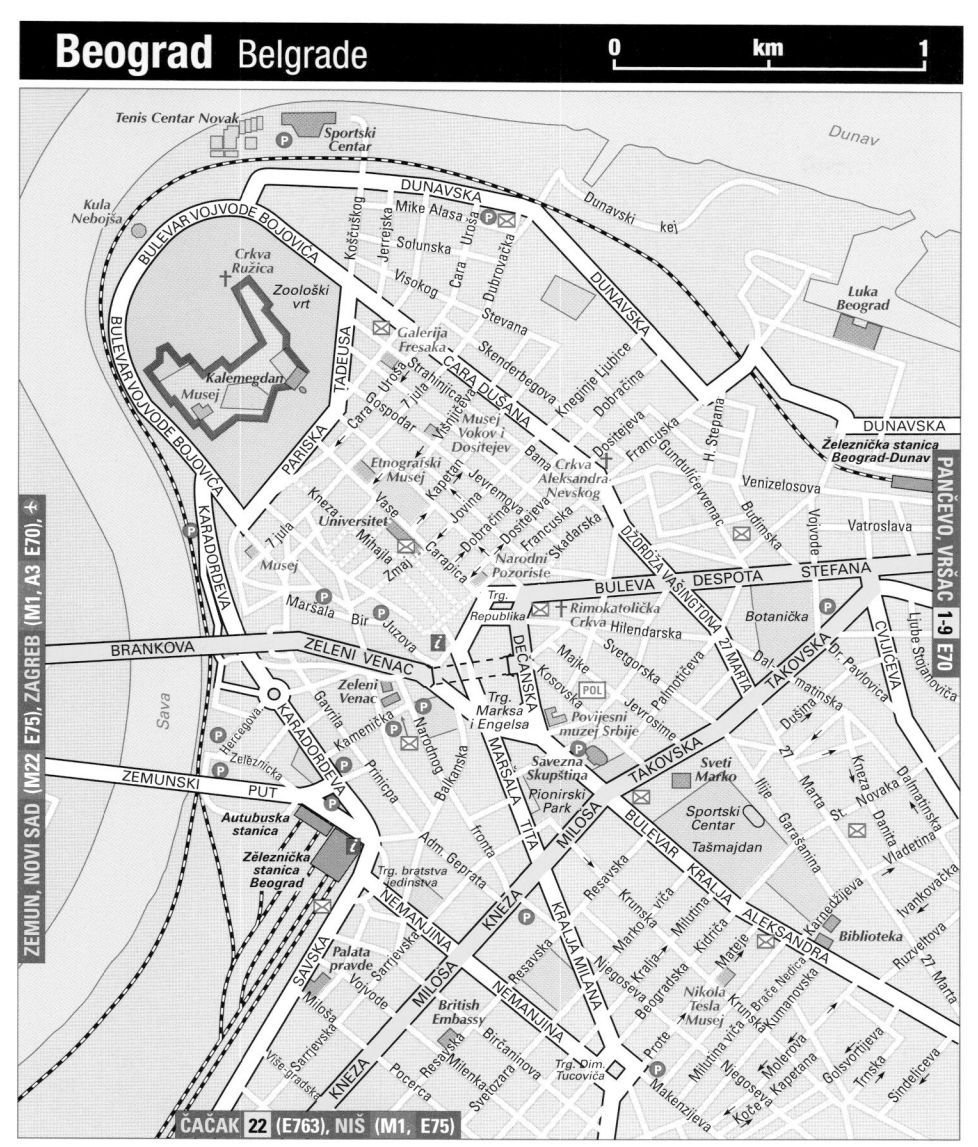

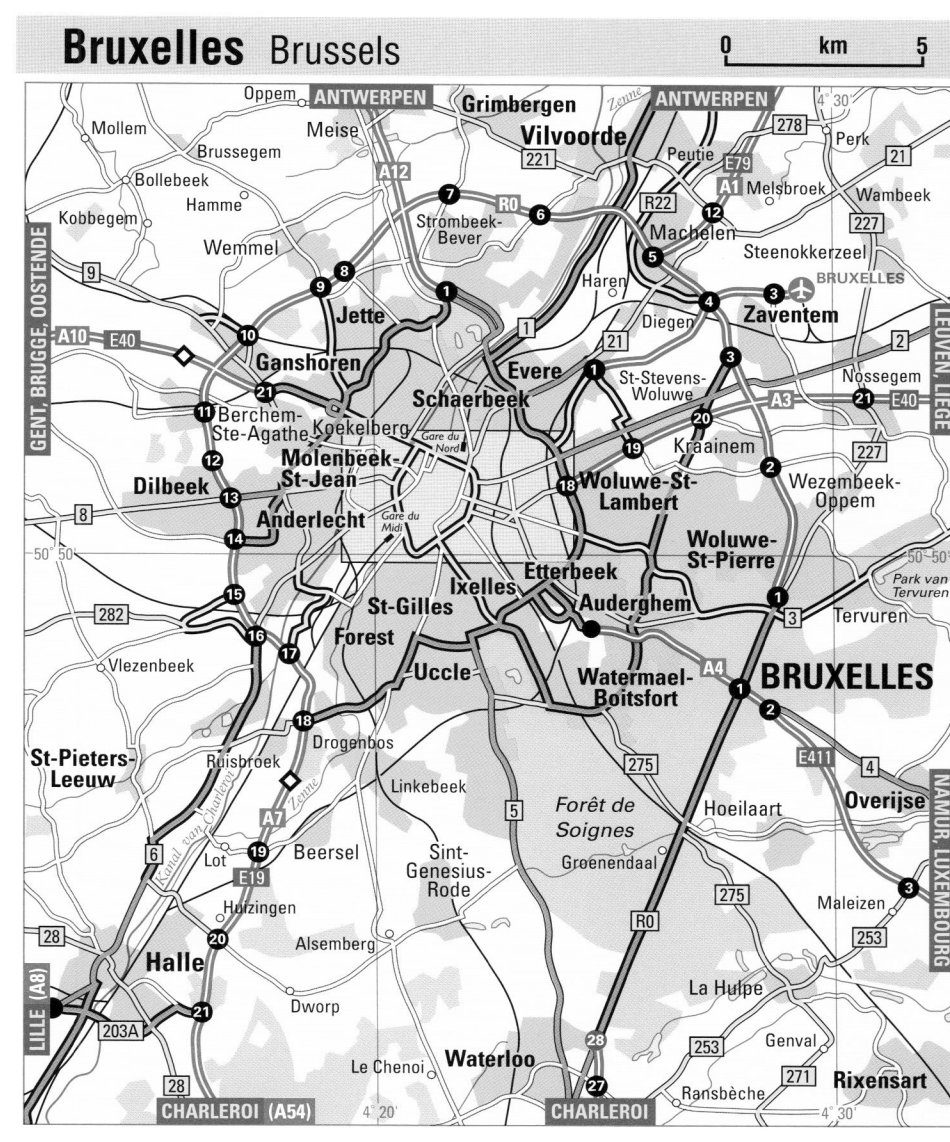

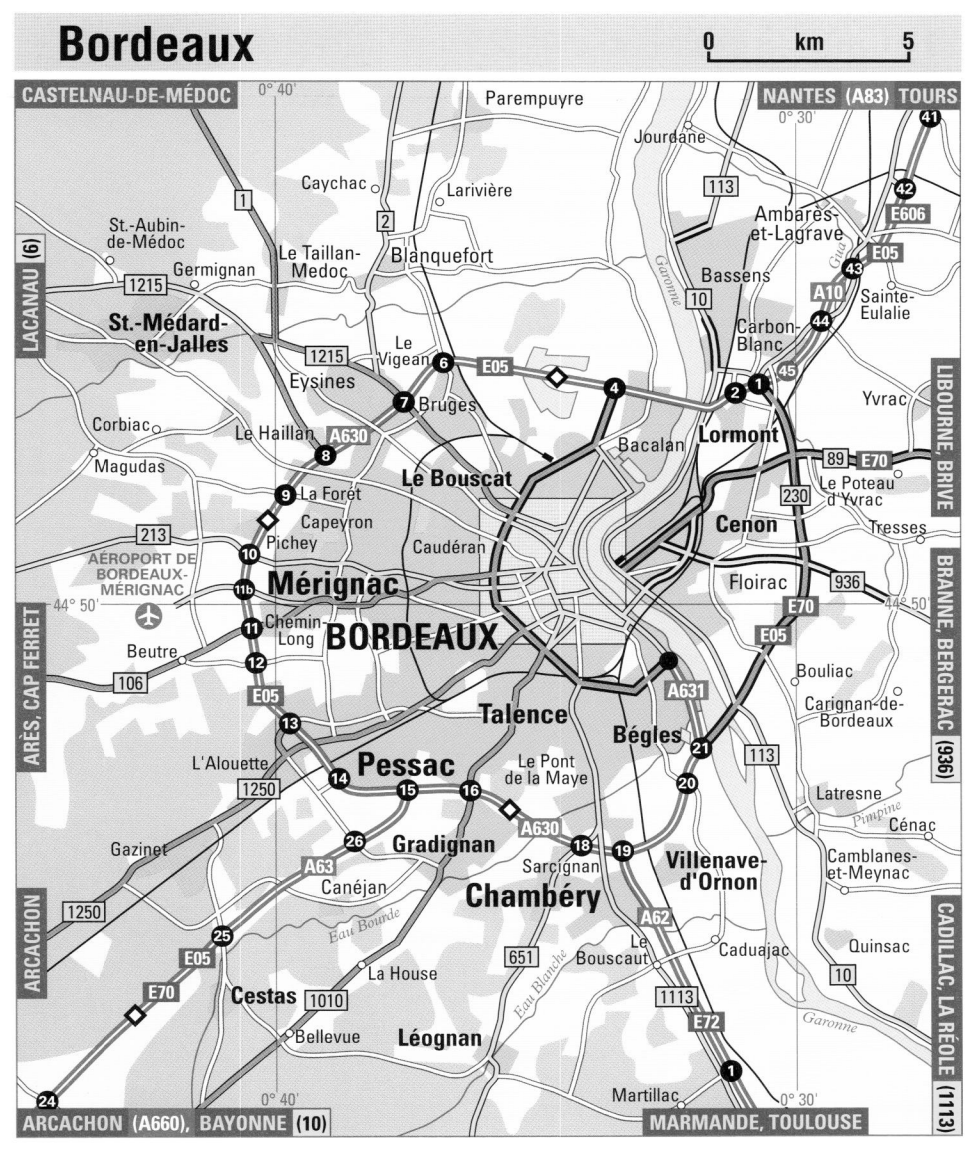

Bruxelles Brussels

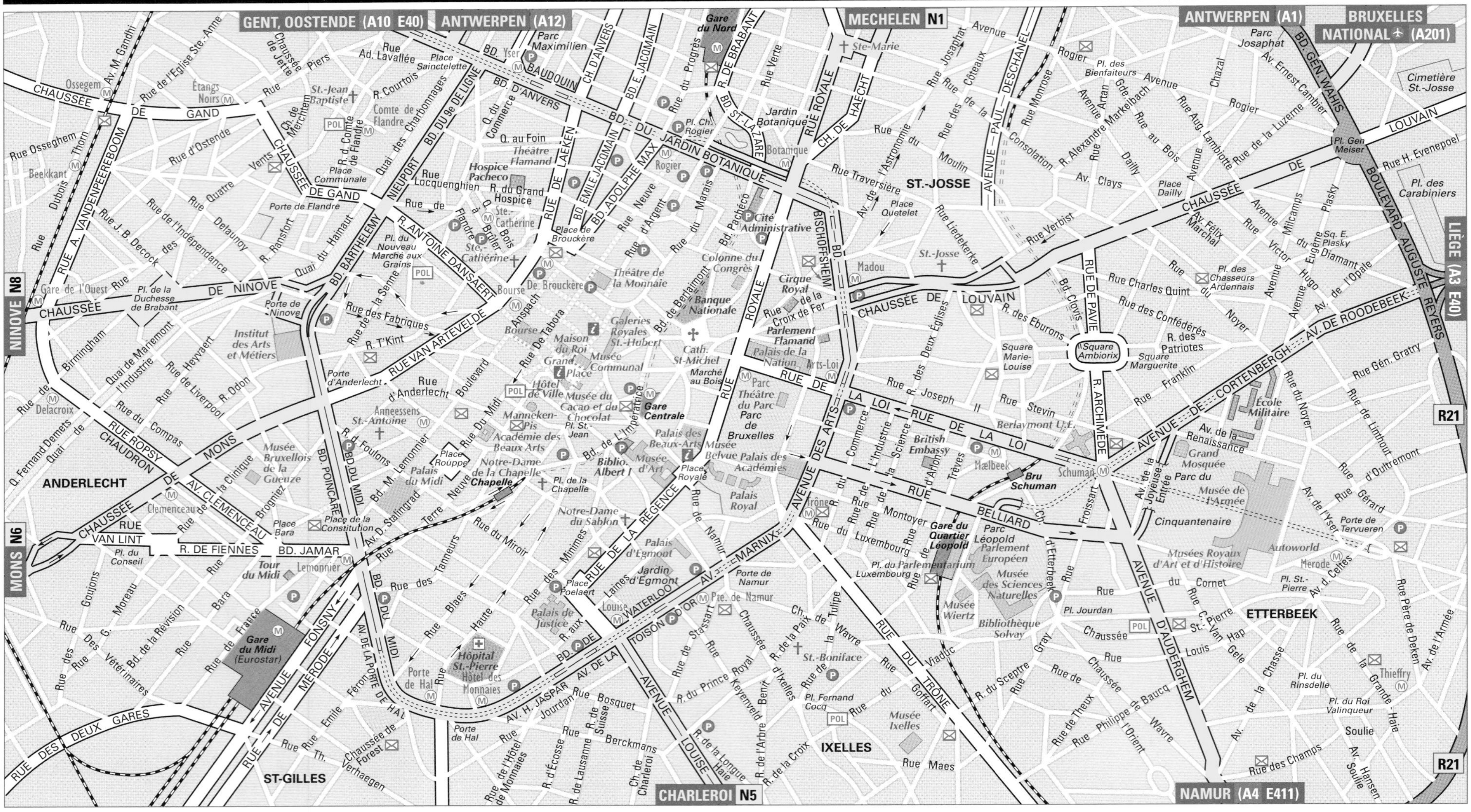

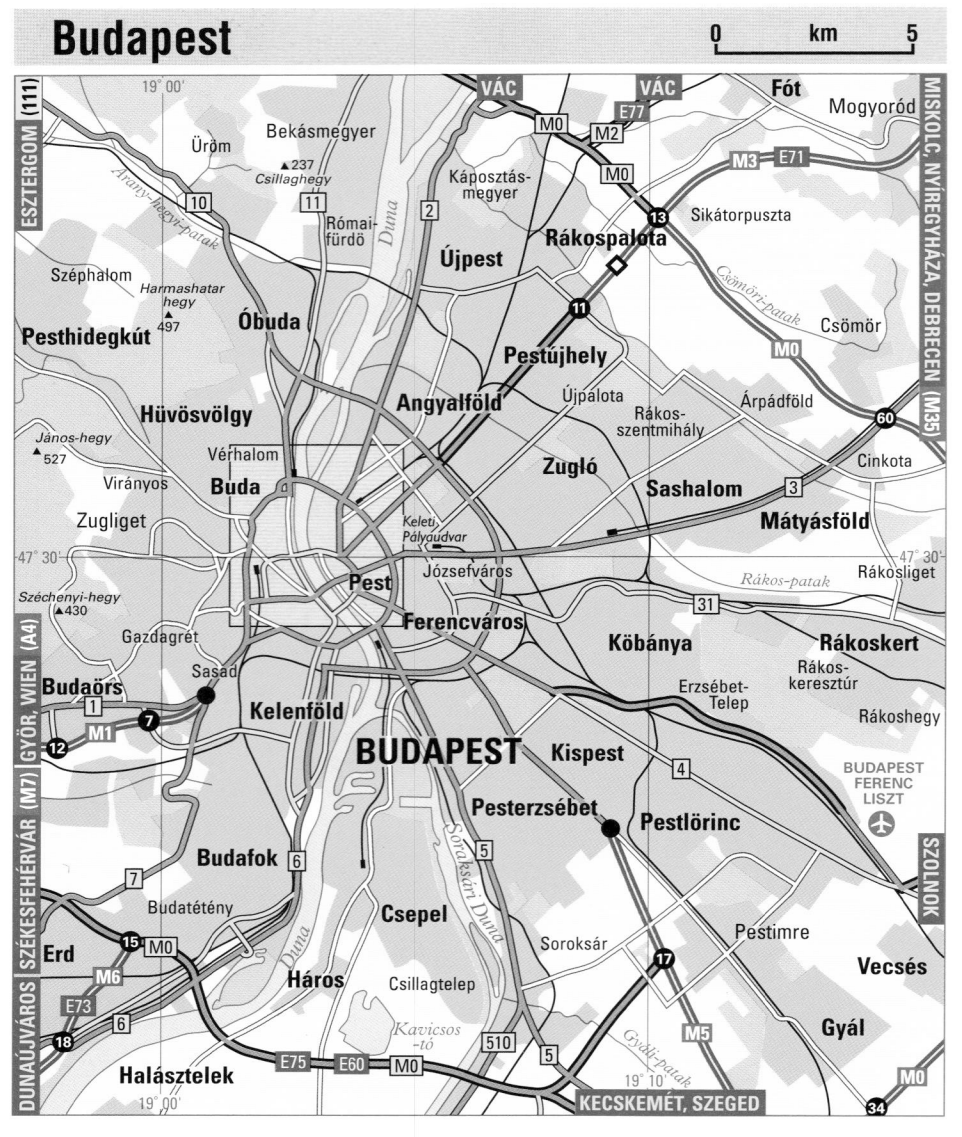

Budapest

Budapest

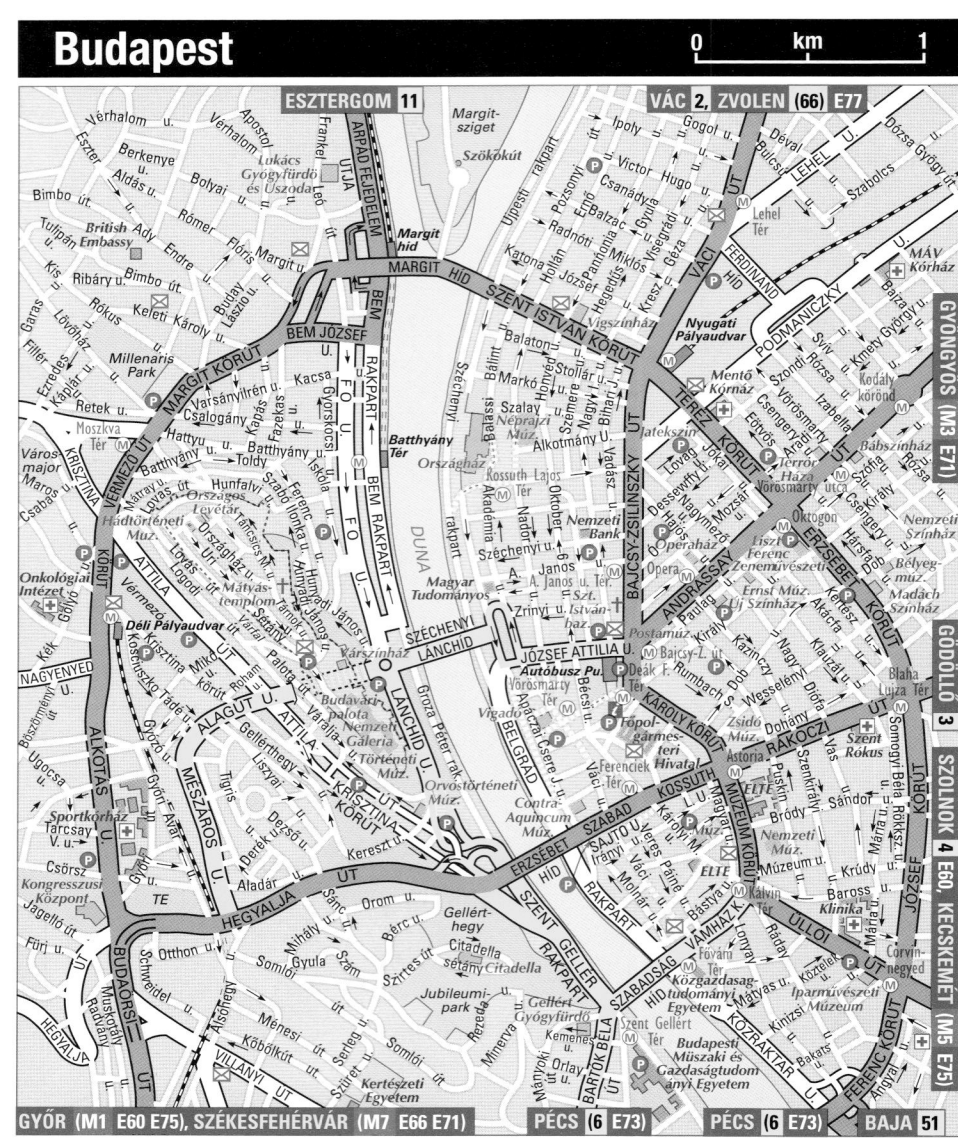

Dublin

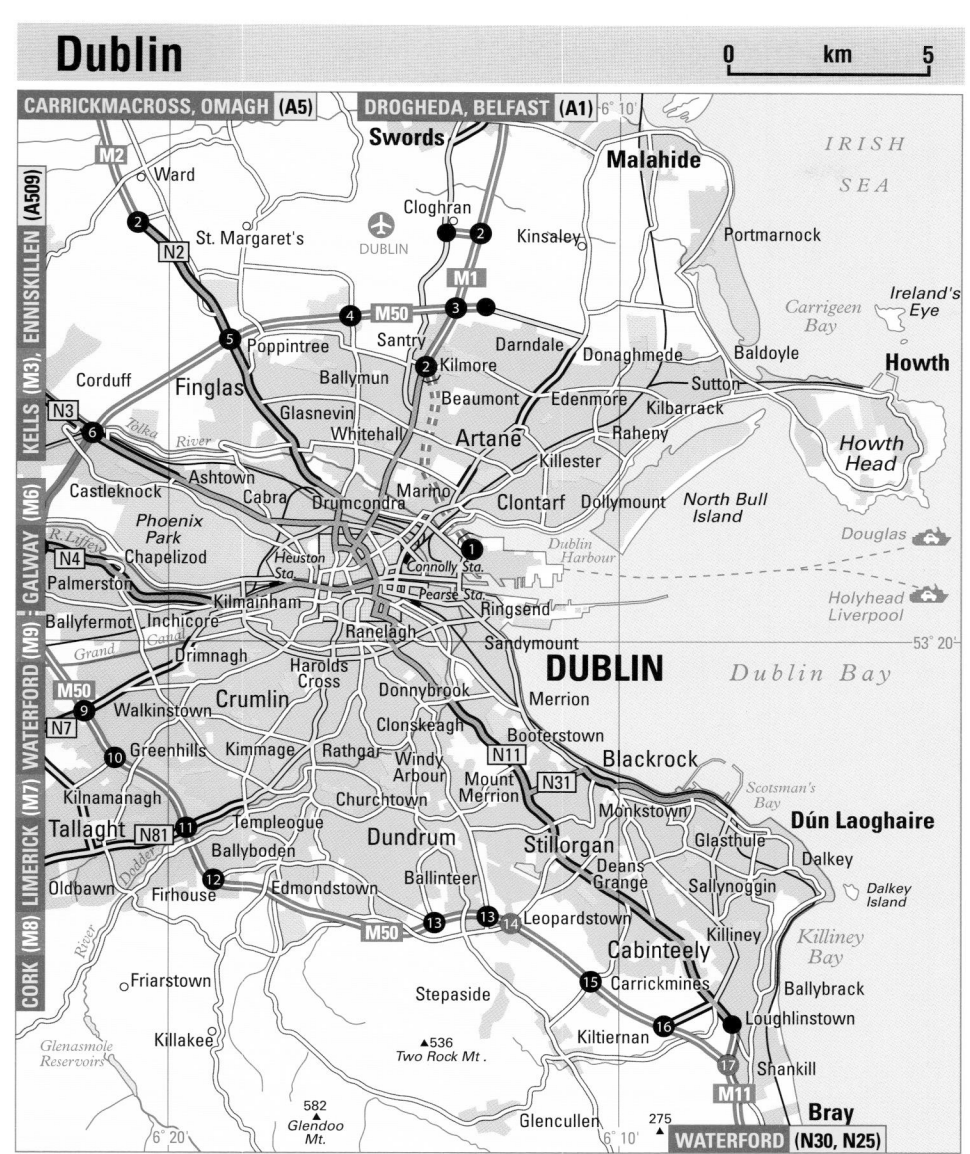

Dublin

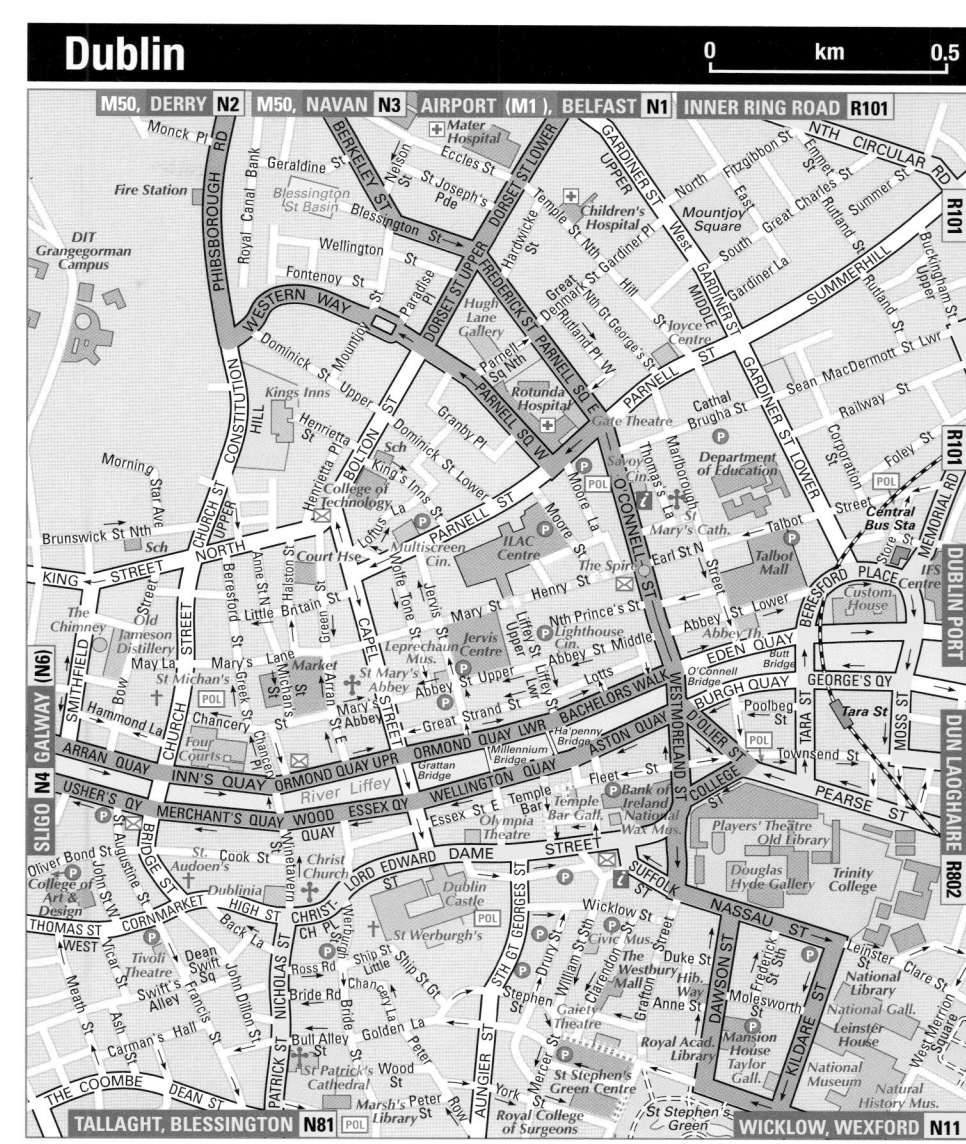

Düsseldorf

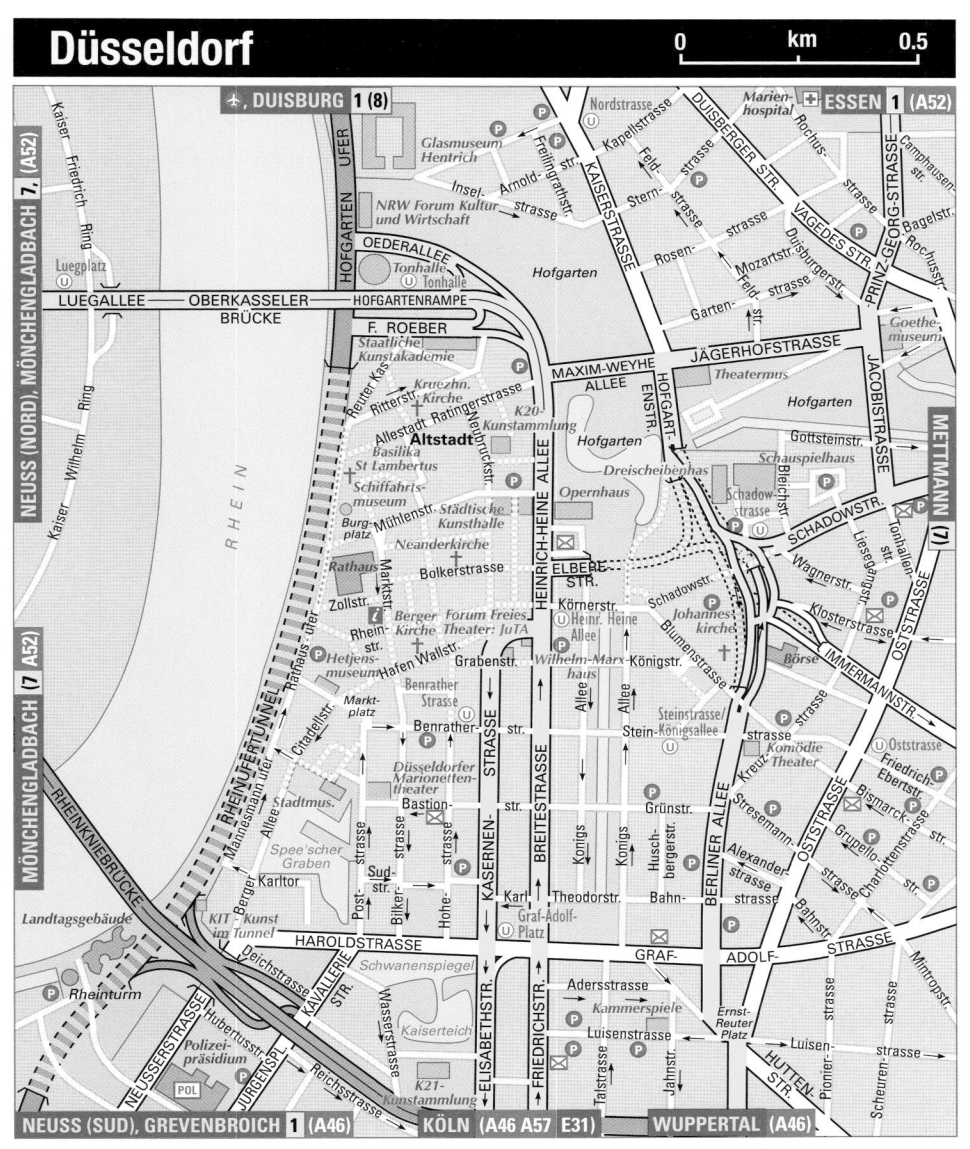

Edinburgh

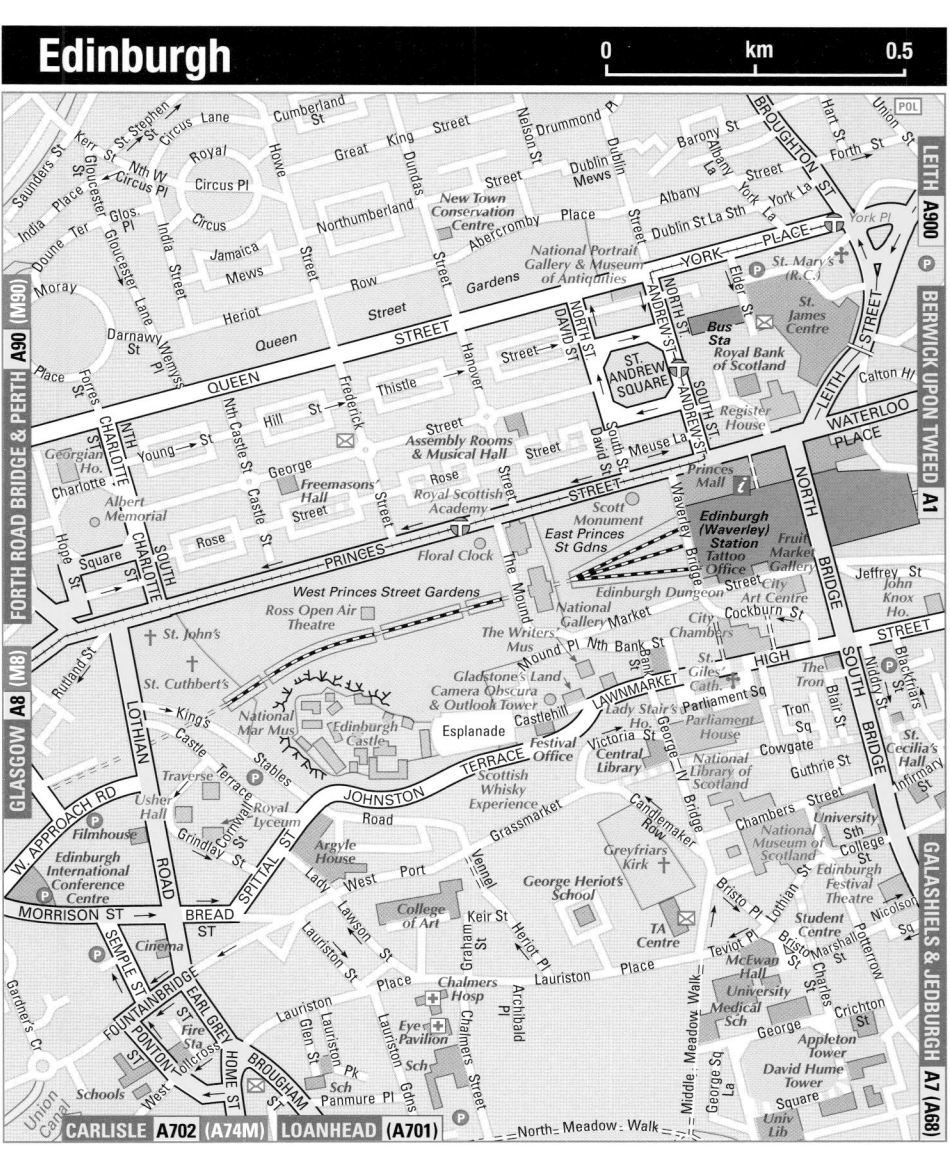

For **Cologne** see page 132

For **Copenhagen** see page 132

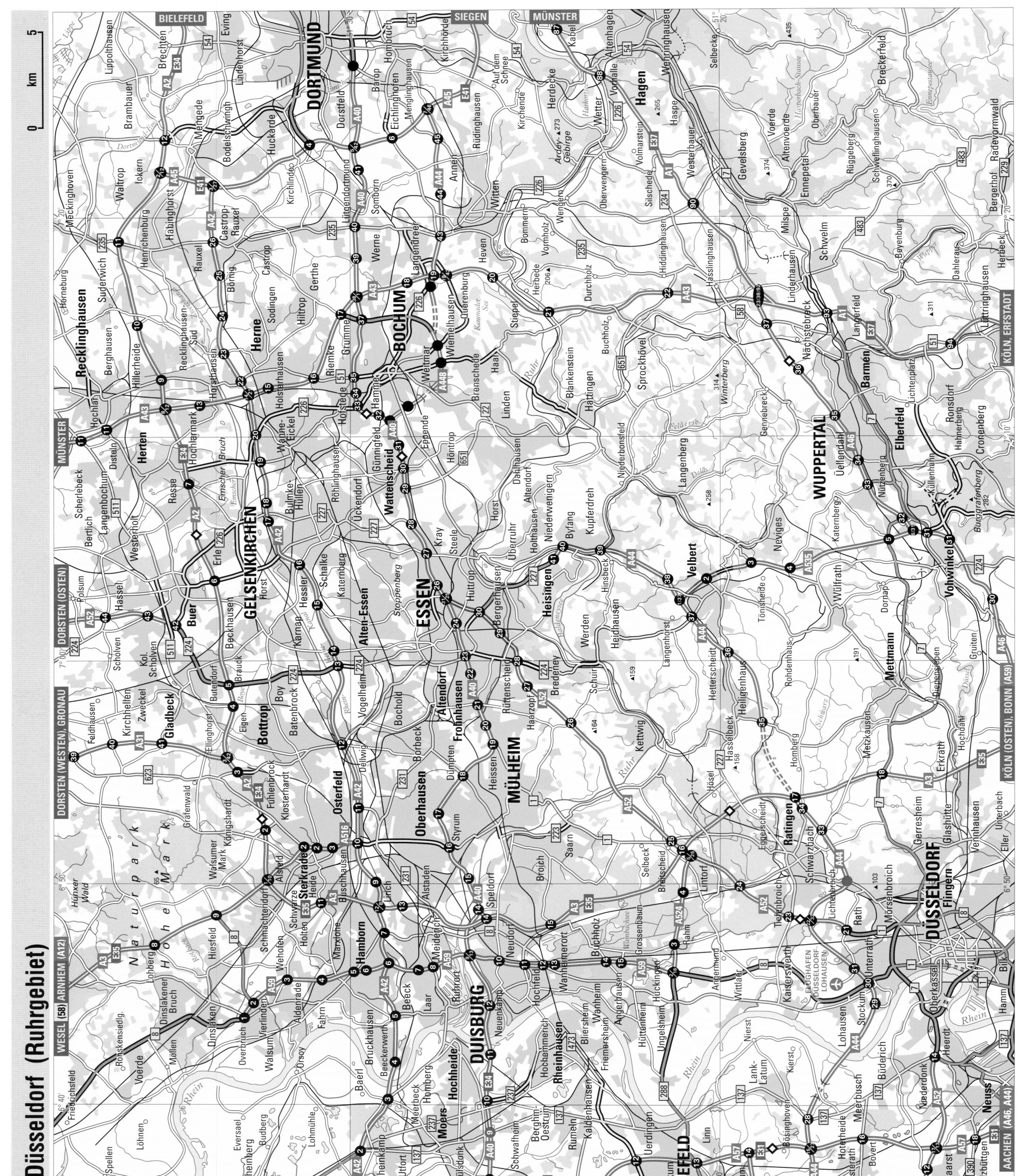

Düsseldorf (Ruhrgebiet)

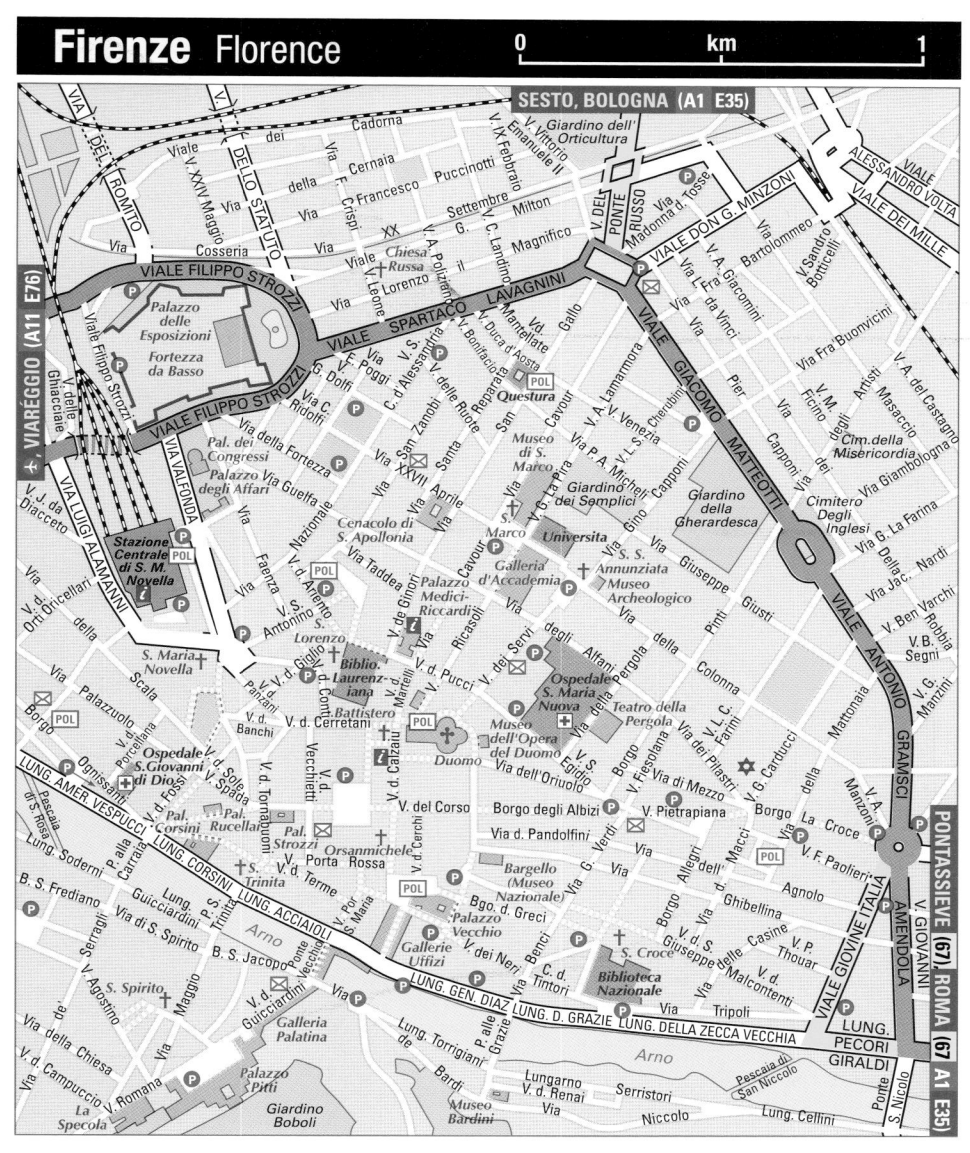

Firenze Florence

0 km 1

SESTO, BOLOGNA (A1 E35)

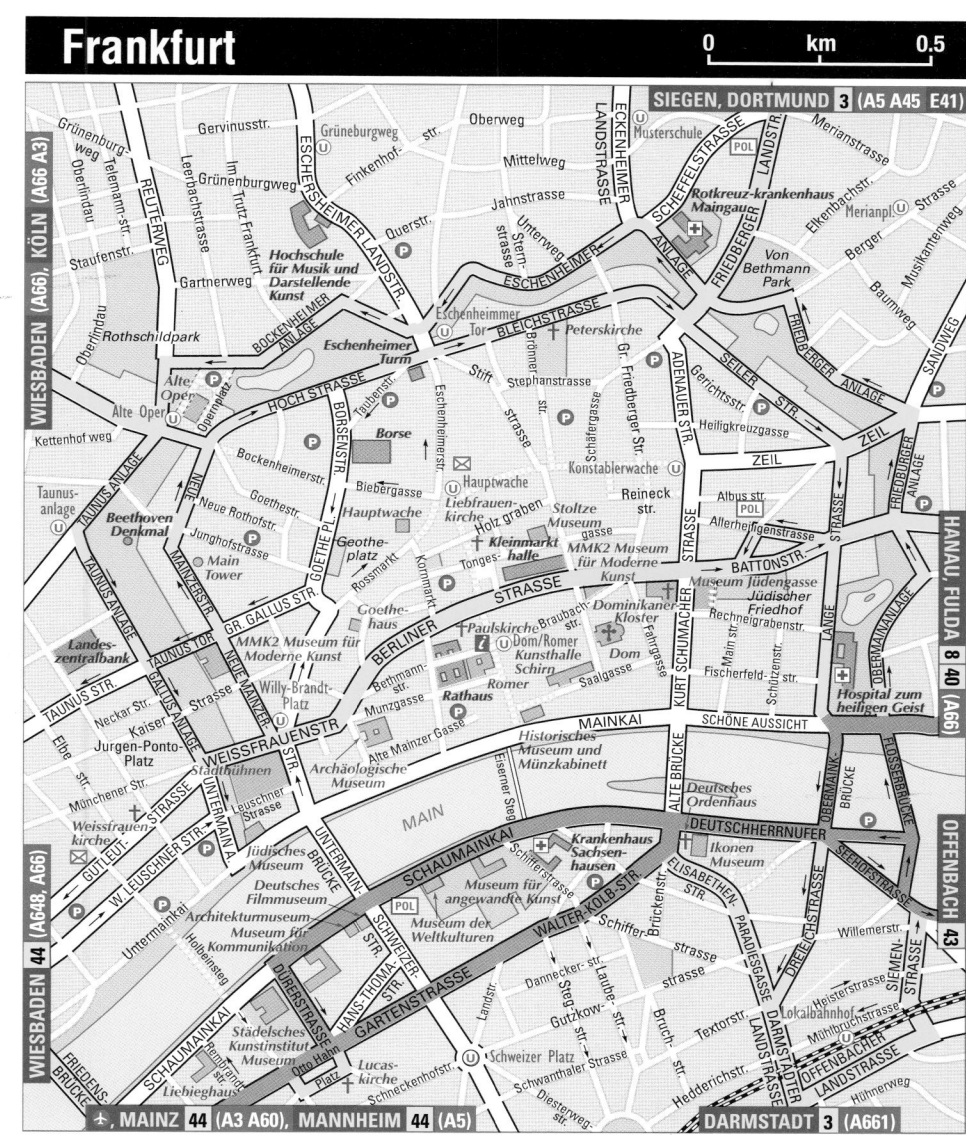

Frankfurt

0 km 0.5

SIEGEN, DORTMUND 3 (A5 A45 E41)

MAINZ 44 (A3 A60), MANNHEIM 44 (A5)

DARMSTADT 3 (A661)

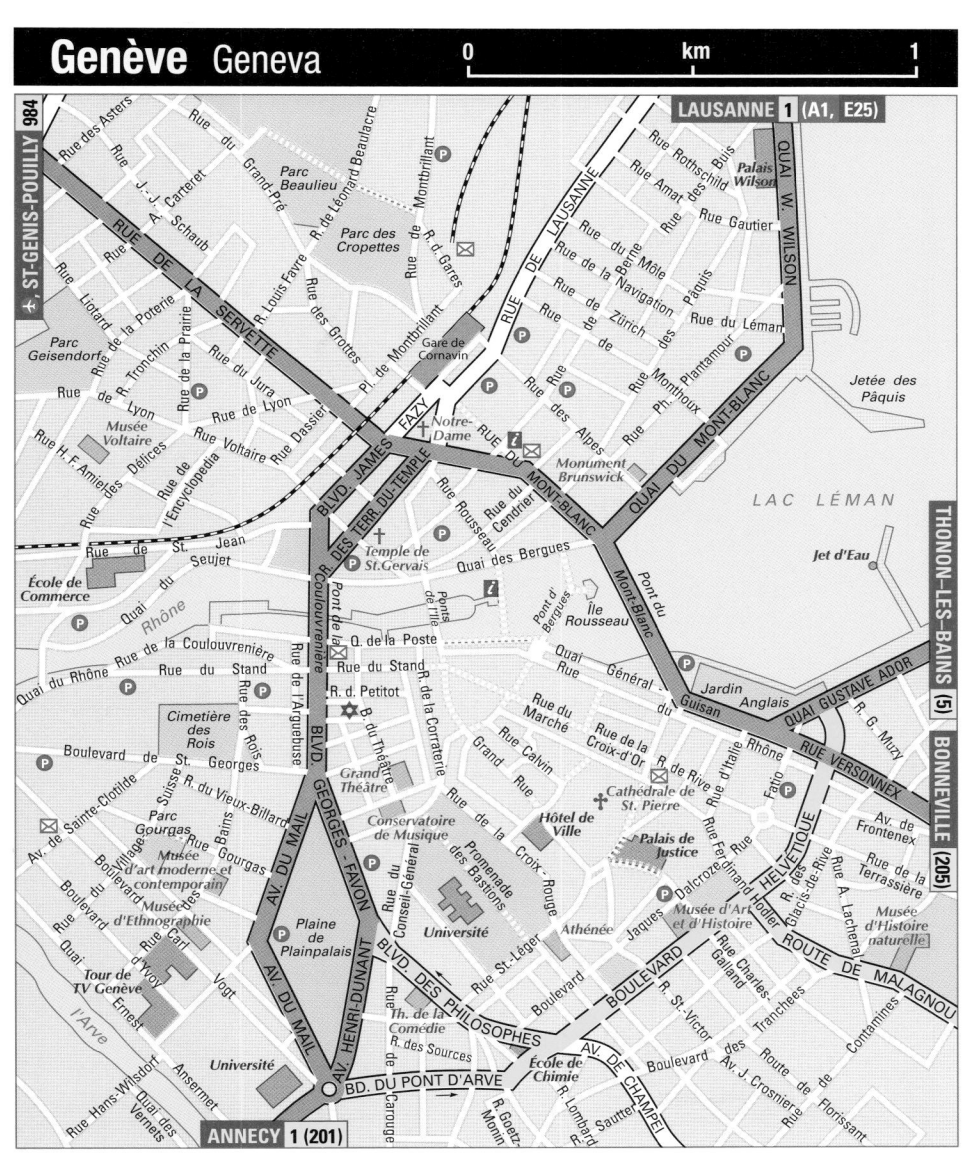

Genève Geneva

0 km 1

LAUSANNE 1 (A1, E25)

ANNECY 1 (201)

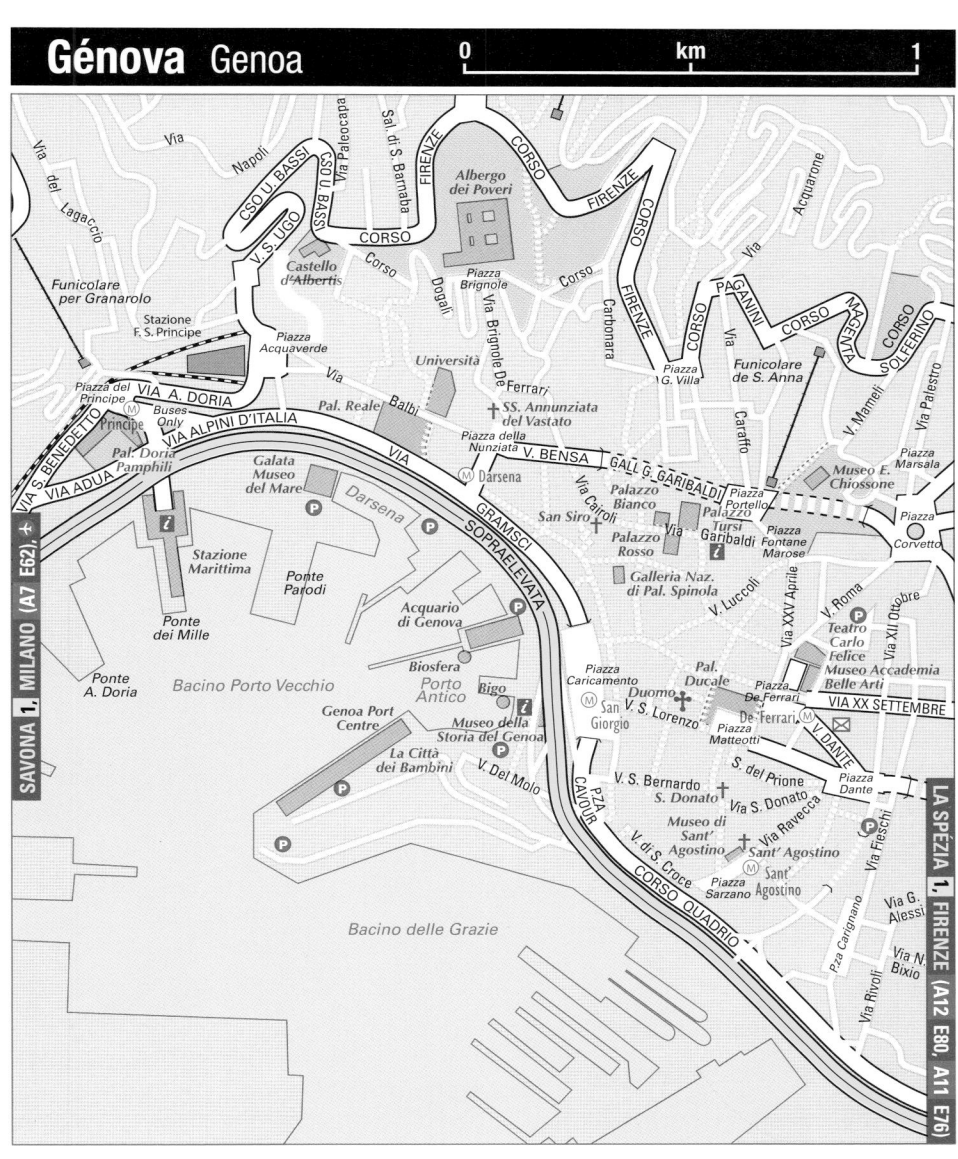

Génova Genoa

0 km 1

Granada

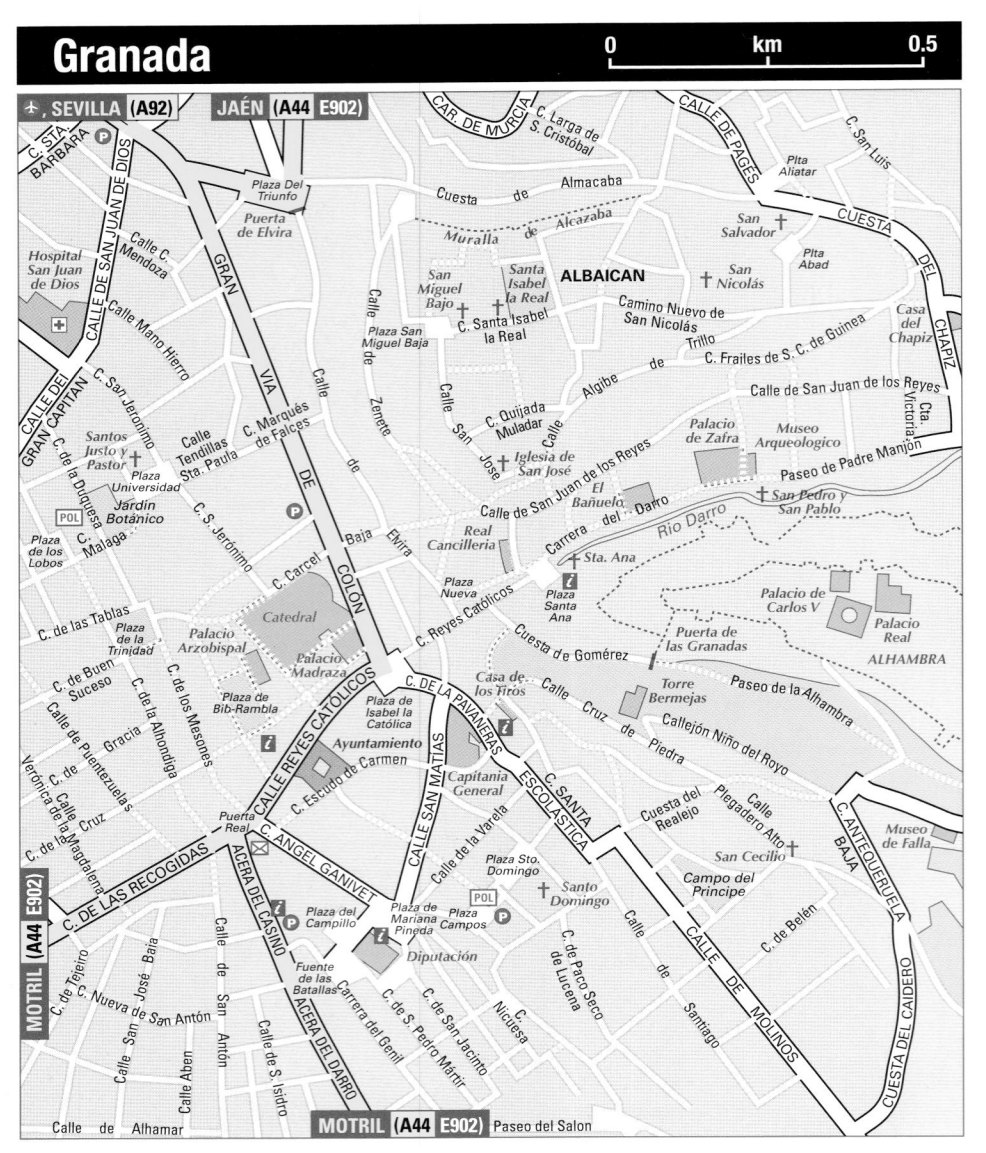

Göteborg Gothenburg

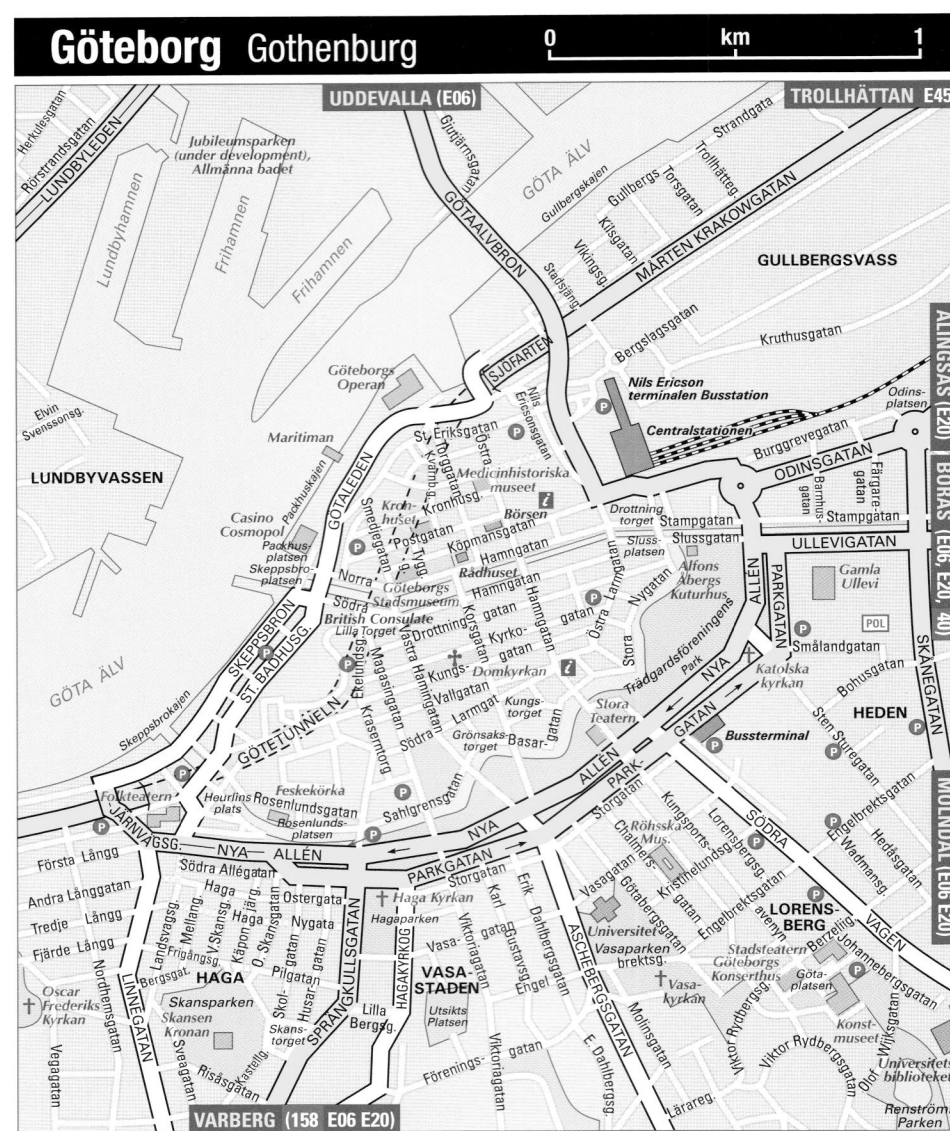

Hamburg

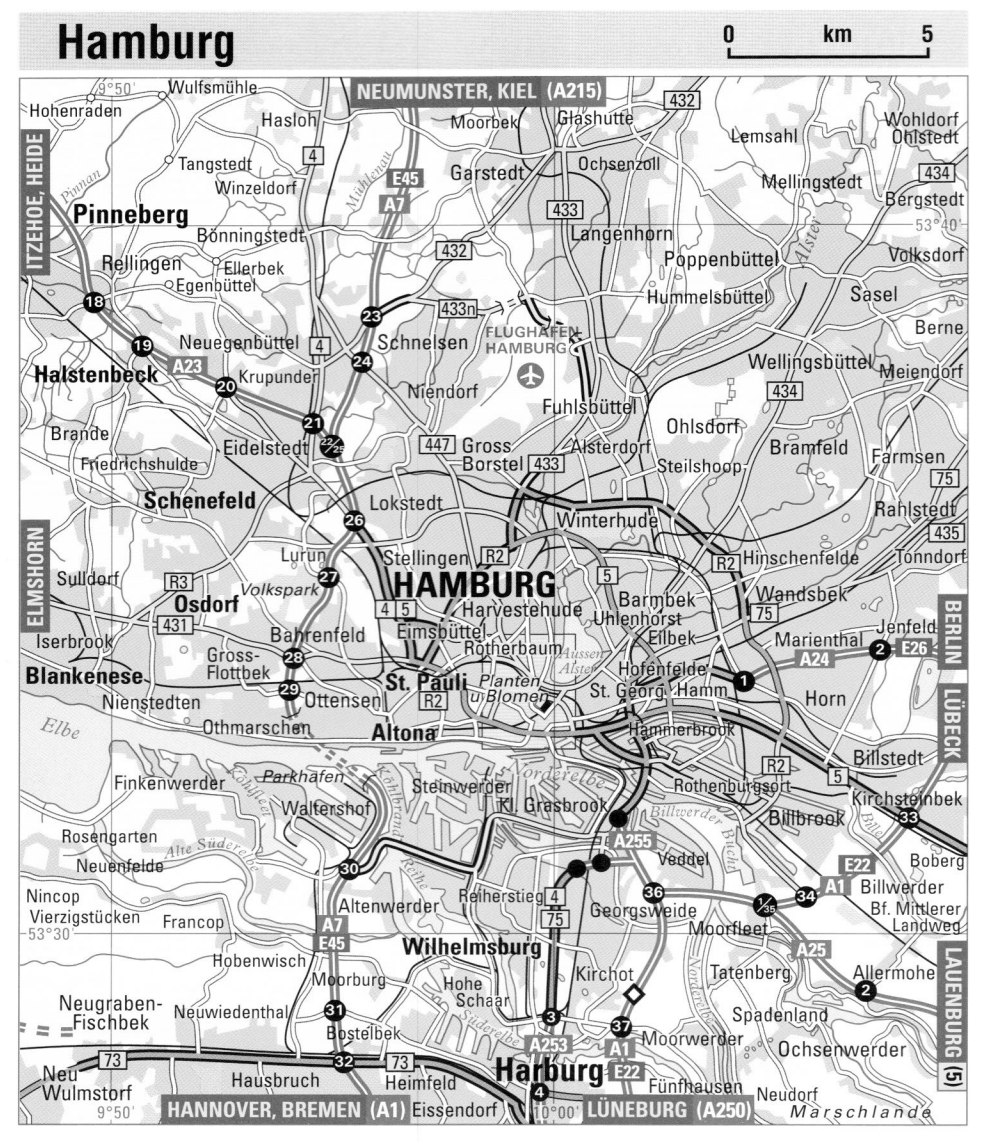

Hamburg

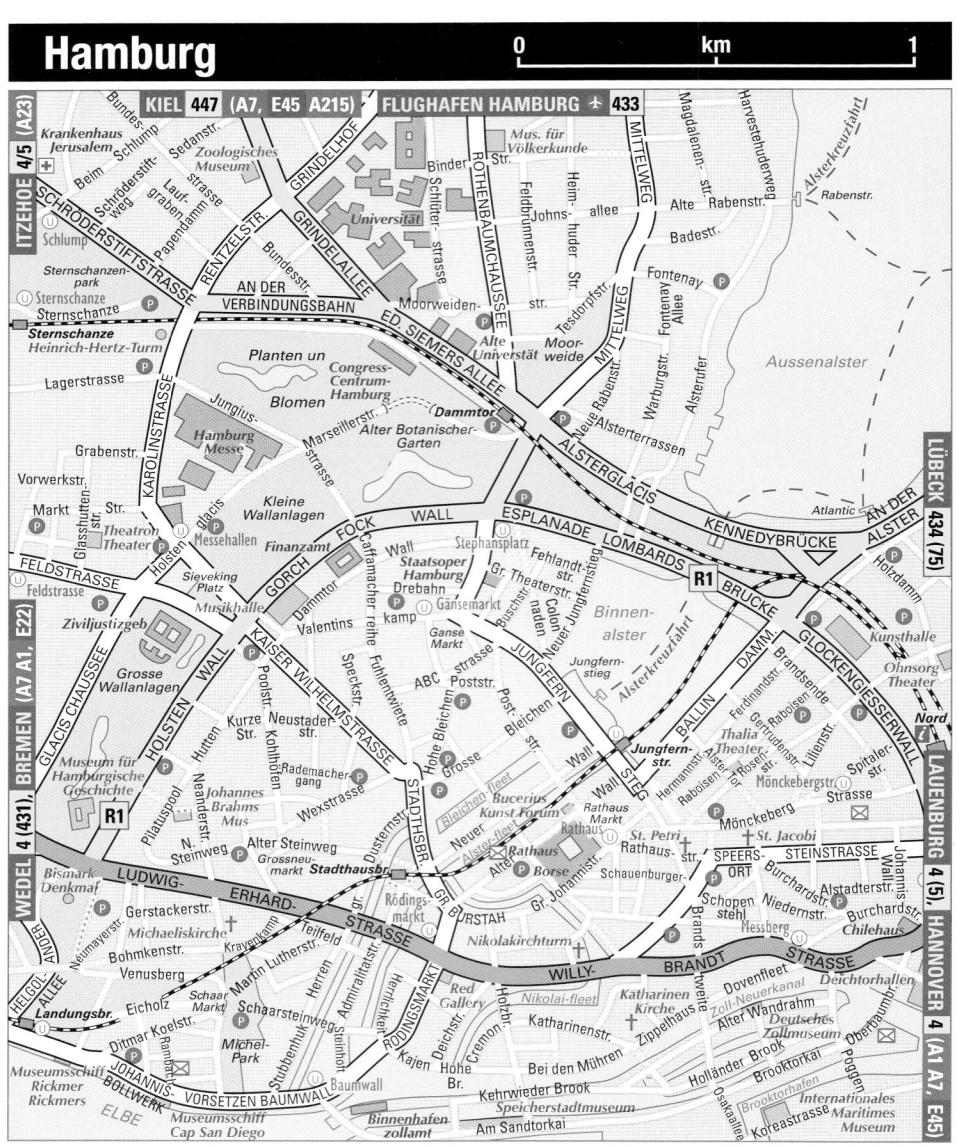

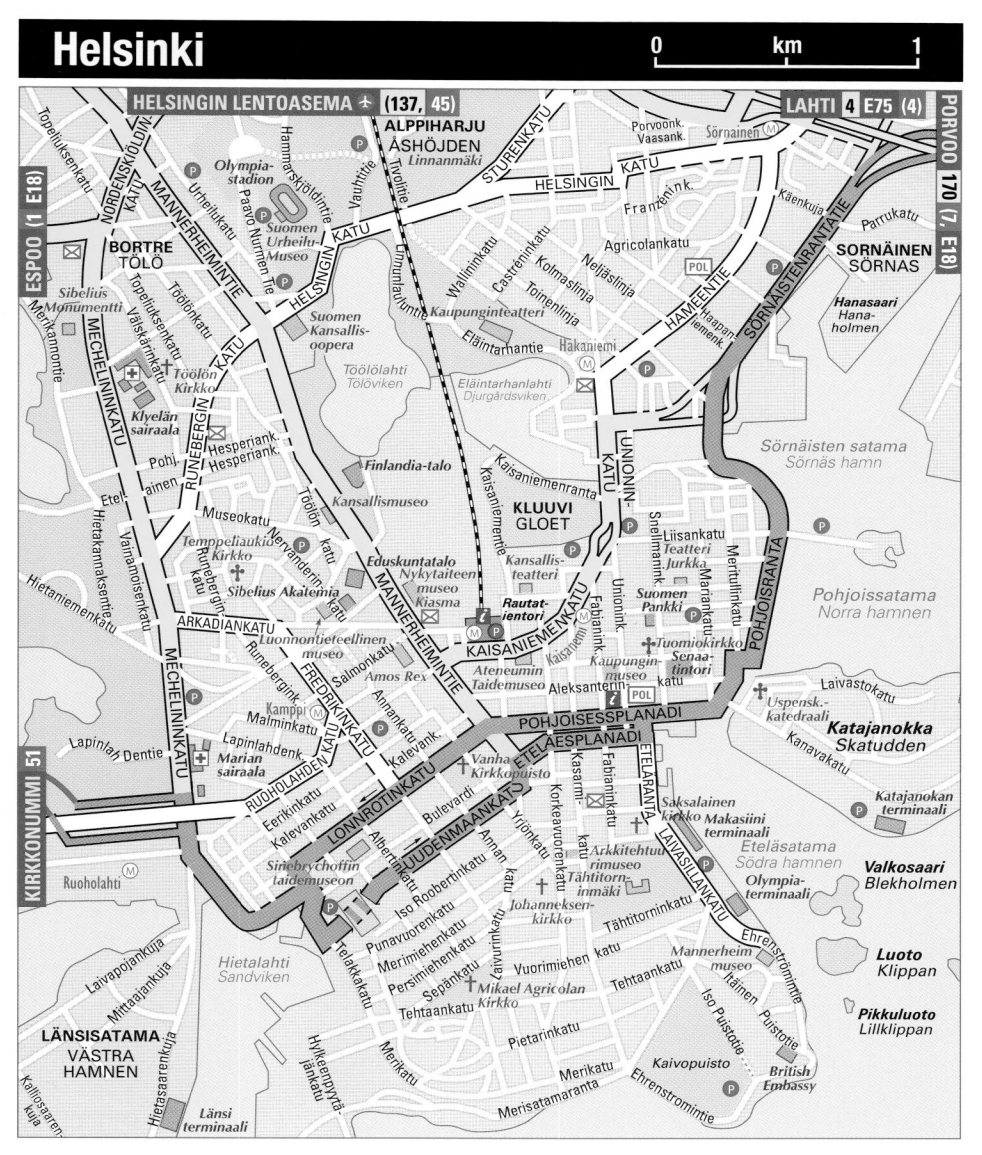

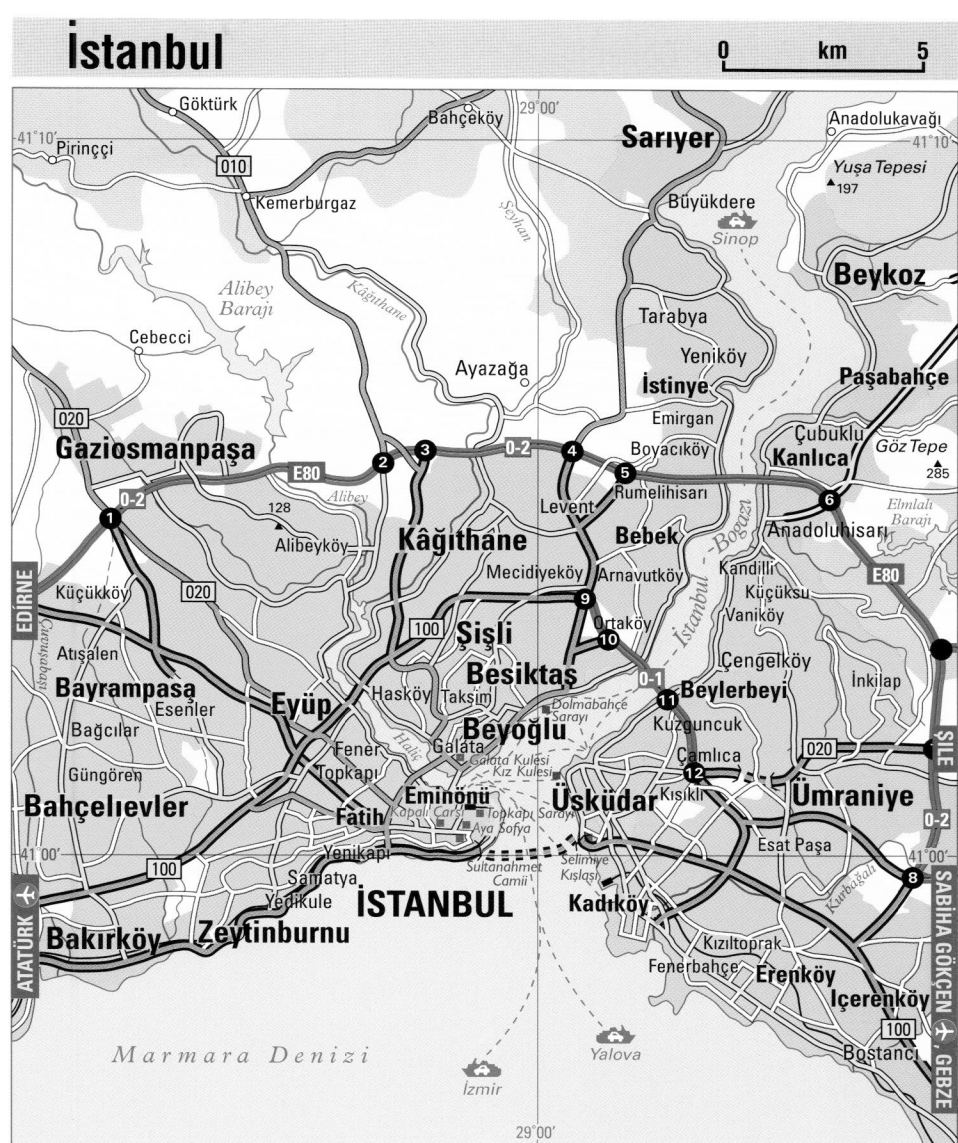

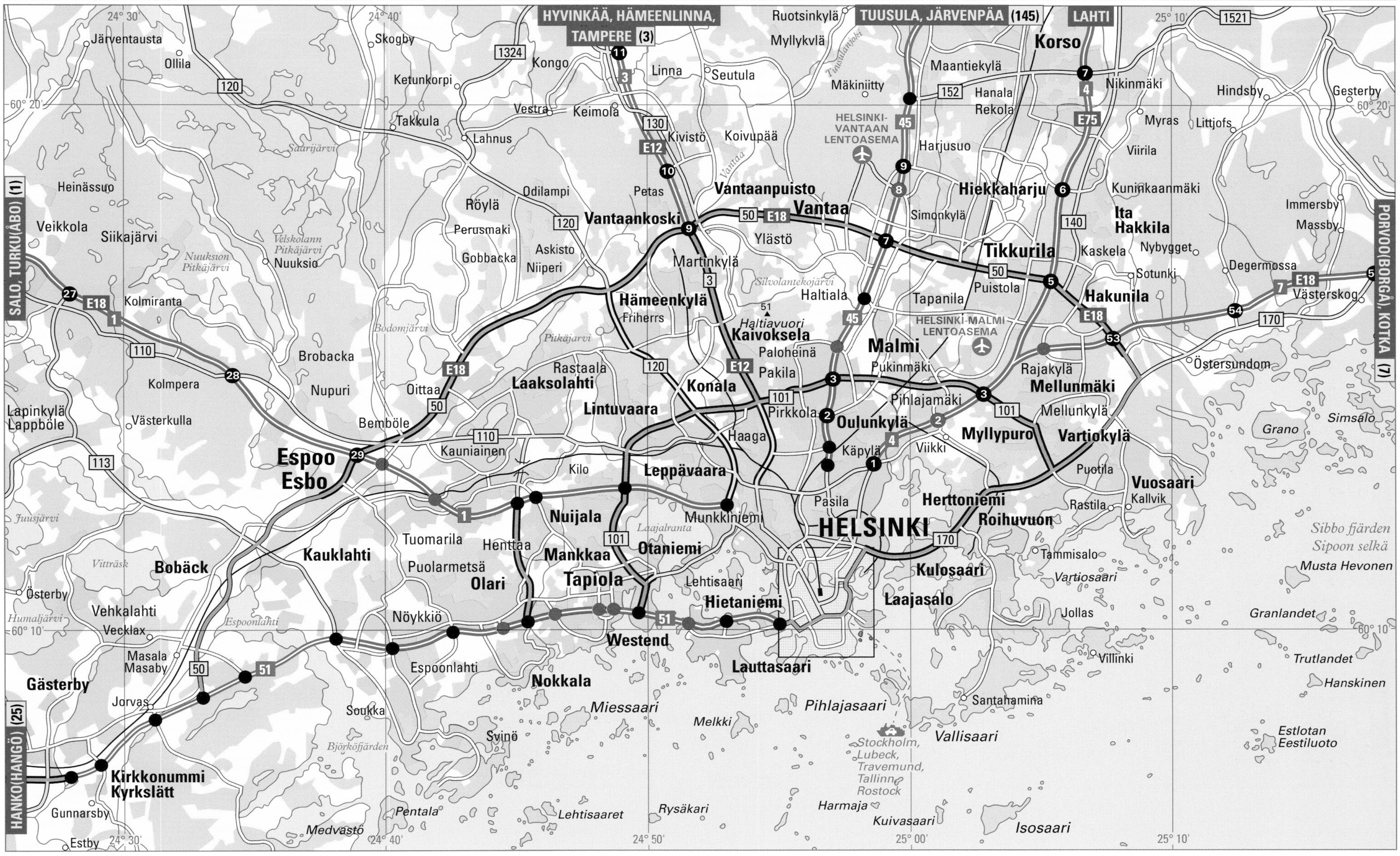

København Copenhagen

0 km 5

Köln Cologne

0 km 1

København Copenhagen

0 km 1

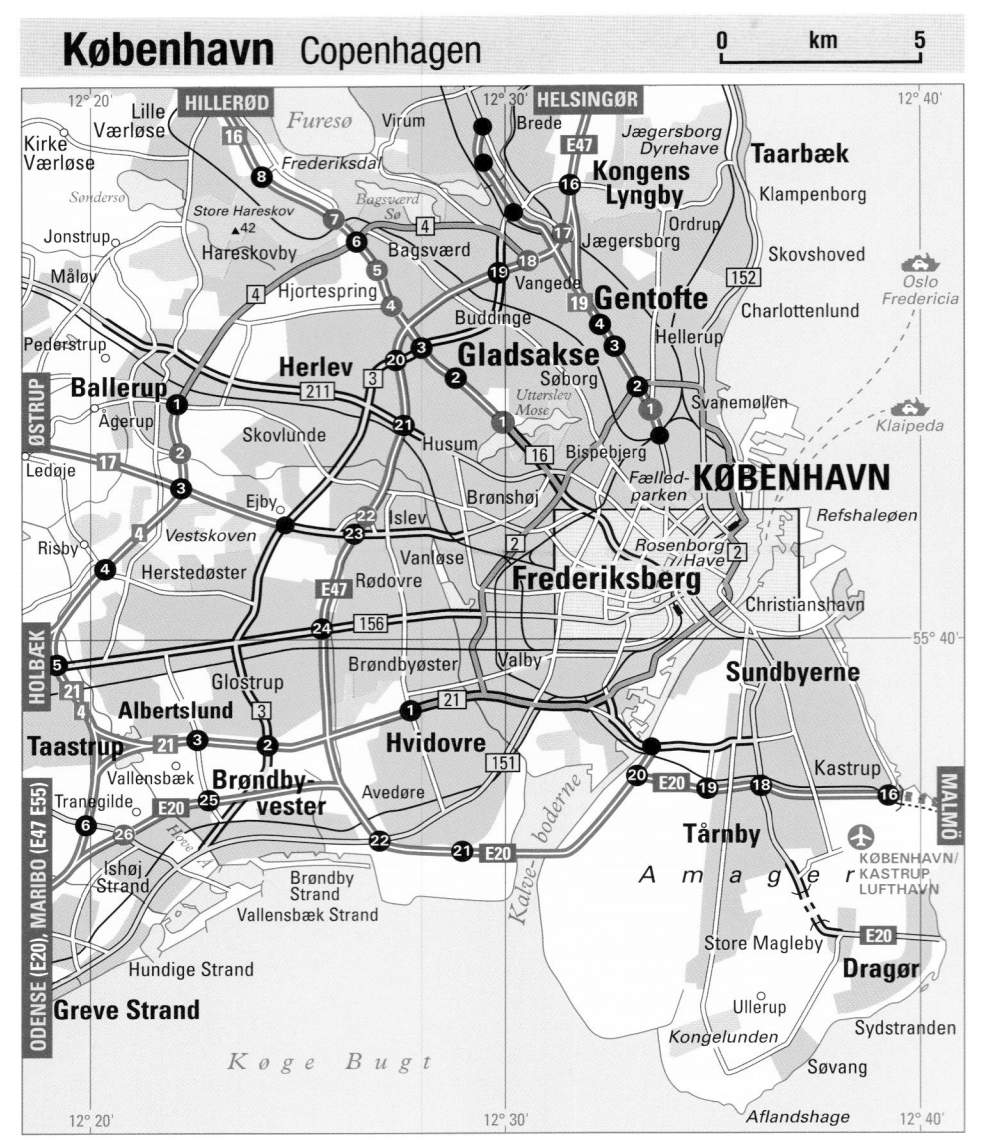

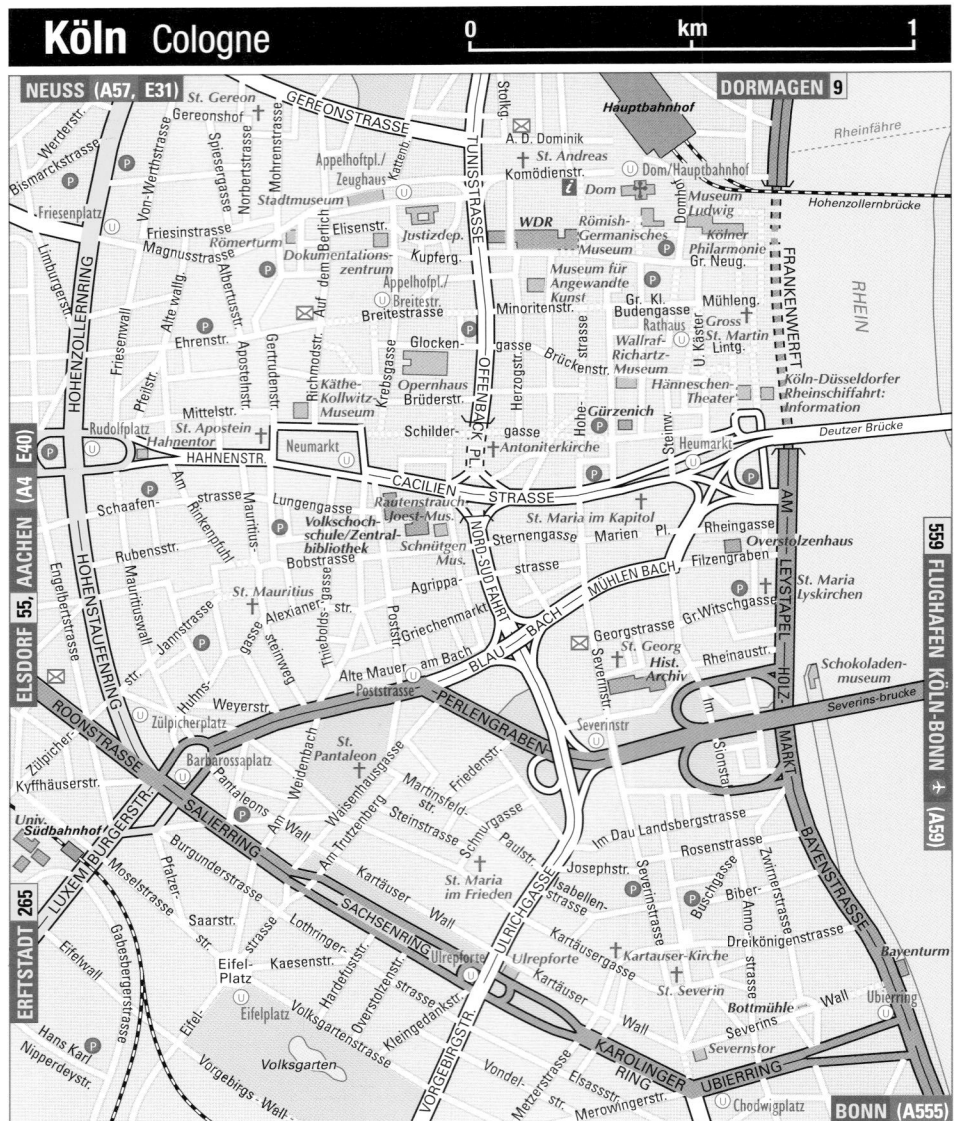

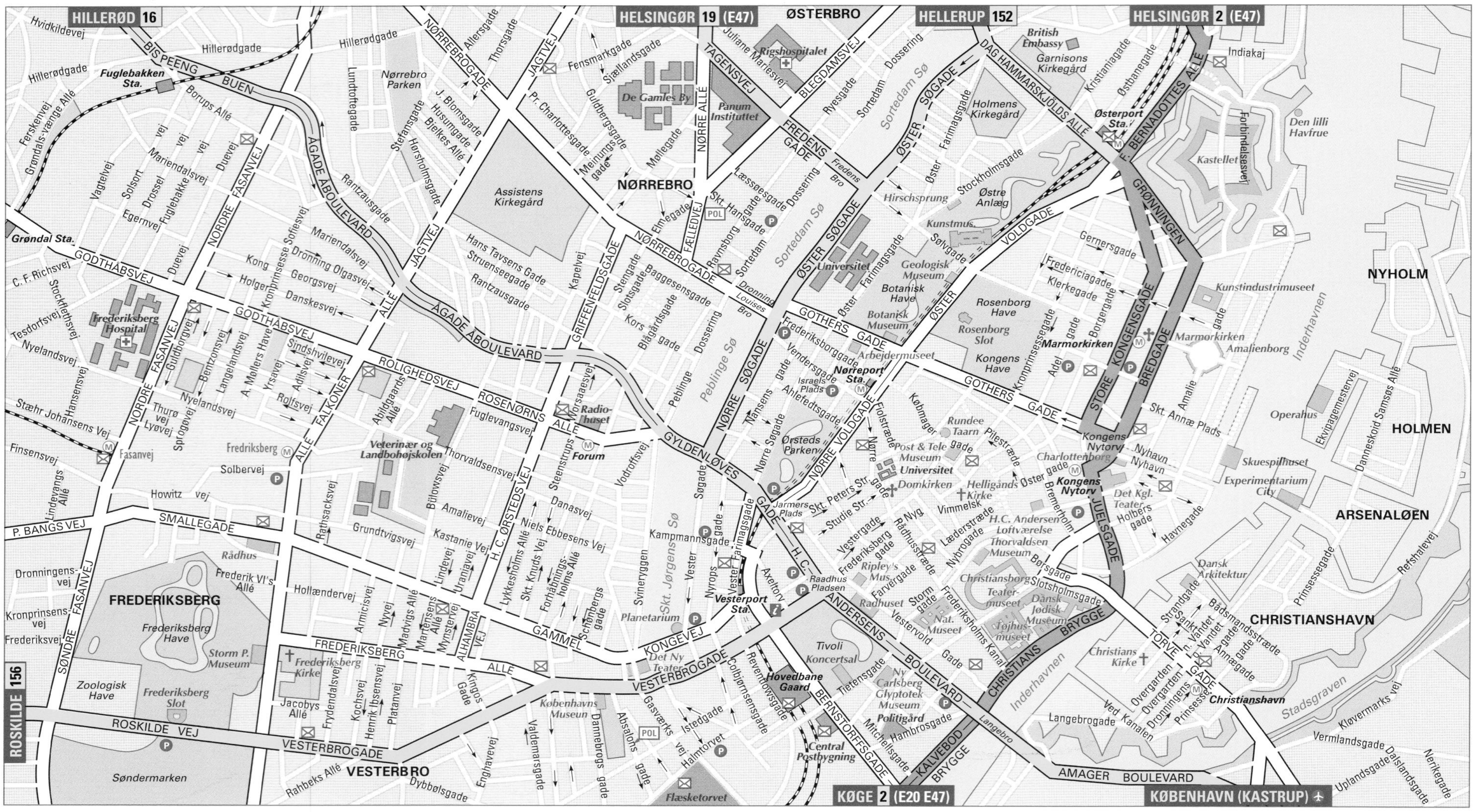

Lisboa Lisbon

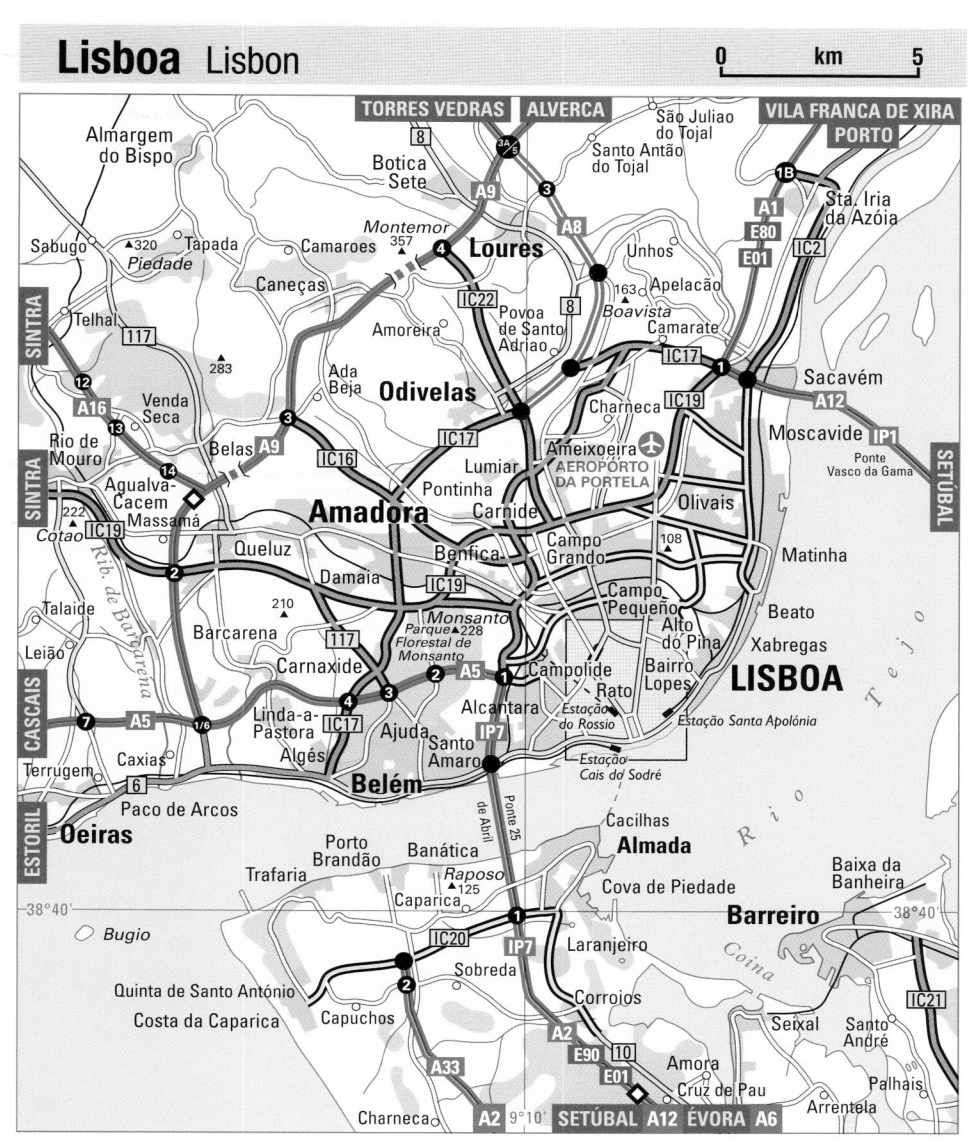

Lisboa Lisbon

London

London

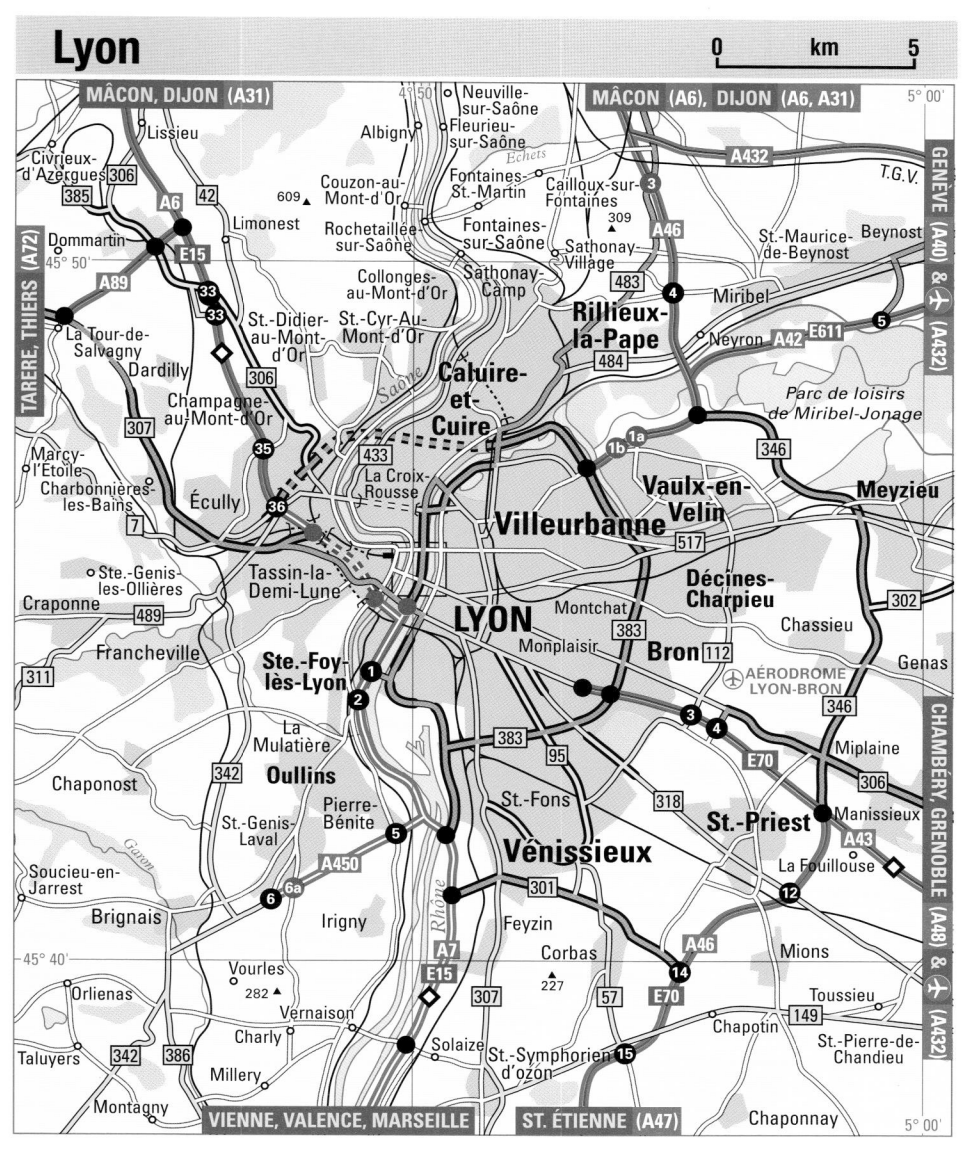

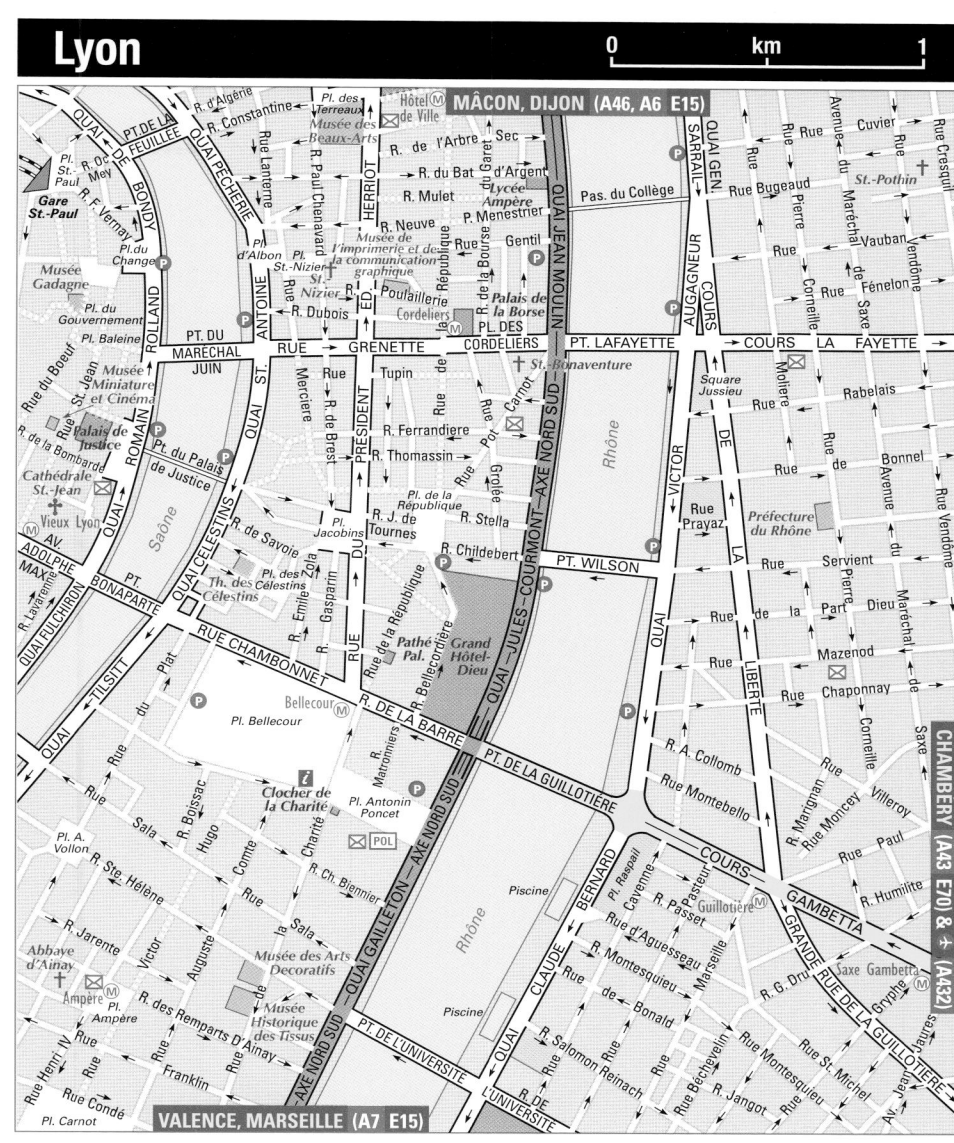

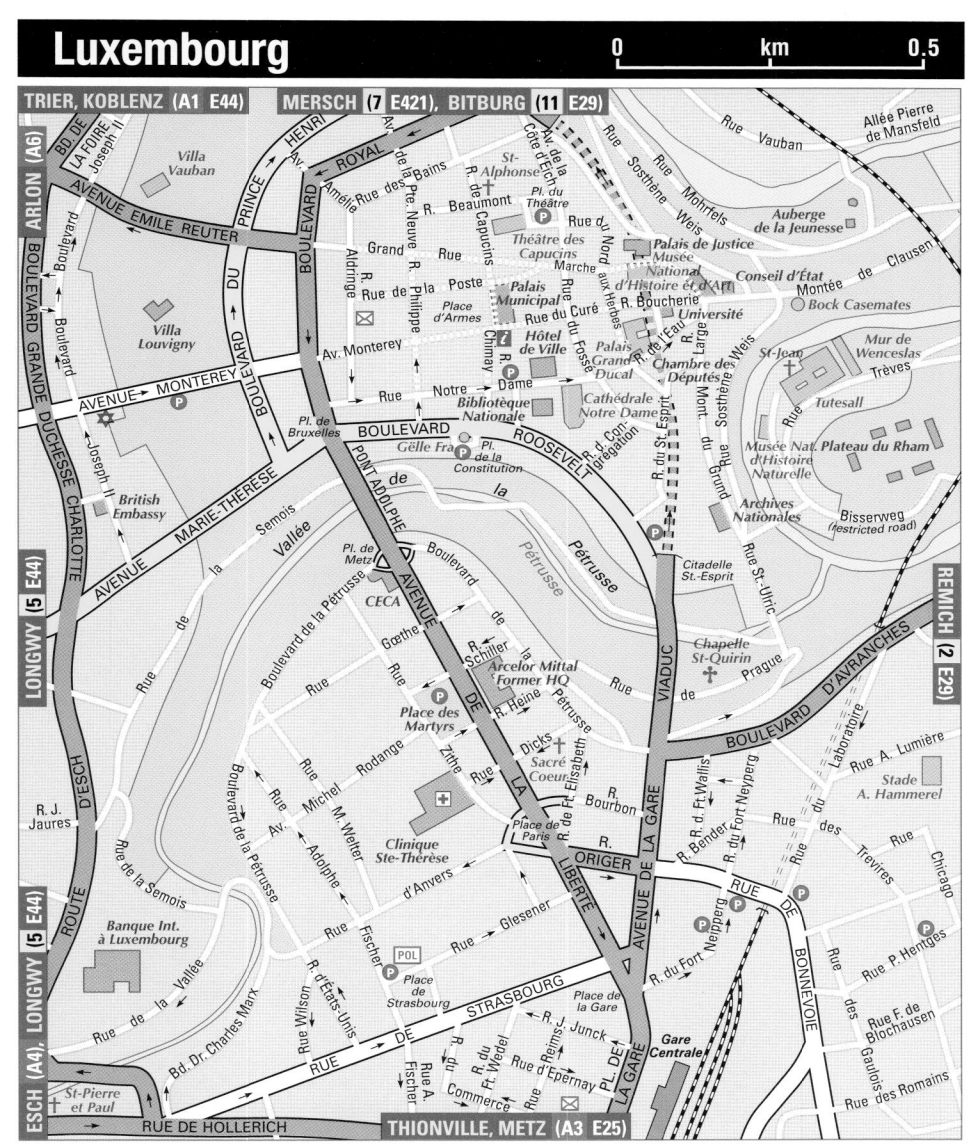

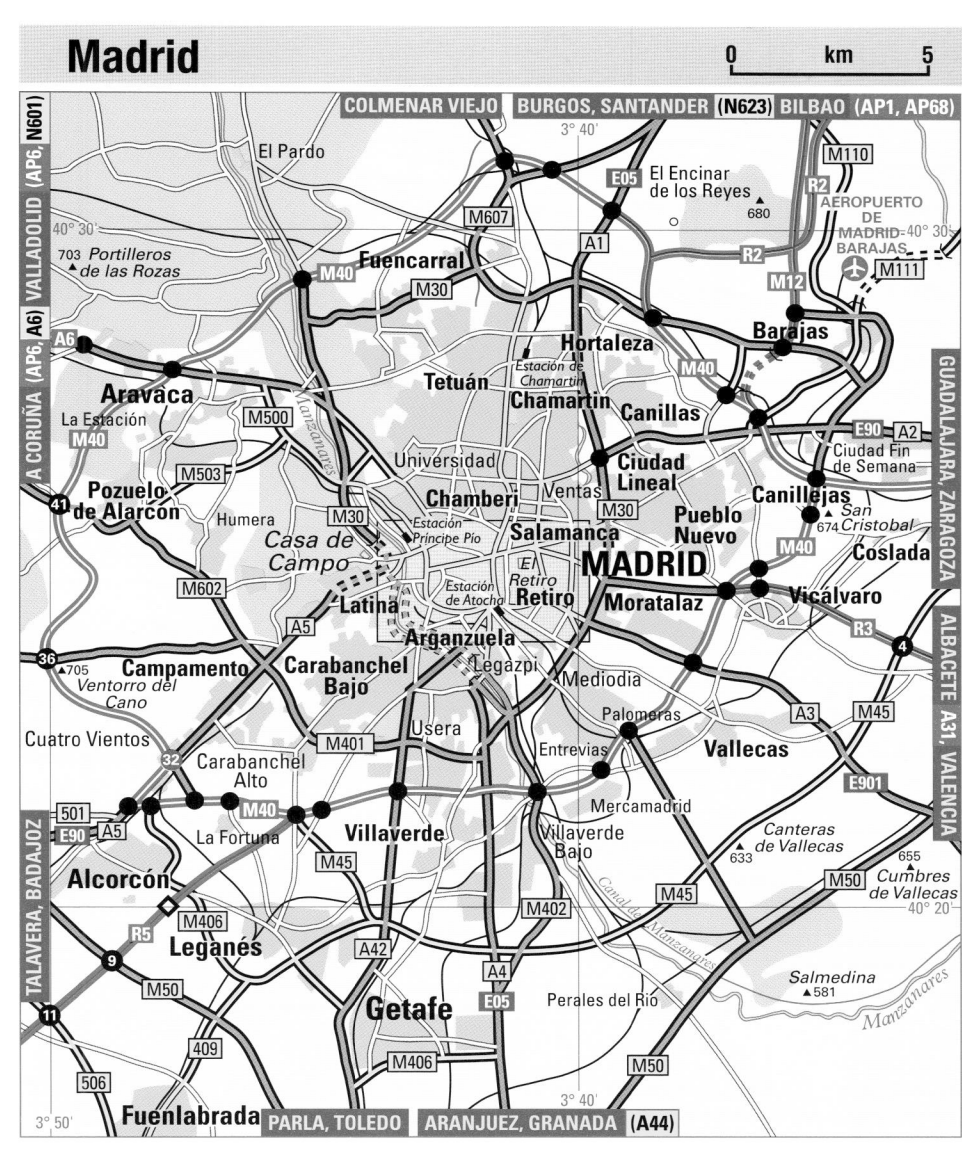

Madrid

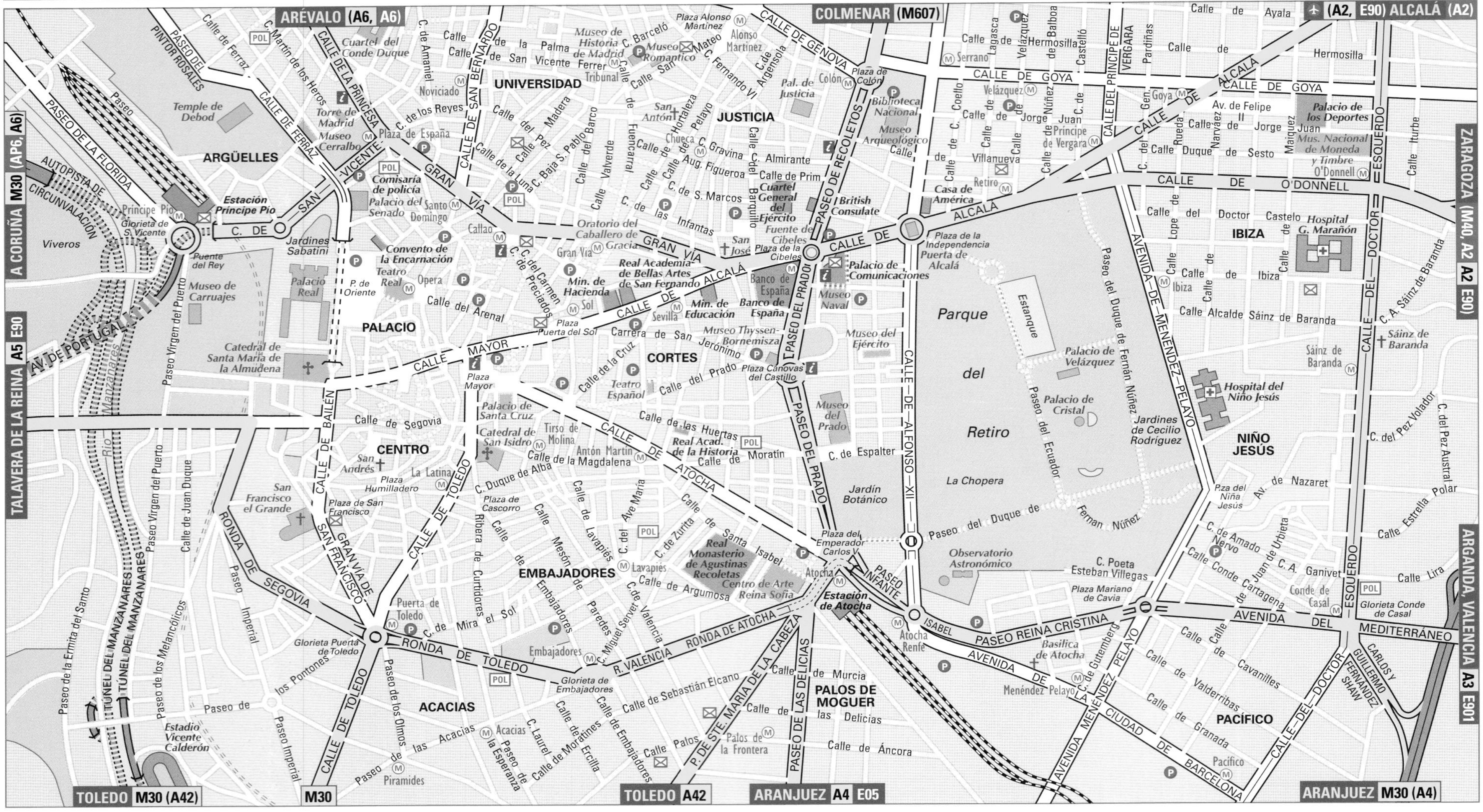

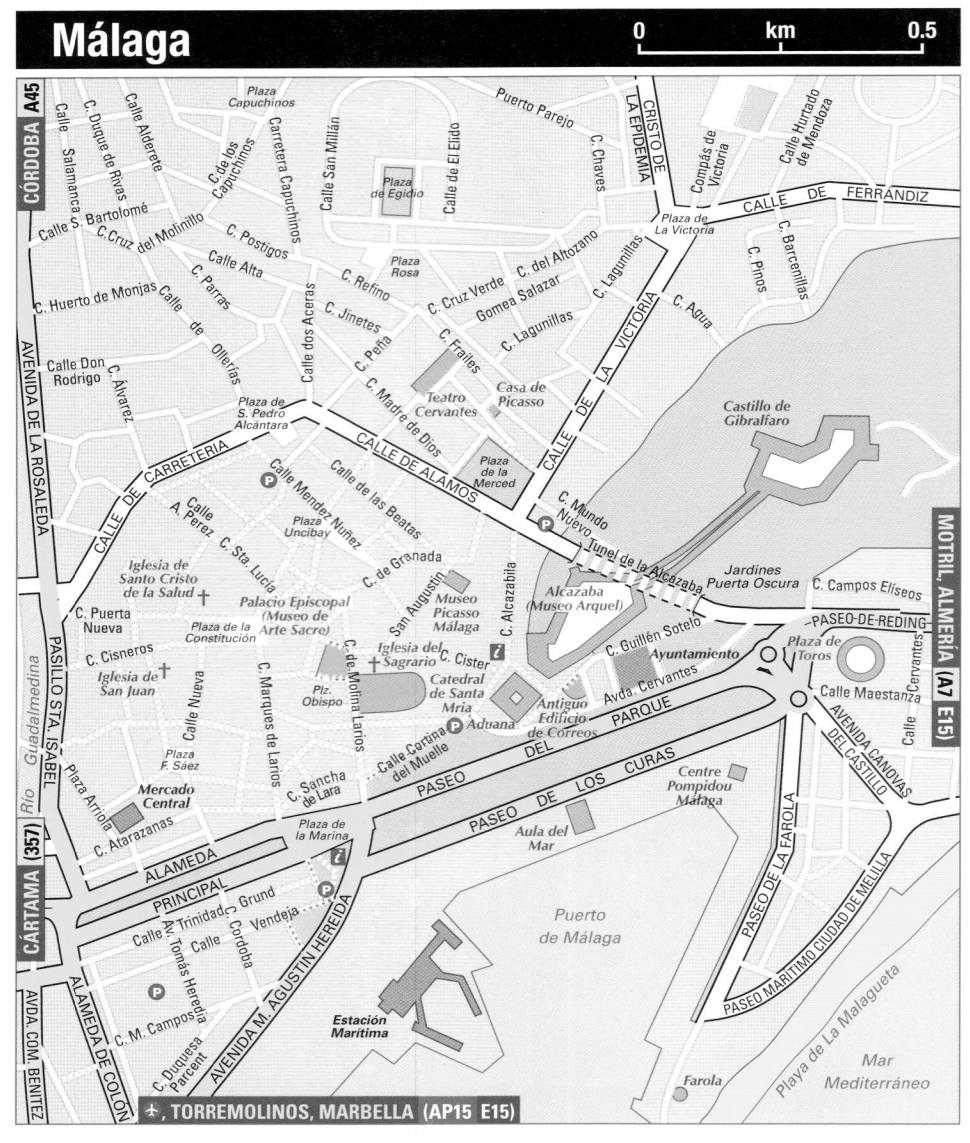

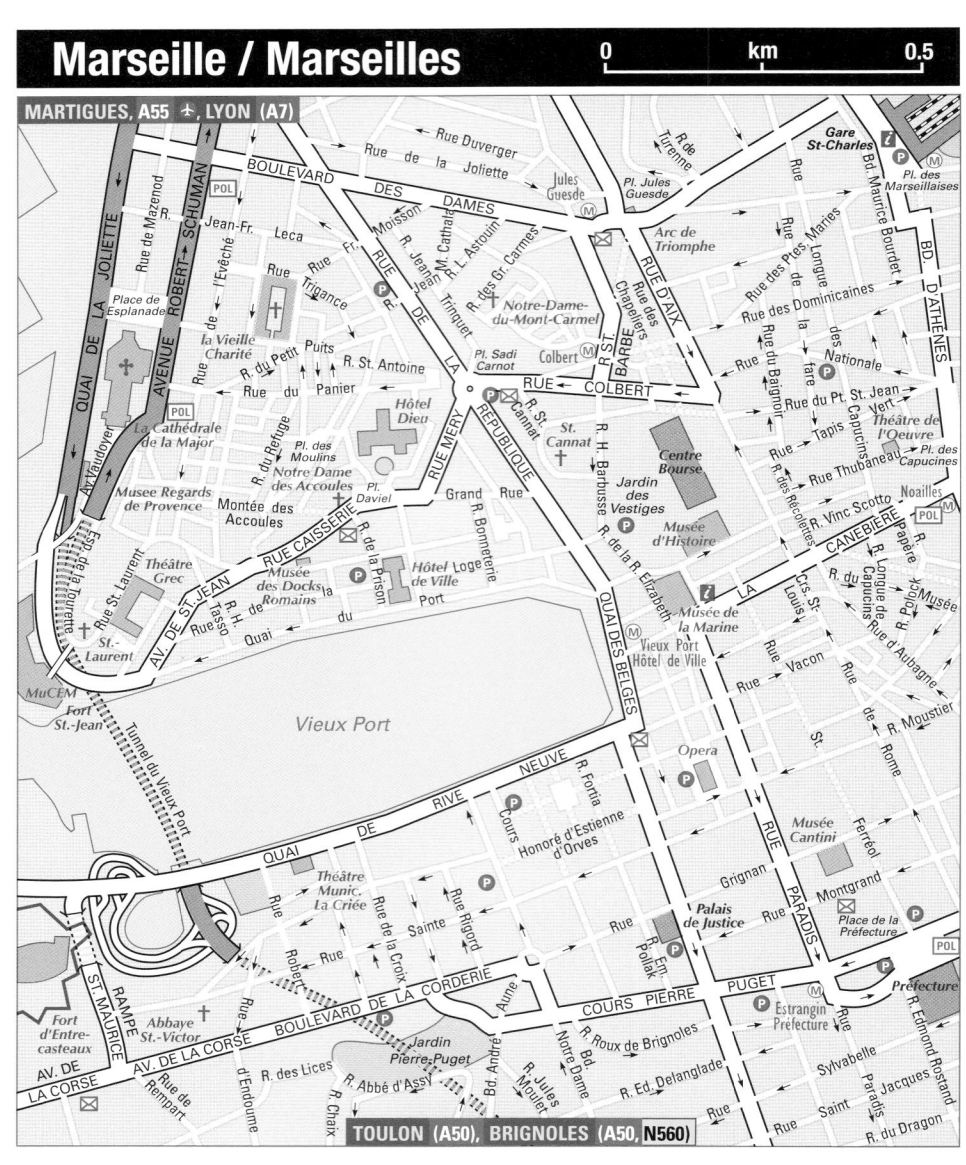

Milano Milan

0 km 5

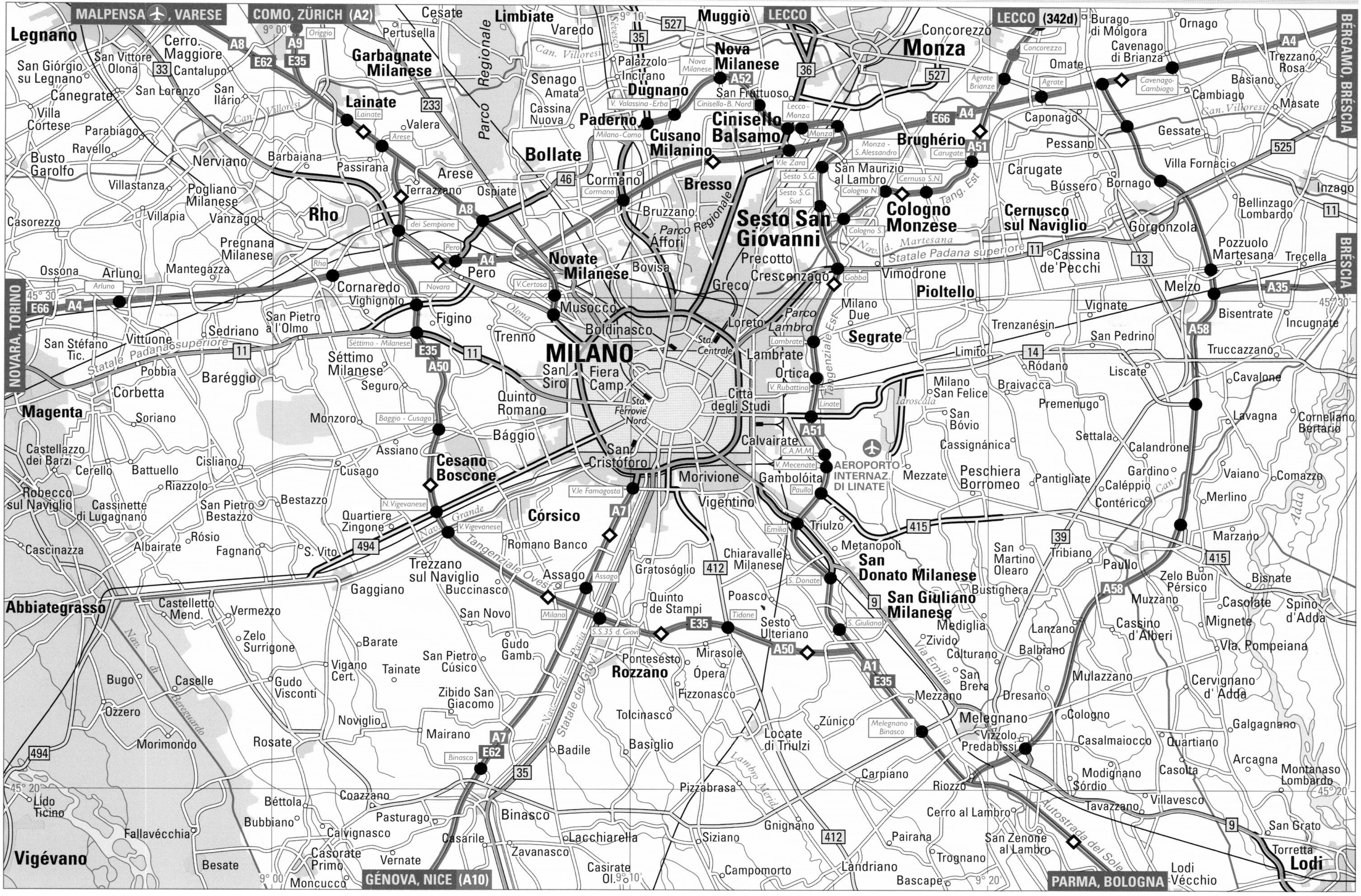

MALPENSA ✈ VARESE | COMO, ZÜRICH (A2) | LECCO | LECCO (342d) | BERGAMO, BRESCIA

Legnano · San Giórgio su Legnano · Cerro Maggiore · Canegrate · San Vittore Olona · Villa Córtese · San Lorenzo · San Ilário · Parabiago · Busto Garolfo · Casorezzo · Ravello · Pregnana Milanese · Vanzago · Arluno · Ossona · Mantegazza

Pertusella · Cesate · Garbagnate Milanese · Bollate · Rho · Novate Milanese · Pero · Arese · Ospiate · Terrazzano · Cornaredo · Vighignolo · Figino · Trenno · Settimo Milanese · Cornaredo

Limbiate · Varedo · Senago · Cassina Nuova · Paderno · Cusano Milanino · Cormano · Bresso · Bruzzano · Parco Affori · Musocco · Boldinasco · Baggio

Muggió · Nova Milanese · Dugnano · Cinisello Balsamo · Sesto San Giovanni · Precotto · Greco · Crescenzago · Loreto · Bovisa

Monza · Brughério · Cologno Monzese · Cernusco sul Naviglio · Vimodrone · Pioltello · Segrate · Limito

MILANO · San Siro · Fiera Camp. · Quinto Romano · Bággio · Cesano Boscone · Córsico · Trezzano sul Naviglio · Buccinasco · Assago · Gaggiano · Rozzano

Concorezzo · Burago di Mólgora · Ornago · Omate · Cavenago di Brianza · Trezzano Rosa · Básiano · Masate · Cambiago · Caponago · Pessano · Carugate · Bússero · Bornago · Gorgonzola · Pozzuolo Martesana · Trecella · Melzo · Inzago · Bellinzago Lombardo · Vignate · Liscate · Truccazzano · Ródano · Bisentrate · Incugnate · Cavalone · Cassignánica · Cassina de' Pecchi

Magenta · Corbetta · Castellazzo dei Barzi · Cisliano · Bestazzo · Cusago · Quartiere Zingone · S. Vito · Romano Banco

Abbiategrasso · Castelletto Mend. · Albairate · Cassinetta di Lugagnano · Cascinazza · Rósio · Fagnano · S. Novo · Gudo Gambaredo · Gratosóglio · Assago

ABBIATEGRASSO 494 | GÉNOVA, NICE (A10) | PARMA, BOLOGNA | Lodi Vécchio · Lodi

---

Milano Milan

0 km 1

MALPENSA ✈ VARESE (A8) | VARESE 233 | COMO 35 MONZA (36) | BÉRGAMO 11 (525)

ABBIATEGRASSO 494 | GÉNOVA (A7 E62) | PAVIA 35 | LODI 9 PARMA (A51, A1)

Piazzale Lotto · Lido di Milano · Velodromo Vigorelli · CityLife · Tre Torri · Parco Sempione · Arco della Pace · Acquario · Arena · Castello Sforzesco · Cairoli · Foro Buonaparte · Duomo · Galleria Vittorio Emanuele II · Teatro alla Scala · Museo Poldi-Pezzoli · Giardini Pubblici Indro Montanelli · Museo di Storia Naturale · Palazzo di Brera · S. Maria delle Grazie · S. Ambrogio · Università Cattolica · Policlinico · Porta Romana · Porta Genova · Porta Ticinese · Corso Buenos Aires

LINATE ✈ BRÉSCIA (11)

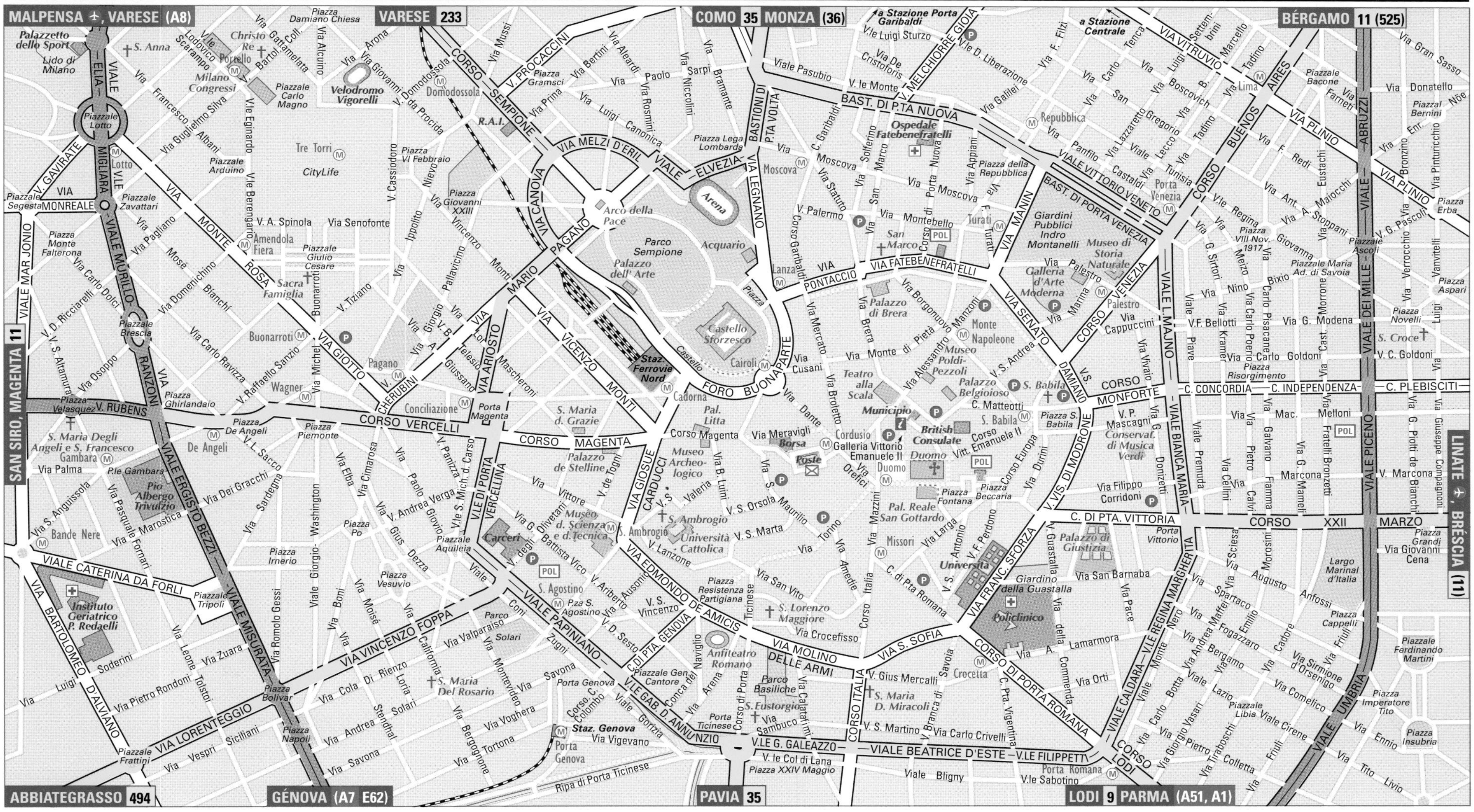

Moskva Moscow

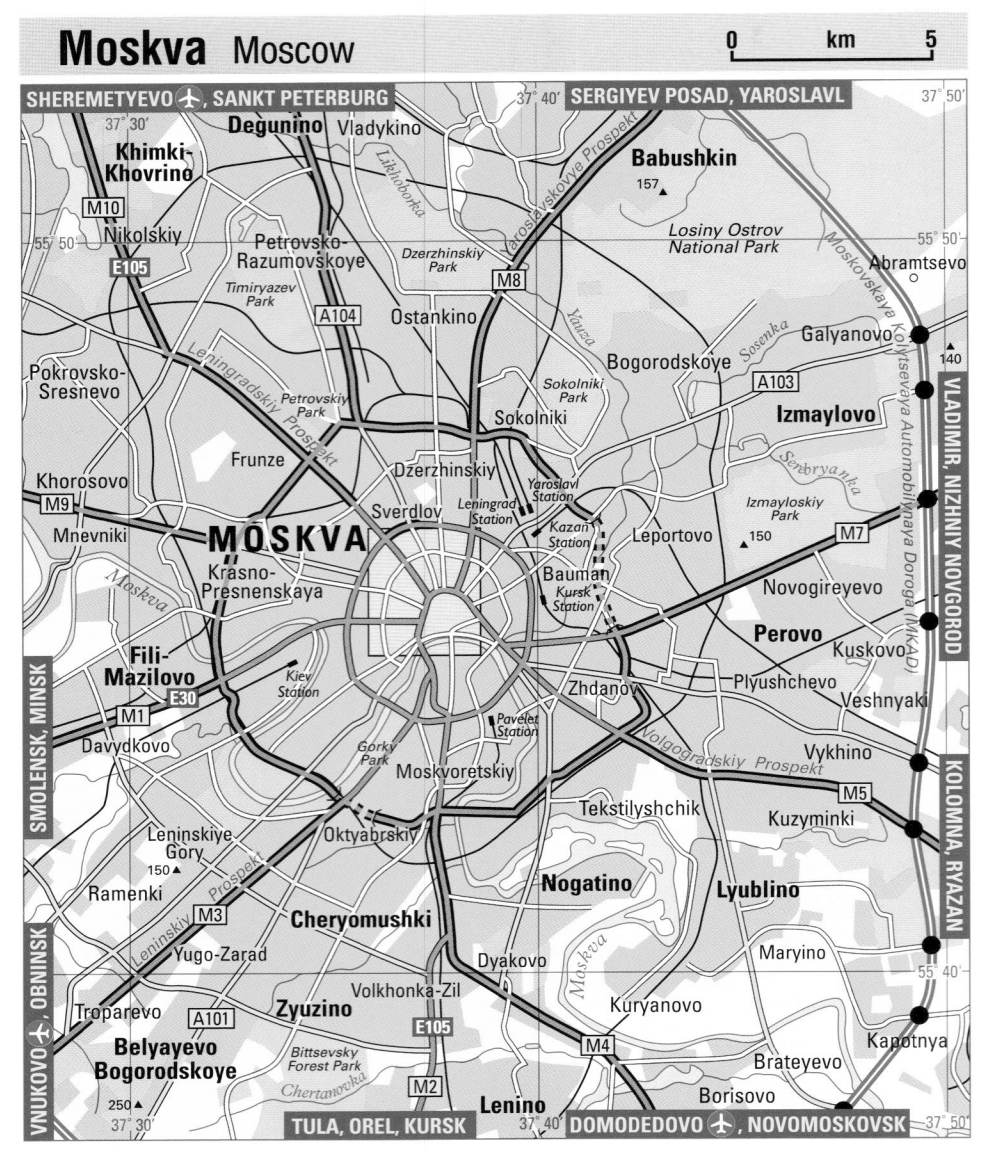

Moskva Moscow

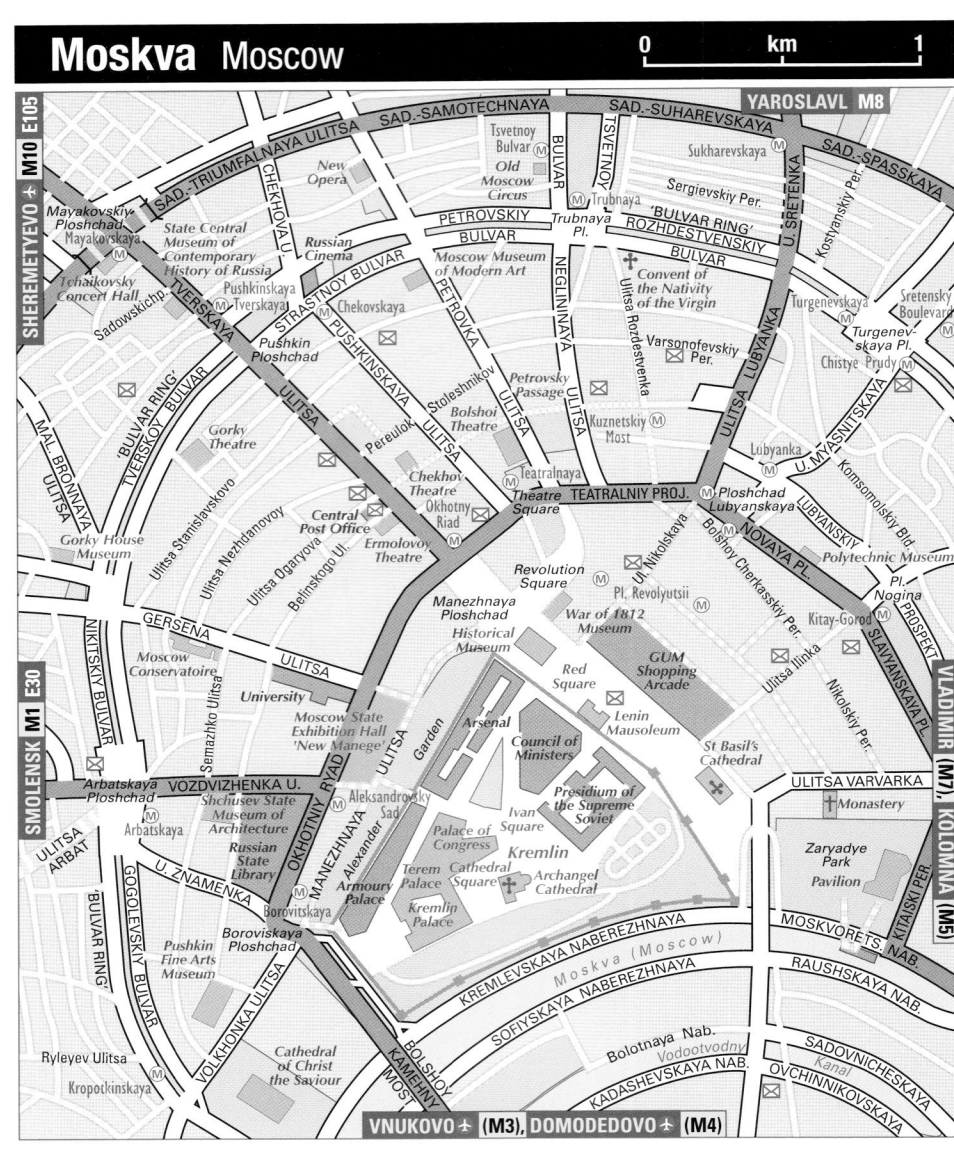

München Munich

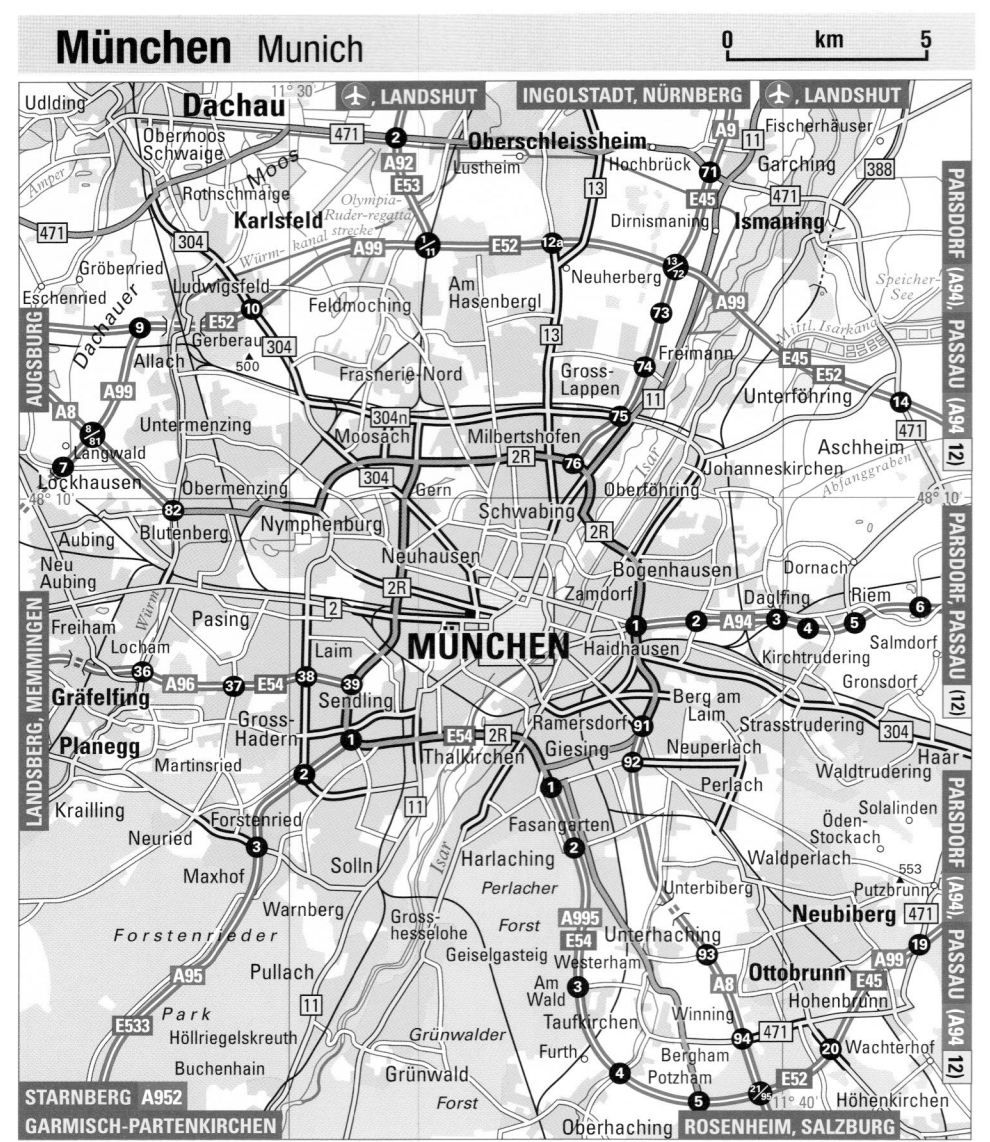

München Munich

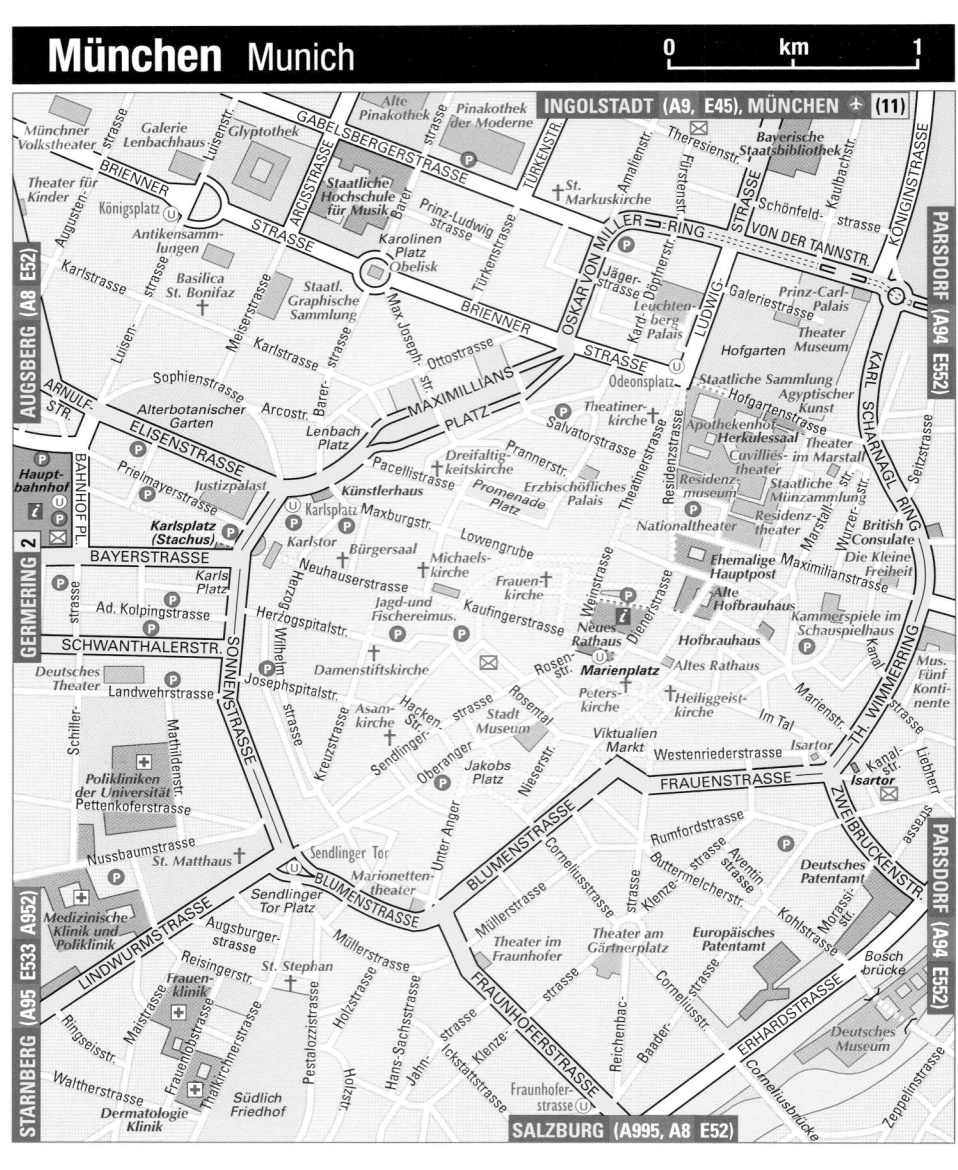

Nápoli Naples

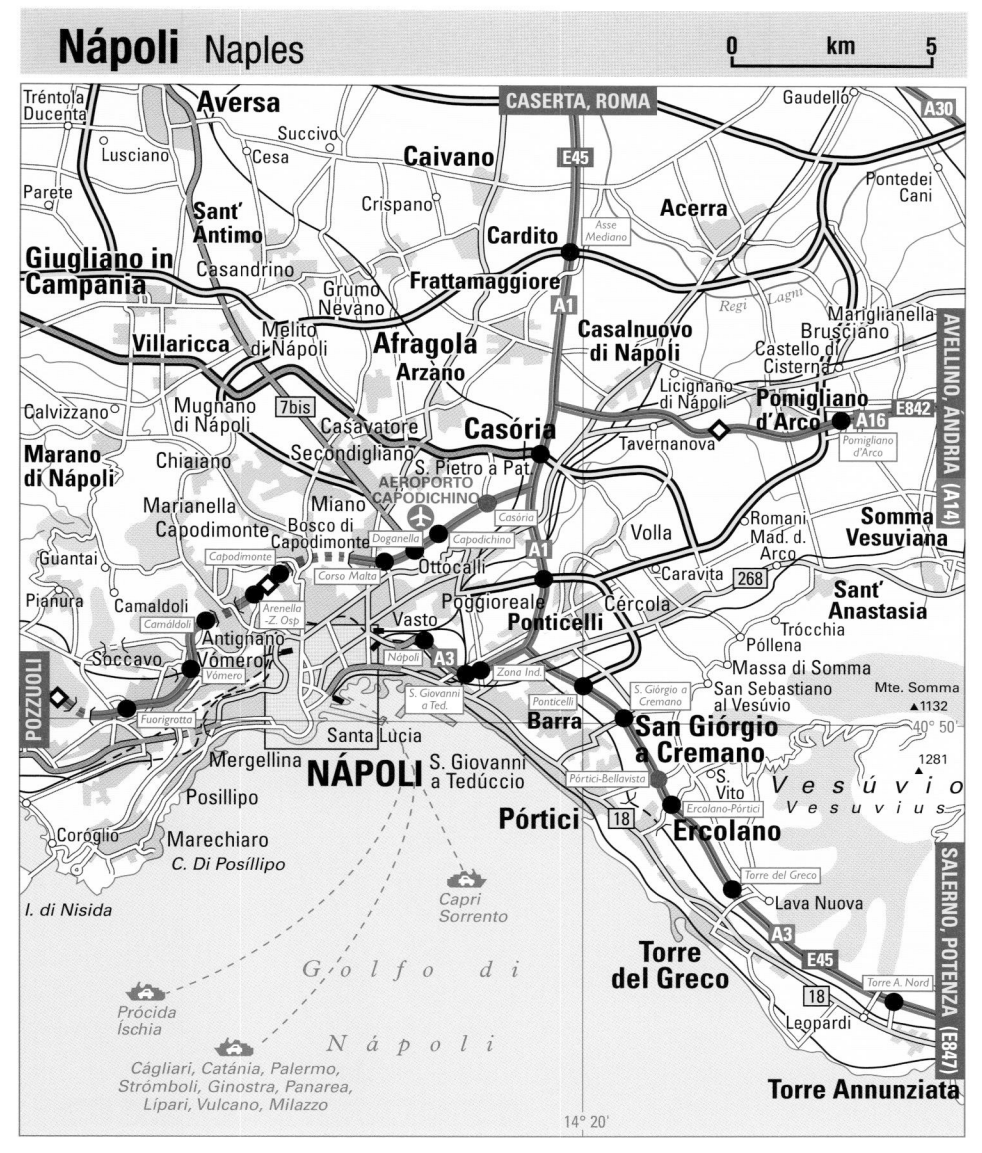

Nápoli Naples

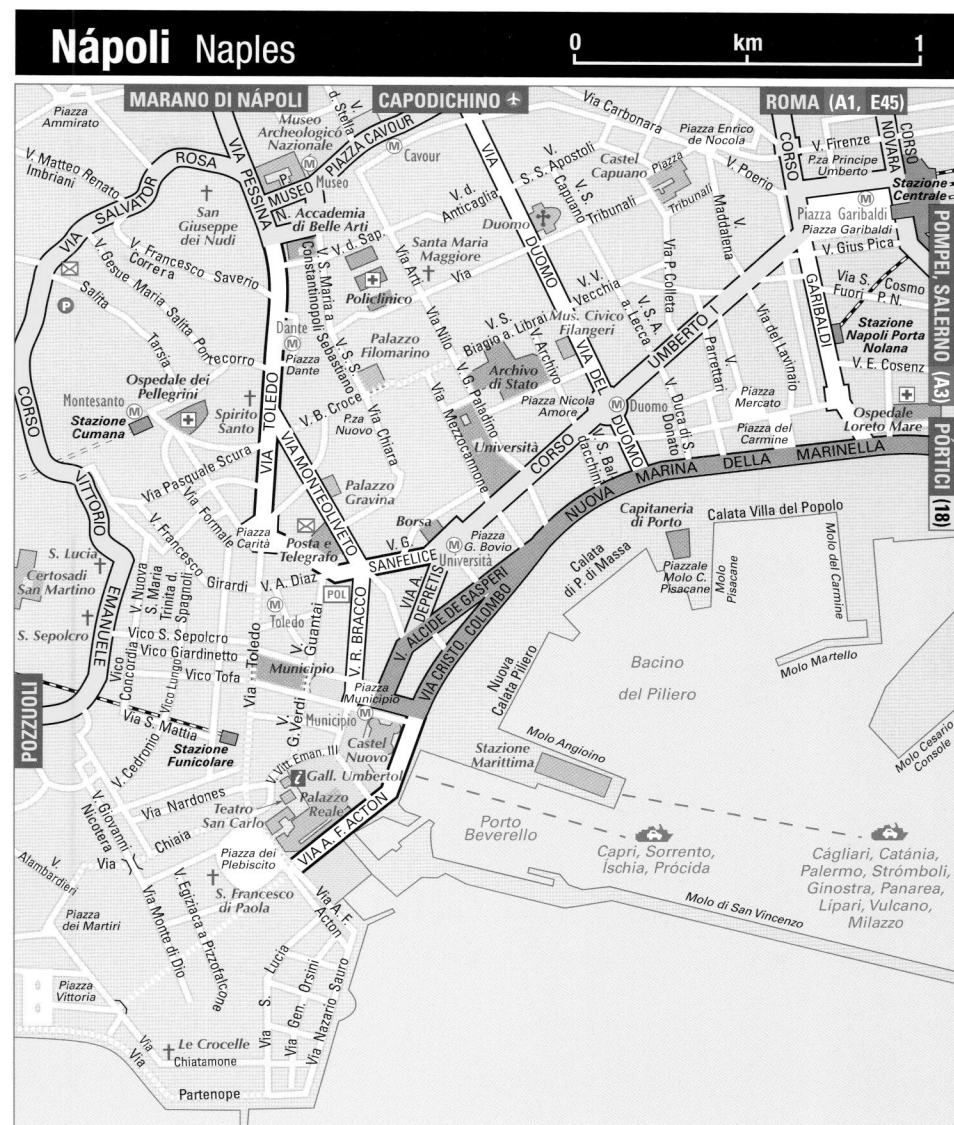

Oslo

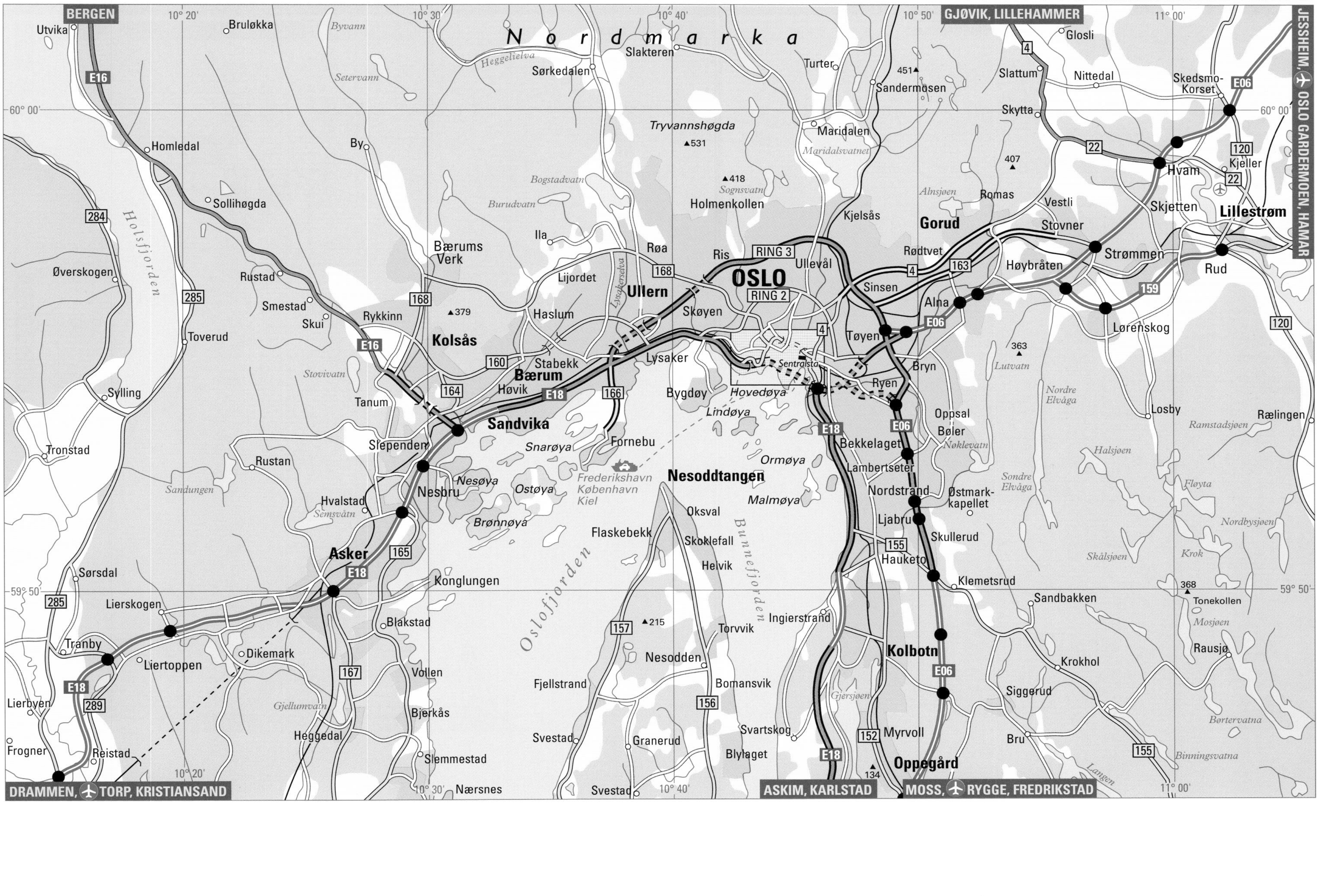

Oslo

0 km 0.5

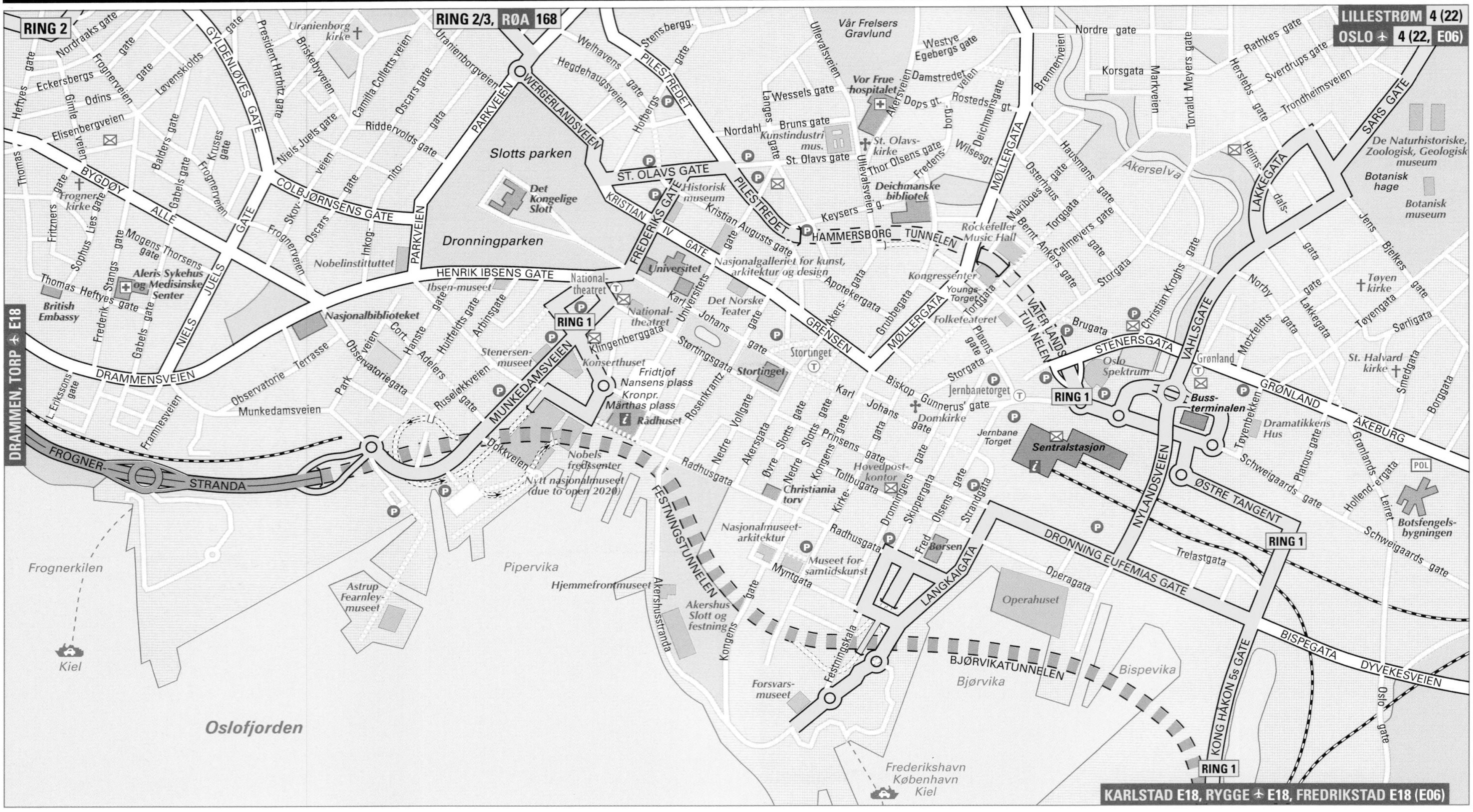

RING 2 | RING 2/3, RØA 168 | LILLESTRØM 4 (22) | OSLO ✈ 4 (22, E06)

Oslofjorden

Frognerkilen

Pipervika

Bjørvika | *Bispevika*

Slotts parken

Det Kongelige Slott

Dronningparken

Nasjonalbiblioteket

National-theatret

Universitet

Stortinget

Rådhuset

Akershus Slott og festning

Operahuset

Sentralstasjon

Buss-terminalen

BJØRVIKATUNNELEN

FESTNINGSTUNNELEN

HAMMERSBORG TUNNELEN

DRONNING EUFEMIAS GATE

RING 1

KARLSTAD E18, RYGGE ✈ E18, FREDRIKSTAD E18 (E06)

DRAMMEN, TORP ✈ E18

Kiel

Frederikshavn København Kiel

Paris

0 km 1

BOULEVARD PÉRIPHÉRIQUE

AV. DE LA PTE. DE CHAMPERRET

ARGENTEUIL (909) | ROUEN D14 A15 | ✈ CHARLES DE GAULLE, LILLE (A1, E15 E19) | MEAUX (N3)

ST-GERMAIN-EN-LAYE N13 (A14)

ROUEN (A13 E05)

VERSAILLES 910 | ✈ ORLY (A6), LE MANS (A10 A11 E50) | REIMS (A4 E50)

NOISY-LE-SEC (A3)

Arc de Triomphe

AVENUE FOCH

AVENUE DES CHAMPS ÉLYSÉES

Place de la Concorde

Jardin des Tuileries

Musée du Louvre

Tour Eiffel

Champ de Mars

Hôtel des Invalides

Palais du Luxembourg

Panthéon

Notre Dame

Île de la Cité

Gare du Nord

Gare de l'Est

Gare de Lyon

Sacré Cœur

Seine

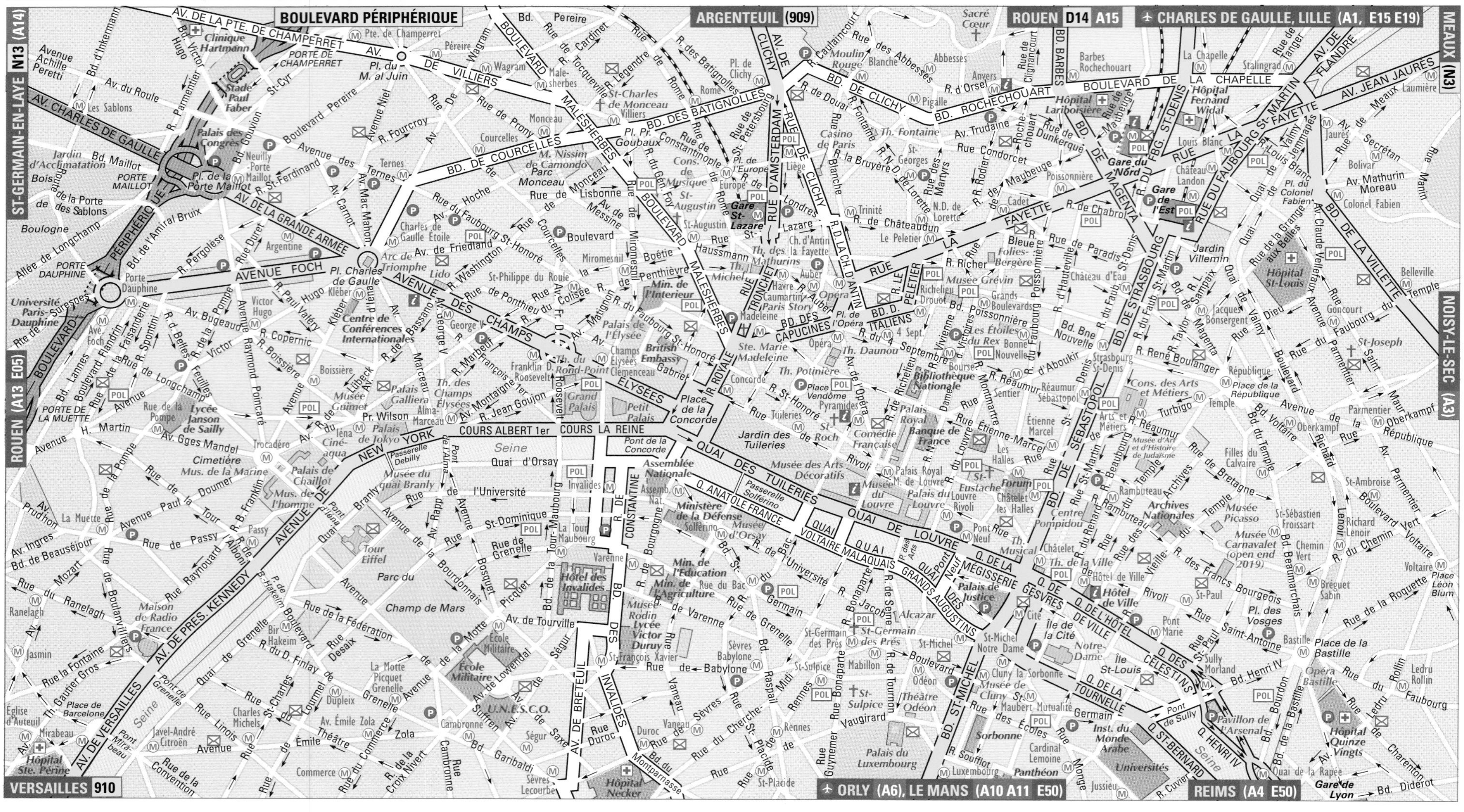

Paris

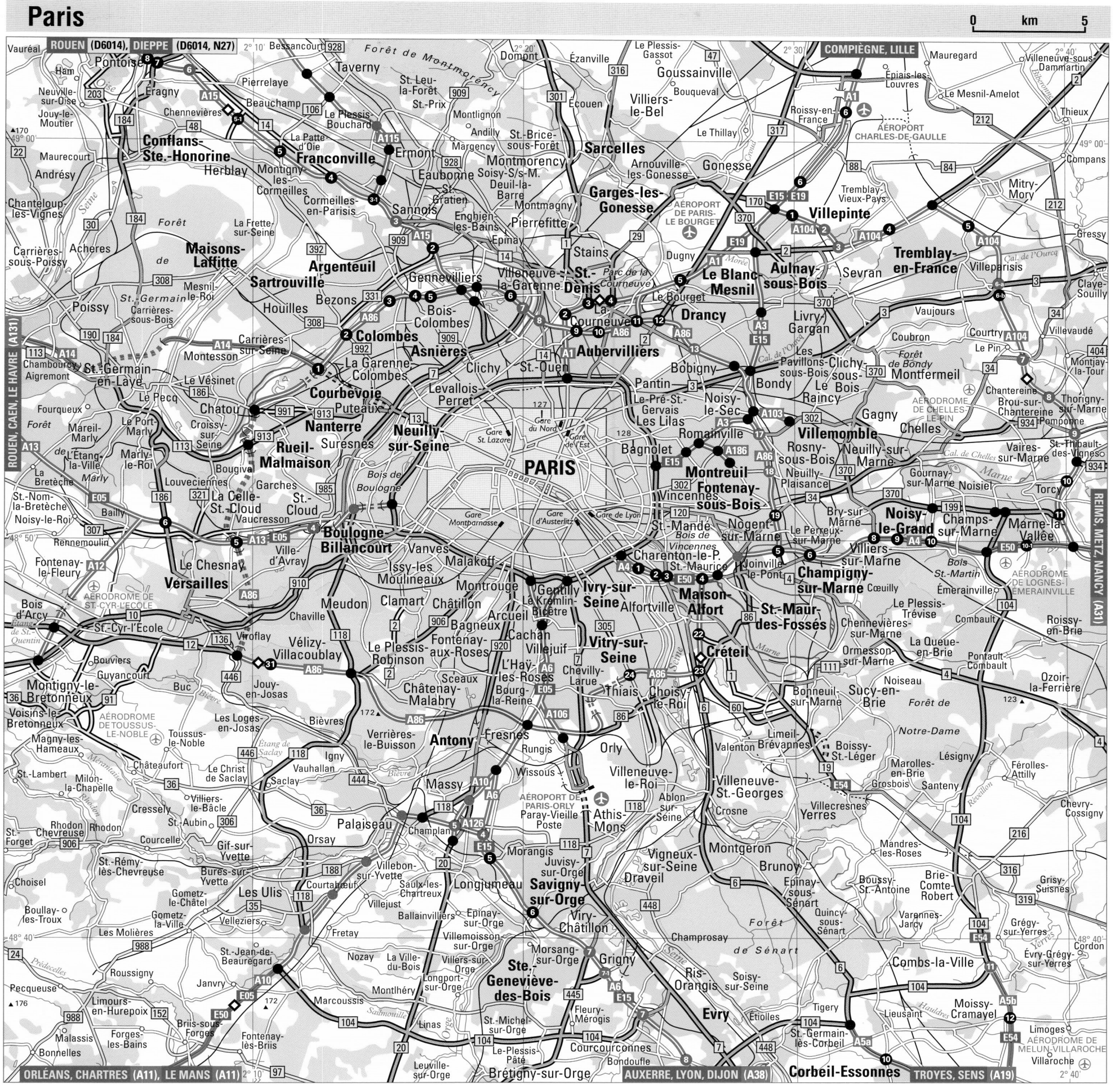

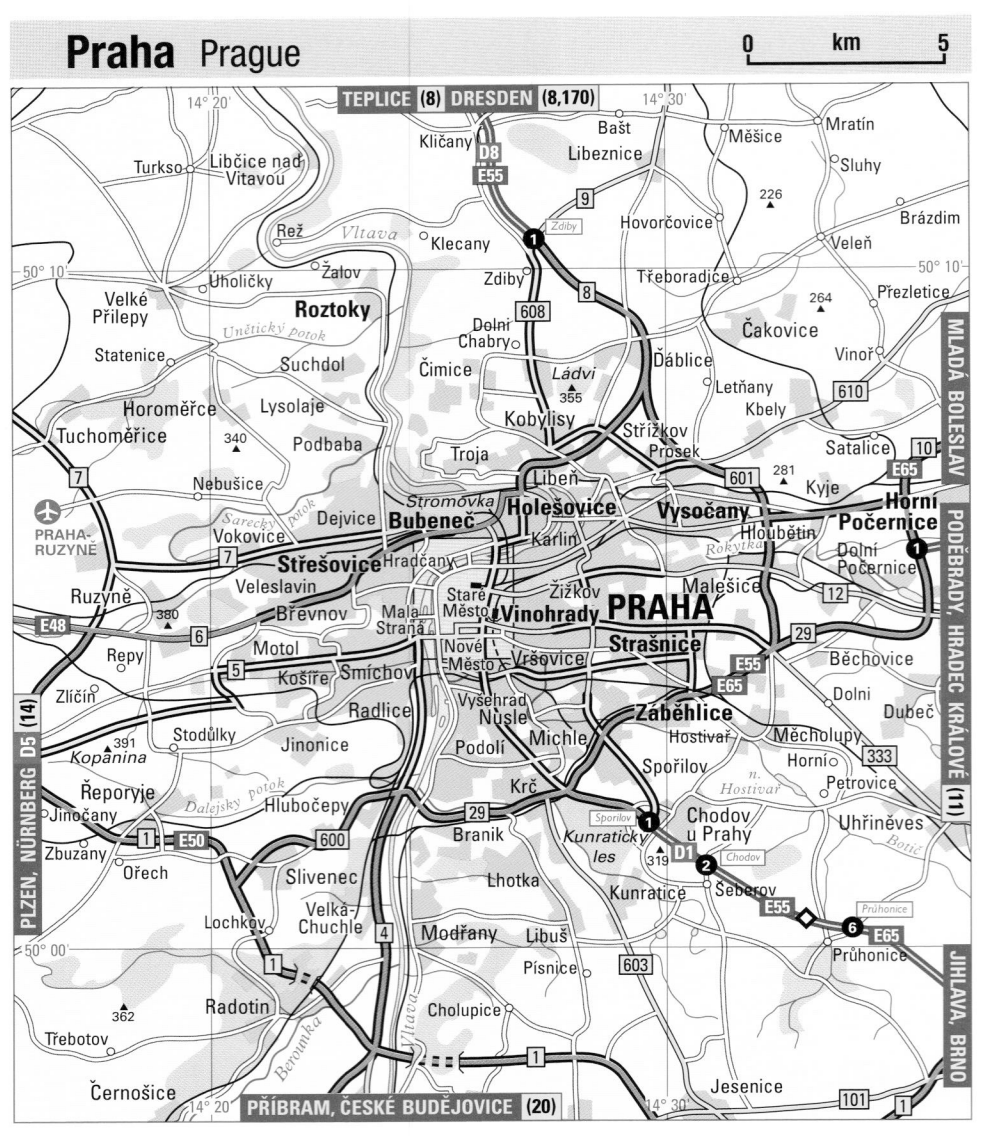

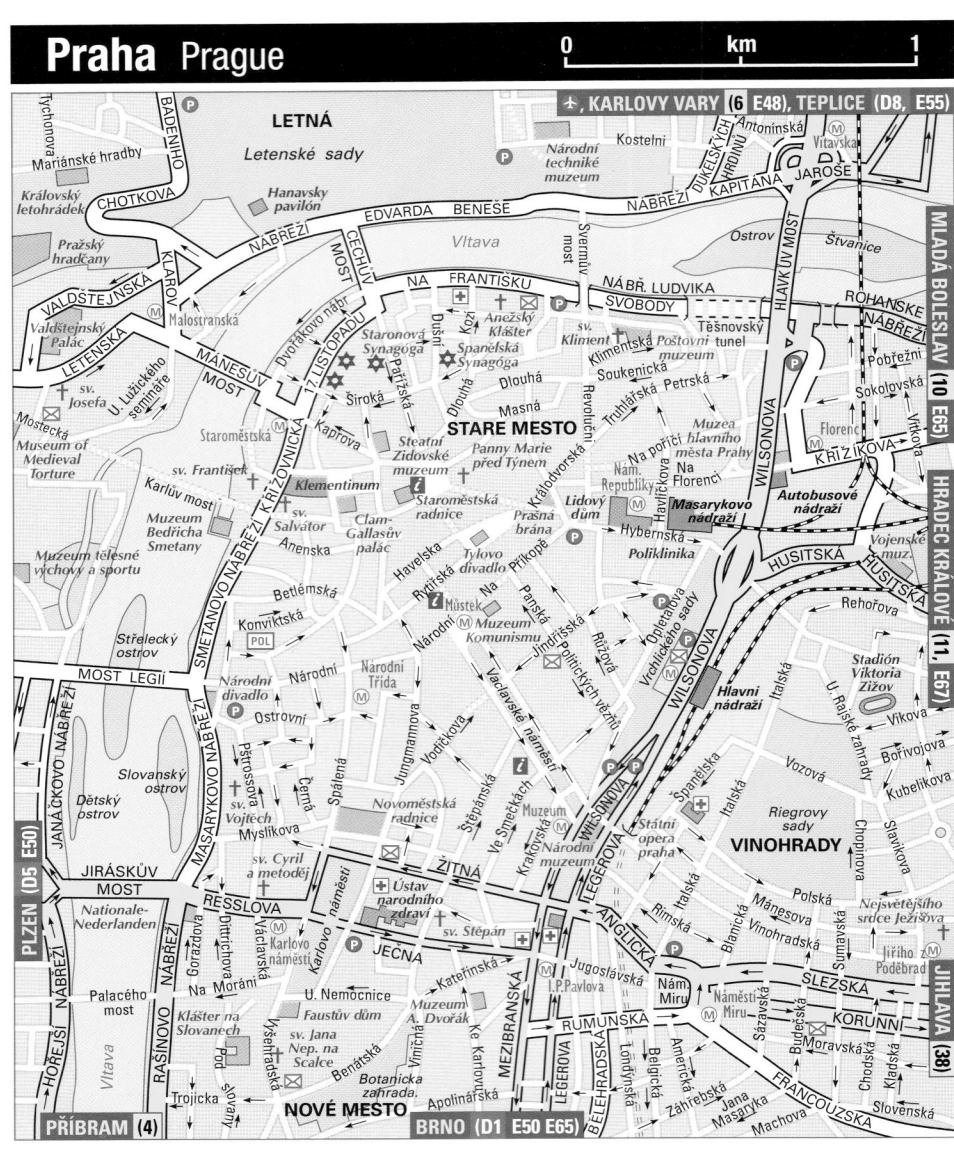

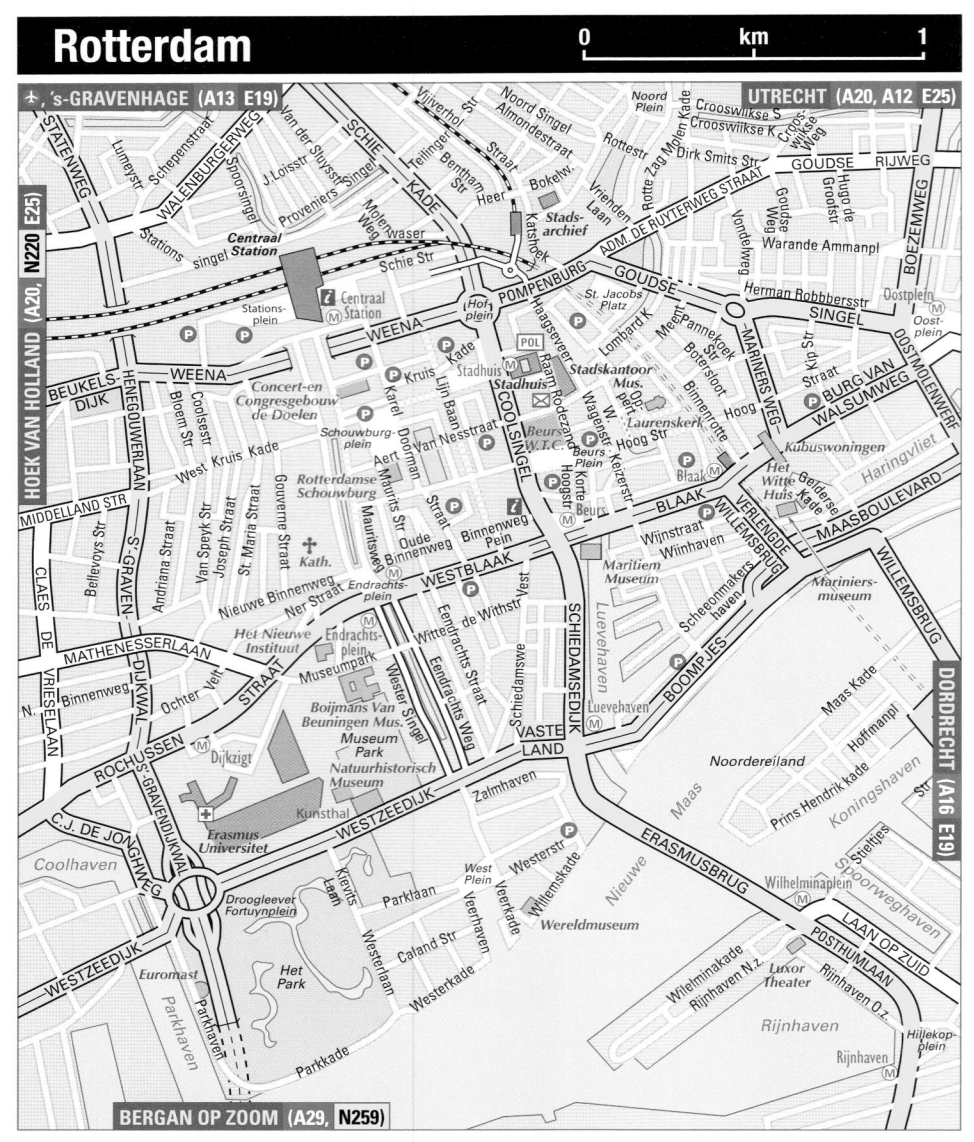

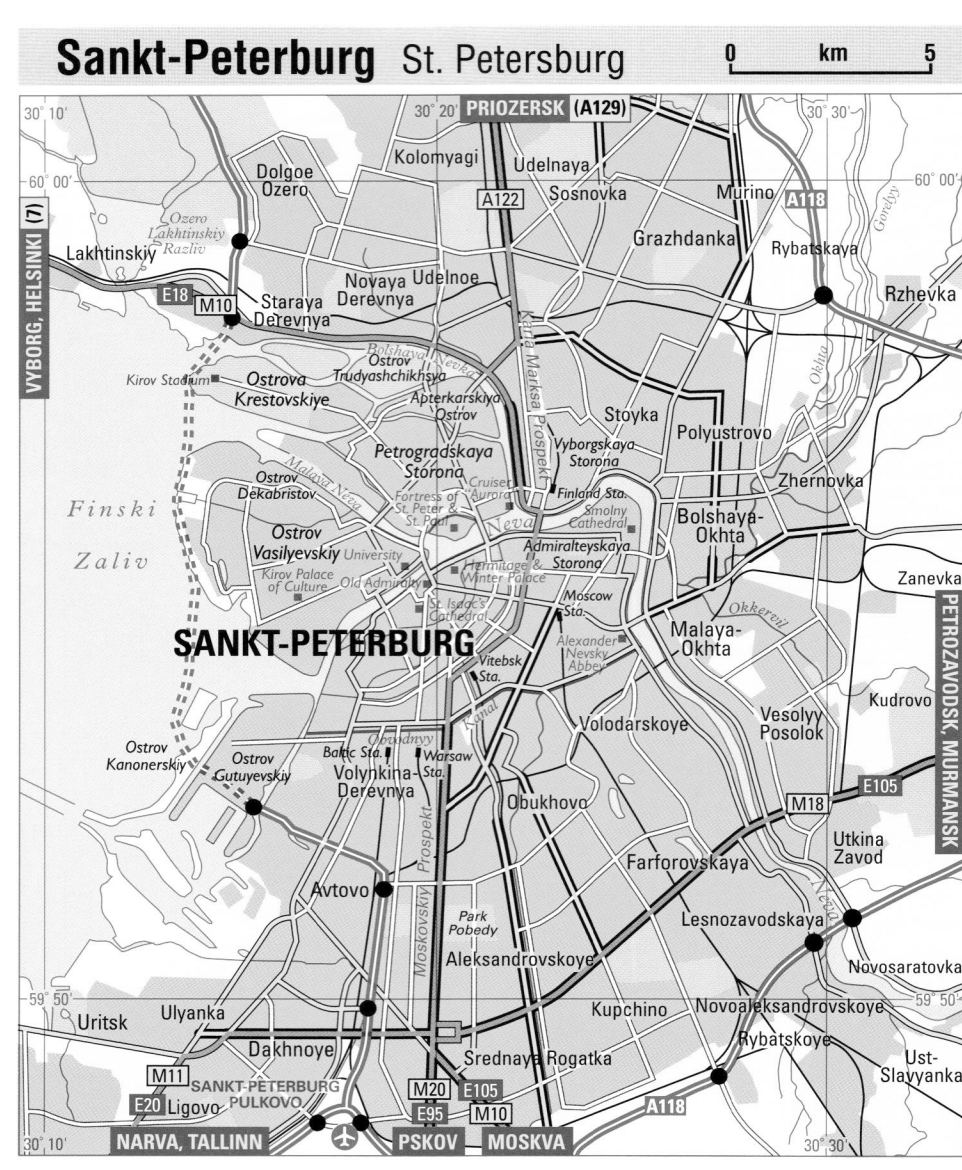

For **Rome** see page 143

Roma Rome

0   km   5

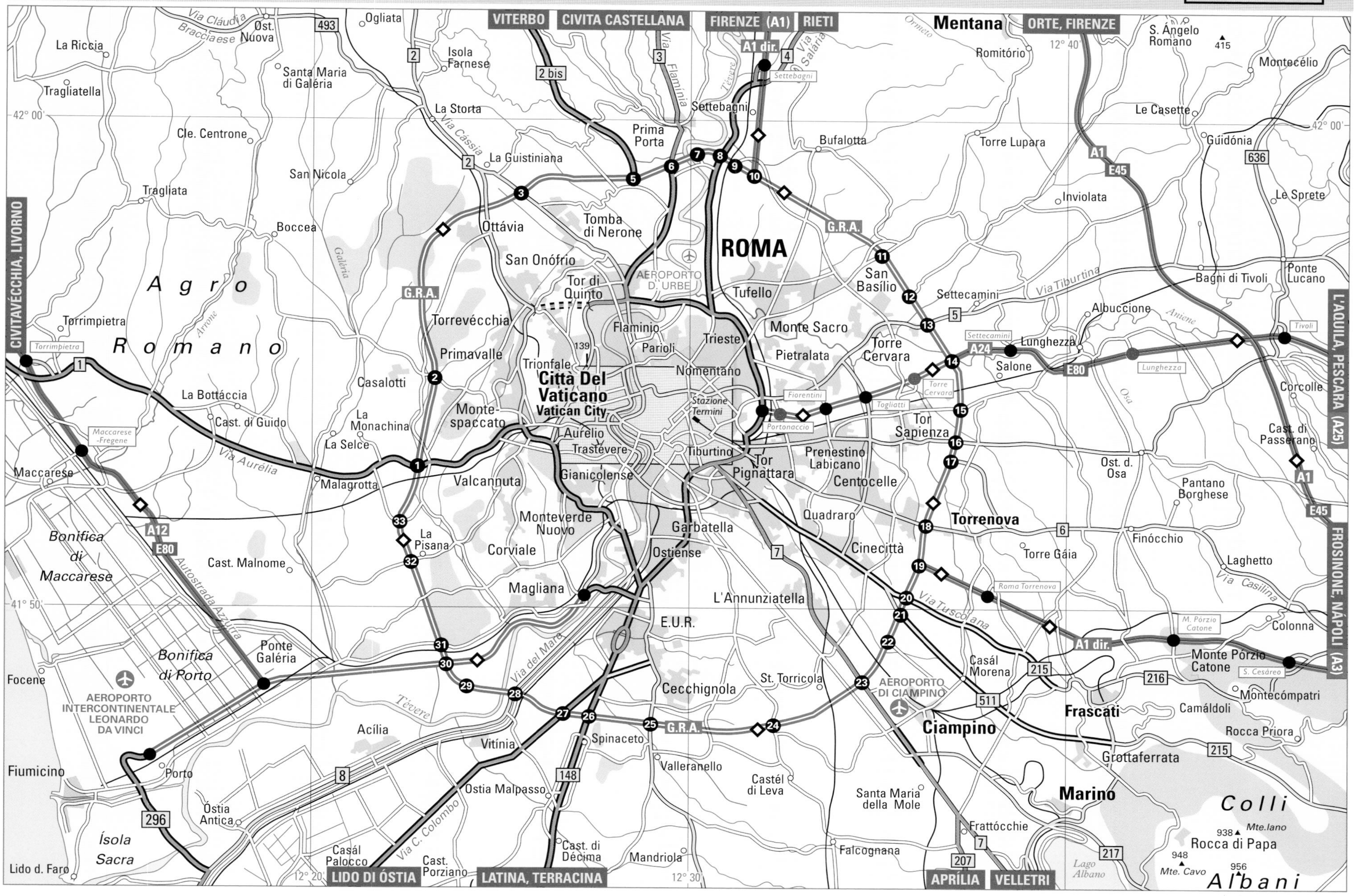

VITERBO · CIVITA CASTELLANA   FIRENZE (A1) · RIETI   Mentana   ORTE, FIRENZE

CIVITAVÉCCHIA, LIVORNO

La Riccia · Ogliata · Ost. Nuova · S. Angelo Romano · Montecélio
Tragliatella · Santa Maria di Galéria · Isola Farnese · Romitório · 415 · Guidónia · Le Casette
La Storta · Prima Porta · Settebagni · Bufalotta · Torre Lupara · Ponte Lucano
San Nicola · La Giustiniana · ROMA · Inviolata · Le Sprete
Boccea · Ottávia · Tomba di Nerone · G.R.A. · Bagni di Tivoli
Tragliata · Torrevécchia · San Onófrio · AEROPORTO D. URBE · Tufello · San Basilio · Settecamini · Albuccione · Tívoli
Tor di Quinto · Flaminio · Monte Sacro · Torre Cervara · Lunghezza · Corcolle
Primavalle · Trieste · Pietralata · Salone · L'AQUILA, PESCARA (A25)
Monte-spaccato · Città Del Vaticano · Parioli · Nomentano · Stazione Termini · Tor Sapienza · Cast. di Passerano
La Monachina · Casalotti · Aurélio · Trastévere · Portonaccio · Prenestino Labicano · Torrenova · FROSINONE, NAPOLI (A3)
Malagrotta · Valcannuta · Gianicolense · Tor Pignattara · Centocelle · Torre Gáia · Finócchio
La Pisana · Monteverde Nuovo · Garbatella · Quadraro · Cinecittà · Monte Pórzio Catone · Colonna
Corviale · Ostiense · Casál Morena · Frascati · Montecómpatri
Magliana · L'Annunziatella · St. Torricola · Camáldoli · Rocca Priora
Ponte Galéria · E.U.R. · Cecchignola · AEROPORTO DI CIAMPINO · Ciampino · Grottaferrata
Bonifica di Porto · Acília · Vitinia · Spinaceto · Valleranello · Marino · Colli
AEROPORTO INTERCONTINENTALE LEONARDO DA VINCI · Castél di Leva · Santa Maria della Mole · Frattócchie · Albani
Fiumicino · Porto · Ostia Antica · Ostia Malpasso · Mandriola · Cast. di Décima · Falcognana · Rocca di Papa
Ísola Sacra · Lido d. Faro · Casál Palocco · Cast. Porziano · Mte. Cavo
LIDO DI OSTIA · LATINA, TERRACINA · APRÍLIA · VELLETRI

Restricted Zones (ZTL)

Roma Rome

0   km   1

TERNI (3)   VITERBO (2)   FIRENZE 4 (A1 dir, A1 E35)

CIVITAVÉCCHIA 1 (A12 E80)   FROSINONE 6 (A1 E45)

Galleria Nazionale d'Arte Moderna e Contemporanea · Bioparco
Museo Naz. di Villa Giulia · Villa Borghese · Museo e Gall. Borghese
CITTÀ DEL VATICANO Vatican City · Musei Vaticani · Piazza San Pietro · S. Pietro in Vaticano · Stazione Vaticana
Porta del Popolo · Piazza del Popolo · Galoppatoio · MACRO · Villa Albani · Villa Torlonia
Castel S. Angelo · Mausoleo di Augusto · Piazza di Spagna · British Embassy
Pantheon · Fontana di Trevi · Piazza della Repubblica · Stazione Centrale Roma-Termini
Piazza Navona · Palazzo Venezia · Palazzo del Quirinale · Sapienza Università di Roma
Campo d. Fiori · Monte Palatino · Colosseo · Policlinico
Villa Doria Pamphili · S. Maria in Trastevere · Monte Palatino · Circo Massimo · S. Giovanni in Laterano
'LEONARDO DA VINCI' (A12)   LATINA 148

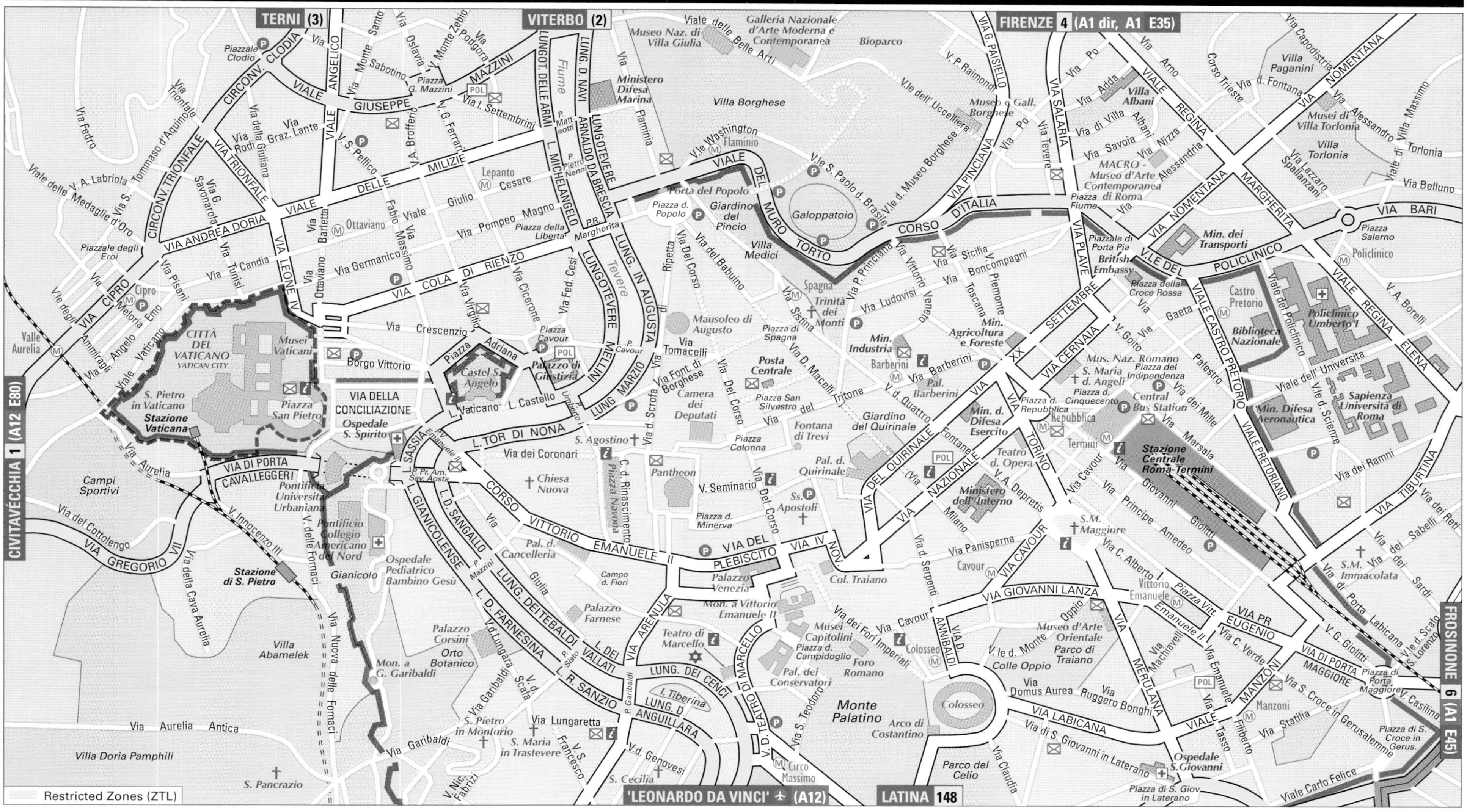

Sevilla Seville

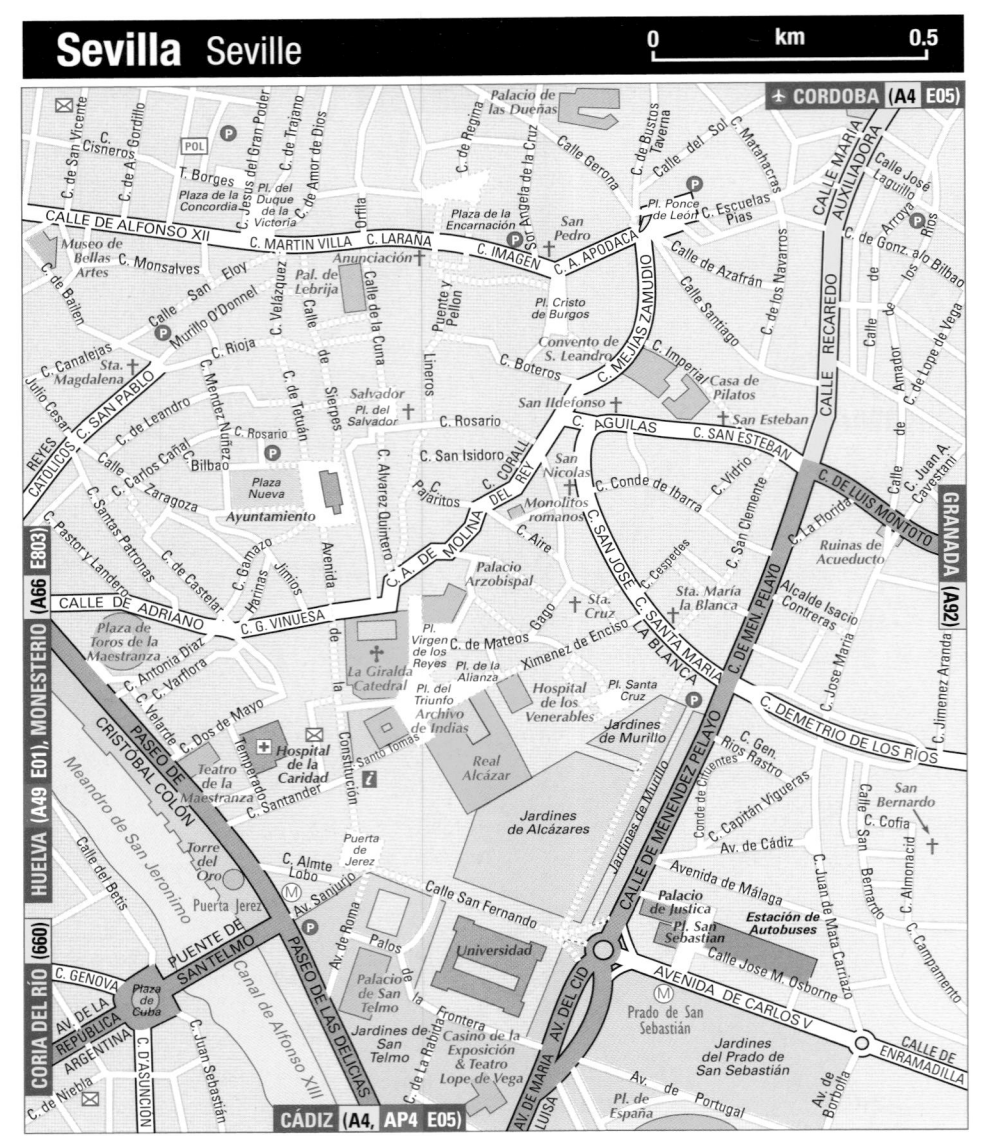

Stuttgart

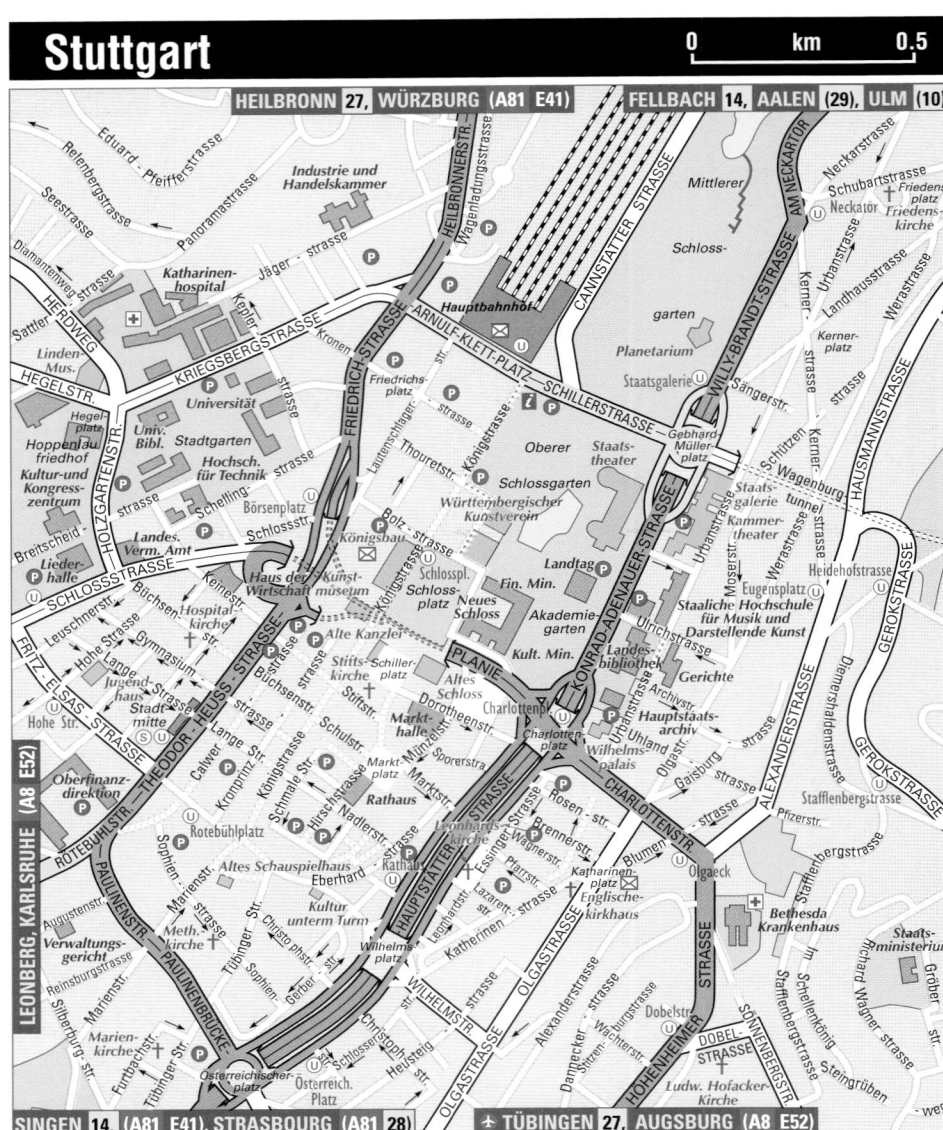

Strasbourg

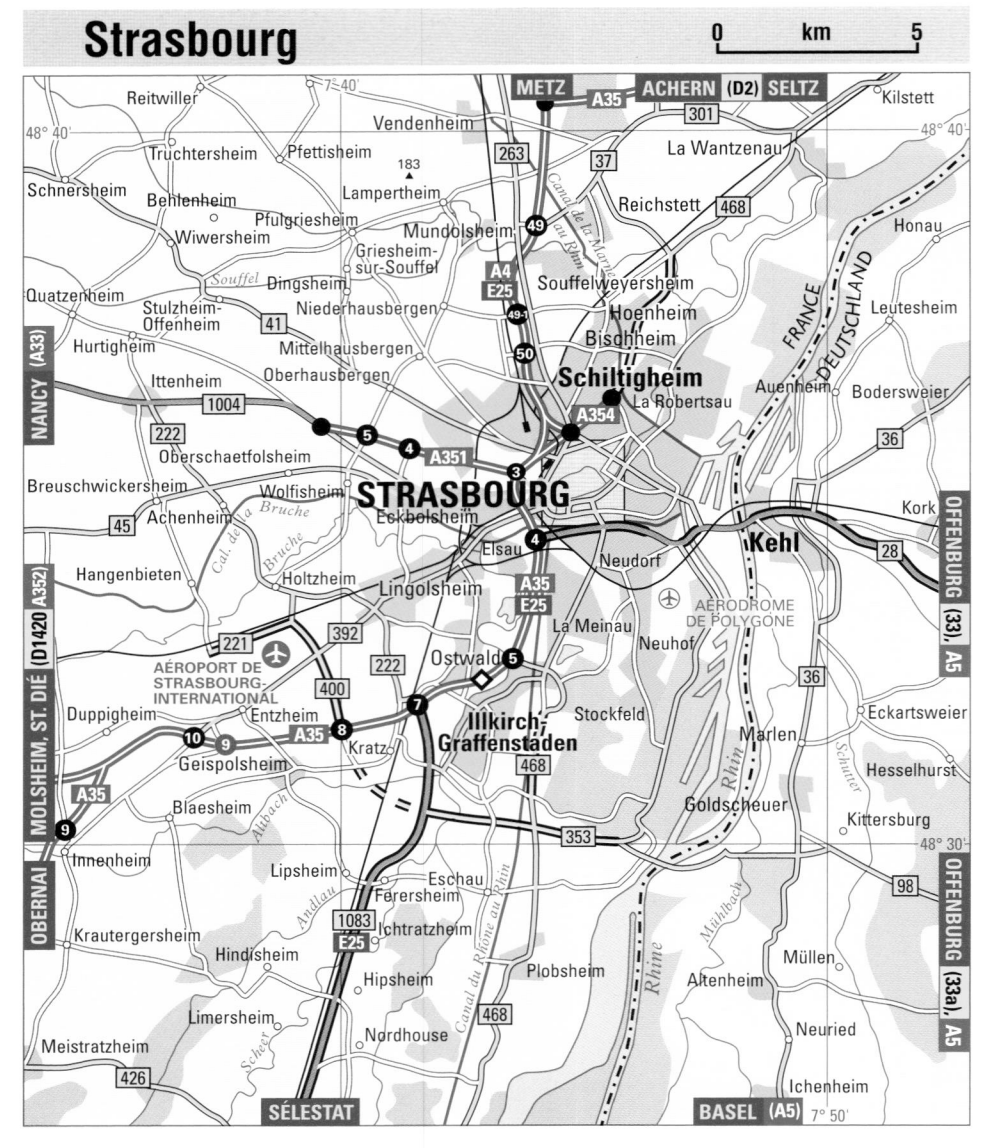

Strasbourg

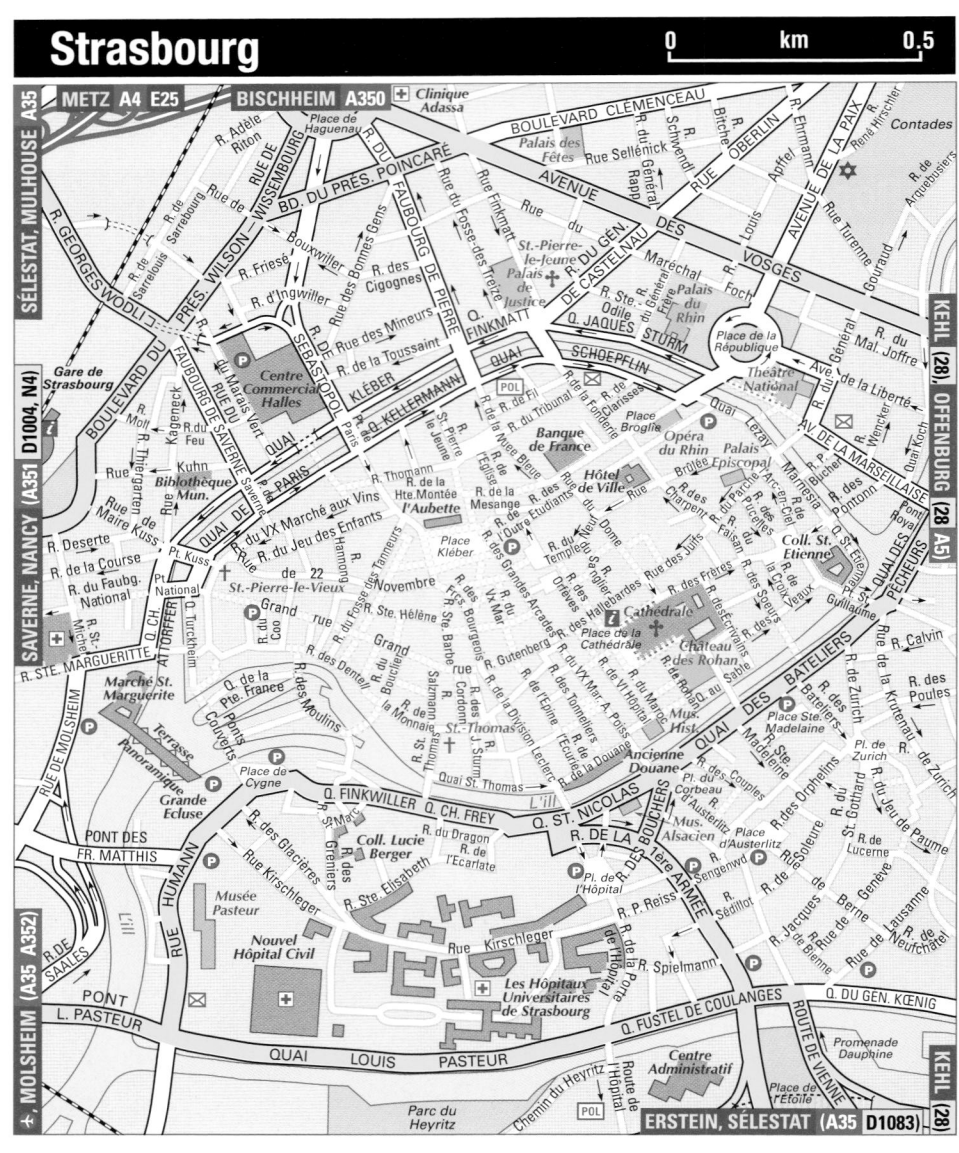

Stockholm

0   km   5

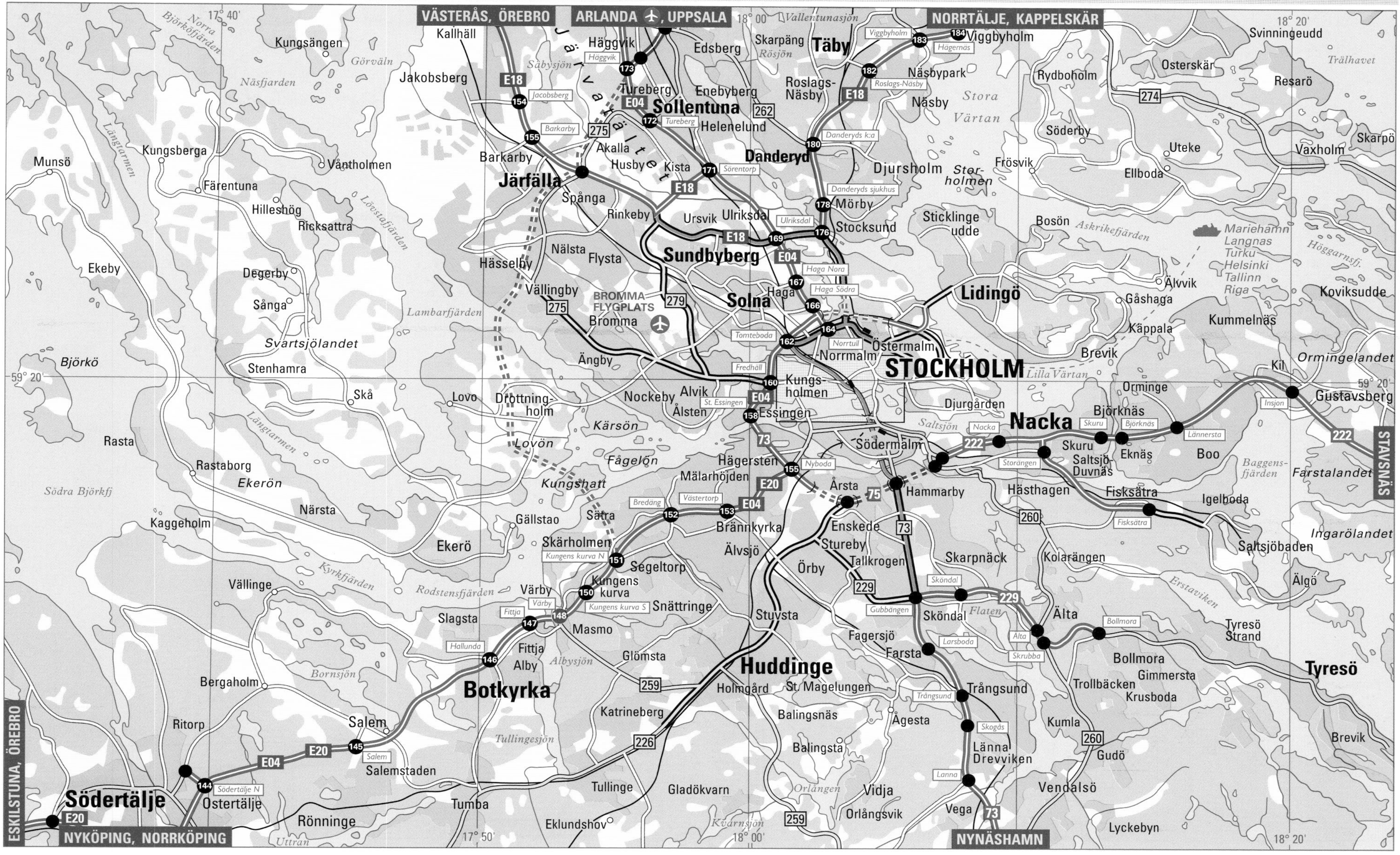

VÄSTERÅS, ÖREBRO | ARLANDA ✈, UPPSALA | NORRTÄLJE, KAPPELSKÄR

Kallhäll
Kungsängen
Görväln
Häggvik 173
Skarpäng
Täby
Viggbyholm 183
Viggbyholm 184
Svinningeudd
Näsfjarden
Näsbyholmen
Norra Björköfjärden
Edsberg
Rösjön
Näsbypark 182
Österskär
Trälhavet
Resarö
Sabysjön
Jakobsberg 154
E18
Tureberg
Eneberg
Roslags-Näsby
E18
Näsby
Stora Värtan
Rydboholm
Söderby
274
Uteke
Skarpö
Sollentuna 172
262
E04
Helenelund
180
Danderyds k:a
Skärpo
Jakobsberg
Barkarby 155
Akalla
Kista 171
Sörentorp
Danderyd
Mörby 178
Djursholm
Storholmen
Frösvik
Sticklinge udde
Bosön
Askrikefjärden
Mariehamn
Langnäs
Turku
Ellboda
Vaxholm
Järfälla
Spånga
Husby
Rinkeby
Ursvik
Ulriksdal
169
Ulriksdal
176
Stocksund
Mörby
Helsinki
Tallinn
Riga
Gåshaga
Koviksudde
Nälsta
Flysta
Sundbyberg
E04
Haga Nora
167
Haga Södra
Lidingö
Brevik
Älvvik
Kummelnäs
Hässelby
Vällingby
275
BROMMA FLYGPLATS
Bromma
279
Solna
166
164
Tomteboda
162
Norrtull
Östermalm
Lilla Värtan
Käppala
Ormingelandet
Ängby
Alvik
St. Essingen
E04
160
Kungsholmen
158
Essingen
Fredhäll
Norrmalm
STOCKHOLM
Djurgården
Nacka
Björknäs
Skuru
Lännersta
Insjön
Gustavsberg
222
STAVSNÄS
Drottningholm
Nockeby
Ålsten
73
Nyboda
Södermalm
Saltsjön
Nacka
222
Björknäs
Skuru
Saltsjö Duvnäs
Eknäs
Boo
Färstalandet
Baggensfjärden
Lovön
Kärsön
Fågelön
Hägersten
Mälarhöjden
155
Årsta
75
Hammarby
Storängen
Hästhagen
260
Fisksätra
Fisksätra
Igelboda
Ingarölandet
Kungshatt
Bredäng
Västertorp
E20
153
Bränkyrka
73
Enskede
Stureby
Tallkrogen
Skarpnäck
Kolarängen
Erstaviken
Saltsjöbaden
Älgö
Gällstao
Satra
152
Skärholmen
151
Segeltorp
Älvsjö
Örby
229
Skondal
Skondal
229
Älta
Bollmora
Tyresö Strand
Ekerö
Kungens kurva N
Kungens kurva
150
Kungens kurva S
Snättringe
Stuvsta
Fagersjö
Skondal
Larsboda
Flaten
Alta
Skrubba
Bollmora
Gimmersta
Krusboda
Tyresö
Vällinge
Värby 147 148
Fittja
Masmo
Glömsta
Holmgård
St. Mägelungen
Farsta
Trångsund
Trångsund
Agesta
Kumla
260
Gudö
Bergaholm
146
Alby
Botkyrka
Albysjön
Katrineberg
Balingsnäs
Balingsta
Skogås
Länna Dreviken
Vendalsö
Brevik
Ritorp
Salem
226
E04
E20
145
Salem
Tumba
Tullinge
Gladökvarn
259
Orlången
Orlångsvik
Lönna
Vega
73
Lyckebyn
Södertälje
144
Södertälje N
Östertälje
Rönninge
Eklundshov
Kvarnsjön
Vidja
E20
NYKÖPING, NORRKÖPING | NYNÄSHAMN
ESKILSTUNA, ÖREBRO

Stockholm

0   km   1

VÄSTERÅS (E04, E18)

Karlbergs Slott
Karlberg
STADSHAGEN
Kungsholmen
NORRMALM
Vasaparken
Observatoriemuseet
Sabbatsbergs sjukhus
Strindbergsmuseet
Johanneskyrkan
Kungliga Biblioteket
Humlegården
ÖSTERMALM
VALHALLAVÄGEN
Karla plan
Stadion
KUNGSGATAN
Östermalmstorg
H. Eleonora kyrka
Historiska museet
Sankt Eriks sjukhus
Sankt Görans sjukhus
Barnklinik
Dansens hus
Hötorget
Konserthuset
Dramatiske teater
Armé museet
MARIEBERG
DROTTNINGHOLMSVÄGEN
Kronobergs parken
Polishuset
Raduset
KUNGSHOLMEN
Arlanda Express
City Terminalen
T-Centralen
Klara kyrka
Kulturhuset
Kungsträdgården
Karl XII Torg
Berzelii Park
Medelhavsmuseet
Operan
Nationalmuseum
SKEPPSHOLMEN
Moderna museet/ Arkitektur-och design centrum
RIDDARHOLMEN
Riddarholmskyrkan
GAMLA STAN
Postmus.
Storkyrkan
Tyska kyrkan
Kungliga Slottet
Mälaren
Riddarfjärden
SÖDERMALM
Söder Mälarstrand
LÅNGHOLMEN
Långholmskanalen
Saltsjön
Kastellholmen
Strömmen
NYNÄSHAMN 73 (73) | GUSTAVSBERG 222 (222)

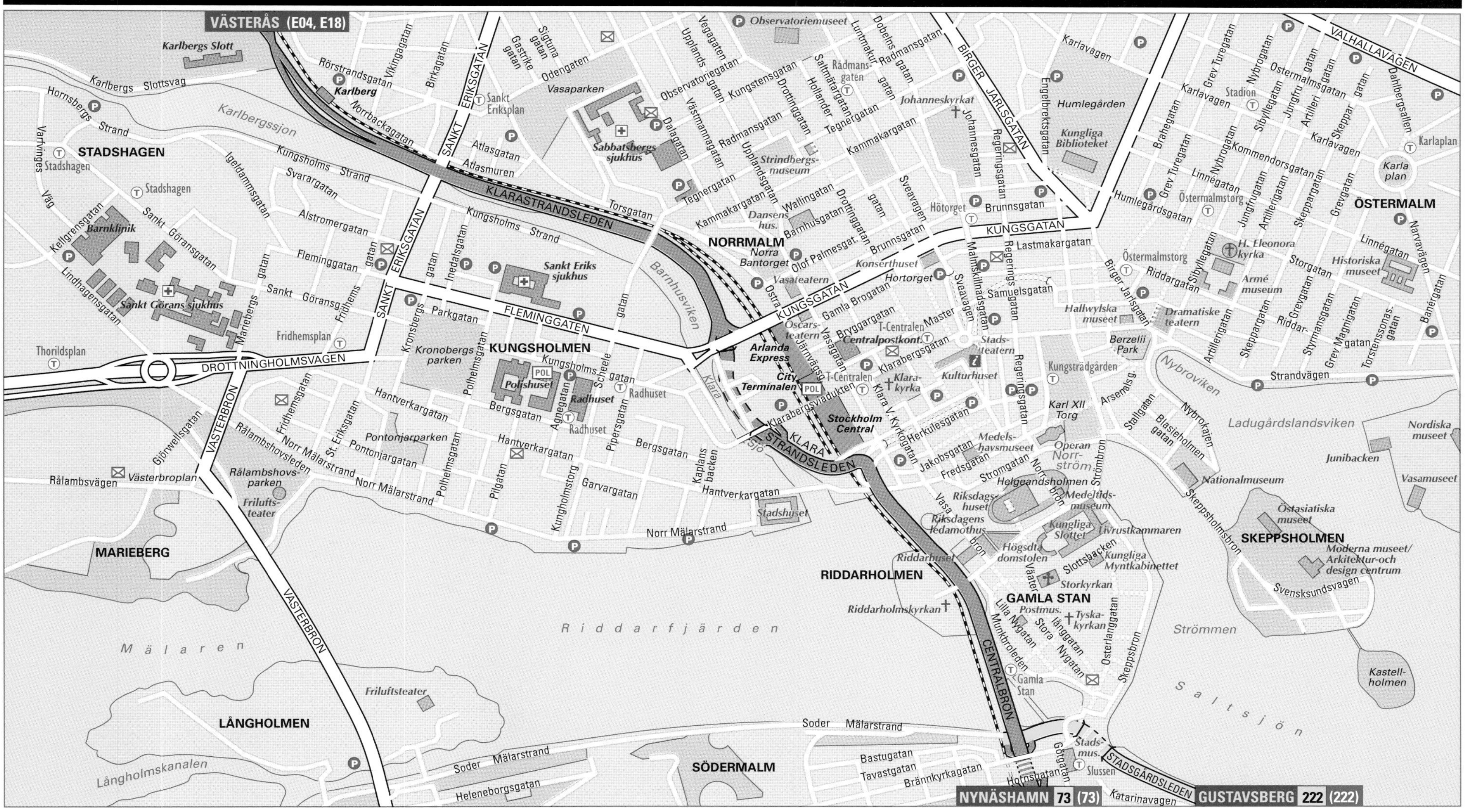

Torino Turin

0   km   5

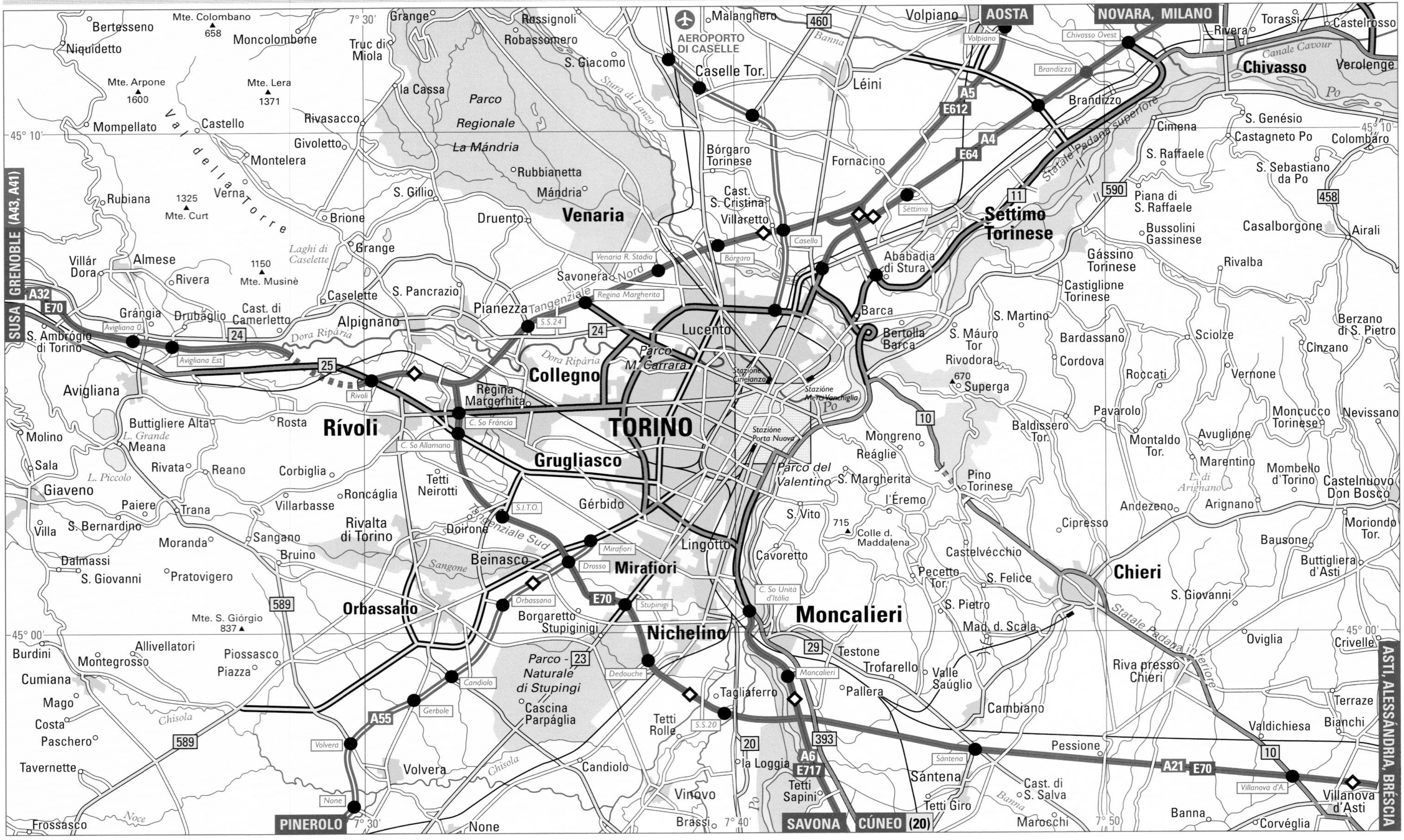

Bertesseno, Niquidetto, Mte. Colombano 658, Moncolombone, Truc di Miola, Grange, Russignoli, Robassomero, Malanghero, 460, Volpiano, **AOSTA**, **NOVARA, MILANO**, Torasso, Castelrosso

Mte. Arpone 1600, Mte. Lera 1371, la Cassa, S. Giacomo, AEROPORTO DI CASELLE, Caselle Tor., Léini, Volpiano, Chivasso Ovest, Rivera, **Chivasso**, Verolenge

Mompellato, Castello, Rivasacco, Parco Regionale, A5, E612, Brandizzo, Cimena, S. Genésio, Castagneto Po, Colombaro, 45° 10'

Rubiana, 1325, Mte. Curt, Givoletto, La Mándria, Bórgaro Torinese, Fornacino, A4, E64, Statale Padana Superiore, S. Raffaele, S. Sebastiano da Po, Casalborgone, Airali, 458

Villár Dora, Almese, Rivera, 1150 Mte. Musinè, Laghi di Caselette, Grange, S. Gillio, Cast. S. Cristina, Villaretto, 11, 590, Piana di S. Raffaele, Bussolini Gassinese, Casalborgone

Val della Torre, Montelera, Brione, Savonera Nord, Venaria R. Stadio, Bórgaro, **Settimo Torinese**, Gássino Torinese, Rivalba

S. Ambrógio di Torino, Grángia, Drubáglio, Caselette, S. Pancrazio, Pianezza, Tangenziale, Regina Margherita, Barca, Bertolla Barca, S. Máuro Tor., Rivodora, Castiglione Torinese, Cordova, Berzano di S. Pietro

SUSA GRENOBLE (A43, A41), A32, E70, A32, 24, Avigliana O., Avigliana Est, 25, Alpignano, S.S.24, Dora Riparia, Lucento, **TORINO**, Superga, 670, S. Martino, Bardassano, Roccati, Cinzano, Scioize

Avigliana, Buttigliera Alta, L. Grande Meana, Rosta, Rívoli, C. So Fráncia, Regina Margherita, Parco M. Catrara, Stazione Smistamento, Stazione Porta Nuova, Po, Mongreno, Reáglie, Pino Torinese, 10, Baldissero Tor., Pavarolo, Vernone, Avuglione, Montaldo Tor., Moncucco Torinese, Nevissano

Molino, Sala, Giaveno, L. Piccolo, Rivata, Reano, Corbiglia, Tetti Neirotti, **Collegno**, C. So Allamano, **Grugliasco**, Gérbido, Parco del Valentino, S. Margherita, l'Éremo, S. Vito, Colle d. Maddalena, Pecetto Tor., Cipresso, Marentino, Mombello d'Torino, Bausone, Castelnuovo Don Bosco

Villa, S. Bernardino, Paiere, Trana, Villarbasse, Roncáglia, Rivalta di Torino, Dojrone, S.I.T.O, Tangenziale Sud, Drosso, **Mirafiori**, Lingotto, Cavoretto, 715, S. Felice, Castelvécchio, S. Giovanni, Buttigliera d'Asti

Dalmassi, S. Giovanni, Moranda, Sangano, Bruino, Beinasco, Orbassano, **Orbassano**, Borgaretto, Stupinigi, Mirafiori, C. So Unità d'Italia, S. Pietro, Mad. d. Scala, **Chieri**, Moriondo Tor., Moriondo Tor.

Burdini, Cumiana, Allivellatori, Montegrosso, Piossasco, Piazza, Mte. S. Giórgio 837, 589, A55, Gerbole, **Nichelino**, E70, **Moncalieri**, 29, Testone, Trofarello, Valle Saúglio, Cambiano, Riva presso Chieri, Oviglia, Crivelle, 45° 00', ASTI, ALESSÁNDRIA, BRÉSCIA

Mago, Costa Paschero, Tavernette, Candiolo, Volvera, 589, Volvera, Parco Naturale di Stupingi, Cascina Parpáglia, 23, Dedouche, Pallera, Santena, Cast. di S. Salva, Pessione, A21, E70, 10, Valdichiesa, Bianchi, Terraze

Frossasco, **PINEROLO**, None, Vinovo, Tetti Sapini, Brassi, la Loggia, 20, 393, Tetti Rolle, S.S.20, A6, E217, Moncalieri, Tagliaferro, Sántena, Tetti Giro, Marocchi, Banna, Villanova d'A., **SAVONA CÚNEO (20)**, Corvéglia

Venézia Venice

0   km   0.5

MESTRE, PÁDOVA (A4 E70)

Marittima, Stazione Marittima (Main cruise and Ferry Port), Stazione FF. SS. S. Lucia, Degli Scalzi, Ponte d. Scalzi, Canal Grande, Canale di S. Chiara, Rio di S. Maria Maggiore, Fond. Cossetti, Piazzale Roma, Autorimessa, Sant' Andrea, Giardino Papadopoli, Palazzo Papadopoli, Canal Grande, C. S. Degola, Campo C. S. Degola, Strada Nuova, R. Terrà Barba Fruttarol, C. Stella, Testa, Fondamenta Nuove

Ex Chiesa di S. Maria Maggiore, Fond. delle Burchielle, Fond. Rio Novo, Riva di Biasio, S. Stae, Campo S. Stae, Ca' d'Oro, Santa Maria dei Miracoli, Ospedale Civile, S. Maria della Pianta

Rio Terrà dei Pensieri, Fond. Rizzi, Fond. dei Ceren, Lista di Bari, Campo N. Sauro, Ca' Pesaro, Palazzo Corner della Regina, Campo S. Apostoli, Sal. S. G. Crisostomo, Poste Telegrafi, S. S. Giovani e Paolo

Fond. S. Marta, Rio Terrà dei Secchi, Briati, Rio Terrà della Scoazzera, Carmini, Scuola del Carmini, Ca' Rezzonico, Campo S. Barnaba, Galleria Accademia, Campo S. Margherita, Campo S. Angelo, Campo S. Stefano, Campo Morosini, Teatro La Fenice, C. Larga 22. Marzo, Piazza San Marco, S. Marco (Basilica), Palazzo Ducale, Ponte dei Sospiri, Riva degli Schiavoni, S. Giovanni in Bragora

San Nicolò dei Mendicoli, Angelo Raffaele, S. Sebastiano, Ospedale G. B. Giustinian, Pte. Accademia, Collezione Guggenheim, Punta della Dogana, Palazzo Dogana di Mare, S. Maria della Salute, Zattere, Canale della Giudecca, Isola di San Giorgio Maggiore, Campo San Giorgio, San Giorgio Maggiore, Bacino di San Marco, Canale di San Marco

Stazione Marittima (San Basilio), Fond. Zattere, Gesuiti, Fond. Zattere dei Gesuiti, S. Agnese, R. Terrà S. Vio, Fond. Zattere Spirito Santo, Fondamenta Beata Giuliana di Collalto

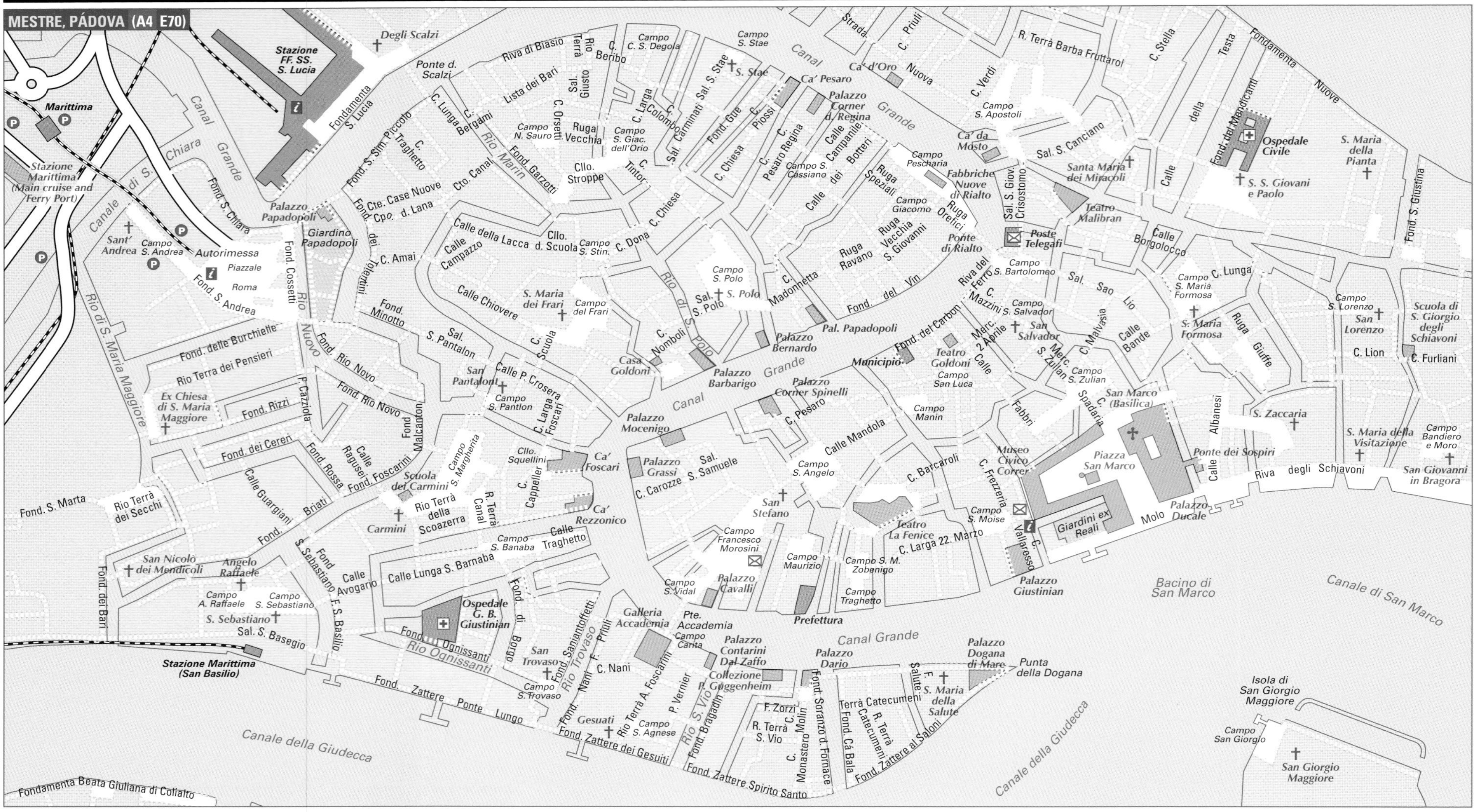

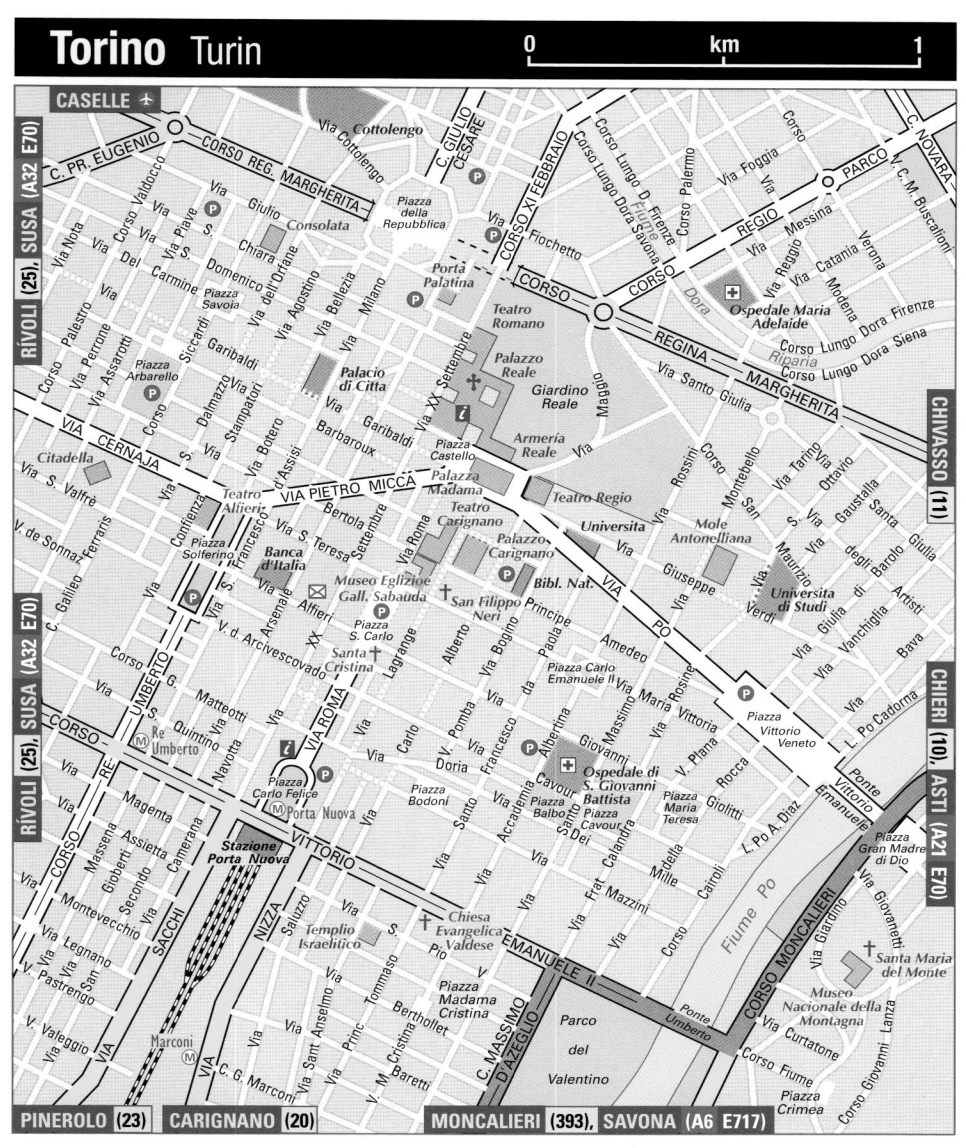

Torino Turin

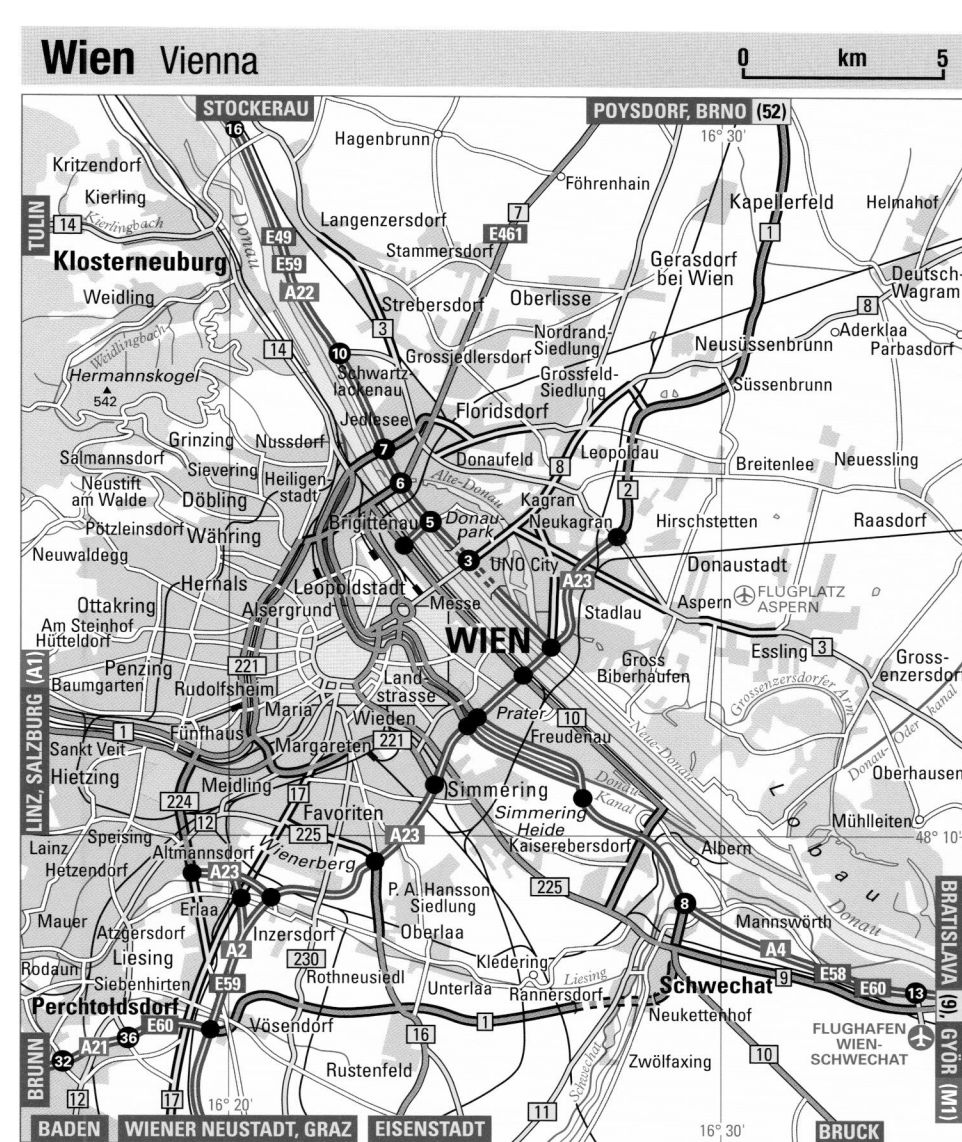

Wien Vienna

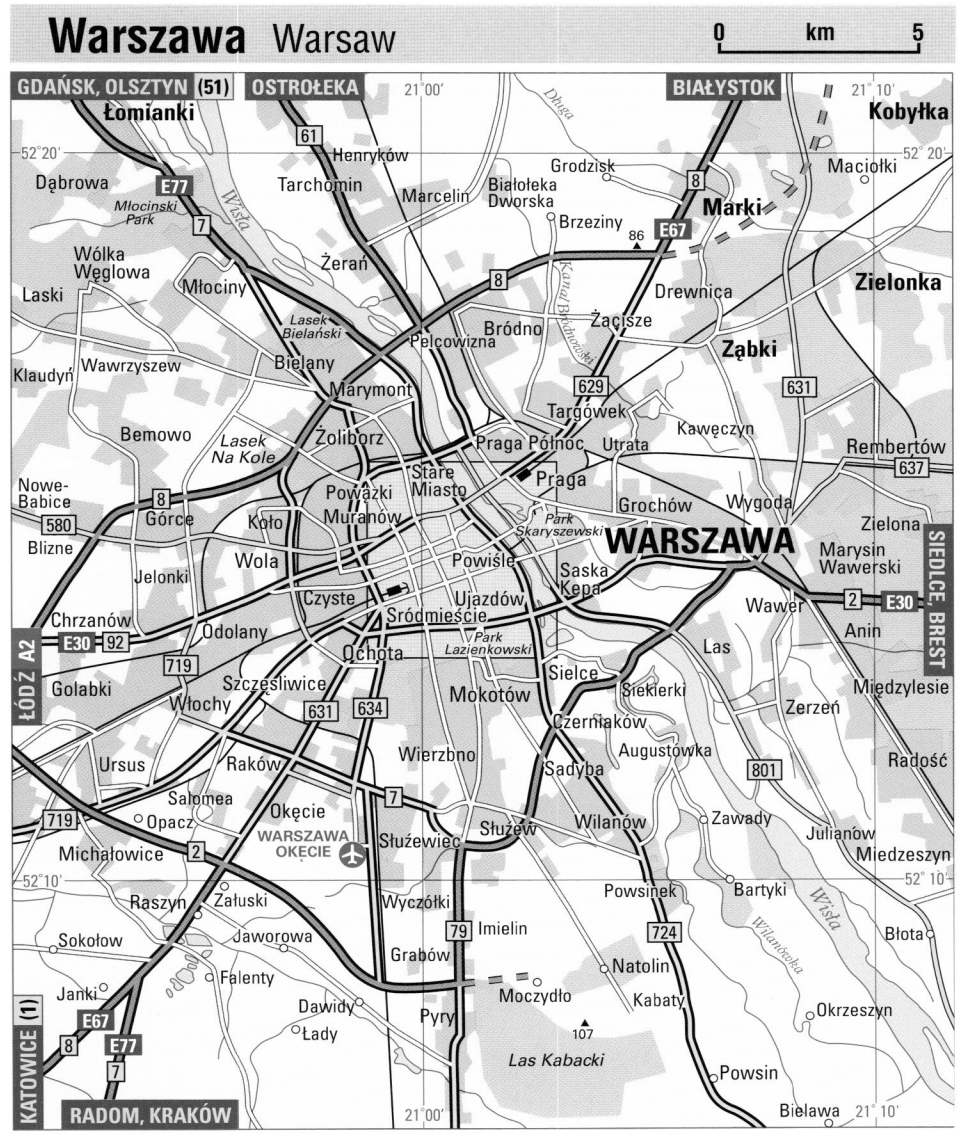

Warszawa Warsaw

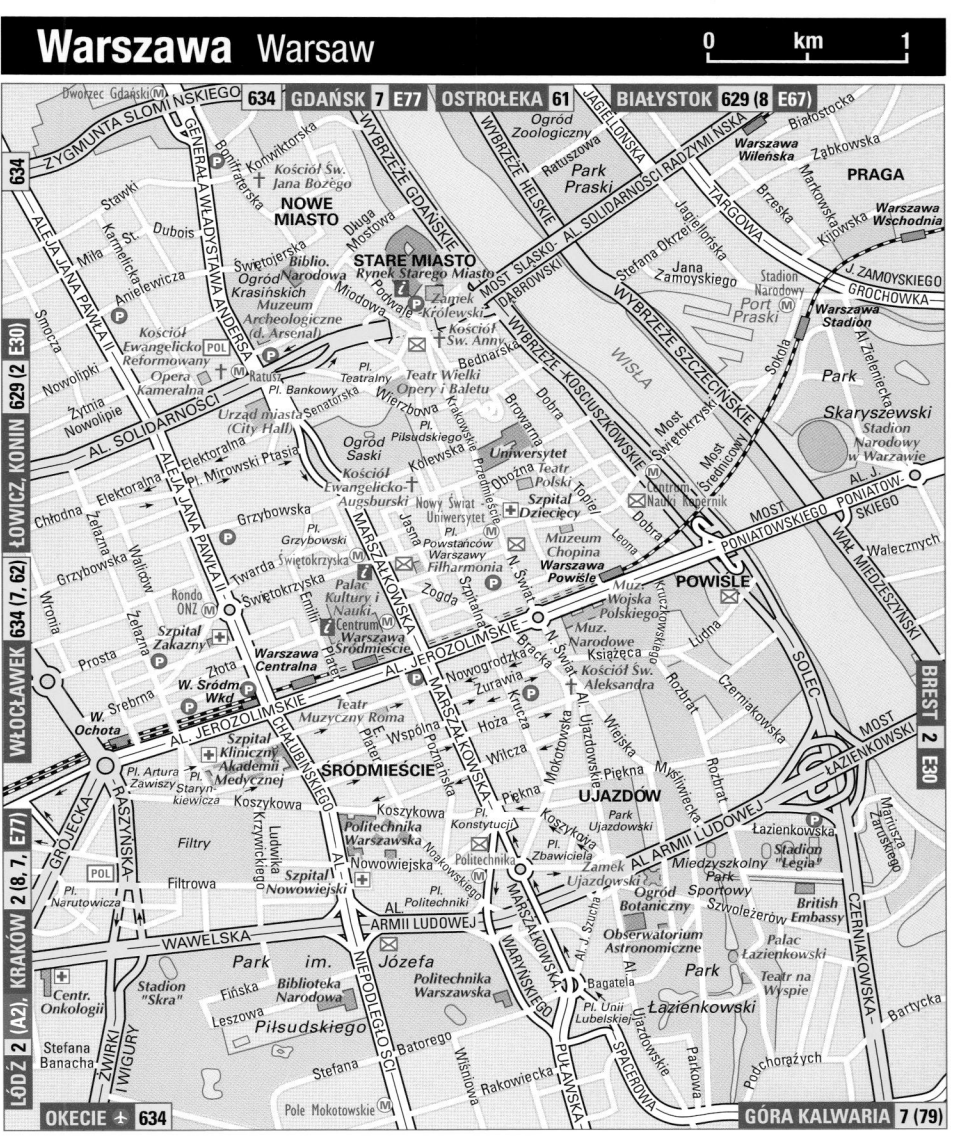

Warszawa Warsaw

Wien Vienna

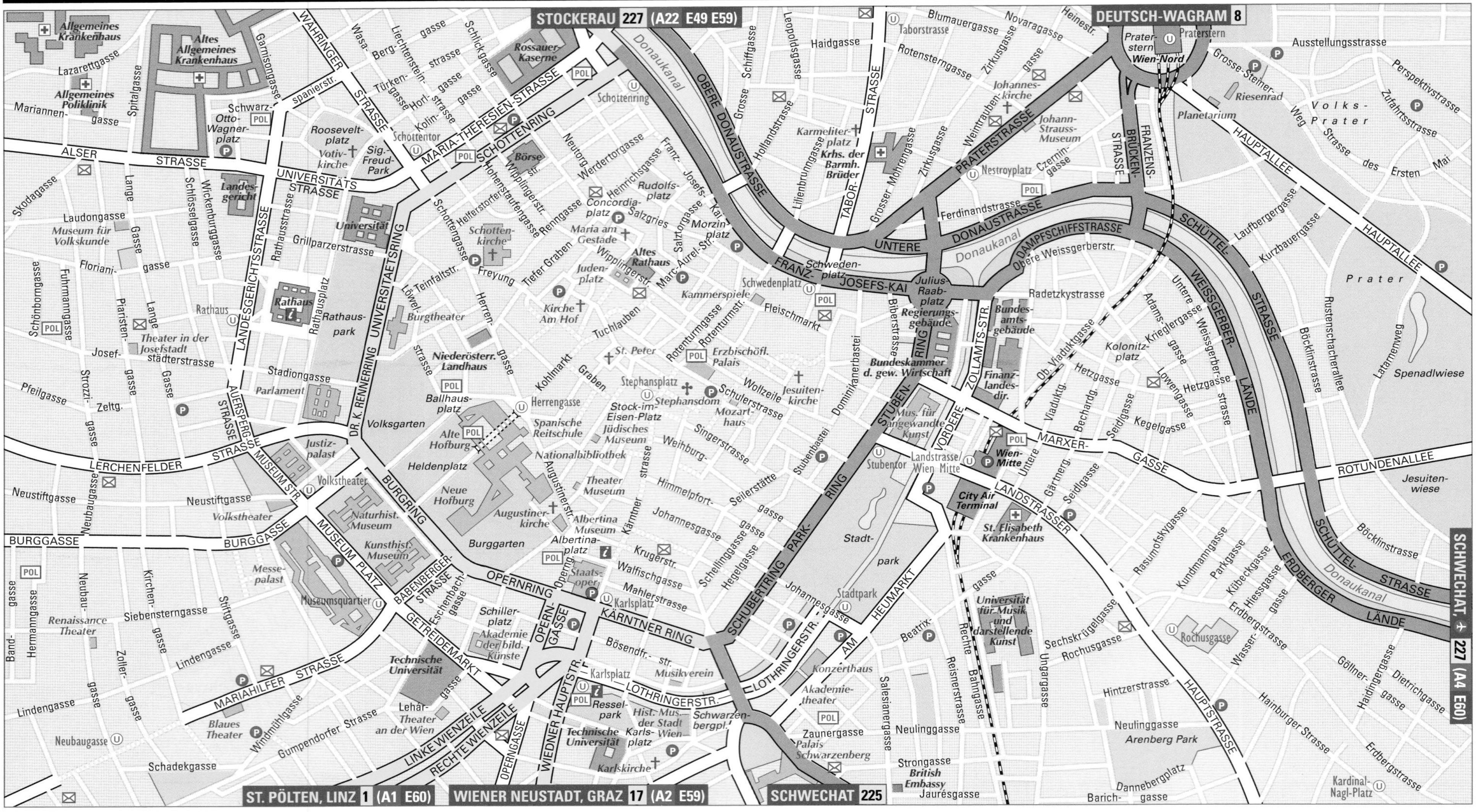

Zagreb

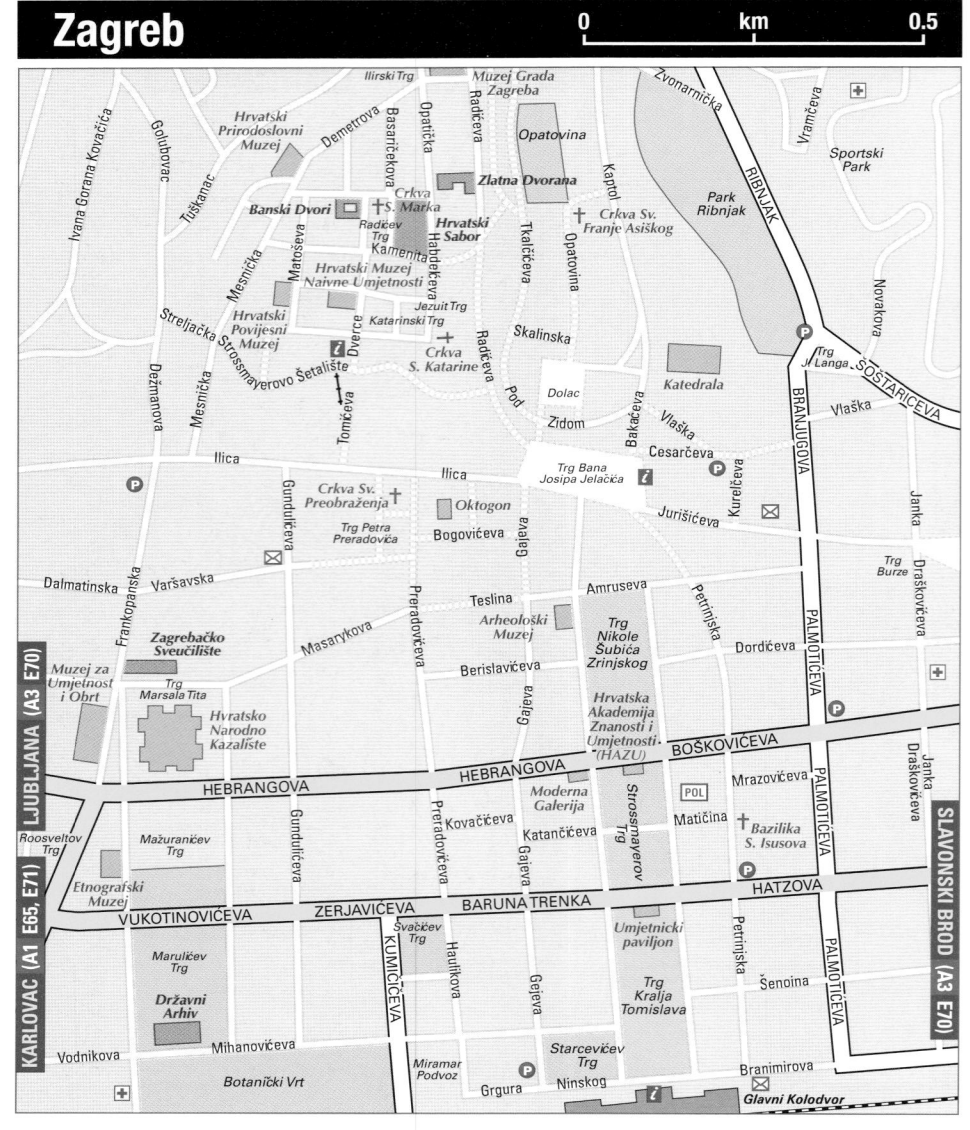

Zürich

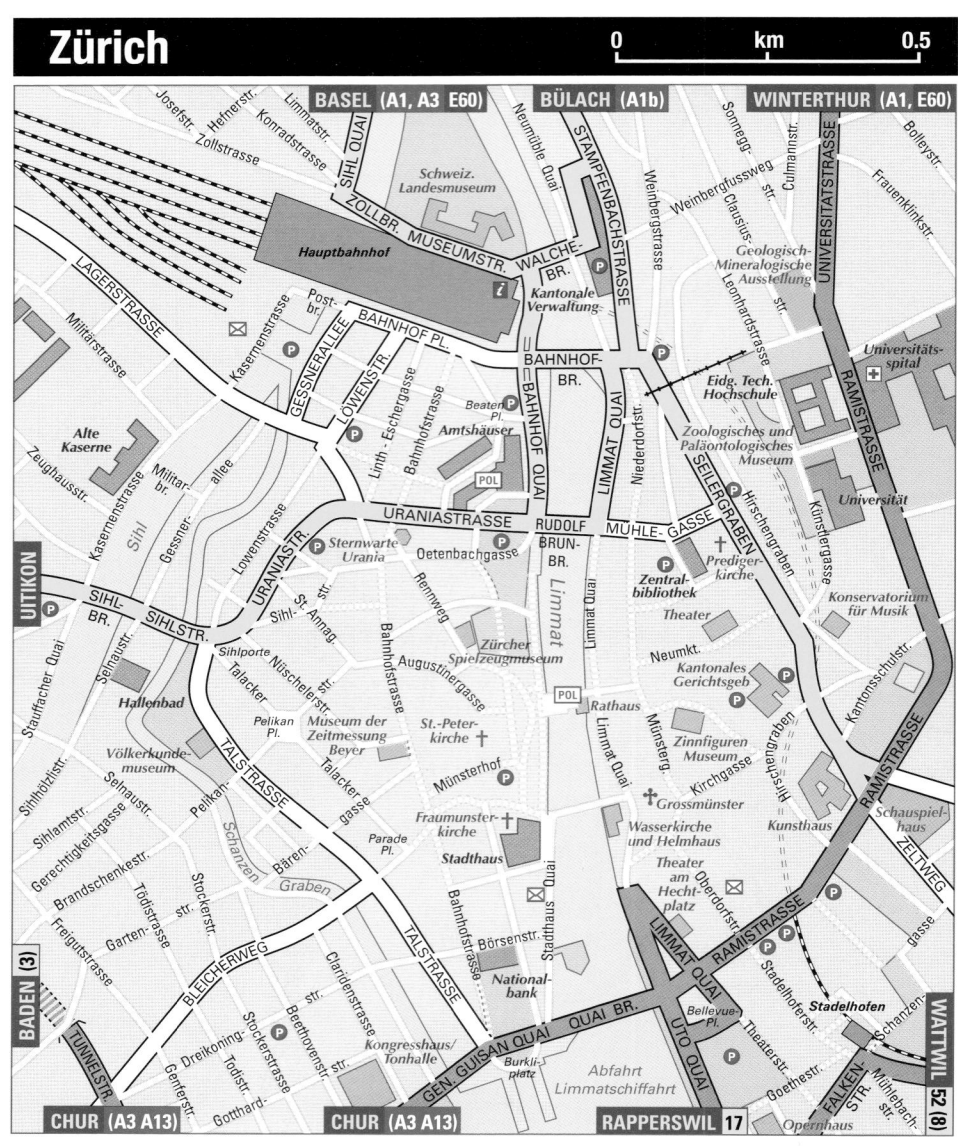

	English	Français	Deutsch	Italiano
A	Austria	Autriche	Österreich	Austria
AL	Albania	Albanie	Albanien	Albania
AND	Andorra	Andorre	Andorra	Andorra
B	Belgium	Belgique	Belgien	Belgio
BG	Bulgaria	Bulgarie	Bulgarien	Bulgaria
BIH	Bosnia-Herzegovin	Bosnia-Herzegovine	Bosnien-Herzegowina	Bosnia-Herzogovina
BY	Belarus	Belarus	Weissrussland	Bielorussia
CH	Switzerland	Suisse	Schweiz	Svizzera
CY	Cyprus	Chypre	Zypern	Cipro
CZ	Czechia	République Tchèque	Tschechische Republik	Repubblica Ceca
D	Germany	Allemagne	Deutschland	Germania
DK	Denmark	Danemark	Dänemark	Danimarca
E	Spain	Espagne	Spanien	Spagna
EST	Estonia	Estonie	Estland	Estonia
F	France	France	Frankreich	Francia
FIN	Finland	Finlande	Finnland	Finlandia
FL	Liechtenstein	Liechtenstein	Liechtenstein	Liechtenstein
FO	Faeroe Islands	Îles Féroé	Färoër-Inseln	Isole Faroe
GB	United Kingdom	Royaume Uni	Grossbritannien und Nordirland	Regno Unito
GBZ	Gibraltar	Gibraltar	Gibraltar	Gibilterra
GR	Greece	Grèce	Greichenland	Grecia
H	Hungary	Hongrie	Ungarn	Ungheria
HR	Croatia	Croatie	Kroatien	Croazia
I	Italy	Italie	Italien	Italia
IRL	Ireland	Irlande	Irland	Irlanda
IS	Iceland	Islande	Island	Islanda
KOS	Kosovo	Kosovo	Kosovo	Kosovo
L	Luxembourg	Luxembourg	Luxemburg	Lussemburgo
LT	Lithuania	Lituanie	Litauen	Lituania
LV	Latvia	Lettonie	Lettland	Lettonia
M	Malta	Malte	Malta	Malta
MC	Monaco	Monaco	Monaco	Monaco
MD	Moldova	Moldavie	Moldawien	Moldavia
MK	Macedonia	Macédoine	Makedonien	Macedonia
MNE	Montenegro	Monténégro	Montenegro	Montenegro
N	Norway	Norvège	Norwegen	Norvegia
NL	Netherlands	Pays-Bas	Niederlande	Paesi Bassi
P	Portugal	Portugal	Portugal	Portogallo
PL	Poland	Pologne	Polen	Polonia
RO	Romania	Roumanie	Rumanien	Romania
RSM	San Marino	Saint-Marin	San Marino	San Marino
RUS	Russia	Russie	Russland	Russia
S	Sweden	Suède	Schweden	Svezia
SK	Slovakia	République Slovaque	Slowak Republik	Repubblica Slovacca
SLO	Slovenia	Slovénie	Slowenien	Slovenia
SRB	Serbia	Serbie	Serbien	Serbia
TR	Turkey	Turquie	Türkei	Turchia
UA	Ukraine	Ukraine	Ukraine	Ucraina

A

Aabenraa DK 39 D2
Aabybro DK 38 B2
Aach D 71 A4
Aachen D 50 C2
Aalborg DK 38 B2
Aalen D 61 B6
Aalestrup D 38 C2
Aalsmeer NL 49 A5
Aalst B 49 C5
Aalten NL 50 B2
Aalter B 49 B4
Äänekoski FIN 3 E26
Aapajärvi FIN 113 E16
Agapınar TR 118 C5
Aarau CH 70 A3
Aarberg CH 70 A2
Aarburg CH 70 A2
Aardenburg NL 49 B4
Aars DK 38 C2
Aarschot B 49 C5
Aarup DK 39 D3
Aba H 74 A3
Abádanes E 95 B4
Abades E 94 B2
Abadin E 86 A3
Abádszalók H 75 A5
Abaliget H 74 B3
Abana TR 16 A7
A Baña E 86 B2
Abanilla E 101 A4
Abano Terme I 72 C1
Abarán E 101 A4
Abasár H 65 C6
Abbadia San Salvatore I 81 D5
Abbaue D 45 B5
Abbehausen D 43 B5
Abbekås S 41 D3
Abbeville F 48 C2
Abbey IRL 20 A3
Abbeydorney IRL 20 B2
Abbeyfeale IRL 20 B2
Abbeyleix IRL 21 B4
Abbey Town GB 25 D4
Abbiategrasso I 70 C3
Abborrträsk S 115 B16
Abbots Bromley GB 27 C4
Abbotsbury GB 29 C5
Abda H 64 C3
Abejar E 89 C4
Abela P 98 B2
Abelvær N 114 C8
Abenberg D 62 A1
Abenójar E 100 A1
Abensberg D 62 B2
Aberaeron GB 28 A3
Abercarn GB 29 B4
Aberchirder GB 23 D6
Aberdare GB 29 B4
Aberdaron GB 26 C1
Aberdeen GB 23 D6
Aberdulais GB 28 B4
Aberdyfi GB 26 C1
Aberfeldy GB 25 B4
Aberffraw GB 26 B1
Aberfoyle GB 24 B3
Abergavenny GB 29 B4
Abergele GB 26 B2
Abergynolwyn GB 26 C2
Aberporth GB 28 A3
Abersoch GB 26 C1
Abertillery GB 29 B4
Abertura E 93 B5
Aberystwyth GB 26 C1
Abetone I 81 B4
Abfaltersbach A 72 B2
Abide
Çanakkale TR 118 B1
Kütahya TR 118 D4
Abiego E 90 A2
Abild DK 39 E1
Abingdon-on-Thames GB 31 C2
Abington GB 25 C4
Abisko S 112 D7
Abiul P 92 B2
Abla E 101 B3
Ablis F 58 B2
A Bola E 87 B3
Abondance F 70 B1
Abony H 75 A5
Aboyne GB 23 D6
Abrantes P 92 B2
Abreiro P 87 C3
Abreschviller F 60 B3
Abrest F 68 B3
Abriès F 79 B5
Abrud RO 11 C7
Absdorf A 64 B1
Abtenau A 72 A3
Abtsgmünd D 61 B5
Abusejo E 93 A4
Aby
Kronoberg S 40 B4
Östergötland S 37 D3
Åbyggeby S 36 B4
Åbytorp S 37 C2
A Cañiza E 87 B2
A Capela E 86 A2
Acate I 109 B3
Accadia I 103 B8
Accéglio I 79 B5
Accettura I 104 C2
Acciaroli I 106 A2

Accous F 76 D2
Accrington GB 26 B3
Accrimoli I 82 D2
Acedera E 93 B5
Acehúche E 93 B4
Acered E 95 A5
Acerenza I 104 C1
Acerno I 103 C8
Acerra I 103 C7
Aceuchal E 93 C4
Acharacle GB 24 B2
Acharnes GR 117 D5
Achavanich GB 23 C5
Achene B 49 C6
Achenkirch A 72 A1
Achensee A 72 A1
Achenthal A 72 A1
Achentrias GR 117 H7
Achern D 61 B4
Acheux-en-Amienois F 48 C3
Achiltibuie GB 22 C3
Achim D 43 B6
Achladokambos GR 117 E4
Achnasheen GB 22 D3
Achnashellach GB 22 D3
Achosnich GB 24 B1
Aci Castello I 109 B4
Aci Catena I 109 B4
Acilia I 102 B5
Acıpayam TR 119 E4
Acireale I 109 B4
Acle GB 30 B5
Agria GR 116 C4
Agreda E 89 C5
A Coruña E 86 A2
Acquacadda I 110 C1
Acqua Doria F 102 B1
Acquanegra sul Chiese I 71 C5
Acquapendente I 81 D5
Acquasanta Terme I 82 D2
Acquasparta I 102 A5
Acquaviva I 81 C5
Acquaviva delle Fonti I 104 C2
Acquaviva Picena I 82 D2
Acquigny F 58 A2
Acqui Terme I 80 B2
Acri I 106 B3
Acs H 64 C4
Acsa H 65 C5
Acsteszér H 74 A2
Acy-en-Multien F 59 A3
Ada SRB 75 C5
Adak S 115 B15
Ådalsbruk N 34 B3
Adamas GR 117 F6
Adamsfjord N 113 B15
Adamuz E 100 A1
Adana TR 16 C7
Ådåndi H 74 B3
Adare IRL 20 B3
Adaševci SRB 85 A4
Adeanueva de Ebro E 89 B5
Adelboden CH 70 B2
Adelebsen D 51 B5
Adélfia I 104 B2
Adelmannsfelden D 61 B6
Adelsheim D 61 A5
Adelsö S 37 C4
Ademuz E 96 A1
Adenau D 50 C2
Adendorf D 44 B2
Adinkerke B 48 B3
Adjud RO 11 C9
Adliswil CH 70 A3
Admont A 63 C5
Ådneram N 33 C3
Adony H 74 A3
Adorf
Hessen D 51 B4
Sachsen D 52 C2
Adradas E 89 C4
Adrall E 91 A4
Adrano I 109 B3
Adria I 82 A1
Adrigole IRL 20 C2
Adwick le Street GB 27 B4
Adzaneta E 96 A2
Aesch CH 70 A2
A Estrada E 86 B2
Afandou GR 119 F3
Afarnes N 114 E4
Affing D 62 B1
Affoltern CH 70 A3
Affric Lodge GB 22 D3
Afjord N 114 D7
Aflenz Kurort A 73 A5
A Fonsagrada E 86 A3
Afragóla I 103 C7
Afritz A 72 B3
Afyonkarahisar TR 118 C5
Ágasegyháza H 75 B4
Agay F 79 C5
Agazzano I 80 B3
Agde F 78 C2
Agdenes N 114 D6
Agen F 77 B3
Agerbæk DK 39 D1
Agerskov DK 39 D2
Agger DK 38 C1
Aggius I 110 B2

Aggsbach Dorf A 63 B6
Aggsbach Markt A 63 B6
Aggtelek H 65 B6
Aghalee GB 19 B5
Aghia GR 116 C4
Aghia Anna GR 116 D5
Aghia Galini GR 117 G6
Aghia Marina GR 119 G1
Aghia Paraskevi GR 118 C1
Aghia Pelagia GR 117 F4
Aghia Triada GR 117 E3
Aghiokambos GR 116 C4
Aghios Efstratios GR 116 C6
Aghios Kirikos GR 119 E1
Aghios Matheos GR 116 C1
Aghios Mironas GR 117 G7
Aghios Nikolaos GR 117 G7
Aghios Petros GR 116 D2
Aghios Theodori GR 117 E5
Agiči BIH 83 B5
Agira I 109 B3
Aglientu I 110 A2
Agnières F 79 B4
Agno CH 70 C3
Agnone I 103 B7
Agolada E 86 B2
Agon Coutainville F 57 A4
Agordo I 72 B2
Agost E 96 C2
Agramón E 101 A4
Agramunt E 91 B4
Agreda E 89 C5
Agria GR 116 C4
Agrigento I 108 B2
Agrinio GR 116 D3
Agrón E 100 B2
Agrópoli I 103 C7
Aguadulce
Almería E 101 C3
Sevilla E 100 B1
Agualada E 86 A2
Agua Longa P 87 C2
A Guarda E 87 C2
Aguarón E 89 C5
Aguas E 90 A2
Aguas Belas P 92 B2
Aguas de Busot E 96 C2
Aguas de Moura P 92 C2
Aguas Frias P 87 C3
Aguas Santas P 87 C2
Aguaviva E 90 C2
Aguaviva de la Vega E 89 C4
A Gudiña E 87 B3
Agudo E 94 D2
Agueda P 92 A2
Aguessac F 78 B2
Agugliano I 82 C2
Aguiar P 92 C3
Aguiar da Beira P 87 D3
Aguilafuente E 94 A2
Aguilar de Campóo E 88 B2
Aguilar de la Frontera E 100 B1
Aguilas E 101 B4
Agunnaryd S 40 C4
Ahat TR 118 D4
Ahaus D 50 A2
Åheim N 114 E2
Ahigal E 93 A4
Ahigal de Villarino E 87 C4
Ahillones E 99 A5
Ahlbeck
Mecklenburg-Vorpommern D 45 B6
Mecklenburg-Vorpommern D 45 B6
Ahlen D 50 B3
Ahlhorn D 43 C5
Ahmetbey TR 118 A2
Ahmetler TR 119 D4
Ahmetli TR 119 D2
Ahoghill GB 19 B5
Ahrensbök D 44 A2
Ahrensburg D 44 B2
Ahrenshoop D 44 A4
Ahun F 68 B2
Ahus S 41 D4
Ahvensalmi FIN 113 F17
Aibar E 89 B5
Aich D 62 B3
Aichach D 62 B2
Aidone I 109 B3
Aiello Cálabro I 106 B3
Aigen im Mühlkreis A 63 B4
Aigle CH 70 B1
Aignan F 76 C3
Aignay-le-Duc F 59 C5
Aigre F 67 C5
Aigrefeuille-d'Aunis F 66 B4
Aigrefeuille-sur-Maine F 66 A3
Aiguablava E 91 B6
Aiguebelette F 69 C6
Aigueperse F 68 B3
Aigues-Mortes F 78 C3
Aigues-Vives F 78 C1
Aiguilles F 79 B5
Aiguillon F 77 B3
Ailefroide F 79 B5
Ailiant-sur-Tholon F 59 C4
Ailly-sur-Noye F 58 A3
Ailly-sur-Somme F 58 A3

Aime F 69 C6
Ainaži LV 6 C8
Ainet A 72 B2
Ainsa E 90 A3
Airaines F 48 D2
Aird GB 24 B2
Aird Asaig Tairbeart GB 22 D2
Airdrie GB 25 C4
Aire-sur-l'Adour F 76 C2
Aire-sur-la-Lys F 48 C3
Airole I 80 C1
Airolo CH 70 B3
Airvault F 67 B4
Aisey-sur-Seine F 59 C5
Aïssey F 69 A6
Aisy-sur-Armançon F 59 C5
Aith
Orkney GB 23 B6
Shetland GB 22 A7
Aitona E 90 B3
Aitrach D 61 C6
Aiud RO 11 C7
Aix-en-Othe F 59 B4
Aix-en-Provence F 79 C4
Aixe-sur-Vienne F 67 C6
Aix-les-Bains F 69 C5
Aizenay F 66 B3
Aizkraukle LV 7 C8
Aizpute LV 6 C6
Ajac F 77 C5
Ajaccio F 102 B1
Ajain F 68 B1
Ajaureforsen S 115 B12
Ajdovščina SLO 72 C3
Ajka H 74 A2
Ajo E 89 A3
Ajofrin E 94 C3
Ajuda P 93 C3
Akanthou CY 120 A2
Akarca TR 119 D4
Akasztó H 75 B4
Akçakoca TR 118 A6
Akçaova TR 118 A4
Akçay TR 119 F4
Aken D 52 B2
Åkernes N 33 D4
Åkernes S 36 B4
Åkersberga S 37 C5
Åkers Styckebruk S 37 C4
Åkervik N 115 B10
Akhisar TR 118 D2
Åkirkeby DK 41 D4
Akköy TR 119 E2
Akkrum NL 42 B2
Akören TR 119 E7
Åkra N 32 C3
Akranes IS 111 C3
Åkrehamn N 33 C2
Akrotiri CY 120 B1
Aksaray TR 16 B7
Akşehir TR 119 D6
Akseki TR 119 E6
Aksla N 32 A3
Aksu TR 119 F5
Aktsyabrski BY 7 E10
Akureyri IS 111 B7
Åkvåg N 33 D6
Akyazı TR 118 B5
Ala I 71 C6
Alaca TR 16 A7
Alacaatlı TR 118 C3
Alaçam TR 16 A7
Alaçatı TR 119 D1
Ala di Stura I 70 C2
Alaejos E 94 A1
Alagna Valsésia I 70 C2
Alagón E 90 B1
Alaior E 97 B4
Alájar E 99 B4
Alakurtti RUS 3 C29
Alakylä FIN 113 E13
Alameda E 100 B1
Alameda de la Sagra E 94 B3
Alamedilla E 100 B2
Alamillo E 100 A1
Alaminos E 95 B4
Ala-Nampa FIN 113 F15
Alanäs S 115 C12
Alandroal P 92 C3
Alange E 93 C4
Alaniemi FIN 3 D26
Alanís E 99 A5
Alansbro S 115 E14
Alanya TR 119 F7
Alap H 74 B3
Alaquàs E 96 B2
Alaraz E 94 B1
Alarcón E 95 C4
Alar del Rey E 88 B2
Alaró E 97 B2
Alaşehir TR 119 D3
Alássio I 80 B2
Alatoz E 96 B1
Alatri I 103 B6
Alavus FIN 3 E25
Alba
E 95 B5
I 80 B2
Alba Adriática I 82 D2
Albacete E 95 D5

Alba de Tormes E 94 B1
Alba de Yeltes E 93 A4
Albaida E 96 C2
Alba-Iulia RO 11 C7
Albæk DK 38 B3
Albaladejo E 101 A3
Albala del Caudillo E 93 B4
Albalat E 96 B2
Albalate de Cinca E 90 B3
Albalate del Arzobispo E 90 B2
Albalate de las Nogueras E 95 B4
Albalate de Zorita E 95 B4
Alban F 77 C5
Albánchez E 101 B3
Albanchez de Ubeda E 100 B2
Albano Laziale I 102 B5
Albanyà E 91 A5
Albaredo d'Adige I 71 C6
Albares E 95 B3
Albarracin E 95 B5
Albatana E 101 A4
Albatarrec E 90 B3
Albatera E 101 A5
Albbruck D 61 C4
Albedin E 100 B1
Albelda de Iregua E 89 B4
Albenga I 80 B2
Albens F 69 C5
Alberga
Södermanland S 37 C3
Södermanland S 37 D3
Albergaria-a-Nova P 87 D2
Albergaria-a-Velha P 92 A2
Albergaria dos Doze P 92 B2
Alberge P 92 C2
Alberic E 96 B2
Albernoa P 98 B3
Alberobello I 104 C3
Alberoni I 72 C2
Albersdorf D 43 A6
Albersloh D 50 B3
Albert F 48 C3
Albertirsa H 75 A4
Albertville F 69 C6
Albi F 77 C5
Albidona I 106 B3
Albinia I 102 A4
Albino I 71 C4
Albinshof D 45 B5
Albires E 88 B1
Albisola Marina I 80 B2
Albocàcer E 90 C3
Albolote E 100 B2
Albondón E 100 C2
Alborea E 96 B1
Albox E 101 B3
Albrechtice nad Vltavou CZ 63 A5
Albstadt D 61 B5
Albufeira P 98 B2
Albuñol E 100 C2
Albuñuelas E 100 C2
Alburquerque E 93 B3
Alby
Öland S 41 C6
Västernorrland S 115 E12
Alcácer do Sal P 92 C2
Alcáçovas P 92 C2
Alcadozo E 101 A4
Alcafoces P 93 B3
Alcains P 92 B3
Alcalá de Guadaira E 99 B5
Alcalá de Gurrea E 90 A2
Alcalá de Henares E 95 B3
Alcalá de la Selva E 90 C2
Alcalá del Júcar E 96 B1
Alcalá de los Gazules E 99 C5
Alcalá del Río E 99 B5
Alcalá del Valle E 99 C5
Alcalá la Real E 100 B2
Alcamo I 108 B1
Alcampell E 90 B3
Alcanadre E 89 B4
Alcanar E 90 C3
Alcanede P 92 B2
Alcanena P 92 B2
Alcañices E 87 C4
Alcántara E 93 B4
Alcantarilha P 98 B2
Alcantarilla E 101 B4
Alcañz E 90 C2
Alcaracejos E 100 A1
Alcara il Fusi I 109 A3
Alcaraz E 101 A3
Alcaria Ruiva P 98 B3
Alcarraz E 90 B3
Alcaudete E 100 B1
Alcaudete de la Jara E 94 C2
Alcázar de San Juan E 95 C3
Alcazarén E 88 C2
Alcester GB 29 A6
Alcoba E 94 C2
Alcobaça P 92 B1
Alcobendas E 94 B3
Alcocer E 95 B4
Alcocéber E 90 C3
Alcochete P 92 C2
Alcoentre P 92 B1

Alcolea
Almería E 100 C3
Córdoba E 100 B1
Alcolea de Calatrava E 94 D2
Alcolea de Cinca E 90 B3
Alcolea del Pinar E 95 A4
Alcolea del Rio E 99 B5
Alcollarin E 93 B5
Alconchel E 93 C3
Alconera E 93 C4
Alcontar E 101 B3
Alcora E 96 A2
Alcorcón E 94 B3
Alcorisa E 90 C2
Alcossebre E 96 A3
Alcoutim P 98 B3
Alcover E 91 B4
Alcoy E 96 C2
Alcsutdoboz H 74 A3
Alcubierre E 90 B2
Alcubilla de Avellaneda E 89 C3
Alcubilla de Nogales E 88 B1
Alcubillas E 100 A2
Alcublas E 96 B2
Alcúdia E 97 B3
Alcudia de Guadix E 100 B2
Alcuéscar E 93 B4
Aldbrough GB 27 B5
Aldeacentenera E 93 C5
Aldeadávila de la Ribera E 87 C4
Aldea del Cano E 93 B4
Aldea del Fresno E 94 B2
Aldea del Obispo E 87 D4
Aldea del Rey E 100 A2
Aldea de Trujillo E 93 B5
Aldealcorvo E 94 A3
Aldealuenga de Santa Maria E 89 C3
Aldeamayor de San Martin E 88 C2
Aldeanueva de Barbarroya E 94 C1
Aldeanueva del Camino E 93 A5
Aldeanueva del Codonal E 94 A2
Aldeanueva de San Bartolomé E 94 C1
Aldeapozo E 89 C4
Aldeaquemada E 100 A2
Aldea Real E 94 A2
Aldearrubia E 94 A1
Aldeaseca de la Frontera E 94 B1
Aldeasoña E 88 C2
Aldeatejada E 94 B1
Aldeavieja E 94 B2
Aldeburgh GB 30 B5
Aldehuela E 96 A1
Aldehuela de Calatañazor E 89 C4
Aldeia da Serra P 92 C3
Aldeia do Bispo P 93 A4
Aldeia do Mato P 92 B2
Aldeia Gavinha P 92 B1
Aldeire E 100 B2
Aldenhoven D 50 C2
Aldersbach D 62 B4
Aldershot GB 31 C3
Aldudes F 76 C1
Åled S 40 C2
Aledo E 101 B4
Alegria E 89 B4
Aleksandrovac
Srbija SRB 85 B6
Srbija SRB 85 C6
Aleksandrów Kujawski PL 47 C4
Aleksandrów Łódzki PL 55 B4
Aleksa Šantić SRB 75 C4
Ålem S 40 C6
Alençon F 57 B6
Alenquer P 92 B1
Alenya F 91 A5
Aléria F 102 A2
Alès F 78 B3
Áles I 110 C1
Alessándria I 80 B2
Alessándria della Rocca I 108 B2
Alessano I 107 B5
Alet-les-Bains F 77 D5
Alexandria
GB 24 C3
RO 11 E8
Alezio I 107 A5
Alézreal E 92 C1
Alfajarin E 90 B2
Alfambra
E 90 C1
P 98 B2
Alfándega da Fé P 87 C4
Alfarela de Jafes P 87 C3
Alfarelos P 92 A2
Alfarim P 92 C1

Alfarnate E 100 C1
Alfaro E 89 B5
Alfarrás E 90 B3
Alfaz del Pi E 96 C2
Alfedena I 103 B7
Alfeizarão P 92 B1
Alfeld
Bayern D 62 A2
Niedersachsen D 51 B5
Alfena P 87 C2
Alferce P 98 B2
Alfhausen D 43 C4
Alfonsine I 81 B6
Alford
Aberdeenshire GB 23 D6
Lincolnshire GB 27 B6
Alforja E 90 B3
Alfoz E 86 A3
Alfreton GB 27 B4
Alfta S 36 A3
Alfundão P 98 A2
Algaida E 97 B2
Algar E 99 C5
Ålgård N 33 D2
Algarinejo E 100 B1
Algarrobo E 100 C1
Algatocín E 99 C5
Algeciras E 99 C5
Algemesi E 96 B2
Algenás S 92 C1
Algete E 95 B3
Alghero I 110 B1
Älghult S 40 B5
Alginet E 96 B2
Algodonales E 99 C5
Algodor
E 94 C3
P 98 B3
Algora E 95 B4
Algoso P 87 C4
Algoz P 98 B2
Älgsjö S 115 C14
Alguaire E 90 B3
Alguazas E 101 A4
Algutsrum S 41 C6
Algyö H 75 B5
Alhama de Almeria E 101 C3
Alhama de Aragón E 89 C5
Alhama de Granada E 100 C2
Alhama de Murcia E 101 B4
Alhambra E 100 A2
Alhandra P 92 C1
Alhaurin de la Torre E 100 C1
Alhaurin el Grande E 100 C1
Alhendin E 100 B2
Alhóndiga E 95 B4
Ália I 108 B2
Aliaga E 90 C2
Aliağa TR 118 D1
Aliaguilla E 96 B1
Alibunar SRB 85 A6
Alicante E 96 C2
Alicún de Ortega E 100 B2
Alife I 103 B7
Alija del Infantado E 88 B1
Alijó P 87 C3
Alimena I 109 B3
Alingsås S 40 B2
Alinyà E 91 A4
Aliseda E 93 B4
Ali Terme I 109 A4
Aliveri GR 116 D6
Alixan F 79 B4
Aljaraque E 99 B3
Aljezur P 98 B2
Aljorra E 101 B4
Aljubarrota P 92 B2
Aljucen E 93 B4
Aljustrel P 98 B2
Alken B 49 C6
Alkmaar NL 42 C1
Alkoven A 63 B5
Allaines F 58 B2
Allaire F 57 C3
Allanche F 68 C2
Allariz E 87 B3
Allassac F 67 C6
Allauch F 79 C4
Alleen N 33 D4
Allègre F 68 C3
Allein I 70 C2
Allemont F 79 A5
Allendale Town GB 25 D5
Allendorf D 51 C4
Allentsteig A 63 B6
Allepuz E 90 C2
Allersberg D 62 A2
Allershausen D 62 B2
Alleuze F 68 C2
Allevard F 69 C6
Allgood GB 25 D5
Allinge DK 41 D4
Allmannsdorf D 61 C5
Allo E 89 B4
Alloa GB 25 B4
Allogny F 68 A2
Allones
Eure et Loire F 58 B2
Maine-et-Loire F 67 A5
Allonnes F 57 C6

Aab–Als

Allons F 76 B2
Allos F 79 B5
Allstedt D 52 B1
Alltwalis GB 28 B3
Allumiere I 102 A4
Almaceda P 92 B3
Almacelles E 90 B3
Almáchar E 100 C1
Almada P 92 C1
Almadén E 100 A1
Almadén de la Plata E 99 B4
Almadenejos E 100 A1
Almadrones E 95 B4
Almagro E 100 A2
Almajano E 89 C4
Almansa E 96 C1
Almansil P 98 B2
Almanza E 88 B1
Almaraz E 93 B5
Almargen E 99 C5
Almarza E 89 C4
Almásfüzitő H 64 C4
Almassora E 96 B2
Almazán E 89 C4
Almazul E 89 C4
Alme D 51 B4
Almedina E 100 A3
Almedinilla E 100 B1
Almeida
E 87 C4
P 93 A4
Almeirim P 92 B2
Almelo NL 42 C3
Almenar E 90 B3
Almenara E 96 B2
Almenar de Soria E 89 C4
Almendra P 87 D3
Almendral E 93 C4
Almendral de la Cañada E 94 B2
Almendralejo E 93 C4
Almere NL 42 C2
Almería E 101 C3
Almerimar E 101 C3
Almese I 70 C2
Almexial P 98 B3
Älmhult S 40 C4
Almiropotamos GR 117 D6
Almiros GR 116 C4
Almodóvar P 98 B2
Almodóvar del Campo E 100 A1
Almodóvar del Pinar E 95 C5
Almodóvar del Río E 99 B5
Almofala P 87 D3
Almogia E 100 C1
Almoharin E 93 B4
Almonacid de la Sierra E 89 C5
Almonacid de Toledo E 94 C3
Almonaster la Real E 99 B4
Almondsbury GB 29 B5
Almonte E 99 B4
Almoradí E 101 A5
Almoraima E 99 C5
Almorox E 94 B2
Almoster P 92 B2
Almsele S 115 C14
Älmsta S 36 C5
Almudena E 101 A4
Almudévar E 90 A2
Almuñécar E 100 C2
Almuradiel E 100 A2
Almusafes E 96 B2
Almvik S 40 B6
Alness GB 23 D4
Alnmouth GB 25 C6
Alnwick GB 25 C6
Aloppe S 36 C4
Alora E 100 C1
Alos d'Ensil E 91 A4
Alosno E 99 B3
Alozaina E 100 C1
Alpedrete de la Sierra E 95 B3
Alpedrinha P 92 A3
Alpen D 50 B2
Alpera E 96 C1
Alphen aan de Rijn NL 49 A5
Alpiarça P 92 B2
Alpignano I 70 C2
Alpirsbach D 61 B4
Alpu TR 118 C5
Alqueva P 98 A3
Alquézar E 90 A3
Als DK 38 C3
Alsasua E 89 B4
Alsdorf D 50 C2
Alselv DK 39 D1
Alsfeld D 51 C5
Alskog S 37 E5
Alsleben D 52 B1
Alsónémedi H 75 A4
Alsótold H 65 C5

Alsóújlak H 74 A1
Alstad N 112 E4
Alstätte D 50 A2
Alsterbro S 40 C5
Alstermo S 40 C5
Alston GB 25 D5
Alsvåg N 112 D4
Alsvik N 112 E3
Alta N 113 C12
Älta S 37 C5
Altamura I 104 C2
Altarejos E 95 C4
Altaussee A 63 C4
Altavilla Irpina I . . . 103 B7
Altavilla Silentina I . . 103 C8
Altdöbern D 53 B4
Altdorf
  CH 70 B3
  D 62 B3
Altdorf bei Nürnberg
  D 62 A2
Alte P 98 B2
Altea E 96 C2
Altedo I 81 B5
Altena D 50 B3
Altenau D 51 B6
Altenberg D 53 C3
Altenberge D 50 A3
Altenbruch D 43 B5
Altenburg D 52 C2
Altenfelden A 63 B4
Altengronau D 51 C5
Altenheim D 60 B3
Altenhundem D 50 B4
Altenkirchen
  Mecklenburg-
  Vorpommern D . . . 45 A5
  Radom D 50 C3
Altenkunstadt D 52 C1
Altenmarkt
  A 63 C4
  D 62 B3
Altenmarkt im Pongall
  A 72 A3
Altensteig D 61 B4
Altentreptow D 45 B5
Altenwalde D 43 B5
Alten-weddingen D . . 52 A1
Alter do Chão P 92 B3
Altfraunhofen D 62 B3
Altheim
  A 63 B4
  D 61 A5
Althofen A 73 B4
Altluluk TR 118 C1
Altnova TR 118 C1
Altıntaş TR 118 C5
Altınyaka TR 119 F5
Altınyayla TR 119 E4
Altkirch F 60 C3
Altlandsberg D 45 C6
Altlewin D 45 C6
Altmannstein D 62 B2
Altmorschen D 51 B5
Altmunster A 63 C4
Altnaharra GB 23 C4
Alto Campoó E 88 A2
Altofonte I 108 A2
Altomonte I 106 B3
Alton
  Hampshire GB 31 C3
  Staffordshire GB . . . 27 C4
Altopaško I 81 C4
Altötting D 62 B3
Altreichenau D 63 B4
Alt Ruppin D 45 C4
Altshausen D 61 C5
Altstätten CH 71 A4
Altura E 96 B2
Altusried D 61 C6
Alūksne LV 7 C9
Alunda S 36 B5
Alustante E 95 B5
Alva GB 25 B4
Alvaiázere P 92 B2
Alvalade P 98 B2
Älvängen S 38 B5
Alvarenga P 87 D2
Alvares P 92 A2
Alvdal N 114 E7
Älvdalen S 34 A6
Alverca P 92 C1
Alversund N 32 B2
Alvesta S 40 C4
Alvignac F 77 B4
Alvignano I 103 B7
Alvik N 32 B3
Alvik S 36 B1
Alvimare F 58 A1
Alviobeira P 92 B2
Alvkarleby S 36 B4
Alvkarleöbruk S 36 B4
Alvor P 98 B2
Alvorge P 92 B2
Alvøy N 32 B2
Älvros S 115 E11
Alvsbacka S 35 C5
Älvsbyn S 3 D24
Alvsered S 40 B2
Alwernia PL 55 C4
Alwinton GB 25 C5
Alyth GB 25 B4
Alytus LT 6 D8
Alzénau D 51 C5
Alzey D 61 A4
Alzira E 96 B2
Alzonne F 77 C5
Amadora P 92 C1
Amål S 35 C4
Amalfi I 103 C7
Amaliada GR 117 E3
Amance F 60 C2
Amancey F 69 A6
Amándola I 82 D2
Amantea I 106 B3
Amarante P 87 C2
Amareleja P 98 A3
Amares P 87 C2
Amaseno I 103 B6
Amasra TR 118 A7
Amasya TR 16 A7
Amatrice I 103 A6
Amay B 49 C6
Ambarnyy RUS 3 D30
Ambazac F 67 B6
Ambelonas GR 116 C4
Amberg D 62 A2
Ambérieu-en-Bugey
  F 69 C5
Ambérieux-en-Dombes
  F 69 B4
Ambert F 68 C3
Ambés F 76 A2
Ambjörby S 34 B5
Ambjörnarp S 40 B3
Amble GB 25 C6
Ambleside GB 26 A3
Ambleteuse F 48 C2
Ambleve F 67 A5
Ambrières-les-Vallées
  F 57 B5
Amden CH 71 A4
Amel B 50 C2
Amélia I 102 A5
Amélie-les-Bains-Palalda
  F 91 A5
Amelinghausen D . . . 44 B2
Amendoa P 92 B2
Amendoeira P 98 B3
Améndola I 104 B1
Améndolara I 106 B3
Amer E 91 A5
A Merca E 87 B3
Ameronguen NL 49 A6
Amersfoort NL 49 A6
Amersham GB 31 C3
Amesbury GB 29 B6
Amfiklia GR 116 D4

Amfilochia GR 116 D3
Amfipoli GR 116 B5
Amfissa GR 116 D4
Amièira P 98 A3
Amieira P 92 B3
Amieiro P 92 A2
Amiens F 58 A3
Amindeo GR 116 B3
Åminne S 40 B3
Åmli N 33 D5
Amlwch GB 26 B1
Ammanford GB 28 B4
Ammarnäs S 115 B13
Ammeberg S 37 D1
Amorbach D 61 A5
Amorebieta E 89 A4
Amorgos GR 117 F7
Amorosa P 87 C2
Amorosi I 103 B7
Åmot
  Buskerud N 34 C1
  Telemark N 33 C4
  S 36 B3
Åmotfors S 34 C4
Åmotsdal N 33 C5
Amou F 76 C2
Ampezzo I 72 B2
Ampfing D 62 B3
Ampflwang A 63 B4
Amplepuis F 69 C4
Amposta E 90 C3
Ampudia E 88 C2
Ampuero E 89 A3
Amriswil CH 71 A4
Amsele S 115 C16
Amstelveen NL 49 A5
Amsterdam NL 42 C1
Amstetten A 63 B5
Amtzell D 61 C5
Amulree GB 25 B4
Amurrio E 89 A4
Amusco E 88 B2
Anacapri I 103 C7
Anadia P 92 A2
Anadon E 90 C1
Anafi GR 117 F7
Anagni I 102 B6
Anamur TR 16 C6
Ananyiv UA 11 C10
Anascaul IRL 20 B1
Anäset S 3 D24
Ana-Sira N 33 D3
Anastazewo PL 47 C4
Anaya de Alba E 94 B1
Ança P 92 A2
Ancaster GB 27 C5
Ancede P 87 C2
Ancenis F 66 A3
Ancerville F 59 B6
Anchuras E 94 C2
Ancona I 82 C2
Ancora P 87 C2
Ancrum GB 25 C5
Ancy-le-Franc F 59 C5
Andalo I 71 B5
Andalsnes N 114 E4
Andance F 69 C4
Andau A 64 C3
Andebu N 35 C2
Andeer CH 71 B4
Andelfingen CH 61 C4
Andelot-Blanchville F . 59 B6
Andelot-en-Montagne
  F 69 B5
Andenes N 112 C5
Andenne B 49 C6
Anderlues B 49 C5
Andermatt CH 70 B3
Andernach D 50 C3
Andernos-les-Bains F . 76 B1
Anderslöv S 40 B3
Anderstorp S 40 B3
Andijk NL 42 C2
Andoain E 89 A4
Andocs H 74 B2
Andoain E 60 B3
Andolsheim F 60 B3
Andorra La Vella AND . 91 A4
Andosilla E 89 B5
Andover GB 31 C2
Andratx E 97 B2
Andreapol RUS 7 C12
Andreas GB 26 A1
Andréspol PL 55 B4
Andrest F 76 C3
Andretta I 103 C8
Andrezieux-Bouthéon
  F 69 C4
Andria I 104 B2
Andrijevica MNE 85 D4
Andritsena GR 117 E3
Andros GR 117 E6
Andrychów PL 55 D4
Andújar E 100 A1
Anduze F 78 B2
Åneby N 34 B2
Åneby S 40 B4
Añes E 89 A4
Anet F 58 B2
Anfo I 71 C5
Anga S 37 E5
Ånge S 115 E12
Angeja P 92 A2
Ängelholm S 41 C2
Angelokastro GR 116 D3
Anger A 73 A5
Angermünde D 45 B6
Angern A 64 B2
Angerville F 58 B3
Anghiari I 82 C1
Angle GB 28 B2
Anglès E 91 B5
Anglès F 77 C5
Anglesola E 91 B4
Angles sur l'Anglin F . . 67 B5
Anglisides CY 120 B2
Anglure F 59 B4
Ango S 37 C3
Angueira P 87 C4
Anguiano E 89 B4
Anguillara Sabazia I . . 102 A5
Anguillara Véneta I . . 72 C1
Anholt DK 38 C4
Aniane F 78 C2
Aniche F 49 C4
Animskog S 35 D4
Anina RO 10 B6
Anixi GR 116 C3
Anjalankoski FIN . . . 3 F27
Ankara TR 118 C7
Ankaran SLO 72 C3
Ankarsrum S 40 B6
Ankerlia N 112 C8
Anklam D 45 B5
Ankum D 43 C4
Anlauftal A 72 A3
Anlezy F 68 B3
Ann S 115 D9
Annaberg A 63 C6
Annaberg-Buchholz
  D 52 C3
Annaberg im Lammertal
  A 72 A3
Annaburg D 52 B3
Annahütte D 53 B4
Annalong GB 19 B6

Annan GB 25 D4
Anndalsvågen N 115 B9
Anneberg
  Halland S 38 B5
  Jönköping S 40 B4
Annecy F 69 C6
Annelund S 40 B3
Annemasse F 69 B6
Annerstad S 40 C3
Annestown IRL 21 B4
Annevoie-Rouillon B . . 49 C5
Annonay F 69 C4
Annot F 79 C5
Annweiler D 60 A3
Ano Poroia GR 116 A5
Añora E 100 A1
Ano Siros GR 117 E6
Anould F 60 B2
Anquela del Ducado
  E 95 B4
Anröchte D 51 B4
Ans DK 39 C2
Ansager DK 39 D1
Ansbach D 62 A1
Anse F 69 C4
Anseroeul B 49 C4
Ansfelden A 63 B5
Ansião P 92 B2
Ansó E 76 D2
Ansoain E 76 D1
Anstruther GB 25 B5
Antalya TR 119 F5
Antas E 101 B4
Antegnate I 71 C4
Antequera E 100 B1
Anterselva di Mezzo I . 72 B2
Antibes F 79 C6
Antigüedad E 88 C2
Antillo I 109 B4
Antirio GR 117 D3
An t-Ob GB 22 D1
Antoing B 49 C4
Antonin P 54 B2
Antrain F 57 B4
Antrim GB 19 B5
Antrodoco I 102 A6
Antronapiana I 70 B3
Anttis S 113 E11
Antuzede P 92 A2
Antwerp = Antwerpen
  B 49 B5
Antwerpen = Antwerp
  B 49 B5
Anversa d'Abruzzi I . . 103 B6
Anvin F 48 C3
Anzat-le-Luguet F . . . 68 C3
Anzi I 104 C1
Anzio I 102 B5
Anzola d'Emilia I . . . 81 B5
Aoiz E 76 D1
Aosta I 70 C2
Apalhão P 92 B3
Apátfalva H 75 B5
Apatin SRB 75 C4
Apc H 65 C5
Apécchio I 82 C1
Apeldoorn NL 50 A1
Apen D 43 B4
Apenburg D 44 C3
Apensen D 43 B6
A Peroxa E 86 B3
Apiro I 82 C2
Apliki CY 120 B2
Apolda D 52 B1
Apolonia GR 117 F6
A Pontenova E 86 A3
Apostag H 75 B3
Appelbo S 34 B6
Appennino I 82 D2
Appenzell CH 71 A4
Appiano I 71 B6
Appingedam NL 42 B3
Appleby-in-Westmorland
  GB 26 A3
Applecross GB 22 D3
Appledore GB 28 B3
Appoigny F 59 C4
Apremont-la-Forêt F . . 60 B1
Aprica I 71 B5
Apricena I 103 B8
Aprigliano I 106 B3
Aprilia I 102 B5
Apt F 79 C4
Apúlia P 87 C2
Aquiléia I 72 C3
Aquilónia I 103 C8
Aquino I 103 B6
Ar S 37 E5
Arabayona E 94 A1
Arabba I 72 B1
Araç TR 16 A6
Aracena E 99 B4
Arachova GR 116 D4
Aračinovo SRB 75 C4
Arad RO 75 B6
Aradac SRB 75 C5
Aradhippou CY 120 B2
Aragnouet F 76 D3
Aragona I 108 B2
Aramits F 76 C2
Aramon F 78 C3
Aranda de Duero E . . 89 C3
Aranda de Moncayo
  E 89 C5
Arandelovac SRB . . . 85 B5
Aranjuez E 95 B3
Arañuel E 96 A2
Aranzueque E 95 B3
Aras de Alpuente E . . 96 B1
Arauzo de Miel E . . . 89 C3
Arazede P 92 A2
Árbatax I 110 C2
Arbeca E 90 B3
Arberg D 62 A1
Arbesbach A 63 B5
Arboga S 37 C2
Arbois F 69 B5
Arbon CH 71 A4
Arborea I 110 C1
Arbório I 70 C3
Årbostad N 112 C7
Arbrå S 36 A3
Arbroath GB 25 B5
Arbúcies E 91 B5
Arbuniel E 100 B2
Arbus I 110 C1
Arcachon F 76 B1
Arce I 103 B6
Arcen NL 50 B2
Arc-en-Barrois F 59 C5
Arces-Dilo F 59 B4
Arcévia I 82 C1
Arcey F 70 A1
Archangelos GR 119 F3
Archena E 101 A4
Archez E 100 C1
Archiac F 67 C4
Archidona E 100 B1
Archiestown GB 23 D5
Archivel E 101 A4
Arcidosso I 81 D5
Arcille I 81 D5
Arcis-sur-Aube F . . . 59 B5
Arco I 71 C5
Arcones E 94 A3
Arcos E 89 B3
Arcos de Jalón E . . . 89 C4
Arcos de la Frontera
  E 99 C5
Arcos de la Sierra E . . 95 B4
Arcos de Valdevez P . . 87 C2
Arcozelo P 92 A3
Arcs-sur-Tille F 69 A5
Arcusa E 90 A3

Arcy-sur-Cure F 59 C4
Ardagh IRL 20 B2
Årdal N 33 B3
Ardala S 35 D5
Ardales E 100 C1
Ardalstangen N 32 A4
Ardara
  I 110 B1
  IRL 18 B3
Ardarroch GB 22 D3
Ardbeg GB 24 C1
Ardcharnich GB 22 D3
Ardchyle GB 24 B3
Ardee IRL 19 C5
Arden DK 38 C2
Ardentes F 68 B1
Ardenza I 81 C4
Ardersier GB 23 D4
Ardes F 68 C3
Ardessie GB 22 D3
Ardez CH 71 B5
Ardfert IRL 20 B2
Ardgay GB 23 D4
Ardglass GB 19 B6
Ardgroom IRL 20 C2
Ardhasig GB 22 D2
Ardino BG 116 A7
Ardisa E 90 A2
Ardkearagh IRL 20 C1
Ardlui GB 24 B3
Ardlussa GB 24 B2
Ardón E 88 B1
Ardooie B 49 C4
Ardore I 106 C3
Ardrahan IRL 20 A3
Ardre S 37 E5
Ardres F 48 C2
Ardrishaig GB 24 B2
Ardrossan GB 24 C3
Åre S 115 D10
Åre S 33 C2
Areia Branca P 92 B1
Arenäs S 35 C3
Arenales de San Gregorio
  E 95 C3
Arenas E 100 C1
Arenas de Iguña E . . . 88 A2
Arenas del Rey E . . . 100 C2
Arenas de San Juan
  E 95 C3
Arenas de San Pedro
  E 93 B5
Arendal N 33 D5
Arendonk B 49 B6
Arengosse F 76 B2
Arentorp S 35 D4
Arenys de Mar E . . . 91 B5
Arenys de Munt E . . . 91 B5
Arenzano I 80 B2
Areo E 91 A4
Areopoli GR 117 F4
Ares E 86 A2
Arês S 70 C2
Ares del Maestrat E . . 90 C2
Aresvika N 114 D5
Arette F 76 C2
Aretxabaleta E 89 A4
Arevalillo E 93 A5
Arévalo E 94 A2
Arez P 92 B3
Arezzo I 81 C5
Arfeuilles F 68 B3
Argalasti GR 116 C5
Argallón E 99 A5
Argamasilla de Alba
  E 95 C3
Argamasilla de Calatrava
  E 100 A1
Arganda E 95 B3
Arganil P 92 A2
Argasion GR 117 E2
Argegno I 71 C4
Argelès-Gazost F . . . 76 C2
Argelès-sur-Mer F . . . 91 A6
Argenta I 81 B5
Argentan F 57 B5
Argentat F 77 A4
Argentera I 79 B5
Argenteuil F 58 B3
Argenthal D 50 D3
Argentiera I 110 B1
Argentière F 70 C1
Argenton-Château F . . 67 B4
Argenton-sur-Creuse
  F 67 B6
Argentré F 57 B5
Argentré-du-Plessis
  F 57 B4
Argés E 94 C2
Argentá I 72 C1
Arginónta GR 119 E1
Argithani TR 119 D6
Argos GR 117 E4
Argos Orestiko GR . . . 116 B3
Argostoli GR 117 D2
Argote E 89 B4
Arguedas E 89 B5
Argueil F 58 A2
Arholma S 36 C6
Árhus DK 39 C3
Ariano Irpino I 103 B8
Ariano nel Polésine I . . 82 B1
Aribe E 76 D1
Aridea GR 116 B4
Arienzo I 103 B7
Arild S 41 C2
Arileod GB 24 B1
Arilje SRB 85 C5
Arinagour GB 24 B1
Ariño E 90 B2
Arinthod F 69 B5
Arisaig GB 24 B2
Arisgotas E 94 C3
Aritzo I 110 C2
Ariza E 89 C4
Arjäng S 35 C3
Arjeplog S 115 A14
Arjona E 100 B1
Arjonilla E 100 B1
Arkasa GR 119 G2
Arkelstorp S 41 C4
Arklow IRL 21 B5
Arkösund S 37 D3
Ärla S 37 C3
Arlanc F 68 C3
Arlanzón E 89 B3
Arlebosc F 78 A3
Arlena di Castro I . . . 102 A4
Arles F 78 C3
Arles-sur-Tech F 91 A5
Arló H 65 B6
Arlon B 60 A1
Armação de Pera P . . 98 B2
Armadale
  Highland GB 22 D3
  West Lothian GB . . . 25 C4
Armagh GB 19 B5
Armamar P 87 C3
Armenistis GR 117 E8
Armeno I 70 C3
Armenteros E 93 A5
Armentières F 48 C3
Armilla E 100 B2
Armiñón E 89 B4
Armoy GB 19 A5
Armuña de Tajuña E . . 95 B3
Armutlu
  Bursa TR 118 B3
  İzmir TR 119 D2
Arnac-Pompadour F . . 67 C6
Arnafjord N 32 A3
Arnage F 57 C6
Arnas F 69 B4
Arnäs S 35 D5
Arnay-le-Duc F 69 A4
Arnborg DK 39 C2
Arnbruck D 62 A3
Arne GB 29 C5
Arneberg
  Hedmark N 34 B4
  Hedmark N 34 B2
Arneburg D 44 C4
Arnedillo E 89 B4

Arnedo E 89 B4
Arneguy F 76 C1
Arnés E 90 C3
Arnes IS 111 A4
Årnes
  Akershus N 34 B3
  Troms N 112 C7
Arnfels A 73 B5
Arnhem NL 50 B1
Arnissa GR 116 B3
Arno S 37 D4
Arnold GB 27 B4
Arnoldstein A 72 B3
Arnsberg D 50 B4
Arnschwang D 62 A3
Arnsdorf D 53 B3
Årnset N 114 D6
Arnside GB 26 A3
Arnstadt D 51 C6
Arnstein D 51 D5
Arnstorf D 62 B3
Arnum DK 39 D1
Aroche E 99 B4
Arolla CH 70 B2
Arolsen D 51 B5
Åros N 35 C2
Arosa
  CH 71 B4
  P 87 C2
Ærøskøbing DK 39 E3
Ärøysund N 35 C2
Arouca P 87 D2
Arøysund N 35 C2
Arpajon F 58 B3
Arpajon-sur-Cère F . . 77 B5
Arpino I 103 B6
Arquata del Tronto I . . 82 D2
Arques F 48 C3
Arques-la-Bataille F . . 58 A2
Arquillos E 100 A2
Arraia-Maeztu E 89 B4
Arraiolos P 92 C2
Arrancourt F 60 B2
Arras F 48 C3
Arrasate E 89 A4
Årre DK 39 D1
Arreau F 77 D3
Arredondo E 88 A3
Arren-Marsous F 76 C2
Arriate E 99 C5
Arrifana P 98 B2
Arrigorriaga E 89 A4
Arriondas E 88 A1
Arroba de los Montes
  E 94 C2
Årø DK 39 D1
Arrochar GB 24 B3
Arromanches-les-Bains
  F 57 A5
Arronches P 92 B3
Arroniz E 89 B4
Arrou F 58 B2
Arroya E 88 B2
Arroyo de Cuéllar E . . 88 C2
Arroyo de la Luz E . . . 93 B4
Arroyo del Ojanco E . . 100 A3
Arroyo de San Servan
  E 93 C4
Arroyomolinos de León
  E 99 A4
Arroyomolinos de
  Montánchez E 93 B4
Arsac F 76 B2
Ars-en-Ré F 66 B3
Arsiè I 72 C1
Arsiero I 71 C6
Årslev DK 39 D3
Ársoli I 102 A6
Ars-sur-Moselle F . . . 60 A2
Arsunda S 36 B3
Artà E 97 B3
Arta GR 116 C3
Artajona E 89 B5
Artegna I 72 B3
Arteixo E 86 A2
Artemare F 69 C5
Arten I 72 B1
Artena I 102 B5
Artern D 52 B1
Artés E 91 B4
Artesa de Segre E . . . 91 B4
Arth CH 70 A3
Arthez-de-Béarn F . . . 76 C2
Arthon-en-Retz F . . . 66 A3
Arthurstown IRL 21 B5
Artieda E 90 A2
Artix F 76 C2
Artotina GR 116 D4
Artsyz UA 11 C10
Artziniega E 89 A3
Aruá F 87 B3
Arudy F 76 C2
Arundel GB 31 D3
Arveyres F 76 B2
Arvidsjaur S 115 B16
Arvieux F 79 B5
Arvika S 35 C4
Aryd
  Blekinge S 41 C5
  Kronoberg S 40 C4
Arzachena I 110 A2
Arzacq-Arraziguet F . . 76 C2
Arzana I 110 C2
Arzano F 56 C2
Arzberg D 52 C2
Aržignano I 71 C6
Arzila P 92 A2
Arzl im Pitztal A 71 A5
Arzúa E 86 A2
Aš CZ 52 C2
As B 49 B6
Ås
  S 40 B2
  S 115 D11
Aša CZ 64 A2
Åsa S 40 B2
Asaa DK 38 B3
Aşağıçiğil TR 119 D6
Åsarna S 115 E11
Åsarp S 40 A3
Asarum S 41 C4
Åsbro S 37 C2
Asby S 40 B5
Åsbygri IS 111 A9
Ascain F 76 C1
Ascea I 106 A2
Ascha D 62 A3
Aschach an der Donau
  A 63 B5
Aschaffenburg D 51 D5
Aschbach Markt A . . . 63 B5
Ascheberg
  Nordrhein-
  Westfalen D 50 B3
  Schleswig-Holstein D 44 A2
Aschendorf D 43 B4
Aschersleben D 52 B1
Asciano I 81 C5
Ascó E 90 B3
Áscoli Piceno I 82 D2
Áscoli Satriano I 104 B1
Ascona CH 70 B3
Ascot GB 31 C3
Ascoux F 58 B3
Åse N 112 C5
Aseda S 40 B5
Åsele S 115 C14
Åsen
  N 114 D8
  S 34 A5
Asendorf D 43 C6
Asenovgrad BG 11 E8
Asensbruk S 35 D4
Åseral N 33 D4
Asfeld F 59 A5
Åsgårdstrand N 35 C2
Ásgarður IS 111 B1

Asgate CY 120 B2
Ash
  Kent GB 31 C5
  Surrey GB 31 C3
Ashammar S 36 B3
Ashbourne
  GB 27 B4
  IRL 21 A5
Ashburton GB 28 C4
Ashby-de-la-Zouch
  GB 27 C4
Ashchurch GB 29 B5
Asheim N 114 F8
Ashford GB 31 C4
Ashington GB 25 C6
Ashley GB 26 C3
Ashmyany BY 7 D8
Ashton Under Lyne
  GB 26 B3
Ashwell GB 30 B3
Asiago I 71 C6
Asipovichy BY 7 E10
Aska FIN 113 E15
Askeaton IRL 20 B3
Asker N 34 C2
Askersund S 37 D1
Askilje S 115 C14
Askim N 35 C3
Askland N 33 D5
Asköping S 37 C3
Askvoll N 32 A2
Asljunga S 41 C3
Asnæs DK 39 D4
As Neves E 87 B2
As Nogais E 86 B3
Åsola I 71 C5
Asolo I 72 C1
Asos GR 116 D2
Asotthalom H 75 B4
Aspach Markt A 64 C2
Aspang Markt A 73 A6
Aspariegos E 88 C1
Asparn an der Zaya A . 64 B2
Aspatria GB 26 A2
Aspberg S 35 C5
Aspe E 101 A5
Aspet F 77 C3
Aspö S 41 C5
As Pontes de García
  Rodríguez E 86 A3
Aspres-sur-Buëch F . . 79 B4
Aspsele S 115 D15
Assafora P 92 C1
Asse B 49 C5
Assebakte N 113 C14
Assel D 43 B6
Asselborn L 50 C1
Assémini I 110 C1
Assen NL 42 C3
Assenede B 49 B4
Assens
  Aarhus Amt. DK . . . 38 C3
  Fyns Amt. DK 39 D2
Assesse B 49 C6
Assisi I 82 C1
Asskard N 114 D5
Assling D 62 C3
Asso I 71 C4
Assoro I 109 B3
Assumar P 92 B3
Asta N 34 A3
Astaffort F 77 B3
Astakos GR 116 D3
Asten NL 50 B1
Asti I 80 B2
Astipalea GR 119 F1
Astorga E 86 B4
Astorp S 41 C2
Åsträsk S 115 C16
Astudillo E 88 B2
Asuni I 110 C1
Ásványráró H 64 C3
Aszód H 65 C5
Aszófő H 74 B2
Atabey TR 119 E5
Atalaia P 92 B3
Atalandi GR 116 D4
Atalho P 92 C2
Átány H 65 C6
Atanzón E 95 B3
Ataquines E 94 A2
Atarfe E 100 B2
Atça TR 119 E3
Ateca E 89 C5
A Teixeira E 87 B3
Atella I 104 C1
Atessa I 103 A7
Ath B 49 C4
Athboy IRL 19 C5
Athea IRL 20 B2
Athenry IRL 20 A3
Athens = Athina GR . . 117 E5
Atherstone GB 27 C4
Athienou CY 120 B2
Athies F 59 A3
Athies-sous-Laon F . . 59 A4
Athina = Athens GR . . 117 E5
Athleague IRL 20 A3
Athlone IRL 21 A4
Athna CY 120 A2
Athy IRL 21 B5
Atienza E 95 A4
Atina I 103 B6
Atkár H 65 C5
Atlanti TR 119 D6
Atna N 114 F7
Atorp S 35 C6
Åträsk S 3 D24
Atri I 103 A6
Atripalda I 103 C7
Atsiki GR 116 C6
Attendorn D 50 B3
Attichy F 59 A4
Attigliano I 102 A5
Attigny F 59 A5
Attleborough GB 30 B5
Atvidaberg S 37 D2
Au
  Steiermark A 63 C6
  Vorarlberg A 71 A4
  Bayern D 62 B2
  Bayern D 62 B3
Aub D 61 A6
Aubagne F 79 C4
Aubange B 60 A1
Aubel B 50 C1
Aubenas F 78 B3
Aubenton F 59 A5
Auberive F 59 C6
Aubeterre-sur-Dronne
  F 67 C5
Aubiet F 77 C3
Aubigné F 67 B4
Aubigny F 66 B3
Aubigny-au-Bac F . . . 49 C4
Aubigny-en-Artois F . . 48 C3
Aubigny-sur-Nère F . . 68 A2
Aubin F 77 B5
Aubonne CH 69 B6
Aubrac F 78 B1
Aubusson F 68 C2
Auch F 77 C3
Auchencairn GB 25 D4
Auchinleck GB 24 C3
Auchterarder GB 25 B4
Auchtermuchty GB . . . 25 B4
Auchy-au-Bois F 48 C3
Audenge F 76 B1
Auderville F 57 A4
Audheim N 114 E3
Audincourt F 70 A1
Audlem GB 26 C3
Audruicq F 48 C3
Audun-le-Roman F . . . 60 A1
Audun-le-Tiche F 60 A1

Aue
  Nordrhein-Westfalen
  D 50 B4
  Sachsen D 52 C2
Auerbach
  Bayern D 62 A2
  Sachsen D 52 C2
Auffach A 72 A2
Augher GB 19 B4
Aughnacloy GB 19 B5
Aughrim IRL 21 B5
Augignac F 67 C5
Augsburg D 62 B1
Augusta I 109 B4
Augusten-borg DK . . . 39 E2
Augustfehn D 43 B4
Augustów PL 6 E7
Aukrug D 43 A6
Auktsjaur S 115 B16
Auldearn GB 23 D5
Aulendorf D 61 C5
Auletta I 103 C8
Aulla I 81 B3
Aullène F 102 B2
Aulnay F 67 B4
Aulnoye-Aymeries F . . 49 C4
Ault F 48 C2
Aultbea GB 22 D3
Aulum DK 39 C1
Aulus-les-Bains F . . . 77 D4
Auma D 52 C1
Aumale F 58 A2
Aumetz F 60 A1
Aumont-Aubrac F . . . 78 B2
Aunay-en-Bazois F . . . 68 A3
Aunay-sur-Odon F . . . 57 A5
Aune N 115 C10
Auneau F 58 B2
Auneuil F 58 A2
Aups F 79 C5
Aura F 51 C5
Auray F 56 C3
Aurdal N 32 B6
Aure N 114 D5
Aurich D 43 B4
Aurignac F 77 C3
Aurillac F 77 B5
Auritz F 76 D1
Auritz-Burguete F . . . 76 D1
Aurlandsvangen N . . . 32 B4
Auronzo di Cadore I . . 72 B2
Auros F 76 B2
Auroux F 78 B2
Aurskog N 34 C3
Aursmoen N 34 C3
Ausonia I 103 B6
Aussernvillgraten A . . 72 B2
Austad N 33 D4
Austbygda N 32 B5
Áustis I 110 B2
Austmarka N 34 B4
Austre Moland N 33 D5
Austre Vikebygd N . . . 33 C2
Austrheim N 32 B1
Auterive F 77 C4
Autheuil-Authouillet
  F 58 A2
Authon F 79 B5
Authon-du-Perche F . . 58 B1
Autol E 89 B5
Autreville F 60 B1
Autrey-lès-Gray F . . . 69 A5
Autti FIN 113 F16
Autun F 69 B4
Auty-le-Châtel F 58 C3
Auvelais B 49 C5
Auvillar F 77 B3
Auxerre F 59 C4
Auxi-le-Château F . . . 48 C3
Auxon F 59 B4
Auxonne F 69 A5
Auxy F 69 B4
Auzances F 68 B2
Auzon F 68 C3
Ava S 115 D16
Availles-Limouzine F . . 67 B5
Avaldsnes N 33 C2
Avallon F 68 A3
Avantas GR 116 B7
Avaviken S 115 B15
Avebury GB 29 B6
A Veiga E 87 B3
Aveiras de Cima P . . . 92 B2
Aveiro P 92 A2
Avelgem B 49 C4
Avellino I 103 C7
Avenches CH 70 B2
A-Ver-o-Mar P 87 C2
Aversa I 103 C7
Avesnes-le-Comte F . . 48 C3
Avesnes-sur-Helpe F . . 49 C4
Avesta S 36 B3
Avetrana I 105 C3
Avezzano I 103 A6
Avià E 91 A4
Aviano I 72 B2
Aviemore GB 23 D5
Avigliana I 80 A1
Avigliano I 104 C1
Avignon F 78 C3
Ávila E 94 B2
Avilés E 88 A1
Avilley F 69 A6
Avintes P 87 C2
Avinyo E 91 B4
Avio I 71 C5
Avioth F 59 A6
Avis P 92 B3
Avize F 59 B5
Avlonari GR 116 D6
Ávola I 109 C4
Avon F 58 B3
Avonmouth GB 29 B5
Avord F 68 A2
Avranches F 57 B4
Avril F 60 A1
Avrillé F 67 A4
Avtovac BIH 84 C3
Awans B 49 C6
Axams A 71 A6
Axat F 77 D5
Axbridge GB 29 B5
Axel NL 49 B4
Ax-les-Thermes F . . . 77 D4
Axmarby S 36 B4
Axmarsbruk S 36 A4
Axminster GB 29 C5
Axvall S 35 D5
Ay F 59 A5
Aya E 89 A4
Ayamonte E 98 B3
Ayancık TR 16 A7
Ayas I 70 C2
Ayaş TR 118 B7
Aydın TR 119 E2
Aydıncık TR 16 C6
Ayelo de Malferit E . . . 96 C2
Ayer CH 70 B2
Ayerbe E 90 A2
Ayette F 48 C3
Áyia Napa CY 120 B2
Áyia Phyla CY 120 B2
Ayia Varvara
  CY 120 A2
Ayios Seryios CY . . . 120 A2
Ayios Theodhoros
  CY 120 A2
Aykirikçi TR 118 C5
Aylesbury GB 31 C3
Aylesham GB 31 C5
Ayllón E 89 C3
Aylsham GB 30 B5
Ayna E 101 A3
Ayódar E 96 A2
Ayora E 96 B1
Ayr GB 24 C3
Ayron F 67 B5
Aysgarth GB 27 A4
Ayton GB 25 C5
Aytos BG 11 E9
Ayvacık TR 118 C1
Ayvalık TR 118 C1

Aywaille B 49 C6
Azaila E 90 B2
Azambuja P 92 B2
Azambujeira P 92 B2
Azanja SRB 85 B5
Azannes-et-Soumazannes
  F 60 A1
Azanuy-Alins E 90 A3
Azaruja P 92 C3
Azay-le-Ferron F 67 B6
Azay-le-Rideau F 67 A5
Azcoitia E 89 A4
Azé F 69 B4
Azeiteiros P 92 B3
Azenhas do Mar P . . . 92 C1
Azinhaga P 92 B2
Azinheira dos Barros
  P 98 A2
Aznalcázar E 99 B4
Aznalcóllar E 99 B4
Azóia P 92 B2
Azpeitia E 89 A4
Azuaga E 99 A5
Azuara E 90 B2
Azuqueca de Henares
  E 95 B3
Azur F 76 C1
Azzano Décimo I 72 C2

B

Baad A 71 A5
Baamonde E 86 A3
Baar CH 70 A3
Bağarası TR 119 E2
Baarle-Nassau B 49 B5
Baarn NL 49 A6
Babadag RO 11 D10
Babaeski TR 118 A2
Babayevo RUS 7 B13
Babenhausen
  Bayern D 61 B6
  Hessen D 51 D4
Babiak PL 54 A3
Babice PL 55 C4
Babigoszcz PL 45 B6
Babimost PL 53 A5
Babina Greda HR . . . 84 A3
Babócsa H 74 B2
Bábolma H 64 C3
Baborów PL 54 C2
Baboszewo PL 47 C6
Babruysk BY 7 E10
Babsk PL 55 B5
Bac GB 22 C2
Bač
  MNE 85 D5
  SRB 75 C4
Bacares E 101 B3
Bacău RO 11 C9
Baccarat F 60 B2
Bacharach D 50 C3
Bačina SRB 85 C6
Backa S 36 B2
Bačka Palanka SRB . . 75 C4
Backaryd S 41 C5
Bačka Topola SRB . . . 75 C4
Backe S 115 D13
Bäckebo S 40 C6
Bäckefors S 35 D4
Bäckhammar S 35 C6
Bački Breg SRB 75 C3
Bački-Brestovac SRB . 75 C4
Bački Monoštor SRB . . 75 C3
Bački Petrovac SRB . . 75 C4
Bački Sokolac SRB . . . 75 C4
Backnang D 61 B5
Bačko Gradište SRB . . 75 C5
Bačko Novo Selo
  SRB 75 C4
Bačko Petrovo Selo
  SRB 75 C5
Bácoli I 103 C7
Bacqueville-en-Caux
  F 58 A2
Bácsalmás H 75 B4
Bácsbokod H 75 B4
Bad Abbach D 62 B3
Badacsonytomaj H . . . 74 B2
Bad Aibling D 62 C3
Badajoz E 93 C4
Badalona E 91 B5
Badalucco I 80 C1
Bad Aussee A 63 C4
Bad Bederkesa D . . . 43 B5
Bad Bergzabern D . . . 60 A3
Bad Berka D 52 C1
Bad Berleburg D 50 B4
Bad Berneck D 52 C1
Bad Bevensen D 44 B2
Bad Bibra D 52 B1
Bad Birnbach D 62 B4
Bad Blankenburg D . . 52 C1
Bad Bleiberg A 72 B3
Bad Brambach D 52 C2
Bad Bramstedt D 44 B1
Bad Breisig D 50 C3
Bad Brückenau D . . . 51 C5
Bad Camberg D 50 C4
Baddeckenstedt D . . . 113 C11
Bad Doberan D 44 A3
Bad Driburg D 51 B5
Bad Dürkheim D 61 A4
Bad Dürrenberg D . . . 52 B2
Bad Dürrheim D 61 B4
Bad Elster D 52 C2
Bad Ems D 50 C3
Baden
  A 64 B2
  CH 70 A3
Bádenas E 90 B1
Baden-Baden D 61 B4
Bad Endorf D 62 C3
Badenweiler D 60 C3
Baderna HR 72 C3
Bad Essen D 50 A4
Bad Fischau A 64 C2
Bad Frankenhausen
  D 52 B1
Bad Freienwalde D . . . 45 C6
Bad Friedrichshall D . . 61 A5
Bad Gandersheim D . . 51 B6
Bad Gastein A 72 A3
Bad Gleichenberg A . . 73 B5
Bad Goisern A 63 C4
Bad Gottleuba D 53 C3
Bad Grund D 51 B6
Bad Hall A 63 B5
Bad Harzburg D 51 B6
Bad Herrenalb D 61 B4
Bad Hersfeld D 51 C5
Bad Hofgastein A . . . 72 A3
Bad Homburg D 51 C4
Bad Honnef D 50 C3
Bad Hönningen D . . . 50 C3
Badia Calavena I 71 C6
Badia Polésine I 81 A5
Badia Pratáglia I 81 C5
Badia Tedalda I 82 C1
Bad Iburg D 50 A4
Bad Inberlahra D 72 A2
Badljevina HR 74 C2
Bad Ischl A 63 C4
Bad Karlshafen D . . . 51 B5
Bad Kemmeriboden
  CH 70 B2
Bądki PL 47 B4
Bad Kissingen D 51 C6
Bad Kleinen D 44 B3
Bad Kohlgrub D 62 C2
Bad König D 61 A5
Bad Königshofen D . . . 51 C6
Badkowo PL 47 C4
Bad Kreuzen A 63 B5

Bad Kreuznach D ... 60 A3
Bad Krozingen D ... 60 C3
Bad Laasphe D ... 51 C4
Bad Langensalza D ... 51 B6
Bad Lauchstädt D ... 52 B1
Bad Lausick D ... 52 B2
Bad Lauterberg D ... 51 B6
Bad Leonfelden A ... 63 B5
Bad Liebenwerda D ... 52 B3
Bad Liebenzell D ... 61 B4
Bad Lippspringe D ... 51 B4
Badljevina HR ... 74 C2
Bad Meinberg D ... 51 B4
Bad Mergentheim D ... 61 A5
Bad Mitterndorf A ... 72 A3
Bad Münder D ... 51 A5
Bad Münstereifel D ... 50 C2
Bad Muskau D ... 53 B4
Bad Nauheim D ... 51 C4
Bad Nenndorf D ... 43 C6
Bad Neuenahr-Ahrweiler
 D ... 50 C3
Bad Neustadt D ... 51 C6
Bad Oeynhausen D ... 51 A4
Badolato I ... 106 C3
Badolatosa E ... 100 B1
Bad Oldesloe D ... 44 B2
Badonviller F ... 60 B2
Bad Orb D ... 51 C5
Badovinci SRB ... 85 B4
Bad Peterstal D ... 61 B4
Bad Pyrmont D ... 51 B5
Bad Radkersburg A ... 73 B5
Bad Ragaz CH ... 71 B4
Bad Rappenau D ... 61 A5
Bad Reichenhall D ... 62 C3
Bad Saarow-Pieskow
 D ... 53 A4
Bad Sachsa D ... 51 B6
Bad Säckingen D ... 70 A2
Bad Salzdetfurth D ... 51 A6
Bad Salzig D ... 50 C3
Bad Salzuflen D ... 51 A4
Bad Salzungen D ... 51 C6
Bad Sankt Leonhard
 A ... 73 B4
Bad Sassendorf D ... 50 B4
Bad Schandau D ... 53 C4
Bad Schmiedeberg D ... 52 B2
Bad Schönborn D ... 61 A4
Bad Schussenried D ... 61 B5
Bad Schwalbach D ... 50 C4
Bad Schwartau D ... 44 B2
Bad Segeberg D ... 44 B2
Bad Soden D ... 51 C4
Bad Soden-Salmünster
 D ... 51 C5
Bad Sooden-Allendorf
 D ... 51 B5
Bad Sulza D ... 52 B1
Bad Sülze D ... 44 A4
Bad Tatzmannsdorf A ... 73 A6
Bad Tennstedt D ... 51 B6
Bad Tölz D ... 62 C2
Badules E ... 90 B1
Bad Urach D ... 61 B5
Bad Vellach A ... 73 B4
Bad Vilbel D ... 51 C4
Bad Vöslau A ... 64 C2
Bad Waldsee D ... 61 C5
Bad Wiessee D ... 62 C2
Bad Wildungen D ... 51 B5
Bad Wilsnack D ... 44 C3
Bad Windsheim D ... 61 A6
Bad Wörishofen D ... 62 B1
Bad Wurzach D ... 61 C5
Bad Zwesten D ... 51 B5
Bad Zwischenahn D ... 43 B5
Baells E ... 90 B3
Baena E ... 100 B1
Baesweiler D ... 50 C2
Baeza E ... 100 B2
Baflo NL ... 42 B3
Bafra TR ... 16 A7
Baga E ... 91 A4
Bagaladi I ... 106 C2
Bagenkop DK ... 39 C3
Baggetorp S ... 37 C3
Bagh a Chaisteil GB ... 22 E1
Bagheria I ... 108 A2
Bagn N ... 32 B6
Bagnacavallo I ... 81 B5
Bagnáia I ... 102 A5
Bagnasco I ... 80 B2
Bagnères-de-Bigorre
 F ... 76 C3
Bagnères-de-Luchon
 F ... 77 D3
Bagni del Másino I ... 71 B4
Bagni di Lucca I ... 81 B4
Bagni di Rabbi I ... 71 B5
Bagni di Tívoli I ... 102 B5
Bagno di Romagna I ... 81 B5
Bagnoles-de-l'Orne F ... 57 B5
Bagnoli dei Trigno I ... 103 B7
Bagnoli di Sopra I ... 72 C1
Bagnoli Irpino I ... 103 C8
Bagnolo Mella I ... 71 C5
Bagnols-en-Forêt F ... 79 C5
Bagnols-sur-Cèze F ... 78 B3
Bagnorégio I ... 102 A5
Bagolino I ... 71 C5
Bagrationovsk RUS ... 47 A6
Bagrdan SRB ... 85 B6
Báguena E ... 95 A5
Bahabón de Esgueva
 E ... 88 C2
Bahillo E ... 88 B2
Bàia delle Zágare I ... 104 B2
Báia Domizia I ... 103 B6
Baia Mare RO ... 11 C7
Baiano I ... 103 C7
Baião P ... 87 C2
Baiersbronn D ... 61 B4
Baiersdorf D ... 62 A2
Baignes-Ste Radegonde
 F ... 67 C4
Baigneux-les-Juifs F ... 59 C5
Baildon GB ... 27 B4
Bailén E ... 100 A2
Băileşti RO ... 11 D7
Bailleul F ... 48 C3
Baillieborough IRL ... 19 C5
Bailleul F ... 48 C3
Bailó E ... 90 A2
Bain-de-Bretagne F ... 57 C4
Bains F ... 78 A2
Bains-les-Bains F ... 60 B2
Bainton GB ... 27 B5
Baio E ... 86 A2
Baiona E ... 87 B2
Bais F ... 57 B5
Baiso I ... 81 B4
Baja H ... 75 B3
Bajánsenye H ... 73 B6
Bajmok SRB ... 75 C4
Bajna H ... 65 C4
Bajovo Polje MNE ... 84 C3
Bajram Curri AL ... 105 A6
Bajša SRB ... 75 C4
Bajzë AL ... 105 A5
Bak H ... 74 B1
Bakar HR ... 73 C4
Bakewell GB ... 27 B4
Bakhmach UA ... 7 F12
Bakio E ... 89 A4
Bakırdaği TR ... 16 B7
Bakka N ... 32 B5
Bakkafjörður IS ... 111 A11
Bakkagerði IS ... 111 B12
Bække DK ... 39 D2
Bakken N ... 34 B3
Baklan TR ... 119 E4
Bakonybél H ... 74 A2
Bakonycsernye H ... 74 A3
Bakonyjákó F ... 74 A2
Bakonyszentkirály H ... 74 A2

Bakonyszombathely
 H ... 74 A2
Bakov nad Jizerou
 CZ ... 53 C4
Bąkowiec PL ... 55 B6
Baks H ... 75 B5
Baksa H ... 74 C3
Bala TR ... 30 A2
Bala GB ... 26 C2
Balâ TR ... 16 B6
Balaguer E ... 90 B3
Balassagyarmat H ... 65 B5
Balástya H ... 75 B5
Balatonakali H ... 74 B2
Balatonalmádi H ... 74 A3
Balatonboglár H ... 74 B2
Balatonbozsok H ... 74 B3
Balatonederics H ... 74 B2
Balatonfenyves H ... 74 B2
Balatonföldvár H ... 74 B2
Balatonfüred H ... 74 A3
Balatonfüzfö H ... 74 A3
Balatonkenese H ... 74 A3
Balatonkiliti H ... 74 B3
Balatonlelle H ... 74 B2
Balatonszabadi H ... 74 B3
Balatonszemes H ... 74 B2
Balatonszentgyörgy
 H ... 74 B2
Balazote E ... 101 A3
Balbeggie GB ... 25 B4
Balbigny F ... 69 C4
Balboa E ... 86 B4
Balbriggan IRL ... 19 C5
Balchik BG ... 11 E10
Balçova TR ... 119 D2
Baldock GB ... 31 C3
Bale HR ... 82 A2
Baleira E ... 86 A3
Baleizao P ... 98 A3
Balen B ... 49 B6
Balerna CH ... 70 C4
Balestrand N ... 32 A3
Balestrate I ... 108 A2
Balfour GB ... 23 B6
Bälganet S ... 41 C5
Balgari BG ... 11 E9
Balıkesir TR ... 118 C2
Balıklıçeşme TR ... 118 B1
Bälinge S ... 36 C4
Balingen D ... 61 B4
Balingsta S ... 36 C4
Balintore GB ... 23 D5
Balizac F ... 76 B2
Baljevac SRB ... 85 C5
Balk NL ... 42 C2
Balkbrug NL ... 42 C3
Balla IRL ... 18 C2
Ballachulish GB ... 24 B2
Ballaghaderreen IRL ... 18 C3
Ballancourt-sur-Essonne
 F ... 58 B3
Ballantrae GB ... 24 C3
Ballao I ... 110 C2
Ballasalla GB ... 26 A1
Ballater GB ... 23 D5
Ballen DK ... 39 D3
Ballenstedt D ... 52 B1
Ballerias E ... 90 B2
Balleroy F ... 57 A5
Ballerup DK ... 41 D2
Ballesteros de Calatrava
 E ... 100 A2
Balli TR ... 118 B2
Ballina IRL ... 18 B2
Ballinalack IRL ... 19 C4
Ballinamore IRL ... 19 B4
Ballinascarty IRL ... 20 C3
Ballinasloe IRL ... 20 A3
Ballindine IRL ... 18 C3
Balling DK ... 38 C1
Ballingarry
 Limerick IRL ... 20 B3
 Tipperary IRL ... 21 B4
Ballingeary IRL ... 20 C2
Ballinhassig IRL ... 20 C3
Ballinluig GB ... 25 B4
Ballino I ... 71 C5
Ballinrobe IRL ... 18 C2
Ballinskelligs IRL ... 20 C1
Ballinspittle IRL ... 20 C3
Ballintra IRL ... 18 B3
Ballivor IRL ... 19 C5
Ballobar E ... 90 B3
Ballon
 F ... 58 B1
 IRL ... 21 B5
Bállószög H ... 75 B4
Ballstad N ... 112 D2
Ballum DK ... 39 D1
Ballybay IRL ... 19 B5
Ballybofey IRL ... 19 B4
Ballyboghil IRL ... 19 C5
Ballybunion IRL ... 20 B2
Ballycanew IRL ... 21 B5
Ballycarry GB ... 19 B6
Ballycastle
 GB ... 19 A5
 IRL ... 18 B2
Ballyclare GB ... 19 B6
Ballyconneely IRL ... 18 C1
Ballycotton IRL ... 20 C3
Ballycroy IRL ... 18 B2
Ballydehob IRL ... 20 C2
Ballyferriter IRL ... 20 B1
Ballygawley GB ... 19 B4
Ballygowan GB ... 19 B6
Ballyhaunis IRL ... 18 C3
Ballyheige IRL ... 20 B2
Ballyjamesduff IRL ... 19 C4
Ballylanders IRL ... 20 B3
Ballylynan IRL ... 21 B4
Ballymahon IRL ... 21 A4
Ballymena GB ... 19 B5
Ballymoe IRL ... 18 C3
Ballymoney GB ... 19 A5
Ballymote IRL ... 18 B3
Ballynacorra IRL ... 20 C3
Ballynagore IRL ... 21 A4
Ballynahinch GB ... 19 B6
Ballynure GB ... 19 B6
Ballyragget IRL ... 21 B4
Ballyshannon IRL ... 18 B3
Ballyvaughan IRL ... 20 A2
Ballyvourney IRL ... 20 C2
Ballywalter GB ... 19 B6
Balmaclellan GB ... 24 C3
Balmaseda E ... 89 A3
Balmedie GB ... 23 D6
Balmuccia I ... 70 C3
Balna-paling GB ... 23 D4
Balneario de Panticosa
 E ... 76 D2
Balotaszállás H ... 75 B4
Balsareny E ... 91 B4
Balsorano-Nuovo I ... 103 B6
Bålsta S ... 37 C4
Balsthal CH ... 70 A2
Balta
 RO ... 11 B10
 UA ... 11 B10
Baltanás E ... 88 C2
Baltar E ... 87 C3
Baltasound GB ... 22 A8
Bălţi MD ... 11 C9
Baltimore IRL ... 20 D2
Baltinglass IRL ... 21 B5
Baltiysk RUS ... 47 A5
Baltów PL ... 55 B6
Balugães P ... 87 C2
Bælum DK ... 38 C3
Balve D ... 50 B3
Balvi LV ... 7 C9
Balvicar GB ... 24 B2
Balya TR ... 118 C2
Balzo I ... 82 D2
Bamberg D ... 62 A1
Bamburgh GB ... 25 C6
Banatska Palanka SRB ... 85 B6

Banatski Brestovac
 SRB ... 85 B5
Banatski Despotovac
 SRB ... 75 C5
Banatski Dvor SRB ... 75 C5
Banatski-Karlovac
 SRB ... 85 A6
Banatsko Aranđjelovo
 SRB ... 75 B5
Banatsko-Novo Selo
 SRB ... 85 B5
Banaz TR ... 118 D4
Banbridge GB ... 19 B5
Banbury GB ... 30 B2
Banchory GB ... 23 D6
Bande
 B ... 87 B3
 E ... 87 B3
Bandholm DK ... 39 E4
Bandırma TR ... 118 B2
Bandol F ... 79 C4
Bandon IRL ... 20 C3
Bañeres E ... 96 C2
Banff GB ... 23 D6
Bangor
 F ... 66 A1
 Down GB ... 19 B6
 Gwynedd GB ... 26 B1
 IRL ... 18 B2
Bangsund N ... 114 C8
Banie PL ... 45 B6
Banja SRB ... 85 C4
Banja Koviljača SRB ... 85 B4
Banjaloka SLO ... 73 C4
Banja Luka BIH ... 84 B2
Banjani SRB ... 85 B4
Banja Vrućica BIH ... 84 B2
Banje KOS ... 85 D5
Banjska KOS ... 85 D5
Banka SK ... 64 B3
Bankekind S ... 37 D2
Bankend GB ... 25 C4
Bankeryd S ... 40 B4
Bankfoot GB ... 25 B4
Banloc RO ... 75 C6
Bannalec F ... 56 C2
Bannes F ... 59 B4
Bannockburn GB ... 25 B4
Bañobárez E ... 87 D4
Bañon E ... 90 C1
Bañon F ... 79 B4
Baños E ... 93 A5
Baños de Gigonza E ... 99 C5
Baños de la Encina
 E ... 100 A2
Baños de Molgas E ... 87 B3
Baños de Rio Tobia
 E ... 89 B4
Baños de Valdearados
 E ... 89 C3
Bánov CZ ... 64 B3
Banova Jaruga HR ... 74 C1
Bánovce nad Bebravou
 SK ... 64 B4
Banovići BIH ... 84 B3
Banovići Selo BIH ... 84 B3
Bánréve H ... 65 B6
Bansin D ... 45 B6
Banská Belá SK ... 65 B4
Banská Bystrica SK ... 65 B5
Banská Štiavnica SK ... 65 B4
Banstead GB ... 31 C3
Banteer IRL ... 20 B3
Bantheville F ... 59 A6
Bantry IRL ... 20 C2
Bantzenheim F ... 60 C3
Banyalbufar E ... 97 B2
Banyoles E ... 91 A5
Banyuls-sur-Mer F ... 91 A6
Bapaume F ... 48 C3
Bar
 MNE ... 105 A5
 UA ... 11 B9
Barabhas GB ... 22 C2
Baraći BIH ... 84 B1
Baracs H ... 74 B3
Baracska H ... 74 A3
Barahona E ... 95 A4
Barajas de Melo E ... 95 B4
Barakaldo E ... 89 A4
Baralla E ... 86 B3
Barañain E ... 76 D1
Baranda SRB ... 85 A5
Baranello I ... 103 B7
Baranow Sandomierski
 PL ... 55 C6
Baraqueville F ... 77 B5
Barasoain E ... 89 B5
Barbacena P ... 92 C3
Barbadás E ... 87 B3
Barbadillo de Herreros
 E ... 89 B3
Barbadillo del Mercado
 E ... 89 B3
Barbadillo del Pez E ... 89 B3
Barban HR ... 82 A3
Barbarano Vicento I ... 71 C6
Barbariga HR ... 82 B2
Barbaros TR ... 118 B2
Barbastro E ... 90 A3
Barbatona E ... 95 A4
Barbâtre F ... 66 B2
Barbazan F ... 77 C3
Barbeitos E ... 86 A3
Barbentane F ... 78 C3
Barberino di Mugello
 I ... 81 B5
Barbezieux-St Hilaire
 F ... 67 C4
Barbonne-Fayel F ... 59 B4
Barbotan-les-Thermes
 F ... 76 C2
Barby F ... 52 B1
Bárcabo E ... 90 A3
Barca de Alva P ... 87 C3
Barcarrota E ... 93 C4
Barcellona-Pozzo di Gotto
 I ... 109 A4
Barcelona E ... 91 B5
Barcelonette F ... 79 B5
Barcelos P ... 87 C2
Bárcena del Monasterio
 E ... 86 A4
Bárcena de Pie de
 Concha E ... 88 A2
Barchfeld D ... 51 C6
Barcin PL ... 46 C3
Barcino PL ... 46 A2
Barco P ... 92 A3
Barcones E ... 89 C4
Barcs H ... 74 C2
Barczewo PL ... 47 B6
Bardejov SK ... 65 A4
Bårdesø DK ... 39 D3
Bardi I ... 81 B3
Bardney GB ... 27 B5
Bardo PL ... 54 C1
Bardolino I ... 71 C5
Bardonécchia I ... 79 A5
Bardoňovo SK ... 65 B4
Barèges F ... 76 D3
Barenstein D ... 52 C3
Barentin F ... 58 A1
Barenton F ... 57 B5
Barevo BIH ... 84 B2
Barfleur F ... 57 A4
Barga I ... 81 B4
Bargas E ... 94 C2
Barge I ... 79 B6
Bargemon F ... 79 C5
Barghe I ... 71 C5
Bargoed GB ... 29 B4
Bargrennan GB ... 24 C3
Bargteheide D ... 44 B2
Barham GB ... 31 C5

Bari I ... 104 B2
Barić Draga HR ... 83 B4
Barilović HR ... 73 C5
Bari Sardo I ... 110 C2
Barisciano I ... 103 A6
Barjac F ... 78 B3
Barjols F ... 79 C4
Barjon F ... 59 C5
Bárkáker N ... 35 C2
Barkald N ... 114 F7
Barkowo
 Dolnośląskie PL ... 54 B1
 Pomorskie PL ... 46 B3
Bårlad RO ... 11 C9
Bar-le-Duc F ... 59 B6
Barles F ... 79 B5
Barletta I ... 104 B2
Barlinek PL ... 45 C7
Barmouth GB ... 26 C1
Barmstedt D ... 43 B6
Barnard Castle GB ... 27 A4
Barnarp S ... 40 B4
Bärnau D ... 62 A3
Bärnbach A ... 73 A5
Barneberg D ... 52 A1
Barnenitz D ... 45 C4
Barnet GB ... 31 C3
Barnetby le Wold GB ... 27 B5
Barneveld NL ... 49 A6
Barneville-Carteret F ... 57 A4
Barnoldswick GB ... 26 B3
Barnowko PL ... 45 C6
Barnsley GB ... 27 B4
Barnstädt D ... 52 B1
Barnstaple GB ... 28 B3
Barnstorf D ... 43 C5
Barntrup D ... 51 B5
Baron F ... 58 A3
Baronissi I ... 103 C7
Barqueiro P ... 92 B2
Barquinha P ... 92 B2
Barr
 F ... 60 B3
 GB ... 24 C3
Barra P ... 92 A2
Barracas E ... 96 A2
Barraco E ... 94 B2
Barrado E ... 93 A5
Barrafranca I ... 109 B3
Barrancos P ... 98 A3
Barrax E ... 95 C4
Barrbaar D ... 62 B1
Barre-des-Cevennes F ... 78 B2
Barreiro P ... 92 C1
Barreiros E ... 86 A3
Barrême F ... 79 C5
Barret-le-Bas F ... 79 B4
Barrhead GB ... 24 C3
Barrhill GB ... 24 C3
Barrio de Nuesra Señora
 E ... 88 B1
Barrow-in-Furness
 GB ... 26 A2
Barrow upon Humber
 GB ... 27 B5
Barruecopardo E ... 87 C4
Barruelo de Santullán
 E ... 88 B2
Barry GB ... 29 B4
Bårse DK ... 39 D4
Barsinghausen D ... 51 A5
Barssel D ... 43 B4
Bar-sur-Aube F ... 59 B5
Bar-sur-Seine F ... 59 B5
Barth D ... 45 A4
Bartholomä D ... 61 B5
Barton upon Humber
 GB ... 27 B5
Bartoszyce PL ... 47 A6
Barúmini I ... 110 C1
Baruth D ... 52 A3
Barvaux B ... 49 C6
Barver D ... 43 C5
Barwatd PL ... 65 A5
Barwice PL ... 46 B2
Barysaw BY ... 7 D10
Barzana E ... 88 A1
Bârzava RO ... 10 C6
Bárzio I ... 71 C4
Bas E ... 91 A5
Bašaid SRB ... 75 C5
Basabeasca MD ... 11 C10
Basauri E ... 89 A4
Baschi I ... 82 D1
Baschurch GB ... 26 C3
Basconcillos del Tozo
 E ... 88 B3
Bascones de Ojeda E ... 88 B2
Basécles B ... 49 C4
Basel CH ... 70 A2
Basélice I ... 103 B7
Basildon GB ... 31 C4
Basingstoke GB ... 31 C2
Baška
 CZ ... 65 A4
 HR ... 83 B3
Baška Voda HR ... 84 C1
Bäsksjö S ... 115 C14
Baslow GB ... 27 B4
Başmakçı TR ... 119 E5
Basovizza I ... 72 C3
Bassacutena I ... 110 A2
Bassano del Grappa I ... 72 C1
Bassano Romano I ... 102 A5
Bassecourt CH ... 70 A2
Bassella E ... 91 A4
Bassevuovdde N ... 113 D14
Bassou F ... 59 C4
Bassoues F ... 76 C3
Bassum D ... 43 C5
Båstad S ... 40 C2
Bastardo I ... 82 D1
Bastelica F ... 102 A2
Bastelicaccia F ... 102 B1
Bastia
 F ... 102 A2
 I ... 82 C1
Bastogne B ... 50 C1
Baston GB ... 30 B3
Bastuträsk S ... 115 C17
Bata H ... 74 B3
Batajnica SRB ... 85 B5
Batalha P ... 92 B2
Bátaszék H ... 74 B3
Batea E ... 90 B3
Batelov CZ ... 63 A6
Baterno E ... 94 D2
Bath GB ... 29 B5
Bathgate GB ... 25 C4
Batida H ... 75 B5
Batignano I ... 81 D5
Batina HR ... 74 C3
Bátka SK ... 65 B6
Batković BIH ... 85 B4
Batlava KOS ... 85 D6
Batley GB ... 27 B4
Batočina SRB ... 85 B6
Batonyterenye H ... 65 C5
Batrina HR ... 74 C2
Båtsfjord N ... 113 B18
Battaglia Terme I ... 72 C1
Bätterkinden CH ... 70 A2
Battice B ... 50 C1
Battipáglia I ... 103 C7
Battle GB ... 31 D4
Battonya H ... 75 B6
Batuša SRB ... 85 B6
Bátya H ... 74 B3
Bau I ... 110 C1
Baud F ... 56 C2
Baudour F ... 49 C4
Baugé F ... 67 A4
Baugy F ... 68 A2
Bauma CH ... 70 A3
Baume-les-Dames F ... 69 A6
Baumholder D ... 60 A3

Baunatal D ... 51 B5
Baunei I ... 110 B2
Bauska LV ... 6 C8
Bautzen D ... 53 B4
Bavanište SRB ... 85 B5
Bavay F ... 49 C4
Bavilliers F ... 60 C2
Bavorov CZ ... 63 A5
Bawdsey GB ... 31 B5
Bawinkel D ... 43 C4
Bawtry GB ... 27 B4
Bayat TR ... 118 D5
Bayel F ... 59 B5
Bayeux F ... 57 A5
Bayındır TR ... 119 D2
Bayon F ... 60 B2
Bayonne F ... 76 C1
Bayons F ... 79 B5
Bayramiç TR ... 118 C1
Bayreuth D ... 52 D1
Bayrischzell D ... 62 C3
Baza E ... 101 B3
Bazas F ... 76 B2
Baziege F ... 77 C4
Bazoches-les-Gallerandes
 F ... 58 B3
Bazoches-sur-Hoëne
 F ... 58 B1
Bazzano I ... 81 B5
Beaconsfield GB ... 31 C3
Beade E ... 87 B2
Beadnell GB ... 25 C6
Beaminster GB ... 29 C5
Bearsden GB ... 24 C3
Beas E ... 99 B4
Beasain E ... 89 A4
Beas de Segura E ... 101 A3
Beattock GB ... 25 C4
Beaubery F ... 69 B4
Beaucaire F ... 78 C3
Beaufort
 F ... 69 C6
 IRL ... 20 B2
Beaufort-en-Vallée F ... 67 A4
Beaugency F ... 58 C2
Beaujeu
 Alpes-de-Haute-
 Provence F ... 79 B5
 Rhône F ... 69 B4
Beaulac F ... 76 B2
Beaulieu
 F ... 68 A2
 GB ... 31 D2
Beaulieu-sous-la-Roche
 F ... 66 B3
Beaulieu-sur-Dordogne
 F ... 77 B4
Beaulieu-sur-Mer F ... 80 C1
Beaulon F ... 68 B3
Beauly GB ... 23 D4
Beaumaris GB ... 26 B1
Beaumesnil F ... 58 A1
Beaumetz-lès-Loges F ... 48 C3
Beaumont
 B ... 49 C5
 F ... 77 B3
Beaumont-de-Lomagne
 F ... 77 C3
Beaumont-du-Gâtinais
 F ... 58 B3
Beaumont-en-Argonne
 F ... 59 A6
Beaumont-Hague F ... 57 A4
Beaumont-la-Ronce F ... 58 C1
Beaumont-le-Roger F ... 58 A1
Beaumont-sur-Oise F ... 58 A3
Beaumont-sur-Sarthe
 F ... 57 B6
Beaune F ... 69 A4
Beaune-la-Rolande F ... 58 B3
Beaupréau F ... 66 A4
Beauraing B ... 49 C5
Beaurepaire F ... 69 C5
Beaurepaire-en-Bresse
 F ... 69 B5
Beaurières F ... 79 B4
Beauvais F ... 58 A3
Beauval F ... 48 C3
Beauville F ... 77 B3
Beauvoir-sur-Mer F ... 66 B2
Beauvoir-sur-Niort F ... 67 B4
Beba Veche RO ... 75 B5
Bebertal D ... 52 A1
Bebington GB ... 26 B2
Bebra D ... 51 C5
Bebrina HR ... 84 A2
Beccles GB ... 30 B5
Becedas E ... 93 A5
Beceite E ... 90 C3
Bečej SRB ... 75 C5
Becerreá E ... 86 B3
Becerril de Campos E ... 88 B2
Bécherel F ... 57 B4
Bechhofen D ... 61 A6
Bechyně CZ ... 63 A5
Bečići MNE ... 105 A4
Beckfoot GB ... 25 D4
Beckingham GB ... 27 B5
Beckington GB ... 29 B5
Beckum D ... 50 B4
Bečov nad Teplou CZ ... 52 C2
Becsehely H ... 74 B1
Bedale GB ... 27 A4
Bedames E ... 89 A3
Bédar E ... 101 B4
Bédarieux F ... 78 C2
Bédarrides F ... 78 B3
Bedburg D ... 50 C2
Beddgelert GB ... 26 B1
Beddingestrand S ... 41 D3
Bédée F ... 57 B4
Bederkesa D ... 43 B5
Bedford GB ... 31 B3
Będków PL ... 55 B4
Bedlington GB ... 25 C6
Bedlno PL ... 55 A4
Bedmar E ... 100 B2
Bédoin F ... 79 B4
Bedónia I ... 81 B3
Bedretto CH ... 70 B3
Bedsted DK ... 38 C1
Bedum NL ... 42 B3
Bedwas GB ... 29 B4
Bedworth GB ... 30 B2
Będzin PL ... 55 C4
Beekbergen NL ... 50 A1
Beek en Donk NL ... 50 B1
Beelen D ... 50 B4
Beelitz D ... 52 A2
Beer GB ... 29 C5
Beerfelde D ... 45 C6
Beerfelden D ... 61 A4
Beernem B ... 49 B4
Beeskow D ... 53 A4
Beetsterzwaag NL ... 42 B3
Beetzendorf D ... 44 C3
Begaljica SRB ... 85 B5
Bégard F ... 56 B2
Begejci SRB ... 75 C5
Begijar E ... 100 B2
Begijnendijk B ... 49 B5
Begndal N ... 32 B4
Begues E ... 91 B4
Begur E ... 91 B6
Beho B ... 50 C1
Behram TR ... 118 C1
Behringen D ... 51 B6
Beilen NL ... 42 C3
Beilngries D ... 62 A2
Beine-Nauroy F ... 59 A5
Beinwil CH ... 70 A3
Beiseförth D ... 51 B5
Beith GB ... 24 C3
Beitostølen N ... 32 A5
Beiuş RO ... 11 C7

Beja P ... 98 A3
Béjar E ... 93 A5
Bekçiler TR ... 119 F4
Békés H ... 75 B6
Békéscsaba H ... 75 B6
Bekilli TR ... 119 D4
Bekkarfjord N ... 113 B16
Bela SK ... 65 A4
Bélâbre F ... 67 B6
Bela Crkva SRB ... 85 B6
Belalcázar E ... 93 C5
Belanovica SRB ... 85 B5
Belcaire F ... 77 D4
Bełchatów PL ... 55 B4
Belchite E ... 90 B2
Belcoo GB ... 19 B4
Belecke D ... 51 B4
Beled H ... 74 A2
Belej HR ... 83 B3
Beleño E ... 88 A1
Bélesta F ... 77 D4
Belev RUS ... 7 E13
Belevi TR ... 119 D2
Belfast GB ... 19 B6
Belford GB ... 25 C6
Belfort F ... 60 C2
Belgentier F ... 79 C4
Belgern D ... 52 B3
Belgioioso I ... 71 C4
Belgodère F ... 102 A2
Belgooly IRL ... 20 C3
Belgorod RUS ... 7 F14
Belgrade = Beograd
 SRB ... 85 B5
Belhade F ... 76 B2
Belica HR ... 74 B1
Beli Manastir HR ... 74 C3
Belin-Béliet F ... 76 B2
Belinchón E ... 95 B3
Belišće HR ... 74 C3
Bělkovice-Laštany
 CZ ... 64 A3
Bella I ... 104 C1
Bellac F ... 67 B6
Bellágio I ... 71 C4
Bellananagh IRL ... 19 C4
Bellano I ... 71 C4
Bellária I ... 82 B1
Bellavary IRL ... 18 C2
Belleek GB ... 18 B3
Bellegarde
 F ... 78 C3
 Loiret F ... 58 C3
Bellegarde-en-Diois F ... 79 B4
Bellegarde-en-Marche
 F ... 68 C2
Bellegarde-sur-Valserine
 F ... 69 B5
Belle-Isle-en-Terre F ... 56 B2
Bellême F ... 58 B1
Bellenaves F ... 68 B3
Bellentre F ... 70 C1
Belleville F ... 69 B4
Belleville-sur-Vie F ... 66 B3
Bellevaux F ... 69 B6
Bellevesvre F ... 69 B5
Belley F ... 69 C5
Bellheim D ... 61 A4
Bellinge DK ... 39 D3
Bellingham GB ... 25 C5
Bellinzago Novarese I ... 70 C3
Bellinzona CH ... 70 B4
Bell-lloc d'Urgell E ... 90 B3
Bello E ... 95 B5
Bellpuig d'Urgell E ... 91 B4
Bellreguart E ... 96 C2
Bellsbank GB ... 24 C3
Belltall E ... 91 B4
Belluno I ... 72 B2
Bélmez E ... 99 A5
Bélmez de la Moraleda
 E ... 100 B2
Belmont GB ... 22 A8
Belmont-de-la-Loire F ... 69 B4
Belmonte
 Asturias E ... 86 A4
 Cuenca E ... 95 C4
 P ... 92 A3
Belmonte de San José
 E ... 90 C2
Belmonte de Tajo E ... 95 B3
Belmont-sur-Rance F ... 78 C1
Belmullet IRL ... 18 B1
Belobreşca RO ... 85 B6
Beloeil B ... 49 C4
Belogradchik BG ... 11 E7
Belokorovichi UA ... 11 A10
Belorado E ... 89 B3
Belotić SRB ... 85 B4
Bělotin CZ ... 64 A3
Belozersk RUS ... 7 B14
Belp CH ... 70 B2
Belpasso I ... 109 B3
Belpech F ... 77 C4
Belper GB ... 27 B4
Belsay GB ... 25 C6
Belsk Duży PL ... 55 B5
Beltinci SLO ... 73 B6
Beltra IRL ... 18 C2
Belturbet IRL ... 19 B4
Beluša SK ... 64 A4
Belušić SRB ... 85 C6
Belvedere Maríttimo I ... 106 B2
Belver de Cinca E ... 90 B3
Belver de los Montes
 E ... 88 C1
Belvès F ... 77 B3
Belvezet F ... 78 B2
Belvis de la Jara E ... 94 C2
Belvis de Monroy E ... 93 B5
Bely RUS ... 7 D11
Belz
 F ... 56 C2
 UA ... 11 A7
Belzig D ... 52 A2
Bembibre E ... 86 B4
Bembridge GB ... 31 D2
Bemmel NL ... 50 B1
Bemposta
 Bragança P ... 87 C4
 Santarém P ... 92 B2
Benabarre E ... 90 A3
Benacazón E ... 99 B4
Benaguacil E ... 96 B2
Benahadux E ... 101 C3
Benalmádena E ... 100 C1
Benalúa de Guadix E ... 100 B2
Benalúa de las Villas
 E ... 100 B2
Benalup E ... 99 C5
Benamargosa E ... 100 C1
Benamaurel E ... 101 B3
Benameji E ... 100 B1
Benamocarra E ... 100 C1
Benaocaz E ... 99 C5
Benaoján E ... 99 C5
Benarrabá E ... 99 C5
Benasque E ... 90 A3
Benátky nad Jizerou
 CZ ... 53 C4
Benavente
 E ... 88 B1
 P ... 92 C2
Benavides de Órbigo E ... 88 B1
Benavila P ... 92 B2

Bendorf D ... 50 C3
Benedikt SLO ... 73 B5
Benejama E ... 101 A5
Benejúzar E ... 101 A5
Benešov CZ ... 63 A5
Bénestroff F ... 60 B2
Bénévent-l'Abbaye F ... 67 B6
Benevento I ... 103 B7
Benfeld F ... 60 B3
Benfica P ... 92 B2
Bengtsfors S ... 35 C4
Benia de Onis E ... 88 A1
Beničanci HR ... 74 C3
Benicarló E ... 90 C3
Benicássim E ... 96 A3
Benidorm E ... 96 C2
Benifaió E ... 96 B2
Beniganim E ... 96 C2
Benington GB ... 27 B6
Benisa E ... 96 C3
Benkovac HR ... 83 B4
Benllech GB ... 26 B1
Benneckenstein D ... 51 B6
Bénodet F ... 56 C1
Benquerencia de la
 Serena E ... 93 C5
Bensafrim P ... 98 B2
Bensdorf D ... 44 C4
Benshausen D ... 51 C6
Bensheim D ... 61 A4
Bentley GB ... 31 C3
Bentwisch D ... 44 A4
Beočin SRB ... 75 C4
Beograd = Belgrade
 SRB ... 85 B5
Beragh GB ... 19 B4
Berane MNE ... 85 D4
Beranga E ... 89 A3
Berat AL ... 105 C5
Bérat F ... 77 C4
Beratzhausen D ... 62 A2
Bérbaltavár H ... 74 A1
Berbegal E ... 90 B2
Berberana E ... 89 B3
Bercedo E ... 89 A3
Bercel H ... 65 C5
Bercenay-le-Hayer F ... 59 B4
Berceto I ... 81 B4
Berchem B ... 49 C4
Berchidda I ... 110 B2
Berching D ... 62 A2
Berchtesgaden D ... 62 C4
Bérchules E ... 100 C2
Bercianos de Aliste E ... 87 C4
Berck F ... 48 C2
Berclaire d'Urgell E ... 90 B3
Berdoias E ... 86 A4
Berducedo E ... 86 A4
Berdún E ... 90 A2
Berdychiv UA ... 11 B10
Bere Alston GB ... 28 C3
Bereguardo I ... 70 C4
Berehomet UA ... 11 B8
Berehove UA ... 11 B7
Berek BIH ... 74 C2
Beremend H ... 74 C3
Bere Regis GB ... 29 C5
Berestechko UA ... 11 A8
Berettyóújfalu H ... 10 C6
Berezhany UA ... 11 B8
Berezivka UA ... 11 C11
Berezna UA ... 7 F11
Berg
 D ... 62 A2
 N ... 114 B9
 S ... 37 D3
Berga
 Sachsen-Anhalt D ... 51 B7
 Thüringen D ... 52 C2
 E ... 91 A4
 S ... 40 B6
Bergama TR ... 118 C2
Bérgamo I ... 71 C4
Bergara E ... 89 A4
Bergby S ... 36 B4
Berge
 Brandenburg D ... 45 C4
 Niedersachsen D ... 43 C4
 Telemark N ... 33 C5
 Telemark N ... 33 C5
Bergeforsen S ... 115 E14
Bergen
 Mecklenburg-
 Vorpommern D ... 45 A5
 Niedersachsen D ... 44 C1
 Niedersachsen D ... 44 C2
 N ... 32 B2
Bergen op Zoom NL ... 49 B5
Bergerac F ... 77 B3
Bergères-lès-Vertus F ... 59 B5
Bergeyk NL ... 49 B6
Berghausen D ... 61 B4
Bergheim D ... 50 C2
Berg im Gau D ... 62 B2
Bergisch Gladbach D ... 50 C3
Bergkamen D ... 50 B3
Bergkvara S ... 40 C6
Berglern D ... 62 B2
Bergneustadt D ... 50 B3
Bergsäng S ... 34 B5
Bergshamra S ... 37 C5
Bergsjö S ... 115 F14
Bergs slussar S ... 37 D2
Bergtheim D ... 61 A6
Bergues F ... 48 B3
Bergum NL ... 42 B2
Bergün Bravuogn CH ... 71 B4
Bergwitz D ... 52 B2
Berhida H ... 74 A3
Beringel P ... 98 A3
Beringen
 B ... 49 B6
 CH ... 70 A3
Berja E ... 100 C3
Berkåk N ... 114 E7
Berkeley GB ... 29 B5
Berkenthin D ... 44 B2
Berkhamsted GB ... 31 C3
Berkheim D ... 61 B6
Berkhof D ... 43 C6
Berkovici BIH ... 84 C3
Berkovitsa BG ... 11 E7
Berlanga E ... 99 A5
Berlanga de Duero E ... 89 C4
Berlevåg N ... 113 B18
Berlikum NL ... 42 B2
Berlin D ... 45 C5
Bermeo E ... 89 A4
Bermillo de Sayago E ... 87 C4
Bern CH ... 70 B2
Bernalda I ... 104 C2
Bernardos E ... 94 A2
Bernartice
 Jihočeský CZ ... 63 A5
 Vychodočeský CZ ... 53 C5
Bernau
 Baden-Württemberg
 D ... 61 C4
 Bayern D ... 62 C3
 Brandenburg D ... 45 C5
Bernay F ... 58 A1
Bernburg D ... 52 B1
Berndorf A ... 64 C2
Berne D ... 43 B5
Bernecebaráti H ... 65 B4
Bernhardsthal A ... 64 B2
Bernkastel-Kues D ... 60 A3
Bernolákovo SK ... 64 B3
Bernsdorf D ... 53 B4
Bernstadt D ... 53 B4
Bernstein A ... 73 A6
Bernués E ... 90 A2
Beromünster CH ... 70 A3
Beroun CZ ... 63 A5
Berovo MK ... 116 A4

Berre-l'Etang F ... 79 C4
Berriedale GB ... 23 C5
Berriew GB ... 26 C2
Berrocal E ... 99 B4
Bersenbrück D ... 43 C4
Bershad' UA ... 11 B10
Bertamiráns E ... 86 B2
Berthåga S ... 36 C4
Berthelming F ... 60 B2
Bertincourt F ... 48 C3
Bertinoro I ... 82 B1
Bertogne B ... 49 C6
Bertrix B ... 59 A6
Berufjörður IS ... 111 C11
Berville-sur-Mer F ... 58 A1
Berwick-upon-Tweed
 GB ... 25 C5
Berzasca RO ... 10 D6
Berzence H ... 74 B2
Berzocana E ... 93 B5
Besalú E ... 91 A5
Besançon F ... 69 A6
Besande E ... 88 B2
Besenfeld D ... 61 B4
Besenyötelek H ... 65 C6
Besenyszög H ... 75 A5
Beshenkovichi BY ... 7 D10
Besigheim D ... 61 B5
Běšiny CZ ... 63 A4
Beška SRB ... 75 C5
Beşkonak TR ... 119 E6
Besle F ... 57 C4
Besnyő H ... 74 A3
Bessais-le-Fromental
 F ... 68 B2
Bessan F ... 78 C2
Besse-en-Chandesse
 F ... 68 C2
Bessèges F ... 78 B3
Bessé-sur-Braye F ... 58 C1
Bessines-sur-Gartempe
 F ... 67 B6
Best NL ... 49 B6
Bestorp S ... 37 D2
Betanzos E ... 86 A2
Bétera E ... 96 B2
Beteta E ... 95 B4
Béthenville F ... 59 A5
Bethesda GB ... 26 B1
Béthune F ... 48 C3
Beton-Bazoches F ... 59 B4
Bettembourg L ... 60 A2
Betterdorf L ... 60 A2
Bettna S ... 37 D3
Béttola I ... 80 B3
Bettona I ... 82 C1
Betws-y-Coed GB ... 26 B2
Betxi E ... 96 B2
Betz F ... 59 A3
Betzdorf D ... 50 C3
Beuil F ... 79 B5
Beulah GB ... 29 A4
Beuzeville F ... 58 A1
Bevagna I ... 82 D1
Bevens-bruk S ... 37 C1
Beveren B ... 49 B5
Beverley GB ... 27 B5
Beverstedt D ... 43 B5
Beverungen D ... 51 B5
Beverwijk NL ... 42 C1
Bex CH ... 70 B2
Bexhill GB ... 31 D4
Beyazköy TR ... 118 A2
Beychevelle F ... 76 A2
Beydağ TR ... 119 D3
Beyeğaç TR ... 119 E3
Beykoz TR ... 118 A4
Beynat F ... 77 A4
Beypazarı TR ... 118 B6
Beyşehir TR ... 119 E6
Bezas E ... 95 B5
Bezau A ... 71 A4
Bezdan SRB ... 75 C3
Bèze F ... 69 A5
Bezenet F ... 68 B2
Bezhetsk RUS ... 7 C14
Béziers F ... 78 C2
Bezzecca I ... 71 C5
Biadki PL ... 54 B2
Biała
 Łódzkie PL ... 55 B4
 Opolskie PL ... 54 C2
Biała Podlaska PL ... 6 E7
Biała Rawska PL ... 55 B5
Białe Błota PL ... 46 B3
Białobłoty PL ... 54 A2
Białobrzegi PL ... 55 B5
Białogard PL ... 46 A2
Białośliwie PL ... 46 B3
Białowąs PL ... 46 B2
Biały Bór PL ... 46 B2
Białystok PL ... 6 E7
Biancavilla I ... 109 B3
Bianco I ... 106 C3
Biandrate I ... 70 C3
Biar E ... 101 A5
Biarritz F ... 76 C1
Bias F ... 76 B1
Biasca CH ... 70 B3
Biatorbágy H ... 74 A3
Bibbiena I ... 81 C5
Bibbona I ... 81 C4
Biberach
 Baden-Württemberg
 D ... 61 B4
 Baden-Württemberg
 D ... 61 B5
Bibinje HR ... 83 B4
Bibione I ... 72 C3
Biblis D ... 61 A4
Bibury GB ... 29 B6
Biccari I ... 103 B8
Bicester GB ... 31 C2
Bichl D ... 62 C2
Bichlbach A ... 71 A5
Bicorp E ... 96 B2
Bicos P ... 98 B2
Bicske H ... 74 A3
Bidache F ... 76 C1
Bidart F ... 76 C1
Biddinghuizen NL ... 42 C2
Biddulph GB ... 26 B3
Bideford GB ... 28 B3
Bidford-on-Avon GB ... 29 A6
Bidjovagge N ... 113 C11
Bie S ... 37 C3
Bieber D ... 51 C5
Biebersdorf D ... 53 A3
Biedenkopf D ... 51 C4
Biel/Bienne CH ... 70 A2
Bielany Wrocławskie
 PL ... 54 B1
Bielawa PL ... 54 C1
Bielawy PL ... 55 A4
Biel/Bienne CH ... 70 A2
Bielefeld D ... 51 A4
Biella I ... 70 C3
Biélsa E ... 90 A3
Bielsk PL ... 47 C5
Bielsko-Biała PL ... 65 A5
Bielsk Podlaski PL ... 6 E7
Bienenbüttel D ... 44 B2
Bieniów PL ... 53 B5
Bienservida E ... 101 A3
Bienvenida E ... 93 C4
Bierdzany PL ... 54 C3
Bierné F ... 57 C5
Biersted DK ... 38 B2
Bierun PL ... 55 C4
Bierutów PL ... 54 B2
Bierwart B ... 49 C6
Bierzwina PL ... 46 B1
Bierzwnik PL ... 46 B1
Biescas E ... 90 A2
Biesenthal D ... 45 C5

Biesiekierz PL 46 A2
Bietigheim-Bissingen
D 61 B5
Bièvre B 49 D6
Biezuń PL 47 C5
Biga TR 118 B2
Bigadiç TR 118 C3
Biganos F 76 B2
Bigas P 87 D3
Bigastro E 101 A5
Bigbury GB 28 C4
Biggar GB 25 C4
Biggin Hill GB 31 C4
Biggleswade GB 30 B3
Bignasco CH 70 B3
Biguglia F 102 A2
Bihać BIH 83 B4
Biharnagybajom H 75 A6
Bijela MNE 105 A4
Bijeljani BIH 84 C3
Bijeljina BIH 85 B4
Bijelo Polje MNE 85 C4
Bijuesca E 89 C5
Bilaj HR 83 B4
Bila Tserkva UA 11 B11
Bilbao E 89 A4
Bilcza PL 55 C5
Bildudalur IS 111 B2
Bileća BIH 84 D3
Bilecik TR 118 B4
Biled RO 75 C5
Bilgoraj PL 11 A7
Bilhorod-Dnistrovskyy
UA 11 C11
Bilina CZ 53 C3
Bilisht AL 116 B2
Bilje HR 74 C3
Billdal S 38 B4
Billerbeck D 50 B3
Billericay GB 31 C4
Billesholm S 41 C2
Billingborough GB 30 B3
Billinge S 41 D3
Billingham GB 27 A4
Billinghay GB 27 B5
Billingsfors S 35 D4
Billingshurst GB 31 C3
Billom F 68 C3
Billsta S 115 D15
Billund DK 39 D2
Bilopillya UA 7 F13
Bilovec CZ 64 A4
Bilstein D 50 B4
Bilthoven NL 49 A6
Bilto N 112 C10
Bilzen B 49 C6
Biña SK 64 B4
Binaced E 90 B3
Binasco I 71 C4
Binbrook GB 27 B5
Binche B 49 C5
Bindlach D 52 D1
Bindslev DK 38 B3
Binefar E 90 B3
Bingen D 50 D3
Bingham GB 27 C5
Bingley GB 27 B4
Bingsjö S 36 A2
Binic F 56 B3
Binz D 45 A5
Bioče MNE 105 A5
Biograd na Moru HR . . . 83 C4
Bionaz I 70 C2
Bioska SRB 85 C4
Birda RO 75 C6
Birdlip GB 29 B5
Biri N 34 B2
Birkeland N 33 D5
Birkenfeld
Baden-Württemberg
D 61 B4
Rheinland-Pfalz D . . . 60 A3
Birkenhead GB 26 B2
Birkerød DK 41 D2
Birkfeld A 73 A5
Birkirkara M 107 C5
Birmingham GB 27 C4
Birr IRL 21 A4
Birresborn D 50 C2
Birstein D 51 C5
Biržai LT 6 C8
Birzebbugia M 107 C5
Bisáccia I 103 B8
Bisacquino I 108 B2
Bisbal de Falset E 90 B3
Biscarosse F 76 B1
Biscarosse Plage F . . . 76 B1
Biscarrués E 90 A2
Biscéglie I 104 B2
Bischheim F 60 B3
Bischofsheim D 51 C5
Bischofshofen A 72 A3
Bischofswerda D 53 B4
Bischofswiesen D 62 C3
Bischofszell CH 71 A4
Bischwiller F 60 B3
Bisenti I 103 A6
Bishop Auckland GB . . . 27 A4
Bishop's Castle GB 26 C3
Bishops Lydeard GB . . . 29 B4
Bishop's Stortford
GB 31 C4
Bishop's Waltham
GB 31 D2
Bisignano I 106 B3
Bisingen D 61 B4
Biskupice-Oławskie
PL 54 B2
Biskupiec PL 47 B5
Bismark D 44 C3
Bismo N 114 F5
Bispgården S 115 D13
Bispingen D 44 B1
Bissen L 60 A2
Bissendorf D 50 A4
Bisserup DK 39 D4
Bistango I 80 B2
Bistarac Donje BIH . . . 84 B3
Bistrica
BIH 84 B2
MNE 85 D4
SRB 85 C4
Bistrica ob Sotli SLO . . 73 B5
Bistrița RO 11 C8
Bisztynek PL 47 A6
Bitburg D 60 A2
Bitche F 60 A3
Bitetto I 104 B2
Bitola MK 116 A3
Bitonto I 104 B2
Bitschwiller F 60 C3
Bitterfeld D 52 B2
Bitti I 110 B2
Biville-sur-Mer F 48 D2
Bivona I 108 B2
Biwer L 60 A2
Bizeljsko SLO 73 C5
Bizovac HR 74 C3
Bjæn N 112 C10
Bjärnum S 41 C3
Bjärred S 41 D3
Bjästa S 115 D15
Bjelland
Vest-Agder N 33 D3
Vest-Agder N 33 D4
Bjelovar HR 74 C1
Bjerkreim N 33 D3
Bjerkvik N 112 D6
Bjerreby DK 39 E3
Bjerregrav DK 38 C2
Bjerringbro DK 39 C2
Bjøberg N 32 B5
Bjøllånes N 112 F3
Björbo S 36 B1
Björg IS 111 B8
Björkåsen N 112 D5
Björke
Gävleborg S 36 B4

Björke continued
Östergötland S 37 D2
Bjørkelangen N 34 C2
Björketorp S 40 B2
Björkholmen S 112 F8
Björkliden S 112 D7
Björklinge S 36 B4
Björkö S 36 C6
Björkö S 38 B4
Björköby S 40 B4
Björkvik S 37 D3
Bjørn N 115 A9
Bjørna S 115 D15
Bjørneborg S 35 C6
Bjørnerod S 35 C3
Bjørnevatn N 113 C18
Bjørnlunda S 37 C4
Bjørnstad N 113 C19
Bjørsäter S 37 D3
Bjurberget S 34 B4
Bjurholm S 115 D16
Bjursås S 36 B2
Bjurtjärn S 35 C6
Bjuv S 41 C2
Blace SRB 85 C6
Blachownia PL 54 C3
Blackburn GB 26 B3
Blackpool GB 26 B2
Blackstad S 40 B6
Blackwater IRL 21 B5
Blackwaterfoot GB 24 C2
Blacy F 59 B5
Bladåker S 36 B5
Blaenau Ffestiniog
GB 26 C2
Blaenavon GB 29 B4
Blaengarw GB 29 B4
Blagaj
BIH 83 A5
BIH 84 C2
Blagdon GB 29 B5
Blagnac F 77 C4
Blagoevgrad BG 11 E7
Blaichach D 61 C6
Blain F 66 A3
Blainville-sur-l'Eau F . . 60 B2
Blair Atholl GB 25 B4
Blairgowrie GB 25 B4
Blajan F 77 C3
Blakeney GB 29 B5
Blakstad N 33 D5
Blámont F 60 B2
Blanca E 101 A4
Blancos E 87 C3
Blandford Forum GB . . 29 C5
Blanes E 91 B5
Blangy-sur-Bresle F . . . 58 A2
Blankaholm S 40 B6
Blankenberge B 49 B4
Blankenburg D 51 B6
Blankenfelde D 45 C5
Blankenhain D 52 C1
Blankenheim D 50 C2
Blanquefort F 76 B2
Blansko CZ 64 A2
Blanzac F 67 C5
Blanzy F 69 B4
Blaricum NL 49 A6
Blarney IRL 20 C3
Blascomillán E 94 B1
Blascosancho E 94 B2
Błaszki PL 54 B3
Blatná CZ 63 A4
Blatné SK 64 B3
Blatnice CZ 64 B3
Blatnika BIH 84 B2
Blato HR 84 D1
Blato na Cetini HR 84 C1
Blatten CH 70 B2
Blattnicksele S 115 B14
Blatzheim D 50 C2
Blaubeuren D 61 B5
Blaufelden D 61 A5
Blaustein D 61 B5
Blaydon GB 25 D6
Blaye F 76 A2
Blaye-les-Mines F 77 B5
Blázquez E 93 C5
Bleckede D 44 B2
Blecua E 90 A2
Bled SLO 73 B4
Bleiburg A 73 B4
Bleicherbach D 51 C5
Bleicherode D 51 B6
Bleik N 112 C4
Bleikvassli N 115 B10
Bléneau F 59 C3
Blentarp S 41 D3
Blera I 102 A5
Blérancourt F 59 A4
Bléré F 67 A5
Blesle F 68 C3
Blessington GB 21 A5
Blet F 68 B2
Bletchley GB 31 C3
Bletterans F 69 B5
Blidö S 37 C5
Blidsberg S 40 B3
Blieskastel D 60 A3
Bligny-sur-Ouche F . . . 69 A4
Blikstorp S 35 D6
Blinisht AL 105 B6
Blinja HR 73 C6
Blizanówek PL 54 B3
Bliżyn PL 55 B5
Blois F 58 C2
Blokhus DK 38 B2
Blokzijl NL 42 C2
Blomberg D 33 C5
Blombacka S 35 C5
Blomskog S 35 C4
Blomstermåla S 40 C6
Blönduós IS 111 B5
Blonie PL 55 A5
Blonville-sur-Mer F . . . 57 A6
Blötberget S 36 B2
Blovice CZ 63 A4
Bloxham GB 31 B2
Błoński UA 11 D10
Bludenz A 71 A4
Bludov CZ 64 A2
Blumberg D 61 C4
Blyberg S 34 A6
Blyth
Northumberland
GB 25 C6
Nottinghamshire GB . . 27 B4
Blyth Bridge GB 25 C4
Blythburgh GB 30 B5
Blythe Bridge GB 26 C3
Bø
Nordland N 112 D3
Telemark N 33 C6
Boal E 86 A4
Boan MNE 85 D4
Boario Terme I 71 C5
Boat of Garten GB 23 D5
Boa Vista P 92 B2
Boğazkale TR 16 A7
Boğazlıyan TR 16 B7
Boba H 74 A2
Bobadilla
Logroño E 89 B4
Málaga E 100 B1
Bobadilla del Campo
E 94 A1
Bobadilla del Monte
E 94 B3
Böbingen D 61 B5
Bóbbio I 80 B3
Bóbbio Pellice I 79 B6
Bobigny F 58 B3
Bobingen D 62 B1
Böblingen D 61 B5
Bobolice PL 46 B2
Boboras E 87 B2
Bobowa PL 11 B12
Bobrová CZ 64 A2
Bobrowice PL 53 B5
Bobrówko PL 46 C1

Boca de Huérgano E . . 88 B2
Bocairent E 96 C2
Bočar SRB 75 C5
Bocchigliero I 106 B3
Boceguillas E 89 C3
Bochnia PL 55 D5
Bocholt
B 49 B6
D 50 B2
Bochov CZ 52 C3
Bochum D 50 B3
Bockara S 40 B6
Bockenem D 51 A6
Bockfliess A 64 B2
Bockhorn D 43 B5
Bočna SLO 73 B4
Bocognano F 102 A2
Boconád H 65 C6
Boczów PL 45 C6
Boda S 36 A2
Böda S 41 B7
Boda
Stockholm S 36 B5
Värmland S 35 C5
Västernorrland S . . 115 E13
Bodafors S 40 B4
Boda Glasbruk S 40 C5
Bodajk H 74 A3
Boddam
Aberdeenshire GB . . 23 D7
Shetland GB 22 B7
Boddin D 44 B3
Bödefeld-Freiheit D . . . 51 B4
Boden S 3 D24
Bodenmais D 62 A4
Bodenteich D 44 C2
Bodenwerder D 51 B5
Bodiam GB 31 C4
Bodinnick GB 28 C3
Bodio CH 70 B3
Bodjani SRB 75 C4
Bodmin GB 28 C3
Bodø N 112 E3
Bodonal de la Sierra
E 99 A4
Bodrum TR 119 E2
Bodstedt D 45 A4
Bodzanów PL 47 C6
Bodzanowice PL 54 C3
Bodzechów PL 55 C5
Bodzentyn PL 55 C5
Boecillo E 88 C2
Boëge F 69 B6
Boën F 68 C4
Bogács H 65 C6
Bogadmindszent H . . . 74 C3
Bogajo E 87 D4
Bogarra E 101 A3
Bogarre E 100 B2
Bogatić SRB 85 B4
Bogatynia PL 53 C4
Bogdaniec PL 45 C7
Bogé AL 105 A5
Boge S 37 E5
Bogen
D 62 B3
Nordland N 112 D5
Nordland N 112 E4
S 34 B4
Bogense DK 39 D3
Bogetići MNE 84 D3
Bognanco Fonti I 70 B3
Bognelv N 113 B11
Bognes N 112 D5
Bogno CH 70 B4
Bognor Regis GB 31 D3
Bogoria PL 55 C6
Bograngen S 34 B4
Boguchwały PL 47 B6
Bogumiłowice PL 55 B4
Boguslav UA 11 B11
Boguszów-Gorce PL . . 53 C6
Bogutovac SRB 85 C5
Bogyiszló H 74 B3
Bohain-en-Vermandois
F 49 D4
Böheimkirchen A 64 B1
Bohinjska Bistrica
SLO 72 B3
Böhlen D 52 B2
Böhmenkirch D 61 B5
Bohmte D 43 C5
Bohonal de Ibor E 93 B5
Böhönye H 74 B2
Bohumin CZ 65 A4
Boiro E 86 B2
Bois-d'Amont F 69 B6
Boisseron F 78 C3
Boitzenburg D 45 B5
Boixols E 91 A4
Boizenburg D 44 B2
Bojadła PL 53 B5
Bojano I 103 B7
Bojanowo PL 54 B1
Bøjden DK 39 D3
Bojkovice CZ 64 A3
Bojná SK 64 B4
Bojnice SK 65 B4
Boka SRB 75 C5
Böklund D 43 A6
Bokod H 74 A3
Bököny H 75 A4
Bokros H 75 B5
Boksitogorsk RUS . . . 7 B12
Bol HR 83 C5
Bolaños de Calatrava
E 100 A2
Bolayır TR 118 B1
Bolbec F 58 A1
Bölcske H 75 B3
Boldekow D 45 B5
Boldog H 65 C5
Boldva H 65 B6
Bolea E 90 A2
Bolekhiv UA 11 B7
Bolesławiec PL 53 B5
Boleszkowice PL 45 C6
Bolewice PL 46 C2
Bolgheri I 81 C4
Bolhrad UA 11 D10
Boliden S 3 D24
Bolimów PL 55 A5
Boliqueime P 98 B2
Boljevci SRB 85 B5
Boljkovci SRB 85 B5
Bolkhov RUS 7 E14
Bolków PL 53 C6
Bollebygd S 40 B2
Bollène F 78 B3
Bólliga E 95 B4
Bollnäs S 36 A3
Bollstabruk S 115 E14
Bollullos E 99 B4
Bollullos par del Condado
E 99 B4
Bologna I 81 B5
Bologne F 59 B6
Bolognetta I 108 B2
Bologoye RUS 7 C13
Bolótana I 110 B1
Bolsena I 102 A4
Bolshaya Vradiyevka
UA 11 C11
Bolsover GB 27 B4
Bolstad S 35 D4
Bolsward NL 42 B2
Boltaña E 90 A3
Boltenhagen D 44 B3
Boltigen CH 70 B2
Bolton GB 26 B3
Bolu TR 118 B6
Bolungarvík IS 111 A2
Bolvadin TR 118 D6
Bóly H 74 C3
Bolzaneto I 80 B2
Bolzano I 71 B6
Bómari I 103 A7
Bomarzo I 102 A5
Bombarral P 92 B1
Bömenzien D 44 C3
Bomlitz D 43 C6
Bømlo N 33 C2
Bøn N 34 B3

Bona F 68 A3
Bonaduz CH 71 B4
Bonanza E 99 C4
Bonar E 88 B1
Bonarbridge GB 23 D4
Bonárcado I 110 B1
Bonares E 99 B4
Bonäs S 36 A1
Bonassola I 80 B3
Bonawe GB 24 B2
Bondal N 32 C5
Bondeno I 81 B5
Bondorf D 61 B4
Bondstorp S 40 B3
Bône E 101 A4
Bonete E 101 A4
Bonifacio F 102 B2
Bonigen CH 70 B2
Bonin PL 46 A2
Bonn D 50 C3
Bonnánaro I 110 B1
Bonnåsjøen N 112 E4
Bonnat F 68 B1
Bonndorf D 61 C4
Bonnétable F 58 B1
Bonnétage F 70 A1
Bonneuil-les-Eaux F . . 58 A3
Bonneuil-Matours F . . 67 B5
Bonneval F 58 B2
Bonneval-sur-Arc F . . . 70 C2
Bonneville F 69 B6
Bonnières-sur-Seine
F 58 A2
Bonnieux F 79 C4
Bönnigheim D 61 A5
Bonny-sur-Loire F 68 A2
Bono
E 90 A3
I 110 B2
Bonorva I 110 B1
Bønsnes N 34 B2
Bonyhád H 74 B3
Boom B 49 B5
Boos F 58 A2
Boostedt D 44 A2
Bootle
Cumbria GB 26 A2
Merseyside GB 26 B2
Bopfingen D 61 B6
Boppard D 50 C3
Boqueixón E 86 B2
Bor
CZ 62 A3
S 40 B4
SRB 11 D7
TR 16 C7
Boran-sur-Oise F 58 A3
Borås S 40 B2
Borba P 92 C3
Borbona I 102 A6
Borča SRB 85 B5
Borci BIH 84 C3
Borculo NL 50 A2
Bordány H 75 B4
Bordeaux F 76 B2
Bordeira P 98 B2
Bordesholm D 44 A2
Borðeyri IS 111 B4
Bordighera I 80 C1
Bording DK 39 C2
Bordón E 90 C2
Bore I 81 B3
Borehamwood GB 31 C3
Borek Strzeliński PL . . 54 C2
Borek Wielkopolski
PL 54 B2
Boreland GB 25 C4
Borello I 82 B1
Borgafjäll S 115 C12
Borgarnes IS 111 C4
Borgentreich D 51 B5
Börger D 43 C4
Borger NL 42 C3
Borggård S 37 D2
Borghamn S 37 D1
Borghetto di Vara I . . . 81 B3
Borghetto d'Arróscia
I 80 B2
Borghetto Santo Spirito
I 80 B2
Borgholm S 41 C6
Borghorst D 50 A3
Bórgia I 106 C3
Borgloon B 49 C6
Børglum DK 38 B2
Borgo F 102 A2
Borgo alla Collina I . . . 81 C5
Borgo a Mozzano I . . . 81 C4
Borgoforte I 81 A4
Borgofranco d'Ivrea I . 70 C2
Borgomanero I 70 C3
Borgomasino I 70 C2
Borgo nuovo Val Tidone
I 80 B3
Borgo Pace I 82 C1
Borgorose I 102 A6
Borgo San Dalmazzo
I 80 B1
Borgo San Lorenzo I . . 81 C5
Borgosésia I 70 C3
Borgo Val di Taro I . . . 81 B3
Borgo Valsugana I 71 B6
Borgo Vercelli I 70 C3
Borgstena S 40 B3
Borgue GB 24 D3
Borgund N 32 A4
Borgvik S 35 C4
Borisova RUS 7 F14
Borja E 90 A2
Bork D 50 B3
Borken D 50 B2
Borkenes N 112 D5
Børkop DK 39 D2
Borkowice PL 55 B6
Borkowo PL 47 C6
Borkum D 42 B3
Borlänge S 36 B2
Borlu TR 118 D3
Bormes-les-Mimosas
F 79 C5
Bórmio I 71 B5
Bormujos E 99 B4
Borna D 52 B2
Borne NL 50 A2
Bornes P 87 C3
Borne Sulinowo PL . . . 46 B2
Bornheim D 50 C2
Bornhöved D 44 A2
Börnicke D 45 C5
Bornos E 99 C5
Borobia E 89 C5
Borodino RUS 7 D13
Borohrádek CZ 53 C6
Boronów PL 54 C3
Bórore I 110 B1
Boroszów PL 54 C3
Borota H 75 B4
Boroughbridge GB 27 A4
Borovany CZ 63 B5
Borovichi RUS 7 B13
Borovnica SLO 73 C4
Borovo HR 75 C4
Borovsk RUS 7 D14
Borowa PL 54 B2
Borowie PL 55 B6
Borox E 94 B3
Borrby S 41 D4
Borre
DK 41 E2
N 35 C2
Borredá E 91 A4
Borrenes E 86 B4
Borriol E 96 A2
Borris
DK 39 D1
IRL 21 B5
Borris-in-Ossory IRL . . 21 B4
Borrisokane IRL 20 B3

Borrisoleigh IRL 21 B4
Borrowdale GB 26 A2
Borrud N 34 C4
Børsa N 11 C8
Borsdorf D 52 B2
Børselv N 113 B14
Borsfa H 74 B1
Borský Mikuláš SK . . . 64 B3
Borsodivánka H 65 C6
Borsodnádasd H 65 B6
Börte N 33 C4
Bort GB 26 C1
Bort-les-Orgues F 68 C2
Börtnan S 115 E10
Børtnes N 32 B6
Borup DK 39 D4
Boryslav UA 11 A7
Boryspil UA 11 A11
Borysov CH 60 B2
Borzęcin PL 46 C1
Borzęciczki PL 54 B2
Borzęcin PL 55 A5
Borzna UA 7 F12
Borzonasca I 80 B3
Borzyszkowy PL 46 A3
Borzytuchom PL 46 A3
Bosal I 110 B1
Bosàca SK 64 B3
Bosanci HR 73 C5
Bosanska Dubica BIH . . 74 C1
Bosanska Gradiška
BIH 74 C2
Bosanska Kostajnica
BIH 74 C1
Bosanska Krupa BIH . . 83 B5
Bosanski Brod BIH 84 A3
Bosanski Novi BIH 83 A5
Bosanski Petrovac
BIH 83 B5
Bosanski Šamac BIH . . 84 A3
Bosansko Grahovo
BIH 83 B5
Bošány SK 64 B4
Bösárkány H 64 C3
Bosau D 44 A2
Bósca I 75 B4
Boscastle GB 28 C3
Bosco I 80 B2
Bosco Chiesanuova I . . 71 C6
Bösdorf D 44 A2
Bösel D 43 B4
Bosham GB 31 D3
Bösingfeld D 51 A5
Bosjön S 34 C5
Boskoop NL 49 A5
Boskovice CZ 64 A2
Bošnjaci HR 84 A3
Bošnjane SRB 85 C6
Bossast E 77 D3
Bossolasco I 80 B2
Boštanj SLO 73 B5
Boston GB 27 C5
Bostrak N 33 C5
Bötajica BIH 84 B3
Bøte By DK 44 A3
Bothel GB 26 A2
Boticas P 87 C3
Botilsäter S 35 C5
Botngård N 114 D6
Botoš SRB 75 C5
Botoşani RO 11 C9
Botricello I 107 C3
Bottendorf D 51 B4
Bottesford GB 27 C5
Bottnaryd S 40 B3
Bottrop D 50 B2
Botunje SRB 85 B5
Boturić SRB 85 C5
Bötzingen D 60 B3
Bouaye F 66 A3
Bouça P 87 C3
Boucau F 76 C1
Bouchain F 49 C4
Bouchoir F 58 A3
Bouesse F 67 B6
Bouguenais F 66 A3
Bouhy F 68 A3
Bouillargues F 78 C3
Bouillon B 59 A6
Bouilly F 59 B4
Bouin F 66 B3
Boulay-Moselle F 60 A2
Boulazac F 67 C5
Boule-d'Amont F 91 A5
Bouligny F 60 A1
Boulogne-sur-Gesse
F 77 C3
Boulogne-sur-Mer F . . 48 C2
Bouloire F 58 C1
Bouquemaison F 48 C3
Bourbon-Lancy F 68 B3
Bourbon-l'Archambault
F 68 B3
Bourbonne-les-Bains
F 60 C1
Bourbourg F 48 C3
Bourbriac F 56 B2
Bourcefranc-le-Chapus
F 66 C3
Bourdeaux F 79 B4
Bouresse F 67 B5
Bourg F 76 A2
Bourg-Achard F 58 A1
Bourganeuf F 68 C1
Bourg-Argental F 69 C4
Bourg-de-Péage F 79 A4
Bourg-de-Thizy F 69 B4
Bourg-de-Visa F 77 B3
Bourg-en-Bresse F . . . 69 B5
Bourges F 68 A2
Bourg-et-Comin F 59 A4
Bourg-Lastic F 68 C2
Bourg-Madame F 91 A4
Bourgneuf-en-Retz F . . 66 A3
Bourgogne F 59 A5
Bourgoin-Jallieu F 69 C5
Bourg-St Andéol F 78 B3
Bourg-St Maurice F . . . 70 C1
Bourgtheroulde F 58 A1
Bourgueil F 67 A5
Bourmont F 60 B1
Bourne GB 30 B3
Bournemouth GB 29 C6
Bourneville F 58 A1
Bournezeau F 66 B3
Bourran F 77 B3
Bourret F 77 C4
Bourron-Marlotte F . . . 58 B3
Bourton-on-The-Water
GB 29 B6
Boussac F 68 B2
Boussens F 77 C3
Boutersem B 49 C5
Bouttencourt F 48 D2
Bouvières F 79 B4
Bouvron F 66 A3
Bouxwiller F 60 B3
Bouzas E 87 B2
Bouzonville F 60 A2
Bova I 106 D2
Bovalino Marina I 106 C3
Bovallstrand S 35 D3
Bova Marina I 106 D2
Bovec SLO 72 B3
Bóveda E 86 B3
Bovenau D 44 A1
Bovenden D 51 B5
Boverdal N 114 F4
Boves
F 58 A3
I 80 B1
Bóves I 80 B1
Bovey Tracey GB 28 C4
Bovino I 103 B8
Bovolenta I 72 C1
Bovolone I 71 C6
Bowes GB 27 A4
Bowmore GB 24 C1

Bowness-on-Windermere
GB 26 A3
Box GB 29 B5
Boxberg
Baden-Württemberg
D 61 A5
Sachsen D 53 B4
Boxholm S 37 D2
Boxmeer NL 50 B1
Boxtel NL 49 B6
Boyabat TR 16 A7
Boyalica TR 118 B4
Boyle IRL 18 C3
Bozan TR 118 C6
Božava HR 83 B3
Bozburun TR 119 F3
Bozcaada TR 118 C1
Bozdoğan TR 119 E3
Bozel F 70 C1
Bozepole Wielkie PL . . 46 A3
Boževac SRB 85 B6
Božice CZ 64 B2
Boži Dar CZ 52 C2
Bozkır TR 119 E7
Bozouls F 78 B1
Bozova TR 119 C5
Bozüyük TR 118 C5
Bózzolo I 81 A4
Bra I 80 B1
Braås S 40 B5
Brabrand DK 39 C3
Bracadale GB 22 D2
Bracciano I 102 A5
Bracieux F 58 C2
Bräcke S 115 E12
Brackenheim D 61 A5
Brackley GB 30 B2
Bracklin IRL 19 C5
Bracknell GB 31 C3
Brackwede D 51 B4
Braco GB 25 B4
Brad RO 11 C7
Bradford GB 27 B4
Bradford on Avon GB . . 29 B5
Bradina BIH 84 C3
Brådland N 33 D3
Brædstrup DK 39 D2
Brae GB 22 A7
Braemar GB 23 D5
Braemore GB 22 D3
Braga P 87 C2
Bragança P 87 C4
Braide I 80 C2
Brăila RO 11 D9
Braine F 59 A4
Braine-le-Comte B 49 C5
Braintree GB 31 C4
Braives B 49 C6
Brake D 43 B5
Brakel
B 49 C4
D 51 B5
Bräkne-Hoby S 41 C5
Brålanda S 35 D4
Bralin PL 54 B2
Brallo di Pregola I 80 B3
Bram F 77 C5
Bramafan F 79 C5
Bramberg am Wildkogel
A 72 A2
Bramdrupdam DK 39 D2
Bramming DK 39 D1
Brampton GB 25 D5
Bramsche D 43 C4
Branca I 82 C1
Brancaleone Marina
I 106 D3
Brancaster GB 30 B4
Brand
Nieder Österreich A . . 63 B6
Vorarlberg A 71 A4
Brandbu N 34 B2
Brande DK 39 D2
Brande-Hornerkirchen
D 43 B6
Brandenberg A 72 A1
Brandenburg D 45 C4
Brand-Erbisdorf D 52 C3
Brandis D 52 B2
Brando F 102 A2
Brandomil E 86 A2
Brandon GB 30 B4
Brandshagen D 45 A5
Brandval N 34 B4
Brandýs nad Labem
CZ 53 C4
Branice CZ 54 C2
Braničevo SRB 85 B6
Braniewo PL 47 A5
Branik SLO 72 C3
Brankovina SRB 85 B4
Branky CZ 64 A3
Branne F 76 B2
Brannenburg-Degerndorf
D 62 C2
Brantôme F 67 C5
Branzi I 71 B4
Bras d'Asse F 79 C5
Braskereidfoss N 34 B3
Braslaw BY 7 D9
Braşov RO 11 D8
Brasparts F 56 B2
Brassac F 77 C5
Brassac-les-Mines F . . 68 C3
Brasschaat B 49 B5
Bras-sur-Meuse F 60 A1
Brassy F 68 A3
Břasy CZ 63 A4
Braszewice PL 54 B3
Bratislava SK 64 B3
Brattfors S 35 C6
Brattvåg N 114 E3
Bratunac BIH 85 B4
Braubach D 50 C3
Braunau A 62 B3
Braunfels D 51 C4
Braunlage D 51 B6
Braunsbedra D 52 B1
Braunschweig D 51 A6
Bray IRL 21 A5
Bray Dunes F 48 B3
Bray-sur-Seine F 59 B3
Bray-sur-Somme F . . . 48 D3
Brazatortas E 100 A1
Brazey-en-Plaine F . . . 69 A5
Brbinj HR 83 B4
Brčko BIH 84 B3
Brdani SRB 85 C5
Brdów PL 47 C4
Brea de Tajo E 95 B3
Brécey F 57 B4
Brechen D 50 C4
Brechin GB 25 B5
Brecht B 49 B5
Brecketfeld D 50 B3
Břeclav CZ 64 B2
Brecon GB 29 B4
Brécy F 68 A2
Breda
E 91 B5
NL 49 B5
Bredaryd S 40 B3
Bredbyn S 115 D15
Breddin D 44 C4
Bredebro DK 39 D1
Bredelar D 51 B4
Bredenfelde D 45 B5
Bredsjö S 36 C1
Bredstedt D 43 A6
Bredsten DK 39 D2
Bredträsk S 115 D15
Bredviken S 115 A11
Bree B 49 B6
Bregana HR 73 C5
Breganze I 72 C1
Bregenz A 71 A4
Bréhal F 57 B4
Brehna D 52 B2
Breiðdalsvík IS 111 D11
Breil-sur-Roya F 80 B1
Breisach D 60 B3
Breitenbach
CH 70 A2

Breitenbach continued
D 51 C5
Breitenberg D 63 B4
Breitenfelde D 44 B2
Breitengussbach D 51 D6
Breivikbotn N 113 B11
Brejning DK 39 D2
Brekken N 114 E8
Brekkestø N 33 D5
Brekkvasselv N 115 C10
Brekstad N 114 D6
Breland N 33 D4
Bremanger N 114 F1
Bremen D 43 B5
Bremerhaven D 43 B5
Bremervörde D 43 B6
Bremgarten CH 70 A3
Bremsnes N 114 D4
Brem-sur-Mer F 66 B3
Brenderup DK 39 D2
Brenes E 99 B5
Brengova SLO 73 B5
Brenna PL 65 A4
Breno I 71 C5
Brénod F 69 B5
Brés F 61 B4
Brescello I 81 B4
Bréscia I 71 C5
Breskens NL 49 B4
Bresle F 58 A3
Bresnica SRB 85 C5
Bressana I 80 A3
Bressanone I 72 B1
Bressuire F 67 B4
Brest
BY 6 E7
F 56 B1
HR 72 C3
Brestač SRB 85 B4
Brestanica SLO 73 B5
Brestova HR 82 A3
Brestovac HR 74 C2
Bretenoux F 77 B4
Breteuil
Eure F 58 B1
Oise F 58 A3
Brétigny-sur-Orge F . . 58 B3
Bretten D 61 A4
Bretteville-sur-Laize
F 57 A5
Brettheim D 61 A6
Breuil-Cervínia I 70 C2
Breukelen NL 49 A6
Brevik
N 35 C1
Stockholm S 37 C5
Västra Götaland S . . 37 D1
Breza BIH 84 B3
Brežice SLO 73 C5
Bréziers F 79 B5
Brezna SRB 85 C5
Breznica HR 73 B6
Breznica Našička HR . . 74 C3
Březnice CZ 63 A4
Brezno SK 65 B5
Brezolles F 58 B2
Březová nad Svitavou
CZ 64 A2
Brezovápod Bradlom
SK 64 B3
Brezovica
SK 65 A6
SLO 73 B4
Brezovo Polje Selo
BIH 84 B3
Briançon F 79 B5
Briançonnet F 79 C5
Briare F 58 C3
Briatexte F 77 C4
Briático I 106 C2
Briaucourt F 59 B6
Bribir HR 73 C4
Bricquebec F 57 A4
Bridgend
Argyll & Bute GB . . . 24 C1
Bridgend GB 29 B4
Bridge of Cally GB . . . 25 B4
Bridge of Don GB 23 D6
Bridge of Earn GB 25 B4
Bridge of Orchy GB . . . 24 B3
Bridgnorth GB 26 C3
Bridgwater GB 29 B5
Břidličná CZ 64 A3
Bridlington GB 27 A5
Bridport GB 29 C5
Briec F 56 B1
Brie-Comte-Robert F . . 58 B3
Brienne-le-Château F . . 59 B5
Brienon-sur-Armançon
F 59 C4
Brienz CH 70 B3
Brienza I 104 C1
Briesen D 45 C6
Brietlingen D 44 B2
Brieva de Cameros E . . 89 B4
Briey F 60 A1
Brig CH 70 B2
Brigg GB 27 B5
Brighouse GB 27 B4
Brightlingsea GB 31 C5
Brighton GB 31 D3
Brignogan-Plage F . . . 56 B1
Brignoles F 79 C5
Brigstock GB 30 B3
Brihuega E 95 B4
Brijuni HR 82 B2
Brillon-en-Barrois F . . . 59 B6
Brilon D 51 B4
Brimnes N 32 B3
Brinches P 98 A3
Bríndisi I 105 C3
Brinje HR 73 C5
Brinon-sur-Beuvron
F 68 A3
Brinon-sur-Sauldre F . . 68 A2
Brinyan GB 23 B5
Brioude F 68 C3
Brioux-sur-Boutonne
F 67 B4
Briouze F 57 B5
Brisighella I 81 B5
Brissac-Quincé F 67 A4
Brissago CH 70 B3
Bristol GB 29 B5
Brive-la-Gaillarde F . . . 77 A4
Briviesca E 89 B3
Brixham GB 28 C4
Brixlegg A 72 A1
Brjánslækur IS 111 B2
Brka BIH 84 B3
Brnaze HR 83 C5
Brněnec CZ 64 A2
Brno CZ 64 A2
Bro S 37 C4
Broadclyst GB 29 C4
Broad Haven IRL 18 B2
Broadstairs GB 31 C5
Broadstone GB 29 C5
Broadway GB 29 A6
Broager DK 39 E2
Broaryd S 40 B3
Broby S 41 C3
Bročanac BIH 84 C2
Brocēni LV 6 C7
Bröckel D 44 C1
Brockel D 43 B6
Brockenhurst GB 31 D2
Broczyno PL 46 B2

Brod MK 116 A3
Brodalen S 35 D3
Brodarevo SRB 85 C4
Broddbo S 36 C3
Brodek u Přerova CZ . . 64 A3
Broden-bach D 50 C3
Brodick GB 24 C2
Brod na Kupi HR 73 C4
Brodnica F 47 B5
Brodnica Graniczna
PL 47 A4
Brody
Lubuskie PL 53 A5
Lubuskie PL 53 B4
Mazowieckie PL 47 C6
UA 11 A8
Broglie F 58 B1
Brójce F 53 A5
Brokind S 37 D2
Brolo I 109 A3
Brome D 44 C2
Bromley GB 31 C4
Bromölla S 41 C4
Bromont-Lamothe F . . 68 C2
Brömsebro S 41 C5
Bromsgrove GB 29 A5
Bromyard GB 29 A5
Bronchales E 95 B5
Bronco E 93 A4
Brønderslev DK 38 B2
Broni I 80 A3
Brønnøysund N 114 B9
Brøns DK 39 D1
Bronte I 109 B3
Bronzani Mejdan BIH . . 84 B1
Bronzolo I 71 B6
Broons F 57 B3
Broquies F 78 B1
Brora GB 23 C5
Brørup DK 39 D2
Brösarp S 41 D4
Brossac F 67 C4
Brostrud N 32 B5
Brotas P 92 C2
Bröttjärna S 36 B2
Broto E 90 A2
Brottby S 37 C5
Brøttum N 34 A2
Brou F 58 B2
Brouage F 66 C3
Brough GB 26 A3
Broughshane GB 19 B5
Broughton-in-Furness
GB 26 A2
Broumov CZ 53 C6
Broût-Vernet F 68 B3
Brouvelieures F 60 B2
Brouwershaven NL . . . 49 B4
Brovary UA 11 A11
Brovst DK 38 B2
Brownhills GB 27 C4
Brozas E 93 B4
Brozzo I 71 C5
Brtnice CZ 63 A6
Brtonigla HR 72 C3
Bruay-la-Buissière F . . 48 C3
Bruchhausen-Vilsen
D 43 C6
Bruck D 62 A3
Brück D 52 A2
Bruck an der
Grossglocknerstrasse
A 72 A2
Bruck an der Leitha A . . 64 B2
Bruck an der Mur A . . . 73 A5
Brückl A 73 B4
Bruckmühl D 62 C2
Brue-Auriac F 79 C4
Brüel D 44 B3
Bruen CH 70 B3
Bruère-Allichamps F . . 68 B2
Bruff IRL 20 B3
Bruflat N 32 B6
Brugg CH 70 A3
Brugge B 49 B4
Brüggen D 50 B2
Brühl D 50 C2
Bruinisse NL 49 B5
Brûlon F 57 C5
Brumano I 71 C4
Brumath F 60 B3
Brummen NL 50 A2
Brumov-Bylnice CZ . . . 64 A4
Brumunddal N 34 B2
Brunau D 44 C3
Brunehamel F 59 A5
Brünen D 50 B2
Brunete E 94 B2
Brunflo S 115 D11
Brunico I 72 B1
Brunkeberg N 33 C5
Brunn D 45 B5
Brunnen CH 70 B3
Brunsbüttel D 43 B6
Brunssum NL 50 C1
Bruntál CZ 64 A3
Brus SRB 85 C6
Brušane HR 83 B4
Brusasco I 80 A2
Brusno SK 65 B5
Brusque F 78 C1
Brussels = Bruxelles
B 49 C5
Brusson I 70 C2
Brüssow D 45 B6
Brusy PL 46 B3
Bruton GB 29 B5
Bruvno HR 83 B4
Bruvoll N 34 B3
Bruxelles = Brussels
B 49 C5
Bruyères F 60 B2
Bruz F 57 B4
Bruzaholm S 40 B5
Brvéen GB 55 A5
Brwice SRB 85 C5
Brzeg PL 54 C2
Brzeg Dolny PL 54 B1
Brześć Kujawski PL . . . 47 C4
Brzeszcze PL 55 D4
Brzezie PL 46 B2
Brzeziny
Łódzkie PL 55 B4
Wielkopolskie PL . . . 54 B3
Brzeźnica PL 53 B5
Brzeźnica Nowa PL . . . 55 B4
Brzeźno PL 46 B1
Brzotin SK 65 B6
Brzozie Lubawskie
PL 47 B5
Bua S 40 B2
Buarcos P 92 A2
Buavåg N 33 C2
Bubbio I 80 B2
Bubry F 56 C2
Buca TR 119 D2
Buca TR 119 E5
Bucak TR 119 E5
Bučany SK 64 B3
Buccheri I 109 B3
Buccino I 103 C8
Bucelas P 92 C1
Buch
Bayern D 61 B6
Bayern D 62 B2
Buchach UA 11 B8
Bucharest = Bucureşti
RO 11 D9
Buchbach D 62 B3
Buchboden A 71 A4
Buchen D 61 A5
Büchen D 44 B2
Buchenberg D 61 C6

Buchères F 59 B5
Buchholz D 44 B1
Buchloe D 62 B1
Buchlovice CZ 64 A3
Buchlyvie GB 24 B3
Bucholz D 44 B4
Buchs CH 71 A4
Buchy F 58 A2
Bückeburg D 51 A5
Buckfastleigh GB 28 C4
Buckhaven GB 25 B4
Buckie GB 23 D6
Buckingham GB 31 B3
Buckley GB 26 B2
Bückwitz D 44 C4
Bučovice CZ 64 A3
Bucsa H 75 A6
Bucureşti = Bucharest RO 11 D9
Bucy-lés-Pierrepont F 59 A4
Buczek PL 55 B4
Bud N 114 E3
Budakalasz H 65 C5
Budakeszi H 75 A3
Budal N 114 E7
Budaörs H 75 A3
Budapest H 75 A4
Búðardalur IS 111 B4
Budča SK 65 B5
Buddusò I 110 B2
Bude GB 28 C3
Budeč CZ 63 A6
Büdelsdorf D 43 A6
Budens P 98 B2
Budia E 95 B4
Budimlić-Japra BIH 83 B5
Büdingen D 51 C5
Budinšćina HR 73 B6
Budišov CZ 64 A3
Budleigh Salterton GB 29 C4
Budmerice SK 64 B3
Budoni I 110 B2
Búdrio I 81 B5
Budva MNE 105 A4
Budyněnad Ohří CZ 53 C4
Budziszewice PL 55 B4
Budzyń PL 46 C2
Bue N 33 D2
Bueña E 95 B5
Buenache de Alarcón E 95 C4
Buenache de la Sierra E 95 B5
Buenaventura E 94 B2
Buenavista de Valdavia E 88 B2
Buendia E 95 B4
Bueu E 87 B2
Buezo E 89 B3
Bugac H 75 B4
Bugarra E 96 B2
Bugeat F 68 C1
Buggerru I 110 C1
Bugojno BIH 84 B2
Bugøyfjord N 113 C18
Bugøynes N 113 C18
Bugyi H 75 A4
Buharkent TR 119 E3
Bühl
Baden-Württemberg D 61 B4
Bayern D 61 C6
Bühlertal D 61 B4
Bühlertann D 61 A5
Buia I 72 B3
Builth Wells GB 29 A4
Buin N 32 B6
Buis-les-Baronnies F 79 B4
Buitenpost NL 42 B3
Buitrago del Lozoya E 94 B3
Bujalance E 100 B1
Bujaraloz E 90 B2
Buje HR 72 C3
Bujedo E 89 B3
Bük H 74 A1
Buk PL 46 C2
Bükkösd H 74 B2
Bükkzsérc H 65 C6
Bukovci SLO 73 B5
Bukowiec PL 53 A6
Bukowina Tatrzańska PL 65 A6
Bukownica PL 54 B3
Bukowno PL 55 C4
Bülach CH 70 A3
Búland IS 111 D7
Buldan TR 119 D3
Bulgnéville F 60 B1
Bulgurca TR 119 D2
Bülkau D 43 B5
Bulken N 32 B3
Bulkowo PL 47 C6
Bullas E 101 A4
Bulle CH 70 B2
Büllingen B 50 C2
Bulqizë AL 116 A2
Buna BIH 84 C2
Bunahowen IRL 18 B2
Bunbeg IRL 18 A3
Bunclody IRL 21 B5
Buncrana IRL 19 A4
Bunde D 43 B4
Bünde D 51 A4
Bundoran IRL 18 B3
Bunessan GB 24 B1
Bungay GB 30 B5
Bunge S 37 E6
Bunić HR 83 B4
Bunmahon IRL 21 B4
Bunnyconnellan IRL 18 B2
Buño E 86 A2
Buñol E 96 B2
Bunratty IRL 20 B3
Bunsbeek B 49 C5
Buñuel E 89 C5
Bünyan TR 16 B7
Bunyola E 97 B2
Buonabitácolo I 104 C1
Buonalbergo I 103 B7
Buonconvento I 81 C5
Buonvicino I 106 B2
Burano I 72 C2
Burbach D 50 C4
Burcei I 110 C2
Burdons-sur-Rognon F 59 B6
Burdur TR 119 E5
Bureå S 3 D24
Burela E 86 A3
Büren D 51 B4
Büren an der Aare CH 70 A2
Burford GB 29 B6
Burg
Cottbus D 53 B4
Magdeburg D 52 A1
Schleswig-Holstein D 43 B6
Burgas BG 11 E9
Burgau
A 73 A6
D 61 B6
P 98 B2
Burg auf Fehmarn D 44 A3
Burgbernheim D 61 A6
Burgdorf
CH 70 A2
D 44 C2
Burgebrach D 62 A1
Bürgel D 52 C1
Burgess Hill GB 31 D3
Burghaslach D 61 A6
Burghausen D 62 B3
Burghead GB 23 D5
Burgheim D 62 B2
Burgh le Marsh GB 27 B6
Búrgio I 108 B2
Burgkirchen D 62 B3
Burgkunstadt D 52 C1
Burglengenfeld D 62 A3
Burgo P 87 D2
Burgoberbach D 61 A6
Burgohondo E 94 B2
Burgos E 88 B3
Burgsinn D 51 C5
Burgstädt D 52 C2
Burgstall D 44 C3
Burg Stargard D 45 B5
Burgsvik S 37 E5
Burgui E 76 D2
Burguillos E 99 B5
Burguillos del Cerro E 93 C4
Burguillos de Toledo E 94 C3
Burhaniye TR 118 C1
Burhave D 43 B5
Burie F 67 C4
Burjassot E 96 B2
Burk D 61 A6
Burkhardtsdorf D 52 C2
Burlada E 76 D1
Burladingen D 61 B5
Burlage D 43 B4
Burness GB 23 B6
Burnham GB 31 C3
Burnham Market GB 30 B4
Burnham-on-Crouch GB 31 C4
Burnham-on-Sea GB 29 B5
Burniston GB 27 A5
Burnley GB 26 B3
Burntisland GB 25 B4
Burón E 88 A1
Buronzo I 70 C3
Burovac SRB 85 B6
Burow D 45 B5
Burravoe GB 22 A7
Burrel AL 105 B6
Burret F 77 D4
Burriana E 96 B2
Burry Port GB 28 B3
Bürs A 71 A4
Bursa TR 118 B4
Burseryd S 40 B3
Bürstadt D 61 A4
Burton GB 26 A3
Burton Agnes GB 27 A5
Burton Bradstock GB 29 C5
Burton Latimer GB 30 B3
Burton upon Stather GB 27 B5
Burton upon Trent GB 27 C4
Burujón E 94 C2
Burwell GB 30 B4
Burwick GB 23 C6
Bury GB 26 B3
Buryn UA 7 F12
Bury St Edmunds GB 30 B4
Burzenin PL 54 B3
Busachi I 110 B1
Busalla I 80 B2
Busana I 81 B4
Busano I 70 C2
Busca I 80 B1
Busch D 44 C3
Buševec HR 73 C6
Bushat AL 105 B5
Bushey GB 31 C3
Bushmills GB 19 A5
Bušince SK 65 B5
Buskhyttan S 37 D3
Busko-Zdrój PL 55 C5
Busot E 96 C2
Busovača BIH 84 B2
Busquístar E 100 C2
Bussang F 60 C2
Busseto I 81 B4
Bussière-Badil F 67 C5
Bussière-Poitevine F 67 B5
Bussolengo I 71 C5
Bussoleno I 70 C2
Bussum NL 49 A6
Busto Arsizio I 70 C3
Büsum D 43 A5
Butera I 109 B3
Butgenbach B 50 C2
Butler's Bridge IRL 19 B4
Butryny PL 47 B6
Bütschwil CH 70 A4
Buttermere GB 26 A2
Buttevant IRL 20 B3
Buttle S 37 E5
Buttstädt D 52 B1
Butzbach D 51 C4
Bützfleth D 43 B6
Bützow D 44 B3
Buxières-les-Mines F 68 B2
Buxtehude D 43 B6
Buxton GB 27 B4
Buxy F 69 B4
Büyükçekmece TR 118 A3
Büyükkariştiran TR 118 A2
Büyükorhan TR 118 C3
Buzançais F 67 B6
Buzancy F 59 A5
Buzău RO 11 D9
Buzet HR 72 C3
Buziaş RO 75 C6
Buzsák H 74 B2
Buzy F 76 C2
By S 36 B3
Byala BG 11 E8
Byaroza BY 6 E8
Byczyna PL 54 B3
Bydalen S 115 D10
Bydgoszcz PL 47 B4
Bygdin N 32 A5
Bygland N 33 D4
Byglandsfjord N 33 D4
Bygstad N 32 A2
Bykhaw BY 7 E11
Bykle N 33 C4
Bylderup-Bov DK 39 E2
Bylnice CZ 64 A4
Byrkjedal N 33 D3
Byrkjelo N 114 F3
Byrum DK 38 B3
Byšice CZ 53 C4
Byske S 3 D24
Býškovice CZ 64 A3
Bysław PL 46 B3
Bystré CZ 64 A2
Bystřice CZ 63 A5
Bystřice CZ 65 A4
Bystřice nad Pernštejnem CZ 64 A2
Bystřice pod Hostýnem CZ 64 A3
Bystrzyca Kłodzka PL 54 C1
Bytča SK 65 A4
Bytnica PL 53 A5
Bytom PL 54 C3
Bytom Odrzański PL 53 B5
Bytów PL 46 A3
Byxelkrok S 41 B7
Bzenec CZ 64 B3
Bzince SK 64 B3

C

Çağa TR 118 B7
Cabacos P 92 B2
Cabaj-Čápor SK 64 B4
Cabana E 86 A2
Cabanac-et-Villagrains F 76 B2
Cabañaquinta E 88 A1
Cabanas P 98 B3
Cabañas del Castillo E 93 B5
Cabañas de Yepes E 95 C3
Cabanelles E 91 A5
Cabanes E 96 A3
Cabanillas E 89 B5
Čabar HR 73 C4
Cabasse F 79 C5
Cabdella E 91 A4
Cabeceiras de Basto P 87 C2
Cabeço de Vide P 92 B3
Cabella Ligure I 80 B3
Cabeza del Buey E 93 C5
Cabeza la Vaca E 99 A4
Cabezamesada E 95 C3
Cabezarados E 100 A1
Cabezarrubias del Puerto E 100 A1
Cabezas del Villar E 94 B1
Cabezas Rubias E 98 B3
Cabezón E 88 C2
Cabezón de la Sal E 88 A2
Cabezón de Liébana E 88 A2
Cabezuela E 94 A3
Cabezuela del Valle E 93 A5
Cabo de Gata E 101 C3
Cabo de Palos E 101 B5
Cabolafuenta E 95 A4
Cabourg F 57 A5
Cabra
E 100 B1
P 92 A3
Cabrach GB 23 D5
Cabra del Santo Cristo E 100 B2
Cábras I 110 C1
Cabreiro P 87 C2
Cabreiros E 86 A3
Cabrejas E 95 B4
Cabrela P 92 C2
Cabrillas E 87 D4
Cabuna HR 74 C2
Cacabelos E 86 B4
Čačak SRB 85 C5
Cáccamo I 108 B2
Caccuri I 107 B3
Cacela P 98 B3
Cacém P 92 C1
Cáceres E 93 B4
Cachafeiro E 86 B2
Cachopo P 98 B3
Čachtice SK 64 B3
Cacin E 100 B2
Čačinci HR 74 C2
Cadafais P 92 C1
Cadalen F 77 C5
Cadalso E 93 A4
Cadaqués E 91 A6
Cadaval P 92 B1
Cadavedo E 86 A4
Čadavica BIH 84 B1
Čadca SK 65 A4
Cadéac F 77 D3
Cadelbosco di Sopra I 81 B4
Cadenazzo CH 70 B3
Cadenberge D 43 B6
Cadenet F 79 C4
Cadeuil F 66 C4
Cádiar E 100 C2
Cadillac F 76 B2
Cádiz E 99 C4
Čadjavica HR 74 C2
Cadouin F 77 B3
Cadours F 77 C4
Cadrete E 90 B2
Caen F 57 A5
Caerleon GB 29 B5
Caernarfon GB 26 B1
Caerphilly GB 29 B4
Caersws GB 26 C2
Cafede P 92 B3
Caggiano I 104 C1
Cagli I 82 C1
Cágliari I 110 C2
Čaglin HR 74 C2
Cagnano Varano I 104 B1
Cagnes-sur-Mer F 79 C6
Caher IRL 21 B4
Caherciveen IRL 20 C1
Caherdaniel IRL 20 C1
Cahors F 77 B4
Cahul MD 11 D10
Caiazzo I 103 B7
Caion E 86 A2
Cairndow GB 24 B3
Cairnryan GB 24 D2
Cairo Montenotte I 80 B2
Caister-on-Sea GB 30 B5
Caistor GB 27 B5
Caivano I 103 C7
Cajarc F 77 B4
Čajetina SRB 85 C4
Čajniče BIH 84 C4
Çakırlar TR 119 F5
Çakmak TR 118 C6
Čakovec HR 73 B6
Çakran AL 105 C5
Çal TR 119 D4
Cala E 99 B4
Calabritto I 103 C8
Calaceite E 90 C3
Calacuccia F 102 A2
Cala d'Or E 97 B3
Calaf E 91 B4
Calafat RO 11 D7
Calafell E 91 B4
Cala Galdana E 97 B3
Cala Gonone I 110 B2
Calahonda
Granada E 100 C2
Málaga E 100 C1
Calahorra E 89 B5
Calais F 48 C2
Cala Llonga E 97 C1
Calalzo di Cadore I 72 B2
Cala Millor E 97 B3
Calamocha E 95 B5
Calamonte E 93 C4
Cala Morell E 97 A3
Calanais GB 22 C2
Calañas E 99 B4
Calanda E 90 C2
Calangiánus I 110 B2
Călăraşi RO 11 D9
Cala Ratjada E 97 B3
Calascibetta I 109 B3
Calasetta I 110 C1
Calasparra E 101 A4
Calatafimi I 108 B1
Calatayud E 89 C5
Calatorao E 89 C5
Calau D 53 B3
Calbe D 52 B1
Calcena E 89 C5
Calcinelli I 82 C1
Calco I 71 C4
Caldaro sulla strada del Vino I 71 B6
Caldas da Rainha P 92 B1
Caldas de Boì E 90 A3
Caldas de Malavella E 91 B5
Caldas de Reis E 86 B2
Caldas de San Jorge P 87 D2
Caldas de Vizela P 87 C2
Caldaso de los Vidrios E 94 B2
Caldbeck GB 26 A2
Caldearenas E 90 A2
Caldelas P 87 C2
Calders E 91 B4
Caldes de Montbui E 91 B5
Caldicot GB 29 B5
Caldirola I 80 B3
Caledon GB 19 B5
Calella
Barcelona E 91 B5
Girona E 91 B6
Calenzana F 102 A1
Calera de León E 99 A4
Calera y Chozas E 94 C2
Caleruega E 89 C3
Caleruela E 93 B5
Cales de Mallorca E 97 B3
Calestano I 81 B4
Calfsound GB 23 B6
Calgary GB 24 B1
Calimera I 105 C4
Calitri I 103 C8
Calizzano I 80 B2
Callac F 56 B2
Callan IRL 21 B4
Callander GB 24 B3
Callas F 79 C5
Calliano
Piemonte I 80 A2
Trentino Alto Adige I 71 C6
Callington GB 28 C3
Callosa de Ensarriá E 96 C2
Callosa de Segura E 101 A5
Çallús E 91 B4
Čalma SRB 85 A4
Calmbach D 61 B4
Calne GB 29 B6
Calolziocorte I 71 C4
Calonge E 91 B6
Čalovec SK 64 C3
Calpe E 96 C3
Caltabellotta I 108 B2
Caltagirone I 109 B3
Caltanissetta I 109 B3
Caltavuturo I 108 B2
Çaltılıbük TR 118 C3
Caltojar E 89 C4
Caluire-et-Cuire F 69 C4
Caluso I 70 C2
Calvello I 104 C1
Calvi F 102 A1
Calviá E 97 B2
Calvinet F 77 B5
Calvisson F 78 C3
Calvörde D 44 C3
Calw D 61 B4
Calzada de Calatrava E 100 A2
Calzada de Valdunciel E 94 A1
Calzadilla de los Barros E 93 C4
Cam GB 29 B5
Camaiore I 81 C4
Camarasa E 90 B3
Camarena E 94 B2
Camarès F 78 C1
Camaret-sur-Aigues F 78 B3
Camaret-sur-Mer F 56 B1
Camarillas E 90 C2
Camariñas E 86 A1
Camarma E 95 B3
Camarzana de Tera E 87 B4
Camas E 99 B4
Camastra I 108 B2
Cambados E 86 B2
Cambarinho P 92 A2
Camberley GB 31 C3
Cambil E 100 B2
Cambligeu F 48 C3
Cambo-les-Bains F 76 C1
Camborne GB 28 C2
Cambrai F 49 C4
Cambre E 86 A2
Cambridge GB 30 B4
Cambrils E 91 B4
Cambs D 44 B3
Camburg D 52 B1
Camden GB 31 C3
Cameleño E 88 A2
Camelford GB 28 C3
Çameli TR 119 E4
Camelle E 86 A1
Camerano I 82 C2
Camerino I 82 C2
Camerota I 106 A2
Camigliatello Silano I 106 B3
Caminha P 87 C2
Caminomorisco E 93 A4
Caminreal E 95 B5
Camisano Vicentino I 72 C1
Camlıdere TR 118 B7
Cammarata I 108 B2
Camogli I 80 B3
Camors F 56 C3
Camp IRL 20 B2
Campagna I 103 C8
Campagnano di Roma I 102 A5
Campagnático I 81 D5
Campan F 76 C3
Campana I 107 B3
Campanario E 93 C5
Campanillas E 100 C1
Campano E 99 C4
Campaspero E 88 C2
Campbeltown GB 24 C2
Campello E 96 C2
Campelos P 92 B1
Campi Bisenzio I 81 C5
Campico López E 101 B4
Campíglia Marittima I 81 C4
Campillo de Altobuey E 95 C5
Campillo de Aragón E 95 A5
Campillo de Arenas E 100 B2
Campillo de Llerena E 93 C5
Campillos E 100 B1
Câmpina RO 11 D8
Campi Salentina I 105 C4
Campli I 82 D2
Campo E 90 A3
Campobasso I 103 B7
Campobello di Licata I 108 B2
Campobello di Mazara I 108 B1
Campo da Feira E 86 A3
Campodársego I 72 C1
Campo de Bacerros E 87 B3
Campo de Caso E 88 A1
Campo de Criptana E 95 C3
Campodolcino I 71 B4
Campofelice di Roccella I 108 B2
Campofiorito I 108 B2
Campofórmido I 72 B3
Campofranco I 108 B2
Campofrio E 99 B4
Campogalliano I 81 B4
Campo Ligure I 80 B2
Campolongo I 72 B2
Campo Lugar E 93 B5
Campo Maior P 93 B3
Campomanes E 88 A1
Campomarino I 103 B8
Campo Molino I 79 B6
Campomono F 102 B1
Campo Real E 95 B3
Camporeale I 108 B2
Camporeggiano I 82 C1
Camporrells E 90 B3
Camporrobles E 96 B1
Campos P 87 C3
Camposa P 87 C2
Camposampiero I 72 C1
Camposanto I 81 B5
Campos del Port E 97 B3
Camposines E 90 B3
Campotéjar E 100 B2
Campotosto I 103 A6
Campo Túres I 72 B1
Camprodón E 91 A5
Campsegret F 77 B3
Camrose GB 28 B2
Camuñas E 95 C3
Çamyolu TR 119 F7
Çan TR 118 B2
Cana I 81 D5
Cañada del Hoyo E 95 C5
Cañadajuncosa E 95 C4
Cañada Rosal E 99 B5
Čanak HR 83 B4
Çanakkale TR 118 B1
Canale I 80 B1
Canales
Asturias E 88 B1
Canales *continued*
Castellón de la Plana E 96 B2
Canals E 96 C2
Canal San Bovo I 72 B1
Cañamares E 95 B4
Cañamero E 93 B5
Cañar E 100 C2
Cañate la Real E 99 C5
Cañaveral E 93 B4
Cañaveral de León E 99 A4
Cañaveras E 95 B4
Cañaveruelas E 95 B4
Canazei I 72 B1
Cancale F 57 B4
Cancellara I 104 C1
Cancello ed Arnone I 103 B7
Cancon F 77 B3
Canda E 87 B4
Candamil E 86 A3
Candanchu E 76 D2
Çandarlı TR 118 D1
Candas E 88 A1
Candasnos E 90 B3
Candé F 66 A3
Candela I 104 B1
Candelario E 93 A5
Candeleda E 93 A5
Cándia Lomellina I 70 C3
Candide Casamazzagno I 72 B2
Candin E 86 B4
Candosa P 92 A3
Canecas P 92 C1
Canelli I 80 B2
Canena E 100 A2
Canencia E 94 B3
Canero E 86 A4
Canet F 78 C2
Canet de Mar E 91 B5
Canet d'en Berenguer E 96 B2
Cañete E 95 B5
Cañete de las Torres E 100 B1
Canet-Plage F 91 A6
Canfranc E 76 D2
Cangas
Lugo E 86 A3
Pontevedra E 87 B2
Cangas de Narcea E 86 A4
Cangas de Onís E 88 A1
Canha P 92 C2
Canhestros P 98 A2
Canicatti I 108 B2
Canicattini Bagni I 109 B4
Canicosa de la Sierra E 89 C3
Caniles E 101 B3
Canillas de Aceituno E 100 C1
Canino I 102 A4
Canisy F 57 A4
Cañizal E 94 A1
Cañizo E 88 C1
Canjáyar E 101 C3
Çankırı TR 16 A6
Cannai I 110 C1
Cannara I 82 C1
Cannero Riviera I 70 B3
Cannes F 79 C6
Canneto
Sicilia I 106 C1
Toscana I 81 C4
Canneto sull'Oglio I 71 C5
Cannich GB 22 D4
Cannóbio I 70 B3
Cannock GB 26 C3
Canonbie GB 25 C5
Canosa di Púglia I 104 B2
Can Pastilla E 97 B2
C'an Picafort E 97 B3
Cantalapiedra E 94 A1
Cantalejo E 94 A3
Cantalgallo E 99 A4
Cantalice I 102 A5
Cantalpino E 94 A1
Cantalupo in Sabina I 102 A5
Cantanhede P 92 A2
Cantavieja E 90 C2
Čantavir SRB 75 C4
Canterbury GB 31 C5
Cantiano I 82 C1
Cantillana E 99 B5
Cantiveros E 94 B2
Cantoria E 101 B3
Cantù I 71 C4
Canvey GB 31 C4
Cany-Barville F 58 A1
Canyet de Mar E 91 B5
Caol GB 24 B2
Cáorle I 72 C2
Caorso I 81 A3
Capáccio I 103 C8
Capaci I 108 A2
Capálbio I 102 A4
Capannori I 81 C4
Caparde BIH 84 B3
Caparroso E 89 B5
Capbreton F 76 C1
Capdenac-Gare F 77 B5
Capdepera E 97 B3
Cap-de-Pin F 76 B2
Capel Curig GB 26 B2
Capellades E 91 B4
Capena I 102 A5
Capendu F 77 C5
Capestang F 78 C2
Capestrano I 103 A6
Cap Ferret F 76 B1
Capileira E 100 C2
Capinha P 92 A3
Ca'Pisani I 82 B1
Capistrello I 103 B6
Capizzi I 109 B3
Čaplje BIH 83 B5
Čapljina BIH 84 C2
Capo di Ponte I 71 B5
Caposile I 72 C2
Capoterra I 110 C1
Cappamore IRL 20 B3
Cappeln D 43 C5
Cappoquin IRL 21 B4
Capracotta I 103 B7
Capránica I 102 A5
Caprarola I 102 A5
Capretta I 82 D1
Capri I 103 C7
Capriati a Volturno I 103 B7
Caprino Veronese I 71 C5
Captieux F 76 B2
Cápua I 103 B7
Capurso I 104 B2
Capvern F 77 C3
Carabaña E 95 B3
Carabias E 88 C3
Caracal RO 11 D8
Caracenilla E 95 B4
Caráglio I 80 B1
Caraman F 77 C4
Caramánico Terme I 103 A7
Caranga E 86 A4
Caranguejeira P 92 B2
Caransebeş RO 11 D7
Carantec F 56 B2
Carapelle I 104 B1
Carasco I 80 B3
Carate Brianza I 71 C4
Caravaca de la Cruz E 101 A4
Caravággio I 71 C4
Carbajal E 100 C1
Carbajo E 93 B3
Carballeda E 86 B3
Carballeda de Avia E 87 B2
Carballo E 86 A2
Carbis Bay GB 28 C2
Carbon-Blanc F 76 B2
Carbonera de Frentes E 89 C4
Carboneras E 101 C4
Carboneras de Guadazaón E 95 C5
Carbonero el Mayor E 94 A2
Carboneros E 100 A2
Carbónia I 110 C1
Carbonin I 72 B2
Carbonne F 77 C4
Carbost
Highland GB 22 D2
Highland GB 22 D2
Carcaboso E 93 A4
Carcabuey E 100 B1
Carcaixent E 96 B2
Carcans F 76 A1
Carcans-Plage F 76 A1
Carção P 87 C4
Carcar E 89 B5
Cárcare I 80 B2
Carcassonne F 77 C5
Carcastillo E 89 B5
Carcedo de Burgos E 89 B3
Carcelén E 96 B1
Carcès F 79 C5
Carchelejo E 100 B2
Çardak
Çanakkale TR 118 B1
Denizli TR 119 E4
Cardedeu E 91 B5
Cardeña E 100 A1
Cardenete E 95 C5
Cardeñosa E 94 B2
Cardeto I 109 A4
Cardiff GB 29 B4
Cardigan GB 28 A3
Cardona E 91 B4
Cardosos P 92 B2
Carei RO 11 C7
Carentan F 57 A4
Carentoir F 57 C3
Careri I 106 C3
Carevdar HR 74 B1
Cargèse F 102 A1
Carhaix-Plouguer F 56 B2
Caria P 92 A3
Cariati I 107 B3
Carignan F 59 A6
Carignano I 80 B1
Cariñena E 90 B1
Carini I 108 A2
Cariño E 86 A3
Carínola I 103 B6
Carisbrooke GB 31 D2
Carlabhagh GB 22 C2
Carlepont F 59 A4
Carlet E 96 B2
Carlingford IRL 19 B5
Carlisle GB 25 D5
Carloforte I 110 C1
Carlópoli I 106 B3
Carlow
D 44 B2
IRL 21 B5
Carlton GB 27 C4
Carluke GB 25 C4
Carmagnola I 80 B1
Carmarthen GB 28 B3
Carmaux F 77 B5
Carmena E 94 C2
Cármenes E 88 B1
Carmine I 80 B1
Carmona E 99 B5
Carmonita E 93 B4
Carmyllie GB 25 B5
Carnac F 56 C2
Carndonagh IRL 19 A4
Carnew IRL 21 B5
Carnforth GB 26 A3
Cárnia I 72 B3
Carnlough GB 19 B6
Carno GB 26 C2
Carnon Plage F 78 C2
Carnota E 86 B1
Carnoustie GB 25 B5
Carnwath GB 25 C4
Carolei I 106 B3
Carolinensiel D 43 B4
Carolles F 57 B4
Carona I 71 B4
Caronía I 109 A3
Carovigno I 104 C3
Carovilli I 103 B7
Carpaneto Piacentino I 81 B3
Carpegna I 82 C1
Carpenédolo I 71 C5
Carpentras F 79 B4
Carpi I 81 B4
Carpignano Sésia I 70 C3
Carpineti I 81 B4
Carpineto Romano I 102 B6
Cărpiniş RO 75 C5
Carpino I 104 B1
Carpinone I 103 B7
Carpio E 94 A1
Carquefou F 66 A3
Carqueiranne F 79 C5
Carral E 86 A2
Carranque E 94 B3
Carrapichana P 92 A3
Carrara I 81 B4
Carraroe IRL 20 A2
Carrascalejo E 93 B5
Carrascosa del Campo E 95 B4
Carratraca E 100 C1
Carrazeda de Ansiães P 87 C3
Carrazedo de Montenegro P 87 C3
Carrbridge GB 23 D5
Carregal do Sal P 92 A2
Carreña E 88 A2
Carrick IRL 18 B3
Carrickart IRL 19 A4
Carrickfergus GB 19 B6
Carrickmacross IRL 19 C5
Carrick-on-Shannon IRL 18 C3
Carrick-on-Suir IRL 21 B4
Carrigallen IRL 19 C4
Carrión E 99 B4
Carrión de Calatrava E 94 C3
Carrión de los Condes E 88 B2
Carrizo de la Ribera E 88 B1
Carrizosa E 100 A3
Carro F 79 C4
Carrocera E 88 B1
Carros F 79 C6
Carrouge CH 70 B1
Carrouges F 57 B5
Carrù I 80 B1
Carryduff GB 19 B6
Carry-le-Rouet F 79 C4
Carsóli I 102 A6
Carsphairn GB 24 C3
Cartagena E 101 B5
Cártama E 100 C1
Cartaxo P 92 B2
Cartaya E 98 B3
Carteret F 57 A4
Cartes E 88 A2
Carúnchio I 103 B7
Carviçais P 87 C4
Carvin F 48 C3
Carvoeira P 92 B1
Carvoeiro P 98 B2
Casabermeja E 100 C1
Casa Branca
Portalegre P 92 C3
Setúbal P 98 A2
Casacalenda I 103 B7
Casa Castalda I 82 C1
Casaio E 87 B4
Casa l'Abate I 105 C4
Casalarreina E 89 B4
Casalbordino I 103 A7
Casalborgone I 70 C2
Casalbuono I 104 C1
Casalbuttano ed Uniti I 71 C4
Casàl di Principe I 103 B7
Casalécchio di Reno I 81 B5
Casale Monferrato I 70 C3
Casalina I 82 D1
Casalmaggiore I 81 B4
Casalnuovo Monterotaro I 103 B8
Casaloldo I 71 C5
Casalpusterlengo I 71 C4
Casamássima I 104 C2
Casamicciola Terme I 103 C6
Casamozza F 102 A2
Casarabonela E 100 C1
Casarano I 107 A5
Casar de Cáceres E 93 B4
Casar de Palomero E 93 A4
Casarejos E 89 C3
Casares E 99 C5
Casares de las Hurdes E 93 A4
Casariche E 100 B1
Casarrubios del Monte E 94 B2
Casas de Don Pedro E 93 B5
Casas de Fernando Alonso E 95 C4
Casas de Haro E 95 C4
Casas de Juan Gil E 96 B1
Casas del Juan Núñez E 95 C5
Casas del Puerto E 101 A4
Casas del Rio E 96 B1
Casas de Millán E 93 B4
Casas de Reina E 99 A5
Casas de Ves E 96 B1
Casas-Ibáñez E 96 B1
Casasimarro E 95 C4
Casas Nuevas E 101 B4
Casasola E 94 B2
Casasola de Arión E 88 C1
Casasuertes E 88 A2
Casatejada E 93 B5
Casavieja E 94 B2
Casazza I 71 C4
Cascais P 92 C1
Cascante E 89 C5
Cascante del Rio E 96 A1
Cáscia I 82 D2
Casciana Terme I 81 C4
Cascina I 81 C4
Cáseda E 89 B5
Casekow D 45 B6
Casella I 80 B3
Caselle Torinese I 70 C2
Casemurate I 82 B1
Casenove I 82 D1
Caseres E 90 B3
Caserío Benali E 96 B2
Caserta I 103 B7
Casével P 98 B2
Cashel IRL 21 B4
Casillas E 94 B2
Casillas de Coria E 93 B4
Casina I 81 B4
Casinos E 96 B2
Čáslav CZ 63 A6
Cásola Valsénio I 81 B5
Cásole d'Elsa I 81 C5
Cásoli I 103 A7
Casória I 103 C7
Caspe E 90 B2
Cassàde la Selva E 91 B5
Cassagnas F 78 B2
Cassagnes-Bégonhès F 77 B5
Cassano allo Iónio I 106 B3
Cassano d'Adda I 71 C4
Cassano delle Murge I 104 C2
Cassano Magnago I 70 C3
Cassano Spinola I 80 B2
Cassel F 48 C3
Cassíbile I 109 C4
Cassine I 80 B2
Cassino I 103 B6
Cassis F 79 C4
Cassolnovo I 70 C3
Cassuéjouls F 78 B1
Častá SK 64 B3
Castagnaro I 71 C6
Castagneto Carducci I 81 C4
Castagnola CH 70 B3
Castalla E 96 C2
Castañar de Ibor E 93 B5
Castanheira de Pêra P 92 A2
Cástano Primo I 70 C3
Castasegna CH 71 B4
Castéggio I 80 A3
Casteição P 87 D3
Castejón E 89 B5
Castejón de Monegros E 90 B2
Castejón de Sos E 90 A3
Castejón de Valdejasa E 90 B2
Castèl Baronia I 103 B8
Castel Bolognese I 81 B5
Castelbuono I 109 B3
Casteldáccia I 108 A2
Castel d'Aiano I 81 B4
Castel d'Ario I 71 C5
Castel de Cabra E 90 C2
Casteldelfino I 79 B6
Castél del Monte I 103 A6
Castel del Piano I 81 D5
Castel di Iúdica I 109 B3
Castel di Rio I 81 B5
Castèl di Sangro I 103 B7
Castél di Tora I 102 A5
Castelfidardo I 82 C2
Castelfiorentino I 81 C4
Castelforte I 103 B6
Castelfranco Emília I 81 B5
Castelfranco in Miscano I 103 B8
Castelfranco Véneto I 72 C1
Castèl Frentano I 103 A7
Casteljaloux F 76 B3
Castellabate I 103 C7
Castellammare del Golfo I 108 A1
Castellammare di Stábia I 103 C7
Castellamonte I 70 C2
Castellana Grotte I 104 C3
Castellane F 79 C5
Castellaneta I 104 C2
Castellaneta Marina I 104 C2
Castellar E 100 A2
Castellarano I 81 B4
Castellar de la Frontera E 99 C5
Castellar de la Ribera E 91 A4
Castellar del Vallés E 91 B5
Castellar de Santiago E 100 A2
Castell Arquato I 81 B3
Castell'Azzara I 81 D5
Castellbell i Villar E 91 B4
Castelldans E 90 B3
Castell de Cabres E 90 C3
Castell de Castells E 96 C2
Castelldefels E 91 B4
Castell de Ferro E 100 C2
Castelleone I 71 C4
Castellet E 91 B4
Castelletto di Brenzone I 71 C5
Castellfollit de la Roca E 91 A5
Castellfollit de Riubregos E 91 B4
Castellfort E 90 C2
Castellina in Chianti I 81 C5
Castellina Marittima I 81 C4
Castellóde Farfaña E 90 B3
Castellóde la Plana E 96 B2
Castello d'Empùries E 91 A6
Castello di Fiemme I 71 B6
Castelloli E 91 B4
Castellón de Rugat E 96 C2
Castellote E 90 C2
Castello Tesino I 72 B1
Castellterçol E 91 B5
Castellúcchio I 71 C5
Castellúccio de'Sáuri I 103 B8
Castelluccio Inferiore I 106 B2
Castelmassa I 81 A5
Castelmáuro I 103 B7
Castelmoron-sur-Lot F 77 B3
Castelnaudary F 77 C4
Castelnau-de-Médoc F 76 A2
Castelnau-de-Montmirail F 77 C4
Castelnau-Magnoac F 77 C3
Castelnau-Montratier F 77 B4
Castelnou E 90 B2
Castelnovo ne'Monti I 81 B4
Castelnuovo Berardenga I 81 C5
Castelnuovo della Dáunia I 103 B8
Castelnuovo di Garfagnana I 81 B4
Castelnuovo di Val di Cécina I 81 C4
Castelnuovo Don Bosco I 80 A1
Castelnuovo Scrivia I 80 B2
Castelo Branco
Bragança P 87 C4
Castelo Branco P 92 B3
Castelo de Paiva P 87 C2
Castelo de Vide P 92 B3
Castelo do Neiva P 87 C2
Castelo Mendo P 93 A4
Castelraimondo I 82 C2
Castel San Gimignano I 81 C5
Castèl San Giovanni I 80 A3
Castèl San Pietro Terme I 81 B5
Castelsantángelo I 82 D2
Castél Sant'Elia I 102 A5
Castelsaraceno I 106 A2
Castelsardo I 110 B1
Castelsarrasin F 77 B4
Castelserás E 90 C2
Casteltérmini I 108 B2
Castelvecchio Subéquo I 103 A6
Castelvetrano I 108 B1
Castél Volturno I 103 B6
Castenédolo I 71 C5
Castets F 76 C1
Castiádas I 110 C2
Castiglioncello I 81 C4
Castiglione I 102 A6
Castiglione Chiavarese I 80 B3
Castiglione d'Adda I 71 C4
Castiglione dei Pepoli I 81 B5
Castiglione del Lago I 81 C6
Castiglione della Pescáia I 81 D4
Castiglione delle Stiviere I 71 C5
Castiglione di Sicília I 109 B4
Castiglione d'Órcia I 81 C5
Castiglione Messer Marino I 103 B7
Castiglione Messer Raimondo I 103 A6
Castiglion Fibocchi I 81 C5
Castiglion Fiorentino I 81 C5
Castilblanco E 94 C1
Castilblanco de los Arroyos E 99 B5
Castil de Peones E 89 B3
Castilfrío de la Sierra E 89 C4
Castilgaleu E 90 A3
Castilisar E 90 A1
Castilleja E 99 B4
Castillejar E 101 B3
Castillejo de Martin Viejo E 93 A4
Castillejo de Mesleón E 89 C3
Castillejo de Robledo E 89 C3
Castillo de Bayuela E 94 B2
Castillo de Locubín E 100 B2
Castillonès F 77 B3
Castillon-la-Bataille F 76 B2
Castillon-Len-Couserans F 77 D4
Castillonroy E 90 B3
Castilruiz E 89 C4
Castione CH 70 B4
Castions di Strada I 72 C3
Castirla F 102 A2
Castlebar IRL 18 C2
Castlebellingham IRL 19 C5
Castleblaney IRL 19 B5
Castlebridge IRL 21 B5
Castle Cary GB 29 B5
Castlecomer IRL 21 B4
Castlederg GB 19 B4
Castledermot IRL 21 B5
Castle Douglas GB 25 D4
Castleford GB 27 B4
Castleisland IRL 20 B2
Castlemaine IRL 20 B2
Castlemartyr IRL 20 C3
Castlepollard IRL 19 C4
Castlerea IRL 18 C3
Castleton GB 27 B4
Castletown
Highland GB 23 C5
Isle of Man GB 26 A1
Castletown Bearhaven IRL 20 C2
Castletownroche IRL 20 B3
Castlewellan GB 19 B6
Casto I 71 C5
Castrejón E 88 C1
Castrelo del Valle E 87 B3
Castres F 77 C5
Castricum NL 42 C1
Castries F 78 C2
Castrignano del Capo I 107 B5
Castril E 101 B3
Castrillo de Duero E 88 C3
Castrillo de la Vega E 88 C3
Castrillo de Onielo E 88 C2
Castro
E 88 A2
I 107 A5
Castrocabón E 88 B1
Castro-Caldelas E 87 B3
Castrocaro Terme I 81 B5
Castrocontrigo E 87 B4
Castro Daire P 87 D3
Castro dei Volsci I 103 B6
Castro del Río E 100 B1
Castro de Rey E 86 A3
Castrofilippo I 108 B2

Castrogonzaio E 88 B2
Castrojeriz E 88 B2
Castro Laboreiro P . . .87 B2
Castro Marim P 98 B3
Castromonte E 88 C1
Castromudarra E 88 B1
Castronuevo E 88 C1
Castronuño E 88 C1
Castropol E 86 A3
Castroreale I 109 A4
Castroserracin E 88 C3
Castro-Urdiales E 89 A3
Castroverde E 86 A3
Castro Verde P 98 B2
Castroverde de Campos
E 88 C1
Castroverde de Cerrato
E 88 C2
Castrovillari I 106 B3
Castuera E 93 C5
Catadau E 96 B2
Cataéggio I 71 B4
Çatalca TR 118 A3
Çatallar TR 119 F5
Catánia I 109 B4
Catanzaro I 106 C3
Catanzaro Marina I . .106 C3
Catarroja E 96 B2
Catarruchas E 92 A2
Catcleugh GB 25 C5
Catenanuova I 109 B3
Caterham GB 31 C3
Cati E 90 C3
Čatići BIH 84 B3
Catignano I 103 A6
Catillon F 49 C4
Catoira E 86 B2
Caton GB 26 A3
Catral E 101 A5
Catterick GB 27 A4
Cáttolica I 82 C1
Cáttolica Eraclea I . .108 B2
Catton GB 25 D5
Caudebec-en-Caux F .58 A1
Caudete E 101 A5
Caudete de las Fuentes
E 96 B1
Caudiel E 96 B2
Caudiès-de-Fenouillèdes
F 77 D5
Caudry F 49 C4
Caulkerbush GB 25 D4
Caulnes F 57 B3
Caulónia I 106 C3
Caumont-l'Evente F . .57 A5
Caunes-Minervois F . .77 C5
Cauro F 102 B1
Caussade F 77 B4
Causse-de-la-Selle F . .78 C2
Cauterets F 76 D2
Cava de'Tirreni I 103 C7
Cavaglia I 70 C3
Cavaleiro P 98 B2
Cavalese I 71 B6
Cavallermaggiore I . . .80 B1
Cavallino I 72 C2
Cavan IRL 19 C4
Cavárzere I 72 C2
Çavdarhisar TR 118 C4
Çavdir TR 119 E4
Cavernães P 87 D3
Cavezzo I 81 B5
Cavignac F 76 A2
Cavle HR 73 C4
Cavo I 81 D4
Cavour I 80 B1
Cavtat HR 84 D3
Cawdor GB 23 D5
Çay TR 118 D6
Çaycuma TR 118 A7
Cayeux-sur-Mer F 48 C2
Çayiralan TR 16 B7
Çayirhan TR 118 B6
Caylus F 77 B4
Cayres F 78 B2
Cazalilla E 100 B2
Cazalla de la Sierra E .99 B5
Cazals F 77 B4
Cazanuecos E 88 B1
Cazaubon F 76 C2
Cazaux F 76 B1
Cazavet F 77 C4
Cazères F 77 C4
Cazin BIH 83 B4
Čazis CH 71 B4
Čazma HR 74 C1
Cazo E 88 A1
Cazorla E 100 B3
Cazouls-lès-Béziers
F 78 C2
Cea
  León E 88 B1
  Orense E 86 B3
Ceánuri E 89 A4
Ceauce F 57 B5
Cebolla E 94 C2
Cebreros E 94 B2
Čeccano I 103 B6
Cece H 74 B3
Ceconowo PL 47 A4
Čechtice CZ 63 A6
Čechtin CZ 64 A1
Cécina I 81 C4
Ceclavín E 93 B4
Cedégolo I 71 B5
Cedeira E 86 A2
Cedillo E 92 B3
Cedillo del Condado
E 94 B3
Cedrillas E 90 C2
Cedeira I 86 B1
Cée E 86 B1
Céggia I 72 C2
Cegléd H 75 A4
Céglie Messápica I . .104 C3
Cehegín E 101 A4
Ceilhes-et-Rocozels
F 78 C2
Ceinos de Campos E .88 B1
Ceira P 92 A2
Čejč CZ 64 B2
Cekcyn PL 47 B4
Čela BIH 83 B5
Čelákovice CZ 53 C4
Celano I 103 A6
Celanova E 87 B3
Celbridge IRL 21 A5
Čelebić BIH 83 C5
Celenza Valfortore I .103 B7
Čelić BIH 84 B3
Čelinac BIH 84 B2
Celje SLO 73 B5
Cella E 95 B5
Celldömölk H 74 A2
Celle D 44 C2
Celle Ligure I 80 B2
Celles B 49 C5
Celles-sur-Belle F 67 B4
Cellino San Marco I . .105 C3
Celorico da Beira P . . .92 A3
Celorico de Basto P . .87 C2
Çeltik TR 118 C6
Çeltikçi TR 119 E5
Cemaes GB 26 B1
Cembra I 71 B6
Čemerno BIH 84 C3
Cenad RO 75 B5
Cencenighe Agordino
I 72 B1
Cenei RO 75 C5
Ceneselli I 81 A5
Cenicero E 89 B4

Cenicientos E 94 B2
Čenseau F 69 B6
Centa SRB 85 A5
Centallo I 80 B1
Centelles E 91 B5
Cento I 81 B5
Centúripe I 109 B3
Cepeda la Mora E 94 B1
Čepin HR 74 C3
Čepinski Martinci HR .74 C3
Čepovan SLO 72 B3
Ceprano I 103 B6
Čeralije HR 74 C2
Cerami I 109 B3
Cerano I 70 C3
Cérans Foulletourte
F 57 C6
Ceraso I 106 A2
Cerbaia I 81 C5
Cerbère F 91 A6
Cercadillo E 95 A4
Cercal
  Lisboa P 92 B1
  Setúbal P 98 B2
Čerčany CZ 63 A5
Cercedilla E 94 B3
Cercemaggiore I 103 B7
Cercs E 91 A4
Cerdedo E 86 B2
Cerdedo F 93 A3
Cerdon F 58 C3
Cerea I 71 C6
Ceres
  GB 25 B5
  I 70 C2
Ceres e I 81 A4
Ceresole-Reale I 70 C2
Céret F 79 C4
Cerezo de Abajo E . . .95 A3
Cerezo de Riotirón E .89 B3
Cerfontaine B 49 C5
Cergy F 58 A3
Cerignola I 104 B1
Cérilly F 68 B2
Cerisiers F 59 B4
Cerizay F 67 B4
Çerkeş TR 16 A6
Çerkezköy TR 118 A3
Cerkije SLO 73 B4
Cerknica SLO 73 C4
Cerkno SLO 72 B3
Çermë-Proshkë AL . .105 B5
Cermenate I 74 C3
Černá Hora CZ 64 A2
Cernavodă RO 11 D10
Cernay F 60 C3
Cerne Abbas GB 29 C5
Cernégula E 89 B3
Černik HR 74 C2
Černóbbio I 70 C4
Cernovice CZ 63 A5
Cerqueto I 82 D1
Černošin CZ 62 A3
Cérons F 76 B2
Cerovlje HR 73 C4
Cerovo SK 65 B5
Cerqueto I 82 D1
Cerreto d'Esi I 82 C1
Cerreto Sannita I 103 B7
Cerrigydrudion GB . . .26 B2
Čerrik AL 105 B5
Cerro Muriano E 100 A1
Certaldo I 81 C5
Certosa di Pésio I 80 B1
Cerva P 87 C3
Cervatos de la Cueza
E 88 B2
Červená Řečice CZ . . .63 A6
Červená-Skala SK 65 B6
Červený Kostelec CZ .53 C6
Cervera E 91 B4
Cervera de la Cañada
E 89 C5
Cervera del Llano E . .95 C4
Cervera del Río Alhama
E 89 B5
Cervera de Pisuerga
E 88 B2
Cervéteri I 102 B5
Cérvia I 82 B1
Cerviá les Garriques
E 90 B3
Cervignano del Friuli
I 72 C3
Cervinara I 103 B7
Cervione F 102 A2
Cervon F 68 A3
Cervo E 86 A3
Cesana Torinese I 79 A5
Cesarica HR 83 B4
Cesarò I 109 B3
Cesena I 82 B1
Cesenático I 82 B1
Cēsis LV 7 C8
Česká Bělá CZ 63 A6
Česká Kamenice CZ . .53 C4
Česká Lípa CZ 53 C4
Česká Třebová CZ . . .64 A2
České Budějovice CZ .63 B5
České Velenice CZ . . .63 B5
Český Brod CZ 53 C4
Český Dub CZ 53 C4
Český Krumlov CZ . . .63 B5
Český Těšín CZ 65 A4
Čestobrodica SRB 85 C5
Čestas F 76 B2
Čestobrodica SRB 85 C5
Cesuras E 86 A2
Cetina E 89 C5
Cetin Grad HR 73 C5
Cetinje MNE 105 A4
Cetraro I 106 B2
Ceuta E 99 D5
Ceuti E 101 A4
Ceva I 80 B2
Cévico de la Torre E . .88 C2
Cévico Navero E 88 C2
Cévio CH 70 B3
Çevizli TR 119 E6
Cewice PL 46 A3
Ceyhan TR 16 C7
Ceylan TR 119 F4
Ceyrat F 68 C3
Ceyzériat F 69 B5
Chaam NL 49 B5
Chabanais F 67 C5
Chabeuil F 79 B4
Chabielice PL 55 B4
ChabÓwka PL 65 A5
Chabreloche F 68 C3
Chabris F 67 A6
Chagford GB 28 C4
Chagny F 69 B4
Chagoda RUS 7 B13
Chaherrero E 94 B2
Chailland F 57 B5
Chaillé-les-Marais F . .66 B3
Chailley F 59 B4
Chailluz F 69 A6
Chalabre F 77 D5
Chalais F 67 C5
Chalamont F 69 C5
Châlette-sur-Loing F . .58 B3
Chalindrey F 59 C6
Chalkida GR 116 D5
Challacombe GB 28 B4
Challans F 66 B3

Challes-les-Eaux F . . .69 C5
Chalmazel F 68 C3
Chalmoux F 68 B3
Chalonnes-sur-Loire
F 66 A4
Châlons-en-Champagne
F 59 B5
Chalon-sur-Saône F . .69 B4
Chalupy PL 47 A4
Châlus F 67 C5
Cham
  CH 70 A3
  D 62 B3
Chamberet F 68 C1
Chambéry F 69 C5
Chambilly F 68 B4
Chambley F 60 A1
Chambly F 58 A3
Chambois F 57 B6
Chambon-sur-Lac F . .68 C2
Chambon-sur-Voueize
F 68 B2
Chambord F 58 C2
Chamborigaud F 78 B2
Chamboulive F 68 C1
Chamerau D 62 A3
Chamonix-Mont Blanc
F 70 C1
Chamoux-sur-Gelon
F 69 C6
Champagnac-le-Vieux
F 68 C3
Champagney F 60 C2
Champagnole F 69 B5
Champagny-Mouton
F 67 B5
Champaubert F 59 B4
Champdeniers-St Denis
F 67 B4
Champdieu F 68 C4
Champdôtre F 69 A5
Champeix F 68 C3
Champéry CH 70 B1
Champigné F 57 C5
Champignelles F 59 C4
Champigny-sur-Veude
F 67 A5
Champlitte-et-le-Prelot
F 60 C1
Champoluc I 70 C2
Champoly F 68 C3
Champorcher I 70 C2
Champrond-en-Gâtine
F 58 B2
Champs-sur-Tarentaine
F 68 C2
Champs-sur-Yonne F .59 C4
Champtoceaux F 66 A3
Chamrousse F 69 C5
Chamusca P 92 B2
Chanac F 78 B2
Chanaleiro F 71 B6
Chandler's Ford GB . .31 D2
Chandra GR 117 G8
Chandrexa de Queixa
E 87 B3
Chañe E 88 C2
Changy F 68 B4
Chania GR 117 G6
Channes F 59 C5
Chantada E 86 B3
Chantelle F 68 B3
Chantenay-St Imbert
F 68 B3
Chanteuges F 78 A2
Chantilly F 58 A3
Chantonnay F 66 B3
Chão de Codes P 92 B2
Chaource F 59 B4
Chapa E 86 B2
Chapareillan F 69 C5
Chapel en le Frith GB .27 B4
Chapelle Royale F 58 B2
Chapelle-St Laurent F .67 B4
Charbonnat F 68 B4
Chard GB 29 C5
Charenton-du-Cher F .68 B2
Charlbury GB 31 C2
Charleroi B 49 C5
Charlestown
  GB 28 C3
  IRL 18 C3
Charlestown of Aberlour
GB 23 D5
Charleville IRL 20 B3
Charleville-Mézières
F 59 A5
Charlieu F 68 B4
Charlottenberg S 34 C4
Charlton Kings GB . . .29 B5
Charly F 59 B4
Charmes F 60 B2
Charmes-sur-Rhône
F 78 B3
Charmey CH 70 B2
Charminster GB 29 C5
Charmont-en-Beauce
F 58 B3
Charny F 59 C4
Charolles F 69 B4
Chârost F 68 B2
Charquemont F 70 A1
Charrin F 68 B3
Charroux F 67 B5
Chartres F 58 B2
Charzykowy PL 46 B3
Chasseneuil-sur-
  Bonnieure F 67 C5
Chassigny F 59 C6
Château-Arnoux F 79 B5
Châteaubernard F 67 C4
Châteaubourg F 57 B4
Châteaubriant F 57 C4
Château-Chinon F 68 A3
Château-d'Oex CH . . .70 B2
Château-d'Olonne F . .66 B3
Château-du-Loir F 58 C1
Châteaudun F 58 B2
Châteaugiron F 57 B4
Château-Gontier F . . .57 C5
Château-Landon F 58 B3
Château-la-Vallière F .58 C1
Château-l'Evêque F . . .67 C5
Châteaulin F 56 B1
Châteaumeillant F 68 B2
Châteauneuf
  Nièvre F 68 A3
  Saône-et-Loire F . . .69 B4
Châteauneuf-de-Randon
F 78 B2
Châteauneuf-d'Ille-et-
  Vilaine F 57 B4
Châteauneuf-du-Faou
F 56 B2
Châteauneuf-du-Pape
F 78 B3
Châteauneuf-en-
  Thymerais F 58 B2
Châteauneuf la-Forêt
F 67 C6
Châteauneuf-le-Rouge
F 79 C4
Châteauneuf-sur-
  Charente F 67 C4
Châteauneuf-sur-Cher
F 68 B2
Châteauneuf-sur-Loire
F 58 C3
Châteauneuf-sur-Sarthe
F 57 C5
Châteauponsac F 67 B6
Châteauporcien F 59 A5
Châteauredon F 79 B5
Châteaurenard
  Bouches du Rhône
  F 78 C3
  Loiret F 59 C3
Château-Renault F . . .58 C1
Châteauroux F 68 B1
Châteauroux-les-Alpes
F 79 B5
Château-Salins F 60 B2

Château-Thierry F 59 A4
Châteauvillain F 59 B5
Châtel F 70 B1
Châtelaillon-Plage F . .66 B3
Châtelaudren F 56 B3
Châtel-Censoir F 68 A3
Châtel-de-Neuvre F . .68 B3
Châtelet B 49 C5
Châtelguyon F 68 C3
Châtellerault F 67 B5
Châtel-Montagne F . . .68 B3
Châtel-St Denis CH . . .70 B1
Châtel-sur-Moselle F . .60 B2
Châtelus-Malvaleix F . .68 B2
Châtenois F 60 B1
Châtenois-les-Forges
F 70 A1
Chatham GB 31 C4
Châtillon I 70 C2
Châtillon-Coligny F . . .59 C3
Châtillon-en-Bazois
F 68 A3
Châtillon-en-Diois F . .79 B4
Châtillon-sur-Chalaronne
F 69 B4
Châtillon-sur-Indre F . .67 B6
Châtillon-sur-Loire F . .58 C3
Châtillon-sur-Marne
F 59 A4
Châtillon-sur-Seine F . .59 C5
Châtres F 59 B4
Chatteris GB 30 B4
Chatton GB 25 C6
Chauchina E 100 B2
Chaudes-Aigues F 78 B2
Chaudrey F 59 B5
Chauffailles F 69 B4
Chaulnes F 58 A3
Chaument Gistoux B . .49 C5
Chaumergy F 69 B5
Chaumont F 59 B6
Chaumont-en-Vexin F .58 A2
Chaumont-Porcien F . .59 A5
Chaumont-sur-Aire F . .59 B6
Chaumont-sur-Loire
F 58 C2
Chaunay F 67 B5
Chauny F 59 A4
Chaussin F 69 B5
Chauvigny F 67 B5
Chavagnes-en-Paillers
F 66 B3
Chavanges F 59 B5
Chaves P 87 C3
Chavignon F 59 A4
Chazelles-sur-Lyon F .69 C4
Chazey-Bons F 69 C5
Cheadle
  Greater Manchester
  GB 26 B3
  Staffordshire GB . . .27 C4
Cheb CZ 52 C2
Chebsara RUS 7 B15
Checa E 95 B5
Cheddar GB 29 B5
Cheddleton GB 27 B4
Chef-Boutonne F 67 B4
Chekalin RUS 7 D14
Chekhovo RUS 47 A6
Cheles E 93 C3
Chella E 96 B2
Chelles F 58 B3
Chełm PL 11 A7
Chelmno
  Kujawsko-Pomorskie
  PL 47 B4
  Wielkopolskie PL . . .46 C2
Chelmsford GB 31 C4
Chelmża PL 47 B4
Cheltenham GB 29 B5
Chelva E 96 B1
Chémery F 67 A6
Chemery-sur-Bar F . . .59 A5
Chemillé F 67 A4
Chemin F 69 B5
Chemnitz D 52 C2
Chénerailles F 68 B2
Cheniménil F 60 B2
Chenonceaux F 67 A6
Chenôve F 69 A4
Chepelare BG 116 A6
Chepstow GB 29 B5
Chera E 96 B2
Cherasco I 80 B1
Cherbonnières F 67 C4
Cherbourg F 57 A4
Cherchiara di Calábria
I 106 B3
Cherepovets RUS . . .7 B14
Cherkasy UA 11 B12
Chernihiv UA 7 F11
Chernivtsi UA 11 B8
Chernobyl = Chornobyl
UA 7 F11
Chernyakhovsk RUS . .6 D6
Chéroy F 59 B3
Cherven BY 7 E10
Chervonohrad UA 11 A8
Cherykaw BY 7 E11
Chesham GB 31 C3
Cheshunt GB 31 C3
Chessy-lès-Pres F 59 B4
Cheste E 96 B2
Chester GB 26 B3
Chesterfield GB 27 B4
Chester-le-Street GB . .25 D6
Chevagnes F 68 B3
Chevanceaux F 67 C4
Chevillon F 59 B6
Chevilly F 58 B2
Chew Magna GB 29 B5
Chézery-Forens F 69 B5
Chialamberto I 70 C2
Chiampo I 71 C6
Chianale I 79 B6
Chianciano Terme I . . .81 C5
Chiaramonte Gulfi I . .109 B3
Chiaramonti I 110 B1
Chiaravalle I 82 C2
Chiaravalle Centrale
I 106 C3
Chiaréggio I 71 B4
Chiari I 71 C4
Chiaromonte I 106 A3
Chiasso CH 70 C4
Chiávari I 80 B3
Chiavenna I 71 B4
Chiché F 67 B4
Chichester GB 31 D3
Chiclana de la Frontera
E 99 C4
Chiclana de Segura
E 100 A2
Chiddingfold GB 31 C3
Chieri I 80 A1
Chiesa in Valmalenco
I 71 B4
Chieti I 103 A7
Chieti Scalo I 103 A7
Chiéuti I 103 B8
Chigirin UA 11 B12
Chigwell GB 31 C4
Chiliomodi GR 117 E4
Chillarón de Cuenca
E 95 B4
Chillarón del Rey E . . .95 B4
Chilleurs-aux-Bois F . .58 B3
Chillón E 100 A1
Chilluevar E 100 B2
Chiloeches E 95 B3
Chimay B 49 C5
Chimeneas E 100 B2
Chinchilla de Monte
  Aragón E 96 C1
Chinchón E 95 B3
Chingford GB 31 C4
Chinon F 67 A5
Chióggia I 72 C2
Chiomonte I 79 A5
Chipiona E 99 C4
Chippenham GB 29 B5

Chipping Campden
GB 29 A6
Chipping Norton GB . .31 C2
Chipping Ongar GB . . .31 C4
Chipping Sodbury
GB 29 B5
Chirac F 78 B2
Chirbury GB 26 C2
Chirens F 69 C5
Chirivel E 101 B3
Chirk GB 26 C2
Chirnside GB 25 C5
Chişinău = Khisinev
MD 11 C10
Chişineu Criş RO 75 B6
Chissey-en-Morvan F .69 A4
Chiusa I 71 B6
Chiusa di Pésio I 80 B1
Chiusaforte I 72 B3
Chiusa Scláfani I 108 B2
Chiusi I 81 C5
Chiva E 96 B2
Chivasso I 70 C2
Chlewiska PL 55 B5
Chludowo PL 46 C2
Chlumec nad Cidlinou
CZ 53 C5
Chlum u Třeboně CZ . .63 B5
Chmielnik PL 55 C5
Chobienia PL 53 A5
Chobienice PL 53 A5
Choceń CZ 53 D6
Chocen PL 47 C5
Chochołów PL 65 A5
Chocianów PL 53 B5
Chociw PL 55 B4
Chociwel PL 46 B1
Choczewo PL 46 A3
Chodaków PL 55 A5
Chodecz PL 47 C5
Chodov CZ 52 C2
Chodzież PL 46 C2
Chojna PL 45 C6
Chojnice PL 46 B3
Chojno
  Kujawsko-Pomorskie
  PL 47 C5
  Wielkopolskie PL . . .46 C2
Chojnów PL 53 B5
Cholet F 66 A4
Chomérac F 78 B3
Chomutov CZ 52 C3
Chop UA 11 B7
Chora GR 117 E3
Chora Stakion GR . . .117 G6
Chorges F 79 B5
Choristanco E 86 A2
Chorley GB 26 B3
Chornobyl = Chernobyl
UA 7 F11
Chortkiv UA 11 B8
Chorzele PL 47 B6
Chorzów PL 54 C3
Choszczno PL 46 B1
Chotcza-Józefów PL . .55 B6
Chotěboř CZ 63 A6
Chouilly F 59 A5
Chouto P 92 B2
Chouzy-sur-Cisse F . . .58 C2
Chozas de Abajo E . . .88 B1
Chrast CZ 64 A1
Chrást CZ 63 A4
Chrastava CZ 53 C4
Chřibská CZ 53 C4
Christchurch GB 29 C6
Christiansfeld DK 39 D2
Chroberz PL 55 C5
Chropyně CZ 64 A3
Chrudim CZ 53 D5
Chrzanów PL 55 C4
Chtelnica SK 64 B3
Chudovo RUS 7 B11
Chueca E 94 C3
Chulmleigh GB 28 C4
Chur CH 71 B4
Church Stretton GB . . .26 C3
Churchdown GB 29 B5
Churriana E 100 C1
Churwalden CH 71 B4
Chvalšiny CZ 63 B5
Chwaszczyno PL 47 A4
Chynava CZ 53 C4
Chýnov CZ 63 A5
Ciacova RO 75 C6
Ciadîr-Lunga MD 11 C10
Ciadoncha E 88 B3
Cianciana I 108 B2
Ciano d'Enza I 81 B4
Ciążeń PL 46 C3
Cibakhaza H 75 B5
Ciborro P 92 C2
Cicagna I 80 B3
Cicciano I 103 C7
Cicognolo I 71 C5
Cidadelhe P 87 D3
Cide TR 16 A6
Cidones E 89 C4
Ciechanów
  Dolnośląskie PL . . .54 B1
  Mazowieckie PL . . .47 C6
Ciechocinek PL 47 C4
Cieladz PL 55 B5
Ciemnik PL 46 B1
Ciempozuelos E 95 B3
Ciepielów PL 55 B6
Cierny Balog SK 65 B5
Cierp-Gaud F 77 D3
Cierpice PL 47 C4
Ciervana E 89 A3
Cierznie PL 46 B3
Cieslé PL 47 C6
Cieszanów PL 11 A7
Cieszyn PL 65 A4
Cieutat F 76 C3
Cieza E 101 A4
Cifer SK 64 B3
Çifteler TR 118 C6
Cifuentes E 95 B4
Cigales E 88 C2
Cigliano I 70 C3
Cihanbeyli TR 16 B6
Çıldır TR 105 A4
Cillas E 95 B5
Cilleros E 93 A4
Cilleruelo de Arriba E .88 C3
Cilleruelo de Bezana
E 88 B3
Cimalmotto CH 70 B3
Cimanes del Tejar E . .88 B1
Ciminna I 108 B2
Cimişlia MD 11 C10
Cimolais I 72 B2
Câmpulung RO 11 D8
Çınarcık TR 118 B4
Çınartepe TR 118 A6
Çıncirres E 90 C2
Çine TR 119 E3
Cínfaes P 87 C2
Cingia de Botti I 81 A4
Cíngoli I 82 C2
Cinigiano I 81 D5
Cinobaña SK 65 B5
Cinq-Mars-la-Pile F . . .67 A5
Cinquefrondi I 106 C3
Cintegabelle F 77 C4
Cintruénigo E 89 B5
Ciólkowo PL 47 C5
Ciperez E 87 D4
Cirat E 96 A2
Cirella I 106 B2
Cirencester GB 29 B6
Cirey F 60 B2
Ciria E 89 C5
Ciriè I 70 C2
Cirigliano I 104 C1
Cirò I 107 B3
Cirò Marina I 107 B3
Ciry-le-Noble F 69 B4
Cislău RO 11 D9
Cismon del Grappa I . .72 C1

Cisneros E 88 B2
Cissac-Médoc F 66 C4
Cista CZ 52 C3
Cisterna di Latina I . .102 B5
Cisternino I 104 C3
Cistierna E 88 B1
Citluk BIH 84 C2
Čitov CZ 53 C4
Cittadella I 72 C1
Cittàdel Pieve I 81 D6
Cittàdel Vaticano =
  Vatican City I 102 B5
Cittàdi Castello I 82 C1
Cittaducale I 102 A5
Cittanova I 106 C3
Città Sant'Angelo I . .103 A7
Ciudad Real E 94 D3
Ciudad Rodrigo E 93 A4
Ciutadilla E 91 B4
Cividale del Friuli I . . .72 B3
Civita I 106 B3
Civita Castellana I . . .102 A5
Civitanova Alta I 82 C2
Civitanova Marche I . .82 C2
Civitavécchia I 102 A4
Civitella di Romagna
I 81 B5
Civitella di Tronto I . . .82 D2
Civitella Roveto I 103 B6
Civray F 67 B5
Çivril TR 119 D4
Cizur Mayor E 76 D1
Clabhach GB 24 B1
Clachan GB 22 D2
Clachan na Luib GB . .22 D1
Clacton-on-Sea GB . . .31 C5
Cladich GB 24 B2
Claggan GB 24 B2
Clairvaux-les-Lacs F . .69 B5
Clamecy F 68 A3
Claonaig GB 24 C2
Clarecastle IRL 20 B3
Claregalway IRL 20 A3
Claremorris IRL 18 C2
Clarinbridge IRL 20 A3
Clashmore
  GB 23 D4
  IRL 21 B4
Claudy GB 19 B4
Clausthal-Zellerfeld D .51 B6
Cláut I 72 B2
Clavering GB 31 C4
Claye-Souilly F 58 B3
Cléder F 56 B1
Cleethorpes GB 27 B5
Clefmont F 60 B1
Cléguérec F 56 B2
Clelles F 79 B4
Clémont F 58 A4
Clenze D 44 C2
Cléon-d'Andran F 78 B3
Cléré-les-Pins F 67 A5
Clères F 58 A2
Clermont F 58 A3
Clermont-en-Argonne
F 59 A6
Clermont-Ferrand F . . .68 C3
Clermont-l'Hérault F . .78 C2
Clerval F 69 A6
Clervaux L 50 C2
Cléry-St André F 58 C2
Cles I 71 B6
Clevedon GB 29 B5
Cleveleys GB 26 B2
Cley GB 30 B5
Clifden IRL 18 C1
Clifford GB 29 A4
Clisson F 66 A3
Clitheroe GB 26 B3
Clogh IRL 21 B4
Cloghan
  Donegal IRL 19 B4
  Offaly IRL 21 A4
Clogheen IRL 21 B4
Clogher GB 19 B4
Cloghjordan IRL 20 B3
Clonakilty IRL 20 C3
Clonard IRL 21 A4
Clonaslee IRL 21 A4
Clondalkin IRL 21 A5
Clones IRL 19 B4
Clonmany IRL 19 A4
Clonmel IRL 21 B4
Clonmellon IRL 21 A4
Clonord IRL 21 A4
Clonroche IRL 21 B5
Cloone IRL 19 C4
Cloppenburg D 43 C5
Closeburn GB 25 C4
Clough GB 19 B6
Clova GB 25 B4
Clovelly GB 28 C3
Clowne GB 27 B4
Cloyes-sur-le-Loir F . .58 C2
Cloyne IRL 20 C3
Cluis F 68 B1
Cluj-Napoca RO 11 C7
Clun GB 26 C2
Clunes GB 24 B3
Cluny F 69 B4
Cluses F 69 B6
Clusone I 71 C4
Clydach GB 28 B4
Clydebank GB 24 C3
Coachford IRL 20 C3
Coagh GB 19 B5
Coalisland GB 19 B5
Coalville GB 27 C4
Coaña E 86 A4
Çobanlar TR 118 D5
Cobas E 86 A2
Cóbreces E 88 A2
Cóbh IRL 20 C3
Cobreces E 88 A2
Coca E 94 A2
Cocentaina E 96 C2
Cochem D 50 C3
Cockburnspath GB . . .25 C5
Cockermouth GB 26 A2
Codigoro I 82 B1
Codogno I 71 C4
Codos E 89 C5
Codróipo I 72 C2
Codrongianos I 110 B1
Coelhoso P 87 C4
Coesfeld D 50 B3
Coevorden NL 42 C3
Cofrentes E 96 B1
Cogeces del Monte E .88 C2
Coggeshall GB 31 C4
Cognac F 67 C4
Cognein F 70 C2
Cogolin F 79 C5
Cogollos de Guadix
E 100 B2
Cogollos-Vega E 100 B2
Cogolludo E 95 B3
Coimbra P 92 A2
Coin E 100 C1
Coirós E 86 A2
Čoka SRB 75 C5
Col SLO 73 C4
Colares P 92 C1
Cölbe D 51 C4
Colbitz D 52 A1
Colchester GB 31 C4
Coldingham GB 25 C5
Colditz D 52 B2
Coldstream GB 25 C5
Colebrooke GB 28 C4
Colera E 91 A6
Coleraine GB 19 A5
Colfiorito I 82 C1
Cólico I 71 B4
Coligny F 69 B5

Colindres E 89 A3
Collado-Mediano E . . .94 B2
Collado Villalba E 94 B3
Collagna I 81 B4
Collanzo E 88 A1
Coll de Nargó E 91 A4
Collécchio I 81 B4
Colledimezzo I 103 B7
Colle di Val d'Elsa I . . .81 C5
Colle Isarco I 71 B6
Collelongo I 103 B6
Collepasso I 107 A5
Collepepe I 82 D1
Collesalvetti I 81 C4
Colle Sannita I 103 B7
Collesano I 108 B2
Colli a Volturno I 103 B7
Collin GB 25 C4
Collinée F 56 B3
Collingham
  Nottinghamshire
  GB 27 B5
  West Yorkshire GB . .27 B4
Collinghorst D 43 B4
Cóllio I 71 C5
Collobrières F 79 C5
Collon IRL 19 C5
Collooney IRL 18 B3
Colmar F 60 B3
Colmars F 79 B5
Colmenar E 100 C1
Colmenar de la Sierra
E 95 A3
Colmenar de Oreja E .95 B3
Colmenar Viejo E 94 B3
Colmonell GB 24 C3
Colne GB 26 B3
Colobraro I 106 A3
Cologna Véneta I 71 C6
Cologne = Köln D 50 C2
Cologne al Serio I 71 C4
Colombey-les-deux-
  Églises F 59 B5
Colombres E 88 A2
Colomera E 100 B2
Colomers E 91 A5
Colomiers F 77 C4
Colònia de Sant Jordi
E 97 B3
Colorno I 81 B4
Colos P 98 B2
Cölpin D 45 B5
Colpy GB 23 D6
Colsterworth GB 30 B3
Coltishall GB 30 B5
Colunga E 88 A1
Colwell GB 25 C5
Colwyn Bay GB 26 B2
Colyford GB 29 C4
Comácchio I 82 B1
Coma-ruga E 91 B4
Combarros E 88 B4
Combeaufontaine F . . .60 C1
Comber GB 19 B6
Combloux F 70 C1
Combourg F 57 B4
Combronde F 68 C3
Comeglians I 72 B2
Comillas E 88 A2
Cómiso I 109 C3
Comloşu Mare RO . . .75 C5
Commensacq F 76 B2
Commentry F 68 B2
Commerau D 53 B4
Commercy F 60 B1
Como I 71 C4
Cómpeta E 100 C2
Compiègne F 58 A3
Comporta P 92 C2
Comps-sur-Artuby F . .79 C5
Comrat MD 11 C10
Comrie GB 25 B4
Comunanza I 82 D2
Cona
  Emilia Romagna I . .81 B5
  Veneto I 72 C2
Concarneau F 56 C2
Conceição P 98 B2
Conches-en-Ouche F . .58 B1
Concordia Sagittária
I 72 C2
Concordia sulla Sécchia
I 81 B4
Concots F 77 B4
Condat F 68 C2
Condé-en-Brie F 59 B4
Condeixa P 92 A2
Condé-sur-l'Escaut F . .49 C4
Condé-sur-Marne F . . .59 B5
Condé-sur-Noireau F . .57 B5
Condino I 71 C5
Condom F 77 C3
Condove I 70 C2
Condrieu F 69 C4
Conegliano I 72 C2
Conflans-sur-Lanterne
F 60 C2
Confolens F 67 B5
Conforto E 86 A3
Cong IRL 18 C2
Congleton GB 26 B3
Congosto de Valdavia
E 88 B2
Congostrina E 95 A3
Conil de la Frontera
E 99 C4
Coningsby GB 27 B5
Coniston GB 26 A2
Conlie F 57 B5
Conliège F 69 B5
Conna IRL 20 C3
Connah's Quay GB . . .26 B2
Connaux F 78 B3
Connel GB 24 B2
Connerré F 58 B1
Cononbridge GB 23 D4
Conoplja SRB 75 C4
Conques-sur-Orbiel F .77 C5
Conquista E 100 A1
Conquista de la Sierra
E 93 B5
Consándolo I 81 B5
Consélice I 81 B5
Conselve I 72 C1
Consenvoye F 59 A6
Consett GB 25 D6
Consolação P 92 B1
Constancia P 92 B2
Constanța RO 11 D10
Constanti E 91 B4
Constantina E 99 B5
Consuegra E 95 C3
Consuma I 81 C5
Contarina I 72 C2
Contay F 48 D3
Conthey CH 70 B2
Contigliano I 102 A5
Contis-Plage F 76 B1
Contrada I 103 C7
Contres F 58 C2
Contrexéville F 60 B1
Controne I 103 C8
Contursi Termi I 103 C8
Conty F 58 A3
Conversano I 104 C3
Conwy GB 26 B2
Cookstown GB 19 B5

Coole F 59 B5
Coolgreany IRL 21 B5
Cooneen GB 19 B4
Cootehill IRL 19 B4
Cope E 101 B4
Copenhagen =
  København DK 41 D2
Copertino I 105 C4
Copparo I 81 B5
Coppenbrugge D 51 A5
Corabia RO 11 E8
Córaci I 106 B3
Coralići BIH 83 B4
Corato I 104 B2
Coray F 56 B2
Corbeil-Essonnes F . . .58 B3
Corbera E 96 B2
Corbie F 58 A3
Corbigny F 68 A3
Corbridge GB 25 D5
Corby GB 30 B3
Corconte E 88 A3
Corcubión E 86 B1
Cordenons I 72 C2
Cordes-sur-Ciel F 77 B4
Córdoba E 100 B1
Cordobilla de Lácara
E 93 B4
Cordovado I 72 C2
Corella E 89 B5
Coreses E 88 C1
Corfe Castle GB 29 C5
Corga de Lobão P 87 D2
Cori I 102 B5
Coria E 93 B4
Coria del Río E 99 B4
Corigliano Cálabro I . .106 B3
Corinaldo I 82 C1
Corinth = Korinthos
GR 117 E4
Corio I 70 C2
Cork IRL 20 C3
Corlay F 56 B2
Corleone I 108 B2
Corleto Monforte I . . .103 C8
Corleto Perticara I . . .104 C2
Çorlu TR 118 A2
Cormainville F 58 B2
Cormatin F 69 B4
Cormeilles F 58 A1
Cormery F 67 A5
Cormòns I 72 C3
Cormoz F 69 B5
Cornago E 89 B4
Cornberg D 51 B5
Cornellana E 86 A4
Cornesti MD 11 C10
Corníglio I 81 B4
Cornimont F 60 C2
Corníolo I 81 C5
Cornuda I 72 C2
Cornudella de Montsant
E 90 B3
Cornudilla E 89 B3
Cornus F 78 C2
Çorovodë AL 116 B2
Corpach GB 24 B2
Corps F 79 B4
Corps Nuds F 57 C4
Corral de Almaguer E .95 C3
Corral de Ayllón E 89 C3
Corral de Calatrava
E 100 A1
Corrales E 88 C1
Corral-Rubio E 101 A4
Corran GB 24 B2
Corredoiras E 86 A2
Corréggio I 81 B4
Corréze F 68 C1
Corridónia I 82 C2
Corris GB 26 C2
Corrubedo E 86 B1
Corsico I 71 C4
Corsock GB 25 C4
Cortala F 102 A2
Corteconceptión E 99 B4
Corte de Peleas E 93 C4
Cortegada E 87 B2
Cortegana E 99 B4
Cortemilia I 80 B2
Cortemaggiore I 81 B4
Cortes E 89 C5
Cortes de Aragón E . .90 C2
Cortes de Arenoso E .96 A2
Cortes de Baza E 101 B3
Cortes de la Frontera
E 99 C5
Cortes de Pallás E . . .96 B2
Cortiçadas P 92 C2
Cortico P 87 C3
Cortijo de Arriba E . . .94 C2
Cortijos Nuevos E . . .101 A3
Cortina d'Ampezzo I . .72 B2
Corton GB 30 B5
Cortona I 81 C5
Coruche P 92 C2
Corullón E 86 B4
Çorum TR 16 A7
Corvara in Badia I 72 B1
Corvera E 101 B4
Corwen GB 26 C2
Cosa E 90 C1
Cosenza I 106 B3
Cosham GB 31 D2
Coslada E 95 B3
Cosne-Cours-sur-Loire
F 68 A2
Cosne d'Allier F 68 B2
Cospeito E 86 A3
Cossato I 70 C3
Cossaye F 68 B3
Cossé-le-Vivien F 57 C5
Cossonay CH 69 B6
Costa da Caparica P . .92 C1
Costa de Santo André
P 98 A2
Costalpino I 81 C5
Costa Nova P 92 A2
Costaros F 78 B2
Costești RO 11 D8
Costigliole d'Asti I 80 B2
Costigliole Saluzzo I . .80 B1

Cotherstone GB 27 A4
Cotronei I 107 B3
Cottbus D 53 B4
Cottingham GB 27 B5
Coublanc F 60 C1
Couches F 69 B4
Couço P 92 C2
Coucouron F 78 B2
Coucy-le-Château-
  Auffrique F 59 A4
Couflens F 77 D4
Couhé F 67 B5
Couiza F 77 D5
Coulags GB 22 D3
Coulanges-la-Vineuse
F 59 C4
Coulanges-sur-Yonne
F 68 A3
Couleuvre F 68 B2
Coulmier-le-Sec F 59 C5
Coulommiers F 59 B4
Coulonges-sur-l'Autize
F 67 B4
Coulounieix-Chamiers
F 67 C5
Coulport GB 24 B3
Coupar Angus GB 25 B4
Coupéville F 59 B5
Couptrain F 57 B5

D

Coura P 87 C2
Courcelles B 49 C5
Courcelles-Chaussy
F 60 A2
Courchevel F 70 C1
Cour-Cheverny F 67 A6
Courcôme F 67 C5
Courçon F 66 B4
Cour-et-Buis F 69 C4
Courgenay CH 70 A2
Courmayeur I 70 C1
Courniou F 78 C1
Cournon d'Auvergne
F 68 C3
Cournonterral F 78 C2
Courpière F 68 C3
Coursan F 78 C2
Courseulles-sur-Mer
F 57 A5
Cours-la-Ville F 69 B4
Courson-les-Carrières
F 59 C4
Courtalain F 58 B2
Courtenay F 59 B4
Courtomer F 58 B1
Courville
Eure-et-Loire F . . .58 B2
Marne F 59 A4
Coussac-Bonneval F .67 C6
Coutances F 57 A4
Couterne F 57 B5
Coutras F 76 A2
Couvet CH 70 B1
Couvin B 49 C5
Couzon F 68 B3
Covadonga E 88 A1
Covaleda E 89 C4
Covarrubias E 89 B3
Covas P 87 C2
Cove GB 22 D3
Coventry GB 30 B2
Coverack GB 28 C2
Covigliano I 81 B5
Covilhã P 92 A3
Cowbridge GB 29 B4
Cowdenbeath GB . . .25 B4
Cowes GB 31 D2
Cox F 77 C4
Cózar E 100 A2
Cozes F 66 C4
Cozzano F 102 B2
Craco I 104 C2
Cracow = Kraków PL .55 C4
Craibstone GB 23 D6
Craighouse GB 24 C2
Craignure GB 24 B2
Crail GB 25 B5
Crailsheim D 61 A6
Craiova RO 11 D7
Cramlington GB 25 C6
Cranleigh GB 31 C3
Craon F 57 C5
Craponne F 59 A4
Craponne-sur-Arzon
F 68 C3
Crathie GB 23 D5
Crato P 92 B3
Craughwell IRL 20 A3
Craven Arms GB 26 C3
Crawford GB 25 C4
Crawinkel D 51 C6
Crawley GB 31 C3
Creag Ghoraidh GB .22 D1
Crecente E 87 B2
Crèches-sur-Saône F .69 B4
Crécy-en-Ponthieu F .48 C2
Crécy-la-Chapelle F . .59 B3
Crécy-sur-Serre F . . .59 A4
Crediton GB 29 C4
Creeslough IRL 19 A4
Creetown GB 24 D3
Creeve GB 19 B5
Creglingen D 61 A6
Creil F 58 A3
Creissels F 78 B2
Crema I 71 C4
Cremaux F 68 C3
Crémenes E 88 B1
Cremlingen D 69 C5
Cremona I 81 A4
Creney F 59 B5
Crenšovci SLO 73 B6
Créon F 76 B2
Crepaja SRB 85 A5
Crépey F 60 B1
Crépy F 59 A4
Crépy-en-Valois F . . .59 A3
Cres HR 83 B3
Crescentino I 70 C3
Crespino I 81 B5
Crespos E 94 B2
Cressage GB 26 C3
Cressensac F 77 A4
Cressia F 69 B5
Crest F 79 B4
Cresta CH 71 B4
Créteil F 58 B3
Creully F 57 A5
Creussen D 62 A2
Creutzwald F 60 A2
Creuzburg D 51 B6
Crevalcore I 81 B5
Crèvecœur-le-Grand
F 58 A3
Crévillente E 101 A5
Crévola d'Ossola I . .70 B3
Crewe GB 26 B3
Crewkerne GB 29 C5
Criales E 89 B3
Crianlarich GB 24 B3
Criccieth GB 26 C1
Crickhowell GB 29 B4
Cricklade GB 29 B2
Crieff GB 25 B4
Criel-sur-Mer F 48 C2
Crikvenica HR 73 C4
Crillon F 58 A2
Crimmitschau D 52 C2
Crimond GB 23 D7
Crinitz D 53 B3
Cripán E 89 B4
Criquetot-l'Esneval F .57 A6
Crispiano I 104 C3
Crissolo I 79 B6
Cristóbal E 93 A5
Crivitz D 44 B3
Crna SLO 73 B4
Crna Bara
Srbija SRB 85 B4
Vojvodina SRB . . .75 C5
Crnac HR 74 C2
Crnča SRB 85 B4
Crni Lug
BIH 83 B5
Crni Vrh SLO 73 C4
Crnjelovo Donje BIH .85 B5
Crnomelj SLO 73 C5
Crocketford GB 25 C4
Crocq F 68 C2
Crodo I 70 B3
Croglin GB 25 D5
Crolly IRL 18 A3
Cromarty GB 23 D4
Cromer GB 30 B5
Cronat F 68 B3
Crookhaven IRL 20 C2
Crookstown IRL 20 C3
Croom IRL 20 B3
Cropalati I 106 B3
Cropani I 107 C3
Crosbost GB 22 C2
Crosby GB 26 B2
Crosia I 106 B3
Crossakiel IRL 19 C4
Crosshaven IRL 20 C3
Crosshill GB 24 C3
Crossmolina IRL 18 B2
Crotone I 107 B4

Crottendorf D 52 C2
Crouy F 59 A4
Crowborough GB 31 C4
Crowland GB 30 B3
Crowthorne GB 31 C3
Croyde GB 28 B3
Croydon GB 31 C3
Crozon F 56 B1
Cruas F 78 B3
Cruceni RO 75 B6
Crúden Bay GB 23 D7
Crudgington GB 26 C3
Cruis F 79 B4
Crumlin GB 19 B5
Cruseilles F 69 B6
Crusheen IRL 20 B3
Cruz de Incio E 86 B3
Crvenka SRB 75 C4
Crveny Kamen SK . . .64 A4
Csabacsüd H 75 B5
Csabrendek H 74 A2
Csákánydoroszló H . .74 B1
Csákvár H 74 A3
Császár H 74 A3
Császártöltés H 75 B4
Csávoly H 75 B4
Csemö H 75 A4
Csengöd H 75 B4
Csépa H 75 B5
Csepreg H 74 A1
Cserkeszölö H 75 B5
Csernely H 65 B6
Csesztreg H 74 B1
Csökmö H 75 A6
Csököly H 74 B2
Csokonyavisonta H . .74 B2
Csolyospálos H 75 B4
Csongrád H 75 B5
Csopak H 74 B2
Csorna H 64 C3
Csorvás H 75 B5
Csurgo H 74 B2
Cuacos de Yuste E . .93 A5
Cualedro E 87 C3
Cuanca de Campos E .88 B1
Cuba P 98 A3
Cubel E 95 A5
Cubelles E 91 B4
Cubillos E 89 C4
Cubjac F 67 C5
Cubo de la Solana E .89 C4
Çubuk TR 16 A6
Cuckfield GB 31 C3
Cucuron F 79 C4
Cudillero E 86 A4
Cuéllar E 88 C2
Cuenca E 95 B4
Cuers F 79 C5
Cuevas de Agreda E .89 C5
Cuevas Bajas E 100 B2
Cuevas del Almanzora
E 101 B4
Cuevas del Becerro E 99 C5
Cuevas del Campo
E 100 B3
Cuevas del Valle E . .94 B1
Cuevas de San Clemente
E 89 B3
Cuevas de San Marcos
E 100 B1
Cuges-les-Pins F . . .79 C4
Cúglieri I 110 B1
Cuijk NL 50 B1
Cuinzier F 69 B4
Cuiseaux F 69 B5
Cuisery F 69 B5
Culan F 68 B2
Culemborg NL 49 B6
Cúllar E 101 B3
Cullaville GB 19 B5
Cullera E 96 B2
Cullivoe GB 22 A7
Cullompton GB 29 C4
Cully CH 70 B1
Culoz F 69 C5
Cults GB 23 D6
Cumbernauld GB . . .25 C4
Cumbres de San
Bartolomé E 99 A4
Cumbres Mayores E .99 A4
Cumiana I 80 B1
Cumié SRB 85 B5
Cumnock GB 24 C3
Çumra TR 16 C6
Cúneo I 80 B1
Cunlhat F 68 C3
Çunski HR 83 B3
Cuntis E 86 B2
Cuorgnè I 70 C2
Cupar GB 25 B4
Cupello I 103 A7
Cupra Maríttima I . . .82 C2
Cupramontana I 82 C2
Cuprija SRB 85 C6
Curinga I 106 C3
Curtea de Argeş RO .11 D8
Curtici RO 75 B6
Curtis E 86 A2
Curtis Santa Eulalia E 86 A2
Çurug SRB 75 C5
Cusano Mutri I 103 B7
Cushendall GB 19 A5
Cusset F 68 B3
Cussy-les-Forges F . .68 A4
Custines F 60 B2
Cutanda E 90 C1
Cutro I 107 B3
Cutrofiano I 107 A5
Cuxhaven D 43 B5
Cvikov CZ 53 C4
Cwmbran GB 29 B4
Cybinka PL 53 A4
Czacz PL 54 A1
Czajków PL 54 B3
Czaplinek PL 46 B2
Czarlin PL 47 A4
Czarna-Dąbrówka PL .46 A3
Czarna Woda PL . . .47 B4
Czarna PL 55 C4
Czarnków PL 46 C2
Czarnowo PL 47 B4
Czarnozyly PL 54 B3
Czarny Bór PL 53 C6
Czarny-Dunajec PL . .65 A5
Czarny Las PL 54 B2
Czchow PL 65 A6
Czchowice-Dziedzice
PL 65 A4
Czempiń PL 54 A1
Czermno PL 55 B5
Czernichow PL 55 A4
Czerniejewo PL 46 C3
Czernikowo PL 47 C5
Czersk PL 46 B3
Czerwieńsk PL 53 A5
Czerwionka-Leszczyny
PL 54 C3
Czerwonka PL 47 B6
Częstochowa PL 55 C4
Czeszewo PL 54 A2
Człopa PL 46 B2
Człuchów PL 46 B3
Czołpino PL 46 A3

D

Dağ TR 119 E5
Daaden D 50 C3
Dabas H 75 A4
Dąbie PL 54 A3
Dąbki PL 46 A2
Dabo F 60 B3
Dabrowa PL 46 C3
Dąbrowa Górnicza
PL 55 C4
Dąbrowa Tarnowska
PL 55 C5
Dąbrowice PL 55 A4
Dabrowno PL 47 B6
Dachau D 62 B2
Dačice CZ 63 A6
Daday TR 16 A6
Dagali E 32 B5
Dągebüll D 39 E1
Dagmersellen CH . . .70 A2
Dahlen D 52 B2
Dahlenburg D 44 B2
Dahme D 52 B3
Dahn D 60 A3
Dähre D 44 C2
Daikanvik S 115 B13
Dail bho Dheas 22 C2
Dailly GB 24 C3
Daimiel E 95 C3
Daingean IRL 21 A4
Đakovica KOS 10 E6
Đakovo HR 74 C3
Dal
Akershus N 34 B3
Telemark N 32 C5
Dalaas A 71 A5
Dalabrog GB 22 D1
Dala-Floda S 36 B1
Dala-Husby S 36 B2
Dala-Järna S 36 B1
Dalaman TR 119 F3
Dalarö S 37 C5
Dalbeattie GB 25 D4
Dalby
DK 39 D3
Skåne S 41 D3
Uppsala S 37 C4
Värmland S 34 B4
Dale
Pembrokeshire GB .28 B2
Shetland GB 22 A7
Hordaland N 32 B2
Sogn og Fjordane N .32 A2
Dalen
Akershus N 34 B3
Telemark N 33 C5
Daleszyce PL 55 C5
Dalhalvaig GB 23 C5
Dalheim L 60 A2
Dalhem S 37 E5
Dalías E 100 C3
Dalj HR 75 C3
Dalkeith GB 25 C4
Dalkey IRL 21 A5
Dalmally GB 24 B3
Dalmellington GB . . .24 C3
Dalmose DK 39 D4
Daløy N 32 A1
Dalry
Dumfries & Galloway
GB 24 C3
North Ayrshire GB .24 C3
Dalrymple GB 24 C3
Dalseter N 32 A6
Dalsjöfors S 40 B3
Dalskog S 35 D4
Dals Långed S 35 D4
Dals Rostock S 35 D4
Dalston GB 25 D5
Dalstorp S 40 B3
Dalton-in-Furness GB 26 A2
Daluis F 79 B5
Dalum
D 43 C4
S 40 B3
Dalvík IS 111 B7
Dalwhinnie GB 24 B3
Dalyan TR 119 F3
Damasi GR 116 C4
Damasławek PL 46 C3
Damazan F 76 B3
Damës AL 105 C5
Damgan F 56 C2
Dammartin-les-Lys F .58 B3
Dammartin-en-Goële
F 58 A3
Damme
D 43 C5
Damnica PL 46 A3
Dampierre F 69 A5
Dampierre-sur-Salon
F 69 A5
Damüls A 71 A4
Damville F 58 B2
Damvillers F 59 A6
Danasjö S 115 B13
Danbury GB 31 C4
Dångebo S 40 C5
Dangé-St Romain F . .67 B5
Dangeul F 57 B6
Danilovgrad MNE . .105 A5
Danischenhagen D . .44 A2
Danjoutin F 60 C2
Dannas S 40 B3
Dannemarie F 60 C3
Dannemora S 36 B4
Dannenberg D 44 B3
Dänschendorf D 44 A2
Dány H 75 A4
Daoulas F 56 B1
Darabani RO 11 B9
Darány H 74 C2
Darda HR 74 C3
Dardesheim D 51 B6
Darfeld D 50 A3
Darfo I 71 C5
Dargin PL 46 A2
Dargun D 45 B4
Darlington GB 27 A4
Darłowo PL 46 A2
Darmstadt D 61 A4
Darney F 60 B2
Daroca E 95 A5
Darque P 87 C2
Darragh IRL 20 B2
Dartford GB 31 C4
Dartington GB 28 C4
Dartmouth GB 29 C4
Darton GB 27 B4
Daruvar HR 74 C2
Darvas H 75 A6
Darvel GB 24 C3
Darwen GB 26 B3
Dassel D 51 B5
Dassow D 44 B2
Datça TR 119 F2
Datteln D 50 B3
Dattenfeld D 50 C3
Daugard DK 39 D2
Daugavpils LV 7 D9
Daumeray F 57 C5
Daun D 50 C2
Daventry GB 30 B2
Davle CZ 63 A5
Davor HR 84 A2
Davos CH 71 B4
Davutlar TR 119 E2
Davyd Haradok BY . . .7 E9
Dawlish GB 29 C4
Dax F 76 C1
Dazkırı TR 119 E4
Deal GB 31 C5
Deauville F 57 A6
Deba E 89 A4
Debar MK 116 A2
Debe Wielkie PL 55 A6
Dębica PL 55 C6

Dębnica Kaszubska
PL 46 A3
Dębno PL 45 C6
Dębołęka PL 54 B3
Dębowa Łąka PL . . .47 B5
Debrc SRB 85 B4
Debrecen H 10 C6
Debrznica PL 53 A5
Debrzno PL 46 B3
Debstedt D 43 B5
Decazeville F 77 B5
Dechtice SK 64 B3
Decima I 102 B5
Decimomannu I 110 C1
Děčín CZ 53 C4
Decize F 68 B3
De Cocksdorp NL . . .42 B1
Decollatura I 106 B3
Decs H 74 B3
Dedaj AL 105 A5
Deddington GB 31 C2
Dedeler TR 118 B5
Dedelow D 45 B5
Dedemli TR 119 E7
Dedemsvaart NL 42 C3
Dédestapolcsány H . .65 B6
Dedovichi RUS 7 C10
Deeping St Nicholas
. . . . .30 B3
Deftera CY 120 A2
Dég H 74 B3
Degaña E 86 B4
Degeberga S 41 D4
Degerby FIN 36 B7
Degerfors S 37 C1
Degerhamn S 41 C6
Degernes N 35 C3
Deggendorf D 62 B3
Deggingen D 61 B5
Dego I 80 B2
Degolados P 93 B3
De Haan B 49 B4
Dehesa de Guadix
E 100 B2
Dehesas Viejas E . .100 B2
Deia E 97 B2
Deining D 62 A2
Deinze B 49 C4
Déiva Marina I 80 B3
Dej RO 11 C7
Deje S 35 C5
De Koog NL 42 B1
Delabole GB 28 C3
Delary S 40 C3
Delbrück D 51 B4
Delden NL 50 A2
Deleitosa E 93 B5
Delekovec HR 74 B1
Delémont CH 70 A2
Delft NL 49 A5
Delfzijl NL 42 B3
Délia I 108 B2
Delianuova I 106 C2
Deliblato SRB 85 B6
Deliceto I 103 B8
Delitzsch D 52 B2
Dellach I 72 B3
Delle F 70 A1
Delme F 60 B2
Delmen-horst D 43 B5
Delnice HR 73 C4
Delsbo S 115 F13
Delvin IRL 19 C4
Delvinë AL 116 C2
Demandice SK 65 B4
Demen D 44 B3
Demidov RUS 7 D11
Demigny F 69 B4
Demirci TR 118 C3
Demirköy TR 118 A2
Demirtaş TR 118 B4
Demmin D 45 B5
Demonte I 79 B6
Demyansk RUS 7 C12
Denain F 49 C4
Denbigh GB 26 B2
Den Burg NL 42 B1
Dender-monde B 49 B5
Denekamp NL 42 C3
Den Ham NL 42 C3
Den Helder NL 42 C1
Denholm GB 25 C5
Denia E 96 C3
Denizli TR 119 E4
Denkendorf D 62 B2
Denklingen D 50 C3
Den Oever NL 42 C2
Denta RO 75 C6
Derbent TR 119 D3
Derby GB 27 C4
Dereköy TR 118 A2
Derenberg D 51 B6
Derinkuyu TR 16 B7
Dermbach D 51 C6
Dermulo I 71 B6
Deronje SRB 75 C4
Derrygonnelly GB . . .19 B4
Derrylin GB 19 B4
Derry/Londonderry
. . . . .19 B4
Dersingham GB 30 B4
Deruta I 82 D1
Dervaig GB 24 B1
Derval F 57 C4
Derveni GR 117 D4
Derventa BIH 84 B2
Dervock GB 19 A5
Descartes F 67 B5
Desenzano del Garda
I 71 C5
Deset N 34 A3
Deševa BIH 84 C3
Desfina GR 116 D4
Desimirovac SRB . . .85 B5
Desio I 71 C4
Deskati GR 116 C4
Deskle SLO 72 B3
Desná CZ 53 C5
Dešov CZ 63 B6
Despotovac SRB . . .85 B6
Despotovo SRB 75 C4
Dessau D 52 B2
Deštná CZ 63 A5
Destriana E 87 B4
Desulo I 110 C2
Desvres F 48 C2
Deszk H 75 B5
Detmold D 51 B4
Dětřichov CZ 64 A3
Dettelbach D 61 A6
Dettingen
Baden-Württemberg
D 61 B5
Baden-Württemberg
D 61 B5
Dettwiller F 60 B3
Detva SK 65 B5
Deurne NL 50 B1
Deutschkreutz A 64 C2
Deutschlandsberg A .73 B5
Deutsch Wagram A . .64 B2
Deva RO 11 D7
Dévaványa H 75 A5
Devecikonağı TR . . .118 C3
Devecser H 74 A2
Develi TR 16 B7
Deventer NL 50 A2
Devil's Bridge GB . . .26 C2
Devin BG 116 A6
Devínska Nova Ves
SK 64 B3
Devizes GB 29 B6
Devonport GB 28 C3
Devrek TR 118 A6
Devrekâni TR 16 A6
Đevrske HR 83 C4

De Wijk NL 42 C3
Dewsbury GB 27 B4
Deza E 89 C4
Dežanovac HR 74 C2
Dezzo I 71 C5
Dhali CY 120 A2
Dherinia CY 120 A2
Dhèrmi AL 105 C5
Diamante I 106 B2
Dianalund DK 39 D4
Diano d'Alba I 80 B2
Diano Marina I 80 C2
Dicomano I 81 C5
Didcot GB 31 C2
Didim TR 119 E2
Didimoticho GR 118 A1
Die F 79 B4
Diebling F 60 A2
Dieburg D 61 A4
Diego del Carpio E . .94 B1
Diekirch L 60 A2
Diélette F 57 A4
Diemelstadt D 51 B5
Diémoz F 69 C5
Dienten am Hochkönig
A 72 A2
Diepenbeck B 49 C6
Diepholz D 43 C5
Dieppe F 58 A2
Dierberg D 45 B4
Dierdorf D 50 C3
Dieren NL 50 A1
Dierhagen D 44 A4
Diesdorf D 44 C2
Diessen D 62 C2
Diest B 49 C6
Dietenheim D 61 B6
Dietfurt D 62 A2
Dietikon CH 70 A3
Dietzenbach D 51 C4
Dieue-sur-Meuse F . .59 A6
Dieulefit F 79 B4
Dieulouard F 60 B2
Dieuze F 60 B2
Diever NL 42 C3
Diez D 50 C4
Diezma E 100 B2
Differdange L 60 A1
Digermulen N 112 D4
Dignac F 67 C5
Dignano I 72 B2
Digne-les-Bains F . . .79 B5
Digny F 58 B2
Digoin F 68 B3
Dijon F 69 A5
Dikanäs S 115 B13
Dikili TR 118 C1
Diksmuide B 48 B3
Dilar E 100 B2
Dillenburg D 50 C4
Dillingen
Bayern D 61 B6
Saarland D 60 A2
Dilsen B 50 B1
Dimaro I 71 B5
Dimitrovgrad BG 11 E8
Dimitsana GR 117 E4
Dinami I 106 C3
Dinan F 57 B3
Dinant B 49 C5
Dinar TR 119 D5
Dinard F 57 B3
Dinek TR 118 C6
Dingden D 50 B2
Dingelstädt D 51 B6
Dingle
IRL 20 B1
S 35 D3
Dingolfing D 62 B3
Dingtuna S 37 C3
Dingwall GB 23 D4
Dinkelsbühl D 61 A6
Dinkelscherben D . . .62 B1
Dinklage D 43 C5
Dinslaken D 50 B2
Dinxperlo NL 50 B2
Diö S 40 C4
Diósgyör H 65 B6
Diósjeno H 65 C5
Diou F 68 B3
Dippen GB 24 C2
Dipperz D 51 C5
Dippoldiswalde D . . .53 C3
Dirdal N 33 D3
Dirksland NL 49 B5
Dirlewang D 61 B6
Dischingen D 61 B6
Disentis CH 70 B3
Diso I 107 A5
Dispilió GR 116 B3
Diss GB 30 B5
Dissen D 51 A4
Ditzingen D 61 B5
Ditzum D 43 B4
Divača SLO 72 C3
Dives-sur-Mer F 57 A5
Divín SK 65 B5
Divion F 48 C3
Divišov CZ 63 A5
Divjakë AL 105 C5
Divonne les Bains F .69 B6
Dixmont F 59 B4
Dizy-le-Gros F 59 A5
Djatlovo = ...111 C11
Djupivogur IS 111 C11
Djupvasshytta N . . .114 F5
Djura S 36 B1
Djurås S 36 B2
Djurmo S 36 B2
Djursdala S 40 B5
Dlouhá Loucka CZ . .64 A3
Długowola PL 55 B6
Dmitriyev Lgovskiy
RUS 7 E13
Dmitrov RUS 7 C14
Dmitrovsk-Orlovskiy
RUS 7 E13
Dno RUS 7 C10
Doade E 86 B3
Doğanhisar TR 119 D6
Dobanovci SRB 85 B5
Dobbertin D 44 B4
Dobbiaco I 72 B2
Dobczyce PL 55 C5
Dobele LV 6 C7
Döbeln D 52 B3
Doberlug-Kirchhain D 52 B3
Dobern D 53 B4
Dobersberg A 63 B6
Dobiegniew PL 46 C1
Dobieszyn PL 55 B6
Doboj BIH 84 B3
Dobošnica BIH 84 B3
Doboz H 75 B6
Dobra
Wielkopolskie PL . .54 B3
Zachodnio-Pomorskie
PL 45 B6
Zachodnio-Pomorskie
PL 45 B7
Dobřany SK 63 A4
Dobre
Kujawsko-Pomorskie
PL 47 C4
Mazowieckie PL . .55 C6
Dobre Miasto PL . . .47 B6
Dobreta-Turnu-Severin
RO 11 D7
Dobri H 74 B1
Dobrica SRB 75 C5
Dobrich BG 11 E9
Dobri Do SRB 85 C6
Dobříš CZ 63 A5
Dobro E 89 B3
Dobrodzień PL 54 C3
Dobromani BIH 84 D3
Dobrosołowo PL 47 C4
Dobroszyce PL 54 B2
Dobrota MNE 105 A4

Dobrovnik SLO 73 B6
Dobrush BY 7 E11
Dobruška CZ 53 C6
Dobrzany PL 46 B1
Dobrzen Wielki PL . .54 C2
Dobrzyca
Wielkopolskie PL . .46 B2
Wielkopolskie PL . .54 B2
Zachodnio-Pomorskie
PL 46 A1
Dobrzyńnad Wisłą
PL 47 C5
Dobšiná SK 65 B6
Dobwalls GB 28 C3
Dochamps B 49 C6
Docking GB 30 B4
Docksta S 115 D15
Doddington GB 25 C5
Döderhult S 40 B6
Doesburg NL 50 A2
Doetinchem NL 50 B2
Dogliani I 80 B1
Dogueno P 98 B3
Doische B 49 C5
Dois Portos P 92 B1
Dojč SK 64 B3
Dokka N 34 B2
Dokkedal DK 38 C3
Dokkum NL 42 B2
Dokležovje SLO 73 B6
Doksy CZ 53 C4
Dokuz TR 119 D7
Dolancourt F 59 B5
Dolceácqua I 80 C1
Dol-de-Bretagne F . .57 B4
Dole F 69 A5
Delemo N 33 D5
Dolenja vas SLO 73 C4
Dolenjske Toplice
SLO 73 C5
Dolfor GB 26 C2
Dolgarrog GB 26 B2
Dolgellau GB 26 C2
Doliana GR 116 C2
Dolianova I 110 C2
Dolice PL 45 B7
Doljani HR 83 B5
Döllach im Mölltal A . .72 B2
Dolle D 44 C3
Dollnstein D 62 B2
Dollot F 59 B4
Dollstadt D 51 B6
Dolná Strehová SK . .65 B5
Dolné Saliby SK 64 B3
Dolni Benešov CZ . . .64 A4
Dolni Bousov CZ 53 C5
Dolní Kralovice CZ . .63 A6
Dolní Újezd CZ 64 A2
Dolní Žandov CZ 52 C2
Dolný Kubin SK 65 A5
Dolo I 72 C2
Dolores E 96 C2
Dolovo SRB 85 B5
Dölsach A 72 B2
Dolsk PL 54 B2
Dolwyddelan GB 26 B2
Domaljevac BIH 84 A3
Domanic TR 118 C4
Domaniža SK 65 A4
Domanovići BIH 84 C2
Domašov CZ 54 C2
Domaszék H 75 B4
Domaszków PL 54 C1
Domaszowice PL . . .54 B2
Domat-Ems CH 71 B4
Domažlice CZ 62 A3
Dombås N 114 E6
Dombasle-sur-Meurthe
F 60 B2
Dombegyház H 75 B6
Dombóvár H 74 B3
Domène F 69 C5
Domérat F 68 B2
Domfessel F 60 B3
Domfront F 57 B5
Domfront-en-Champagne
F 57 B6
Domingão P 92 B2
Domingo Pérez
Granada E 100 B2
Toledo E 94 C2
Dömitz D 44 B3
Dommartin F 59 B5
Dommartin-le-Franc
F 59 B5
Domme F 77 B4
Dommitzsch D 52 B2
Domodóssola I 70 B3
Domokos GR 116 C4
Domoszló H 65 C6
Dompaire F 60 B2
Dompierre-du-Chemin
F 57 B4
Dompierre-sur-Besbre
F 68 B3
Dompierre-sur-Mer F .66 B3
Domrémy-la-Pucelle
F 60 B1
Dömsöd H 75 A4
Domsure F 69 B5
Dómus de Maria I . .110 D1
Domusnóvas I 110 C1
Domvena GR 116 D4
Domžale SLO 73 B4
Donado E 87 B4
Donaghadee GB 19 B6
Donaueschingen D . .61 C4
Donauwörth D 62 B1
Don Benito E 93 C5
Doncaster GB 27 B4
Donegal IRL 18 B3
Donestebe-Santesteban
E 76 C1
Donges F 66 A2
Dongo I 71 B4
Donington GB 30 B3
Doniños E 86 A2
Donja Bebrina HR . .84 A3
Donja Brela HR 84 C1
Donja Dubica BIH . . .84 A3
Donja Dubrava HR . .74 B1
Donja Kupčina HR . .73 C5
Donja Mutnica SRB .85 C6
Donja Satornja SRB .85 B5
Donja Stubica HR . . .73 C5
Donja Brišnik BIH . . .84 C2
Donje Ljupče KOS . . .85 D6
Donje Stative HR . . .73 C5
Donji-Andrijevci HR .74 C3
Donji Kazanci BIH . .84 C1
Donji Koričáni BIH . .84 B2
Donji Malovan BIH . .84 C2
Donji Miljević BIH . . .84 B2
Donji Mosti HR 74 B1
Donji Poljci HR 73 C5
Donji-Rujani BIH 84 C1
Donji Srb HR 83 B5
Donji Svilaj BIH 84 B3
Donji Tovarnik SRB . .85 B4
Donji Vakuf BIH 84 B2
Donnalucata I 109 C3
Donnemarie-Dontilly
F 59 B4
Donnersbach A 73 A4
Donnersbachwald A . .73 A4
Donnerskirchen A . . .64 C2
Donorático I 81 C4
Donostia-San Sebastián
E 76 C1
Donovaly SK 65 B5
Donzenac F 67 C6
Donzère F 78 B3
Donzy F 68 A3
Doonbeg IRL 20 B2
Doorn NL 49 A6
Dor E 86 A1
Dorchester GB 29 C5

Dørdal N 33 D6
Dordrecht NL 49 B5
Dörenthe D 50 A3
Dores GB 23 D4
Dorfen D 62 B3
Dorfgastein A 72 A3
Dormhaeck D 43 C6
Dorf Mecklenburg D .44 B3
Dorgali I 110 B2
Dorking GB 31 C3
Dormagen D 50 B2
Dormänd H 65 C6
Dornava SLO 73 B5
Dornbirn A 71 A4
Dornburg D 52 B1
Dorndorf D 51 C6
Dornecy F 68 A3
Dornes F 68 B3
Dornhan D 61 B4
Dornie GB 22 D3
Dornoch GB 23 D4
Dornum D 43 B4
Dorog H 65 C4
Dorogobuzh RUS 7 D12
Dorohoi RO 11 C9
Dorotea S 115 C13
Dörpen D 43 C4
Dorsten D 50 B2
Dortan F 69 B5
Dortmund D 50 B3
Doruchów PL 54 B3
Dörverden D 43 C6
Dörzbach D 61 A5
Dos Aguas E 96 B2
Dosbarrios E 95 C3
Dösemealtı TR 119 E5
Dos Hermanas E 99 B5
Dospat BG 116 A6
Dos-Torres E 100 A1
Dötlingen D 43 C5
Dottignies B 49 C4
Dottington CH 70 B2
Dotzheim D 50 C4
Douai F 49 C4
Douarnenez F 56 B1
Douchy F 59 C4
Douchy-les-Mines F .49 C4
Doucier F 69 B5
Doudeville F 58 A1
Doué-la-Fontaine F . .67 A4
Douglas
Isle of Man GB . . .26 A1
South Lanarkshire
GB 25 C4
Doulaincourt-Saucourt
F 59 B6
Doulevant-le-Château
F 59 B5
Doullens F 48 C3
Dounby GB 23 B5
Doune GB 24 B3
Dounreay GB 23 C5
Dour B 49 C4
Dourdan F 58 B3
Dourgne F 77 C5
Dournazac F 67 C5
Douro Calvo P 92 A3
Douvaine F 69 B6
Douvres-la-Délivrande
F 57 A5
Douzy F 59 A6
Dover GB 31 C5
Dovje SLO 72 B3
Dovre N 114 F6
Downham Market GB 30 B4
Downhill GB 19 A5
Downpatrick GB 19 B6
Dowra IRL 18 B3
Doxato GR 116 A6
Doyet F 68 B2
Dozule F 57 A5
Dråb SRB 85 C4
Drachten NL 42 B3
Draga SLO 73 C4
Drăgăşani RO 11 D8
Dragatuš SLO 73 C5
Dragichyn BY 7 E8
Draginja SRB 85 B4
Dragocvet SRB 85 C6
Dragolovci BIH 84 B2
Dragoni I 103 B7
Dragør DK 41 D2
Dragotina HR 73 C6
Dragozetići HR 83 A3
Dragsmark S 35 D3
Draguignan F 79 C5
Drahnsdorf D 52 B3
Drahonice CZ 63 A4
Drahovce SK 64 B3
Drama GR 116 A6
Drammen N 35 C2
Drangedal N 33 D6
Drangsnes IS 111 B4
Dransfeld D 51 B5
Dranske D 45 A5
Draperstown GB 19 B5
Drasburg A 64 C2
Drávaszabolcs H 74 C3
Dravograd SLO 73 B5
Drawno PL 46 B1
Drawsko Pomorskie
PL 46 B1
Drayton GB 30 B5
Draženov CZ 62 A3
Draževac SRB 85 B5
Dražice HR 73 C4
Drebkau D 53 B4
Dreieich D 51 C4
Dreisen D 61 A4
Dren KOS 85 C5
Drena I 71 C5
Drenovac SRB 85 C6
Drenovci HR 84 B3
Drensteinfurt D 50 B3
Dretyń PL 46 A2
Dřevohostice CZ 64 A3
Drevsjø N 114 F9
Drewitz D 44 C4
Drezdenko PL 46 C1
Drežnica HR 83 A4
Drežnik-Grad HR . . .83 B4
Drietona SK 64 B3
Driffield GB 27 A5
Drimnin GB 24 B2
Drimoleague IRL 20 C2
Dringenberg D 51 B5
Drini BIH 84 B2
Drinjača BIH 85 B4
Driopida GR 117 E6
Drivstua N 114 E7
Drlace SRB 85 B4
Drnholec CZ 64 B2
Drniš HR 83 C5
Drnje HR 74 B1
Drnovice CZ 64 A2
Dro I 71 C5
Drøbak N 35 C2
Drobin PL 47 C6
Drochia MD 11 B9
Drochtersen D 43 B6
Drogheda IRL 19 C5
Drohobych UA 11 B7
Droitwich Spa GB . . .29 A5
Drołtowice PL 54 B2
Dromahair IRL 18 B3
Dromcolliher IRL 20 B3
Dromore
Down GB 19 B5
Tyrone GB 19 B4
Dromore West IRL . .18 B3
Dronero I 79 B6
Dronfield GB 27 B4
Drongan GB 24 C3
Dronninglund DK . . .38 B3
Dronrijp NL 42 B2
Dronten NL 42 C2

Drosendorf A 63 B6
Drösing A 64 B2
Drottningholm S 37 C4
Droué F 58 B2
Drulingen F 60 B3
Drumbeg GB 22 C3
Drumcliff IRL 18 B3
Drumgask GB 23 D4
Drumkeeran IRL 18 B3
Drummore GB 24 D3
Drumnadrochit GB . .23 D4
Drumquin GB 19 B4
Drumshanbo IRL 18 B3
Drumsna IRL 19 C4
Drunen NL 49 B6
Druskininkai LT 6 D7
Druten NL 49 B6
Druya BY 7 D9
Drużetići SRB 85 B5
Drvar BIH 83 B5
Drvenik HR 84 C2
Drwalew PL 55 B6
Drymen GB 24 B3
Drzewce PL 54 A2
Drzewica PL 55 B5
Dualchi I 110 B1
Duas Igrejas P 87 C4
Dub SRB 85 C4
Dubá CZ 53 C4
Dubăsari MD 11 C10
Duben D 53 B3
Dübendorf CH 70 A3
Dubi CZ 53 C3
Dubica HR 74 C1
Dublin IRL 21 A5
Dubna RUS 7 C14
Dubňany CZ 64 B3
Dubnica nad Váhom
SK 64 B4
Dubnik SK 64 C4
Dubna S 11 A8
Dubona SRB 85 B5
Dubovic BIH 83 B5
Dubranec HR 73 C5
Dubrava HR 74 C1
Dubrave BIH 84 B3
Dubravica
HR 73 C5
SRB 85 B6
Dubrovnik HR 84 D3
Dubrovytsya UA 7 F9
Ducey F 57 B4
Duchcov CZ 53 C3
Ducherow D 45 B5
Dučina SRB 85 B5
Duclair F 58 A1
Dudar H 74 A2
Duddington GB 30 B3
Duderstadt D 51 B6
Dudley GB 26 C3
Dueñas E 88 C2
Duesund N 32 B2
Dueville I 72 C1
Duffel B 49 B5
Duffield GB 27 C4
Dufftown GB 23 D5
Duga Poljana SRB . .85 C5
Duga Resa HR 73 C5
Dugi Rat HR 83 C5
Dugny-sur-Meuse F . .60 A1
Dugo Selo HR 73 C6
Duino I 72 C3
Duisburg D 50 B2
Dukat AL 105 C5
Dukhovshchina RUS . .7 D12
Dukovany CZ 64 A2
Duleek IRL 19 C5
Dülmen D 50 B3
Dulovo BG 11 E9
Dulpetorpet N 34 B4
Dulverton GB 29 B4
Dumbarton GB 24 C3
Dümerek TR 118 C6
Dümmer D 44 B2
Dumlupınar TR 118 D4
Dümpelfeld D 50 C2
Dunaalmás H 65 C4
Dunabogdány H 65 C5
Dunafalva H 74 B3
Dunaföldvár H 74 B3
Dunaharaszti H 75 A4
Dunakeszi H 65 C5
Dunakömlöd H 74 B3
Dunapataj H 75 B3
Dunaszekcsö H 74 B3
Dunaszentgyörgy H . .74 B3
Dunatetétlen H 75 B4
Dunaújváros H 74 B3
Dunavecse H 75 B3
Dunbar GB 25 B5
Dunbeath GB 23 C5
Dunblane GB 24 B4
Dunboyne IRL 21 A5
Dundalk IRL 19 B5
Dundee GB 25 B5
Dundrennan GB 25 D4
Dundrum GB 19 B6
Dunfanaghy IRL 19 A4
Dunfermline GB 25 B4
Dungannon GB 19 B5
Dungarvan IRL 21 B4
Dungiven GB 19 B5
Dunglow IRL 18 B3
Dungourney IRL 20 C3
Dunino PL 46 A2
Dunion SRB 85 C6
Dunkeld GB 25 B4
Dunker S 37 C3
Dunkerque = Dunkirk
F 48 B3
Dunkineely IRL 18 B3
Dunkirk = Dunkerque
F 48 B3
Dun Laoghaire IRL . .21 A5
Dunlavin IRL 21 A5
Dunleer IRL 19 C5
Dun-le-Palestel F . . .67 B6
Dun-les-Places F . . .68 A4
Dunlop GB 24 C3
Dunloy GB 19 A5
Dunmanway IRL 20 C2
Dunmore IRL 18 C3
Dunmore East IRL . .21 B5
Dunmurry GB 19 B5
Dunnet GB 23 C5
Dunningen D 61 B4
Dunoon GB 24 C3
Dunsaghlin IRL 21 A5
Dunstable GB 31 C3
Dun-sur-Auron F 68 B2
Dun-sur-Meuse F . . .59 A6
Dunvegan GB 22 D2
Duplek SLO 73 B5
Dupnitsa BG 11 E7
Durach D 61 C6
Durak TR 118 C3
Durakovac KOS 85 D5
Durana E 89 B4
Durance F 76 B3
Durankulak BG 11 E10
Durban-Corbières F . .78 D1
Durbuy B 49 C6

Dúrcal E 100 C2
Đurđjenovac HR 74 C3
Đurđevac HR 74 B2
Đurđjevik BIH 84 B3
Düren D 50 C2
Durham GB 25 D6
Đurinci SRB 85 B5
Durlach D 61 B4
Đurmanec HR 73 B5
Durness GB 22 C4
Dürnkrut A 64 B2
Dürrboden CH 71 B4
Dürrenboden CH 70 B3
Durrës AL 105 B5
Durrow IRL 21 B4
Durrus IRL 20 C2
Dursunbey TR 118 C3
Durtal F 57 C5
Durup DK 38 C1
Durusu TR 118 A3
Dusina BIH 84 C2
Dusnik N 75 B3
Dusocin PL 47 B4
Düsseldorf D 50 B2
Dusslingen D 61 B5
Duszniki PL 46 C2
Duszniki-Zdrój PL 54 C1
Dutovlje SLO 72 C3
Duvebo S 40 A4
Duved S 115 D9
Đúzağac TR 118 D5
Düzce TR 118 B6
Dvärsätt S 115 D11
Dvor HR 83 A5
Dvorce CZ 64 A3
Dvorniky SK 64 B3
Dvory nad Žitavou SK 64 C4
Dvůr Králóvénad Labem CZ 53 C5
Dyatkovo RUS 7 E13
Dybvad DK 38 B3
Dyce GB 23 D6
Dygowo PL 46 A1
Dyhérnfurth GB 25 B4
Dymchurch GB 31 C5
Dymer UA 11 A11
Dyrnes N 114 D4
Dywity PL 47 B6
Džaníci BIH 84 C2
Dziadowa Kłoda PL 54 B2
Działdowo PL 47 B6
Działoszyce PL 55 C5
Działoszyn PL 54 B3
Dziemiany PL 46 A3
Dzierżążnia PL 47 C6
Dzierzgoń PL 47 B5
Dzierzgowo PL 47 B6
Dzierżoniów PL 54 C1
Dzisna BY 7 D10
Dziwnów PL 45 A6
Dzyarzhynsk BY 7 E9
Dzyatlava BY 7 E8

E

Ea E 89 A4
Eaglesfield GB 25 C4
Ealing GB 31 C3
Eardisley GB 29 A4
Earls Barton GB 30 B3
Earl Shilton GB 30 B2
Earlston GB 25 C5
Easington GB 27 B6
Easky IRL 18 B3
Eastbourne GB 31 D4
East Calder GB 25 C4
East Dereham GB 30 B4
Easter Skeld GB 22 A7
East Grinstead GB 31 C4
East Ilsley GB 31 C2
East Kilbride GB 24 C3
Eastleigh GB 31 D2
East Linton GB 25 C5
East Markham GB 27 B5
Easton GB 29 C5
East Wittering GB 31 D3
Eaton Socon GB 30 B3
Eaux-Bonnes F 76 C2
Eauze F 76 C3
Ebberup DK 39 D2
Ebbs A 62 C3
Ebbw Vale GB 29 B4
Ebeleben D 51 B6
Ebeltoft DK 39 C3
Ebene Reichenau A 72 B3
Eben im Pongau A 72 A3
Ebensee A 63 C4
Ebensfeld D 51 C6
Eberbach D 61 A4
Ebergötzen D 51 B6
Ebern D 51 C6
Eberndorf A 73 B4
Ebersbach D 53 B4
Ebersberg D 62 B2
Ebersdorf
  Bayern D 52 C1
  Niedersachsen D 43 B6
Eberstein A 73 B4
Eberswalde D 45 C5
Ebnat-Kappel CH 71 A4
Éboli I 103 C8
Ebrach D 61 A6
Ebreichsdorf A 64 C2
Ebreuil F 68 B3
Ebstorf D 44 B2
Ecclefechan GB 25 C4
Eccleshall GB 26 C3
Eccabat TR 118 B1
Echallens CH 70 B1
Echauri E 76 D1
Echinos GR 116 A7
Échiré F 67 B4
Échirolles F 69 C5
Echourgnac F 76 A3
Echt NL 50 B1
Echte D 51 B6
Echternach L 60 A2
Écija E 99 B5
Ečka SRB 75 C5
Eckartsberga D 52 B1
Eckelshausen D 51 C4
Eckental D 62 A2
Eckernförde D 44 A1
Eckerö FIN 36 B6
Eckington GB 27 B4
Éclaron F 59 B5
Écommoy F 58 C1
Écouché F 57 B5
Ecouis F 58 A2
Ecséd H 65 C5
Ecsegfalva H 75 A5
Écueillé F 67 A6
Ed S 35 D3
Eda glasbruk S 34 C4
Edam NL 42 C2
Edane S 35 C4
Edderton GB 23 D4
Ede NL 49 A6
Edebäck S 34 B5
Edebo S 36 B5
Edelény H 65 B6
Edelschrott A 73 A5
Edemissen D 44 C2
Edenbridge GB 31 C4
Edenderry IRL 21 A4
Edenkoben D 61 A4
Edesheim D 61 A4
Edessa GR 116 B4
Edewecht D 43 B4
Edgeworthstown IRL 19 C4
Edinburgh GB 25 C4
Edinet MD 11 B9
Edland N 33 C4
Edolo I 71 B5

Edøy N 114 D5
Edremit TR 118 C2
Edsbro S 36 C5
Edsbruk S 40 A6
Edsbyn S 36 A2
Edsele S 115 D13
Edsleskog S 35 C4
Edsvalla S 35 C5
Eekloo B 49 B4
Eemshaven NL 42 B3
Eerbeek NL 50 A1
Eersel NL 49 B6
Eferding A 63 B5
Effiat F 68 B3
Eftelot N 35 C1
Egeln D 52 B1
Eger H 65 C6
Egerbakta H 65 C6
Egersund D 39 E2
Egerszólát H 65 C6
Egervár H 74 B1
Egg
  A 71 A4
  D 61 B6
Eggby S 35 D5
Eggedal N 32 B6
Eggenburg A 64 B1
Eggenfelden D 62 B3
Eggesin D 45 B6
Eggum N 112 D2
Egham GB 31 C3
Eghezée B 49 C5
Egiertowo PL 47 A4
Egilsstaðir IS 111 B11
Egina GR 117 E5
Eginio GR 116 B4
Egio GR 117 D4
Egletons F 68 C2
Egling D 62 C2
Eglinton GB 19 A4
Eglisau CH 61 C4
Égliseneuve-d'Entraigues F 68 C2
Eglofs D 61 C5
Egmond aan Zee NL 42 C1
Egna I 71 B6
Egosthena GR 117 D5
Egremont GB 26 A2
Egtved DK 39 D2
Éguilles F 79 C4
Éguilly-sous-Bois F 59 B5
Éguzon-Chantôme F 67 B6
Egyek H 65 C6
Egyházasrádóc H 74 A1
Ehekirchen D 62 B2
Ehingen D 61 B5
Ehra-Lessien D 44 C2
Ehrang D 60 A2
Ehrenfriedersdorf D 52 C2
Ehrenhain D 52 C2
Ehrenhausen A 73 B5
Ehringshausen D 51 C4
Ehrwald A 71 A5
Eibar E 89 A4
Eibelstadt D 61 A6
Eibenstock D 52 C2
Eibergen NL 50 A2
Eibiswald A 73 B5
Eichenbarleben D 52 A1
Eichendorf D 62 B3
Eichstätt D 62 B2
Eickelborn D 50 B4
Eide
  Hordaland N 32 B3
  Møre og Romsdal N 114 E4
Eidet N 112 C7
Eidfjord N 32 B4
Eidsberg N 35 C3
Eidsbugarden N 32 A5
Eidsdal N 114 E4
Eidsfoss N 35 C2
Eidskog N 34 B4
Eidsvåg
  Hordaland N 32 B2
  Møre og Romsdal N 114 E5
Eidsvoll N 34 B3
Eikefjord N 114 F2
Eikelandsosen N 32 B2
Eiken N 33 D4
Eikesdal N 114 E5
Eikstrand N 35 C1
Eilenburg D 52 B2
Eilsleben D 52 A1
Eina N 34 B2
Einbeck D 51 B6
Eindhoven NL 49 B6
Einsiedeln CH 70 A3
Einville-au-Jard F 60 B2
Eisenach D 51 C6
Eisenberg
  Rheinland-Pfalz D 61 A4
  Thüringen D 52 C1
Eisenerz A 73 A4
Eisenhüttenstadt D 53 A4
Eisenkappel A 73 B4
Eisenstadt A 64 C2
Eisentratten A 72 B3
Eisfeld D 51 C6
Eisleben D 52 B1
Eislingen D 61 B5
Eitensheim D 62 B2
Eiterfeld D 51 C5
Eitorf D 50 C3
Eivindvik N 32 B2
Eivissa = Ibiza E 97 C1
Eixo P 92 A2
Ejby DK 39 D2
Ejea de los Caballeros E 90 A1
Ejstrupholm DK 39 D2
Ejulve E 90 C2
Eke B 49 C4
Ekeby
  Gotland S 37 E5
  Skåne S 41 D2
  Uppsala S 36 B5
Ekeby-Almby S 37 C2
Ekenäs S 35 D5
Ekenässjön S 40 B5
Ekerö S 37 C4
Eket S 41 C3
Eketorp S 41 C6
Ekevik S 37 D3
Ekkerøy N 113 B19
Ekshärad S 34 B5
Eksingedal N 32 B2
Eksjö S 40 B4
Eksta S 37 E5
Ekträsk S 115 C16
El Alamo
  Madrid E 94 B3
  Sevilla E 99 B4
El Algar E 101 B5
El Almendro E 98 B3
El Alquián E 101 C3
Élancourt F 58 B2
El Arahal E 99 B5
El Arenal E 99 B5
El Arguellite E 101 A3
Elassona GR 116 C4
El Astillero E 88 A3
Elati GR 116 C3
Elazig TR 16 B7
Zelazno PL 54 C1
El Ballestero E 101 A3
Elbasan AL 116 A2
El Berrón E 88 A1
El Berrueco E 95 B3
Elbeuf F 58 A1
El Bing’egerde D 51 B6
Elblag PL 47 A5
El Bodón E 93 A4
El Bonillo E 95 D4
El Bosque E 99 C5
El Bullaque E 94 C2
El Burgo E 100 C1
El Burgo de Ebro E 90 B2
El Burgo de Osma E 89 C3

El Burgo Ranero E 88 B1
El Buste E 89 C5
El Cabaco E 93 A4
El Callejo E 89 A3
El Campillo E 99 B4
El Campillo de la Jara E 94 C1
El Cañavete E 95 C4
El Carpio E 100 B1
El Carpio de Tajo E 94 C2
El Casar E 95 B3
El Casar de Escalona E 94 C2
El Centenillo E 100 A2
El Cerro E 93 A5
El Cerro de Andévalo E 99 B4
Elche E 96 C2
Elche de la Sierra E 101 A3
Elchingen D 61 B6
El Comenar E 99 C5
El Coronil E 99 B5
El Crucero E 86 A4
El Cubo de Tierra del Vino E 88 C1
El Cuervo E 99 C4
Elda E 101 A5
Eldena D 44 B3
Eldingen D 44 C2
Elefsina GR 117 D5
El Ejido E 101 C3
Elek H 75 B6
Elemir SRB 75 C5
El Escorial E 94 B2
El Espinar E 94 B2
Eleftheroupoli GR 116 B6
El Frago E 90 A2
El Franco E 86 A4
El Frasno E 89 C5
Elgå N 114 E8
El Garrobo E 99 B4
El Gastor E 99 C5
Elgin GB 23 D5
Elgoibar E 89 A4
Elgol GB 22 D2
El Gordo E 93 B5
El Grado E 90 A3
El Granado E 98 B3
El Grao de Castelló E 96 B3
El Grau E 96 C2
Elgshøa N 34 A4
El Higuera E 100 B1
El Hijate E 101 B3
El Hontanar E 96 A1
Elhovo BG 11 E9
El Hoyo E 100 A2
Elie GB 25 B5
Elizondo E 76 C1
Elk PL 6 E7
Ellenberg D 61 A6
Ellesmere GB 26 C3
Ellesmere Port GB 26 B3
Ellezelles B 49 C4
Ellingen D 62 A2
Ellmau A 72 A2
Ellon GB 23 D6
Ellös S 35 D3
Ellrich D 51 B6
Ellwangen D 61 B6
Elm
  CH 71 B4
  D 43 B6
Elmadağ TR 16 B6
El Madroño E 99 B4
El Maillo E 93 A4
Elmalı TR 119 F4
El Masnou E 91 B5
El Mirón E 93 A5
El Molar E 95 B3
El Molinillo E 94 C2
El Morell E 91 B4
Elmshorn D 43 B6
Elmstein D 60 A3
El Muyo E 89 C3
Elnesvågen N 114 E4
El Olmo E 88 C3
Elorrio E 89 A4
Elöszállás H 74 B3
Elouda GR 117 G7
Éloyes F 60 B2
El Palo E 100 C1
El Pardo E 94 B3
El Payo E 93 A4
El Pedernoso E 95 C4
El Pedroso E 99 B5
El Peral E 95 C5
El Perelló
  Tarragona E 90 C3
  Valencia E 96 B2
Elphin GB 22 C3
El Picazo E 95 C4
El Pinell de Bray E 90 B3
El Piñero E 88 C1
El Pla de Santa Maria E 91 B4
El Pobo E 90 C2
El Pobo de Dueñas E 95 B5
El Pont d'Armentera E 91 B4
El Port de la Selva E 91 A6
El Port de Llançà E 91 A6
El Port de Sagunt E 96 B2
El Prat de Llobregat E 91 B5
El Provencio E 95 C4
El Puente E 89 A3
El Puerto E 86 A4
El Puerto de Santa Maria E 99 C4
El Real de la Jara E 99 B4
El Real de San Vicente E 94 B2
El Robledo E 94 C2
El Rocio E 99 B4
El Rompido E 99 B3
El Ronquillo E 99 B4
El Royo E 89 C4
El Rubio E 100 B1
El Sabinar E 101 A3
El Saler E 96 B2
El Salobral E 101 A4
El Saucejo E 99 B5
Els Castells E 91 A4
El Serrat AND 91 A4
El Temple E 90 B2
Eltmann D 51 D6
El Tormillo E 90 B2
El Torno E 93 A5
Eltville D 50 C4
El Valle de las Casas E 88 B1
Elvas P 93 C3
Elvebakken N 113 C12
El Vellón E 95 B3
Elven F 56 C3
El Vendrell E 91 B4
Elverum N 34 B3
El Villar de Arnedo E 89 B4
Elvington GB 27 B5
El Viso E 100 A1
El Viso del Alcor E 99 B5
Ely GB 30 B4
Elzach D 61 B4
Elze D 51 A5

Emådalen S 36 A1
Embleton GB 25 C6
Embonas GR 119 F2
Embrun F 79 B5
Embún E 90 A2
Emden D 43 B4
Emecik TR 119 F2
Emet TR 118 C4
Emirdağ TR 118 C6
Emlichheim D 42 C3
Emmaboda S 40 C5
Emmaljunga S 41 C3
Emmeloord NL 42 C2
Emmen
  CH 70 A3
  NL 42 C3
Emmendingen D 60 B3
Emmer-Compascuum NL 43 C4
Emmerich D 50 B2
Emmern D 51 A5
Emöd H 65 C6
Empoli I 81 C4
Emsbüren D 43 C4
Emsdetten D 50 A3
Emsfors S 40 B6
Emskirchen D 62 A1
Emstek D 43 C5
Emsworth GB 31 D3
Emyvale IRL 19 B5
Enånger S 115 F14
Encamp AND 91 A4
Encarnação P 92 C1
Encinas de Abajo E 94 B1
Encinas de Esgueva E 88 C2
Encinasola E 99 A4
Encinas Reales E 100 B1
Encio E 89 B3
Enciso E 89 B4
Enden N 114 F7
Endingen D 60 B3
Endrinal E 93 A5
Endröd H 75 B5
Enebakk N 34 C3
Eneryda S 40 C4
Enese H 64 C3
Enez TR 116 B8
Enfield IRL 21 A5
Eng A 72 A1
Engelberg CH 70 B3
Engelhartszell A 63 B4
Engelskirchen D 50 C3
Engen D 61 C4
Enger N 34 B2
Engerdal N 114 F8
Engerneset N 34 A4
Enge-sande D 39 E1
Engesvang DK 39 C2
Enghien B 49 C5
Engstingen D 61 B5
Engter D 43 C5
Enguera E 96 C2
Enguidanos E 95 C5
Enkenbach D 60 A3
Enkhuizen NL 42 C2
Enklinge FIN 36 B7
Enköping S 37 C4
Enna I 109 B3
Ennezat F 68 C3
Ennigerloh D 50 B4
Enningdal N 35 D3
Ennis IRL 20 B3
Enniscorthy IRL 21 B5
Enniskean IRL 20 C3
Enniskillen GB 19 B4
Ennistimon IRL 20 B2
Enns A 63 B5
Eno FIN 3 E29
Enontekiö FIN 113 D12
Ens NL 42 C2
Enschede NL 50 A2
Ensdorf D 62 A2
Ensisheim F 60 C3
Enstaberga S 37 D3
Enstone GB 31 C2
Entlebuch CH 70 A3
Entracque I 80 B1
Entradas P 98 B2
Entrácque I 88 A3
Entrambasaguas E 88 A3
Entrambasmestas E 88 A3
Entraygues-sur-Truyère F 77 B5
Entre-os-Rios P 87 C2
Entrevaux F 79 C5
Entrin Bajo E 93 C4
Entroncamento P 92 B2
Entzheim F 60 B3
Envermeu F 58 A2
Enviken S 36 B2
Enying H 74 B3
Enzingerboden A 72 A2
Enzklösterle D 61 B4
Épagny F 59 A4
Épalinges CH 70 B1
Epanomi GR 116 B4
Epe
  D 50 A3
  NL 42 C2
Épernay F 59 A4
Épernon F 58 B2
Epfig F 60 B3
Épierre F 69 C6
Épila E 90 B1
Épinac F 69 B4
Épinal F 60 B2
Episcopia I 106 A3
Episkopi CY 120 B1
Epitalio GR 117 E3
Epoisses F 69 A4
Eppenbrunn D 60 A3
Eppendorf D 52 C3
Epping GB 31 C4
Eppingen D 61 A4
Epsom GB 31 C3
Epworth GB 27 B5
Eraclea I 72 C2
Eraclea Mare I 72 C2
Erba I 71 C4
Erbach
  Baden-Württemberg D 61 B5
  Hessen D 61 A4
Erbalunga F 102 A2
Erbendorf D 62 A3
Érchie I 105 C3
Ercolano I 103 C7
Érd H 74 A3
Erdek TR 118 B2
Erdemli TR 16 C7
Erdevik SRB 85 A4
Erdötelek H 65 C6
Erdut HR 75 C4
Erdweg D 62 B2
Erégli
  Konya TR 16 C7
  Zonguldak TR 118 A6
Erenkaya TR 119 F7
Eresfjord N 114 E5
Eresos GR 116 C7
Eretria GR 116 D5
Erfde D 43 A6
Erfjord N 33 C3
Erfstadt D 50 C2
Erfurt D 52 C1
Érgli LV 7 C8
Ergoldsbach D 62 B3
Eriboll GB 22 C4
Érice I 108 A1
Ericeira P 92 C1
Eğridir TR 119 E5
Eriksberg S 115 B12
Eriksmåla S 40 C5
Eringsboda S 40 C5
Eriswil CH 70 A2
Erithres GR 117 D5

Erkelenz D 50 B2
Erkner D 45 C5
Erkrath D 50 B2
Erla E 90 A2
Erlangen D 62 A2
Erli I 80 B2
Erlsbach A 72 B2
Ermelo NL 42 C2
Ermenak TR 16 C6
Ermenek TR 16 C6
Ermenonville F 58 A3
Ermesinde P 87 C2
Ermezinde P 87 C2
Ermidas P 98 A2
Ermioni GR 117 E5
Ermoupoli GR 117 E6
Ermsleben D 52 B1
Erndtebrück D 50 C4
Ernée F 57 B5
Ernestinovo HR 74 C3
Ernstbrunn A 64 B2
Erolzheim D 61 B6
Erquelinnes B 49 C5
Erquy F 56 B3
Erratzu E 76 C1
Erres E 72 C1
Ersa F 102 A2
Érsekcsanád H 75 B3
Érsekë AL 116 B2
Érsekvadkert H 65 C5
Enafors S 115 D9
Ersa I 60 B3
Erstfeld CH 70 B3
Ertebølle DK 38 C2
Ertingen D 61 B5
Ervedal
  Coimbra P 92 A2
  Portalegre P 92 B3
Ervenik HR 83 B4
Ervidel P 98 B2
Ervy-le-Châtel F 59 B4
Erwitte D 51 B4
Erxleben D 52 A1
Erzsébet H 74 B3
Esbjerg DK 39 D1
Esbly F 58 B3
Escacena del Campo E 99 B4
Escairón E 86 B3
Escalada E 88 B3
Escalante E 89 A3
Escalaplano I 110 C2
Escalona E 94 B2
Escalona del Prado E 94 A2
Escalonilla E 94 C2
Escalos de Baixo P 92 B3
Escalos de Cima P 92 B3
Escamilla E 95 B4
Es Caná E 97 B1
Escañuela E 100 B1
Es Castell E 97 B4
Escatrón E 90 B2
Eschach D 61 C5
Eschau D 61 A5
Eschede D 44 C2
Eschenau D 62 A2
Eschenbach D 62 A2
Eschenz CH 61 C4
Eschershausen D 51 B5
Esch-sur-Alzette L 60 A1
Esch-sur-Sûre L 60 A1
Eschwege D 51 B6
Eschweiler D 50 C2
Escobasa de Almazán E 89 C4
Escoeuilles F 48 C2
Escombreras E 101 B5
Escos F 76 C1
Escource F 76 B1
Escragnolles F 79 C5
Escrick GB 27 B4
Escurial E 93 B5
Escurial de la Sierra E 93 A5
Esens D 43 B4
Esgos E 87 B3
Esher GB 31 C3
Eskdalemuir GB 25 C4
Eskifjörður IS 111 B12
Eskilhem S 37 E5
Eskilsäter S 35 D5
Eskilstrup DK 39 E4
Eskilstuna S 37 C3
Eskipazar TR 118 B7
Eskişehir TR 118 C5
Eslarn D 62 A3
Eslava E 89 B5
Eslida E 96 B2
Eslohe D 50 B4
Eslöv S 41 D3
Esme TR 119 D3
Es Mercadal E 97 B4
Es Migjorn Gran E 97 B4
Espa N 34 B3
Espalion F 78 B1
Esparragalejo E 93 C4
Esparragosa del Caudillo E 93 C5
Esparragosa de la Serena E 93 C5
Esparreguera E 91 B4
Esparron F 79 C4
Espe N 32 B3
Espedal N 33 D3
Espejo
  Alava E 89 B3
  Córdoba E 100 B1
Espeland N 32 B2
Espelkamp D 43 C5
Espeluche F 78 B3
Espera E 99 C5
Esperança P 93 B3
Espéraza F 77 D5
Espéria I 103 B6
Espevær N 33 C2
Espiel E 100 A1
Espinama E 88 A2
Espinasses F 79 B5
Espinelves E 91 B5
Espinhal P 92 A2
Espinho P 87 C2
Espinilla E 88 A2
Espinosa de Cerrato E 88 C3
Espinosa de los Monteros E 89 A3
Espinoso del Rey E 94 C2
Espírito Santo P 98 B3
Espluga de Francolí E 91 B4
Esplús E 90 B3
Espolla E 91 A5
Espoo FIN 6 A8
Esporles E 97 B2
Es Port d'Alcúdia E 97 B3
Esposende P 87 C2
Espot E 91 A4
Es Pujols E 97 C1
Esquedas E 90 A2
Esquivias E 94 B3
Essay F 57 B6
Essen
  B 49 B5
  Niedersachsen D 43 C4
  Nordrhein-Westfalen D 50 B3
Essertaux F 58 A3
Essingen D 61 B6
Esslingen D 61 B5
Essoyes F 59 B5
Estact E 91 A4
Estadilla E 90 A3
Estagel F 78 D1
Estaing F 77 B5
Estaires F 78 B1
Estang F 76 C2
Estarreja P 92 A2
Estavayer-le-Lac CH 70 B1
Este I 72 C1

Esteiro E 86 A2
Estela P 87 C2
Estella E 89 B4
Estellencs E 97 B2
Estepa E 100 B1
Estépar E 88 B3
Estepona E 99 C5
Esternay F 59 B4
Esterri d'Aneu E 91 A4
Esterwegen D 43 C4
Estissac F 59 B4
Estivadas E 87 B3
Estivareilles F 68 B2
Estivella E 96 B2
Estói P 98 B3
Estopiñán E 90 B3
Estoril P 92 C1
Estoublon F 79 C5
Estrela P 93 C3
Estremera E 95 B3
Estremoz P 92 C3
Estuna S 36 C5
Esyres F 67 A5
Esztergom H 65 C4
Étables-sur-Mer F 56 B3
Étain F 60 A1
Étalans F 69 A6
Etalle B 60 A1
Étampes F 58 B3
Étang-sur-Arroux F 69 B4
Étaples F 48 C2
Etauliers F 67 C4
Etili TR 118 C1
Etne N 33 C2
Etoliko GR 116 D3
Eton GB 31 C3
Étréaupont F 59 A4
Étréchy F 58 B3
Étrépagny F 58 A2
Étretat F 57 A6
Étroeungt F 49 C4
Étroubles I 70 C2
Ettal D 62 C2
Ettelbruck L 60 A2
Etten NL 49 B5
Ettenheim D 60 B3
Ettington GB 29 A6
Ettlingen D 61 B4
Ettringen D 62 B1
Etxarri-Aranatz E 89 B4
Etyek H 74 A3
Eu F 48 C2
Euerdorf D 51 C6
Eulate E 89 B4
Eupen B 50 C2
Europoort NL 49 B5
Euskirchen D 50 C2
Eutin D 44 A2
Évanges-les-Bains F 68 B2
Évaux-les-Bains F 68 B2
Evciler
  Afyon TR 119 D4
  Çanakkale TR 118 C1
Evenskjær N 112 D5
Evenstad N 34 A3
Evercreech GB 29 B5
Everöd S 41 D4
Eversberg D 51 B4
Everswinkel D 50 B3
Evertsberg S 34 A5
Evesham GB 29 A6
Évian-les-Bains F 69 B6
Evisa F 102 A1
Evje N 33 D4
Evolène CH 70 B2
Évora P 92 C2
Évoramonte P 92 C3
Evran F 57 B4
Évrecy F 57 A5
Evron F 57 B5
Évry F 58 B3
Ewell GB 31 C3
Ewersbach D 50 C4
Excideuil F 67 C6
Exeter GB 29 C4
Exmes F 57 B6
Exminster GB 29 C4
Exmouth GB 29 C4
Eydehamn N 33 D5
Eye
  Peterborough GB 30 B3
  Suffolk GB 30 B5
Eyemouth GB 25 C5
Eyguières F 79 C4
Eygurande F 68 C2
Eylie F 77 D3
Eymet F 77 B3
Eymoutiers F 68 C1
Eynsham GB 31 C2
Eyrarbakki IS 111 D4
Eystrup D 43 C6
Ezaro E 86 B1
Ezcároz E 76 D1
Ezine TR 118 C1
Ezmoriz P 87 D2

F

Fabara E 90 B3
Fábbrico I 81 B4
Fabero E 86 B4
Fábiánsebestyén H 75 B5
Fåborg DK 39 D3
Fabrègues F 78 C2
Fabrezan F 78 C1
Fabrízia I 106 C3
Facha P 87 C2
Facinas E 99 C5
Fačkov SK 65 A4
Fadagosa P 92 B3
Fadd H 74 B3
Faédis I 72 B3
Faenza I 81 B5
Fafe P 87 C2
Fagagna I 72 B3
Fágáras RO 11 D8
Fagelberget S 115 C11
Fagerheim N 32 B4
Fagerhøy N 34 A1
Fagerhult S 40 B5
Fagerlund N 34 B2
Fagernes
  Oppland N 32 B6
  Troms N 112 C8
Fagersanna S 35 D6
Fagersta S 36 C2
Fåglavik S 35 D4
Fagnano Castello I 106 B3
Fagnières F 59 B5
Fagurhólsmýri IS 111 D5
Fahrenzhausen D 62 A2
Fai della Paganella I 71 B6
Faido CH 70 B3
Fains-Véel F 59 B6
Fairford GB 29 B6
Fairlie GB 24 C3
Fakenham GB 30 B4
Fåker S 115 D11
Fåkovce SK 65 B5
Fakse DK 39 D5
Fakse Ladeplads DK 39 D5
Falaise F 57 B5
Falcade I 72 B1
Falces E 89 B5
Fălciu RO 11 C10
Falconara I 108 B2
Falconara Marittima I 82 C2
Falcone I 109 A3
Faldingworth GB 27 B5

Falerum S 37 D3
Fălești MD 11 C9
Falkenberg
  Bayern D 62 A3
  Bayern D 62 B3
  Brandenburg D 52 B3
  S 40 C2
Falkensee D 45 C5
Falkenstein
  Bayern D 62 A3
  Sachsen D 52 C2
Falkenthal D 45 C5
Falkirk GB 25 B4
Falkland GB 25 B4
Falköping S 35 D5
Fall D 62 C2
Falla S 37 D2
Fallingbostel D 43 C6
Falmouth GB 28 C2
Falset E 90 B3
Fălticeni RO 11 C9
Falun S 36 B2
Famagusta CY 120 A2
Fammestad N 32 B1
Fanano I 81 B4
Fanári GR 116 C3
Fanjeaux F 77 C5
Fano I 82 C2
Fântânele RO 11 C7
Fão P 87 C2
Fara in Sabina I 102 A5
Faramontanos de Tábara E 88 C1
Fara Novarese I 70 C3
Farasdues E 90 A1
Fårbo S 40 B6
Fareham GB 31 D2
Färentuna S 37 C4
Färgelanda S 35 D3
Färila S 115 F12
Faringdon GB 31 C2
Faringe S 36 C5
Färjestaden S 41 C6
Farkadona GR 116 C4
Farkasfa H 73 B6
Farlete E 90 B2
Färlöv S 41 C4
Farmos H 75 A4
Fárná SK 65 C4
Farnborough GB 31 C3
Farnham GB 31 C3
Farnroda D 51 C6
Faro P 98 B3
Fårö S 37 E6
Fårösund S 37 E6
Farra d'Alpago I 72 B2
Farranfore IRL 20 B2
Farre DK 39 C2
Farsala GR 116 C4
Farsø DK 38 C2
Farsund N 33 D3
Farum DK 41 D2
Fårup DK 38 C2
Fasana I 103 C8
Fasano I 104 C3
Fáskrúðsfjörður IS 111 C11
Fassberg D 44 B2
Fastiv UA 11 A10
Fastnäs S 34 B5
Fatesh RUS 7 E13
Fátima P 92 B2
Fatmomakke S 115 C12
Fättjaur S 115 B12
Faucogney-et-la-Mer F 60 C2
Fauguerolles F 76 B3
Faulenrost D 45 B4
Faulquemont F 60 A2
Fauquembergues F 48 C3
Fauske N 112 E4
Fauville-en-Caux F 58 A1
Fauvillers B 60 A1
Fåvang N 34 A2
Favara
  E 96 B2
  I 108 B2
Favareta E 96 B2
Faverges F 69 C6
Faverney F 60 C2
Faversham GB 31 C4
Favignana I 108 B1
Fawley GB 31 D2
Fay-aux-Loges F 58 C3
Fayence F 79 C5
Fayl-Billot F 60 C1
Fayón E 90 B3
Fécamp F 58 A1
Feda N 33 D3
Fedje N 32 B1
Feeny GB 19 B4
Fegen S 40 B3
Fegyvernek H 75 A5
Fehrbellin D 45 C4
Fehring A 73 B5
Feichten A 71 A5
Feiring N 34 B3
Feistritz im Rosental A 73 B4
Feke TR 16 C7
Feketić SRB 75 C4
Felanitx E 97 B3
Feld am See A 72 B3
Feldbach A 73 B5
Feldberg D 45 B5
Feldkirch A 71 A4
Feldkirchen in Kärnten A 73 B4
Feldkirchen-Westerham D 62 C2
Felgueiras P 87 C2
Felitto I 103 C8
Félix E 101 C3
Felixstowe GB 31 C5
Felizzano I 80 B2
Felletin F 68 C2
Fellingsbro S 37 C2
Felnac RO 75 B6
Felnémet H 65 C6
Felpéc H 74 A2
Fels am Wagram A 64 B1
Felsberg D 51 B5
Felsőszentmárton H 74 C2
Felsőszolca H 65 B6
Felsted DK 39 E2
Feltre I 72 B1
Femsjö S 40 C3
Fenagh IRL 19 B4
Fene E 86 A2
Fenestrelle I 79 A6
Fénétrange F 60 B3
Feneu F 57 C5
Fengersfors S 35 D4
Fenit IRL 20 B2
Fensmark DK 39 D4
Fenwick GB 24 C3
Feolin Ferry GB 24 C1

Fermoy IRL 20 B3
Fernancaballero E 94 C3
Fernán Nuñez E 100 B1
Fernán Peréz E 101 C3
Fernão Ferro P 92 C1
Fernay-Voltaire F 69 B6
Ferndown GB 29 C6
Ferness GB 23 D5
Fernhurst GB 31 C3
Ferns IRL 21 B5
Ferpécle CH 70 B2
Ferrals-les-Corbières F 78 C1
Ferrandina I 104 C2
Ferrara I 81 B5
Ferrara di Monte Baldo I 71 C5
Ferreira E 86 A3
Ferreira do Alentejo P 98 A2
Ferreira do Zêzere P 92 B2
Ferreiras do Abajo E 87 C4
Ferreras de Arriba E 87 C4
Ferreries E 97 B4
Ferreruela E 90 B1
Ferreruela de Tabara E 87 C4
Ferbane IRL 21 A4
Ferdinandovac HR 74 B2
Ferdinandshof D 45 B5
Fère-Champenoise F 59 B4
Fère-en-Tardenois F 59 A4
Ferentillo I 102 A5
Ferentino I 102 B6
Féres GR 116 B8
Feria E 93 C4
Feričanci HR 74 C2
Ferizli TR 118 B5
Ferla I 109 B3
Ferlach A 73 B4
Ferleiten A 72 A2
Fermil P 87 C3
Fermo I 82 C2
Fermoselle E 87 C4
Ferret CH 70 C2
Ferrette F 70 A2
Ferriere I 80 B3
Ferrières
  Hautes-Pyrénées F 76 C2
  Loiret F 58 C3
  Oise F 58 A3
Ferrières-sur-Sichon F 68 B3
Ferrol E 86 A2
Ferryhill GB 27 A4
Fertörakos H 64 C2
Fertöszentmiklós H 64 C2
Ferwerd NL 42 B2
Festieux F 59 A4
Festøy N 114 E3
Festvåg N 112 E3
Fetesti RO 11 D9
Fethard
  Tipperary IRL 21 B4
  Wexford IRL 21 B5
Fethiye TR 119 F4
Fetsund N 34 C3
Fettercairn GB 25 B5
Feucht D 62 A2
Feuchtwangen D 61 A6
Feudingen D 50 C4
Feuges F 59 B5
Feuquières F 58 A2
Feurs F 69 C4
Fevik N 33 D5
Ffestiniog GB 26 C2
Fiamignano I 102 A6
Fiano I 70 C2
Ficarazzi I 108 A2
Ficarolo I 81 B5
Fichtelberg D 52 C1
Fidenza I 81 B4
Fidjeland N 33 D3
Fieberbrunn A 72 A2
Fier AL 105 C5
Fiera di Primiero I 72 B1
Fierzë AL 105 A6
Fiesch CH 70 B3
Fiesso Umbertiano I 81 B5
Figari F 102 B2
Figeac F 77 B5
Figeholm S 40 B6
Figgjo N 33 D2
Figline Valdarno I 81 C5
Figols E 90 A3
Figueira da Foz P 92 A2
Figueira de Castelo Rodrigo P 87 D4
Figueira dos Caveleiros P 98 A2
Figueiredo P 92 B3
Figueiredo de Alva P 87 D3
Figueirós Vinhos P 92 B2
Figueres E 91 A5
Figueroles E 96 A2
Figueruela de Arriba E 87 C4
Filadélfia I 106 C3
Fil'akovo SK 65 B5
Filderstadt D 61 B5
Filey GB 27 A5
Filiași RO 11 D7
Filiates GR 116 C2
Filiatra GR 117 E3
Filipstad S 35 C6
Filisur CH 71 B4
Fillan N 114 D5
Filotio I 117 E7
Filottrano I 82 C2
Filskov DK 39 D2
Filton GB 29 B5
Filtvet N 35 C2
Filzmoos A 72 A3
Finale Emilia I 81 B5
Finale Ligure I 80 B2
Fiñana E 101 B3
Finby FIN 36 B7
Fincham GB 30 B4
Finchingfield GB 31 C4
Findhorn GB 23 D5
Findochty GB 23 D6
Finike TR 119 F5
Finkenberg A 72 A1
Finnea IRL 19 C4
Finneidfjord N 115 A10
Finnerödja S 35 D6
Finnsnes N 112 C7
Finntorp S 35 C4
Finócchio I 102 B5
Finsjö S 40 B6
Finsland N 33 D4
Finspång S 37 D2
Finsterwalde D 53 B3
Finsterwolde NL 43 B4
Finstown GB 23 B5
Fionnphort GB 24 B1
Fiorenzuola d'Arda I 81 B3
Firenze = Florence I 81 C5
Firenzuola I 81 B5
Firmi F 77 B5
Firminy F 69 C4
Firmo I 106 B3
Fischamend Markt A 64 B2
Fischbach
  A 73 A5
  D 60 A3
Fischbeck D 44 C4
Fischen D 61 C6
Fishbourne GB 31 D2
Fishguard GB 28 A3
Fiskardo GR 116 D2
Fiskebäckskil S 35 D3
Fiskebøl N 112 D3
Fismes F 59 A4
Fisterra E 86 B1
Fitero E 89 B5
Fitjar N 32 C2
Fiuggi I 102 B6
Fiumata I 102 A6
Fiumefreddo Brúzio I 106 B3
Fiumefreddo di Sicilia I 109 B4
Fiumicino I 102 B5
Fivemiletown GB 19 B4
Fivizzano I 81 B4
Fjälkinge S 41 D4
Fjällåsen S 112 E9
Fjällbacka S 35 D3
Fjæra N 32 C3
Fjärdhundra S 36 C3
Fjellerup DK 38 C3
Fjerritslev DK 38 B2
Fjordgard N 112 C6

Fjugesta S 37 C1
Flå N 32 B6
Flåbygd N 33 C5
Flaça E 91 A5
Flaçà F 69 B4
Fladungen D 51 C6
Flaine F 70 B1
Flåm N 32 B4
Flamatt CH 70 B2
Flamborough GB 27 A5
Flammersfeld D 50 C3
Flassans-sur-Issole F 79 C5
Flatdal N 33 C5
Flatebø N 32 B3
Flateby N 34 C3
Flateland N 33 C4
Flateyri IS 111 A2
Flatøydegard N 32 B6
Flatråker N 32 C2
Flattach A 72 B3
Flatvarp S 37 E3
Flauenskjold DK 38 B3
Flavigny-sur-Moselle F 60 B2
Flavy-le-Martel F 59 A4
Flawil CH 71 A4
Flayosc F 79 C5
Flechtingen D 44 C3
Fleckeby D 44 A1
Fleet GB 31 C3
Fleetmark D 44 C3
Fleetwood GB 26 B2
Flehingen D 61 A4
Flekke N 32 A2
Flekkefjord N 33 D3
Flen S 37 C3
Flensburg D 39 E2
Fleringe S 37 E5
Flerohopp S 40 C5
Flers F 57 B5
Flesberg N 32 C6
Fleurance F 77 C3
Fleuré F 67 B5
Fleurier CH 69 B6
Fleurus B 49 C5
Fleury
  Hérault F 78 C2
  Yonne F 59 C4
Fleury-les-Aubrais F 58 C2
Fleury-sur-Andelle F 58 A2
Fleury-sur-Orne F 57 A5
Fléron B 50 C1
Flieden D 51 C5
Flimby GB 26 A2
Flims CH 71 B4
Flines-lèz-Raches F 49 C4
Flint GB 26 B2
Flirey F 60 B1
Flirsch A 71 A5
Flisa N 34 B4
Flisby S 40 B4
Fliseryd S 40 B6
Flix E 90 B3
Flixecourt F 48 C3
Flize F 59 A5
Flobecq B 49 C4
Floby S 35 C5
Floda S 40 B2
Flodden GB 25 C5
Flogny-la-Chapelle F 59 C4
Flöha D 52 C3
Flonheim D 61 A4
Florac F 78 B2
Floreffe B 49 C5
Florence = Firenze I 81 C5
Florennes B 49 C5
Florensac F 78 C2
Florentin F 77 C5
Florenville B 59 A6
Flores de Avila E 94 B1
Floreşti MD 11 C10
Floridia I 109 B4
Florina GR 116 B3
Florø N 114 F2
Flörsheim D 51 C4
Floss D 62 A3
Fluberg N 34 B2
Flúðir IS 111 C5
Flühli CH 70 B3
Flumet F 69 C6
Fluminimaggiore I 110 C1
Flums CH 71 A4
Flyeryd S 41 C5
Flygsfors S 40 C5
Foča BIH 84 C3
Foça TR 118 D1
Fochabers GB 23 D5
Focşani RO 11 D9
Foel GB 26 C2
Foeni RO 75 C5
Fogdö S 37 C3
Fóggia I 104 B1
Föglö FIN 36 B7
Fohnsdorf A 73 A4
Foiano della Chiana I 81 C5
Foix F 77 D4
Fojnica
  BIH 84 C2
  BIH 84 C3
Fokino RUS 7 E13
Fokstua N 114 E6
Földeák H 75 B5
Foldereid N 114 C9
Földes H 75 A6
Folegandros GR 117 F6
Folelli F 102 A2
Folgaria I 71 C6
Folgosinho P 92 A3
Folgoso de la Ribera E 86 B4
Folgoso do Courel E 86 B3
Foligno I 82 D1
Folkärna S 36 B3
Folkestad N 114 E3
Folkestone GB 31 C5
Follafoss N 114 D8
Folldal N 114 E6
Follebu N 34 A2
Follina I 72 C2
Föllinge S 115 D11
Follónica I 81 D4
Fölsbyn S 35 C4
Foncebadón E 86 B4
Foncine-le-Bas F 69 B6
Fondevila E 87 C2
Fondi I 103 B6
Fondo I 71 B6
Fonelas E 100 B2
Fonfría
  Teruel E 90 C1
  Zamora E 87 C4
Fonnes N 32 B1
Fonni I 110 B2
Fontaine F 59 B5
Fontaine de Vaucluse F 79 C4
Fontaine-Française F 69 A5
Fontaine-le-Dun F 58 A1
Fontan F 80 B1
Fontanarejo E 94 C2
Fontane I 80 B1
Fontanélice I 81 B5
Fontanières F 68 B2
Fontanosas E 94 C2
Fonteblanda I 102 A4
Fontenay-le-Comte F 66 B4
Fontenay-Trésigny F 59 B3
Fontevrault-l'Abbaye F 67 A5
Fontiveros E 94 B2
Fontoy F 60 A1
Fontpédrouse F 91 A5
Fontstown IRL 21 A5
Fonyód H 74 B2
Fonz E 90 A3
Fonzaso I 72 B1
Fóppolo I 71 B4
Föra S 41 B6

Forbach
  D 61 B4
  F 60 A2
Forcall E 90 C2
Forcalquier F 79 C4
Forcarei E 86 B2
Forchheim D 62 A2
Forchtenau A 64 C2
Forchtenberg D 61 A5
Ford GB 24 B2
Førde
  Hordaland N 33 C2
  Sogn og Fjordane N 32 A2
Førdesbruk D 52 B1
Førdesfjorden N 33 C2
Fordham GB 30 B4
Fordingbridge GB 29 C6
Fordon PL 47 B4
Fordongiánus I 110 C1
Forenza I 104 C1
Foresta di Búrgos I 110 B1
Forfar GB 25 B5
Forges-les-Eaux F 58 A2
Foria I 106 A2
Forío I 103 C6
Forjães P 87 C2
Førland N 33 D4
Forlì I 81 B6
Forlimpópoli I 82 B1
Formazza I 70 B3
Formby GB 26 B2
Formerie F 58 A2
Fórmia I 103 B6
Formigine I 81 B4
Formigliana I 70 C3
Formiguères F 91 A5
Fornalutx E 97 B2
Fornása S 37 D2
Fornelli I 110 B1
Fornells E 97 A4
Fornes de Montes E 87 B2
Fornes E 100 C2
Forneset N 112 C8
Forni Avoltri I 72 B2
Forni di Sopra I 72 B2
Forni di Sotto I 72 B2
Forno
  Piemonte I 70 C3
  Piemonte I 79 A6
Forno Alpi-Gráie I 70 C2
Forno di Zoldo I 72 B2
Fornos de Algodres P 92 A3
Fornovo di Taro I 81 B4
Foros do Arrão P 92 B2
Forráskút H 75 B4
Forres GB 23 D5
Forríolo E 87 B3
Fors S 36 B3
Forsand N 33 D3
Forsbacka S 36 B3
Forserum S 40 B4
Forshaga S 35 C5
Forsheda S 40 B3
Forsinain GB 23 C5
Førslev DK 39 D4
Forsmark
  Uppsala S 36 B5
  Västerbotten S 115 B12
Forsmo S 115 D14
Forsnäs S 115 A15
Forsnes N 114 D5
Forssa FIN 3 F25
Forssjöbruk S 37 D3
Forst D 53 B4
Forsvik S 37 D1
Fort Augustus GB 22 D4
Fortezza I 72 B1
Forth GB 25 C4
Fort-Mahon-Plage F 48 C2
Fortrie GB 23 D6
Fortrose GB 23 D4
Fortuna E 101 A4
Fortuneswell GB 29 C5
Fort William GB 24 B2
Forvik N 115 B9
Fos F 77 D3
Fosdinovo I 81 B4
Foss N 32 B6
Fossacésia I 103 A7
Fossano I 80 B1
Fossato di Vico I 82 C1
Fossbakken N 112 D6
Fosse-la-Ville B 49 C5
Fossombrone I 82 C1
Fos-sur-Mer F 78 C3
Foth I 65 C5
Fouchères F 59 B5
Fouesnant F 56 C1
Foug F 60 B1
Fougères F 57 B4
Fougerolles F 60 C2
Foulain F 59 B6
Fountainhall GB 25 C5
Fouras F 66 C3
Fourchambault F 68 A3
Fourmies F 49 C5
Fourna GR 116 C3
Fournels F 78 B2
Fourni GR 119 E1
Fournols F 68 C3
Fourques F 91 A5
Fourquevaux F 77 C4
Fours F 68 B3
Fowey GB 28 C3
Foxdale GB 26 A1
Foxford IRL 18 C2
Foyers GB 23 D4
Foynes IRL 20 B2
Foz E 86 A3
Foza I 72 C1
Foz do Arelho P 92 B1
Foz do Giraldo P 92 B3
Frabosa Soprana I 80 B1
Frades de la Sierra E 93 A5
Fraga E 90 B3
Fragagnano I 104 C3
Frailes E 100 B2
Fraire B 49 C5
Fraize F 60 B2
Framlingham GB 30 B5
Frammersbach D 51 C5
Framnes N 35 C2
França P 87 C4
Francaltroff F 60 B2
Francavilla al Mare I 103 A7
Francavilla di Sicília I 109 B4
Francavilla Fontana I 104 C3
Francavilla in Sinni I 106 A3
Francescas F 77 B3
Franco P 87 C3
Francofonte I 109 B3
Francos E 89 C3
Frändefors S 35 D4
Frangy F 69 B5
Frankenau D 51 B4
Frankenberg
  Hessen D 51 B4
  Sachsen D 52 C3
Frankenburg A 63 B4
Frankenfels A 63 C6
Frankenmarkt A 63 C4
Frankenthal D 61 A4
Frankfurt
  Brandenburg D 45 C6
  Hessen D 51 C4
Frankowo PL 47 A5
Frankrike S 115 D10
Fränsta S 115 E13
Františkovy Lázně CZ 52 C2
Franzburg D 45 A4
Frasdorf D 62 C3

Fraserburgh GB 23 D6
Frashër AL 116 B2
Frasne F 69 B6
Frasnes-lez-Anvaing F 49 C4
Frasseto F 102 B2
Frastanz A 71 A4
Fratel P 92 B3
Fratta Todina I 82 D1
Frauenau D 63 B4
Frauenfeld CH 70 A3
Frauenkirchen A 64 C2
Frauenstein D 52 C3
Frauental A 73 B5
Frayssinet F 77 B4
Frayssinet-le-Gélat F 77 B4
Frechas P 87 C3
Frechen D 50 C2
Frechilla E 88 B2
Freckenhorst D 50 B3
Fredeburg D 50 B4
Fredelsloh D 51 B5
Fredeng N 34 B2
Fredericia DK 39 D2
Frederiks DK 39 C2
Frederikshavn DK 38 B3
Frederikssund DK 39 D5
Frederiksværk DK 39 D5
Fredrika S 115 C15
Fredriksberg S 36 B6
Fredriksdal S 40 B4
Fredrikstad N 35 C2
Fregenal de la Sierra E 99 A4
Fregene I 102 B5
Freiberg D 52 C3
Freiburg
  Baden-Württemberg D 60 C3
  Niedersachsen D 43 B6
Freienhagen D 51 B5
Freienhufen D 53 B3
Freienstein I 51 C5
Freihung D 62 A2
Freilassing D 62 C3
Freisen D 60 A3
Freising D 62 B2
Freistadt A 63 B5
Freital D 52 B3
Freixedas P 93 A3
Freixo de Espada à Cinta P 87 C4
Fréjus F 79 C5
Fremdingen D 61 B6
Frenštát pod Radhoštěm CZ 64 A4
Freren D 43 C4
Freshford IRL 21 B4
Freshwater GB 31 D2
Fresnay-sur-Sarthe F 57 B6
Fresneda de la Sierra E 95 B4
Fresneda de la Sierra Tirón E 89 B3
Fresnedillas E 94 B2
Fresnes-en-Woevre F 60 A1
Fresne-St Mamès F 69 A5
Fresno Alhándiga E 94 B1
Fresno de la Ribera E 88 C1
Fresno de la Vega E 88 B1
Fresno de Sayago E 87 C5
Fresnoy-Folny F 58 A2
Fresnoy-le-Grand F 59 A4
Fressenville F 48 C2
Freswick N 32 A3
Fréteval F 58 C2
Fretigney F 69 A5
Freudenberg
  Baden-Württemberg D 61 A5
  Nordrhein-Westfalen D 50 C3
Freudenstadt D 61 B4
Freux B 49 D6
Frévent F 48 C3
Freyburg D 52 B1
Freyenstein D 44 B4
Freyming-Merlebach F 60 A2
Freystadt D 62 A2
Freyung D 63 B4
Frías de Albarracín E 95 B5
Fribourg CH 70 B2
Frick CH 70 A3
Fridafors S 41 C4
Fridaythorpe GB 27 A5
Friedberg
  Bayern D 62 B1
  Hessen D 51 C4
Friedeburg D 43 B4
Friedewald D 51 C5
Friedland
  Brandenburg D 53 A4
  Mecklenburg-Vorpommern D 45 B5
  Niedersachsen D 51 B5
Friedrichroda D 51 C6
Friedrichsdorf D 51 C4
Friedrichshafen D 61 C5
Friedrichskoog D 43 A5
Friedrichstadt D 43 A6
Friedrichswalde D 45 B5
Friesach A 73 B4
Friesack D 45 C4
Friesenheim D 60 B3
Friesoythe D 43 B4
Friggesund S 115 F13
Frigiliana E 100 C2
Frihetsli N 112 D8
Frillesås S 40 B2
Frinnaryd S 40 B4
Frinton-on-Sea GB 31 C5
Friockheim GB 25 B5
Friol E 86 A3
Fristad S 40 B3
Fritzlar D 51 B5
Frizington GB 26 A2
Frödinge S 40 B6
Froges F 69 C5
Frohburg D 52 B2
Frohnhausen D 50 C4
Frohnleiten A 73 A5
Froissy F 58 A3
Frombork PL 47 A5
Frome GB 29 B5
Frómista E 88 B2
Fröndenberg D 50 B3
Fronsac F 76 B2
Front I 70 C2
Fronteira P 92 B3
Frontenhausen D 62 B3
Frontignan F 78 C2
Frontnas F 77 C4
Fröseke S 40 C5
Frosinone I 103 B6
Frosolone I 103 B7
Frosta N 114 D7
Frøstrup DK 38 B1
Frosunda S 37 C5
Frouard F 60 B2
Frøyrå S 37 C2
Frøyset N 32 B1
Fruges F 48 C3
Frutigen CH 70 B2
Frýdek-Místek CZ 65 A4
Frýdlant
  CZ 53 C5
Frýdlant nad Ostravicí CZ 65 A4
Frygnowo PL 47 B6
Fryšták CZ 64 A3
Fucécchio I 81 C4
Fuencaliente
  Ciudad Real E 94 C3
  Ciudad Real E 100 A1
Fuencemillán E 95 B3
Fuendejalón E 90 B1
Fuengirola E 100 C1

Fuenlabrada E 94 B3
Fuenlabrada de los Montes E 94 C2
Fuensalida E 94 B2
Fuensanta E 101 B4
Fuensanta de Martos E 100 B2
Fuente-Álamo E 101 A4
Fuente-Álamo de Murcia E 101 B4
Fuentealbilla E 96 B1
Fuente al Olmo de Iscar E 88 C2
Fuentecén E 88 A2
Fuente de Cantos E 99 A4
Fuente del Arco E 99 A5
Fuente del Conde E 100 B1
Fuente del Maestre E 93 C4
Fuente de Santa Cruz E 94 A2
Fuente el Fresno E 94 C3
Fuente el Saz de Jarama E 95 B3
Fuente el Sol E 94 A2
Fuenteguinaldo E 93 A4
Fuentelapeña E 94 A1
Fuentelcésped E 89 C3
Fuentelespino de Haro E 95 C4
Fuentelespino de Moya E 96 B1
Fuente Obejuna E 99 A5
Fuente Palmera E 99 B5
Fuentepelayo E 94 A2
Fuentepinilla E 89 C4
Fuenterrobles de Salvatierra E 93 A5
Fuenterrobles E 96 B1
Fuentes E 95 C5
Fuentesauco E 88 C2
Fuentesaúco E 94 A1
Fuentes de Andalucía E 99 B5
Fuentes de Ebro E 90 B2
Fuentes de Jiloca E 89 C5
Fuentes de la Alcarria E 95 B4
Fuentes de León E 99 A4
Fuentes de Nava E 88 B2
Fuentes de Oñoro E 93 A4
Fuentes de Ropel E 88 B1
Fuentespalda E 90 C3
Fuentespina E 89 C3
Fuente-Tójar E 100 B1
Fuente Vaqueros E 100 B2
Fuentidueña E 88 C2
Fuentidueña de Tajo E 95 B3
Fuerte del Rey E 100 B2
Fügen A 72 A1
Fuglebjerg DK 39 D4
Fuglevik N 35 C2
Fuhrberg D 44 C1
Fulda D 51 C5
Fulgatore I 108 B1
Fulnek CZ 64 A3
Fülöpszállás H 75 B4
Fully CH 70 B2
Fulpmes A 71 A6
Fulunäs S 34 A5
Fumay F 49 D5
Fumel F 77 B3
Funäsdalen S 115 E9
Fundão P 92 A3
Fundres I 72 B1
Funzie GB 22 A8
Furadouro P 87 D2
Füre N 32 A2
Fürstenau D 43 C4
Furstenau D 51 B5
Fürstenberg D 45 B5
Fürstenfeld A 73 A6
Fürstenfeldbruck D 62 B2
Fürstenstein D 63 B4
Fürstenwalde D 45 C6
Fürstenwerder D 45 B5
Fürstenzell D 63 B4
Fürth
  Bayern D 62 A1
  Hessen D 61 A4
Furth im Wald D 62 A3
Furtwangen D 61 B4
Furuby S 40 C5
Furudal S 36 A2
Furuflaten N 112 C9
Furulund S 41 D3
Furusjö S 40 B4
Fusa N 32 B2
Fuscaldo I 106 B3
Fusch an der Grossglocknerstrasse A 72 A2
Fushë Arrëz AL 105 A6
Fushë-Krujë AL 105 B5
Fusina I 72 C2
Fusio CH 70 B3
Füssen D 62 C1
Fustiñana E 89 B5
Futog SRB 75 C4
Futrikelv N 112 C8
Füzesabony H 65 C6
Füzesgyarmat H 75 A6
Fužine HR 73 C4
Fylling S 40 C2
Fynshav DK 39 E2
Fyresdal N 33 C5

G

Gaalkacy
Gaaldorf A 73 A4
Gabaldón E 95 C5
Gabarret F 76 C3
Gabčíkovo SK 64 C3
Gabin PL 47 C5
Gabriac F 78 B1
Gabrovo BG 11 E8
Gaby I 70 C2
Gacé F 58 B1
Gacko BIH 84 C3
Gäddede S 115 C11
Gadebusch D 44 B3
Gádheim D 70 B3
Gádor E 101 C3
Gádoros H 75 B5
Gael F 57 B3
Găeşti RO 11 D8
Gaeta I 103 B6
Gafanhoeira P 92 C2
Gaflenz A 63 C5
Gagarin RUS 7 D13
Gaggenau D 61 B4
Gagliano Castelferrato I 109 B3
Gagliano del Capo I 107 B5
Gagnet S 36 B2
Gaibanella E 81 B5
Gaildorf D 61 B5
Gaillac F 77 C4
Gaillefontaine F 58 A2
Gaillon F 58 A2
Gainsborough GB 27 B5
Gairloch GB 22 D3
Gairlochy GB 24 B3
Gáiro I 110 C2
Gaj
  HR 74 C2
  SRB 85 B6
Gaja-la-Selve F 77 C4
Gajanejos E 95 B4
Gajary SK 64 B3
Gajdobra SRB 75 C4
Galan F 77 C3
Galanta SK 64 B3
Galapagar E 94 B2
Galápagos E 95 B3
Galaroza E 99 B4
Galashiels GB 25 C5
Galatás GR 117 E5
Galați RO 11 D10
Galatina I 107 A5
Galatista GR 116 B5
Galátone I 107 A5
Galaxidi GR 117 D4
Galdakao E 89 A4
Galeata I 81 C5
Galende E 87 B4
Galera E 101 B3
Galéria F 102 A1
Galgamácsa H 65 C5
Galgate GB 26 B3
Galgon F 76 B2
Galinduste E 93 A5
Galinoporni CY 120 A3
Galisteo E 93 B4
Galizes P 92 A3
Galków PL 55 B4
Gallarate I 70 C3
Gallardon F 58 B2
Gallegos de Argañán E 93 A4
Gallegos del Solmirón E 93 A5
Galleguillos de Campos E 88 B1
Galleno I 81 C4
Galliate I 70 C3
Gallicano I 81 B4
Gállio I 72 C1
Gallipoli = Gelibolu TR 118 B1
Gallipoli I 107 A4
Gällivare S 112 E9
Gallizien A 73 B4
Gallneukirchen A 63 B5
Gallocanta E 95 B5
Gällstad S 40 B3
Galluccio I 103 B7
Gallur E 90 B1
Galmisdale GB 24 B1
Galston GB 24 C3
Galta N 33 C2
Galtelli I 110 B2
Galten DK 39 C2
Galtür A 71 B5
Galve de Sorbe E 95 A3
Galveias P 92 B2
Gálvez E 94 C2
Galway IRL 20 A2
Gamaches F 48 D2
Gámbara I 71 C5
Gambárie I 106 C2
Gambassi Terme I 81 C4
Gambatesa I 103 B7
Gambolò I 70 C3
Gaming A 63 C6
Gamla Uppsala S 36 C4
Gamleby S 40 B6
Gamlingay GB 30 B3
Gammelgarn S 37 E5
Gammelstad S 3 D25
Gammertingen D 61 B5
Gams CH 71 A4
Gamvik
  Finnmark N 113 A17
  Finnmark N 113 B11
Gan F 76 C2
Gáname E 87 C4
Ganda di Martello I 71 B5
Gandarela P 87 C2
Ganddal N 33 D2
Ganderkesee D 43 B5
Gandesa E 90 B3
Gandía E 96 C2
Gandino I 71 C4
Gandrup DK 38 B3
Gånghester S 40 B3
Gangi I 109 B3
Gangkofen D 62 B3
Gannat F 68 B3
Gannay-sur-Loire F 68 B3
Gänserdorf A 64 B2
Ganzlin D 44 B4
Gap F 79 B5
Gara H 75 B4
Garaballa E 96 B1
Garaguso I 104 C1
Garbayuela E 94 C1
Garbhallt GB 24 B2
Garbsen D 43 C6
Garching D 62 B2
Garciaz E 93 B5
Garcihernández E 94 B1
Garcillán E 94 B2
Garcinarro E 95 B4
Garcisobaco E 99 C5
Garda I 71 C5
Gardanne F 79 C4
Gårdás S 34 B5
Gárdby S 41 C6
Gardeja PL 47 B4
Gardelegen D 44 C3
Gardermoen N 34 B3
Gardiki GR 116 D3
Garding D 43 A5
Gardone Riviera I 71 C5
Gardone Val Trómpia I 71 C5
Gárdony H 74 A3
Gardouch F 77 C4
Gårdsjö S 37 D1
Gårdskär S 36 B4
Gards Köpinge S 41 D4
Garein F 76 B2
Garelochhead GB 24 B3
Garéscio I 80 B2
Garforth GB 27 B4
Gargaliani GR 117 E3
Gargaligas E 93 B5
Garganta la Olla E 93 A5
Gargantiel E 100 A1
Gargellen A 71 B4
Gargilesse-Dampierre F 67 B6
Gargnano I 71 C5
Gargnäs S 115 B14
Gárgoles de Abajo E 95 B4
Gargrave GB 26 B3
Garitz D 52 B2
Garlasco I 70 C3
Garlieston GB 24 D3
Garlin F 76 C2
Garlitos E 94 D1
Garmisch-Partenkirchen D 62 C2
Garnat-sur-Engièvre F 68 B3
Garpenberg S 36 B3
Garphyttan S 37 C1
Garray E 89 C4
Garrel D 43 C5
Garriguella E 91 A6
Garrison GB 18 B3
Garrovillas E 93 B4
Garrucha E 101 B4
Gars-am-Kamp A 63 B6
Garsås S 36 B1
Garsdale Head GB 26 A3
Gärsnäs S 41 D4
Garstang GB 26 B3
Gartow D 44 B3
Gartz D 45 B6
Garvagh GB 19 B5
Garvão P 98 B2
Garve GB 22 D4
Garwolin PL 55 B6
Garz D 45 A5
Garzyn PL 54 B1
Gasawa PL 46 C3
Gåsborn S 34 C6
Gaschurn A 71 B4
Gascueña E 95 B4
Gasny F 58 A2
Gasocin PL 47 C6
Gastes F 76 B1
Gastouni GR 117 E3
Gastouri GR 116 C1

Gata
  E 93 A4
  HR 83 C5
Gata de Gorgos E 96 C3
Gatchina RUS 7 B11
Gatehouse of Fleet GB 24 D3
Gátér H 75 B4
Gateshead GB 25 D6
Gátova E 96 B2
Gattendorf A 64 B2
Gatteo a Mare I 82 B1
Gattinara I 70 C3
Gattorna I 80 B3
Gaucín E 99 C5
Gaulstad N 114 D9
Gaupne N 32 A4
Gautefall N 33 C5
Gauting D 62 B2
Gauto S 115 A13
Gava E 91 B5
Gavardo I 71 C5
Gavarnie F 76 D2
Gavi I 80 B2
Gaviáo P 92 B3
Gavirate I 70 C3
Gävle S 36 B4
Gavoi I 110 B2
Gavorrano I 81 D4
Gavray F 57 B4
Gavrio GR 117 E6
Gävunda S 34 B6
Gaweinstal A 64 B2
Gaworzyce PL 53 B5
Gaydon GB 30 B2
Gayton GB 30 B4
Gazipaşa TR 119 F7
Gazoldo degli Ippoliti I 71 C5
Gazzuolo I 81 A4
Gbelce SK 65 C4
Gdańsk PL 47 A4
Gdinj HR 84 C1
Gdov RUS 7 B9
Gdów PL 65 A6
Gdynia PL 47 A4
Gea de Albarracín E 95 B5
Geary GB 22 D2
Géaudot F 59 B5
Geaune F 76 C2
Gebesee D 51 B6
Gebiz TR 119 E5
Gebze TR 118 B4
Géderlak H 75 B3
Gedern D 51 C5
Gedinne B 49 D5
Gediz TR 118 D4
Gèdre F 76 D3
Gedser DK 44 A3
Gedsted DK 38 C2
Geel B 49 B5
Geesthacht D 44 B2
Geetbets B 49 C6
Gefell D 52 C1
Gehrden D 51 A5
Gehren D 52 C1
Geilenkirchen D 50 C2
Geilo N 32 B5
Geinsheim D 61 A4
Geisa D 51 C5
Geiselhöring D 62 B3
Geiselwind D 61 A6
Geisenfeld D 62 B2
Geisenhausen D 62 B3
Geisenheim D 50 D4
Geisingen D 61 C4
Geislingen D 61 B5
Geistthal A 73 A5
Geiterygghytta N 32 B4
Geithain D 52 B2
Geithus N 34 C1
Gela I 109 B3
Geldermalsen NL 49 B6
Geldern D 50 B2
Geldrop NL 49 B6
Geleen NL 50 C1
Gelembe TR 118 C2
Gelendost TR 119 D6
Gelibolu = Gallipoli TR 118 B1
Gelida E 91 B4
Gelnhausen D 51 C5
Gelnica SK 65 B6
Gelsa E 90 B2
Gelse H 74 B1
Gelsenkirchen D 50 B3
Gelsted DK 39 D2
Geltendorf D 62 B1
Gelterkinden CH 70 A2
Gelting D 39 E2
Gelu RO 75 B6
Gelves E 99 B4
Gembloux B 49 C5
Gemeaux F 69 A5
Gémenos F 79 C4
Gemerská Poloma SK 65 B6
Gemert NL 50 B1
Gemla S 40 C4
Gemlik TR 118 B4
Gemmenich B 50 C1
Gemona del Friuli I 72 B3
Gémozac F 67 C4
Gemund D 50 C2
Gemünden
  Bayern D 51 C5
  Hessen D 51 C4
  Rheinland-Pfalz D 60 A3
Genappe B 49 C5
Génave E 101 A3
Genazzano I 102 B5
Gençay F 67 B5
Gencsapáti H 74 A1
Gendringen NL 50 B2
Genelard F 69 B4
Genemuiden NL 42 C2
Generalski Stol HR 73 C5
Genève = Geneva CH 69 B6
Genevad S 40 C3
Geneviéres F 60 C1
Gengenbach D 61 B4
Genillé F 67 A6
Genk B 49 C6
Genlis F 69 A5
Gennep NL 50 B1
Genner DK 39 D2
Gennes F 67 A4
Genoa = Génova I 80 B2
Génova = Genoa I 80 B2
Genowefa PL 54 A3
Gensingen D 60 A3
Gent = Ghent B 49 B4
Genthin D 44 C4
Gentioux F 68 C1
Genzano di Lucánia I 104 C2
Genzano di Roma I 102 B5
Georgenthal D 51 C6
Georgsmarienhütte D 50 A4
Gera D 52 C2
Geraards-bergen B 49 C4
Gerace I 106 C3
Geraci Sículo I 109 B3
Geráki GR 117 F4
Gérardmer F 60 B2
Geras A 63 B6
Gerberoy F 58 A2
Gerbéviller F 60 B2
Gerbini I 109 B3
Gerbstedt D 52 B1
Gerði IS 111 C9
Gerede TR 118 B7
Gerena E 99 B4
Geretsried D 62 C2
Gérgal E 101 B3
Gergy F 69 B4
Gerindote E 94 C2
Gerjen H 74 B3

Gerlos A 72 A2
Germay F 59 B6
Germencik TR 119 E2
Germering D 62 B2
Germersheim D 61 A4
Gérnyeç AL 105 C5
Gernika-Lumo E 89 A4
Gernrode D 52 B1
Gernsbach D 61 B4
Gernsheim D 61 A4
Geroda D 51 C5
Gerola Alta I 71 B4
Geroldsgrun D 52 C1
Gerolsbach D 62 B2
Gerolstein D 50 C2
Gerolzhofen D 61 A6
Gerovo HR 73 C4
Gerpinnes B 49 C5
Gersfeld D 51 C5
Gerstetten D 61 B6
Gersthofen D 62 B1
Gerstungen D 51 C6
Gerswalde D 45 B5
Gerzat F 68 C3
Gerze TR 16 A7
Gerzen D 62 B3
Geseke D 51 B4
Geslau D 61 A6
Gespunsart F 59 A5
Gesté F 66 A3
Gestorf D 51 A5
Gesualda I 103 C8
Gesunda S 36 B1
Geta FIN 36 B6
Getafe E 94 B3
Getinge S 40 C2
Getxo E 89 A4
Geversdorf D 43 B6
Gevgelija MK 116 A4
Gevora del Caudillo E 93 C4
Gevrey-Chambertin F 69 A4
Gex F 69 B6
Gey D 50 C2
Geyikli TR 118 C1
Geysir IS 111 C5
Geyve TR 118 B5
Gföhl A 63 B6
Ghedi I 71 C5
Ghent = Gent B 49 B4
Gheorgheni RO 11 C8
Ghigo I 79 B6
Ghilarza I 110 B1
Ghisonaccia F 102 A2
Ghisoni F 102 A2
Gialtra GR 116 D4
Giannitsa GR 116 B4
Giardini Naxos I 109 B4
Giarratana I 109 B3
Giarre I 109 B4
Giat F 68 C2
Giaveno I 80 A1
Giazza I 71 C6
Giba I 110 C1
Gibellina Nuova I 108 B1
Gibostad N 112 C7
Gibraléon E 99 B4
Gibraltar GBZ 99 C5
Gic H 74 A2
Gideå S 115 D16
Gideåkroken S 115 C14
Gidle PL 55 C4
Giebelstadt D 61 A5
Gieboldehausen D 51 B6
Gielniów PL 55 B5
Gielow D 45 B4
Gien F 58 C3
Giengen D 61 B6
Giens F 79 C5
Giera RO 75 C5
Gieselwerder D 51 B5
Giessen D 51 C4
Gieten NL 42 B3
Giethoorn NL 42 C2
Giffaumont-Champaubert F 59 B5
Gifford GB 25 C5
Gifhorn D 44 C2
Gige H 74 B2
Giglio Porto I 102 A3
Gignac F 78 C2
Gijón = Xixón E 88 A1
Gilena E 100 B1
Gilford GB 19 B5
Gillberga S 35 C4
Gilleleje DK 41 C2
Gilley F 69 A6
Gilley-sur-Loire F 68 B3
Gillingham
  Dorset GB 29 B5
  Medway GB 31 C4
Gilocourt F 59 A3
Gilserberg D 51 C5
Gilze NL 49 B5
Gimat S 115 D15
Gimo S 36 B5
Gimont F 77 C3
Ginasservis F 79 C4
Gingelom B 49 C6
Gingst D 45 A5
Ginosa I 104 C2
Ginzling A 72 A1
Gióia dei Marsi I 103 B6
Gióia del Colle I 104 C2
Gióia Sannitica I 103 B7
Gióia Táuro I 106 C2
Gioiosa Iónica I 106 C3
Gioiosa Marea I 109 A3
Giosla E 22 C2
Giovinazzo I 104 B2
Girifalco I 106 C3
Giromagny F 60 C2
Girona E 91 A5
Gironcourt-sur-Vraine F 60 B1
Gironella E 91 A4
Gironville-sous-les-Côtes F 60 B1
Girvan GB 24 C3
Gislaved S 40 B3
Gislev DK 39 D3
Gislinge DK 39 D4
Gisors F 58 A2
Gissi I 103 A7
Gistad S 37 D2
Gistel B 48 B3
Gistrup DK 38 C3
Giswil CH 70 B3
Githio GR 117 F4
Giugliano in Campania I 103 C7
Giulianova I 82 D2
Giulvăz RO 75 C5
Giurgiu RO 11 E8
Give DK 39 D2
Givet F 49 C5
Givors F 69 C4
Givry
  B 49 C5
  F 69 B4
Givry-en-Argonne F 59 B6
Givskud DK 39 D2
Gizałki PL 54 A2
Gizeux F 67 A5
Giźycko PL 6 D7
Gizzeria I 106 C3
Gizzeria Lido I 106 C3
Gjedved DK 39 D2
Gjegjan AL 105 B6
Gjerde N 32 B3
Gjerlev DK 38 C3
Gjermundshamn N 32 B2
Gjerrild DK 39 C3
Gjerstad N 33 D5
Gjesås N 34 B4
Gjøl DK ...

Gjesvær N 113 A14
Gjirokastër AL 116 B2
Gjøfjell N 35 C2
Gjøl DK 38 B2
Gjøra N 114 E6
Gjøvik N 34 B2
Gladbeck D 50 B2
Gladenbach D 51 C4
Gladstad N 114 B8
Glamis GB 25 B5
Glamoč BIH 84 B1
Glamsbjerg DK 39 D3
Gland CH 69 B6
Glandorf D 50 A3
Glanegg A 73 B4
Glanshammar S 37 C2
Glarus CH 70 A4
Glasgow GB 24 C3
Glashütte
  Bayern D 62 C2
  Sachsen D 53 C3
Glastonbury GB 29 B5
Glatzau A 73 B5
Glauchau D 52 C2
Glava S 35 C4
Glavatiĉevo BIH 84 C3
Glavičice BIH 85 B4
Glavnik KOS 85 D6
Gledica SRB 85 C5
Glein
  A 73 A4
  N 115 A9
Gleinstätten A 73 B5
Gleisdorf A 73 A5
Glenamoy IRL 18 B2
Glenarm GB 19 B6
Glenbeigh IRL 20 B2
Glenbrittle GB 22 D2
Glencoe GB 24 B2
Glencolumbkille IRL 18 B3
Glendalough IRL 21 A5
Glenealy IRL 21 B5
Glenelg GB 22 D3
Glenfinnan GB 24 B2
Glengarriff IRL 20 C2
Glenluce GB 24 D3
Glennamaddy IRL 18 C3
Glenrothes GB 25 B4
Glenties IRL 18 B3
Glesborg DK 39 C3
Glesien D 52 B2
Gletsch CH 70 B3
Glewitz D 45 A4
Glifada GR 117 E5
Glimåkra S 41 C4
Glin IRL 20 B2
Glina HR 73 C6
Glinde D 44 B2
Glinojeck PL 47 C6
Glinsk IRL 20 A2
Gliwice PL 54 C3
Glödnitz A 73 B4
Gloggnitz A 64 C1
Głogoczów PL 65 A5
Głogonj SRB 85 B5
Glogovac SRB 85 B6
Glogów PL 53 B6
Głogówek PL 54 C2
Glomel F 56 B2
Glomfjord N 112 F2
Glommen S 40 C2
Glomsträsk S 115 B16
Glonn D 62 C2
Glorenza I 71 B5
Gloria P 92 B2
Glosa GR 116 C5
Glossop GB 27 B4
Gloucester GB 29 B5
Głowaczów PL 55 B6
Główczyce PL 46 A3
Glowe D 45 A5
Głowno PL 55 B4
Gložan SRB 75 C4
Glubczyce PL 54 C2
Głuchołazy PL 54 C2
Głuchów PL 55 B5
Głuchowo PL 54 A1
Glücksburg D 39 E2
Glückstadt D 43 B6
Glumina BIH 84 B4
Glumsø DK 39 D4
Glušci SRB 85 B4
Glusk BY 7 E10
Głuszyca PL 53 C6
Glyngøre DK 38 C1
Glyn Neath GB 29 B4
Gmünd
  Kärnten A 72 B3
  Nieder Österreich A 63 B5
Gmund D 62 C2
Gmunden A 63 C4
Gnarp S 115 E14
Gnarrenburg D 43 B6
Gnesau A 72 B3
Gnesta S 37 C4
Gniew PL 47 B4
Gniewkowo PL 47 C4
Gnoien D 45 B4
Gnojnice BIH 84 C2
Gnojno PL 55 C5
Gnosall GB 26 C3
Gnosjö S 40 B3
Göbel TR 118 B3
Göçbeyli TR 118 C2
Goch D 50 B2
Gochsheim D 51 C6
Göd H 65 C5
Godalming GB 31 C3
Godby FIN 36 B6
Goðdalir IS 111 B6
Goddelsheim D 51 B4
Godech BG 11 E7
Godegård S 37 D2
Godelheim D 51 B5
Goderville F 58 A1
Godiasco I 80 B3
Godič SLO 73 B4
Godkowo PL 47 A5
Godmanchester GB 30 B3
Gödöllő H 65 C5
Gödre H 74 B2
Godshill GB 31 D2
Godzikowice PL 54 C2
Godziszewo PL 47 A4
Goes NL 49 B4
Goetzenbrück F 60 B3
Góglio I 70 B3
Gogolin PL 54 C3
Göhren D 45 A5
Góis P 92 A2
Góito I 71 C5
Goizueta E 89 A5
Gójsk PL 47 C5
Gökçedağ TR 118 C3
Gökçen TR 119 D2
Gökçeören TR 119 D3
Gökçeyazı TR 118 C2
Göktepe TR 119 E3
Gol N 32 B5
Gola
  HR 74 B2
  N 34 A1
Golańcz PL 46 C3
Gołaszyn PL 54 B1
Golbey F 60 B2
Gölby FIN 36 B6
Gölcük
  Kocaeli TR 118 B4
  Niğde TR 16 B7
Golčův Jenikov CZ 63 A6
Gołczewo PL 45 B6
Goldach CH 71 A4
Goldbach D 51 C5

Goldbeck D 44 C3
Goldberg D 44 B4
Goldelund D 43 A6
Goldenstedt D 43 C5
Gołębiewo PL 47 A4
Golegã P 92 B2
Goleniów PL 45 C6
Golfo Aranci I 110 B2
Gölhisar TR 119 E4
Golina PL 54 A3
Gölle H 74 B3
Göllersdorf A 64 B2
Golling an der Salzach
A 63 C4
Gölmarmara TR 118 D2
Golnice PL 53 B5
Golnik SLO 73 B4
Gölova TR 119 F5
Gölpazarı TR 118 B5
Gols A 64 C2
Golspie GB 23 D5
Golssen D 52 B3
Golubac SRB 85 B6
Golub-Dobrzyń PL . . .47 B5
Goluchów PL 54 B2
Golzow D 52 A2
Gomagoi I 71 B5
Gómara E 89 C4
Gomaringen D 61 B5
Gömbe TR 119 F4
Gömeç TR 118 C1
Gomel = Homyel BY . .7 E11
Gomes Aires P 98 B2
Gómezserracin E 88 C2
Gommern D 52 A1
Gomulin PL 55 B4
Gonäs S 36 B2
Goncelin F 69 C5
Gończyce PL 55 B6
Gondomar
E 87 B2
P 87 C2
Gondrecourt-le-Château
F 60 B1
Gondrin F 76 C3
Gönen
Balıkesir TR 118 B2
İsparta TR 119 E5
Gonfaron F 79 C5
Goñi E 76 D1
Goni
GR 116 C4
I 110 C2
Gonnesa I 110 C1
Gonnosfanádiga I . . .110 C1
Gönyü H 64 C3
Gonzaga I 81 B4
Goodrich GB 29 B5
Goodwick GB 28 A1
Gooik B 49 C5
Goole GB 27 B5
Goor NL 50 A2
Göpfritz an der Wild
A 63 B6
Goppenstein CH 70 B2
Göppingen D 61 B5
Gor E 100 B3
Góra
Dolnośląskie PL . . .54 B1
Mazowieckie PL . . .47 C6
Gorafe E 100 B2
Góra Kalwaria PL 55 B6
Gorawino PL 46 B1
Goražde BIH 84 C3
Gordaliza del Pino E . .88 B1
Gördes TR 118 D3
Gørding DK 39 D1
Gordola CH 70 B3
Gordon GB 25 C5
Gordoncillo E 88 B1
Gorebridge GB 25 C4
Gorenja Vas SLO 73 B4
Gorenje Jelenje HR . .73 C4
Gorey
GB 57 A3
IRL 21 B5
Gorgonzola I 71 C4
Gorica HR 83 B4
Gorican HR 74 B1
Gorinchem NL 49 B5
Goring GB 31 C2
Goritsy RUS 7 C14
Göritz D 45 B5
Gorizia I 72 C3
Górki PL 47 C5
Gorleben D 44 B3
Gorleston-on-sea GB .30 B5
Gørlev DK 39 D4
Görlitz D 53 B4
Görlitz F 89 A4
Görmin D 45 B5
Górna Grupa PL 47 B4
Gorna Oryahovitsa
BG 11 E8
Gornja Gorevnica
SRB 85 C5
Gornja Klina KOS 85 D5
Gornja Ploča HR 83 B4
Gornja Radgona SLO .73 B5
Gornja Sabanta SRB .85 C6
Gornja Trešnjevica
SRB 85 B5
Gornje Tuzla BIH 84 B3
Gornje Polje MNE 84 D3
Gornje Ratkovo BIH . .84 B1
Gornji Grad SLO 73 B4
Gornji Humac HR 83 C5
Gornji Jasenjani BIH . .84 C2
Gornji Kamengrad
BIH 83 B5
Gornji Kneginec HR . .73 B6
Gornji Kokoti MNE . . .105 A5
Gornji Kosinj HR 83 B4
Gornji Milanovac
SRB 85 B5
Gornji Podgradci BIH .84 A2
Gornji Ravno BIH 84 C2
Gornji Sjenicak HR . . .73 C5
Gornji Vakuf BIH 84 C2
Górno PL 55 C5
Görömböly H 65 B6
Górowo Iławeckie
PL 47 A6
Gorran Haven GB 28 C3
Gorredijk NL 42 B3
Gorron F 57 B5
Gorseinon GB 28 B3
Gort IRL 20 A3
Gortin GB 19 B4
Görzke D 52 A2
Gorzkowice PL 55 B4
Górzno
Kujawsko-Pomorskie
PL 47 B5
Zachodnio-Pomorskie
PL 46 B1
Gorzów Śląski PL 54 B3
Gorzów Wielkopolski
PL 45 C7
Górzyca PL 45 C6
Gorzyce PL 54 D3
Gorzyń PL 46 C1
Gorzyno PL 46 A3
Gosaldo I 72 B1
Gosau A 63 C4
Gosberton GB 30 B3
Gościcino PL 47 A4
Gościęcin PL 54 C3
Gościm PL 46 C1
Gościno PL 46 A1
Gosdorf A 73 B5
Gosforth GB 26 A3
Goslar D 51 B6
Goslice PL 47 C5
Gospić HR 83 B4
Gosport GB 31 D2

Gössäter S 35 D5
Gossau CH 71 A4
Goss Ilsede D 51 A6
Gössnitz D 52 C2
Gössweinstein D 62 A2
Gostimë AL 105 C6
Gostkow PL 55 B4
Göstling an der Ybbs
GB 63 C5
Gostomia PL 46 B2
Gostycyn PL 46 B3
Gostyń PL 54 B2
Gostynin PL 47 C5
Goszczyn PL 55 B5
Göteborg = Gothenburg
S 38 B4
Götene S 35 D5
Gotha D 51 C6
Gothem S 37 E5
Gothenburg = Göteborg
S 38 B4
Gotse Delchev BG . .116 A5
Gottersdorf D 62 B3
Göttingen D 51 B5
Gottne S 115 D15
Götzis A 71 A4
Gouarec F 56 B2
Gouda NL 49 A5
Goudhurst GB 31 C4
Goumenissa GR 116 B4
Goura GR 117 E4
Gourdon F 77 B4
Gourgançon F 59 B5
Gourin F 56 B2
Gournay-en-Bray F . . .58 A2
Gourock GB 24 C3
Gouveia P 92 A3
Gouvy B 50 C1
Gouzeacourt F 49 C4
Gouzon F 68 B2
Govedari HR 84 D2
Goveg S 81 A4
Gowarczów PL 55 B5
Gowerton GB 28 B3
Gowidlino PL 46 A3
Gøwran IRL 21 B4
Goyatz D 53 A4
Göynük
TR 118 B5
Antalya TR 119 F5
Gozdnica PL 53 B5
Gozdowo PL 47 C5
Gozee B 49 C5
Graal-Müritz D 44 A4
Grab BIH 84 D3
Grabenstätt D 62 C3
Grabhair D 22 C2
Grabo S 38 B5
Grabovac
BIH 84 C1
SRB 85 B5
Grabovci SRB 85 B4
Grabow D 44 B3
Grabow D 55 A4
Grabów nad Pilicą PL .55 B6
Grabów nad Prosną
PL 54 B3
Grabowno PL 46 B3
Grabs CH 71 A4
Gračac HR 83 B4
Gračanica
BIH 84 B3
KOS 85 D6
Graçay F 68 A1
Gracen AL 105 B5
Grad SLO 73 B6
Gradac
BIH 84 D3
HR 84 C2
MNE 85 C4
SRB 85 C5
Gradačac BIH 84 B3
Gradec HR 74 C1
Gradefes E 88 B1
Grades A 73 B4
Gradil P 92 C1
Gradina
HR 74 C2
MNE 85 C4
Gradisca d'Isonzo I . . .72 C3
Gradište HR 74 C3
Grado
E 86 A4
I 72 C3
Grafenau D 63 B4
Gräfenberg D 62 A2
Gräfenhainichen D . . .52 B2
Grafenschlag A 63 B6
Grafenstein A 73 B4
Gräfenthal D 52 C1
Grafentonna D 51 B6
Grafenwöhr D 62 A2
Grafing D 62 B2
Gräfsnäs S 40 A2
Gragnano I 103 C7
Graiguenamanagh
IRL 21 B5
Grain GB 31 C4
Grainau D 71 A6
Graja de Iniesta E 95 C5
Grajera E 89 C3
Gram DK 39 D2
Gramais A 71 A5
Gramat F 77 B4
Gramatneusiedl A 64 B2
Grambow D 45 B6
Gramkow D 44 B3
Grammichele I 109 B3
Gramsh AL 116 B2
Gramzow D 45 B6
Gran N 34 B2
Granada E 100 B2
Granard IRL 19 C4
Grañas E 86 A3
Granátula de Calatrava
E 100 A2
Grancey-le-Château
F 59 C6
Grandas de Salime E .86 A4
Grandcamp-Maisy F . .57 A4
Grand-Champ F 56 C3
Grand Couronne F . . .58 A2
Grand-Fougeray F . . .57 C4
Grândola P 98 A2
Grandpré F 59 A5
Grandrieu
F 49 C5
B 78 B2
Grandson CH 70 B1
Grandvilliers F 70 A1
Grandvilliers F 58 A2
Grañén E 90 B2
Grängärde S 36 B1
Grange IRL 18 B3
Grangemouth GB 25 B4
Grange-over-Sands
GB 26 A3
Grängesberg S 36 B1
Granges-de Crouhens
F 77 D3
Granges-sur-Vologne
F 60 B2
Gräningen D 44 C4
Granítola-Torretta I . .108 B1
Granja
Évora P 98 A3
Porto P 87 C2
Granja de Moreruela
E 88 C1
Granja de Torrehermosa
E 93 C5
Gränna S 40 B4
Grannäs
Västerbotten S . . .115 B13
Västerbotten S . . .115 B14
Granö S 115 C16
Granollers E 91 B5
Granowiec PL 54 B2

Granowo PL 54 A1
Gransee D 45 B5
Gransherad N 33 C6
Grantham GB 27 C5
Grantown-on-Spey
GB 23 D5
Grantshouse GB 25 C5
Granville F 57 B4
Granvin N 32 B3
Grærup Strand DK . . .39 D1
Gräsås S 40 C2
Grasbakken N 113 B17
Grasberg D 43 B6
Grasmere GB 26 A2
Gräsmyr S 115 D16
Grasö S 36 B5
Grassano I 104 C2
Grassau D 62 C3
Grasse F 79 C5
Grassington GB 27 A4
Græsted DK 41 C2
Gråsten DK 39 E2
Grästorp S 35 D4
Gratkorn A 73 A5
Gråträsk S 115 B16
Gratwein A 73 A5
Graulhet F 77 C4
Graus E 90 A3
Grávalos E 89 B5
Gravedona I 71 B4
Gravelines F 48 B3
Gravellona Toce I 70 C3
Gravendal S 36 B1
Gravens DK 39 D2
Gravesend GB 31 C4
Graveson F 78 C3
Gravina in Puglia I . . .104 C2
Gray F 69 A5
Grayrigg GB 26 A3
Grays GB 31 C4
Grayshott GB 31 C3
Grayvoron RUS 7 F13
Graz A 73 A5
Grazalema E 99 C5
Grążawy PL 47 B5
Grazzano Visconti I . . .80 B3
Greåker N 35 C3
Great Dunmow GB . . .31 C4
Great Malvern GB 29 A5
Great Torrington GB . .28 C3
Great Waltham GB . . .31 C4
Great Yarmouth GB . . .30 B5
Grebbestad S 35 D3
Grebenstein D 51 B5
Grebocice PL 53 B6
Grębocin PL 47 B4
Greding D 62 A2
Gredstedbro DK 39 D1
Greencastle IRL 19 A4
Greenhead GB 25 D5
Greenisland GB 19 B6
Greenlaw GB 25 C5
Greenock GB 24 C3
Greenway GB 28 B3
Greenwich GB 31 C4
Grefrath D 50 B2
Greifenburg A 72 B3
Greiffenberg D 45 B5
Greifswald D 45 A5
Grein A 63 B5
Greipstad N 33 D4
Greiz D 52 C2
Grenaa DK 38 C3
Grenade F 77 C4
Grenade-sur-l'Adour
F 76 C2
Grenchen CH 70 A2
Grendi N 33 D4
Grenivik IS 111 B7
Grenoble F 69 C5
Gréoux-les-Bains F . . .79 C4
Gresenhorst D 44 A4
Gressoney-la-Trinité
I 70 C2
Gressoney-St-Jean I . .70 C2
Gressthal D 51 C6
Gressvik N 35 C2
Gresten A 63 C6
Gretna GB 25 D4
Greussen D 51 B6
Greve in Chianti I 81 C5
Greven
Mecklenburg-
Vorpommern D . . .44 B2
Nordrhein-Westfalen
D 50 A3
Grevena GR 116 B3
Grevenbroich D 50 B2
Grevenbrück D 50 B4
Grevenmacher L 60 A2
Grevesmühlen D 44 B3
Grevestrand DK 41 D2
Grevie S 41 C2
Greystoke GB 26 A3
Greystones IRL 21 A5
Grez-Doiceau B 49 C5
Grèzec F 77 B4
Grez-en-Bouère F 57 C5
Grezzana I 71 C6
Grgar SLO 72 B3
Grgurevci SRB 85 A4
Gries A 71 A6
Griesbach D 63 B4
Griesheim D 61 A4
Gries in Sellrain A 71 A6
Grieskirchen A 63 B4
Griffen A 73 B4
Grignan F 78 B3
Grignano I 72 B1
Grignols F 76 B2
Grignon F 69 C6
Grijota E 88 B2
Grijpskerk NL 42 B3
Gril AL 105 A5
Grillby S 37 C4
Grimaud F 79 C5
Grimbergen B 49 C5
Grimma D 52 B2
Grimmen D 45 A5
Grimmialp CH 70 B2
Grimsås S 40 B3
Grimsby GB 27 B5
Grimslöv S 40 C4
Grímsstaðir IS 111 B9
Grimstad N 33 D5
Grimstorp S 40 B4
Grindavík IS 111 D3
Grindelwald CH 70 B3
Grindheim N 33 D4
Grindsted DK 39 D1
Griñón E 94 B3
Gripenberg S 40 B4
Gripsholm S 37 C4
Grisolles F 77 C4
Grisslehamn S 36 B5
Gritley GB 23 C6
Grizebeck GB 26 A2
Grndina BIH 84 B1
Gröbming D 72 A3
Gröbzig D 52 B1
Grocka SRB 85 B5
Gröditz D 52 B3
Gródki PL 47 B6
Grodków PL 54 C2
Grodziec PL 54 A3
Grodzisk Mazowiecki
PL 55 A5
Grodzisk Wielkopoiski
PL 54 A1
Groenlo NL 50 A2
Groesbeek NL 50 B1
Groete HR 83 C5
Groitzsch D 52 B2
Groix F 56 C2
Grójec PL 55 B5
Grom PL 47 B6
Gromiljca BIH 84 C3
Grömitz D 44 A2
Gromnik PL 65 A6

Gromo I 71 C4
Gronau
Niedersachsen D . .51 A5
Nordrhein-Westfalen
D 50 A3
Grønbjerg DK 39 C1
Grönenbach D 61 C6
Grong N 114 C9
Grönhögen S 41 C6
Groningen
D 52 B1
NL 42 B3
Grønnestrand DK 38 B2
Grono CH 71 B4
Grönskåra S 40 B5
Gropello Cairoli I 70 C3
Grorud N 34 C2
Grósio I 71 B5
Grošnica SRB 85 C5
Grossalmerode D 51 B5
Grossarl A 72 A3
Gross Berkel D 51 A5
Grossbodungen D 51 B6
Gross-botwar D 61 B5
Grossenbrode D 44 A3
Grossenehrich D 51 B6
Grossengottern D 51 B6
Grossenhain D 52 B3
Grossenkneten D 43 C5
Grossenlüder D 51 C5
Grossensee D 44 B2
Grossenzersdorf A . . .64 B2
Grosseto I 81 D5
Gross-Gerau D 61 A4
Grossgerungs A 63 B5
Grossglobnitz A 63 B6
Grossharbersdorf D . .62 A1
Grossharras A 64 B2
Grosshartmansdorf
D 52 C3
Grosshöchstetten
CH 70 B2
Gross Kreutz D 45 C4
Grosskrut A 64 B2
Gross Lafferde D 51 A6
Gross Leuthen D 53 A4
Grosslohra D 51 B6
Grossmehring D 62 B2
Gross Muckrow D 53 A4
Gross Oesingen D . . .44 C2
Grossostheim D 61 A5
Grosspertholz A 63 B5
Grosspetersdorf A . . .73 A6
Grosspostwitz D 53 B4
Grossraming A 63 C5
Grossräschen D 53 B4
Gross Reken D 50 B3
Grossrinderfeld D 61 A5
Grossröhrsdorf D 53 B4
Gross Sarau D 44 B2
Gross Särchen D 53 B4
Grossschirma I 52 C3
Gross Schönebeck D . 45 C5
Grossschweinbarth A .64 B2
Grosssiegharts A 63 B6
Grosssölk A 72 A3
Gross Umstadt D 61 A4
Grosswarasdorf A 74 A1
Gross Warnow D 44 B3
Gross-Weikersdorf A .64 B1
Gross-Welle D 44 B4
Gross Wokern D 44 B4
Grostenquin F 60 B2
Grosuplje SLO 73 C4
Grotli N 114 E4
Grötlingbo S 37 E5
Grottáglie I 104 C3
Grottaminarda I 103 B8
Grottammare I 82 D2
Grotte di Castro I 81 D5
Grotteria I 106 C3
Gróttole I 104 C2
Grouw NL 42 B2
Grov N 112 D6
Grova N 33 C5
Grove E 86 B2
Grua N 34 B2
Grube D 44 A3
Grubišno Polje HR . . .74 C2
Gruda BIH 105 A4
Grude BIH 84 C2
Grudusk PL 47 B6
Grudziądz PL 47 B4
Grue N 34 B4
Gruissan F 78 C2
Grullos E 86 A4
Grumo Áppula I 104 B2
Grums S 35 C5
Grünau im Almtal A . . .63 C4
Grünberg D 51 C4
Grünburg A 63 C5
Grundarfjörður IS 111 C2
Gründau D 51 C5
Gründelhardt D 61 A5
Grundforsen S 34 A4
Grundlsee A 63 C4
Grundsund S 35 D3
Grunewald D 53 B3
Grüngräbchen D 53 B3
Grunow D 53 A4
Grünstadt D 61 A4
Gruvberget S 36 A3
Gruyères CH 70 B2
Gruža SRB 85 C5
Grybów PL 65 A6
Grycksbo S 36 B2
Gryfice PL 45 B7
Gryfino PL 45 B6
Gryfów Śląski PL 53 B5
Gryllefjord N 112 C6
Grymyr N 34 B2
Gryt S 37 D3
Grytgöl S 37 D2
Grythyttan S 37 C1
Grytnäs S 37 D4
Grzanica PL 46 B3
Grzybno PL 45 B6
Grzywna PL 47 B4
Gschnitz A 71 A6
Gschwend D 61 B5
Gstaad CH 70 B2
Gsteig CH 70 B2
Guadahortuna E 100 B2
Guadalajara E 95 B3
Guadalaviar E 95 B5
Guadalcanal E 99 A5
Guadalcázar E 100 B1
Guadalix de la Sierra
E 94 B3
Guadálmez E 100 A1
Guadalupe E 93 B5
Guadarrama E 94 B2
Guadiaro E 99 C5
Guadix E 100 B2
Guagnano I 105 C3
Guagno F 102 A1
Guájar-Faragüit E . . .100 C2
Gualchos E 100 C2
Gualdo Tadino I 82 C1
Guardköv PL 54 C2
Guardo I 103 B6
Guarda P 92 A3
Guardamar del Segura
E 96 C2
Guardão P 92 A2
Guardavalle I 106 C3
Guardea I 102 A5
Guárdia I 103 C8
Guàrdia E 90 B3
Guardiagrele I 103 A7
Guárdia Sanframondi
I 103 B7
Guardias Viejas E . . .100 C3
Guardiola de Berguedà
E 91 A4

Guardo E 88 B2
Guareña E 93 C4
Guaro E 100 C1
Guarromán E 100 A2
Guasila I 110 C2
Guastalla I 81 B4
Gübbhögen S 115 C12
Gúbbio I 82 C1
Guben D 53 B4
Gubin PL 53 B4
Guča SRB 85 C5
Gudå N 114 D8
Gudavac BIH 83 B5
Guddal N 32 A2
Güdel N 34 B3
Gudhem S 35 D5
Gudhjem DK 41 D4
Gudow D 44 B2
Güdül TR 118 B7
Gudvangen N 32 B3
Guebwiller F 60 C3
Guéjar-Sierra E 100 B2
Guéméné-Penfao F . . .57 C4
Guémené-sur-Scorff
F 56 B2
Güeñes E 89 A3
Guer F 57 C3
Guérande F 66 A2
Guéret F 68 B1
Guérigny F 68 A3
Guesa E 76 D1
Gueugnon F 68 B4
Guglionesi I 103 B7
Gühlen Glienicke D . . .45 B4
Guia P 92 B2
Guichen F 57 C4
Guidizzolo I 71 C5
Guidónia-Montecélio
I 102 B5
Guijo de Coria E 93 A4
Guijo de Santa Bábera
E 93 A5
Guijuelo E 93 A5
Guildford GB 31 C3
Guillaumes F 79 B5
Guillena E 99 B4
Guillestre F 79 B5
Guillos F 76 B2
Guilsfield GB 26 C1
Guilvinec F 56 C1
Guimarães P 87 C2
Guincho P 92 C1
Guînes F 48 C2
Guingamp F 56 B2
Guipavas F 56 B1
Guisborough GB 27 A4
Guiscard F 59 A4
Guiscriff F 56 B2
Guise F 59 A4
Guisona E 91 B4
Guîtres F 76 B2
Gujan-Mestras F 76 B1
Gulbene LV 7 C9
Gülçayır TR 118 C6
Guldborg DK 39 E4
Gullabo S 40 C5
Gullane GB 25 B5
Gullbrandstorp S 40 C2
Gulleråsen S 36 A2
Gullhaug N 35 C2
Gullspång S 35 D6
Gulsvik N 34 B1
Gumiel de Hizán E . . .88 C3
Gummersbach D 50 B3
Gümüldür TR 119 D1
Gümüshacıköy TR . . .16 A7
Gümüsova TR 118 B5
Gundelfingen D 61 B6
Gundel-fingen D 60 B3
Gundelsheim D 61 A5
Gunderschoffen F 60 B3
Gundertshausen A . . .62 B3
Gundinci HR 74 C3
Gündoğmuş TR 119 F7
Güney
Burdur TR 119 E4
Denizli TR 119 D4
Gunja HR 84 B3
Günlüce TR 119 F3
Gunnarn S 115 B14
Gunnarskog S 34 C4
Gunnebo S 40 B6
Gunnislake GB 28 C3
Günselsdorf A 64 C2
Guntersblum D 61 A4
Guntersdorf A 64 B2
Guntin E 86 B3
Günyüzü TR 118 C6
Günzburg D 61 B6
Gunzenhausen D 62 A1
Güre
Balıkesir TR 118 C1
Uşak TR 118 D4
Gurk A 73 B4
Gurrea de Gállego E . .90 A2
Gürsu TR 118 B4
Gušće HR 74 C1
Gusev RUS 6 D7
Gusinje MNE 105 A5
Gusmar AL 105 C5
Gúspini I 110 C1
Gusselby S 37 C2
Güssing A 73 A6
Gusswerk A 63 C6
Gustav Adolf S 34 B5
Gustavsberg S 37 C5
Gustavsfors S 35 C4
Güstrow D 44 B4
Gusum S 37 D3
Gutcher GB 22 A7
Gutenstein A 63 C6
Gütersloh D 51 B4
Guttannen CH 70 B3
Guttaring A 73 B4
Guttau D 53 B4
Güttingen CH 61 C5
Gützkow D 45 B5
Guzów PL 55 A5
Gvardeysk RUS 6 D6
Gvarv N 33 C6
Gvozd MNE 85 D4
Gvozdansko HR 73 C6
Gwda Wielka PL 46 B2
Gwennap GB 28 C2
Gy F 69 A5
Gyál H 75 A4
Gyarmat H 74 A2
Gyékényes H 74 B2
Gyé-sur-Seine F 59 B5
Gylling DK 39 D3
Gyoma H 75 B6
Gyömöre H 74 A2
Gyömrő H 75 A4
Gyón H 75 A4
Gyöngyfa H 74 C2
Gyöngyös H 65 C5
Gyöngyöspata H 65 C5
Gyönk H 74 B3
Györ H 64 C3
Györszemere H 74 A2
Gypsera CH 70 B2
Gysinge S 36 B3
Gyttorp S 37 C1
Gyula H 75 B6
Gyulafirátót H 74 A2
Gyulaj H 74 B3

H

Haacht B 49 C5
Haag
Nieder Österreich A . .63 B5
Ober Österreich A . . .63 B4
D 62 B3
Haaksbergen NL 50 A2
Haamstede NL 49 B4
Haapajärvi FIN 3 E26
Haapsalu EST 6 B7
Haarlem NL 42 C1
Haaksma F 76 C2
Habay B 60 A1
Habo S 40 B4
Håbol S 35 D4
Habry CZ 63 A6
Habsheim F 60 C3
Hachenburg D 50 C3
Hackås S 115 E11
Hacketstown IRL 21 B5
Hackthorpe GB 26 A3
Hadamar D 50 C4
Hädanberg S 115 D15
Haddington GB 25 C5
Hädeborp S 40 B3
Hadersdorf am Kamp
A 63 B6
Haderslev DK 39 D2
Haderup DK 39 C1
Hadim TR 119 F7
Hadleigh
Essex GB 31 C4
Suffolk GB 30 B4
Hadlow GB 31 C4
Hadmersleben D 52 A1
Hadsten DK 39 C3
Hadsund DK 38 C3
Hadyach UA 7 F13
Hadžići BIH 84 C3
Hafnarfjörður IS 111 D3
Hafslo N 32 A4
Haganj HR 74 C1
Hagby S 40 C6
Hage D 43 B4
Hægebostad N 33 D4
Hægeland N 33 D4
Hagen
Niedersachsen D . .43 B5
Nordrhein-Westfalen
D 50 B3
Hagenbach D 61 A4
Hagenow D 44 B3
Hagetmau F 76 C2
Hagfors S 34 B5
Häggenäs S 115 D11
Hagondange F 60 A2
Hagsta S 36 B4
Haguenau F 60 B3
Hahnbach D 62 A2
Hahnslätten D 50 C4
Hahót H 74 B1
Haiger D 50 C4
Haigerloch D 61 B4
Hailsham GB 31 D4
Hainburg D 64 B2
Hainfeld A 63 B6
Hainichen D 52 C3
Hajdúböszörmény H . .10 C6
Hajdúdorog H 10 C6
Hajdúnánás H 10 C6
Hajdúszoboszló H 75 A6
Hajnáčka SK 65 B5
Hajnówka PL 6 E7
Hajós H 75 B4
Håkafot S 115 C11
Hakkas S 113 F10
Håkkårby S 36 B2
Halaszi H 64 C3
Halberstadt D 52 B1
Halberton GB 29 C4
Hald Ege DK 39 C2
Haldem D 43 C5
Halden N 35 C3
Haldensleben D 52 A1
Halenbeck D 44 B4
Halesowen GB 26 C3
Halesworth GB 30 B5
Halfing D 62 C3
Halhjem N 32 B2
Håliden S 34 B5
Halifax GB 27 B4
Halikko FIN 6 A7
Halinaoja FIN 3 F27
Halin FIN 3 F27
Halkirk GB 23 C5
Hall S 37 E5
Hälla S 115 D14
Hallabrottet S 37 C2
Halland GB 31 D4
Hällaryd S 41 C4
Hällaryd S 40 B2
Hallaryd S 40 C3
Hällberga S 37 C3
Hällbybrunn S 37 C3
Halle
B 49 C5
Nordrhein-Westfalen
D 51 A4
Sachsen-Anhalt D . .52 B1
Hälleberga S 40 C5
Hällefors S 36 C1
Hälleforsnäs S 37 C3
Hallein A 62 C4
Hällekis S 35 D5
Hallen S 115 D11
Hallenberg D 51 B4
Hällevadsholm S 35 D3
Hällevik S 41 C4
Hälleviksstrand S 35 D3
Hallingby N 34 B2
Hallingeberg S 40 B6
Hallingen N 32 B6
Hall in Tirol A 71 A6
Hällnäs S 115 A15
Hallormsstaður IS . . .111 B11
Hallsberg S 37 C2
Hållsta S 37 C3
Hallstahammar S 37 C3
Hallstatt A 72 A3
Hallstavik S 36 B5
Halltorp S 40 C6
Halluin F 49 C4
Halmstad S 40 C2
Hals DK 38 B3
Halsa N 114 D5
Halstead GB 31 C4
Haltdålen N 114 E8
Haltern D 50 B3
Halterkotz D 50 B2
Halvarsgårdarna S . . .36 B2
Halver D 50 B3
Halvrimmen DK 38 B2
Ham F 59 A4
Hamar N 34 B3
Hamarhaug N 32 B2
Hamarøy N 112 E4
Hambach F 60 A3
Hambergen D 43 B5
Hambergsund S 35 D3
Hambledon GB 31 D2
Hambuhren D 44 C1
Hamburg D 44 B1
Hamdibey TR 118 C2
Hämeenlinna FIN 3 F26
Hamersleben D 52 A1
Hamidiye TR 118 C5
Hamina FIN 3 F27
Hamlagro N 32 B3
Hamm
Nordrhein-Westfalen
D 50 B3

Hammar S 37 D1
Hammarland FIN 36 B6
Hammarö S 35 C5
Hammarstrand S 115 D13
Hamme B 49 B5
Hammel DK 39 C2
Hammelburg D 51 C5
Hammelspring D 45 B5
Hammenhög S 41 D4
Hamminkeln D 50 B2
Hamnavoe GB 22 A7
Hamneda S 40 C3
Hamnsund N 113 B19
Hamoir B 49 C6
Hamont B 49 B6
Hámor H 65 B6
Hamra
Gävleborg S 115 F12
Gotland S 37 F5
Hamrångefjärden S . . .36 B4
Hamstreet GB 31 C4
Hamsund N 112 D4
Han
MNE 84 D3
TR 118 C5
Hanaskog S 41 C4
Hanau D 51 C4
Händelöp S 40 B6
Handlová SK 65 B4
Hanerau-Hademarschen
D 43 A6
Hånger S 40 B3
Hanhimaa FIN 113 E14
Han i Hotit A 105 A5
Hankensbüttel D 44 C2
Han Knežica BIH 83 A5
Hanko FIN 6 B7
Hannover D 51 A5
Hannut B 49 C6
Han Pijesak BIH 84 B3
Hansnes N 112 C8
Hanstedt D 44 B2
Hanstholm DK 38 B1
Hantsavichy BY 7 E9
Hanušovice CZ 54 C1
Haparanda S 3 D26
Haradok BY 7 D10
Harads S 3 C24
Häradsbäck S 40 C4
Häradsbygden S 36 B2
Harbo S 36 B4
Harboøre DK 38 C1
Harburg
Bayern D 62 B1
Hamburg D 44 B1
Hårby DK 39 D3
Harc H 74 B3
Hardegarijp NL 42 B2
Hardegsen D 51 B5
Hardelot Plage F 48 C2
Hardenbeck D 45 B5
Hardenberg NL 42 C3
Harderwijk NL 49 A6
Hardheim D 61 A5
Hardt D 61 B4
Hareid N 114 E3
Haren
D 43 C4
NL 42 B3
Harestua N 34 B2
Harfleur F 57 A6
Harg S 36 B5
Hargicourt F 49 D4
Hargnies F 49 C5
Hargshamn S 36 B5
Härja S 40 A3
Harkány H 74 C3
Härkeberga S 37 C4
Harkebrügge D 43 B4
Harlech GB 26 C1
Harleston GB 30 B5
Harlingen NL 42 B2
Harlösa S 41 D3
Harlow GB 31 C4
Harmancik TR 118 C4
Härmänger S 115 F14
Harmånli BG 11 F8
Härnösand S 115 E14
Haro E 89 B4
Haroldswick GB 22 A8
Háromfa H 74 B2
Haroué F 60 B2
Harpenden GB 31 C3
Harplinge S 40 C2
Harpstedt D 43 C5
Harrogate GB 27 B4
Harrow GB 31 C3
Härryda S 38 B5
Harsefeld D 43 B6
Harsewinkel D 50 B4
Hârşova RO 11 D9
Harstad N 112 D5
Harsum D 51 A5
Harsvik N 114 C7
Hartberg A 73 A5
Hartburn GB 25 C6
Hartha D 52 B2
Hartland GB 28 C3
Hartlepool GB 27 A4
Hartmanice CZ 63 A4
Hartmannsdorf A 73 A5
Harvassdal N 115 B11
Harwell GB 31 C2
Harwich GB 31 C5
Harzgerode D 52 B1
Häselgehr A 71 A5
Haselünne D 43 C4
Haskovo BG 11 F8
Hasköy TR 118 A1
Haslach an der Mühl
A 63 B5
Hasle DK 41 D4
Haslemere GB 31 C3
Haslev DK 39 D4
Hasloch D 61 A5
Hasparren F 76 C1
Hassela S 115 E13
Hasselfelde D 51 B6
Hasselfors S 37 C1
Hasselt
B 49 C6
NL 42 C3
Hassfurt D 51 C6
Hässleholm S 41 C3
Hasslö S 41 C5
Hässleholm S 41 C3
Hasslö S 41 C5
Hästbo S 36 B3
Hastière-Lavaux B . . .49 C5
Hastigrow GB 23 C5
Hastings GB 31 D4
Hästveda S 41 C3
Hasvik N 113 B11
Hatfield
Hertfordshire GB . .31 C3
South Yorkshire GB .27 B5
Hatherleigh GB 28 C3
Hathersage GB 27 B4
Hatlestrand N 32 B2
Hattem NL 42 C3
Hatten
D 43 B5
F 60 B3
Hattfjelldal N 115 B10
Hatting DK 39 D2
Hattingen D 50 B3
Hattstadt F 60 B3
Hattula FIN 3 F26
Hatvan H 65 C5

Hatvik N 32 B2
Hau D 50 B2
Haudainville F 59 A6
Hauganes IS 111 B7
Haugastøl N 32 B4
Hauge N 33 D3
Haugesund N 33 C2
Haughom N 33 D3
Haugsdorf A 64 B2
Haukedal N 32 A3
Haukeland N 32 B2
Haukeligrend N 33 C4
Haukeliseter N 32 C4
Haukipudas FIN 3 D26
Haulerwijk NL 42 B3
Haunersdorf D 62 B3
Haus N 32 B2
Hausach D 61 B4
Hausham D 62 C2
Hausmannstätten A . .73 B5
Hausvik N 33 D3
Hautajärvi FIN 113 F18
Hautefort F 67 C6
Hauterives F 69 C5
Hauteville-Lompnès
F 69 C5
Haut-Fays B 49 C6
Hautmont F 49 C4
Hautrage B 49 C4
Hauzenberg D 63 B4
Havant GB 31 D3
Havdhem S 37 E5
Havdrup DK 39 D5
Havelange B 49 C6
Havelberg D 44 C4
Havelte NL 42 C3
Haverfordwest GB . . .28 B3
Haverhill GB 30 B4
Havering GB 31 C4
Häverud S 35 D4
Havířov CZ 65 A4
Havixbeck D 50 B3
Havlíčkův Brod CZ . . .63 A6
Havndal DK 38 C3
Havneby DK 39 D1
Havnebyen DK 39 D4
Havøysund N 113 A13
Havran TR 118 C2
Havrebjerg DK 39 D4
Havsa TR 118 A1
Havstenssund S 35 D3
Hawarden GB 26 B2
Hawes GB 26 A3
Hawick GB 25 C5
Hawkhurst GB 31 C4
Hawkinge GB 31 C5
Haxey GB 27 B5
Hayange F 60 A2
Haydarlı TR 119 D5
Haydon Bridge GB . . .25 D5
Hayle GB 28 C2
Haymana TR 118 C7
Hay-on-Wye GB 29 A4
Hayrabolu TR 118 A2
Haysyn UA 11 B10
Hayvoron UA 11 B10
Haywards Heath GB . .31 D3
Hazebrouck F 48 C3
Hazlov CZ 52 C2
Heacham GB 30 B4
Headcorn GB 31 C4
Headford IRL 20 A2
Heanor GB 27 B4
Héas F 76 D3
Heathfield GB 31 D4
Hebden Bridge GB . . .26 B3
Heberg S 40 C2
Heby S 36 C3
Hechingen D 61 B4
Hecho E 76 D2
Hechtel B 49 B6
Hechthausen D 43 B6
Heckelberg D 45 C5
Heckington GB 27 C5
Hecklingen D 52 B1
Hed S 37 C2
Hedalen N 34 B1
Hedared S 40 B2
Heddal N 33 C6
Hédé F 57 B4
Hede S 115 E10
Hedekas S 35 D3
Hedemora S 36 B2
Hedenäset S 3 C25
Hedensted DK 39 D2
Hedersleben D 52 B1
Hedesunda S 36 B4
Hedge End GB 31 D2
Hedon GB 27 B5
Heede D 43 C4
Heek D 50 A3
Heemstede NL 42 C1
Heerde NL 42 C3
Heerenveen NL 42 C2
Heerhugoward NL 42 C1
Heerlen NL 50 C1
Heeze NL 49 B6
Heggenes N 32 A6
Hegra N 114 D8
Hegyeshalom H 64 C3
Hegyközség H 74 A1
Heia N 115 C9
Heide D 43 A6
Heidelberg D 61 A4
Heiden D 50 B2
Heidenau D 53 C3
Heidenheim D 61 B6
Heidenreichstein A . . .63 B6
Heikendorf D 44 A2
Heilam GB 22 C4
Heiland N 33 D5
Heilbad Heiligenstadt
D 51 B6
Heilbronn D 61 A5
Heiligenblut A 72 A2
Heiligendamm D 44 A3
Heiligendorf D 44 C2
Heiligengrabe D 44 B4
Heiligenhaus D 50 B2
Heiligenkreuz A 73 B6
Heiligenstadt D 62 A2
Heiligenstedten D 43 A6
Heilingen D 52 C1
Heiligoo NL 42 C1
Heilsbronn D 62 A1
Heim N 114 D6
Heimburg D 51 B6
Heimdal N 114 D7
Heinämäki FIN 3 E26
Heinebach D 51 B5
Heinerscheid L 50 C2
Heinersdorf D 45 C6
Heining D 63 B4
Heiningen D 61 B5
Heinola FIN 3 F27
Heinsberg D 50 B2
Heist-op-den-Berg B . .49 B5
Hejde S 37 E5
Hejls DK 39 D2
Hejnice CZ 53 C5
Heldrungen D 52 B1
Helechosa E 94 C2
Helensburgh GB 24 B3
Helfenberg A 63 B5
Helgen N 33 C6
Helgeroa N 33 D6
Hella
IS 111 D5
N 32 A3
Helland N 112 D4
Hellas S 35 D5
Helle N 33 D3
Helleland N 33 D3
Hellendoorn NL 42 C3
Hellenthal D 50 C2
Hellesøy N 32 B1
Hellesylt N 114 E3
Hellevoetsluis NL 49 B5
Helligskogen N 112 C9

Hellin E 101 A4
Hellissandur IS 111 C2
Hellnar IS 111 C2
Hellum DK 38 B3
Hellvi S 37 E5
Helm-brechts D 52 C1
Helmond NL 49 B6
Helmsdale GB 23 C5
Helmsley GB 27 A4
Helmstedt D 51 A6
Hel'pa SK 65 B5
Helsa D 51 B5
Helsby GB 26 B3
Helsinge DK 41 C2
Helsingør DK 41 C2
Helsinki FIN 6 A8
Helston GB 28 C2
Hemau D 62 A2
Hemavan S 115 B12
Hemel Hempstead
  GB 31 C3
Hemer D 50 B3
Héming F 60 B2
Hemmet DK 39 D1
Hemmingstedt D 43 A6
Hemmoor D 43 B6
Hemnes N 35 C3
Hemnesberget N . . .115 A10
Hemse S 37 E5
Hemsedal N 32 B5
Hemslingen D 43 B6
Hemsworth GB 27 B4
Hen N 32 B6
Henån S 35 D3
Hendaye F 76 C1
Hendek TR 118 B5
Hendungen D 51 C6
Henfield GB 31 D3
Hengelo
  Gelderland NL 50 A2
  Overijssel NL 50 A2
Hengersberg D 62 B4
Hengoed GB 29 B4
Hénin-Beaumont F . .48 C3
Henley-on-Thames
  GB 31 C3
Hennan S 115 E12
Henneberg D 51 C6
Hennebont F 56 C2
Henne Strand DK 39 D1
Hennigsdorf D 45 C5
Hennset N 114 D5
Hennstedt
  Schleswig-Holstein
    D 43 A6
  Schleswig-Holstein D. 43 A6
Henrichemont F 68 A2
Henryków PL 54 C2
Henrykowo PL 47 A6
Hensås N 32 A5
Henstedt-Ulzburg D . .44 B1
Heppenheim D 61 A4
Herad
  Buskerud N 32 B6
  Vest-Agder N 33 D3
Heradsbygd N 34 B3
Heraklion = Iraklio
  GR 117 G7
Herálec CZ 64 A2
Herand N 32 B3
Herbault F 58 C2
Herbern D 50 B3
Herbertstown IRL . . .20 B3
Herbeumont B 59 A6
Herbignac F 66 A2
Herbisse F 59 B5
Herbolzheim D 60 B3
Herborn D 50 C4
Herbrechtingen D 61 B6
Herby PL 54 C3
Herceg-Novi MNE . .105 A4
Hercegovac HR 74 C2
Hercegovacka Goleša
  SRB 85 C4
Hercegszántó H 75 C3
Herchen D 50 C3
Herdal N 114 F3
Herefoss N 33 D5
Hereke TR 118 B4
Herencia E 95 C3
Herend H 74 A2
Herent B 49 C5
Herentals B 49 B5
Herepian F 78 C2
Herfølge DK 41 D2
Herford D 51 A4
Herguijuela E 93 B5
Héric F 66 A3
Héricourt F 60 C2
Hérimoncourt F 70 A1
Heringsdorf D 44 A3
Herisau CH 71 A4
Hérisson F 68 B2
Herk-de-Stad B 49 C6
Herlufmagle DK 39 D4
Hermagor A 72 B3
Hermannsburg D 44 C2
Hermansverk N 32 A3
Hermanův Mestec
  CZ 53 D5
Herment F 68 C2
Hermeskeil D 60 A2
Hermisende E 87 C4
Hermonville F 59 A4
Hermsdorf D 52 C1
Hernani E 76 C1
Hernansancho E 94 B2
Herne D 50 B3
Herne Bay GB 31 C5
Hernes N 34 B3
Herning DK 39 C1
Herøya N 35 C1
Herramélluri E 89 B3
Herräng S 36 B5
Herre N 33 C6
Herrenberg D 61 B4
Herrera E 100 B1
Herrera de Alcántara
  E 92 B3
Herrera del Duque E .94 C1
Herrera de los Navarros
  E 90 B1
Herrera de Pisuerga
  E 88 B2
Herreros del Suso E . .94 B1
Herrestad S 35 D3
Herrhamra S 37 D4
Herritslev DK 44 A3
Herrljunga S 40 A3
Herrnhut D 53 B4
Herrsching D 62 B2
Hersbruck D 62 A2
Herscheid D 50 B3
Herselt B 49 B5
Herso GR 116 A4
Herstal B 49 C6
Herstmonceux GB . . .31 D4
Herten D 50 B3
Hertford GB 31 C4
Hervás E 93 A5
Herve B 49 C6
Herxheim D 61 A4
Herzberg
  Brandenburg D 45 C4
  Brandenburg D 52 B3
  Niedersachsen D . . .51 B6
Herzebrock D 50 B4
Herzfelde D 45 C5
Herzlake D 43 C4
Herzogenaurach D . . .62 A1
Herzogenbuchsee CH .70 A2
Herzogenburg A 63 B6
Herzsprung D 44 B4
Hesby N 33 C2
Hesdin F 48 C3

Hesel D 43 B4
Heskestad N 33 D3
Hessdalen N 114 E8
Hesselager DK 39 D3
Hesseng N 113 C18
Hessisch Lichtenau
  D 51 B5
Hessisch-Oldendorf
  D 51 A5
Hestra S 40 B3
Heswall GB 26 B2
Hetlevik N 32 B2
Hettange-Grande F . .60 A2
Hetton-le-Hole GB . . .25 D6
Hettstedt D 52 B1
Heuchin F 48 C3
Heudicourt-sous-les-
  Côtes F 60 B1
Heunezel F 60 B2
Heugueville F 57 A6
Heves H 65 C6
Héviz H 74 B2
Hexham GB 25 D5
Heysham GB 26 A3
Heytesbury GB 29 B5
Hidas H 74 B3
Hieflau A 63 C5
Hiendelaencina E 95 A4
Hiersac F 67 C4
High Bentham GB . . .26 A3
Highclere GB 31 C2
High Hesket GB 25 D5
Highley GB 26 C3
High Wycombe GB . . .31 C3
Higuera de Arjona E .100 B2
Higuera de Calatrava
  E 100 B1
Higuera de la Serena
  E 93 C5
Higuera de la Sierra
  E 99 B4
Higuera de Vargas E .93 C4
Higuera la Real E 99 A4
Higuera de Llerena E .93 C5
Higueruela E 96 C1
Híjar E 90 B2
Hilchenbach D 50 B4
Hildburghausen D . . .51 C6
Hilden D 50 B2
Hilders D 51 C5
Hildesheim D 51 A5
Hilgay GB 30 B4
Hillared S 40 B3
Hille D 51 A4
Hillegom NL 49 A5
Hillerød DK 41 D2
Hillerstorp S 40 B3
Hillesheim D 50 C2
Hillestad N 35 C2
Hillmersdorf D 52 B3
Hillsborough GB 19 B5
Hillswick GB 22 A7
Hiltpoltstein D 62 A2
Hiltpoltstein D 62 A2
Hilvarenbeek NL 49 B6
Hilversum NL 49 A6
Himarë AL 116 B1
Himbergen D 44 B2
Himesháza H 74 B3
Himmelberg A 73 B4
Himmelpforten D 43 B6
Himod H 74 A2
Hinckley GB 30 B2
Hindås S 40 B2
Hindelang D 71 A5
Hindelbank CH 70 A2
Hinderavåg N 33 C2
Hindhead GB 31 C3
Hinjosa del Valle E . . .93 C4
Hinnerup DK 39 C3
Hinneryd S 40 C3
Hinojal E 93 B4
Hinojales E 99 B4
Hinojos E 99 B4
Hinojosa del Duque E .93 C5
Hinojosas de Calatrava
  E 100 A1
Hinterhornbach A 71 A5
Hinterriss A 71 A6
Hintersee
  A 63 C4
  D 45 B6
Hinterstoder A 63 C5
Hintertux A 72 A1
Hinterweidenthal D . .60 A3
Hinwil CH 70 A3
Hios GR 116 D8
Hippolytushoef NL . .42 C1
Hirschaid D 62 A2
Hirschau D 62 A3
Hirschfeld D 52 B3
Hirschhorn D 61 A4
Hirsingue F 60 C3
Hirson F 59 A5
Hirtshals DK 38 B2
Hirzenhain D 51 C5
Hisarcık TR 118 C4
Hishult S 41 C3
Hitchin GB 31 C3
Hitra N 114 D5
Hittarp S 41 C2
Hittisau A 71 A4
Hittun N 32 A1
Hitzacker D 44 B3
Hjallerup DK 38 B3
Hjällstad S 34 B5
Hjältevad S 40 B5
Hjärnarp S 41 C2
Hjartdal N 33 C5
Hjellestad N 32 B2
Hjelmeland N 33 C3
Hjelset N 114 E6
Hjerkinn N 114 E6
Hjerm DK 38 C1
Hjerpsted DK 39 D1
Hjo S 35 D6
Hjordkær DK 39 D2
Hjørring DK 38 B2
Hjorted S 40 B6
Hjortkvarn S 37 D2
Hjortnäs S 36 B1
Hjortsberga S 40 C4
Hjukse N 33 C6
Hjuksebø N 33 C6
Hjulsjö S 36 C1
Hlinik nad Hronom
  SK 65 B4
Hlío IS 111 A10
Hlohovec SK 64 B3
Hlubokánad Vltavou
  CZ 63 A5
Hlučín CZ 64 A4
Hlukhiv UA 7 F12
Hlyboka UA 11 C8
Hlybokaye BY 7 D9
Hniezdne SK 65 A6
Hnilec SK 65 B6
Hnúšťa SK 65 B5
Hobol H 74 B2
Hobro DK 38 C2
Hobscheid L 60 A1
Hocalar TR 119 D4
Hochdonn D 43 A6
Hochdorf CH 70 A3
Hochfelden F 60 B3
Hochspeyer D 60 A3
Höchst im Odenwald
  D 61 A5
Höckendorf D 52 C3
Hockenheim D 61 A4
Hoddesdon GB 31 C4
Hodejov SK 65 B5
Hodenhagen D 43 C6
Hódkovice CZ 53 C5
Hódmezóvásárhely
  H 75 B5
Hodnet GB 26 C3

Hodonin CZ 64 B3
Hodslavice CZ 64 A4
Hoedekenskerke NL . .49 B4
Hoegaarden B 49 C5
Hoek van Holland NL .49 B5
Hoenderlo NL 50 A1
Hof
  D 52 C1
  N 35 C2
Hofbieber D 51 C5
Hoff GB 26 A3
Hofgeismar D 51 B5
Hofheim
  Bayern D 51 C6
  Hessen D 51 C4
Hofkirchen im Mühlkreis
  A 63 B5
Höfn IS 111 C10
Hofors S 36 B3
Hofsós IS 111 B6
Hofstad N 114 C7
Höganäs S 41 C2
Högbo S 36 B3
Hogdal S 35 C3
Högfors S 36 C2
Högklint S 37 E5
Högsäter S 35 D4
Högsby S 40 B6
Høgset D 37 C2
Hogstad S 37 D2
Högyész H 74 B3
Hohenau A 64 B2
Hohenberg A 63 C6
Hohenbucko D 52 B3
Hohenburg D 62 A2
Hohendorf D 45 A4
Hohenems A 71 A4
Hohenhameln D 51 A6
Hohenhausen D 51 A4
Hohenkirchen D 43 B4
Hohenlockstedt D 43 B6
Hohenmölsen D 52 B2
Hohennauen D 44 C4
Hohen Neuendorf D . .45 C5
Hohenseeden D 52 A2
Hohentauern A 73 A4
Hohentengen D 70 A3
Hohenwepel D 51 B5
Hohenwestedt D 43 A6
Hohenwutzen D 45 C6
Hohenzieritz D 45 B5
Hohn D 43 A6
Hohne D 44 C2
Hohnstorf D 44 B2
Højer DK 39 E1
Højslev Stby DK 38 C2
Hok S 40 B4
Hökerum S 40 B3
Hokksund N 35 C5
Hökön S 40 C4
Hol N 32 B5
Hola Pristan UA 11 C12
Hólar IS 111 B6
Holašovice CZ 63 B5
Holbæk
  Aarhus Amt. DK . . .38 C3
  Vestsjællands Amt.
    DK 39 D4
Holbeach GB 30 B4
Holdenstedt D 44 C2
Holdhus N 32 B2
Holdorf D 43 C5
Holeby DK 44 A3
Holen N 35 C2
Hølervasseter N 32 B6
Holešov CZ 64 A3
Holguera E 93 B4
Holíč SK 64 B3
Holice
  CZ 53 C4
  SK 64 C3
Höljes S 34 B4
Hollabrunn A 64 B2
Hollandstoun GB 23 B6
Høllen N 33 D4
Hollfeld D 52 D1
Hollókő H 65 C5
Hollstadt D 51 C6
Hollum NL 42 B2
Hollviksnäs S 41 D2
Holm
  N 114 B9
  NL 42 B2
Hólmavik IS 111 B4
Holmbukt N 113 B10
Holmedal S 35 C3
Holmegil N 35 C3
Holmen N 34 B2
Holme-on-Spalding-Moor
  GB 27 B5
Holmes Chapel GB . . .26 B3
Holmestrand N 35 C2
Holmfirth GB 27 B4
Holmfoss N 113 C19
Holmsbu N 35 C2
Holmsjö S 41 C5
Holmsund S 3 E24
Holmsveden S 36 B3
Holmudden S 37 E6
Hölö S 37 C4
Holøydal N 114 E8
Holsbybrunn S 40 B5
Holseter N 34 A1
Holsljunga S 40 B3
Holstebro DK 39 C1
Holsted DK 39 D1
Holsworthy GB 28 C3
Holt
  D 39 E2
  Norfolk GB 30 B5
  Wrexham GB 26 B3
  IS 111 D6
  N 33 D5
Holten NL 50 A2
Holtwick D 50 A3
Holum N 33 D4
Holwerd NL 42 B2
Holycross IRL 21 B4
Holyhead GB 26 B1
Holýšov CZ 62 A4
Holywell GB 26 B2
Holywood GB 19 B6
Holzdorf D 52 B3
Holzhausen D 51 A4
Holzheim D 61 B6
Holzkirchen D 62 C2
Holzminden D 51 B5
Homberg
  Hessen D 51 B5
  Hessen D 51 C5
Homburg D 60 A3
Hommelstø N 115 B9
Hommersåk N 33 D2
Homokmegy H 75 B4
Homokszentgyörgy
  H 74 B2
Homrogd H 65 B6
Homyel = Gomel BY . .7 E11
Honaz TR 119 D4
Hondarribia E 76 C1
Hondón de los Frailes
  E 101 A5
Hondschoote F 48 C3
Hönebach D 51 C5
Hønefoss N 34 B2
Honfleur F 57 A6
Høng DK 39 D4
Honiton GB 29 C4
Hönningen D 50 C2
Honningsvåg N 113 A14
Hönö S 38 B4
Honrubia E 95 C4
Hontalbilla E 88 C2
Hontheim D 50 C2
Hontianske-Nemce
  SK 65 B4
Hontoria de la Cantera
  E 88 B3
Hontoria del Pinar E . .89 C3

Hontoria de Valdearados
  E 89 C3
Hoofddorp NL 49 A5
Hoogerheide NL 49 B5
Hoogeveen NL 42 C3
Hoogezand-Sappemeer
  NL 42 B3
Hoogkarspel NL 42 C2
Hoogkerk NL 42 B3
Hoogstede D 42 C2
Hoogstraten B 49 B5
Hook GB 31 C3
Hooksiel D 43 B5
Höör S 41 D3
Hoorn NL 42 C2
Hope GB 26 B2
Hopen N 112 E4
Hope under Dinmore
  GB 29 A5
Hopfgarten D 52 C1
Hopfgarten in Defereggen
  A 72 B2
Hopseidet N 113 B16
Hopsten D 43 C4
Hoptrup DK 39 D2
Hora Svatého Sebestiána
  CZ 52 C3
Horažďovice CZ 63 A4
Horb am Neckar D . . .61 B4
Horbelev DK 39 E5
Hørby DK 38 B3
Hörby S 41 D3
Horcajada de la Torre
  E 95 B4
Horcajo de los Montes
  E 94 C2
Horcajo de Santiago
  E 95 C3
Horcajo-Medianero E .93 A5
Horche E 95 B3
Horda S 40 B4
Hordabø N 32 B1
Hordalia N 32 B2
Hordvik N 32 B2
Hořesedly CZ 52 C3
Horezu RO 11 D8
Horgen CH 70 A3
Horgoš SRB 75 B4
Hořice CZ 53 C5
Horjul SLO 73 B4
Horka D 53 B4
Hörken S 36 B1
Horki BY 7 D11
Horle S 40 B4
Horn
  A 63 B6
  D 51 B4
  N 34 B2
  S 40 B5
Horna E 101 A4
Hornachos E 93 C4
Hornachuelos E 99 B5
Horná Marikova SK . .64 A4
Hornanes N 32 C2
Horná Streda SK 64 B3
Horná Strubna SK . . .65 B4
Horná Súca SK 64 B3
Hornbæk
  Aarhus Amt. DK . . .38 C2
  Frederiksværk DK . .41 C2
Hornberg D 61 B4
Hornburg D 51 A6
Horncastle GB 27 B5
Horndal S 36 B3
Horndean GB 31 D2
Horne
  Fyns Amt. DK 39 D3
  Ribe Amt. DK 39 D1
Hörnebo S 35 D6
Horneburg D 43 B6
Hörnefors S 115 D16
Horní Becva CZ 64 A4
Horní Benešov CZ . . .64 A3
Horní Cerekev CZ . . .63 A6
Horní Jiřetín CZ 52 C3
Horní Lomná CZ 65 A4
Horní Maršov CZ 53 C5
Hornindal N 114 F3
Hørning DK 39 C3
Hörningsholm S 37 C4
Horní Planá CZ 63 B5
Horní Slavkov CZ 52 C2
Horní Vltavice CZ 63 B4
Hornnes N 33 D4
Horno D 53 B4
Hornos E 101 A3
Hornoy-le-Bourg F . . .58 A2
Hornsea GB 27 B5
Hornsjø N 34 A2
Hornslet DK 39 C3
Hornstein A 64 C2
Hørnum D 39 E1
Hornum DK 38 C2
Horný Tisovnik SK . . .65 B5
Horodenka UA 11 B8
Horodnya UA 7 F11
Horodok
  Khmelnytskyy UA . .11 B9
  Lviv UA 11 B7
Horodyshche UA 11 B11
Horokhiv UA 11 A8
Horovice CZ 63 A4
Horred S 40 B2
Hörröd S 41 D4
Hörsching A 63 B5
Horsens DK 39 D2
Horsham GB 31 C3
Hørsholm DK 41 D2
Horslunde DK 39 E4
Horst
  D 43 B6
  NL 50 B2
Horstel D 50 A3
Horsten D 43 B4
Horstmar D 50 A3
Hort H 65 C5
Horta P 87 C3
Horten N 35 C2
Hortezuela E 89 C4
Hortiguela E 89 B3
Hortobágy H 75 A6
Horton in Ribblesdale
  GB 26 A3
Hørve DK 39 D4
Hörvik S 41 C4
Horwich GB 26 B3
Hosanger N 32 B2
Hösbach D 51 C5
Hosena D 53 B4
Hosenfeld D 51 C5
Hosingen L 50 C2
Hospental CH 70 B3
Hospital IRL 20 B3
Hossegor F 76 C1
Hosszuhetény H 74 B3
Hostal de Ipiés E 90 A2
Hoštálková CZ 64 A3
Hostalric E 91 B5
Hostens F 76 B2
Hostěradice CZ 64 B2
Hostinné CZ 53 C5
Hostomice CZ 63 A5
Hostouň CZ 62 A3
Hotagen S 115 D11
Hoting S 115 C13
Hotolisht AL 116 A2
Hotton B 49 C6
Houdain F 48 C3
Houdan F 58 B2
Houdelaincourt F 60 B1
Houeillès F 76 B3
Houffalize B 50 C1
Houghton-le-Spring
  GB 25 D6
Houlberg D 39 C2
Houlgate F 57 A5
Hounslow GB 31 C3
Hourtin F 66 C2
Hourtin-Plage F 66 C2
Houten NL 49 A6
Houthalen B 49 B6
Houyet B 49 C5
Hov
  DK 39 D3

Hov continued
  N 34 B2
Hova S 35 D6
Høvåg N 33 D5
Hovborg DK 39 D1
Hovda N 32 B5
Hovden N 33 C4
Hove GB 31 D3
Hovedgård DK 39 D2
Hovelhof D 51 B4
Hoven N 39 D1
Hovet N 32 B5
Hovingham GB 27 A5
Hovmantorp S 40 C5
Hovsta S 37 C2
Howden GB 27 B5
Howe D 44 B2
Höxter D 51 B5
Hoya D 43 C6
Hoya-Gonzalo E 95 D5
Hoyanger N 32 A3
Hoyerswerda D 53 B4
Høyjord N 35 C2
Hoylake GB 26 B2
Høylandet N 114 C9
Hoym D 52 B1
Høymyr N 32 C6
Hoyocasero E 94 B2
Hoyo de Manzanares
  E 94 B3
Hoyo de Pinares E . . .94 B2
Hoyos E 93 A4
Hoyos del Espino E . .93 A5
Hrabušice SK 65 B6
Hradec Králové CZ . . .53 C5
Hradec nad Moravicí
  CZ 64 A3
Hrádek CZ 64 B2
Hrádek nad Nisou CZ .53 C4
Hradište SK 65 B4
Hrafnagil IS 111 B7
Hrafnseyri IS 111 B2
Hranice
  Severomoravsky
    CZ 64 A3
  Západoceský CZ . . .52 C2
Hranovnica SK 65 B6
Hrasnica BIH 84 C3
Hrastnik SLO 73 B5
Hrebenka UA 11 A12
Hřensko CZ 53 C4
Hriňová SK 65 B5
Hrisoupoli GR 116 B6
Hrochov CZ 64 A2
Hrochův Tynec CZ . . .53 D5
Hrodna BY 6 E7
Hrodzyanka BY 7 E10
Hronov CZ 53 C6
Hronský Benadík SK .65 B4
Hrotovice CZ 64 A2
Hrtkovci SRB 85 B4
Hrun IS 111 A5
Hrušov SK 65 B5
Hrušovany nad
  Jevišovkou CZ 64 B2
Hrvaćani BIH 84 B2
Hrvace HR 83 C5
Hrymayliv UA 11 B9
Hückel-hoven D 50 B2
Hückeswagen D 50 B3
Hucknall GB 27 B4
Hucqueliers F 48 C2
Huddersfield GB 27 B4
Huddinge S 37 C4
Huddunge S 36 B3
Hude D 43 B5
Hudiksvall S 115 F14
Huélago E 100 B2
Huélamo E 95 B5
Huelgoat F 56 B2
Huelma E 100 B2
Huelva E 99 B4
Huéneja E 100 B3
Huércal-Overa E 101 B4
Huerta de Abajo E . . .89 B3
Huerta del Rey E 89 C3
Huerta de
  Valdecarabanos E . .95 C3
Huertahernando E . . .95 B4
Huesa E 100 B2
Huesca E 90 A2
Huéscar E 101 B3
Huete E 95 B4
Huétor Tájar E 100 B1
Hüfingen D 61 C4
Hufthamar N 32 B1
Hugh Town GB 28 D1
Huglfing D 62 C2
Huissen NL 50 B1
Huittinen FIN 3 F25
Huizen NL 49 A6
Hulín CZ 64 A3
Hüls D 50 B2
Hulsig DK 38 B3
Hulst NL 49 B5
Hult S 40 B5
Hulta S 40 A6
Hulteby S 35 C6
Hultsfred S 40 B5
Hultsjö S 40 B5
Humanes E 95 B3
Humberston GB 27 B5
Humble DK 39 E3
Humenné SK 10 B6
Humilladero E 100 B1
Hümmelbæk DK 41 D2
Hummelsta S 37 C3
Humpolec CZ 63 A6
Humshaugh GB 25 C5
Hundåla N 115 B9
Hundested DK 39 D4
Hundorp N 34 A1
Hundvåg N 33 C2
Hundvin N 32 B2
Hunedoara RO 11 D7
Hünfeld D 51 C5
Hungen D 51 C4
Hungerford GB 31 C2
Hunndalen N 34 B2
Hunnebostrand S 35 D3
Hunstanton GB 30 B4
Huntingdon GB 30 B3
Huntley GB 29 B5
Huntly GB 23 D6
Huparlac F 77 B5
Huppy F 48 D2
Hurbanovo SK 64 C4
Hürbel D 61 B5
Hurdal N 34 B3
Hurezani RO 11 D7
Hurlford GB 24 C3
Hurstbourne Tarrant
  GB 31 C2
Hurstpierpoint GB . . .31 D3
Hürth D 50 C2
Hurum DK 32 A5
Hurup DK 38 C1
Húsafell IS 111 C5
Húsavík IS 111 A8
Husbands Bosworth
  GB 30 B2
Husby
  D 39 E2
  DK 38 C1
Husey IS 111 B11
Husi RO 11 C10
Husína BIH 84 B3
Husínec CZ 63 A4
Husinish GB 22 D1
Huskvarna S 40 B4
Husnes N 32 C2
Husøy N 112 C6
Hustad N 114 E4
Hüsten D 50 B4
Hustopeče CZ 64 B2
Hustopeče nad Bečvou
  CZ 64 A3

Husum
  D 43 A6
  S 115 D16
Husvika N 115 B9
Huta PL 46 C2
Hutovo BIH 84 D2
Hüttenberg A 73 B4
Hüttlingen D 61 B6
Huttoft GB 27 B6
Hutton Cranswick GB .27 B5
Hüttschlag A 72 A3
Huttwil CH 70 A2
Huy B 49 C6
Hüyük TR 119 E6
Hval N 34 B2
Hvåle N 32 B6
Hvaler N 35 C3
Hvalpsund DK 38 C2
Hvammstangi IS 111 B5
Hvammur IS 111 B6
Hvanneyri IS 111 C4
Hvar HR 83 C5
Hvarnes N 35 C2
Hvaragerði IS 111 D4
Hvidbjerg DK 38 C1
Hvide Sande DK 39 D1
Hvittingfoss N 35 C2
Hybe SK 65 A5
Hycklinge S 40 B5
Hydra GR 117 E5
Hyen N 114 F2
Hyères F 79 C5
Hyères Plage F 79 C5
Hylestad N 33 C4
Hylke DK 39 D2
Hyllestad N 32 A2
Hyllstofta S 41 C3
Hyltebruk S 40 C3
Hynish GB 24 B1
Hynnekleiv N 33 D5
Hythe
  Hampshire GB 31 D2
  Kent GB 31 C5
Hyvinkää FIN 3 F26

I

Iam RO 85 A6
Iaşi RO 11 C9
Iasmos GR 116 A7
Ibahernando E 93 B5
Ibbenbüren D 50 A3
Ibeas de Juarros E . . .89 B3
Ibestad N 112 D6
Ibi E 96 C2
Ibiza = Eivissa E 97 C1
Ibriktepe TR 118 A1
Ibros E 100 A2
Ibstock GB 27 C4
İçel TR 16 C7
Ichenhausen D 61 B6
Ichnya UA 11 A12
Ichtegem B 49 B4
Ichtershausen D 51 C6
Idanha-a-Novo P 93 B3
Idar-Oberstein D 60 A3
Idd N 35 C3
Idiazábal E 89 B4
Idivuoma S 113 D10
Idkerberget S 36 B2
Idön S 36 B5
Idre S 115 F9
Idrija SLO 73 C4
Idritsa RUS 7 D10
Idstein D 50 C4
Idvor SRB 75 C5
Iecca Mare RO 75 C5
Ielsi I 103 B7
Ieper = Ypres B 48 C3
Ierapetra GR 117 G7
Ierissos GR 116 B5
Ifjord N 113 B16
Ig SLO 73 C4
Igal H 74 B2
Igea E 89 B4
Igea Marina I 82 B1
Igelfors S 37 D2
Igersheim D 61 A5
Iggesund S 115 F14
Iglarevo KOS 85 D5
Iglesias E 88 B3
Iglésias I 110 C1
Igls A 71 A6
Igny-Comblizy F 59 A4
Igorre E 89 A4
Igoumenitsa GR 116 C2
Igries E 90 A2
Igualada E 91 B4
Igüeña E 86 B4
Iguerande F 68 B4
Iharosberény H 74 B2
Ihl'any SK 65 A6
Ihlienworth D 43 B5
Ihringen D 60 B3
Ihrlerstein D 62 B2
Ihsaniye TR 118 C5
Ii FIN 3 D26
Iijärvi FIN 113 C16
Iisalmi FIN 3 E27
Ijmuiden NL 42 C1
IJsselmuiden NL 42 C2
IJzendijke NL 49 B4
Ikast DK 39 C2
Ikervár H 74 A1
İkizdere TR 16 A9
Ilandža SRB 75 C5
Ilanz CH 71 B4
Ilava SK 64 B4
Ilawa PL 47 B5
Il Castagno I 81 C4
Ilche E 90 B3
Ilchester GB 29 C5
Ilfeld D 51 B6
Ilfracombe GB 28 B3
Ilgaz TR 16 A6
Ilgın TR 119 D6
Ilhavo P 87 A2
Ilica TR 118 C2
Ilidža BIH 84 C3
Ilijaš BIH 84 C3
Ilirska Bistrica SLO . .73 C4
Ilkeston GB 27 C4
Ilkley GB 27 B4
Illana E 95 B4
Illano E 86 A4
Illar E 100 C3
Illats F 76 B2
Illertissen D 61 B6
Illescas E 94 B3
Ille-sur-Têt F 91 A5
Illfurth F 60 C3
Illichivsk UA 11 C11
Illiers-Combray F 58 B2
Illkirch-Graffenstaden
  F 60 B3
Illmersdorf D 52 B3
Illmitz A 64 C2
Illora E 100 B2
Illueca E 89 C5
Ilmajoki FIN 3 E25
Ilmenau D 51 C6
Ilok HR 75 C4
Ilomantsi FIN 3 E29
Ilow PL 47 C6
Ilowa PL 53 B5
Ilowo-Osada PL 47 B6
Ilsede D 51 A6
Ilsenburg D 51 B6
Ilshofen D 61 A5
Ilz A 73 A5
Ilža PL 55 B6
Imamoğlu TR 16 C7
Imatra FIN 3 F28
Imielin PL 55 C4
Imingen N 32 B5
Immeln S 41 C4

Immenhausen D 51 B5
Immenstadt D 61 C6
Immingham GB 27 B5
Imola I 81 B5
Imon E 95 A4
Imotski HR 84 C2
Impéria I 80 C2
Imphy F 68 B3
Imroz TR 116 B7
Imsland N 33 C2
Imst A 71 A5
Inagh IRL 20 B2
Inari FIN 113 D15
Inca E 97 B2
Inchnadamph GB 22 C4
Incinillas E 89 B3
Indal S 115 E14
Indre Arna N 32 B2
Indre Brenna N 113 B14
İneada TR 118 A2
İneboin TR 16 A6
İnecik TR 118 B2
İnegöl TR 118 B4
Inerthal CH 70 A3
Infiesto E 88 A1
Ingatorp S 40 B5
Ingedal N 35 C3
Ingelheim D 50 D4
Ingelmunster B 49 C4
Ingelstad S 40 C4
Ingleton GB 26 A3
Ingolfsland N 32 C5
Ingolstadt D 62 B2
Ingrandes
  Maine-et-Loire F . . .66 A4
  Vienne F 67 B5
Ingwiller F 60 B3
İnhisar TR 118 B5
İniesta E 95 C5
İnishannon IRL 20 C3
İnishcrone IRL 18 B2
İnke H 74 B2
İnnellan GB 24 C3
İnnerleithen GB 25 C4
İnnermessan GB 24 D3
İnnertkirchen CH 70 B3
İnnervillgraten A 72 B2
İnnsbruck A 71 A6
İnnset N 112 D7
İnnvik N 114 F3
İnönü TR 118 C5
İnowłódz PL 55 B5
İnowrocław PL 47 C4
İns CH 70 A2
İnsch GB 23 D6
İnsjön S 36 B2
İnstow GB 28 B3
İntepe TR 118 B1
İnterlaken CH 70 B2
İntragna CH 70 B3
İnverallochy GB 23 D7
İnveran
  GB 23 B4
  IRL 20 A2
İnveraray GB 24 B2
İnverbervie GB 25 B5
İnvergarry GB 22 D4
İnvergordon GB 23 D4
İnverkeilor GB 25 B5
İnverkeithing GB 25 B4
İnvermoriston GB 22 D4
İnverness GB 23 D4
İnveruno I 70 C3
İnverurie GB 23 D6
İoannina GR 116 C2
İolanda di Savóia I . . .81 B5
İon Corvin RO 11 D9
İos GR 117 F7
İpati GR 116 D4
İpsala TR 118 B1
İpswich GB 30 B5
İrdning A 73 A4
İregszemcse H 74 B3
İrgoli I 110 B2
İrig SRB 85 A4
İronbridge GB 26 C3
İrrel D 60 A2
İrsina I 104 C2
İrsta S 37 C3
İrthlingborough GB . . .30 B3
İruela E 87 B4
İrún E 76 C1
İrurita E 76 C1
İrurzun E 76 C1
İrvine GB 24 C3
İrvinestown GB 19 B4
İsaba E 76 D2
İsabela E 87 B3
İsafjörður IS 111 A2
İsane N 114 F2
İsaszeg H 75 A4
İsbister GB 22 A7
İscar E 88 C2
İscehisar TR 118 C5
İschgl A 71 A5
İschia I 103 C6
İschia di Castro I 102 A4
İschitella I 104 B1
İsdes F 58 C3
İse N 35 C3
İselle I 70 B3
İseltwald CH 70 B2
İsen D 62 B2
İsenbüttel D 44 C2
İseo I 71 C5
İserlohn D 50 B3
İsérnia I 103 B7
İsfjorden N 114 E4
İsigny-sur-Mer F 57 A4
İşıklı TR 119 D4
İsili I 110 C2
İskilip TR 16 A7
İsla Canela E 98 B3
İsla Cristina E 98 B3
İslares E 89 A3
İsleham GB 30 B4
İsle of Whithorn GB . .24 E3
İsmaning D 62 B2
İsna H 74 B2
İsnestoften N 113 B11
İsny D 61 C6
İsoba E 88 A1
İsokylä
  FIN 113 F16
İsokyrö FIN 3 E25
İsola F 79 B6
İsola d'Asti I 80 B2
İsola del Gran Sasso
  d'Itália I 103 A6
İsola della Scala I 71 C6
İsola delle Fémmine
  I 108 A2
İsola del Liri I 103 B6
İsola di Capo Rizzuto
  I 107 C4
İsona E 91 A4
İspagnac F 78 B2
İsparta TR 119 E5
İsperih BG 11 E9
İspica I 109 C3
İssanno I 50 B2
İssigeac F 77 B3
İssogne I 70 C2
İssoire F 68 C3
İssoncourt F 59 B6
İssoudun F 68 B1
İssum D 50 B2
İs-sur-Tille F 69 A5
İssy-l'Evêque F 68 B4

Istán E 100 C1
İstanbul TR 118 A3
İstebna PL 65 A4
İstia d'Ombrone I 81 D5
İstok KOS 85 D5
İstres F 78 C3
İstvándi H 74 B2
İtea GR 116 D4
İthaki GR 117 D2
İtoiz E 76 D1
İtrabo E 100 C2
İtri I 103 B6
İttireddu I 110 B1
Íttiri I 110 B1
İtzehoe D 43 B6
İvalo FIN 113 D16
İván H 74 A1
İvanava BY 7 E8
İvančice CZ 64 A2
İvančna Gorica SLO . .73 C4
İvancsa H 74 A3
İvanec HR 73 B6
İvanić Grad HR 73 C6
İvanjica SRB 85 C5
İvanjska BIH 84 B2
İvanka SK 64 B4
İvano-Frankivsk UA . .11 B8
İvanovice na Hané
  CZ 64 A3
İvanska HR 74 C1
İvatsevichy BY 7 E8
İvaylovgrad BG 116 A8
İveland N 33 D4
İvoz Ramet B 49 C6
İvrea I 70 C2
İvrindi TR 118 C2
İvry-en-Montagne F . .69 A4
İvry-la-Bataille F 58 B2
İvybridge GB 28 C4
İwaniska PL 55 C6
İwiny PL 53 B5
İwuy F 49 C4
İxworth GB 30 B4
İzarra E 89 B4
İzbica Kujawska PL . .47 C4
İzbište SRB 85 A6
İzeda P 87 C4
İzegem B 49 C4
İzernore F 69 B5
İzmayil UA 11 D10
İzmir TR 119 D2
İzmit = Kocaeli TR . . .118 B4
İznájar E 100 B1
İznalloz E 100 B2
İznatoraf E 100 A2
İznik TR 118 B4
İzola SLO 72 C3
İzsák H 75 B4
İzsófalva H 65 B6
İzyaslav UA 11 A9

J

Jabalquinto E 100 A2
Jablanac HR 83 B3
Jablanica BIH 84 C2
Jablonec nad Jizerou
  CZ 53 C5
Jablonec nad Nisou
  CZ 53 C5
Jablonica SK 64 B3
Jablonka PL 65 A5
Jablonna PL 55 A5
Jablonné Podještědi
  CZ 53 C4
Jablonov nad Turňou
  SK 65 B6
Jablonowo Pomorskie
  PL 47 B5
Jablunkov CZ 65 A4
Jabučje SRB 85 B5
Jabuka
  Srbija SRB 85 C4
  Vojvodina SRB 85 B5
Jabukovac HR 73 C6
Jaca E 90 A2
Jáchymov CZ 52 C2
Jacobidrebber D 43 C5
Jade D 43 B5
Jäderfors S 36 B3
Jadraque E 95 B4
Jaén E 100 B2
Jagare BIH 84 B2
Jagel D 43 A6
Jagenbach A 63 B6
Jægerspris DK 39 D4
Jagodina SRB 85 C6
Jagodnjak HR 74 C3
Jagstheim D 61 A6
Jagstzell D 61 A6
Jahodna BIH 84 B3
Jajce BIH 84 B2
Ják H 74 A1
Jakabszállás H 75 B4
Jäkkvik S 115 A14
Jakovlje HR 73 C5
Jakobsnes S 113 C19
Jaksice PL 47 C4
Jakšić HR 74 C2
Jakubany SK 65 A6
Jalance E 96 B1
Jalasjärvi FIN 3 E25
Jalhay B 50 C1
Jaligny-sur-Besbre F .68 B3
Jallais F 66 A4
Jalón E 96 C2
Jâlons F 59 B5
Jamena SRB 84 B4
Jamilena E 100 B2
Jämjö S 41 C5
Jamnička Kiselica
  HR 73 C5
Jamno PL 46 A2
Jamoigne B 59 A6
Jämsä FIN 3 F26
Jämshög S 41 C4
Janakkala FIN 3 F26
Jandelsbrunn D 63 B4
Jänickendorf D 52 A3
Janikowo PL 47 C4
Janja BIH 85 B4
Janjina HR 84 D2
Janki
  Łódzkie PL 55 B4
  Mazowieckie PL . . .55 A5
Jankov CZ 63 A5
Jankowo Dolne PL . . .46 C3
Jánoshalma H 75 B4
Jánosháza H 74 A2
Jánossomorja H 64 C3
Janovice nad Uhlavou
  CZ 63 A4
Janów PL 55 C4
Janowiec Wielkopolski
  PL 46 C3
Janowo PL 47 B6
Jänsmässholmen
  S 115 D10
Janville F 58 B2
Janzé F 57 C4
Jarabá SK 65 B5
Jaraczewo PL 54 B2
Jarafuel E 96 B1
Jaraicejo E 93 B5
Jaraíz de la Vera E . . .93 A5
Jarak SRB 85 B4
Jarandilla de la Vera
  E 93 A5
Jaray E 89 C4

Järbo S 36 B3
Jard-sur-Mer F 66 B3
Jaren N 34 B2
Jargeau F 58 C3
Jarkovac SRB 75 C5
Järlåsa S 36 C4
Jarmen D 45 B5
Järna S 37 C4
Jarnac F 67 C4
Järnäs S 115 D16
Järnforsen S 40 B5
Jarny F 60 A1
Jarocin PL 54 B2
Jaroměř CZ 53 C5
Jaroměřice nad Rokytnou CZ 64 A1
Jaroslav CZ 64 B2
Jaroslavice CZ 64 B2
Jarosław PL 11 A7
Jarosławiec PL 46 A2
Jarošov nad Nežárkou CZ 63 A6
Järpås S 35 D4
Järpen S 115 D10
Jarrow GB 25 D6
Järso FIN 36 B6
Järvenpää FIN 7 A8
Jarvorník CZ 54 C1
Järvsö S 115 F13
Jarzé F 67 A4
Jaša Tomic SRB 75 C5
Jasenak BIH 83 B3
Jasenice HR 83 B4
Jasenovac HR 74 C1
Jasenovo
  Srbija SRB 85 C4
  Vojvodina SRB 85 B6
Jasień PL 53 B5
Jasienica PL 53 B5
Jasika SRB 85 C6
Jaslo PL 10 B6
Jásova SK 65 C4
Jasserron F 69 B5
Jastarnia PL 47 A4
Jastrebarsko HR 73 C5
Jastrowie PL 46 B2
Jastrzębia-Góra PL 47 A4
Jastrzębie Zdrój PL 54 C3
Jászals-Lószentgyörgy H 75 A5
Jászapáti H 75 A5
Jászárokszállás H 65 C5
Jászberény H 75 A4
Jászdózsa H 65 C6
Jászfényszaru H 75 A4
Jászjakóhalma H 75 A5
Jászkarajenő H 75 A5
Jászkisér H 75 A5
Jászladány H 75 A4
Jászszentlászló H 75 B4
Jásztelek H 75 A5
Játar E 100 C2
Jättendal S 115 F14
Jatznick D 45 B5
Jaun CH 70 B2
Jausiers F 79 B5
Jávea E 96 C3
Jävenitz D 44 C3
Javerlhac F 67 C5
Javier E 90 A1
Javorani BIH 84 B2
Javorina SK 65 A6
Javron F 57 B5
Jawor PL 53 B6
Jaworzno PL 55 C4
Jaworzyna Śl. PL 54 C1
Jayena E 100 C2
Jażow PL 75 C6
Jebel RO 75 C6
Jebjerg DK 38 C2
Jedburgh GB 25 C5
Jedlinsk PL 55 B6
Jednia PL 55 B6
Jednia Letnisko PL 55 B6
Jedovnice CZ 64 A2
Jędrychów PL 47 B5
Jędrzejów PL 55 C5
Jedwabno PL 47 B6
Jeesiö FIN 113 E15
Jeglownik PL 47 A5
Jegun F 77 C3
Jēkabpils LV 7 C8
Jektevik N 32 C2
Jektvik N 112 F2
Jelakci SRB 85 C5
Jelcz-Laskowice PL 54 B2
Jelenec SK 64 B4
Jelenia Góra PL 53 C5
Jelgava LV 6 C7
Jelka SK 64 B3
Jelling DK 39 D2
Jels DK 39 D2
Jelsa
  HR 83 C5
  N 33 C3
Jelšava SK 65 B6
Jemgum D 43 B4
Jemnice CZ 63 A6
Jena D 52 C1
Jenaz CH 71 B4
Jenbach A 72 A1
Jenikow PL 45 B7
Jennersdorf A 73 B6
Jenny S 40 B6
Jerchel D 44 C3
Jeres del Marquesado E 100 B2
Jerez de la Frontera E 99 C4
Jerez de los Caballeros E 99 A4
Jerica E 96 B2
Jerichow D 44 C4
Jerka PL 54 A1
Jermenovci SRB 75 C6
Jerslev DK 38 B3
Jerte E 93 A5
Jerup DK 38 B3
Jerxheim D 51 A6
Jerzmanowice PL 55 C4
Jerzu I 110 C2
Jerzwałd PL 47 B5
Jesberg D 51 C5
Jesenice
  Středočeský CZ 52 C3
  Středočeský CZ 53 D4
  SLO 73 B4
Jeseník CZ 54 C2
Jesenké SK 65 B6
Jésol I 72 C2
Jessen D 52 B2
Jessenitz D 44 B3
Jessheim N 34 B3
Jessnitz D 52 B2
Jesteburg D 44 B1
Jeumont F 49 C5
Jevenstedt D 44 A1
Jever D 43 B4
Jevičko CZ 64 A2
Jevišovice CZ 64 B1
Jevnaker N 34 B2
Jezerane HR 83 A4
Jezero
  BIH 84 B2
  HR 83 A4
Jeziorany PL 47 B6
Jezów PL 55 B4
Jičín CZ 53 C5
Jičiněves CZ 53 C5
Jihlava CZ 63 A6
Jijona E 96 C2
Jilemnice CZ 53 C5
Jílové E 52 C3
Jílové u Prahy CZ 63 A5
Jimbolia RO 75 C5
Jimena E 100 B2

Jimena de la Frontera E 99 C5
Jimera de Libar E 99 C5
Jimramov CZ 64 A2
Jince CZ 63 A4
Jindřichovice CZ 52 C2
Jindřichův Hradec CZ 63 A6
Jirkov CZ 52 C3
Jistebnice CZ 63 A5
Joachimsthal D 45 C5
João da Loura P 92 C2
Jobbágyi H 65 C5
Jochberg A 72 A2
Jockfall S 113 F11
Jódar E 100 B2
Jodoigne B 49 C5
Joensuu FIN 3 E28
Joesjö S 115 B11
Joeuf F 60 A1
Jõgeva EST 7 B9
Johanngeorgenstadt D 52 C2
Johannishus S 41 C5
Johanniskirchen D 62 B3
Johansfors S 40 C5
John o'Groats GB 23 C5
Johnstone GB 24 C3
Johnstown IRL 21 B4
Jõhvi EST 7 B9
Joigny F 59 C4
Joinville F 59 B6
Jokkmokk S 112 F8
Jöllenbeck D 51 A4
Jomala FIN 36 B6
Jönåker S 37 D3
Jonava LT 6 D8
Jonchery-sur-Vesle F 59 A4
Jondal N 32 B3
Jondalen N 33 C6
Joniškis LT 6 C7
Jönköping S 40 B4
Jonkowo PL 47 B6
Jønnbu N 33 C6
Jonsberg S 37 D3
Jonsered S 38 B5
Jonstorp S 41 C2
Jonzac F 67 C4
Jorba E 91 B4
Jordanów PL 65 A5
Jordanowo PL 46 C1
Jordanów Śląski PL 54 C1
Jordbro S 37 C5
Jordet N 34 A4
Jordøse DK 39 D3
Jork D 43 B6
Jorlanda S 38 B4
Jörmlien S 115 C10
Jormvattnet S 115 C11
Jörn S 115 B17
Jørpeland N 33 C3
Jorquera E 96 B1
Jošan HR 83 B4
Jošanička Banja SRB 85 C5
Jošavka BIH 84 B2
Josipdol HR 73 C5
Josipovac HR 74 C3
Jössefors S 35 C4
Josselin F 56 C3
Jøssund N 114 C7
Jostedal N 114 F4
Jošvafő H 65 B6
Jou P 87 C3
Jouarre F 59 B4
Joué-lès-Tours F 67 A5
Joué-sur-Erdre F 66 A3
Joure NL 42 C2
Joutseno FIN 3 F28
Joutsijärvi FIN 113 F16
Joux-la-Ville F 59 C4
Jouy F 58 B2
Jouy-le-Châtel F 59 B4
Jouy-le-Potier F 58 C2
Joyeuse F 78 B3
Joze F 68 C3
Józefów PL 55 A6
Juankoski FIN 3 E28
Juan-les-Pins F 79 C6
Juban AL 105 A5
Jübek D 43 A6
Jubera E 89 B4
Jubrique E 99 C5
Jüchsen D 51 C6
Judaberg N 33 C2
Judenburg A 73 A4
Juelsminde DK 39 D3
Jugon-les-Lacs F 56 B3
Juillac F 67 C6
Juillan F 76 C3
Juist D 43 B4
Jukkasjärvi S 112 E9
Jule N 115 C10
Julianadorp NL 42 C1
Julianstown IRL 19 C5
Jülich D 50 C2
Julouville F 57 B4
Jumeaux F 68 C3
Jumièges F 58 A1
Jumilhac-le-Grand F 67 C6
Jumilla E 101 A4
Juncosa E 90 B3
Juneda E 90 B3
Jung S 35 D5
Jungingen D 61 B5
Junglingster L 60 A2
Juniville F 59 A5
Junosuando S 113 E11
Junqueira P 87 C3
Junsele S 115 D13
Juoksengi S 113 F12
Juoksenki FIN 113 F12
Juprelle B 49 C6
Jurata PL 47 A4
Jurbarkas LT 6 D7
Jurjevo HR 83 B3
Jūrmala LV 6 C7
Juromenha P 93 C3
Jursla S 37 D3
Jussac F 77 B5
Jussey F 60 C1
Jussy F 59 A4
Juta H 74 B2
Jüterbog D 52 B3
Juuka FIN 3 E28
Juvigny-le-Terte F 57 B4
Juvigny-sous-Andaine F 57 B5
Juzennecourt F 59 B5
Jyderup DK 39 D4
Jyväskylä FIN 3 E26

K
Kaamanen FIN 113 C16
Kaamasmukka FIN 113 C15
Kaaresuvanto FIN 113 D11
Kaarssen D 44 B3
Kaatscheuvel NL 49 B5
Kaba H 75 A6
Kåbdalis S 115 A17
Kačarevo SRB 85 B5
Kačikol KOS 85 D6
Kács H 65 C6
Kadaň CZ 52 C3
Kadarkút H 74 B2
Kadınhanı TR 119 D7
Kaduy RUS 7 B14
Kafása S 37 D2
Kåfjord N 113 C12
Kåfjordbotn N 112 C9
Kågeröd S 41 D3
Kahl D 51 C5
Kahla D 52 C1
Kainach bei Voitsberg A 73 A5
Kaindorf A 73 A5
Kainulasjärvi S 113 F11
Kairala FIN 113 E16

Kaisepakte S 112 D8
Kaisersesch D 50 C3
Kaiserslautern D 60 A3
Kaisheim D 62 B1
Kajaani FIN 3 D27
Kajárpéc H 74 A2
Kajdacs H 74 B3
Kakanj BIH 84 B3
Kakasd H 74 B3
Kaklik TR 119 E4
Kakolewo PL 54 B1
Kál H 65 C6
Kalače MNE 85 D5
Kalajoki FIN 3 D25
Kalak N 113 B16
Kalamata GR 117 E4
Kalambaka GR 116 C3
Kalamira GR 116 B4
Kalandra GR 116 C5
Kalanti S 115 E13
Kalavrita GR 117 D4
Kalbe D 44 C3
Kalce SLO 73 C4
Káld H 74 A2
Kale
  Antalya TR 119 F4
  Denizli TR 119 E4
Kalecik TR 16 A6
Kalefeld D 51 B6
Kalenić SRB 85 C5
Kalety PL 54 C3
Kalevala RUS 3 D29
Kalhovd N 32 B5
Kali GR 83 B4
Kalimnos GR 119 F2
Kaliningrad RUS 47 A6
Kalinkavichy BY 7 E10
Kalinovac HR 74 B2
Kalinovik BIH 84 C3
Kalinovo SK 65 B5
Kalirachi GR 116 C8
Kaliska
  Pomorskie PL 47 A4
  Pomorskie PL 47 A4
Kalisko PL 55 B4
Kalisz PL 54 B3
Kalisz Pomorski PL 46 B1
Kalix S 3 D25
Kaljord N 112 D4
Kalkan TR 119 F4
Kalkar D 50 B2
Kalkım TR 118 C2
Kall
  D 50 C2
  S 115 D10
Källby S 35 D5
Kållered S 38 B5
Kållerstad S 40 B3
Kallinge S 41 C5
Kallmet i Madh AL 105 B5
Kallmünz D 62 A2
Kallsedet S 115 D9
Källvik S 37 D4
Kallmthout B 49 B5
Kalná SK 65 B4
Kalocsa H 75 B3
Kalokhorio CY 120 B2
Kalo Nero GR 117 E3
Kaloni GR 118 D1
Kaloz H 74 B3
Kals A 72 A2
Kalsdorf A 73 B5
Kaltbrunn CH 70 A4
Kaltenbach A 72 A1
Kaltenkirchen D 44 B1
Kaltennordheim D 51 C6
Kaluga RUS 7 D14
Kalundborg DK 39 D4
Kaluš UA 11 B8
Kaluszyn PL 55 A6
Kalv S 40 B3
Kalvåg N 114 F1
Kalvehave DK 41 D2
Kalwang A 73 A4
Kalwaria-Zebrzydowska PL 65 A5
Kalyazin RUS 7 C14
Kam H 74 A1
Kaman TR 16 B6
Kamares GR 117 F6
Kambos CY 120 A1
Kamen D 50 B3
Kamenari MNE 84 D3
Kamenec-Podil'sky UA 11 B9
Kamenica SK 65 A6
Kamieni Krajeński PL 46 B3
Kamienna Góra PL 53 C6
Kamień Pomorski PL 45 B6
Kaminka UA 11 B12
Kamiros Skala GR 119 F2
Kampen NL 42 C2
Kampinos PL 55 A5
Kamp-Lintfort D 50 B2
Kampor HR 83 B3
Kamyanka-Buz'ka UA 11 A8
Kamýk nad Vltavou CZ 63 A5
Kanal SLO 72 B3
Kanalia GR 116 C4
Kandalaksha RUS 3 C30
Kandanos GR 117 G5
Kandel D 61 A4
Kandern D 60 C3
Kandersteg CH 70 B2
Kandira TR 118 A5
Kandyty PL 47 A6
Kanfanar HR 82 A3
Kangasala H 3 F26
Kangos S 113 E10
Kangosjärvi FIN 113 E12
Kaniów PL 53 B4
Kanjiža SRB 75 B5
Kankaanpää FIN 3 F25
Kannus FIN 3 D25
Kanturk IRL 20 B3
Kaonik SRB 85 C6
Kapaklı TR 118 A2

Karaburun TR 118 D1
Karacabey TR 118 B3
Karaçaköy TR 118 A3
Karacaören TR 119 D5
Karacasu TR 119 E3
Karachev RUS 7 E13
Karácsond H 65 C6
Karád H 74 B2
Karahallı TR 119 D4
Karahalli TR 16 C7
Karaman
  Balıkesir TR 118 C3
  Karaman TR 16 C6
Karamanlı TR 119 E4
Karamürsel TR 118 B4
Karan SRB 85 C4
Karancslapujto H 65 B5
Karanovac H 85 B5
Karapınar TR 119 E2
Karapinar TR 16 C6
Karasjok N 113 C14
Karasu TR 118 A5
Karataş
  Adana TR 16 C7
  Manisa TR 119 D3
Karavostasi CY 120 A1
Karbenning S 36 B3
Karberg S 37 D1
Kårböle S 115 F12
Karbunara AL 105 C5
Karby
  D 44 A1
  DK 38 C1
Kårby S 40 B6
Karby S 37 C5
Karcag H 75 A5
Karczew PL 55 A6
Karczów PL 54 C2
Karczowiska PL 53 B6
Kardamena GR 119 F2
Kardamila GR 116 D8
Kardamili GR 117 F4
Kardašova Řečice CZ 63 A5
Kardis S 113 F12
Karditsa GR 116 C3
Kärdla EST 6 B7
Kardoskút H 75 B5
Kardzhali BG 15 C10
Karesuando S 113 D11
Kargı TR 16 A7
Kargowa PL 53 A5
Karigasniemi FIN 113 C14
Karise DK 41 D2
Karistos GR 117 D6
Karkkila FIN 6 A8
Karlholmsbruk S 36 B4
Karlino PL 46 A1
Karl Liebknecht RUS 7 F13
Karlobag HR 83 B4
Karlovac HR 73 C5
Karlovasi GR 119 E1
Karlovčic SRB 85 B5
Karlovo BG 11 E8
Karlovy Vary CZ 52 C2
Karlowice P 54 C2
Karlsborg S 37 D1
Karlshamn S 41 C5
Karlshöfen D 43 B6
Karlshus N 35 C2
Karlskoga S 37 C1
Karlskrona S 41 C5
Karlsrud N 32 B5
Karlsruhe D 61 A4
Karlstad S 35 C5
Karlstadt D 51 D5
Karlstetten A 63 B6
Karlstift A 63 B5
Karlstorp S 40 B5
Karmacs H 74 B2
Karmin PL 54 B2
Kärna S 38 B4
Karnobat BG 11 E9
Karojba HR 82 A3
Karow D 44 B4
Karpacz PL 53 C5
Karpathos GR 119 G2
Karpenisi GR 116 D3
Karpuzlu TR 119 E2
Kärrbo S 37 C3
Karrebaeksminde DK 39 D4
Karshult S 40 B3
Karsin PL 46 B3
Kårsta S 37 C5
Karstädt D 44 B3
Kartal TR 118 B4
Kartitsch A 72 B2
Kartuzy PL 47 A4
Karup DK 39 C2
Karviná CZ 54 C2
Kås DK 38 B2
Kaş TR 119 F4
Kaşaba TR 119 F4
Kasaba TR 64 A3
Käseberga S 41 D4
Kasejovice CZ 63 A4
Kasfjord N 112 D5
Kashin RUS 7 C14
Kašina HR 73 C6
Kasina-Wielka PL 65 A6
Kåskinen FIN 3 E24
Kašperské Hory CZ 63 A4
Kassándria GR 116 B5
Kassándrino GR 116 B5
Kassel D 51 B5
Kassiopi GR 116 C1
Kastamonu TR 16 A6
Kastav HR 73 C4
Kasteli GR 117 G5
Kastellaun D 50 C3
Kasteli-Stari HR 83 C5
Kaštel Zegarski HR 83 B4
Kasterlee B 49 B5
Kastl D 62 A2
Kastlösa S 41 C6
Kastorf D 44 B2
Kastoria GR 116 B3
Kastori GR 117 E4
Kastraki GR 117 F7
Kastrosikia GR 116 C2
Kastsyukovichy BY 7 E12
Kaszaper H 75 B5
Katakolo GR 117 E3
Katapola GR 117 F7
Kåtaselet S 115 B15
Katerbow D 45 C4
Katerini GR 116 B4
Kathikas CY 120 B1
Kätkesuando S 113 D11
Katlenburg-Lindau D 51 B6
Káto Achaia GR 117 D3
Káto Pyrgos CY 120 A1
Katouna GR 116 D3
Katovice CZ 63 A4
Katowice PL 55 C4
Katrineberg S 36 A3
Katrineholm S 37 D3
Kattarp S 41 C2
Kattavia GR 119 G2
Katthammarsvik S 37 E5
Kattilstorp S 35 D5
Katwijk NL 49 A5
Katymár H 75 B4
Katy Wrocławskie PL 54 B1
Katzenelnbogen D 50 C3
Katzhütte D 52 C1
Kaub D 50 C3
Kaufbeuren D 62 C1
Kauhajoki FIN 3 E25
Kauhava FIN 3 E25
Kaukonen FIN 113 E14
Kaulsdorf D 52 C1
Kaunas LT 6 D7
Kaunisvaara S 113 E12
Kaupanger N 32 A4
Kautokeino N 113 C12
Kautzen A 63 B6
Kavadarci MK 116 A4
Kavajë AL 105 B5
Kavakköy TR 118 B1
Kavaklı TR 118 A2

Kavaklıdere TR 119 E3
Kavala GR 116 B6
Kavarna BG 11 E10
Kävlinge S 41 D3
Kawcze PL 46 A2
Kaxås S 115 D10
Kaxholmen S 40 B4
Kaymakçı TR 119 D3
Kaymaz TR 118 C6
Kaynarca TR 118 A5
Käyräymö FIN 113 F15
Kayseri TR 16 B7
Kaysersberg F 60 B3
Kazanlak BG 11 E8
Kazár H 65 B5
Kazimierza Wielka PL 55 C5
Kazimierz Biskupi PL 65 B6
Kazimierz PL 46 C2
Kcynia PL 46 B3
Kdyně CZ 62 A4
Kea GR 117 E6
Keadew IRL 18 B3
Keady GB 19 B5
Kecel H 75 B4
Keçiborlu TR 119 E5
Kecskemét H 75 B4
Kėdainiai LT 6 D7
Kėdzierzyn-Koźle PL 54 C3
Keel IRL 18 C1
Keenagh IRL 19 C4
Keerbergen B 49 B5
Kefalos GR 119 F1
Kefken TR 118 A5
Keflavik IS 111 C3
Kegworth GB 27 C4
Kehl D 60 B3
Kehrigk D 53 A3
Keighley GB 27 B4
Keila EST 6 B8
Keillmore GB 24 C2
Keiss GB 23 C5
Keith GB 23 D6
Kelberg D 50 C2
Kelbra D 51 B7
Kelč CZ 64 A3
Kelchsau A 72 A2
Keld GB 26 A3
Kelebia H 75 B4
Kelekçi TR 119 E4
Keles TR 118 C4
Kelheim D 62 B2
Kell D 60 A2
Kellas GB 23 D5
Kellinghusen D 43 B6
Kellokoski FIN 113 F17
Kells
  GB 19 B5
  IRL 19 C5
Kelmis B 50 C2
Kelokedhara CY 120 B1
Kelottijärvi FIN 113 D11
Kelsall GB 26 B3
Kelso GB 25 C5
Kelsterbach D 51 C4
Keltneyburn GB 24 B3
Kelujärvi FIN 113 E16
Kemaliye TR 119 D2
Kemalpaşa TR 119 D2
Kematen A 71 A6
Kemberg D 52 B2
Kemecse H 11 B6
Kemer
  Antalya TR 119 F5
  Burdur TR 119 E5
  Muğla TR 119 F4
Kemerkaya TR 118 D6
Kemeten A 73 A6
Kemi FIN 3 D26
Kemijärvi FIN 113 F16
Keminmaa FIN 3 D26
Kemnath D 62 A2
Kemnay GB 23 D6
Kemnitz
  Brandenburg D 52 A2
  Mecklenburg-Vorpommern D 45 A5
Kempen D 50 B2
Kempsey GB 29 A5
Kempten D 61 C6
Kemptthal CH 70 A3
Kendal GB 26 A3
Kenderes H 75 A5
Kengyel H 75 A5
Kenilworth GB 30 B2
Kenmare IRL 20 C2
Kenmore GB 24 B3
Kennacraig GB 24 C2
Kenyeri H 74 A2
Kenzingen D 60 B3
Kepez TR 118 B1
Kępice PL 46 A2
Kepno PL 54 B3
Kepsut TR 118 C3
Keramoti GR 116 B6
Keränträ-järvi S 113 E12
Kerava FIN 7 A8
Kerecsend H 65 C6
Kerekegyhaza H 75 A4
Kerepestarcsa H 75 A4
Keri GR 117 E2
Kérien F 56 B2
Kerkafalva H 74 B1
Kerken D 50 B2
Kerkrade NL 50 C2
Kerkyra GR 116 C1
Kerlouan F 56 B1
Kernascléden F 56 B2
Kernhof A 63 C6
Kerns CH 70 B3
Kerpen D 50 C2
Kerrysdale GB 22 D3
Kerta H 74 A2
Kerteminde DK 39 D3
Kerzers CH 70 B2
Keşan TR 118 B1
Kesgrave GB 30 B5
Kesh GB 19 B4
Keskin TR 16 B6
Kesselfall A 72 A2
Keswick GB 26 A2
Keszthely H 74 B2
Kétegyháza H 75 B6
Kéthely H 74 B2
Ketrzyn PL 6 D6
Kettering GB 30 B3
Kettlewell GB 26 A3
Kęty PL 65 A5
Ketzin D 45 C4
Keula D 51 B6
Keuruu FIN 3 E26
Kevelaer D 50 B2
Kevermes H 75 B6
Kevi SRB 75 C4
Keyingham GB 27 B5
Keynsham GB 29 B5
Kežmarok SK 65 A6
Kherson UA 11 C12
Khimki RUS 7 D14
Khisinev = Chişinau MD 11 C10
Khmelnik UA 11 B9
Khmelnytskyy UA 11 B9
Khodorov UA 11 B8
Kholm RUS 7 C11
Khorol UA 11 B9
Khotyn UA 11 B9
Khoyniki BY 7 F10
Khovvaya RUS 7 B13
Khust UA 11 B7
Kibaek DK 39 D1
Kiberg N 113 B19
Kicasalih TR 118 A1
Kičevo MK 116 A3
Kidderminster GB 29 A5
Kidlington GB 31 C2
Kidsgrove GB 26 B3
Kidwelly GB 28 B3
Kiefersfelden D 62 C3
Kiel D 44 A2

Kielce PL 55 C5
Kiełczygłów PL 54 B4
Kielder GB 25 C5
Kielpino PL 47 A4
Kiełpiny PL 47 B5
Kierinki FIN 113 E14
Kiernozia PL 55 A4
Kierspe D 50 B3
Kietrz PL 54 C3
Kietz D 45 C6
Kiev = Kyyiv UA 11 A11
Kiezmark PL 47 A4
Kiffisia GR 117 D5
Kifino Selo BIH 84 C3
Kihlanki
  FIN 113 E12
  S 113 E12
Kiistala FIN 113 E14
Kije PL 55 C5
Kijevo HR 83 C5
Kikallen S 32 B2
Kikinda SRB 75 C5
Kil
  Örebro S 37 C2
  Värmland S 35 C5
Kila S 35 C4
Kilafors S 36 A3
Kilb A 63 B6
Kilbaha IRL 20 B2
Kilberry GB 24 C2
Kilbirnie GB 24 C3
Kilboghamn N 112 F2
Kilbotn N 112 D5
Kilb Rabenstein A 63 B6
Kilchattan GB 24 C2
Kilchoan GB 24 B1
Kilcock IRL 21 A5
Kilconnell IRL 20 A3
Kilcoole IRL 21 A5
Kilcormac IRL 21 A4
Kilcreggan GB 24 C3
Kilcullen IRL 21 A5
Kilcurry IRL 19 B5
Kildare IRL 21 A5
Kildinstroy RUS 3 B30
Kildonan GB 23 C5
Kildorrery IRL 20 B3
Kilegrend N 33 C5
Kilen N 33 C5
Kilgarvan IRL 20 C2
Kiliya UA 11 D10
Kilkee IRL 20 B2
Kilkeel GB 19 B5
Kilkelly IRL 18 C3
Kilkenny IRL 21 B4
Kilkhampton GB 28 C3
Kilkieran IRL 20 A2
Kilkinlea IRL 20 B2
Kilkis GR 116 A4
Kill IRL 21 B4
Killadysert IRL 20 B2
Killala IRL 18 B2
Killaloe IRL 20 B3
Killarney IRL 20 B2
Killashandra IRL 19 B4
Killashee IRL 19 C4
Killearn GB 24 B3
Killeberg S 40 C4
Killeigh IRL 21 A4
Killenaule IRL 21 B4
Killimor IRL 20 A3
Killin GB 24 B3
Killinaboy IRL 20 B2
Killinge S 112 E9
Killinick IRL 21 B5
Killorglin IRL 20 B2
Killucan IRL 21 A4
Killybegs IRL 18 B3
Killyleagh GB 19 B6
Kilmacrenan IRL 19 A4
Kilmacthomas IRL 21 B4
Kilmaine IRL 18 C2
Kilmallock IRL 20 B3
Kilmarnock GB 24 C3
Kilmartin GB 24 B2
Kilmaurs GB 24 C3
Kilmeadan IRL 21 B4
Kilmeedy IRL 20 B3
Kilmelford GB 24 B2
Kilmore Quay IRL 21 B5
Kilmuir GB 23 D4
Kilninver GB 24 B2
Kilpisjärvi FIN 112 C9
Kilrea GB 19 B5
Kilrush IRL 20 B2
Kilsmo S 37 C2
Kilsyth GB 24 C3
Kiltoom IRL 20 A3
Kilwinning GB 24 C3
Kimasozero RUS 3 D29
Kimi GR 116 D6
Kimolos GR 117 F6
Kimry RUS 7 D14
Kimstad S 37 D2
Kinbrace GB 23 C5
Kincardine GB 25 B4
Kincraig GB 23 D5
Kindberg A 73 A5
Kindelbruck D 52 B1
Kingarrow IRL 18 B3
Kingisepp RUS 7 B10
Kingsbridge GB 28 C4
Kingsclere GB 31 C2
Kingscourt IRL 19 C5
Kingskerswell GB 28 C4
Kings Langley GB 31 C3
Kingsley GB 31 C2
Kings Lynn GB 30 B4
Kingston
  Greater London GB 31 C3
  Moray GB 23 D5
Kingston Bagpuize GB 31 C2
Kingston upon Hull GB 27 B5
Kingswear GB 28 C4
Kingswood GB 29 B5
Kington GB 29 A4
Kingussie GB 23 D4
Kınık
  Antalya TR 119 F4
  İzmir TR 118 C2
Kinloch
  Highland GB 22 C4
  Highland GB 23 C3
Kinlochbervie GB 22 C3
Kinlochewe GB 22 D3
Kinlochleven GB 24 B3
Kinlochmoidart GB 24 B2
Kinloch Rannoch GB 24 B3
Kinloss GB 23 D5
Kinlough IRL 18 B3
Kinn N 34 B2
Kinna S 40 B2
Kinnared S 40 C3
Kinnarp S 35 D5
Kinne-Kleva S 35 D5
Kinnitty IRL 21 A4
Kinross GB 25 B4
Kinsale IRL 20 C3
Kinsarvik N 32 B3
Kintore GB 23 D6
Kinvarra IRL 20 A3
Kioni GR 117 D2
Kiparissia GR 117 E3
Kipfenburg D 62 B2
Kippen GB 24 B3
Kirazlı TR 118 B1
Kirberg D 50 C4
Kirchbach in Steiermark A 73 B5
Kirchberg
  CH 70 A2
  Baden-Württemberg D 61 A5
  Rheinland-Pfalz D 60 A3
Kirchberg am Wechsel A 63 C6

Kirchberg an der Pielach A 63 B6
Kirchberg in Tirol A 72 A2
Kirchbichl A 72 A2
Kirchdorf
  Bayern D 63 B4
  Mecklenburg-Vorpommern D 44 B3
  Niedersachsen D 43 C5
Kirchdorf an der Krems A 63 C5
Kirchdorf in Tirol A 72 A2
Kirchenlamitz D 52 C1
Kirchenthumbach D 62 A2
Kirchhain D 51 C4
Kirchheim
  Baden-Württemberg D 61 B5
  Bayern D 61 B6
  Hessen D 51 C5
Kirchheimbolanden D 61 A4
Kirchhundem D 50 B4
Kirchlinteln D 43 C6
Kirchschlag A 73 A6
Kirchweidach D 62 B3
Kirchzarten D 60 C3
Kircubbin GB 19 B6
Kireç TR 118 C3
Kırıkkale TR 16 B6
Kırka TR 118 C5
Kırkağaç TR 118 C2
Kirkbean GB 25 D4
Kirkbride GB 25 D4
Kirkby GB 26 B3
Kirkby Lonsdale GB 26 A3
Kirkby Malzeard GB 27 A4
Kirkbymoorside GB 27 A5
Kirkby Stephen GB 26 A3
Kirkcaldy GB 25 B4
Kirkcolm GB 24 D2
Kirkconnel GB 24 C3
Kirkcowan GB 24 D3
Kirkcudbright GB 24 D3
Kirkehamn N 33 D3
Kirke Hyllinge DK 39 D4
Kirkenær N 34 B4
Kirkenes N 113 C19
Kirkham GB 26 B3
Kirkintilloch GB 24 C3
Kirkjubæjarklaustur IS 111 D7
Kirkkonummi FIN 6 A8
Kırklareli TR 118 A2
Kirkmichael GB 25 B4
Kirk Michael GB 26 A1
Kirkoswald GB 24 C3
Kirkpatrick Fleming GB 25 C4
Kirkton of Glenisla GB 25 B4
Kirkwall GB 23 C6
Kirkwhelpington GB 25 C6
Kirn D 60 A3
Kirovohrad UA 11 B12
Kirovsk RUS 3 C30
Kirriemuir GB 25 B5
Kırşehir TR 16 B7
Kirton GB 30 B3
Kirton in Lindsey GB 27 B5
Kirtorf D 51 C5
Kiruna S 112 E9
Kisa S 40 B5
Kisač SRB 75 C4
Kisbér H 74 A3
Kiseljak
  BIH 84 C3
  BIH 84 C3
Kisielice PL 47 B5
Kiskőre H 75 A5
Kisko FIN 6 A8
Kiskőrös H 75 B4
Kiskunfélegyháza H 75 B4
Kiskunhalas H 75 B4
Kiskunlacháza H 75 A3
Kiskunmajsa H 75 B4
Kisláng H 74 B3
Kisslegg D 61 C5
Kissonerga CY 120 B1
Kist D 61 A5
Kistanje HR 83 C4
Kistelek H 75 B4
Kisterenye H 65 B5
Kisújszállás H 75 A5
Kisvárda H 11 B7
Kisvejke H 74 B3
Kiszkowo PL 46 C3
Kiszombor H 75 B5
Kitee FIN 3 E29
Kithnos GR 117 E6
Kiti CY 120 B2
Kitka FIN 3 D27
Kitkiöjoki S 113 E12
Kittelfjäll S 115 B12
Kittendorf D 45 B4
Kittilä FIN 113 E14
Kittlitz D 53 B4
Kittsee A 64 B3
Kitzbühel A 72 A2
Kitzingen D 61 A6
Kiuruvesi FIN 3 E26
Kivertsi UA 11 A8
Kividhes CY 120 B1
Kivik S 41 D4
Kivivaara FIN 3 D28
Kivotos GR 116 B3
Kjøpmannskjaer N 35 C2
Kjellerup DK 39 C2
Kjøllefjord N 113 B16
Kjøpsvik N 112 E5
Kladanj BIH 84 B3
Kläden D 44 C3
Kladnica SRB 85 C5
Kladnice HR 83 C5
Kladno CZ 53 C4
Kladruby CZ 62 A3
Klagenfurt A 73 B4
Klågerup S 41 D3
Klagstorp S 41 D3
Klaipėda LT 6 D6
Klaistow D 52 A2
Klaksvik FO 2 E10
Klana HR 73 C4
Klanac HR 83 B4
Klardorf D 62 A3
Klarup DK 38 B3
Klašnice BIH 84 B2
Klässbol S 35 C4
Klášterec nad Ohří CZ 52 C3
Klášter pod Znievom SK 65 B4
Klatovy CZ 63 A4
Klaus an der Pyhrnbahn A 63 C5
Klazienaveen NL 42 C3
Kłecko PL 46 C3
Kleczew PL 54 A3
Klein Plasten D 45 B4
Klein Sankt Paul A 73 B4
Kleinsölk A 72 A3
Kleinzell A 63 C6
Klejtrup DK 38 C2
Klek SRB 75 C5
Klemensker DK 41 D4
Klenak SRB 85 B4

Klenci pod Cerchovem CZ 62 A3
Klenica PL 53 B5
Klenje SRB 85 B4
Klenoec MK 116 A2
Klenovec SK 65 B5
Klenovica HR 83 A3
Klenovnik HR 73 B6
Kleppe N 33 D2
Kleppestø N 32 B2
Kleptow D 45 B5
Kleszczów PL 55 B4
Kleszczele PL 6 E7
Kleve D 50 B2
Klevshult S 40 B4
Klewki PL 47 B6
Kličevac SRB 85 B6
Kliening A 73 B4
Klietz D 44 C4
Klikuszowa PL 65 A5
Klimkovice CZ 64 A4
Klimontów PL 55 C6
Klimovichi BY 7 E12
Klimpfjäll S 115 B11
Klin RUS 7 C14
Klinča Sela HR 73 C5
Klingenbach A 64 C2
Klingenberg D 61 A5
Klingenmunster D 61 A4
Klingenthal D 52 C2
Klinken D 44 B3
Klintehamn S 37 E5
Klintsy RUS 7 E12
Kliplev DK 39 E2
Klippan S 41 C3
Klis HR 83 C5
Klitmøller DK 38 B1
Klitten S 34 A6
Klixbüll D 39 E1
Kljajićevo SRB 75 C4
Ključ BIH 83 B5
Klobouky CZ 64 B2
Kłobuck PL 54 C3
Kłodawa PL 55 A4
Kłodawa
  Lubuskie PL 45 C7
  Wielkopolskie PL 54 A3
Kłodzko PL 54 C1
Kløfta N 34 B3
Klokkarvik N 32 B2
Klokkerholm DK 38 B3
Klokočov SK 65 A4
Klomnice PL 55 C4
Klonowa PL 54 B3
Kloosterzande NL 49 B5
Klopot S 53 A4
Klos AL 116 A2
Kloštar Ivanić HR 73 C6
Kloster
  D 45 A5
  D 39 C1
Klösterle A 71 A5
Klostermansfeld D 52 B1
Klosterneuburg A 64 B2
Klosters CH 71 B4
Kloten CH 70 A3
Klötze D 44 C3
Klövsjö S 115 E11
Kluczbork PL 54 C3
Kluczewo PL 46 B2
Kluisbergen B 49 C4
Klundert NL 49 B5
Klutz D 44 B3
Klwów PL 55 B5
Klyetsk BY 7 E9
Knaben N 33 D3
Knaften S 115 C15
Knapstad N 35 C3
Knäred S 40 C3
Knaresborough GB 27 A4
Knarvik N 32 B2
Knebel DK 39 C3
Knebworth GB 31 C3
Knesebeck D 44 C2
Knesselare B 49 B4
Kneževo SLO 73 C4
Kneževi Vinogradi HR 74 C3
Kneža SRB 85 C5
Knić SRB 85 C5
Knighton GB 29 A4
Knin HR 83 B5
Knislinge S 41 C4
Knittelfeld A 73 A4
Knivsta S 37 C4
Knock IRL 18 C3
Knocktopher IRL 21 B4
Knokke-Heist B 49 B4
Knowle GB 30 B2
Knurów PL 54 C3
Knutby S 36 C5
Knutsford GB 26 B3
Kobarid SLO 72 B3
København = Copenhagen DK 41 D2
Kobenz A 73 A4
Kobersdorf A 64 C2
Kobiernice PL 54 C1
Kobierzyce PL 54 C1
Kobilje SLO 73 B6
Koblenz
  CH 61 C4
  D 50 C3
Kobryn BY 9 E6
Kobylanka PL 45 B6
Kobylin PL 54 B2
Kobyłka PL 55 A6
Kobylniki PL 47 C6
Kocaali TR 118 A5
Kocaaliler TR 119 E5
Kocaeli = İzmit TR 118 B4
Kočani MK 11 F7
Koçarlı TR 119 E2
Koceljevo SRB 85 B4
Kočerin BIH 84 C2
Kočevje SLO 73 C4
Kočevska Reka SLO 73 C4
Kochel am See D 62 C2
Kocs H 64 C4
Kocsér H 75 A4
Kocsola H 74 B3
Koczała PL 46 B3
Kodal N 35 C2
Kode S 38 B4
Kodersdorf D 53 B4
Kodrab PL 55 B4
Koekelare B 48 B3
Koerich L 60 A1
Koetschette L 60 A1
Koetz D 61 B6
Kofçaz TR 118 A2
Köflach A 73 A5
Køge DK 41 D2
Kohlberg D 62 A3
Kohtla-Järve EST 7 B9
Köinge S 40 B2
Kojetin CZ 64 A3
Kökar FIN 36 C6
Kokava SRB 85 A4
Kokemäki FIN 36 B3
Kokkinotrimithia CY 120 A2
Kokkola FIN 3 E25
Kokori BIH 84 B2
Koksijde B 48 B3
Kola
  BIH 84 B2
  RUS 3 B30
Kołacin PL 55 B4
Kolari
  FIN 113 E13
  SRB 85 B5
Kolárovo SK 64 C3
Kolašin MNE 85 D4
Kolbäck S 37 C3
Kolbacz PL 45 B6
Kolbeinsstaðir IS 111 C3
Kolbermoor D 62 C3
Kolbnitz A 72 B3
Kolby Kås DK 39 D3
Kolczewo PL 45 B6
Kolczygłowy PL 46 A3

Kolding DK 39 D2
Kölesd H 74 B3
Kolgrov N 32 A1
Kolín CZ 53 C5
Kolind DK 39 C3
Kolinec CZ 63 A4
Koljane HR 83 C5
Kølkær DK 39 C2
Kölleda D 52 B1
Kollum NL 42 B3
Köln = Cologne D 50 C2
Koło PL 54 A3
Kołobrzeg PL 46 A1
Kolochau D 52 B3
Kolomyya UA 11 B8
Kolonje AL 105 C5
Kolonowskie PL 54 C3
Koloveč CZ 62 A4
Kolpino RUS 7 B11
Kolpny RUS 7 E14
Kolrep D 44 B4
Kölsillre S 115 E12
Kolsko PL 53 B5
Kolsva S 37 C2
Kolta SK 65 B4
Kolunič BIH 83 B5
Koluszki PL 55 B4
Kolut SRB 75 C3
Kolvereid N 114 C8
Kølvrå DK 39 C2
Komagvær N 113 B19
Koman AL 105 A5
Komarica BIH 84 B2
Komárno SK 64 C4
Komárom H 64 C4
Komatou Yialou CY 120 A3
Komboti GR 116 C3
Komen SLO 72 C3
Komin HR 84 C2
Komiža HR 83 C5
Komjáti H 65 B6
Komjatice SK 64 B4
Komletinci HR 75 C3
Komló H 74 B3
Kömlo H 65 C6
Komoča SK 64 C4
Komorane KOS 85 D5
Komorniki PL 54 A1
Komorzno PL 54 B3
Komotini GR 116 A7
Konak SRB 75 C5
Konakovo RUS 7 C14
Konary PL 55 B6
Konarzyny PL 46 B3
Kondias GR 116 C7
Kondorfa H 73 B6
Kondoros H 75 B5
Kondrovo RUS 7 D13
Køng DK 39 D4
Konga S 40 C5
Köngäs FIN 113 E13
Kongerslev DK 38 C3
Kongsberg N 35 C1
Kongshamn N 33 D5
Kongsmark DK 39 D1
Kongsmoen N 115 C9
Kongsvik N 112 D5
Kongsvinger N 34 B4
Konice CZ 64 A2
Konie PL 55 B5
Koniecpol PL 55 C4
Königsberg D 51 C6
Königsbronn D 61 B6
Königsbrück D 53 B3
Königsbrunn D 62 B1
Konigsdorf D 62 C2
Königsee D 52 C1
Königshorst D 45 C4
Königslutter D 51 A6
Königssee D 62 C3
Königstein
Hessen D 51 C4
Sachsen D 53 C4
Königstetten A 64 B2
Königswartha D 53 B4
Konigswiesen A 63 B5
Königswinter D 50 C3
Königs Wusterhausen
D 52 A3
Konin PL 54 A3
Konispol AL 116 C2
Konitsa GR 116 B2
Köniz CH 70 B2
Konjevići BIH 85 B4
Konjevrate HR 83 C5
Konjic BIH 84 C2
Konjščina HR 73 B6
Könnern D 52 B1
Konnerud N 35 C2
Konopiska PL 54 C3
Konotop
PL 53 B5
UA 7 F12
Końskie PL 55 B5
Konsmo N 33 D4
Konstancin-Jeziorna
PL 55 A6
Konstantynów Łódźki
PL 55 B4
Konstanz D 61 C5
Kontich B 49 B5
Kontiolahti FIN 3 E28
Konya TR 119 E7
Konz D 60 A2
Kópasker IS 111 A9
Kópavogur IS 111 C4
Kopčany SK 64 B3
Koper SLO 72 C3
Kopervik N 33 C2
Kópháza H 64 C2
Kopice PL 54 C2
Kopidlno CZ 53 C5
Köping S 37 C2
Köpingebro S 41 D3
Köpingsvik S 41 C6
Koplik AL 105 A5
Köpmanholmen S 115 D15
Koppang N 34 A3
Koppangen N 112 C9
Kopparberg S 36 C1
Koppelo FIN 113 D16
Koppom S 35 C4
Koprivlen BG 116 A5
Koprivna BIH 84 B3
Koprivnica HR 74 B1
Kopřivnice CZ 64 A4
Köprübaşı TR 118 D3
Koprzywnica PL 55 C6
Kopstal L 60 A2
Kopychyntsi UA 11 B8
Kopytkowo PL 47 B4
Korbach D 51 B4
Körbecke D 50 B4
Korçë AL 116 B2
Korčula HR 84 D2
Korczyców PL 53 A4
Korenevo RUS 7 F13
Korenita SRB 85 B4
Korets UA 11 A9
Korfantów PL 54 C2
Körfez TR 118 B4
Korgen N 115 A10
Korinth DK 39 D3
Korinthos = Corinth
GR 117 E4
Korita
BIH 83 B5
HR 84 D2
Korithi GR 117 E2
Korkuteli TR 119 E5
Körmend H 74 A1
Korne PL 46 A3
Korneuburg A 64 B2
Kornevo RUS 47 A6
Kórnik PL 54 A2
Kornsjø N 35 D3
Környe H 74 A3
Koromačno HR 82 B3
Koroni GR 117 F3
Koronos GR 117 E7
Koronowo PL 46 B3
Körösladány H 75 B6
Köröstarcsa H 75 B6
Korosten UA 11 A10
Korostyshev UA 11 A10
Korpilombolo S 113 F12
Korsberga
Jönköping S 40 B5
Skaraborg S 35 D6
Korshavn N 35 C2
Korskrogen S 115 F12
Korsnäs S 36 B2
Korsør DK 39 D4
Korsun Shevchenkovskiy
UA 11 B11
Kortrijk B 49 C4
Korucu TR 118 C2
Koryčany CZ 64 A3
Koryukovka UA 7 F12
Korzeńsko PL 54 B1
Korzybie PL 46 A2
Kos GR 119 F2
Kosakowo PL 47 A4
Kosanica MNE 85 C4
Kosaya Gora RUS 7 D14
Kösching D 62 B2
Kościan PL 54 A1
Kościelec PL 54 A3
Kościerzyna PL 46 A3
Koserow D 45 A5
Košetice CZ 63 A6
Košice SK 10 B6
Kosjerić SRB 85 C4
Koška HR 74 C3
Koskullskulle S 112 E9
Kosovska Mitrovica
KOS 85 D5
Kosta S 40 C5
Kostajnica HR 74 C1
Kostajnik SRB 85 B4
Kostanica MNE 105 A5
Kostanjevica SLO 73 C5
Kostelec nad Černými
Lesy CZ 53 D4
Kostelec na Hané CZ 64 A3
Kostice CZ 53 C3
Kostkowo PL 47 A4
Kostojevići SRB 85 B4
Kostolac SRB 85 B6
Kostomłoty PL 54 B1
Kostopil UA 11 A9
Kostów PL 54 B3
Kostrzyn
Lubuskie PL 45 C6
Wielkopolskie PL 46 C3
Koszalin PL 46 A2
Koszęcin PL 54 C3
Köszeg H 74 A1
Koszwaly PL 47 A4
Koszyce PL 55 C5
Kot SLO 73 C5
Kotala FIN 113 E17
Kotë AL 105 C5
Kötelek H 75 A5
Köthen D 52 B1
Kotka FIN 7 A9
Kotomierz PL 47 B4
Kotor MNE 105 A4
Kotoriba HR 74 B1
Kotorsko BIH 84 B3
Kotor Varoš BIH 84 B2
Kotovsk UA 11 C10
Kotraža SRB 85 C5
Kotronas GR 117 F4
Kötschach A 72 B2
Kötzting D 62 A3
Koudum NL 42 C2
Kouřim CZ 53 C4
Kout na Šumave CZ 62 A4
Kouvola FIN 3 F27
Kovačevac SRB 85 B5
Kovačica SRB 85 A5
Kovdor RUS 3 C29
Kovel' UA 11 A8
Kovilj SRB 75 C5
Kovin SRB 85 B5
Kovren MNE 85 C4
Kowal PL 47 C5
Kowalewo Pomorskie
PL 47 B4
Kowalów PL 45 C6
Kowary PL 53 C5
Köyceğiz TR 119 F3
Kozan TR 16 C7
Kozani GR 116 B3
Kozarac
BIH 84 B1
HR 73 C5
Kozárovce SK 65 B4
Kozelets UA 11 A11
Kozelsk RUS 7 D13
Kozica HR 84 C2
Koziegłowy PL 55 C4
Kozienice PL 55 B6
Kozina SLO 72 C3
Kozje SLO 73 B5
Kozlu TR 118 A6
Kozluk BIH 85 B4
Koźmin PL 54 B2
Koźminek PL 54 B3
Kozolupy CZ 63 A4
Kożuchów PL 53 B5
Kožuhe BIH 84 B3
Kozyatyn UA 11 B10
Kozyürük TR 118 A1
Krackow D 45 B6
Kraddsele S 115 B13
Krąg PL 46 A2
Kragenæs DK 39 E4
Kragerø N 33 D6
Krągi PL 46 B2
Kragujevac SRB 85 B5
Kraiburg D 62 B3
Krajenka PL 46 B2
Krajišnik SRB 75 C5
Krajková CZ 52 C2
Krajné SK 64 B3
Krajnik Dolny PL 45 B6
Krakača BIH 83 A4
Kräklingbo S 37 E5
Kraków = Cracow PL 55 C4
Krakow am See D 44 B4
Králíky CZ 54 C1
Kraljevica HR 73 C4
Kraljevo SRB 85 C5
Kral'ovany SK 65 A5
Král'ov Brod SK 64 B3
Kralovice CZ 52 D3
Kralupy nad Vltavou
CZ 53 C4
Králův Dvůr CZ 63 A5
Kramfors S 115 E14
Kramsach A 72 A1
Kramsk PL 54 A3
Kråmvik N 32 C5
Kranenburg D 50 B2
Krania GR 116 C3
Krania Elasonas GR 116 C4
Kranichfeld D 52 C1
Kranidi GR 117 E5
Kranj SLO 73 B4
Kranjska Gora SLO 72 B3
Krapanj HR 83 C4
Krapina HR 73 B5
Krapje HR 74 C1
Krapkowice PL 54 C2
Kraselov CZ 63 A4
Krašić HR 73 C5
Krāslava LV 7 D9
Kraslice CZ 52 C2
Krasna PL 55 B5
Krasna Lipa CZ 53 C4
Kraśnik PL 11 A7
Krašnja SLO 73 B4
Krásno SK 65 A4
Krásnohorské Podhradie
SK 65 B6
Krasno Polje HR 83 B4
Krasnozavodsk RUS 7 C15
Krasnystaw PL 11 A7
Krasnyy RUS 7 D11
Krasnyy Kholm RUS 7 B14
Krasocin PL 55 C5
Kraszewice PL 54 B3
Kraszkowice PL 54 B3
Kratigos GR 118 C1
Kraubath A 73 A4
Krausnick D 53 A3
Krautheim D 61 A5
Kravaře CZ 53 C4
Kraváre CZ 64 A4
Kravarsko HR 73 C6
Kraznějov CZ 63 A4
Krčedin SRB 75 C5
Kŭrdzhali BG 116 A7
Krefeld D 50 B2
Kregme DK 39 D5
Krembz D 44 B3
Kremenchuk UA 11 B12
Kremenets UA 11 A8
Kremmen D 45 C5
Kremna SRB 85 C4
Kremnica SK 65 B4
Krempe D 43 B6
Krems A 63 B6
Kremsbrücke A 72 B3
Kremsmünster A 63 B5
Křemže CZ 63 B5
Křenov CZ 64 A2
Krepa PL 54 B3
Krępa Krajeńska PL 46 B2
Krepsko PL 46 B2
Kreševo BIH 84 C3
Kressbronn D 61 C5
Krestena GR 117 E3
Kretinga LT 6 D6
Krettsy RUS 7 B12
Kreuth D 62 C2
Kreuzau D 50 C2
Kreuzlingen CH 61 C5
Kreuztal D 50 C3
Krewelin D 45 C5
Krezluk BIH 84 B2
Krieglach A 73 A5
Kriegsfeld D 60 A3
Kriens CH 70 A3
Krimml A 72 A2
Krimpen aan de IJssel
NL 49 B5
Křinec CZ 53 C5
Kristdala S 40 B6
Kristiansand N 33 D5
Kristianstad S 41 C4
Kristiansund N 114 D4
Kristiinankaupunki
FIN 3 E24
Kristinefors S 34 B4
Kristinehamn S 35 C6
Kriváň SK 65 B5
Křivokát CZ 53 C3
Krivoy Rog = Kryvyy Rih
UA 11 C12
Kriź HR 74 C1
Křižanov CZ 64 A2
Križevci HR 74 B1
Krk HR 83 A3
Krka SLO 73 C4
Krnjača SRB 85 B5
Krnjak HR 73 C5
Krnjeuša BIH 83 B5
Krnjevo SRB 85 B6
Krnov CZ 54 C2
Krobia PL 54 B1
Kroczyce PL 55 C4
Krøderen N 34 B1
Krokees GR 117 F4
Krokek S 37 D3
Krokom S 115 D11
Krokowa PL 47 A4
Krokstad-elva N 34 C1
Kroksund N 35 C3
Krolevets UA 7 F12
Kroměříž CZ 64 A3
Krommenie NL 42 C1
Krompachy SK 65 B6
Kromy RUS 7 E13
Kronach D 52 C1
Kronshagen D 44 A2
Kronshtadt RUS 7 B10
Kröpelin D 44 A3
Kropp D 43 A6
Kroppenstedt D 52 B1
Kropstädt D 52 B2
Krościenko nad
Dunajcem PL 65 A6
Kröslin D 45 A5
Krośnice PL 54 B2
Krośniewice PL 55 A4
Krosno PL 10 B6
Krosno Odrzańskie
PL 53 A5
Krostitz D 52 B2
Krotoszyn PL 54 B2
Krottendorf A 73 A5
Krouna CZ 64 A2
Krowiarki PL 54 C3
Krrabë AL 105 B5
Kršan HR 73 C4
Krško SLO 73 C5
Krstac MNE 84 C3
Krstur SRB 75 B5
Křtiny CZ 64 A2
Kruft D 50 C3
Kruishoutem B 49 C4
Krujë AL 105 B5
Krulyewshchyna BY 7 D9
Krumbach
A 73 A6
D 61 B6
Krumovgrad BG 116 A7
Krün D 71 A6
Krupá CZ 53 C3
Krupa na Vrbasu BIH 84 B2
Krupanj SRB 85 B4
Krupina SK 65 B5
Krupka CZ 53 C3
Krupki BY 7 D10
Kruså DK 39 E2
Krušćica BIH 84 B2
Kruševac SRB 85 C6
Kruševo MK 116 A3
Kruszwica PL 47 C4
Kruszyn PL 47 C5
Krute MNE 105 A5
Krychaw BY 7 E11
Krynica PL 65 A6
Krynica Morska PL 47 A5
Kryvyy Rih = Krivoy Rog
UA 11 C12
Krzęcin PL 46 B1
Krzelów PL 54 B1
Krzepice PL 54 C3
Krzepielów PL 53 B6
Krzeszowice PL 55 C4
Krzeszyce PL 45 C7
Krzynowlaga Mała
PL 47 B6
Krzywiń PL 54 B1
Krzyźanowice PL 54 D3
Krzyźowa PL 65 A5
Krzyż Wielkopolski
PL 46 C2
Ksiaz Wielkopolski
PL 55 C5
Książ Wielkopolski
PL 54 A2
Ktębowiec PL 46 B2
Kübekháza H 75 B5
Küblis CH 71 B4
Kuç AL 105 C5
Kuchary PL 54 B2
Kuchl A 63 C4
Kucice PL 47 C6
Kuciste HR 84 D2
Kućište KOS 85 D5
Kuçovë AL 105 C5
Küçükbahçe TR 118 D1
Küçükköy TR 118 C1
Küçükkuyu TR 118 C1
Kucura SRB 75 C4
Kuczbork-Osada PL 47 B6
Kuddby S 37 D3
Kudowa-Zdrój PL 53 C6
Kufstein A 62 C3
Kuggeboda S 41 C5
Kuggörana S 115 F14
Kühbach D 62 B2
Kuhmo FIN 3 D28
Kuhmoinen FIN 3 F26
Kuhnsdorf A 73 B4
Kuhstedt D 43 B5
Kuinre NL 42 C2
Kuivastu EST 6 B7
Kukës AL 10 E6
Kuklin PL 47 B6
Kukljica HR 83 B4
Kukujevci SRB 85 A4
Kula
Srbija SRB 85 B6
Vojvodina SRB 75 C4
TR 119 D3
Kuldīga LV 6 C6
Kulen Vakuf BIH 83 B5
Kulina BIH 84 B3
Kullstedt D 51 B6
Kulmain D 62 A2
Kulmbach D 52 C1
Kulu TR 16 B6
Kumafşarı TR 119 E4
Kumane SRB 75 C5
Kumanovo MK 10 E6
Kumbağ TR 118 B2
Kumdanlı TR 119 D5
Kumkale TR 118 C1
Kumla S 37 C2
Kumlakyrkby S 36 C3
Kumlinge FIN 36 B7
Kumluca TR 119 F5
Kumrovec HR 73 B5
Kunadacs H 75 B4
Kunágota H 75 B6
Kunbaja H 75 B4
Kunda EST 7 B9
Kundl A 72 A1
Kunes N 113 B15
Kunfehértó H 75 B4
Kungälv S 38 B4
Kungsängen S 37 C4
Kungsäter S 40 B2
Kungsbacka S 38 B5
Kungsgården S 36 B3
Kungshamn S 35 D3
Kungs-Husby S 37 C4
Kungsör S 37 C3
Kunhegyes H 75 A5
Kunmadaras H 75 A5
Kunovice CZ 64 A3
Kunów PL 55 C6
Kunowo
Wielkopolskie PL 54 B2
Zachodnio-Pomorskie
PL 45 B6
Kunštát CZ 64 A2
Kunszállás H 75 B4
Kunszentmárton H 75 B5
Kunszentmiklós H 75 A4
Kunžak CZ 63 A6
Künzelsau D 61 A5
Kuolayarvi RUS 113 F18
Kuopio FIN 3 E27
Kuosku FIN 113 E17
Kup
H 74 A2
PL 54 C2
Kupa H 65 B6
Kupari HR 84 D3
Kupci SRB 85 C6
Kupferzell D 61 A5
Kupinec HR 73 C5
Kupinečki Kraljevac
HR 73 C5
Kupinovo SRB 85 B5
Kupirovo HR 83 B5
Kupjak HR 73 C4
Kuppenheim D 61 B4
Kupres BIH 84 C2
Küps D 52 C1
Kurbnesh AL 105 B6
Kurd H 74 B3
Küre TR 16 A6
Kuressaare EST 6 B7
Kurikka FIN 3 E25
Kuřim CZ 64 A2
Kuřivody CZ 53 C4
Kurki PL 47 B6
Kurort Oberwiesenthal
D 52 C2
Kurort Schmalkalden
D 51 C6
Kurort Stolberg D 51 B6
Kurort Wippra D 52 B1
Kurów PL 11 A7
Kurowice PL 55 B4
Kurravaara S 112 E9
Kursk RUS 7 F14
Kursu FIN 113 F17
Kuršumlija SRB 85 C6
Kuršumlijska Banja
SRB 85 C6
Kurşunlu
Bursa TR 118 B4
Çankırı TR 16 A6
Kurtakko FIN 113 E13
Kürten D 50 B3
Kurucaşile TR 16 A6
Kurzelów PL 55 C4
Kusadak SRB 85 B5
Kuşadası TR 119 E2
Kusel D 60 A3
Kusey D 44 C3
Küsnacht CH 70 A3
Kütahya TR 118 C4
Kutenholz D 43 B6
Kutina HR 74 C1
Kutjevo HR 74 C2
Kutná Hora CZ 53 D5
Kutno PL 55 A4
Kuttara FIN 113 D15
Küttingen CH 70 A3
Kúty SK 64 B3
Kuusamo FIN 3 D28
Kuusankoski FIN 3 F27
Kuvshinovo RUS 7 C13
Kuyucak TR 119 E3
Kuzmin SRB 85 A4
Kuźnia Raciborska
PL 54 C3
Kuźnica Czarnkowska
PL 46 C2
Kuźnica Żelichowska
PL 46 C2
Kvaløysletta N 112 C7
Kvalsund N 113 B12
Kvam
Nord-Trøndelag N 114 C8
Oppland N 114 F6
Kvamsøy N 32 A3
Kvænangsbotn N 113 C11
Kvanndal N 32 B3
Kvänum S 35 D5
Kværndrup DK 39 D3
Kvås N 33 D4
Kvasice CZ 64 A3
Kvelde N 35 C1
Kvenna N 114 E5
Kvernaland N 33 D2
Kvibille S 40 C2
Kvicksund S 37 C3
Kvidinge S 41 C3
Kvikkjokk S 112 F6
Kvikne N 114 E7
Kvilda CZ 63 A4
Kville S 35 D3
Kvillsfors S 40 B5
Kvinesdal N 33 D3
Kvinlog N 33 D3
Kvinnherad N 32 C3
Kvissel DK 38 B3
Kvissleby S 115 E14
Kviteseid N 33 C5
Kvitsøy N 33 C2
Kwakowo PL 46 A3
Kwidzyn PL 47 B4
Kwilcz PL 46 C2
Kyjov CZ 64 B3
Kyleakin GB 22 D3
Kyle of Lochalsh GB 22 D3
Kylerhea GB 22 D3
Kylestrome GB 22 C3
Kyllburg D 50 C2
Kyllini GR 117 E3
Kynšperk nad Ohří
CZ 52 C2
Kyperounda CY 120 B1
Kyrenia CY 120 A2
Kyritz D 44 C4
Kyrkesund S 38 A4
Kyrkhult S 41 C4
Kyrksæterøra N 114 D6
Kysucké Nové Mesto
SK 65 A4
Kythira GR 117 F4
Kythréa CY 120 A2
Kyustendil BG 11 E7
Kyyiv = Kiev UA 11 A11
Kyyjärvi FIN 3 E26

L

Laa an der Thaya A 64 B2
La Adrada E 94 B2
Laage D 44 B4
La Alameda E 100 A2
La Alberca E 93 A4
La Alberca de Záncara
E 95 C4
La Albergueria de
Argañán E 93 A4
La Albuera E 93 C4
La Aldea del Portillo del
Busto E 89 B3
La Algaba E 99 B4
La Aliseda de Tormes
E 93 A5
La Almarcha E 95 C4
La Almolda E 90 B2
La Almunia de Doña
Godina E 89 C5
Laanila FIN 113 D16
La Antillas E 98 B3
La Arena E 86 A4
Laatzen D 51 A5
La Aulaga E 99 B4
La Balme-de-Sillingy
F 69 C6
La Bañeza E 88 B1
La Barca de la Florida
E 99 C5
La Barre-de-Monts F 66 B2
La Barre-en-Ouche F 58 B1
La Barrosa E 99 C4
La Barthe-de-Neste F 77 C3
La Bassée F 48 C3
La Bastide-de-Sèrou
F 77 C4
La Bastide-des-Jourdans
F 79 C4
Labastide-Murat F 77 B4
La Bastide-Puylaurent
F 78 B2
Labastide-Rouairoux
F 77 C5
Labastide-St Pierre F 77 C4
La Bathie F 69 C6
Lábatlan H 65 C4
La Baule-Escoublac
F 66 A2
La Bazoche-Gouet F 58 B1
La Bégude-de-Mazenc
F 78 B3
Labenne F 76 C1
La Bernerie-en-Retz F 66 A2
Labin HR 82 A3
La Bisbal d'Empordà
E 91 B6
Łabiszyn PL 46 C3
Lablachère F 78 B3
Lábod H 74 B2
Laboe D 44 A2
La Boissière F 57 A6
Labouheyre F 76 B2
La Bourboule F 68 C2
La Bóveda de Toro E 88 C1
Łabowa PL 65 A6
La Brède F 76 B2
La Bresse F 60 B2
La Bridoire F 69 C5
La Brillanne F 79 C4
Labrit F 76 B2
Labros E 95 A5
La Bruffière F 66 A3
Labruguière F 77 C5
Labrujo P 87 C2
L'Absie F 67 B4
La Bussière F 58 C3
Laç AL 105 B5
La Caillère F 66 B4
Lacalahorra E 100 B2
La Caletta
Cágliari I 110 C1
Núoro I 110 B2
La Calmette F 78 C3
La Calzada de Oropesa
E 93 B5
La Campana E 99 B5
La Cañada E 94 B2
Lacanau F 76 B1
Lacanau-Océan F 76 A1
Lacanche F 69 A4
La Canourgue F 78 B2
La Capelle F 49 D4
Lacapelle-Marival F 77 B4
Laćarak SRB 85 A4
La Cardanchosa E 99 A5
La Caridad E 86 A4
La Carlota E 100 B1
La Carolina E 100 A2
Lacaune F 78 C1
La Cava E 90 C3
La Cavalerie F 78 B2
Laceby GB 27 B5
Lacedónia I 103 B8
La Celle-en-Moravan
F 69 A4
La Celle-St Avant F 67 A5
La Cerca E 89 B3
Láces I 71 B5
La Chaise-Dieu F 68 C3
La Chaize-Giraud F 66 B3
La Chaize-le-Vicomte
F 66 B3
La Chambre F 69 C6
Lachania GR 119 G2
La Chapelaude F 68 B2
La Chapelle-d'Angillon
F 68 A2
La Chapelle-en-
Aalgaudémar F 79 B5
La Chapelle-en-Vercors
F 79 B4
La Chapelle-Glain F 57 C4
La Chapelle-la-Reine
F 58 B3
La Chapelle-Laurent
F 68 C3
La Chapelle-St Luc F 59 B5
La Chapelle-sur-Erdre
F 66 A3
La Chapelle-Vicomtesse
F 58 C2
La Charce F 79 B4
La Charité-sur-Loire
F 68 A3
La Chartre-sur-le-Loir
F 58 C1
La Châtaigneraie F 67 B4
La Châtre F 68 B1
La Chaussée-sur-Marne
F 59 B5
La Chaux-de-Fonds
CH 70 A1
Lachen CH 70 A3
Lachendorf D 44 C2
La Cheppe F 59 A5
La Chèze F 56 B3
Lachowice PL 65 A5
La Ciotat F 79 C4
Łąck PL 47 C5
Läckeby S 40 C6
Läckö S 35 D5
La Clayette F 69 B4
La Clusaz F 69 C6
Lacock GB 29 B5
La Codosera E 93 B3
La Concha E 88 A3
La Condamine-Châtelard
F 79 B5
Láconi I 110 C2
La Contienda E 99 A4
La Coquille F 67 C5
La Coronada E 93 C5
La Côte-St André F 69 C5
La Cotinière F 66 C3
La Courtine F 68 C2
Lacq F 76 C2
La Crau F 79 C5
La Crèche F 67 B4
La Croix F 67 A5
Lacroix-Barrez F 77 B5
Lacroix-St Ouen F 58 A3
Lacroix-sur-Meuse F 60 B1
La Croix-Valmer F 79 C5
La Cumbre E 93 B5
Łącznik PL 54 C2
Lad H 74 B2
Ladbergen D 50 A3
Lądek-Zdrój PL 54 C1
Ladelund D 39 E2
Ladendorf A 64 B2
Ladignac-le-Long F 67 C6
Ladíspoli I 102 B5
Ladoeiro P 93 B3
Ladon F 58 C3
La Douze F 77 A3
Ladushkin RUS 47 A6
Ladybank GB 25 B4
Laer D 50 A3
La Espina E 86 A4
La Estrella E 94 C1
La Farga de Moles E 91 A4
La Fatarella E 90 B3
La Felipa E 95 C5
La Fère F 59 A4
La Ferrière
Indre-et-Loire F 58 C1
Vendée F 66 B3
La Ferrière-en-Parthenay
F 67 B4
La-Ferté-Alais F 58 B3
La Ferté-Bernard F 58 B1
La Ferté-Frênel F 58 B1
La Ferté-Gaucher F 59 B4
La Ferté-Imbault F 68 A1
La Ferté-Macé F 57 B5
La Ferté-Milon F 59 A4
La Ferté-sous-Jouarre
F 59 B4
La Ferté-St-Aubin F 58 C2
La Ferté-St-Cyr F 58 C2
La Ferté-Vidame F 58 B1
La Ferté Villeneuil F 58 C2
La Feuillie F 58 A2
Lafkos GR 116 C5
La Flèche F 57 C5
La Flotte F 66 B3
Lafnitz A 73 A6
La Font de la Figuera
E 101 A5
La Fouillade F 77 B5
Lafrançaise F 77 B4
La Fregeneda E 87 D4
La Fresneda E 90 C3
La Fuencubierta E 99 B6
La Fuente de San Esteban
E 87 D4
La Fulioala E 91 B4
La Gacilly F 57 C3
La Galera E 90 C3
Lagan S 40 C3
Laganadi I 109 A4
Lagarde F 77 C4
La Garde-Freinet F 79 C5
Lagares
Coimbra P 92 A3
Porto P 87 C2
La Garnache F 66 B3
Lagaro I 81 B5
La Garriga E 91 B5
La Garrovilla E 93 C4
Lagartera E 93 B5
La Gaubretière F 66 B3
Lågbol S 36 B5
Lage D 51 B4
Lägerdorf D 43 B6
Lagg GB 24 C2
Laggan GB 22 D4
Laggartorp S 35 C6
Łagiewniki PL 54 C1
La Gineta E 95 C4
Láglio I 71 C4
Lagnieu F 69 C5
Lagny-sur-Marne F 58 B3
Lago
Calabria I 106 B3
Veneto I 72 C2
Lagôa P 98 B2
Lagoaça P 87 C4
Lagonegro I 106 A2
Lagos
GR 116 A7
P 98 B2
Lagosanto I 82 B1
Łagów
Lubuskie PL 46 C1
Świętokrzyskie PL 55 C6
La Granadella
Alicante E 96 C3
Lleida E 90 B3
La Grand-Combe F 78 B3
La Grande-Croix F 69 C4
La Grande-Motte F 78 C3
La Granja d'Escarp E 90 B3
La Granjuela E 93 C5
Lagrasse F 77 C5
La Grave F 79 A5
La Gravelle F 57 B4
Laguardia E 89 B4
La Guardia E 95 C3
La Guardia de Jaén
E 100 B2
Laguarres E 90 A3
Laguenne F 68 C1
Laguépie F 77 B4
La Guerche-de-Bretagne
F 57 C4
La Guerche-sur-l'Aubois
F 68 B2
La Guérinière F 66 B2
Laguiole F 78 B1
Laguna de Duera E 88 C2
Laguna del Marquesado
E 95 B5
Laguna de Negrillos
E 88 B1
Lagundo I 71 B6
Lagunilla E 93 A4
La Haba E 93 C5
Laharie F 76 B2
La Haye-du-Puits F 57 A4
La Haye-Pesnel F 57 B4
Lahden D 43 C4
La Herlière F 48 C3
La Hermida E 88 A2
La Herrera E 95 D4
Laheycourt F 59 B6
La Higuera E 101 A4
La Hiniesta E 88 C1
Lahnstein D 50 C3
Laholm S 40 C3
La Horcajada E 93 A5
La Horra E 88 C3
Lahr D 60 B3
Lahti FIN 3 F26
La Hulpe B 49 C5
La Hutte F 57 B6
Laichingen D 61 B5
L'Aigle F 58 B1
La Iglesuela E 94 B2
La Iglesuela del Cid E 90 C2
Laignes F 59 C5
Laiguéglia I 80 C2
L'Aiguillon-sur-Mer F 66 B3
Laimbach am Ostrong
A 63 B6
Laina E 95 A4
Lainio S 113 E11
Lairg GB 23 C4
La Iruela E 100 B3
Laissac F 78 B1
Laisvall S 115 A14
Láives I 71 B6
La Javie F 79 B5
Lajkovac SRB 85 B5
La Jonchère-St Maurice
F 67 B6
La Jonquera E 91 A5
Lajoskomárom H 74 B3
Lajosmizse H 75 A4
Lak H 65 B6
Lakenheath GB 30 B4
Laki BG 116 A6
Lakitelek H 75 B5
Lakki GR 117 G5
Lakolk DK 39 D1
Łąkorz PL 47 B5
Lakšárska Nová Ves
SK 64 B3
Lakselv N 113 B13
Laksfors N 115 B10
Laktaši BIH 84 B2
La Lantejuela E 99 B5
Lalapaşa TR 118 A1
L'Albagès E 90 B3
Lalbenque F 77 B4
L'Alcudia E 96 B2
L'Aldea E 90 C3
Lalëz AL 105 B5
Lalín E 86 B2
Lalinde F 77 B3
La Línea de la
Concepción E 99 C5
Lalizolle F 68 B3
La Llacuna E 91 B4
Lalley F 79 B4
Lalling D 62 B4
Lalm N 114 F6
La Londe-les-Maures
F 79 C5
La Loupe F 58 B2
La Louvière B 49 C5
L'Alpe-d'Huez F 79 A5
La Luisiana E 99 B5
Laluque F 76 C1
Lam D 62 A4
La Machine F 68 B3
la Maddalena I 110 A2
Lama dei Peligni I 103 A7
Lamadrid E 88 A2
Lamagistére F 77 B3
La Mailleraye-sur-Seine
F 58 A1
La Malène F 78 B2
Lama Mocogno I 81 B4
La Mamola E 100 C2
La Manresana dels Prats
E 91 B4
Lamarche F 60 B1
Lamarche-sur-Saône
F 69 A5
Lamargelle F 69 A4
Lamarosa P 92 B2
Lamarque F 76 A2
Lamas P 92 A2
La Masadera E 90 B2
Lamas de Moaro P 87 B2
Lamastre F 78 B3
La Mata E 94 C2
La Mata de Ledesma
E 94 A1
La Mata de Monteagudo
E 88 B1
Lambach A 63 B4
Lamballe F 56 B3
Lamberhurst GB 31 C4
Lambesc F 79 C4
Lambia GR 117 E3
Lambley GB 25 D5
Lambourn GB 31 C2
Lamego P 87 C3
La Meilleraye-de-Bretagne
F 66 A3
La Ménitré F 67 A4
L'Ametlla de Mar E 90 C3
Lamia GR 116 D4
Lammhult S 40 B4
La Mojonera E 101 C3
La Mole F 79 C5
La Molina E 91 A4
La Monnerie-le-Montel
F 68 C3
La Morera E 93 C4
La Mothe-Achard F 66 B3
Lamothe-Cassel F 77 B4
Lamothe-Montravel F 76 B3
La Mothe-St Héray F 67 B4
Lamotte-Beuvron F 58 C3
La Motte-Chalançon
F 79 B4
La Motte-du-Caire F 79 B5
La Motte-Servolex F 69 C5
Lampertheim D 61 A4
Lampeter GB 28 A3
L'Ampolla E 90 C3
Lamprechtshausen A 62 C3
Lamsfeld D 53 B4
Lamspringe D 51 B6
Lamstedt D 43 B6
La Mudarra E 88 C2
La Muela E 90 B1
La Mure F 79 B4
Lamure-sur-Azergues
F 69 B4
Lana I 71 B6
Lanaja E 90 B2
Lanarce F 78 B2
Lanark GB 25 C4
La Nava E 99 B4
La Nava de Ricomalillo
E 94 C2
La Nava de Santiago
E 93 B4
Lancaster GB 26 A3
Lanchester GB 25 D6
Lanciano I 103 A7
Lancing GB 31 D3
Lançon-Provence F 79 C4
Lancova Vas SLO 73 B5
Landau
Bayern D 62 B3
Rheinland-Pfalz D 61 A4
Landeck A 71 A5
Landen B 49 C6
Landerneau F 56 B1
Landeryd S 40 B3
Landesbergen D 43 C6
Landete E 96 B1
Landévant F 56 C2
Landévennec F 56 B1
Landeyjahöfn IS 111 D5
Landivisiau F 56 B1
Landivy F 57 B4
Landl A 62 C3
Landön S 115 D11
Landos F 78 B2
Landouzy-le-Ville F 59 A5
Landquart CH 71 B4
Landrecies F 49 C4
Landreville F 59 B5
Landriano I 71 C4
Landsberg D 62 B1
Lands-berg D 52 B2
Landsbro S 40 B4
Landscheid D 50 D2
Landshut D 62 B3
Landskrona S 41 D2
Landstuhl D 60 A3
Lanesborough IRL 19 C4
Lanester F 56 C2
Lanestosa E 89 A3
La Neuve-Lyre F 58 B1
La Neuveville CH 70 A2
Langå DK 39 C2
Langada GR 116 D8
Langadas GR 116 B5
Langa de Duero E 89 C3
Langadia GR 117 E4
Langangen N 35 C1
Långared S 40 A2
Långaröd S 41 D3
Långaryd S 40 B3
Långås S 40 C2
Långasjö S 40 C5
Langau A 63 B6
Langeac F 78 A2
Langeais F 67 A5
Langedijk NL 42 C1
Langeln D 51 B6
Langelsheim D 51 B6
Langemark-Poelkapelle
B 48 C3
Langen
Hessen D 51 D4
Niedersachsen D 43 B5
Langenau D 61 B6
Langenberg D 50 B4
Langenbruck CH 70 A2
Langenburg D 61 A5
Längenfeld A 71 A5
Langenfeld D 50 B2
Langenhorn D 43 A5
Langenlois A 63 B6
Langenlonsheim D 60 A3
Langennaudorf D 52 B3
Langenneufnach D 62 B1
Langenthal CH 70 A2
Langenzenn D 62 A1
Langeoog D 43 B4
Langeskov DK 39 D3
Langesund N 35 C1
Langewiesen D 51 C6
Långflon S 34 A4
Langförden D 43 C5
Langhagen D 44 B4
Länghem S 40 B3
Langhirano I 81 B4
Langholm GB 25 C5
Langholt IS 111 D7
Långlöt S 41 C6
Langnau CH 70 B2
Langø DK 39 E4
Langogne F 78 B2
Langon F 76 B2
Langquaid D 62 B3
Långrådna S 37 D3
Langreo E 88 A1
Langres F 59 C6
Långsele S 115 D14
Långserud S 35 C4
Langset N 34 B3
Långshyttan S 36 B3
Langstrand N 113 B12
Långträsk S 115 B17
Langueux F 56 B3
Languidic F 56 C2
Längvik S 37 C5
Langwarden D 43 B5
Langwathby GB 26 A3
Langwedel D 43 C6
Langweid D 62 B1
Langwies CH 71 B4
Lanheses P 87 C2
Lanięta PL 47 C5
Lanildut F 56 B1
Lanjarón E 100 C2
Lanmeur F 56 B2
Lanna
Jönköping S 40 B3
Örebro S 37 C1
Lännaholm S 36 C4
Lannavaara S 113 D10
Lannéanou F 56 B2
Lannemezan F 77 C3
Lanneuville-sur-Meuse
F 59 A6
Lannilis F 56 B1
Lannion F 56 B2
La Nocle-Maulaix F 68 B3
Lanouaille F 67 C6
Lansjärv S 113 F11
Lanškroun CZ 64 A2
Lanslebourg-Mont-Cenis
F 70 C1
Lanta F 77 C4
Lantadilla E 88 B2
Lanton F 76 B1
Lantosque F 79 C6
La Nuez de Arriba E 88 B3
Lanusei I 110 C2
Lanúvio I 102 B5
Lanvollon F 56 B3
Lánycsók H 74 B3
Lanz D 44 B3
Lanza E 86 A2
Lanzada E 86 B2
Lanzahita E 94 B2
Lanžhot CZ 64 B2
Lanzo Torinese I 70 C2
Laole SRB 85 B6
Laon F 59 A4
Laons F 58 B2
La Paca E 101 B4
La Pacaudière F 68 B3
Lapalisse F 68 B3
La Palma d'Ebre E 90 B3
La Palma del Condado
E 99 B4
La Palme F 78 D2
La Palmyre F 66 C3
La Parra E 93 C4
Łapczyna Wola PL 55 C4
La Pedraja de Portillo
E 88 C2
La Peraleja E 95 B4
La Petit-Pierre F 60 B3
Lapeyrade F 76 B2
Lapeyrouse F 68 B2
Lapford GB 28 C4
La Pinilla E 101 B4
Lapithos CY 120 A2
La Plagne F 70 C1
La Plaza E 86 A4
Laplje Selo KOS 85 D6
Laplume F 77 B3
La Pobla de Lillet E 91 A4
La Pobla de Vallbona
E 96 B2
La Pobla Llarga E 96 B2
La Pola de Gordón E 88 B1
la Porta F 102 A2
La Pouëze F 66 A4
Lapoutroie F 60 B3
La Póveda de Soria
E 89 B4
Lapovo SRB 85 B6
Läppe S 37 C2
Lappeenranta FIN 3 F28
Lappoluobbal N 113 C12
La Preste F 91 A5
La Primaube F 77 B5
Lapseki TR 118 B1
Lapua FIN 3 E25
La Puebla de Almoradie
E 95 C3
La Puebla de Cazalla
E 99 B5
La Puebla de los Infantes
E 99 B5
La Puebla del Río E 99 B4
La Puebla de Montalbán
E 94 C2
La Puebla de Roda E 90 A3
La Puebla de Valdavia
E 88 B2
La Puebla de Valverde
E 96 A2
La Pueblanueva E 94 C2
La Puerta de Segura
E 101 A3
La Punt CH 71 B4
L'Áquila I 103 A6
La Quintana E 100 B1
La Quintera E 99 B5

La Rábita
 Granada E . . . 100 C2
 Jaén E . . . 100 B1
Laracha E . . . 86 A2
Laragh IRL . . . 21 A5
Laragne-Montéglin F . 79 B4
La Rambla E . . . 100 B1
l'Arboç E . . . 91 B4
L'Arbresle F . . . 69 C4
Lårbro S . . . 37 E5
Larceveau F . . . 76 C1
Larche
 Alpes-de-Haute-
 Provence F . . . 79 B5
 Corrèze F . . . 77 A4
Lårdal N . . . 33 C5
Lærdalsøyri N . . . 32 B3
Lardosa P . . . 92 B3
La Reale I . . . 110 A1
Laredo E . . . 89 A3
La Redondela E . . . 98 B3
La Réole F . . . 76 B2
Largentière F . . . 78 B3
L'Argentière-la-Bessée
 F . . . 79 B5
Largs GB . . . 24 C3
Lari I . . . 81 C4
La Riera E . . . 86 A4
La Riera de Gaià E . . . 91 B4
La Rinconada E . . . 99 B4
Lariño E . . . 86 B1
Larino I . . . 103 B7
Larisa GR . . . 116 C4
La Rivière-Thibouville
 F . . . 58 A1
Larkhall GB . . . 25 C4
Larkollen N . . . 35 C2
Larmor-Plage F . . . 56 C2
Larnaca CY . . . 120 B2
Larne GB . . . 19 B6
La Robla E . . . 88 B1
La Roca de la Sierra
 E . . . 93 B4
La Roche CH . . . 70 B2
La Rochebeaucourt-
 Argentine F . . . 67 C5
La Roche-Bernard F . 66 A2
La Roche-Canillac F . 68 C1
La Roche-Chalais F . . 67 C5
La Roche Derrien F . . 56 B2
La Roche-des-Arnauds
 F . . . 79 B4
La Roche-en-Ardenne
 B . . . 49 C6
La Roche-en-Brénil F . 69 A4
La Rochefoucauld F . 67 C5
La Roche-Guyon F . . 58 A2
La Rochelle F . . . 66 B3
La Roche-Posay F . . 67 B5
La Roche-sur-Foron
 F . . . 69 B6
La Roche-sur-Yon F . 66 B3
Larochette F . . . 60 A2
La Rochette F . . . 79 B4
La Roda
 Albacete E . . . 95 C4
 Oviedo E . . . 86 A4
La Roda de Andalucia
 E . . . 100 B1
Laroquebrou F . . . 77 B5
La Roquebrussanne
 F . . . 79 C4
Laroque d'Olmes F . . 77 D4
La Roque-Gageac F . 77 B4
La Roque-Ste Marguerite
 F . . . 78 B2
Laroque-Timbaut F . . 77 B3
Larouco E . . . 87 B3
Larraga E . . . 89 B5
Larrau F . . . 76 C2
Larrazet F . . . 77 C4
Larsnes N . . . 114 E2
La Rubia E . . . 89 C4
Laruns F . . . 76 C2
Larva E . . . 100 B2
Larvik N . . . 35 C2
La Sagrada E . . . 87 D4
La Salceda E . . . 94 A3
Lasalle F . . . 78 B2
La Salle F . . . 79 B5
la Salute di Livenza I . 72 C2
La Salvetat-Peyralés
 F . . . 77 B5
La Salvetat-sur-Agout
 F . . . 78 C1
Las Arenas E . . . 88 A2
La Sarraz CH . . . 69 B6
Lasarte E . . . 89 A4
Låsby DK . . . 39 C2
Las Cabezadas E . . . 95 A3
Las Cabezas de San Juan
 E . . . 99 C5
Las Correderas E . . . 100 A2
Las Cuevas de Cañart
 E . . . 90 C2
La Seca E . . . 88 C2
La Selva del Camp E . 91 B4
La Senia E . . . 90 C3
La Serra E . . . 91 B4
La Seu d'Urgell E . . . 91 A4
La Seyne-sur-Mer F . 79 C4
Las Gabias E . . . 100 B2
Las Herencias E . . . 94 C2
Las Herrerías E . . . 98 B3
Łasin PL . . . 47 B5
Lask PL . . . 55 B4
Laska PL . . . 46 B3
Łaskarzew PL . . . 55 B6
Laško SLO . . . 73 B5
Laskowice PL . . . 47 B4
Las Labores E . . . 95 C3
Las Mesas E . . . 95 C4
Las Minas E . . . 101 A4
Las Navas E . . . 100 B1
Las Navas de la
 Concepción E . . . 99 B5
Las Navas del Marqués
 E . . . 94 B2
Las Navillas E . . . 94 C2
Las Negras E . . . 101 C4
La Solana E . . . 95 D3
La Souterraine F . . . 67 B6
Las Pajanosas E . . . 99 B4
Laspaules E . . . 90 A3
Las Pedroñas E . . . 95 C4
La Spézia I . . . 81 B3
Las Planes d'Hostoles
 E . . . 91 A5
Laspuña E . . . 90 A3
Las Rozas
 Cantabria E . . . 88 B2
 Madrid E . . . 94 B3
Lassan D . . . 45 B5
Lassay-les-Châteaux
 F . . . 57 B5
Lasseube F . . . 76 C2
Lassigny F . . . 58 A3
La Storta I . . . 102 B5
Lastovo HR . . . 84 D1
Lastras de Cuéllar E . 88 C2
Lästringe S . . . 37 D4
Lastrup D . . . 43 C4
Lastva BIH . . . 84 D3
La Suze-sur-Sarthe F . 57 C6
Las Uces E . . . 87 C4
Lasva BIH . . . 84 B3
Las Veguillas E . . . 94 B1
Las Ventas con Peña
 Aguilera E . . . 94 C2
Las Ventas de San Julián
 E . . . 93 A5
Las Villes E . . . 96 A3
Latasa E . . . 76 C1
Látera I . . . 102 A4
Laterza I . . . 104 C2
La Teste F . . . 76 B1
Lathen D . . . 43 C4
Latheron GB . . . 23 C5
La Thuile I . . . 70 C1
Latiano I . . . 105 C3

Latina I . . . 102 B5
Latisana I . . . 72 C3
Látky SK . . . 65 B5
La Toba E . . . 95 B5
La Toledana E . . . 94 C2
La Torre de Cabdella
 E . . . 90 A3
La Torre de Esteban
 Hambrán E . . . 94 B2
La Torre del l'Espanyol
 E . . . 90 B3
La Torresaviñán E . . 95 B4
La Tour d'Aigues F . . 79 C4
La Tour de Peilz CH . 70 B1
La Tour-du-Pin F . . . 69 C5
Latowicz PL . . . 55 A6
La Tranche-sur-Mer F . 66 B3
La Tremblade F . . . 66 C3
La Trimouille F . . . 67 B6
La Trinité F . . . 56 C2
La Trinité-Porhoët F . 56 B3
Latrónico I . . . 106 A3
Latronquière F . . . 77 B5
Latterbach CH . . . 70 B2
La Turballe F . . . 66 A2
Laubert F . . . 78 B2
Laucha D . . . 52 B1
Lauchhammer D . . . 53 B3
Lauchheim D . . . 61 B6
Lauda-Königshofen
 D . . . 61 A5
Laudal N . . . 33 D4
Lauder GB . . . 25 C5
Lauenau D . . . 51 A5
Lauenburg D . . . 44 B2
Lauf D . . . 62 A2
Laufach D . . . 51 C5
Laufen
 CH . . . 70 A2
 D . . . 62 C3
Lauffen D . . . 61 A5
Laugar IS . . . 111 B8
Laugarás IS . . . 111 D5
Laugarbakki IS . . . 111 B5
Laugarvatn IS . . . 111 C5
Lauingen D . . . 61 B6
Laujar de Andarax E . 100 C3
Laukaa FIN . . . 3 E26
Laukeland IS . . . 3 B16
Lauker S . . . 115 B16
Laukvik N . . . 112 E3
La Uña E . . . 88 A1
Launceston GB . . . 28 C3
La Unión E . . . 101 B5
Launois-sur-Vence F . 59 A5
Lauphiem D . . . 61 B5
Lauragh IRL . . . 20 C2
Laureana di Borrello
 I . . . 106 C3
Laurencekirk GB . . . 25 B5
Laurencetown IRL . . 20 A3
Laurenzana I . . . 104 C1
Lauria I . . . 106 A2
Laurière F . . . 67 B6
Laurieston GB . . . 24 D3
Laurino I . . . 103 C8
Lausanne CH . . . 69 B6
Laussonne F . . . 78 B3
Lauta D . . . 53 B4
Lauterach A . . . 71 A4
Lauterbach D . . . 51 C5
Lauterbrunnen CH . . 70 B2
Lauterecken D . . . 60 A3
Lauterhofen D . . . 62 A2
Lautrec F . . . 77 C5
Lauvsnes N . . . 114 C7
Lauvuskylä N . . . 3 D3
Lauzerte F . . . 77 B4
Lauzès F . . . 77 B4
Lauzun F . . . 77 B3
Lavagna I . . . 80 B3
Laval F . . . 57 B5
Le Val d'Uixó E . . . 96 B2
Lavamünd A . . . 73 B4
Lavara GR . . . 118 A1
Lavardac F . . . 76 B3
Lavaris P . . . 92 A2
Lavarone I . . . 71 C6
Lavau F . . . 59 C3
Lavaur F . . . 77 C4
La Vecilla de Curueño
 E . . . 88 B1
La Vega
 Asturias E . . . 88 A1
 Asturias E . . . 88 A1
 Cantabria E . . . 88 A2
Lavelanet F . . . 77 D4
La Velilla E . . . 94 A3
La Velles E . . . 94 A1
Lavello I . . . 104 B1
Lavelsloh D . . . 43 C5
Lavenham GB . . . 30 B4
Laveno I . . . 70 C3
La Ventosa E . . . 95 B4
Lavezzola I . . . 81 B5
Laviano I . . . 103 C8
La Victoria E . . . 100 B1
La Vid E . . . 89 C3
Lavik N . . . 32 A2
La Vilavella E . . . 96 B2
La Vilella Baixa E . . . 90 B3
La Villa de Don Fadrique
 E . . . 95 C3
Lavilledieu F . . . 78 B3
La Villedieu F . . . 67 B4
La Ville Dieu-du-Temple
 F . . . 77 B4
Lavinio-Lido di Enea
 I . . . 102 B5
Lavis I . . . 71 B6
Lavit F . . . 77 C3
Lavoncourt F . . . 60 C1
Lavos P . . . 92 A2
La Voulte-sur-Rhône
 F . . . 78 B3
Lavradio P . . . 92 C1
Lavre P . . . 92 C2
Lavrio GR . . . 117 E6
La Wantzenau F . . . 60 B3
Lawers GB . . . 24 B3
Ławy PL . . . 45 C6
Laxå S . . . 37 D1
Laxamýri IS . . . 111 B8
Laxe E . . . 86 A1
Laxey GB . . . 26 A1
Laxford Bridge GB . . 22 C3
Laxhall S . . . 35 D5
Laxsjö S . . . 115 D11
Laxtjarn S . . . 34 B6
Laxvik S . . . 40 C2
Laxviken S . . . 115 D11
La Yesa E . . . 96 B2
Laza E . . . 87 B3
Lazarevac SRB . . . 85 B5
Lazarev Krst MNE . . 105 A5
Lazarevo SRB . . . 75 C5
Lazise I . . . 71 C5
Łaziska Grn. PL . . . 54 C3
Lazkao E . . . 89 A4
Lázně Bělohrad CZ . . 53 C5
Lázně Bohdaneč CZ . 53 C5
Lázně Kynžvart CZ . . 52 C2
Lazonby GB . . . 26 A3
La Zubia E . . . 100 B2
Łazy PL . . . 46 A2
Lazzaro I . . . 109 B4
Lea GB . . . 27 B5
Leadburn GB . . . 25 C4
Leadhills GB . . . 25 C4
Leap IRL . . . 20 C2
Leatherhead GB . . . 31 C3
Łeba PL . . . 46 A3
Lebach D . . . 60 A2
Le Barp F . . . 76 B2
Le Bar-sur-Loup F . . 79 C5
Lebane SRB . . . 85 C6
Lebbeke B . . . 49 B5

Lébény H . . . 64 C3
Lébény F . . . 69 C4
Le Blanc F . . . 67 B6
Le Bleymard F . . . 78 B2
Lebno PL . . . 47 A4
Leboreiro E . . . 87 B3
Lębork PL . . . 46 A3
Le Boullay-Mivoye F . 58 B2
Le Boulou F . . . 91 A5
Le Bourg F . . . 77 B4
Le Bourg-d'Oisans F . 79 A5
Le Bourget-du-Lac F . 69 C5
Le Bourgneuf-la-Forêt
 F . . . 57 B5
Le Bousquet d'Orb F . 78 C2
Le Brassus CH . . . 69 B6
Le Breuil F . . . 68 B3
Le Breuil-en-Auge F . 57 A6
Lebrija E . . . 99 C4
Lebring A . . . 73 B5
Le Brusquet F . . . 79 B5
Le Bry F . . . 70 B2
Le Bugue F . . . 77 B3
Le Buisson F . . . 77 B3
Lebus D . . . 45 C6
Lebusa D . . . 52 B3
Le Caloy F . . . 76 C2
Le Cap d'Agde F . . . 78 C2
Le Cateau Cambrésis
 F . . . 49 C4
Le Caylar F . . . 78 C2
Le Cayrol F . . . 78 B1
Lecce I . . . 105 C4
Lecco I . . . 71 C4
Lécera E . . . 90 B2
Lećevica HR . . . 83 C5
Lech A . . . 71 A5
Le Chambon-Feugerolles
 F . . . 69 C4
Le Chambon-sur-Lignon
 F . . . 78 A3
Le Château d'Oléron
 F . . . 66 C3
Le Châtelard F . . . 69 C6
Le Châtelet F . . . 68 B2
Le Châtelet-en-Brie F . 58 B3
Lechbruck D . . . 62 C1
Lechena GR . . . 117 E3
Le Chesne F . . . 59 A5
Le Cheylard F . . . 78 B3
Lechlade GB . . . 29 B6
Lechovice CZ . . . 64 B2
Leciñena E . . . 90 B2
Leck D . . . 39 E1
Le Collet-de-Deze F . 78 B2
Le Conquet F . . . 56 B1
Le Creusot F . . . 69 B4
Le Croisic F . . . 66 A2
Le Crotoy F . . . 48 C2
Lectoure F . . . 77 C3
Łęczyca
 Łódzkie PL . . . 55 A4
 Zachodnio-Pomorskie
 PL . . . 45 B7
Ledaña E . . . 95 C5
Ledbury GB . . . 29 A5
Lede B . . . 49 C4
Ledečnad Sazavou
 CZ . . . 63 A6
Ledenice CZ . . . 63 B5
Le Deschaux F . . . 69 B5
Ledesma E . . . 87 C4
Lédignan F . . . 78 C3
Lédigos E . . . 88 B2
Ledmore GB . . . 22 C4
Lednice CZ . . . 64 B2
Lednické-Rovné SK . . 64 A4
Le Donjon F . . . 68 B3
Le Dorat F . . . 67 B6
Łędyczek PL . . . 46 B2
Lędziny PL . . . 55 C4
Leeds GB . . . 27 B4
Leek
 GB . . . 26 B3
 NL . . . 42 B3
Leenaun IRL . . . 18 C2
Leens NL . . . 42 B3
Leer D . . . 43 B4
Leerdam NL . . . 49 B6
Leerhafe D . . . 43 B4
Leese D . . . 43 C6
Leeuwarden NL . . . 42 B2
Leezen D . . . 44 B2
Le Faou F . . . 56 B1
Le Faoüet F . . . 56 B2
Lefka CY . . . 120 A1
Lefkada GR . . . 116 D2
Lefkimis GR . . . 116 C2
Lefkoniko CY . . . 120 A2
Le Folgoet F . . . 56 B1
Le Fossat F . . . 77 C4
Le Fousseret F . . . 77 C4
Le Fugeret F . . . 79 B5
Leganés E . . . 94 B3
Legau D . . . 61 C6
Le Gault-Soigny F . . 59 B4
Legbąd PL . . . 46 B3
Legé F . . . 66 B3
Lège-Cap-Ferret F . . 76 B1
Legionowo PL . . . 55 A5
Léglise B . . . 60 A1
Legnago I . . . 71 C6
Legnano I . . . 70 C3
Legnaro I . . . 72 C1
Legnica PL . . . 53 B6
Łęgowo PL . . . 47 A4
Legrad HR . . . 74 B1
Le Grand-Bornand F . 69 C6
Le Grand-Bourg F . . 67 B6
Le Grand-Lucé F . . . 58 C1
Le Grand-Pressigny
 F . . . 67 B5
Le Grand-Quevilly F . 58 A2
Le Grau-du-Roi F . . . 78 C3
Léguevin F . . . 77 C4
Legutiano E . . . 89 B4
Le Havre F . . . 57 A6
Lehesten D . . . 52 C1
Lehnice SK . . . 64 B3
Lehnin D . . . 52 A2
Le Hohwald F . . . 60 B3
Le Houga F . . . 76 C2
Lehrberg D . . . 61 A6
Lehre D . . . 51 A6
Lehrte D . . . 44 C1
Lehsen D . . . 44 B3
Leibnitz A . . . 73 B5
Leicester GB . . . 30 B2
Leiden NL . . . 49 A5
Leidschendam NL . . 49 A5
Leigh GB . . . 26 B3
Leighlinbridge IRL . . 21 B5
Leighton Buzzard GB . 31 C3
Leignon B . . . 49 C6
Leikanger N . . . 114 F2
Leimen D . . . 61 A4
Leimuiden NL . . . 49 A5
Leinefelde D . . . 51 B6
Leinì I . . . 70 C2
Leintwardine GB . . . 29 A5
Leipojärvi S . . . 112 E10
Leipzig D . . . 52 B2
Leira
 Nordland N . . . 115 A10
 Oppland N . . . 32 B6
Leiråmoen N . . . 112 F3
Leiria P . . . 92 B2
Leirvåg N . . . 32 B2
Leirvik
 Hordaland N . . . 32 C2
 Sogn og Fjordane N . 32 A2
Leisach A . . . 72 B2
Leisnig D . . . 52 B2
Leiston GB . . . 30 B5
Leitholm GB . . . 25 C5
Leitrim IRL . . . 18 C3
Leitza E . . . 76 C1
Leitzkau D . . . 52 A1
Lejkowo PL . . . 46 A2
Lekani GR . . . 116 A6
Łękawa PL . . . 55 B4
Łękawica PL . . . 65 A5
Lekkbibaj AL . . . 105 A5

Lekeitio E . . . 89 A4
Lekenik HR . . . 73 C6
Lekeryd S . . . 40 B4
Leknes N . . . 112 D2
Łęknica PL . . . 53 B4
Leksand S . . . 36 B1
Leksvik N . . . 114 D7
Lekunberri E . . . 76 C1
Lekvattnet S . . . 34 B4
Le Lardin-St Lazare F . 67 C6
Le Lauzet-Ubaye F . . 79 B5
Le Lavandou F . . . 79 C5
Le Lion-d'Angers F . . 57 C5
Lelkowo PL . . . 47 A6
Le Locle CH . . . 70 A1
Le Loroux-Bottereau
 F . . . 66 A3
Le Louroux-Béconnais
 F . . . 57 C5
Lelów PL . . . 55 C4
Le Luc F . . . 79 C5
Le Lude F . . . 57 C6
Lelystad NL . . . 42 C2
Lem
 Ringkøbing DK . . . 39 C1
 Viborg Amt. DK . . . 38 C1
Le Malzieu-Ville F . . 78 B2
Le Mans F . . . 57 B6
Le Mas-d'Azil F . . . 77 C4
Le Massegros F . . . 78 B2
Le Mayet-de-Montagne
 F . . . 68 B3
Lembach F . . . 60 A3
Lemberg F . . . 60 A3
Lembèye F . . . 76 C2
Lemelerveld NL . . . 42 C3
Le Mêle-sur-Sarthe F . 58 B1
Le Ménil F . . . 60 B2
Le Merlerault F . . . 57 B6
Le Mesnil-sur-Oger F . 59 B5
Lemförde D . . . 43 C5
Lemgo D . . . 51 A4
Le Miroir F . . . 69 B5
Lemland FIN . . . 36 B7
Lemmer NL . . . 42 C2
Le Molay-Littry F . . . 57 A5
Le Monastier-sur-Gazeille
 F . . . 78 B2
Le Monêtier-les-Bains
 F . . . 79 B5
Le Mont-Dore F . . . 68 C2
Le Montet F . . . 68 B3
Le Mont-St Michel F . 57 B4
Lempdes F . . . 68 C3
Le Muret F . . . 76 B2
Le Muy F . . . 79 C5
Lemwig DK . . . 38 C1
Lemwerder D . . . 43 B5
Lena N . . . 34 B2
Lenart SLO . . . 73 B5
Lenartovce SK . . . 65 B6
Lencloître F . . . 67 B5
Lend A . . . 72 A3
Lendalfoot GB . . . 24 C3
Lendava SLO . . . 73 B6
Lendery RUS . . . 3 E29
Lendinara I . . . 81 A5
Lendorf A . . . 72 B3
Lendum DK . . . 38 B3
Le Neubourg F . . . 58 A1
Lengefeld D . . . 52 C3
Lengerich
 Niedersachsen D . . 43 C4
 Nordrhein-Westfalen
 D . . . 50 A3
Lenggries D . . . 62 C2
Lengyeltóti H . . . 74 B2
Lenhovda S . . . 40 C5
Lenk CH . . . 70 B2
Lennartsfors S . . . 35 C3
Lennestadt D . . . 50 B4
Lennoxtown GB . . . 24 C3
Leno I . . . 71 C5
Lénola I . . . 103 B6
Le Nouvion-en-Thiérache
 F . . . 49 C4
Lens
 B . . . 49 C4
 F . . . 48 C3
Lensahn D . . . 44 A2
Lens Lestang F . . . 69 C5
Lensvik N . . . 114 D6
Lentellais E . . . 87 B3
Lentföhrden D . . . 44 B1
Lenti H . . . 74 B1
Lentini I . . . 109 B3
Lenungshamar S . . . 35 C4
Lenzburg CH . . . 70 A3
Lenzen D . . . 44 B3
Lenzerheide CH . . . 71 B4
Leoben A . . . 73 A5
Leogang A . . . 72 A2
Leominster GB . . . 29 A5
León E . . . 88 B1
Léon F . . . 76 C1
Leonberg D . . . 61 B5
Léoncel F . . . 79 B4
Leonding A . . . 63 B5
Leonessa I . . . 102 A5
Leonforte I . . . 109 B3
Leonidio GR . . . 117 E4
Leopoldsburg B . . . 49 B6
Leopoldsdorf im
 Marchfeld A . . . 64 B2
Leopoldshagen D . . . 45 B5
Leova MD . . . 11 C10
Le Palais F . . . 66 A1
Le Parcq F . . . 48 C3
Lepe E . . . 98 B3
Le Péage-de-Roussillon
 F . . . 69 C4
Le Pellerin F . . . 66 A3
Lepenac
 MNE . . . 85 D4
 SRB . . . 85 C6
Lepenou GR . . . 116 D3
Le Perthus F . . . 91 A5
Le Perthus F . . . 78 A3
Le Petit-Bornand F . . 69 C6
Lephin GB . . . 22 D2
Lepoglava HR . . . 73 B6
Le Poiré-sur-Vie F . . 66 B3
Le Pont CH . . . 69 B6
Le Pont-de-Montvert
 F . . . 78 B2
Le Porge F . . . 76 B1
Le Porge-Océan F . . 76 B1
Le Portel F . . . 48 C2
Le Pouldu F . . . 56 C2
Le Pouliguen F . . . 66 A2
Leppäjärvi FIN . . . 113 D12
Leppävirta FIN . . . 3 E27
Leppin D . . . 44 C3
le Prese I . . . 71 B5
Lepsény H . . . 74 B3
Le Puy-en-Velay F . . 78 A2
Le Puy-Ste Réparade
 F . . . 79 C4
Le Quesnoy F . . . 49 C4
Léquile I . . . 105 C4
Le Rayol F . . . 79 C5
Lercara Friddi I . . . 108 B2
Lerdal S . . . 35 D3
Leré F . . . 68 A3
Lérici I . . . 81 B3
Lerin E . . . 89 B5
Lerma E . . . 88 B3
Lerm-et-Musset F . . 76 B2
Lermoos A . . . 71 A5
Le Roeulx B . . . 49 C5
Le Rouget F . . . 77 B5
Lérouville F . . . 60 B1
Le Rozier F . . . 78 B2
Lerum S . . . 40 B2
Le Russey F . . . 70 A1
Lervik N . . . 35 C2
Lerwick GB . . . 22 A7
Lés
 E . . . 77 D3

Les Abrets F . . . 69 C5
Les Aix-d'Angillon F . 68 A2
Lešak KOS . . . 85 C5
Lesaka E . . . 76 C1
Les Ancizes-Comps
 F . . . 68 C2
Les Andelys F . . . 58 A2
Les Arcs
 Savoie F . . . 70 C1
 Var F . . . 79 C5
Les-Aubiers F . . . 67 B4
Les Baux-de-Provence
 F . . . 78 C3
Les Bézards F . . . 58 C3
Les Bois CH . . . 70 A1
Les Bordes F . . . 58 C3
Les Borges Blanques
 E . . . 90 B3
Les Borges del Camp
 E . . . 91 B4
Les Brunettes F . . . 68 B3
Les Cabannes F . . . 77 D4
L'Escala E . . . 91 A6
Lescar F . . . 76 C2
L'Escarène F . . . 80 C1
Lesce SLO . . . 73 B4
Lescheraines F . . . 69 C6
Lesconil F . . . 56 C1
Les Contamines-Montjoie
 F . . . 70 C1
Les Coves de Vinroma
 E . . . 90 C3
Les Déserts F . . . 69 C5
Les Deux-Alpes F . . . 79 B5
Les Diablerets CH . . 70 B2
Lesdins F . . . 59 A4
Les Echelles F . . . 69 C5
Le Sel-de-Bretagne F . 57 C4
Le Sentier CH . . . 69 B6
Les Escaldes AND . . 91 A4
Les Essarts F . . . 66 B3
Les Estables F . . . 78 B3
Les Eyzies-de-Tayac
 F . . . 77 B4
Les Gets F . . . 70 B1
Les Grandes-Ventes
 F . . . 58 A2
Les Haudères CH . . . 70 B2
Les Herbiers F . . . 66 B3
Les Hôpitaux-Neufs
 F . . . 69 B6
Lesično SLO . . . 73 B5
Lésina I . . . 103 B8
Lesjaskog N . . . 114 E5
Lesjöfors S . . . 34 C6
Leskovac SRB . . . 85 C6
Leskova Dolina SLO . 73 C4
Leskovec
 CZ . . . 64 A3
 SLO . . . 73 C5
Leskovik AL . . . 116 B2
Leslie GB . . . 25 B4
Les Lucs-sur-Boulogne
 F . . . 66 B3
Les Mages F . . . 78 B3
Lesmahagow GB . . . 25 C4
Les Mazures F . . . 59 A5
Les Mées F . . . 79 B4
Lesmont F . . . 59 B5
Les Mureaux F . . . 58 B2
Leśna PL . . . 53 B5
Lešná SRB . . . 85 B4
Lesneven F . . . 56 B1
Leśniów Wielkopolski
 PL . . . 53 B5
Lesnoye RUS . . . 7 B13
Les Omergues F . . . 79 B4
Les Ormes-sur-Voulzie
 F . . . 59 B4
Les Orres F . . . 79 B5
Le Souquet F . . . 76 C1
Lesparre-Médoc F . . 66 C4
L'Espérance F . . . 59 A4
L'Esperou F . . . 78 B2
Les Pieux F . . . 57 A4
Les Ponts-de-Cé F . . 67 A4
Les Ponts-de-Martel
 CH . . . 70 B1
Les Praz F . . . 70 C1
L'Espunyola E . . . 91 A4
Les Riceys F . . . 59 C5
Les Roches F . . . 78 B3
Les Rosaires F . . . 56 B3
Les Rosiers F . . . 67 A4
Les Rousses F . . . 69 B6
Les Sables-d'Olonne
 F . . . 66 B3
Lessach A . . . 72 A3
Lessay F . . . 57 A4
Lessebo S . . . 40 C5
Les Settons F . . . 68 A4
Lessines B . . . 49 C4
L'Estany E . . . 91 B5
Les Ternes F . . . 78 A1
Lesterps F . . . 67 B5
Les Thilliers en-Vexin
 F . . . 58 A2
Les Touches F . . . 66 A3
Les Trois Moûtiers F . 67 A5
Les Vans F . . . 78 B3
Les Verrières CH . . . 70 B1
Les Vignes F . . . 78 B2
Leswalt GB . . . 24 D2
Leszno
 Mazowieckie PL . . 55 A5
 Wielkopolskie PL . . 54 B1
Leszno Górne PL . . . 53 B5
Letchworth GB . . . 31 C3
Le Teil F . . . 78 B3
Le Teilleul F . . . 57 B5
Le Temple-de-Bretagne
 F . . . 66 A3
Letenye H . . . 74 B1
Le Theil F . . . 58 B1
Le Thillot F . . . 60 C2
Letino I . . . 103 B7
Letohrad CZ . . . 54 C1
Le Touquet-Paris-Plage
 F . . . 48 C2
Le Touvet F . . . 69 C5
Letovice CZ . . . 64 A2
Le Translay F . . . 48 D2
Le Tréport F . . . 48 C2
Letschin D . . . 45 C6
Letterfrack IRL . . . 18 C2
Letterkenny IRL . . . 19 B4
Lettermacaward IRL . 18 B3
Lettoch GB . . . 23 D5
Letur E . . . 101 A4
Letux E . . . 90 B2
Letzlingen D . . . 44 C3
Leucate F . . . 78 D2
Leuchars GB . . . 25 B5
Leuglay F . . . 59 C5
Leuk CH . . . 70 B2
Leukerbad CH . . . 70 B2
Leumrabhagh GB . . . 22 C2
Leuna D . . . 52 B2
Leusden NL . . . 49 A6
Leutenberg D . . . 52 C1
Leutershausen D . . . 61 A6
Leutkirch D . . . 61 C6
Leuven B . . . 49 C6
Leuze-en-Hainaut B . 49 C4
Le Val F . . . 79 C5
Le Val-André F . . . 56 B3
Le Val-d'Ajol F . . . 60 C2
Levan AL . . . 105 C5
Levanger N . . . 114 D8
Levanjska Varoš HR . 74 C3
Lévanto I . . . 80 B3
Levaré F . . . 57 B5
Levata I . . . 71 C5
Leven
 East Yorkshire GB . 27 B5
 Fife GB . . . 25 B5

Leverano I . . . 105 C3
Le Verdon-sur-Mer F . 66 C3
Leverkusen D . . . 50 B2
Levern D . . . 43 C5
Le Vernet F . . . 79 B5
Levet F . . . 68 B2
Levice SK . . . 65 B4
Lévico Terme I . . . 71 B6
Levie F . . . 102 B2
Levier F . . . 69 B6
Le Vigan F . . . 78 C2
Lévignen F . . . 59 A3
le Ville I . . . 82 C1
Levinovac HR . . . 74 C2
Le Vivier-sur-Mer F . . 57 B4
Levoča SK . . . 65 A6
Levroux F . . . 67 B6
Lewes GB . . . 31 D4
Lewin Brzeski PL . . . 54 C2
Lewisham GB . . . 31 C3
Leyburn GB . . . 27 A4
Leyland GB . . . 26 B3
Leysdown-on-Sea GB . 31 C4
Leysin CH . . . 70 B2
Lezajsk PL . . . 11 A7
Lézardrieux F . . . 56 B2
Lézat-sur-Léze F . . . 77 C4
Lezay F . . . 67 B4
Lezhë AL . . . 105 B5
Lézignan-Corbières
 F . . . 78 C1
Lézignan-la-Cèbe F . 78 C2
Ležimir SRB . . . 75 C4
Lézinnes F . . . 59 C5
Lezoux F . . . 68 C3
Lezuza E . . . 95 C5
Lgov RUS . . . 7 F13
Lhenice CZ . . . 63 B5
Lherm F . . . 77 C4
Lhommaizé F . . . 67 B5
L'Hospitalet F . . . 91 A4
L'Hospitalet de l'Infant
 E . . . 90 C3
L'Hospitalet de Llobregat
 E . . . 91 B5
Lhuître F . . . 59 B5
Liancourt F . . . 58 A3
Liart F . . . 59 A5
Liatorp S . . . 40 C4
Liatrie GB . . . 22 D4
Libáň CZ . . . 53 C5
Libceves CZ . . . 53 C3
Líbchov CZ . . . 53 C4
Liber E . . . 86 B3
Liberec CZ . . . 53 C4
Libiąż PL . . . 55 C4
Libina CZ . . . 64 A3
Libochovice CZ . . . 53 C4
Libohová AL . . . 116 B2
Libourne F . . . 76 B2
Libramont B . . . 59 A6
Librazhd AL . . . 116 A2
Librilla E . . . 101 B4
Libros E . . . 96 A1
Licata I . . . 108 B2
Licciana Nardi I . . . 81 B4
Licenza I . . . 102 A5
Lich D . . . 51 C4
Lichères-près-Aigremont
 F . . . 59 C4
Lichfield GB . . . 27 C4
Lichtenau
 A . . . 63 B6
 D . . . 51 B4
Lichtenberg D . . . 52 C1
Lichtenfels D . . . 52 C1
Lichtensteig CH . . . 71 A4
Lichtenstein D . . . 52 C2
Lichtenvoorde NL . . . 50 B2
Lichtervelde B . . . 49 B4
Lička Jesenica HR . . 83 A4
Lickershamn S . . . 37 E5
Ličko Lešce HR . . . 83 B4
Licodia Eubéa I . . . 109 B3
Licques F . . . 48 C2
Lida BY . . . 7 E8
Lidečko CZ . . . 64 A4
Liden S . . . 115 E13
Lidhult S . . . 40 C3
Lidköping S . . . 35 D5
Lido I . . . 72 C2
Lido Azzurro I . . . 104 C3
Lido degli Estensi I . . 82 B1
Lido degli Scacchi I . . 82 B1
Lido della Nazioni I . . 82 B1
Lido di Camaiore I . . 81 C4
Lido di Casalbordino
 I . . . 103 A7
Lido di Castél Fusano
 I . . . 102 B5
Lido di Cincinnato I . . 102 B5
Lido di Classe I . . . 82 B1
Lido di Fermo I . . . 82 C2
Lido di Fondi I . . . 103 B6
Lido di Jésolo I . . . 72 C2
Lido di Licola I . . . 103 C7
Lido di Metaponto I . . 104 C2
Lido di Óstia I . . . 102 B5
Lido di Policoro I . . . 106 A3
Lido di Pompéia I . . . 82 B1
Lido di Savio I . . . 82 B1
Lido di Scanzano I . . 104 C2
Lido di Siponto I . . . 104 B1
Lido di Squillace I . . . 106 C3
Lido di Volano I . . . 82 B1
Lido Riccio I . . . 103 A7
Lidoriki GR . . . 116 D4
Lido Silvana I . . . 104 C3
Lidsjöberg S . . . 115 C12
Lidzbark PL . . . 47 B6
Lidzbark Warmiński
 PL . . . 47 A6
Liebenau
 A . . . 63 B5
 D . . . 43 C6
Liebenwalde D . . . 45 C5
Lieberose D . . . 53 B4
Liebling RO . . . 75 C6
Lieboch A . . . 73 B5
Liège B . . . 49 C6
Lieksa FIN . . . 3 E29
Lienen D . . . 50 A3
Lienz A . . . 72 B2
Liepāja LV . . . 6 C6
Lier B . . . 49 B5
Lierbyen N . . . 34 C2
Liernais F . . . 69 A4
Liesing A . . . 72 B2
Liestal CH . . . 70 A2
Liétor E . . . 101 A4
Lieurac F . . . 77 D4
Lieurey F . . . 58 A1
Liévin F . . . 48 C3
Liezen A . . . 73 A4
Liffol-le-Grand F . . . 60 B1
Lifford IRL . . . 19 B4
Liffré F . . . 57 B4
Ligardes F . . . 77 B3
Lignano Sabbiadoro I . 72 C3
Ligné F . . . 66 A3
Lignières F . . . 68 B2
Ligny-en-Barrois F . . 59 B6
Ligny-le-Châtel F . . . 59 C4
Ligoła Polska PL . . . 54 B2
Ligourio GR . . . 117 E5
Ligowo PL . . . 47 C5
Ligueil F . . . 67 B5
Likavka SK . . . 65 A5
Likenäs S . . . 34 B5
Likhoslavl RUS . . . 7 D13
Lild Strand DK . . . 38 B1
Lilienfeld A . . . 63 B6
Lilienthal D . . . 43 B5

Lilla Edet S . . . 35 D4
Lilla Tjärby S . . . 40 C3
Lille
 B . . . 49 B5
 F . . . 49 C4
Lillebonne F . . . 58 A1
Lillehammer N . . . 34 A2
Lillerød DK . . . 41 D2
Lillers F . . . 48 C3
Lillesand N . . . 33 D5
Lillestrøm N . . . 34 C3
Lillhärad S . . . 115 F11
Lillkyrka S . . . 37 C4
Lillo E . . . 95 C3
Lillögda S . . . 115 C14
Lima S . . . 34 B5
Limanowa PL . . . 65 A6
Limassol CY . . . 120 B2
Limavady GB . . . 19 A5
Limbach-Oberfrohna
 D . . . 52 C2
Limbaži LV . . . 6 C8
Limburg D . . . 50 C4
Limedsforsen S . . . 34 B5
Limenaria GR . . . 116 B6
Limenas Chersonisou
 GR . . . 117 G7
Limerick IRL . . . 20 B3
Limes I . . . 71 C5
Limésy F . . . 58 A1
Limmared S . . . 40 B3
Limni GR . . . 116 D5
Limoges F . . . 67 C6
Limogne-en-Quercy F . 77 B4
Limoise F . . . 68 B3
Limone Piemonte I . . 80 B1
Limone sul Garda I . . 71 C5
Limons F . . . 68 C3
Limours F . . . 58 B3
Limoux F . . . 77 D5
Linares E . . . 100 A2
Linares de Mora E . . 90 C2
Linares de Riofrio E . 93 A5
Linaria GR . . . 116 D6
Linas de Broto E . . . 90 A2
Lincoln GB . . . 27 B5
Lind DK . . . 39 C1
Lindás N . . . 32 B2
Lindau D . . . 71 A4
Lindberget N . . . 34 A3
Lindelse DK . . . 39 E3
Linden D . . . 53 A4
Lindenberg D . . . 45 C6
Lindenberg im Allgäu
 D . . . 61 C5
Lindern D . . . 43 C4
Lindesberg D . . . 37 C2
Lindesnäs S . . . 36 B1
Lindholmen S . . . 37 C5
Lindknud DK . . . 39 D2
Lindö S . . . 37 D3
Lindome S . . . 38 B5
Lindos GR . . . 119 F3
Lindoso P . . . 87 C2
Lindow D . . . 45 C4
Lindsdal S . . . 40 C6
Lindshammar S . . . 40 B5
Lindstedt D . . . 44 C3
Lindved DK . . . 39 D2
Liné CZ . . . 63 A4
Lingbo S . . . 36 A3
Lingen D . . . 43 C4
Linghed S . . . 36 B2
Linghem S . . . 37 D2
Linguaglossa I . . . 109 B4
Linia PL . . . 46 A3
Linie PL . . . 45 B6
Liniewo PL . . . 47 A4
Linken D . . . 45 B6
Linlithgow GB . . . 25 C4
Linneryd S . . . 40 C5
Linnes Hammarby S . 36 C4
Linnich D . . . 50 C2
Linsell S . . . 115 E10
Linslade GB . . . 31 C3
Linthal CH . . . 70 B4
Linyola E . . . 90 B3
Linz
 A . . . 63 B5
 D . . . 50 C3
Liomseter N . . . 32 A6
Lionárisso CY . . . 120 A3
Lioni I . . . 103 C8
Lion-sur-Mer F . . . 57 A5
Lipany SK . . . 65 A6
Lipar SRB . . . 75 C4
Lípari I . . . 106 C1
Lipcani MD . . . 11 B9
Liperi FIN . . . 3 E28
Liphook GB . . . 31 C3
Lipiany PL . . . 45 B6
Lipik HR . . . 74 C2
Lipka PL . . . 46 B3
Lipki Wielkie PL . . . 46 C1
Lipnica PL . . . 46 B3
Lipnica Murowana PL . 65 A6
Lipnik PL . . . 55 C6
Lipník nad Bečvou
 CZ . . . 64 A3
Lipno
 Kujawsko-Pomorskie
 PL . . . 47 C5
 Łódzkie PL . . . 54 B3
Liposthey F . . . 76 B2
Lipovac HR . . . 84 A4
Lipovec CZ . . . 64 A2
Lipovljani HR . . . 74 C1
Lipowiec PL . . . 47 B7
Lipowina PL . . . 47 A6
Lippborg D . . . 50 B4
Lippó H . . . 74 C3
Lippoldsberg D . . . 51 B5
Lippstadt D . . . 51 B4
Lipsko PL . . . 55 B6
Liptál CZ . . . 64 A3
Liptovská-Lúžna SK . 65 B5
Liptovská Osada SK . 65 B5
Liptovská-Teplička
 SK . . . 65 B6
Liptovský Hrádok SK . 65 A5
Liptovský Milkuláš
 SK . . . 65 A5
Lipusz PL . . . 46 A3
Liré F . . . 66 A3
Lisac BIH . . . 84 B2
Lisbellaw GB . . . 19 B4
Lisboa = Lisbon P . . 92 C1
Lisbon = Lisboa P . . 92 C1
Lisburn GB . . . 19 B5
Liscannor IRL . . . 20 B2
Lisdoonvarna IRL . . . 20 A2
Lisewo PL . . . 47 B4
Lisia Góra PL . . . 55 C5
Lisięcice PL . . . 54 C2
Lisieux F . . . 57 A6
Lisjö S . . . 37 C3
Liskeard GB . . . 28 C3
Liskova SK . . . 65 A5
L'Isle CH . . . 69 B6
L'Isle-Adam F . . . 58 A3
L'Isle-de-Noé F . . . 77 C3
L'Isle-en-Dodon F . . 77 C3
L'Isle-Jourdain
 Gers F . . . 77 C4
 Vienne F . . . 67 B5
L'Isle-sur-la-Sorgue F . 79 C4
L'Isle-sur-le-Doubs F . 70 A1
L'Isle-sur-Serein F . . 59 C4
Lisle-sur-Tarn F . . . 77 C4
Lismore IRL . . . 21 B4
Lišnja BIH . . . 84 B2
Lisów
 Lubuskie PL . . . 45 C6

Lisów continued
 Śląskie PL . . . 54 C3
Lisse NL . . . 49 A5
Lissycasey IRL . . . 20 B2
List D . . . 39 D1
Listerby S . . . 41 C5
Listowel IRL . . . 20 B2
Listrac-Médoc F . . . 76 B2
Liszki PL . . . 55 C4
Liszkowo PL . . . 46 B3
Lit S . . . 115 D11
Litava SK . . . 65 B5
Litcham GB . . . 30 B4
Lit-et-Mixe F . . . 76 B1
Litija SLO . . . 73 B4
Litke H . . . 65 B5
Litlabø N . . . 32 C2
Litochoro GR . . . 116 B4
Litoměřice CZ . . . 53 C4
Litomyšl CZ . . . 64 A2
Litovel CZ . . . 64 A3
Litschau A . . . 63 B6
Littlehampton GB . . . 31 D3
Littleport GB . . . 30 B4
Littleton IRL . . . 21 B4
Little Walsingham GB . 30 B4
Litvínov CZ . . . 52 C3
Livadero GR . . . 116 B3
Livadhia CY . . . 120 B2
Livadia GR . . . 116 D4
Livarot F . . . 57 B6
Liveras CY . . . 120 A1
Livernon F . . . 77 B4
Liverovici MNE . . . 85 D4
Liverpool GB . . . 26 B3
Livigno I . . . 71 B5
Livingston GB . . . 25 C4
Livno BIH . . . 84 C1
Livold SLO . . . 73 C4
Livorno I . . . 81 C4
Livorno Ferraris I . . . 70 C3
Livron-sur-Drôme F . 78 B3
Livry-Louvercy F . . . 59 A5
Lixheim F . . . 60 B3
Lixouri GR . . . 117 D2
Lizard GB . . . 28 D2
Lizy-sur-Ourcq F . . . 59 A4
Lizzano I . . . 104 C3
Lizzano in Belvedere
 I . . . 81 B4
Ljesane KOS . . . 85 D5
Ljig SRB . . . 85 B5
Ljørdalen N . . . 34 A4
Ljosland N . . . 33 D4
Ljubija BIH . . . 83 B5
Ljubinje BIH . . . 84 D3
Ljubljana SLO . . . 73 B4
Ljubno ob Savinji
 SLO . . . 73 B4
Ljubovija SRB . . . 85 B4
Ljubuški BIH . . . 84 C2
Ljugarn S . . . 37 E5
Ljung S . . . 40 B3
Ljunga S . . . 37 D3
Ljungaverk S . . . 115 E13
Ljungby S . . . 40 C3
Ljungbyhed S . . . 41 C3
Ljungbyholm S . . . 40 C6
Ljungdalen S . . . 115 E9
Ljungsarp S . . . 40 B3
Ljungsbro S . . . 37 D2
Ljungskile S . . . 35 D3
Ljusdal S . . . 115 F13
Ljusfallshammar S . . 37 D2
Ljusne S . . . 36 A4
Ljusterö S . . . 37 C5
Ljutomer SLO . . . 73 B6
Llagostera E . . . 91 B5
Llanaelhaiarn GB . . . 26 C1
Llanarth GB . . . 28 A3
Llanbedr GB . . . 26 C1
Llanbedrog GB . . . 26 B1
Llanberis GB . . . 26 B1
Llanbrynmair GB . . . 26 C2
Llançà E . . . 91 A6
Llandeilo GB . . . 28 B4
Llandissilio GB . . . 28 B3
Llandovery GB . . . 28 B4
Llandrillo GB . . . 26 C2
Llandrindod Wells
 GB . . . 29 A4
Llandudno GB . . . 26 B2
Llandysul GB . . . 28 B2
Llanelli GB . . . 28 B3
Llanerchymedd GB . . 26 B1
Llanes E . . . 88 A2
Llanfair Caereinion
 GB . . . 26 C2
Llanfairfechan GB . . 26 B2
Llanfyllin GB . . . 26 C2
Llangadog GB . . . 28 B4
Llangefni GB . . . 26 B1
Llangollen GB . . . 26 C2
Llangrannog GB . . . 28 A3
Llangurig GB . . . 29 A4
Llanidloes GB . . . 26 C2
Llanilar GB . . . 28 A3
Llanrhystud GB . . . 28 A3
Llanrwst GB . . . 26 B2
Llansannan GB . . . 26 B2
Llansawel GB . . . 28 A4
Llanstephan GB . . . 28 B3
Llanteno E . . . 89 A3
Llanthony GB . . . 29 B4
Llantrisant GB . . . 29 B4
Llantwit-Major GB . . 29 B4
Llanuwchllyn GB . . . 26 C2
Llanwddyn GB . . . 26 C2
Llanwrda GB . . . 28 B4
Llanwrtyd Wells GB . 28 A4
Llanybydder GB . . . 28 A3
Llanymynech GB . . . 26 C2
Llavorsí E . . . 91 A4
Lleida E . . . 90 B3
Llera E . . . 93 C4
Llerena E . . . 99 A5
Lles E . . . 91 A4
Llessui E . . . 91 A4
Llinars E . . . 91 A4
Lliria E . . . 96 B2
Llivia E . . . 91 A5
Lloret de Mar E . . . 91 B5
Llosa de Ranes E . . 96 B2
Llucena del Cid E . . 96 A2
Llucmajor E . . . 97 B2
Llutxent E . . . 96 C2
Llwyngwril GB . . . 26 C1
Llyswen GB . . . 29 A4
Lnáře CZ . . . 63 A4
Loanhead GB . . . 25 C4
Loano I . . . 80 B2
Loarre E . . . 90 A2
Löbau D . . . 53 B4
Löbejün D . . . 52 B1
Lobenstein D . . . 52 C1
Löberöd S . . . 41 D3
Łobez PL . . . 45 B7
Löbnitz D . . . 45 A4
Lobón E . . . 93 C4
Loburg D . . . 52 A2
Łobżenica PL . . . 46 B3
Locana I . . . 70 C2
Locarno CH . . . 70 B3
Loccum D . . . 43 C6
Loče SLO . . . 73 B5
Lochailort GB . . . 24 B2
Lochaline GB . . . 24 B2
Lochans GB . . . 24 D2
Locharbriggs GB . . . 25 C4
Lochau A . . . 71 A4
Loch Baghasdail GB . 22 D1
Lochcarron GB . . . 22 D3
Lochearnhead GB . . 24 B3
Lochem NL . . . 50 A2
Loches F . . . 67 A5

Lochgelly GB 25 B4
Lochgilphead GB . . . 24 B2
Lochgoilhead GB . . . 24 B3
Lochinver GB 22 C3
Loch nam Madadh
  GB 22 D1
Lochranza GB 24 C2
Ločika SRB 85 C6
Lockenhaus A 73 A6
Lockerbie GB 25 C4
Löcknitz D 45 B6
Locmaria F 66 A1
Locmariaquer F 56 C3
Locminé F 56 C3
Locorotondo I 104 C3
Locquirec F 56 B2
Locri I 106 C3
Locronan F 56 B1
Loctudy F 56 C1
Lodares de Osma E . . 89 C4
Lodé I 110 B2
Lodeinoye Pole RUS . 7 A12
Lodève F 78 C2
Lodi I 71 C4
Løding N 112 E3
Lødingen N 112 D4
Lodosa E 89 B4
Lødøse S 38 A5
Łódź PL 55 B4
Loeches E 95 B3
Løfallstrand N 32 B2
Lofer A 62 C3
Lofsdalen S 115 E10
Loftahammar S 40 B6
Lofthus N 32 B3
Loftus GB 27 A5
Loga N 33 D3
Logatec SLO 73 C4
Løgdeå S 115 D16
Lograto I 71 C5
Logroño E 89 B4
Logrosán E 93 B5
Løgstør DK 38 C2
Løgumgårde DK 39 D1
Løgumkloster DK . . . 39 D1
Lohals DK 39 D3
Lohiniva FIN 113 E14
Lohja FIN 6 A8
Löhlbach D 51 B4
Lohmen
  Mecklenburg-
  Vorpommern D . . . 44 B3
  Sachsen D 53 C4
Löhnberg D 50 C4
Löhne D 43 C5
Lohne D 43 C5
Lohr D 51 C5
Lohra D 51 C4
Lohsa D 53 B4
Loiano I 81 B5
Loimaa FIN 3 F25
Lóiri I 110 B2
Loitz D 45 B5
Loivos P 87 C3
Loivos do Monte P . . 87 C3
Loja E 100 B1
Lojanice SRB 85 B4
Lojsta S 37 E5
Løjt Kirkeby DK . . . 39 D2
Lok SK 65 B4
Lokca SK 65 A5
Løken N 34 C3
Lokeren B 49 B4
Loket CZ 52 C2
Lokhvitsa UA 11 A12
Lokka FIN 113 E16
Løkken
  DK 38 B2
  N 114 D6
Loknya RUS 7 C11
Lökösháza H 75 B6
Lokot RUS 7 E13
Lokve SRB 75 C6
Lollar D 51 C4
L'Olleria E 96 C2
Lölling-Graben A . . . 73 B4
Lom
  BG 11 E7
  N 114 F5
  SK 65 B5
Lombez F 77 C3
Lomello I 80 A2
Łomianki PL 55 A5
Lomma S 41 D3
Lommaryd S 40 B4
Lommatzsch D 52 B3
Lommel B 49 B6
Lommersum D 50 C2
Lomnice CZ 63 A5
Lomnice nad Lužnicí
  CZ 63 A5
Lomnice nad Popelkou
  CZ 53 C5
Lompolo FIN 113 D13
Łomża PL 6 E7
Lonashult S 40 C4
Lønborg DK 39 D1
Londerzeel B 49 B5
Londinières F 58 A2
London GB 31 C3
Lonevåg N 32 B2
Longa GR 117 F3
Longare I 72 C1
Longares E 90 B1
Longarone I 72 B2
Longastrino I 81 B6
Long Bennington GB . 27 C5
Longbenton GB 25 C6
Longchamp-sur-Aujon
  F 59 B5
Longchaumois F 69 B5
Long Eaton GB 27 C4
Longeau F 59 C6
Longecourt-en-Plaine
  F 69 A5
Longeville-les-St Avold
  F 60 A2
Longeville-sur-Mer F . 66 B3
Longford IRL 19 C4
Longframlington GB . 25 C6
Longhope GB 23 C5
Longhorsley GB 25 C6
Longhoughton GB . . . 25 C6
Longi I 109 A3
Long Melford GB . . . 30 B4
Longny-au-Perche F . . 58 B1
Longobucco I 106 B3
Long Preston GB . . . 26 A3
Longré F 67 B4
Longridge GB 26 B3
Longroiva P 87 D3
Long Sutton GB 30 B4
Longtown
  Cumbria GB 25 C5
  Herefordshire GB . 29 B5
Longueau F 58 A3
Longué-Jumelles F . . 67 A4
Longuyon F 60 A1
Longvic F 69 A5
Longvilly B 60 A1
Longwy F 60 A1
Lonigo I 71 C6
Löningen D 43 C4
Lonja HR 74 C1
Lönsboda S 40 C4
Lønset N 114 E6
Lons-le-Saunier F . . 69 B5
Lønstrup DK 38 B2
Looe GB 28 C3
Loone-Plage F 48 B3
Loon op Zand NL . . . 49 B6
Lo Pagán E 101 B5
Lopar HR 83 B3
Lopare BIH 84 B3
Lopera E 100 B1
Lopigna F 102 A1
Loppersum NL 42 B3
Łopuszna PL 65 A5
Łopuszno PL 55 C5
Lor F 59 A5

Lora N 114 E5
Lora de Estepa E . . . 100 B1
Lora del Río E 99 B5
Loranca del Campo E . 95 B4
Lorbé E 86 A2
Lörby S 41 C4
Lorca E 101 B4
Lorch D 50 C3
Lørenfallet N 34 B3
Lørenskog N 34 C2
Loreo I 82 A1
Loreto I 82 C2
Lorgues F 79 C5
Lorica I 106 B3
Lorient F 56 C2
Lorignac F 67 C4
Lőrinci H 65 C5
Loriol-sur-Drôme F . . 78 B3
Lormes F 68 A3
Loro Ciuffenna I . . . 81 C5
Lorqui E 101 A4
Lörrach D 60 C3
Lorrez-le-Bocage F . . 59 B3
Lorris F 59 C3
Lorup D 43 C4
Łoś PL 55 B5
Losacino E 87 C4
Los Alcázares E . . . 101 B5
Los Arcos E 89 B4
Los Barios de Luna E . 88 B1
Los Barrios E 99 C5
Los Caños de Meca
  E 99 C4
Los Cerricos E 101 B3
Los Corrales E 100 B1
Los Corrales de Buelna
  E 88 A2
Los Dolores E 101 B4
Losenstein A 63 C5
Los Gallardos E . . . 101 B4
Losheim
  Nordrhein-Westfalen
  D 50 C2
  Saarland D 60 A2
Los Hinojosos E . . . 95 C4
Los Isidros E 96 B1
Los Molinos E 94 B2
Los Morales E 99 B5
Los Navalmorales E . . 94 C2
Los Navalucillos E . . 94 C2
Losne F 69 A5
Los Nietos E 101 B5
Løsning DK 39 D2
Los Palacios y Villafranca
  E 99 B5
Los Pozuelos de
  Calatrava E 100 A1
Los Rábanos E 89 C4
Los Santos E 93 A5
Los Santos de la Humosa
  E 95 B3
Los Santos de Maimona
  E 93 C4
Lossburg D 61 B4
Losse F 76 B2
Losser NL 50 A3
Lossiemouth GB 23 D5
Lössnitz D 52 C2
Loštice CZ 64 A2
Los Tijos E 88 A2
Lostwithiel GB 28 C3
Los Villares E 100 B2
Los Yébenes E 94 C3
Løten N 34 B3
Lotorp S 37 D2
Lottefors S 36 A3
Löttorp S 41 B7
Lotyń PL 46 B2
Lotzorai I 110 C2
Louargat F 56 B2
Loudéac F 56 B3
Loudun F 67 A5
Loué F 57 C5
Loughborough GB . . . 27 C4
Loughbrickland GB . . 19 B5
Loughrea IRL 20 A3
Louhans F 69 B5
Louisburgh IRL 18 C2
Loukhi RUS 3 C10
Loulay F 67 B4
Loulé P 98 B2
Lourdes F 76 C2
Lourenzá E 86 A3
Loures P 92 C1
Loures-Barousse F . . 77 C3
Louriçal P 92 B1
Lourinhã P 92 B1
Lourmarin F 79 C4
Loury F 58 C3
Lousa
  Bragança P 87 C3
  Castelo Branco P . 92 B3
Lousã P 92 A2
Lousada
  E 86 B3
  P 87 C2
Louth GB 27 B5
Loutra Edipsou GR . . 116 D5
Loutraki GR 117 E4
Loutropoli Thermis
  GR 118 C1
Louverné F 57 B5
Louvie-Juzon F 76 C2
Louviers F 58 A2
Louvigné-du-Désert
  F 57 B4
Louvois F 59 A5
Lova I 72 C2
Lovasberény H 74 A3
Lövåsen S 34 C5
Lövászatona H 74 A2
Lövberga S 115 D12
Lovech BG 11 E8
Lovere I 71 C4
Lóvero I 71 B5
Lovikka S 113 E11
Lovisa FIN 117 A8
Lovništvo...
Lovosice CZ 53 C4
Lovozero RUS 3 C31
Lovran HR 73 C4
Lovreć HR 84 C1
Lovrenc na Pohorju
  SLO 73 B5
Lovrin RO 75 C5
Lövstabruk S 36 B4
Löwenberg D 45 C5
Lowestoft GB 30 B5
Lowick GB 25 C6
Łowicz PL 55 A4
Loxstedt D 43 B5
Lož SLO 73 C4
Loza CZ 63 A4
Łozina PL 54 B2
Lozničko Polje SRB . 85 B4
Loznica SRB 85 B4
Lozovik SRB 85 B6
Lozoya E 94 B3
Lozoyuela E 95 B3
Lozzo di Cadore I . . 72 B2
Luanco E 88 A1
Luarca E 86 A4
Lubaczów PL 11 A7
Lubań PL 53 B5
Lubanów PL 55 B4
Lubars D 52 A2
Lubartów PL 6 E7
Lubasz PL 46 C2
Lubawa PL 47 B5
Lubawka PL 53 C6

Lübbecke D 51 A4
Lübben D 53 B3
Lübbenau D 53 B3
Lübczyna PL 45 B6
Lübeck D 44 B2
Lubenec CZ 52 C3
Lubersac F 67 C6
Lübesse D 44 B3
Lubia E 89 C4
Lubian E 87 B4
Lubiatowo PL 45 B7
Lubichowo PL 47 B4
Lubicz Dolny PL . . . 47 B4
Lubień PL 65 A5
Lubienia PL 55 B6
Lubień Kujawski PL . 47 C5
Lubieszewo PL 46 B1
Lubin
  Dolnośląskie PL . 53 B6
  Zachodnio-Pomorskie
  PL 45 B6
Lublin PL 11 A7
Lubliniec PL 54 C3
Lubmin D 45 A5
Lubniewice PL 46 C1
Lubny UA 11 A12
Lubochnia PL 55 B5
Lubomierz
  Dolnośląskie PL . 53 B5
  Małopolskie PL . . 65 A6
Lubomino PL 47 A6
Luboń PL 54 A1
Łubowo
  Wielkopolskie PL . 46 C3
  Zachodnio-Pomorskie
  PL 46 B2
Lubraniec PL 47 C4
Lubrin E 101 B3
Lubrza PL 54 C2
Lubsko PL 53 B4
Lübtheen D 44 B3
Lubuczewo PL 46 A3
Luby CZ 52 C2
Lübz D 44 B4
Luc F 78 B3
Lucainena de las Torres
  E 101 B3
Lucan IRL 21 A5
Lučani SRB 85 C5
Lúcar E 101 B3
Luçay-le-Mâle F . . . 67 A6
Lucca I 81 C4
Lucciana F 102 A2
Lucé F 58 B2
Luče SLO 73 B4
Lucena
  Córdoba E 100 B1
  Huelva E 99 B4
Lucena del Cid E . . . 96 A2
Lucenay-les-Aix F . . 68 B3
Lucenay-l'Évéque F . 69 A4
Luc-en-Diois F 79 B4
Lucens CH 70 B1
Lucera I 103 B8
Luceram F 80 C1
Lüchow D 44 C3
Luciana E 94 D2
Lucignano I 81 C5
Lucija SLO 72 C3
Lucka D 52 B2
Luckau D 53 B3
Luckenwalde D 52 A3
Lückstedt D 44 C3
Luco dei Marsi I . . . 103 B6
Luçon F 66 B3
Luc-sur-Mer F 57 A5
Ludanice SK 64 B4
Ludbreg HR 74 B1
Lüdenscheid D 50 B3
Lüderitz D 44 C3
Lüdersdorf D 44 B2
Ludgo S 37 D4
Ludlow GB 26 C3
Ludomy PL 46 C2
Ludvika S 36 B2
Ludweiler Warndt D . 60 A2
Ludwigsburg D 61 B5
Ludwigsfelde D 52 A3
Ludwigshafen D 61 A4
Ludwigslust D 44 B3
Ludwigsstadt D 52 C1
Ludza LV 7 C9
Luesia E 90 A1

Lundsberg S 35 C6
Lüneburg D 44 B2
Lunel F 78 C3
Lünen D 50 B3
Lunéville F 60 B2
Lungern CH 70 B3
Lungro I 106 B3
Luninyets BY 7 E9
Linne D 43 C4
Lunner N 34 B2
Lunteren NL 49 A6
Lunz am See A 63 C6
Luogosanto I 110 A2
Łupawa PL 46 A3
Lupión E 100 A2
Lupoglav HR 73 C4
Luppa D 52 B2
Lupsa RO 11 C7
Lurago d'Erba I . . . 71 C4
Lúras I 110 B2
Lurcy-Lévis F 68 B2
Lure F 60 C2
Lurgan GB 19 B5
Luri F 102 A2
Lury-sur-Arnon F . . . 68 A2
Lušci Palanka BIH . . 83 B5
Lusévera I 72 B3
Lushnjë AL 105 C5
Lusignan F 67 B5
Lusigny-sur-Barse F . 59 B5
Lusnić BIH 84 C1
Luso P 92 A2
Lusówko PL 46 C2
Luspebryggan S 112 E8
Lüss D 44 C2
Lussac F 76 B2
Lussac-les-Châteaux
  F 67 B5
Lussac-les-Eglises F . 67 B6
Lussan F 78 B3
Lüssow D 44 B4
Lustenau A 71 A4
Luštěnice CZ 53 C4
Luster N 32 A4
Lutago I 72 B1
Lutherstadt Wittenberg
  D 52 B2
Lütjenburg D 44 A2
Lutnes N 34 A4
Lutocin PL 47 C5
Lutomiersk PL 55 B4
Luton GB 31 C3
Lutry
  CH 70 B1
  PL 47 A6
Lutsk UA 11 A8
Lutter am Barenberge
  D 51 B6
Lutterworth GB 30 B2
Lututów PL 54 B3
Lützen D 52 B2
Lutzow D 44 B3
Luusua FIN 113 F16
Luvos S 112 F7
Luxembourg L 60 A2
Luxeuil-les-Bains F . 60 C2
Luxey F 76 B2
Luz
  Évora P 92 C3
  Faro P 98 B3
  Faro P 98 B2
Luzarches F 58 A3
Luže CZ 64 A2
Luzech F 77 B4
Luzern CH 70 A3
Luzino PL 47 A4
Luz-St Sauveur F . . . 76 D2
Luzy F 68 B3
Luzzi I 106 B3
L'viv UA 11 B8
Lwówek PL 46 C2
Lwówek Śląski PL . . 53 B5
Lyakhavichy BY 7 E9
Lybster GB 23 C5
Lychen D 45 B5
Lychkova RUS 7 C12
Lyckeby S 41 C5
Lycksele S 115 C15
Lydd GB 31 D4
Lydford GB 28 C3
Lydney GB 29 B5
Lyepyel BY 7 D10
Lygna N 34 B2
Lykkja N 32 B5
Lykling N 33 C2
Lyme Regis GB 29 C5
Lymington GB 31 D2
Lympne GB 31 C5
Lyngdal
  Buskerud N 32 C6
  Vest-Agder N . . . 33 D4
Lyngør N 33 D6
Lyngsa DK 38 B3
Lyngseidet N 112 C8
Lyngsnes N 114 C8
Lynmouth GB 28 B4
Lynton GB 28 B4
Lyntupy BY 7 D9
Lyon F 69 C4
Lyons-la-Forêt F . . . 58 A2
Lyozna BY 7 D11
Lyrestad S 35 D6
Lysá nad Labem CZ . . 53 C4
Lysá pod Makytou SK . 64 A4
Lysebotn N 33 D3
Lysekil S 35 D3
Lysice CZ 64 A2
Lysomice PL 47 B4
Lysøysund N 114 D6
Lysvik S 34 B5
Łyszkowice PL 55 A4
Lytham St Anne's GB . 26 B2
Lyuban RUS 7 B11
Lyubertsy RUS 7 D14
Lyubomi UA 11 A8
Lyubytino RUS 7 B12
Lyudinovo RUS 7 E13

M

Maaninkavaara FIN . . 113 F17
Maarheeze NL 50 B1
Maaseik B 50 B1
Maastricht NL 50 C1
Mablethorpe GB 27 B6
Macael E 101 B3
Maçanet de Cabrenys
  E 91 A5
Mação P 92 B2
Macau F 76 A2
Maccagno-Agra I . . . 70 B3
Maccarese I 102 B5
Macchiagódena I . . . 103 B7
Macclesfield GB . . . 26 B3
Macduff GB 23 D6
Maceda E 87 B3
Macedo de Cavaleiros
  P 87 C4
Maceira
  Guarda P 92 A3
  Leiria P 92 B1
Macelj HR 73 B5
Macerata I 82 C2
Macerata Féltria I . . 82 C1
Machault F 59 A5
Machecoul F 66 B3
Mchowo PL 47 B6
Machrihanish GB . . . 24 C2
Machynlleth GB 26 C2
Macieira P 87 C2
Maciejowice PL 55 B6
Macinaggio F 102 A2
Mackenrode D 51 B6
Mačkovci SLO 73 B6
Macomer I 110 B1

Macon B 49 C5
Mâcon F 69 B4
Macotera E 94 B1
Macroom IRL 20 C3
Macugnaga I 70 C2
Mädängsholm S 35 D5
Madaras H 75 B4
Maddaloni I 103 B7
Made NL 49 B5
Madeley GB 26 C3
Maderuelo E 89 C3
Madetkoski FIN 113 E15
Madley GB 29 A5
Madocsa H 74 B3
Madona LV 7 C9
Madonna di Campiglio
  I 71 B5
Madrid E 94 B3
Madridejos E 95 C3
Madrigal de las Altas
  Torres E 94 A1
Madrigal de la Vera E . 93 A5
Madrigalejo E 93 B5
Madrigalejo de Monte
  E 88 B3
Madriguera E 89 C3
Madrigueras E 95 C5
Madroñera E 93 B5
Mael-Carhaix F 56 B2
Maella E 90 B3
Maello E 94 B2
Maesteg GB 29 B4
Mafra P 92 C1
Magacela E 93 C5
Magallón E 89 C5
Magaluf E 97 B2
Magán E 94 C3
Magaña E 89 C4
Magasa I 71 C5
Magaz E 88 C2
Magdeburg D 52 A1
Magenta I 70 C3
Magescq F 76 C1
Maghera GB 19 B5
Magherafelt GB 19 B5
Maghull GB 26 B3
Magilligan GB 19 A5
Magione I 82 C1
Maglaj BIH 84 B3
Maglehem S 41 D4
Magliano de'Marsi I . 103 A6
Magliano in Toscana
  I 102 A4
Magliano Sabina I . . 102 A5
Maglić SRB 75 C4
Maglie I 107 A5
Maglód H 75 A4
Magnac-Bourg F 67 C6
Magnac-Laval F 67 B6
Magnieres F 60 B2
Magnor N 34 C4
Magnuszew PL 55 B6
Magny-Cours F 68 B3
Magny-en-Vexin F . . 58 A2
Magocs H 74 B3
Magoggia...
Maguiresbridge GB . . 19 B4
Magyarbóly H 74 C3
Magyarkeszi H 74 B3
Magyarszék H 74 B3
Mahala MNE 105 A5
Mahmudiye TR 118 C5
Mahora E 95 C5
Mahovo HR 73 C6
Mähring D 62 A3
Maia
  E 76 C1
  P 87 C2
Maiaelrayo E 95 A3
Maials E 90 B3
Maîche F 70 A1
Máida I 106 C3
Maiden Bradley GB . . 29 B5
Maidenhead GB 31 C3
Maiden Newton GB . . 29 C5
Maidstone GB 31 C4
Maienfeld CH 71 A4
Maignelay Montigny
  F 58 A3
Maijanen FIN 113 E14
Maillezais F 66 B4
Mailly-le-Camp F . . . 59 B5
Mailly-le-Château F . 59 C4
Mainar E 90 B1
Mainbernheim D 61 A6
Mainburg D 62 B2
Maintal D 51 C4
Maintenon F 58 B2
Mainvilliers F 58 B2
Mainz D 50 C4
Maiorca P 92 B2
Mairena de Aljarafe E . 99 B5
Mairena del Alcor E . 99 B5
Maisach D 62 B2
Maishofen A 72 A2
Maison-Rouge F 59 B4
Maissau A 64 B1
Maisse F 58 B3
Maizières-lès-Vic F . 60 B2
Maja HR 73 C6
Majadahonda E 94 B3
Majadas E 93 B5
Majavatn N 115 B10
Majs H 74 C3
Majšperk SLO 73 B5
Makarska HR 84 C2
Makkinga NL 42 C3
Maklár H 65 C6
Makó H 75 B5
Makoszyce PL 54 C2
Makov SK 65 A4
Makovac KOS 85 D6
Mąkowarsko PL 46 B3
Maków Podhalański
  PL 65 A5
Makrakomi GR 116 D4
Mala S 115 B15
Mala Bosna SRB 75 B4
Malacky SK 64 B3
Maladzyechna BY . . . 7 D9
Málaga E 100 C1
Malagón E 94 C3
Malaguilla E 95 B3
Malahide IRL 21 A5
Malaja Vishera RUS . 7 B12
Malalbergo I 81 B5
Malanow PL 54 B3
Malaucène F 79 B4
Malaunay F 58 A2
Mala Vyska UA 11 B11
Malborghetto I 72 B3
Malbork PL 47 A5
Malborn D 60 A2
Malbuisson F 69 B6
Malčésine I 71 C5
Malching D 63 B4
Malchin D 45 B4
Malchow D 45 B4
Malcocinado E 99 A5
Malczyce PL 54 B1
Maldegem B 49 B4
Maldon GB 31 C4
Małdyty PL 47 B5
Malè I 71 B5
Malemort F 67 C6
Malente D 44 A2
Målerås S 40 C5
Males GR 117 G7
Malesherbes F 58 B3
Malesina GR 116 D5
Malestroit F 56 C3

Maletto I 109 B3
Malexander S 40 A5
Malfa I 106 C1
Malgrat de Mar E . . . 91 B5
Malhadas P 87 C4
Malia
  CY 120 B1
  GR 117 G7
Malicorne-sur-Sarthe
  F 57 C5
Malijai F 79 B5
Malilĵos SRB 75 C4
Malilla S 40 B5
Mali Lošinj HR 83 B3
Malin IRL 19 A4
Málinec SK 65 B5
Malingsbo S 36 C2
Malinska HR 73 C4
Maliq AL 116 B2
Maljevac HR 73 C5
Malka TR 118 B1
Małki PL 47 B5
Malko Tarnovo BG . . 11 E9
Mallaig GB 22 D3
Mallén E 89 C5
Malléon F 77 C4
Mallersdorf-Pfaffenberg
  D 62 B3
Málles Venosta I . . . 71 B5
Malling DK 39 C3
Mallnitz A 72 B3
Mallow IRL 20 B3
Mallwyd GB 26 C2
Malm N 114 C8
Malmbäck S 40 B4
Malmberget S 112 E9
Malmby S 37 C4
Malmédy B 50 C2
Malmesbury GB 29 B5
Malmköping S 37 C3
Malmö S 41 D3
Malmon S 35 D3
Malmslätt S 37 D2
Malnate I 70 C3
Malo I 71 C6
Maloarkhangelsk
  RUS 7 E14
Małogoszcz PL 55 C5
Maloja CH 71 B4
Małomice PL 53 B5
Måløy N 114 F2
Maloyaroslavets RUS . 7 D14
Malpartida E 93 B4
Malpartida de la Serena
  E 93 C5
Malpartida de Plasencia
  E 93 B4
Malpas
  E 90 A3
  GB 26 B3
Malpica E 92 B3
Malpica de Bergantiños
  E 86 A2
Malpica de Tajo E . . 94 C2
Malsch D 61 B4
Malšice CZ 63 A5
Malta A 72 B3
Maltat F 68 B3
Maltby GB 27 B4
Malung S 34 B5
Malungsfors S 34 B5
Maluszów PL 45 C7
Maluszyn PL 55 C4
Malva E 88 C1
Malvaglia CH 70 B3
Malveira P 92 C1
Malvik N 114 D7
Malyn UA 11 A10
Mamarrosa P 92 A2
Mamer L 60 A2
Mamers F 58 B1
Mamirolle F 69 A6
Mammendorf D 62 B2
Mámmola I 106 C3
Mamoiada I 110 B2
Mamonovo RUS 47 A5
Mamuras AL 105 B5
Maña SK 65 B4
Mancera de Abajo E . 94 B1
Mancha Real E 100 B2
Manchester GB 26 B3
Manchita E 93 C4
Manciano I 102 A4
Manciet F 76 C3
Mandal N 33 D4
Mandanici I 109 A4
Mandas I 110 C2
Mandatoriccio I . . . 107 B3
Mandayona E 95 B4
Mandelieu-la-Napoule
  F 79 C5
Mandello del Lário I . 71 C4
Mandelsloh D 43 C6
Manderfeld B 50 C2
Manderscheid D 50 C2
Mandino Selo BIH . . 84 C2
Mandoudi GR 116 D5
Mandra GR 117 E5
Mandraki GR 119 F2
Mandúria I 104 C3
Mane
  Alpes-de-Haute-
  Provence F 79 C4
  Haute-Garonne F . 77 C3
Manérbio I 71 C5
Mañeru E 89 B5
Manetin CZ 52 B3
Manfredónia I 104 B1
Mangalia RO 11 E10
Manganeses de la
  Lampreana E . . . 88 C1
Manganeses de la
  Polvorosa E . . . 88 B1
Mangen N 34 C3
Manger N 32 B2
Mangiennes F 60 A1
Mango I 80 B2
Mangotsfield GB . . . 29 B5
Mangualde P 92 A3
Manhay B 50 C1
Maniago I 72 B2
Maniche P 92 B1
Manilva E 99 C5
Manisa TR 118 D2
Manises E 96 B2
Mank A 63 B6
Månkarbo S 36 B4
Manlleu E 91 A5
Manna DK 38 B2
Männedorf CH 70 A3
Mannersdorf am
  Leithagebirge A . 64 C2
Mannheim D 61 A4
Manningtree GB 31 C5
Manoppello I 103 A7
Manorbier GB 28 B3
Manorhamilton IRL . . 18 B3
Manosque F 79 C4
Manowo PL 46 A2
Manresa E 91 B4
Månsarp S 40 B4
Manschnow D 45 C6
Mansfeld D 52 B1
Mansfield GB 27 B4
Mansilla de Burgos E . 88 B3
Mansilla de las Mulas
  E 88 B1
Manskog S 35 C4
Mansle F 67 C5
Manso F 102 A1
Manteigas P 92 A3
Mantel D 62 A3
Mantes-la-Jolie F . . 58 B2
Mantes-la-Ville F . . 58 B2
Manthelan F 67 A5
Mantorp S 37 D2
Mántova I 71 C5

Manzal de Arriba E . . 87 B4
Manzanares E 95 C3
Manzanares el Real E . 94 B3
Manzaneda
  León E 87 B4
  Orense E 87 B3
Manzanedo E 88 B3
Manzaneque E 95 C4
Manzanera E 96 A2
Manzanilla E 99 B4
Manzat F 68 C2
Manziana I 102 A5
Manziat F 69 B5
Maó E 97 B4
Maoča BIH 84 B3
Maqueda E 94 B2
Mara E 89 C5
Maramaraereğlisi
  TR 118 B2
Marañón E 88 A1
Maranchón E 95 A4
Maranello I 81 B4
Marano Lagunare I . . 72 C3
Marans F 66 B3
Maratea I 106 B2
Marateca P 92 C2
Marathokambos GR . . 119 E1
Marathonas GR 117 E5
Marathóvouno CY . . . 120 A2
Marazion GB 28 C2
Marbach
  Baden-Württemberg
  D 61 B5
  Hessen D 51 C5
Marbäck S 40 B3
Marbella E 100 C1
Marboz F 69 B5
Marburg D 51 C4
Marcali H 74 B2
Marčana HR 82 B2
Marcaria I 81 A4
Marcelová SK 64 C4
Marcenat F 68 C2
March GB 30 B4
Marchamalo E 95 B3
Marchaux F 69 A6
Marche-en-Famenne
  B 49 C6
Marchegg A 64 B2
Marchena E 99 B5
Marchenoir F 58 C2
Marcheprime F 76 B2
Marciac F 76 C3
Marciana Marina I . . 81 D4
Marcianise I 103 B7
Marcigny F 68 B4
Marcilla E 89 B5
Marcillac-la-Croisille
  F 68 C2
Marcillac-Vallon F . 77 B5
Marcillat-en-Combraille
  F 68 B2
Marcille-sur-Seine F . 59 B4
Marcilly-le-Hayer F . 59 B4
Marcinkowice PL . . . 46 B2
Marciszów PL 53 C6
Marck F 48 C2
Marckolsheim F 60 B3
Marco de Canaveses
  P 87 C2
Mårdsele S 115 C16
Mårdsjö S 115 D12
Mareham le Fen GB . . 27 B5
Marennes F 66 C3
Mareuil F 67 C5
Mareuil-en-Brie F . . 59 B4
Mareuil-sur-Arnon F . 68 B2
Mareuil-sur-Lay F . . 66 B3
Mareuil-sur-Ourcq F . 59 A4
Margam GB 29 B4
Margariti GR 116 C2
Margate GB 31 C5
Margaux F 76 A2
Margerie-Hancourt F . 59 B5
Margès F 79 A4
Margherita di Savóia
  I 104 B2
Margita SRB 75 C6
Margone I 70 C2
Margonin PL 46 C3
Marguerittes F 78 C3
Margut F 59 A6
Maria E 101 B3
Maria Neustift A . . . 63 C5
Marianelund S 40 B5
Marianópoli I 108 B2
Mariánské Lázně CZ . 52 C2
Mariapfarr A 72 A3
Maria Saal A 73 B4
Maria Taferl A 63 B6
Mariazell A 63 C6
Maribo DK 39 E4
Maribor SLO 73 B5
Marieberg S 37 C2
Mariefred S 37 C4
Mariehamn FIN 36 B6
Marieholm S 41 D3
Marielund S 36 B5
Marienbaum D 50 B2
Marienberg D 52 C3
Marienheide D 50 B3
Mariental D 51 A6
Mariestad S 35 D5
Marieux F 48 C3
Marigliano I 103 C7
Marignane F 79 C4
Marigny
  Jura F 69 B5
  Manche F 57 A4
Marigny-le-Châtel F . 59 B4
Marikostinovo BG . . 116 A5
Marina HR 83 C5
Marina del Cantone
  I 103 C7
Marina di Acquappesa
  I 106 B2
Marina di Alberese I . 81 D5
Marina di Amendolara
  I 106 B3
Marina di Campo I . . 81 D4
Marina di Carrara I . 81 B4
Marina di Castagneto-
  Donorático I . . . 81 C4
Marina di Cécina I . 81 C4
Marina di Gáiro I . . 110 C2
Marina di Ginosa I . 104 C2
Marina di Gioiosa Iónica
  I 106 C3
Marina di Grosseto I . 81 D5
Marina di Léuca I . . 107 B5
Marina di Massá I . . 81 B4
Marina di Nováglie I . 107 B5
Marina di Pisa I . . . 81 C4
Marina di Ragusa I . 109 C3
Marina di Ravenna I . 82 B1
Marina di Torre Grande
  I 110 C1
Marina Romea I 82 B1
Marine de Sisco I . . 102 A2
Marinella I 108 B1
Marinella di Sarzana
  I 81 B4
Marineo I 108 B2
Marines F 58 A2
Maringues F 68 C3
Marinha das Ondas P . 92 B1
Marinha Grande P . . 92 B1
Marinhas P 87 C2
Marino I 102 B5

Marjaliza E 94 C3
Markabygd N 114 D8
Markaryd S 40 C3
Markdorf D 61 C5
Markelo NL 50 A2
Market Deeping GB . . 30 B3
Market Drayton GB . . 26 C3
Market Harborough
  GB 30 B3
Markethill GB 19 B5
Market Rasen GB . . . 27 B5
Market Warsop GB . . 27 B4
Market Weighton GB . 27 B5
Markgröningen D . . . 61 B5
Markhausen D 43 C4
Markí PL 55 A6
Markina-Xemein E . . 89 A4
Markinch GB 25 B4
Märkische Buchholz
  D 53 A3
Markitta S 113 E10
Markkleeberg D 52 B2
Marklohe D 43 C6
Marknesse NL 42 C2
Markneukirchen D . . 52 C2
Markopoulo GR 117 E5
Markovac SRB 85 B6
Markowice PL 54 C3
Markranstädt D 52 B2
Marksuhl D 51 C6
Markt Allhau A 73 A6
Markt Erlbach D . . . 61 A6
Marktbreit D 61 A6
Marktheidenfeld D . . 61 A5
Markt Indersdorf D . 62 B2
Marktl D 62 B3
Marktleuthen D 52 C1
Marktoberdorf D . . . 71 A5
Marktredwitz D 52 C2
Markt Rettenbach D . 61 C6
Markt Schwaben D . . 62 B2
Markt-Übelbach A . . 73 A5
Markusica HR 74 C3
Markušovce SK 65 B6
Marl D 50 B3
Marlborough
  Devon GB 28 C4
  Wiltshire GB . . . 29 B6
Marle F 59 A4
Marlieux F 69 B5
Marlow
  D 45 A4
  GB 31 C3
Marma S 36 B4
Marmagne F 69 B4
Marmande F 76 B3
Marmara TR 118 B2
Marmaris TR 119 F3
Marmelete P 98 B2
Marmolejo E 100 A1
Marmoutier F 60 B3
Marnay F 69 A5
Marne D 43 B6
Marnheim D 61 A4
Marnitz D 44 B3
Maroldsweisach D . . 51 C6
Marolles-les-Braults
  F 58 B1
Maromme F 58 A2
Marónia GR 116 B7
Maroslele H 75 B5
Marostica I 72 C1
Marotta I 82 C2
Marpisa GR 117 E7
Marquion F 48 C3
Marquise F 48 C2
Marradi I 81 B5
Marrasjärvi FIN . . . 113 F14
Marraskoski FIN . . . 113 F14
Marratxi E 97 B2
Marrúbiu I 110 C1
Marrum NL 42 B2
Marrupe E 94 B2
Marsac F 77 C5
Marsac-en-Livradois
  F 68 C3
Marságlia I 80 B3
Marsala I 108 B1
Marsberg D 51 B4
Marsciano I 82 C1
Marseillan F 78 C2
Marseille = Marseilles
  F 79 C4
Marseille en Beauvaisis
  F 58 A2
Marseilles = Marseille
  F 79 C4
Mársico Nuovo I . . . 104 C1
Marske-by-the-Sea
  GB 27 A4
Mars-la-Tours F . . . 60 A1
Marsliden S 115 B12
Marson F 59 B5
Märsta S 37 C4
Marstal DK 39 E3
Marstrand S 38 B4
Marta I 102 A4
Martano I 107 A5
Martel F 77 B4
Martelange B 60 A1
Martfeld D 43 C6
Martfú H 75 A5
Martham GB 30 B5
Marthon F 67 C5
Martigné-Briand F . . 67 A4
Martigné-Ferchaud F . 57 C4
Martigny CH 70 B2
Martigny-les-Bains F . 60 B1
Martigues F 79 C4
Martim-Longo P 98 B3
Martin SK 65 A4
Martina CH 71 B5
Martina Franca I . . . 104 C3
Martinamor E 94 B1
Martin de la Jara E . 100 B1
Martinniemi FIN . . . 3 D26
Martin Muñoz de las
  Posadas E 94 B2
Martinsberg A 63 B6
Martinšćica HR 82 B3
Martinshöhe D 60 A3
Martinsicuro I 82 D2
Martinszell D 61 C6
Mártis I 110 B1
Martofte DK 39 D3
Martonvásár H 74 A3
Martorell E 91 B4
Martos E 100 B2
Martres Tolosane F . 77 C3
Martti FIN 113 E17
Marugán E 94 B2
Marúggio I 104 C3
Marvão P 93 B3
Marvejols F 78 B2
Marville F 60 A1
Marwałd PL 47 B5
Marykirk GB 25 B5
Maryport GB 26 A2
Marytavy GB 28 C3
Marzabotto I 81 B5
Marzahna D 52 A2
Marzamemi I 109 C4
Marzocca I 82 C2
Masa E 88 B3
Mas-Cabardès F 77 C5
Máscali I 109 B4
Mascaraque E 94 C3
Mascarenhas P 87 C3
Mascioni I 103 A6
Mas de Barberáns E . 90 C3
Mas de las Matas E . 90 C2
Masegoso E 101 A3

Masegoso de Tajuña E . . .95 B4
Masera I . . .70 B3
Masevaux F . . .60 C2
Masfjorden N . . .32 B2
Masham GB . . .27 A4
Masi N . . .113 C12
Maside E . . .87 B2
Maslacq F . . .76 C2
Maslinica HR . . .83 C5
Maslovare BIH . . .84 B2
Masone I . . .80 B2
Massa I . . .81 B4
Massa Fiscáglia I . . .81 B6
Massa Lombarda I . . .81 B5
Massa Lubrense I . . .103 C7
Massamagrell E . . .96 B2
Massa Marittima I . . .81 C4
Massa Martana I . . .82 D1
Massanassa E . . .96 B2
Massarosa I . . .81 C4
Massat F . . .77 D4
Massay F . . .68 A1
Massbach D . . .51 C6
Masseret F . . .67 C6
Masseube F . . .77 C3
Massiac F . . .68 C3
Massing D . . .62 B3
Massmechelen B . . .50 C1
Masterud N . . .34 B4
Mastocka S . . .40 C3
Masty BY . . .6 E8
Masúa I . . .110 C1
Masueco E . . .87 C4
Masugnsbyn S . . .113 E11
Mašun SLO . . .73 C4
Maszewo
  Lubuskie PL . . .53 A4
  Zachodnio-Pomorskie PL . . .45 B7
Mata de Alcántara E . . .93 B4
Matala GR . . .117 H6
Matalebreras E . . .89 C4
Matallana de Torio E . . .88 B1
Matamala E . . .89 C4
Mataporquera E . . .88 B2
Matapozuelos E . . .88 C2
Mataró E . . .91 B5
Matarocco I . . .108 B1
Mataruge MNE . . .85 C4
Mataruška Banja SRB . . .85 C5
Matélica I . . .82 C2
Matera I . . .104 C2
Mateševo MNE . . .85 D4
Mátészalka H . . .11 C7
Matet E . . .96 B2
Matfors S . . .115 E14
Matha F . . .67 C4
Mathay F . . .70 A1
Matignon F . . .57 B3
Matila de los Caños del Rio E . . .94 B1
Matlock GB . . .87 B4
Matosinhos P . . .87 C2
Matour F . . .69 B4
Mátrafüred H . . .65 C5
Mátraterenye H . . .65 B5
Matre
  Hordaland N . . .32 B2
  Hordaland N . . .32 C2
Matrei am Brenner A . . .71 A6
Matrei in Osttirol A . . .72 A2
Matrice I . . .103 B7
Matsdal S . . .115 B12
Mattarello I . . .71 B6
Mattersburg A . . .64 C2
Mattighofen A . . .62 B4
Mattinata I . . .104 B1
Mattos P . . .92 B2
Mattsee A . . .62 C4
Mattsmyra S . . .36 A2
Matulji HR . . .73 C4
Maubert-Fontaine F . . .59 A5
Maubeuge F . . .49 C4
Maubourguet F . . .76 C3
Mauchline GB . . .24 C3
Maud GB . . .23 D6
Mauer-kirchen A . . .62 B4
Mauern D . . .62 B2
Mauguio F . . .78 C3
Maulbronn D . . .61 B4
Maule F . . .58 B2
Mauléon F . . .67 B4
Mauléon-Barousse F . . .77 D3
Mauléon-Licharre F . . .76 C2
Maulévrier F . . .67 A4
Maum IRL . . .18 C2
Maurach A . . .72 A1
Maure-de-Bretagne F . . .57 C4
Maureilhan F . . .78 C2
Mauriac F . . .68 C2
Mauron F . . .57 B3
Maury F . . .77 D5
Maussane-les-Alpilles F . . .78 C3
Mautern A . . .63 B6
Mauterndorf A . . .72 A3
Mautern im Steiermark A . . .73 A4
Mauthausen A . . .63 B5
Mauthen A . . .72 B3
Mauvezin F . . .77 C3
Mauzé-sur-le-Mignon F . . .67 B4
Maxent F . . .57 C3
Maxey-sur-Vaise F . . .60 B1
Maxial P . . .92 B1
Maxmo FIN . . .113 F11
Maxwellheugh GB . . .25 C5
Mayalde E . . .88 C1
Maybole GB . . .24 C3
Mayen D . . .50 C3
Mayenne F . . .57 B5
Mayet F . . .58 C1
Mayorga E . . .88 B1
Mayres F . . .78 B3
Mayrhofen A . . .72 A1
Mazagón E . . .99 B4
Mazaleón E . . .90 B3
Mazamet F . . .77 C5
Mazan F . . .79 C4
Mazara del Vallo I . . .108 B1
Mazarambroz E . . .94 C2
Mazarete E . . .95 B4
Mazaricos E . . .86 B2
Mazarrón E . . .101 B4
Mažeikiai LT . . .6 C7
Mazères F . . .77 C4
Mazères-sur-Salat F . . .77 C3
Mazières-en-Gâtine F . . .67 B4
Mazin HR . . .83 B4
Mazuby F . . .77 D5
Mazyr BY . . .7 E10
Mazzarino I . . .109 B3
Mazzarrà Sant'Andrea I . . .109 A4
Mazzo di Valtellina I . . .71 B5
Mdzewo PL . . .47 C6
Mealhada P . . .92 A2
Méan B . . .49 C6
Meana Sardo I . . .110 C2
Meaulne F . . .68 B2
Meaux F . . .59 B3
Mebonden N . . .114 D8
Mecerreyes E . . .89 B3
Mechelen B . . .49 B5
Mechernich D . . .50 C2
Mechnica PL . . .54 C3
Mechowo PL . . .45 B7
Mechterstädt D . . .51 C6
Mecidiye TR . . .118 B1
Mecikal PL . . .46 B3
Mecina-Bombarón E . . .100 C2

Mecitözü TR . . .16 A7
Meckenbeuren D . . .61 C5
Meckenheim
  Rheinland-Pfalz D . . .50 C3
  Rheinland-Pfalz D . . .61 A4
Meckesheim D . . .61 A4
Mecseknádasd H . . .74 B3
Meda
  I . . .71 C4
  P . . .87 D3
Medak HR . . .83 B4
Mede I . . .80 A2
Medebach D . . .51 B4
Medelim P . . .93 A3
Medemblik NL . . .42 C2
Medena Selista BIH . . .84 B1
Medesano I . . .81 B4
Medevi S . . .37 D1
Medgidia RO . . .11 D10
Medgyesháza H . . .75 B6
Medhamn S . . .35 C5
Mediaş RO . . .11 C8
Medicina I . . .81 B5
Medinaceli E . . .95 A4
Medina de las Torres E . . .93 C4
Medina del Campo E . . .88 C2
Medina de Pomar E . . .89 B3
Medina de Rioseco E . . .88 C1
Medina Sidonia E . . .99 C5
Medinilla E . . .93 A5
Medja SRB . . .75 C5
Medjedja BIH . . .84 C4
Medulin HR . . .82 B2
Meduno I . . .72 B2
Medvedja SRB . . .85 B6
Medvedja SRB . . .85 C6
Medvedov SK . . .64 C3
Medvide HR . . .83 B4
Medvode SLO . . .73 B4
Medzev SK . . .65 B6
Medžitlija MK . . .116 B3
Meerane D . . .52 C2
Meerle B . . .49 B5
Meersburg D . . .61 C5
Meeuwen B . . .49 B6
Megálo Horio GR . . .119 F2
Megalopoli GR . . .117 E4
Megara GR . . .117 D5
Megève F . . .69 C6
Meggenhofen A . . .63 B4
Megra RUS . . .7 A14
Mehamn N . . .113 A16
Mehedeby S . . .36 B4
Méhkerék H . . .75 B6
Mehun-sur-Yèvre F . . .68 A2
Meigle GB . . .25 B4
Meijel NL . . .50 B1
Meilen CH . . .70 A3
Meilhan F . . .76 B2
Meimoa P . . .93 A3
Meina I . . .70 C3
Meine D . . .44 C2
Meinerzhagen D . . .50 B3
Meiningen D . . .51 C6
Meira E . . .86 A3
Meiringen CH . . .70 B3
Meisenheim D . . .60 A3
Meissen D . . .52 B3
Meitingen D . . .62 B1
Meix-devant-Virton B . . .60 A1
Męka Gruda BIH . . .84 B2
Mel I . . .72 B2
Melbu N . . .112 D3
Melč CZ . . .64 A3
Meldal N . . .114 D6
Méldola I . . .82 B1
Meldorf D . . .43 A6
Melegnano I . . .71 C4
Melenci SRB . . .75 C5
Melendugno I . . .105 C4
Melfi I . . .104 C1
Melfjordbotn N . . .112 F2
Melgaço P . . .87 B2
Melgar de Arriba E . . .88 B1
Melgar de Fernamental E . . .88 B2
Melgar de Yuso E . . .88 B2
Melhus N . . .114 D7
Meliana E . . .96 B2
Melide
  CH . . .70 C3
  E . . .86 B2
Melides P . . .98 A2
Meligalás GR . . .117 E3
Melilli I . . .109 B4
Melinovac HR . . .83 B4
Melisenda I . . .110 C2
Melisey F . . .60 C2
Mélito di Porto Salvo I . . .109 B4
Melk A . . .63 B6
Melksham GB . . .29 B5
Mellanström S . . .115 B15
Mellbystrand S . . .40 C2
Melle
  B . . .49 B4
  D . . .50 A4
  F . . .67 B4
Mellendorf D . . .43 C6
Mellerud S . . .35 D4
Mellieha M . . .107 C5
Mellösa S . . .37 C3
Mellrichstadt D . . .51 C6
Melnik BG . . .116 A5
Mělnické Vtelno CZ . . .53 C4
Mělník CZ . . .53 C4
Melón E . . .87 B2
Melrose GB . . .25 C5
Mels CH . . .71 A4
Melsungen D . . .51 B5
Meltaus FIN . . .113 F14
Meltham GB . . .27 B4
Melton Mowbray GB . . .30 B3
Meltosjärvi FIN . . .113 F13
Melun F . . .58 B3
Melvaig GB . . .22 D3
Melvich GB . . .23 C5
Mélykút H . . .75 B4
Melzo I . . .71 C4
Memaliaj AL . . .116 B1
Membrilla E . . .95 D3
Membrio E . . .93 B3
Memer F . . .77 B4
Memmelsdorf D . . .51 D6
Memmingen D . . .61 C6
Memória P . . .92 B2
Mena UA . . .7 F12
Menággio I . . .71 B4
Menai Bridge GB . . .26 B1
Menasalbas E . . .94 C2
Menat F . . .68 B2
Mendavia E . . .89 B4
Mendaza E . . .89 B4
Mende F . . .78 B2
Menden D . . .50 B3
Menderes TR . . .119 D2
Mendig D . . .50 C3
Mendrisio CH . . .70 C3
Ménéac F . . .56 B3
Menemen TR . . .118 D2
Menen B . . .49 C4
Menesjärvi FIN . . .113 D15
Menetou-Salon F . . .68 A2
Menfi I . . .108 B1
Ménföcsanak H . . .64 C3
Mengamuñoz E . . .94 B2
Mengen
  D . . .61 B5
  TR . . .118 B7
Mengeš SLO . . .73 B4
Mengíbar E . . .100 B2
Mengkofen D . . .62 B3
Menou F . . .68 A2
Mens F . . .79 B4
Menslage D . . .43 C4
Menstrie GB . . .25 B4
Menstråsk S . . .115 B16
Mentana I . . .102 A5
Menton F . . .80 C1
Méntrida E . . .94 B2

Méobecq F . . .67 B6
Méounes-les-Montrieux F . . .79 C4
Meppel NL . . .42 C3
Meppen D . . .43 C4
Mequinenza E . . .90 B3
Mer F . . .58 C2
Mera
  Coruña E . . .86 A2
  Coruña E . . .86 A3
Meráker N . . .114 D8
Merano I . . .71 B6
Merate I . . .71 C4
Mercadillo E . . .89 A3
Mercatale I . . .82 C1
Mercatino Conca I . . .82 C1
Mercato San Severino I . . .103 C7
Mercato Saraceno I . . .82 C1
Merching D . . .62 B1
Merchtem B . . .49 C5
Merdingen D . . .60 B3
Merdrignac F . . .56 B3
Merdžanići BIH . . .84 C2
Meré E . . .88 A2
Mere GB . . .29 B5
Meréville F . . .58 B3
Merfeld D . . .50 B3
Méribel Motraret F . . .69 C6
Meriç TR . . .118 A1
Mérida E . . .93 C4
Mérignac F . . .76 B2
Mering D . . .62 B1
Merkendorf D . . .62 A1
Merklin CZ . . .63 A4
Merksplas B . . .49 B5
Merlánna S . . .37 C3
Merlimont Plage F . . .48 C2
Mern DK . . .39 D5
Mernye H . . .74 B2
Mersch L . . .60 A2
Merseburg D . . .52 B1
Mers-les-Bains F . . .48 C2
Merthyr Tydfil GB . . .29 B4
Mertingen D . . .62 B1
Mértola P . . .98 B3
Méru F . . .58 A3
Merufe P . . .87 B2
Mervans F . . .69 B5
Merville F . . .48 C3
Méry-sur-Seine F . . .59 B4
Merzen D . . .43 C4
Merzifon TR . . .16 A7
Merzig D . . .60 A2
Mesagne I . . .105 C3
Mesão Frio P . . .87 C3
Mesas de Ibor E . . .93 B5
Meschede D . . .50 B4
Meschers-sur-Gironde F . . .66 C4
Meshchovsk RUS . . .7 D13
Meslay-du-Maine F . . .57 C5
Mesna N . . .34 A2
Mesnalien N . . .34 A2
Mesocco CH . . .71 B4
Mésola I . . .82 B1
Mesologi GR . . .116 D3
Mesopotamo GR . . .116 C2
Mesoraca I . . .107 B3
Messac F . . .57 C4
Messancy B . . .60 A1
Messdorf D . . .44 C3
Messei F . . .57 B5
Messejana P . . .98 B2
Messelt N . . .34 A3
Messina I . . .109 A4
Messingen D . . .43 C4
Messini GR . . .117 E4
Messkirch D . . .61 C5
Messlingen S . . .115 E9
Messstetten D . . .61 B5
Mesta GR . . .117 D7
Mestanza E . . .100 A1
Městec Králové CZ . . .53 C5
Mestlin D . . .44 B3
Město Albrechtice CZ . . .54 C2
Město Libavá CZ . . .64 A3
Město Touškov CZ . . .63 A4
Mestre I . . .72 C2
Mesvres F . . .69 B4
Meszegnyő H . . .74 B2
Meta I . . .103 C7
Metajna HR . . .83 B4
Metelen D . . .50 A3
Methana GR . . .117 E5
Methlick GB . . .23 D6
Methven GB . . .25 B4
Methwold GB . . .30 B4
Metković HR . . .84 C2
Metlika SLO . . .73 C5
Metnitz A . . .73 B4
Metslawier NL . . .42 B3
Metsovo GR . . .116 C3
Metten D . . .62 B3
Mettendorf D . . .50 D2
Mettet B . . .49 C5
Mettingen D . . .50 A3
Mettlach D . . .60 A2
Mettlen CH . . .70 B2
Mettmann D . . .50 B2
Metz F . . .60 A2
Metzervisse F . . .60 A2
Metzingen D . . .61 B5
Meulan F . . .58 A2
Meung-sur-Loire F . . .58 C2
Meuselwitz D . . .52 B2
Meuzac F . . .67 C6
Mevagissey GB . . .28 C3
Meximieux F . . .69 C5
Mey GB . . .23 C5
Meyenburg D . . .44 B4
Meymac F . . .68 C2
Meyrargues F . . .79 C4
Meyrueis F . . .78 B2
Meysse F . . .78 B3
Mèze F . . .78 C2
Mézériat F . . .69 B5
Mežica SLO . . .73 B4
Mézidon-Canon F . . .57 A5
Mézières-en-Brenne F . . .67 B6
Mézières-sur-Issoire F . . .67 B5
Mézilhac F . . .78 B3
Mézilles F . . .59 C4
Mézin F . . .76 B3
Mezőberény H . . .75 B6
Mezőcsát H . . .65 C6
Mezőfalva H . . .74 B3
Mezőhegyes H . . .75 B5
Mezőkeresztes H . . .65 C6
Mezőkomárom H . . .74 B3
Mezőkövesd H . . .65 C6
Mezőörs H . . .74 A2
Mézos F . . .76 B1
Mezőszilas H . . .74 B3
Mezőtúr H . . .75 A5
Mezquita de Jarque E . . .90 C2
Mezzano
  Emilia Romagna I . . .81 B6
  Trentino Alto Adige I . . .72 B1
Mezzojuso I . . .108 B2
Mezzoldo I . . .71 B4
Mezzolombardo I . . .71 B6
Mgarr I . . .107 C5
Mglin RUS . . .7 E12
Miajadas E . . .93 B5
Miały PL . . .46 C2
Mianowice PL . . .46 A3
Miasteczko Krajeńskie PL . . .46 B3
Miasteczko Śl. PL . . .54 C3
Miastko PL . . .46 A2
Michałowice PL . . .55 C4

Michałowice PL . . .55 C4
Michalová D . . .61 A6
Michelbach D . . .61 A6
Micheldorf A . . .63 C5
Michelhausen A . . .64 B1
Michelsneukirchen D . . .62 A3
Michelstadt D . . .61 A5
Mickhausen D . . .62 B1
Mickleover GB . . .27 C4
Micleea GB . . .23 B6
Middelburg NL . . .49 B4
Middelfart DK . . .39 D2
Middelharnis NL . . .49 B5
Middelkerke B . . .48 B3
Middelstum NL . . .42 B3
Middlesbrough GB . . .27 A4
Middleton GB . . .24 B1
Middleton Cheney GB . . .30 B2
Middleton-in-Teesdale GB . . .26 A3
Middletown GB . . .19 B5
Middlewich GB . . .26 B3
Middlezoy GB . . .29 B5
Midhurst GB . . .31 D3
Midleton IRL . . .20 C3
Midlum D . . .43 B5
Midsomer Norton GB . . .29 B5
Midtgulen N . . .114 F2
Midwolda NL . . .43 B4
Mid Yell GB . . .22 A7
Miechów PL . . .55 C5
Miedes de Aragón E . . .89 C5
Miedes de Atienza E . . .95 A3
Międzybodzie Bielskie PL . . .65 A5
Międzybórz PL . . .54 B2
Międzychód PL . . .46 C1
Międzylesie PL . . .54 C1
Międzyrzec Podlaski PL . . .6 F7
Międzyrzecz PL . . .46 C1
Międzywodzie PL . . .45 A6
Międzyzdroje PL . . .45 B6
Miejska Górka PL . . .54 B2
Miélan F . . .76 C3
Mielec PL . . .55 C6
Mielęcin PL . . .45 B6
Mielno
  Warmińsko-Mazurskie PL . . .47 B6
  Zachodnio-Pomorskie PL . . .46 A2
Miengo E . . .88 A3
Mieraslompolo FIN . . .113 C16
Miercurea Ciuc RO . . .11 C8
Mieres
  Asturias E . . .88 A1
  Girona E . . .91 A5
Mierzyn PL . . .53 C6
Miesau D . . .60 A3
Miesbach D . . .62 C2
Mieścisko PL . . .46 C3
Mieste D . . .44 C3
Miesterhorst D . . .44 C3
Mieszków PL . . .54 A2
Mieszkowice PL . . .45 C6
Mietków PL . . .54 C1
Migennes F . . .59 C4
Miggiano I . . .107 B5
Migliánico I . . .103 A7
Migliarino I . . .81 B5
Migliónico I . . .104 C2
Mignano Monte Lungo I . . .103 B6
Migné F . . .67 B6
Miguel Esteban E . . .95 C3
Miguelturra E . . .94 D3
Mihajlovac SRB . . .85 D5
Mihald H . . .74 B2
Mihalgazi TR . . .118 B5
Mihaliçcik TR . . .118 C6
Mihályi H . . .74 A2
Mihla D . . .51 B6
Mihohnić HR . . .83 A3
Miholjsko HR . . .73 C5
Mihovljan HR . . .73 B5
Mijares E . . .94 B2
Mijas E . . .100 C1
Mijoska MNE . . .85 D4
Mike H . . .74 B2
Mikhnevo RUS . . .7 D14
Mikines GR . . .117 E4
Mikkeli FIN . . .3 F27
Mikkelvik N . . .112 B8
Mikleuš HR . . .74 C2
Mikołajki Pomorskie PL . . .47 B5
Mikolów PL . . .54 C3
Mikonos GR . . .117 E7
Mikorzyn PL . . .54 B3
Mikro Derio GR . . .116 A8
Mikstat PL . . .54 B2
Mikulášovice CZ . . .53 C4
Mikulov CZ . . .64 B2
Mikulovice CZ . . .54 C2
Milagro E . . .89 B5
Miłakowo PL . . .47 A6
Milan = Milano I . . .71 C4
Miland N . . .32 C5
Milano = Milan I . . .71 C4
Milano Marittima I . . .82 B1
Milas TR . . .119 E2
Milazzo I . . .109 A4
Mildenhall GB . . .30 B4
Milejewo PL . . .47 A5
Milelín CZ . . .53 C5
Miletić SRB . . .75 C4
Miletićevo SRB . . .75 C6
Mileto I . . .106 C3
Milevsko CZ . . .63 A5
Milford IRL . . .19 A4
Milford Haven GB . . .28 B2
Milford on Sea GB . . .31 D2
Milhão P . . .87 C4
Milići BIH . . .84 B3
Miličín CZ . . .63 A5
Milicz PL . . .54 B2
Milín CZ . . .63 A5
Militello in Val di Catánia I . . .109 B3
Miljevina BIH . . .84 C3
Milkowice PL . . .53 B6
Millançay F . . .68 A1
Millares E . . .96 B2
Millas F . . .91 A5
Millau F . . .78 B2
Millesimo I . . .80 B2
Millevaches F . . .68 C2
Millom GB . . .26 A2
Millport GB . . .24 C3
Millstatt A . . .72 B3
Millstreet
  Cork IRL . . .20 B2
  Waterford IRL . . .21 B4
Milltown
  Galway IRL . . .18 C3
  Kerry IRL . . .20 B1
Milltown Malbay IRL . . .20 B2
Milly-la-Forêt F . . .58 B3
Milmarcos E . . .95 A5
Milmersdorf D . . .45 B5
Milna HR . . .83 C5
Milnthorpe GB . . .26 A3
Miločaj SRB . . .85 C5
Miločer MNE . . .85 D4
Milohnići HR . . .73 C4
Milos GR . . .117 F6
Miloševa Ht . . .85 B6
Miloševo SRB . . .85 B6
Milot AL . . .105 B5
Miłowka PL . . .65 A4
Miltach D . . .62 A3
Milton Keynes GB . . .31 B3
Miltzow D . . .45 A5
Milutovac SRB . . .85 C6
Milverton GB . . .29 B4
Milzyn PL . . .47 C4
Mimice HR . . .84 C1
Mimizan F . . .76 B1

Mimizan-Plage F . . .76 B1
Mimoň CZ . . .53 C4
Mina de Juliana P . . .98 B2
Mina de São Domingos P . . .98 B3
Minas de Riotinto E . . .99 B4
Minateda E . . .101 A4
Minaya E . . .95 C4
Minde P . . .92 B2
Mindelheim D . . .61 B6
Mindelstetten D . . .62 B2
Minden D . . .51 A4
Mindszent H . . .75 B5
Minehead GB . . .29 B4
Mineo I . . .109 B3
Minerbe I . . .71 C6
Minerbio I . . .81 B5
Minervino Murge I . . .104 B2
Minglanilla E . . .95 C5
Mingorria E . . .94 B2
Minnesund N . . .34 B3
Miño E . . .86 A2
Miño de San Esteban E . . .89 C3
Minsen D . . .43 B4
Minsk BY . . .7 E9
Mińsk Mazowiecki PL . . .55 A6
Minsterley GB . . .26 C3
Mintlaw GB . . .23 D6
Minturno I . . .103 B6
Mionica
  BIH . . .84 B3
  SRB . . .85 B5
Mios F . . .76 B2
Mira
  E . . .96 B1
  I . . .72 C2
  P . . .92 A2
Mirabel E . . .93 B4
Mirabel-aux-Baronnies F . . .79 B4
Mirabella Eclano I . . .103 B8
Mirabella Imbáccari I . . .109 B3
Miradoux F . . .77 B3
Miraflores de la Sierra E . . .95 B3
Miralrio E . . .95 B4
Miramar P . . .87 C2
Miramare I . . .82 B1
Miramas F . . .78 C3
Mirambeau F . . .67 C4
Mirambel E . . .90 C2
Miramont-de-Guyenne F . . .77 B3
Miranda de Arga E . . .89 B5
Miranda de Ebro E . . .89 B4
Miranda do Corvo P . . .92 A2
Miranda do Douro P . . .87 C4
Mirande F . . .77 C3
Mirandela P . . .87 C3
Mirandilla E . . .93 C4
Miranje HR . . .83 B4
Mirano I . . .72 C2
Miras AL . . .116 B2
Miravet E . . .90 B3
Miré F . . .57 C5
Mirebeau F . . .67 B5
Mirebeau-sur-Bèze F . . .69 A5
Mirecourt F . . .60 B2
Mirepoix F . . .77 C4
Mires GR . . .117 G6
Miribel F . . .69 C5
Mirina GR . . .116 C7
Mirna GR . . .73 C5
Miroslav CZ . . .64 B2
Mirosławiec PL . . .46 B2
Miroslavlje PL . . .54 A1
Mirošov CZ . . .63 A4
Mirotice CZ . . .63 A5
Mirovice CZ . . .63 A5
Mirow D . . .45 B4
Mirsk PL . . .53 C5
Mirzec PL . . .55 B6
Misi FIN . . .113 F15
Misilmeri I . . .108 A2
Miske H . . .75 B4
Miskolc H . . .65 B6
Mislinja SLO . . .73 B5
Missanello I . . .104 C2
Missillac F . . .66 A2
Mistelbach
  A . . .64 B2
  D . . .62 A2
Misten N . . .112 E3
Misterbianco I . . .109 B4
Misterhult S . . .40 B6
Mistretta I . . .109 B3
Misurina I . . .72 B2
Mitchelstown IRL . . .20 B3
Mithimna GR . . .116 C8
Mithoni GR . . .117 F3
Mitilini GR . . .118 C1
Mittelberg
  Tirol A . . .71 B5
  Vorarlberg A . . .71 A6
Mittenwald D . . .71 A6
Mittenwalde D . . .45 C5
Mitterback A . . .63 C6
Mitterdorf im Mürztal A . . .73 A5
Mitter-Kleinarl A . . .72 A3
Mittersheim F . . .60 B2
Mittersill A . . .72 A2
Mitterskirchen D . . .62 B3
Mitterteich D . . .62 A3
Mitton F . . .78 B3
Mittweida D . . .52 C2
Mitwitz D . . .52 C1
Mizhhir'ya UA . . .11 B7
Mjäby S . . .41 C4
Mjävatn N . . .33 D5
Mjöbäck S . . .40 B2
Mjölby S . . .37 D2
Mjølfjell N . . .32 B3
Mjøndalen N . . .34 C2
Mjørlund N . . .34 B2
Mladá Boleslav CZ . . .53 C4
Mladá Vožice CZ . . .63 A5
Mladé Buky CZ . . .53 C5
Mladenovac SRB . . .85 B5
Mladikovine BIH . . .84 B2
Mława PL . . .47 B6
Mlinište BIH . . .84 B1
Młodzieszyn PL . . .55 A5
Młogoszyn PL . . .55 A4
Młynary PL . . .47 A5
Mnichóvice CZ . . .63 A5
Mnichovo Hradiště CZ . . .53 C4
Mniów PL . . .55 B5
Mnisek pod Brdy CZ . . .63 A5
Mníšek PL . . .55 B5
Mníszków PL . . .55 B5
Mo
  Hedmark N . . .34 B3
  Hordaland N . . .32 B2
  Møre og Romsdal N . . .114 E5
  Telemark N . . .33 C4
  Gävleborg S . . .36 A3
  Västra Götaland S . . .35 D3
Moaña E . . .87 B2
Moate IRL . . .21 A4
Mocejón E . . .94 C3
Močenok SK . . .64 B3
Mochales E . . .95 A4
Mochowo PL . . .47 C5
Mochy PL . . .46 C2
Mockern D . . .52 A1
Mockfjärd S . . .36 B1
Möckmühl D . . .61 A5
Mockrehna D . . .52 B2
Moclín E . . .100 B2
Mocsa H . . .64 C4

Modane F . . .70 C1
Modbury GB . . .28 C4
Módena I . . .81 B4
Módica I . . .109 C3
Modigliana I . . .81 B5
Mödling A . . .64 B2
Modliborzyce PL . . .55 B6
Modliszewice PL . . .55 B5
Modliszewko PL . . .46 C3
Modogno I . . .104 B2
Modra SK . . .64 B3
Modran BIH . . .84 B2
Modriča BIH . . .84 B3
Möðrudalur IS . . .111 B10
Modrúgh E . . .94 C2
Modugno I . . .104 B2
Moëlan-sur-Mer F . . .56 C2
Moelfre GB . . .26 B1
Moelv N . . .34 B2
Moen N . . .112 C7
Moena I . . .72 B1
Moerbeke B . . .49 B4
Moers D . . .50 B2
Moffat GB . . .25 C4
Mogadouro P . . .87 C4
Mogata S . . .37 D3
Móggio Udinese I . . .72 B3
Mogielnica PL . . .55 B5
Mogilany PL . . .65 A5
Mogilno PL . . .46 C3
Mogliano I . . .82 C2
Mogliano Véneto I . . .72 C2
Mogor E . . .87 B2
Mógoro I . . .110 C1
Moguer E . . .99 B4
Mohács H . . .74 C3
Moheda S . . .40 B4
Mohedas E . . .93 A4
Mohedas de la Jara E . . .94 C2
Mohelnice CZ . . .64 A2
Mohill IRL . . .19 C4
Möhlin CH . . .70 A2
Moholm S . . .35 D6
Mohorn D . . .52 B3
Mohyliv-Podil's'kyy UA . . .11 B9
Moi N . . .33 D3
Mòia I . . .91 B5
Moià E . . .82 C2
Moimenta da Beira P . . .87 C3
Mo i Rana N . . .115 A11
Moirans F . . .69 C5
Moirans-en-Montagne F . . .69 B5
Moisaküla EST . . .7 B8
Moisdon-la-Rivière F . . .57 C4
Moissac F . . .77 B4
Moita
  Coimbra P . . .92 A2
  Guarda P . . .93 A3
  Santarém P . . .92 B2
  Setúbal P . . .92 C1
Moita dos Ferreiros P . . .92 B1
Moixent E . . .101 A5
Mojácar E . . .101 B4
Mojados E . . .88 C2
Mojkovac MNE . . .85 C4
Mojmírovce SK . . .64 B4
Mojtin SK . . .65 B4
Möklinta S . . .36 B3
Mokošica HR . . .84 D3
Mokra Gora SRB . . .85 C4
Mokronog SLO . . .73 C5
Mokro Pólje HR . . .83 B5
Mokrzyska PL . . .55 C5
Møkster N . . .32 B2
Mol
  B . . .49 B6
  SRB . . .75 C5
Mola di Bari I . . .104 B3
Molai GR . . .117 F4
Molare I . . .80 B2
Molaretto I . . .70 C2
Molas F . . .77 C3
Molassano I . . .80 B2
Molbergen D . . .43 C4
Mold GB . . .26 B2
Molde N . . .114 E4
Moldjord N . . .112 E4
Moledo do Minho P . . .87 C2
Molfetta I . . .104 B2
Molfsee D . . .44 A2
Moliden S . . .115 D15
Molières F . . .77 B4
Molina de Aragón E . . .95 B5
Molina de Segura E . . .101 A4
Molinar F . . .89 A3
Molinaseca E . . .86 B4
Molinella I . . .81 B5
Molinet F . . .68 B3
Molinicos E . . .101 A3
Molini di Túres I . . .72 B1
Molinos de Duero E . . .89 C4
Molinos de Rei E . . .91 B5
Moliterno I . . .104 C1
Molkom S . . .35 C5
Mollans F . . .105 C6
Möllbrücke A . . .72 B3
Mölle S . . .41 C2
Molledo E . . .88 A2
Möllenbeck D . . .45 B5
Mollerussa E . . .90 B3
Mollet de Perelada E . . .91 A6
Mollina E . . .100 B1
Mölln D . . .44 B2
Mollö S . . .37 D1
Mollösund S . . .35 D3
Mölltorp S . . .37 D1
Mölnbo S . . .37 C4
Mölndal S . . .38 B5
Mölnlycke S . . .38 B5
Molompize F . . .68 C3
Moloy F . . .69 A4
Molsheim F . . .60 B3
Moltzow D . . .45 B4
Molve HR . . .74 B1
Molveno I . . .71 B5
Molvizar E . . .100 C2
Mombaróccio I . . .82 C1
Mombeltrán E . . .94 B1
Mombris D . . .51 C5
Mombuey E . . .87 B4
Momchilgrad BG . . .116 A7
Mommark DK . . .39 E3
Momo I . . .70 C3
Monaghan IRL . . .19 B5
Monar Lodge GB . . .22 D4
Monasterace Marina I . . .106 C3
Monasterevin IRL . . .21 A4
Monasterio de Rodilla E . . .89 B3
Monastir I . . .110 C2
Monbahus F . . .77 B3
Monbazillac F . . .77 B3
Moncada E . . .96 B2
Moncalieri I . . .80 A1
Moncalvo I . . .80 A2
Monção P . . .87 B2
Moncarapacho P . . .98 B3
Moncel-sur-Seille F . . .60 B2
Monchegorsk RUS . . .3 C30
Mönchengladbach = München-Gladbach D . . .50 B2
Mönchdorf A . . .63 B5
Mönchhof A . . .64 C2
Monchique P . . .98 B2
Monclar-de-Quercy F . . .77 C4
Moncofa E . . .96 B2
Moncontour F . . .56 B3
Moncoutant F . . .67 B4
Monda E . . .100 C1
Mondariz E . . .87 B2
Mondavio I . . .82 C2
Mondéjar E . . .95 B3
Mondello I . . .108 A2
Mondim de Basto P . . .87 C3
Mondolfo I . . .82 C2
Mondoñedo E . . .86 A3
Mondorf-les-Bains L . . .60 A2
Mondoubleau F . . .58 C1

Mondov ì I . . .80 B1
Mondragon F . . .78 B3
Mondragone I . . .103 B6
Mondsee A . . .63 C4
Monéglia I . . .80 B3
Monegrillo E . . .90 B2
Monein F . . .76 C2
Monesiglio I . . .80 B2
Monési I . . .80 B1
Monesterio E . . .99 A4
Monestier-de-Clermont F . . .79 B4
Monestiés F . . .77 B5
Monéteau F . . .59 C4
Moneygall IRL . . .21 A4
Moneymore GB . . .19 B5
Monfalcone I . . .72 C3
Monfero E . . .86 A2
Monflanquin F . . .77 B3
Monflorite E . . .90 A2
Monforte P . . .92 B3
Monforte da Beira P . . .92 B3
Monforte d'Alba I . . .80 B1
Monforte del Cid E . . .96 C2
Monforte de Lemos E . . .86 B3
Monforte de Moyuela E . . .90 B1
Monghidoro I . . .81 B5
Mongiana I . . .106 C3
Monguelfo I . . .72 B2
Monheim D . . .62 B1
Moniaive GB . . .25 C4
Monifieth GB . . .25 B5
Monikie GB . . .25 B5
Monistrol-d'Allier F . . .78 B2
Monistrol de Montserrat E . . .91 B4
Monistrol-sur-Loire F . . .68 C4
Mönkebude D . . .45 B5
Monkton GB . . .24 C3
Monmouth GB . . .29 B5
Monnaie F . . .67 A5
Monnerville F . . .58 B3
Monnickendam NL . . .42 C2
Monolithos GR . . .119 F2
Monópoli I . . .104 C3
Monor H . . .75 A4
Monóvar E . . .101 A5
Monpazier F . . .77 B3
Monreal
  D . . .50 C3
  E . . .76 D1
Monreal del Campo E . . .95 B5
Monreale I . . .108 A2
Monroy E . . .93 B4
Monroyo E . . .90 C2
Mons B . . .49 C4
Monsaraz P . . .92 C3
Monschau D . . .50 C2
Monségur F . . .76 B3
Monsélice I . . .72 C1
Monshare N . . .32 B2
Monster NL . . .49 A5
Mönsterås S . . .40 B6
Monsummano Terme I . . .81 C4
Montabaur D . . .50 C3
Montafia I . . .80 B2
Montagnac F . . .78 C2
Montagnana I . . .71 C6
Montaigu F . . .66 B3
Montaigu-de-Quercy F . . .77 B4
Montaiguët-en-Forez F . . .68 B3
Montaigut F . . .68 B2
Montaigut-sur-Save F . . .77 C4
Montainville F . . .58 B2
Montalbán E . . .90 C2
Montalbán de Córdoba E . . .100 B1
Montálbano Elicona I . . .109 A4
Montálbano Iónico I . . .104 C2
Montalbo E . . .95 C4
Montalcino I . . .81 C5
Montaldo di Cósola I . . .80 B3
Montalegre P . . .87 C3
Montalieu-Vercieu F . . .69 C5
Montalivet-les-Bains F . . .66 C3
Montallegro I . . .108 B2
Montalto delle Marche I . . .82 D2
Montalto di Castro I . . .102 A4
Montalto Pavese I . . .80 B3
Montalto Uffugo I . . .106 B3
Montalvão P . . .92 B3
Montamarta E . . .88 C1
Montana BG . . .11 E7
Montana-Vermala CH . . .70 B2
Montánchez E . . .93 B4
Montanejos E . . .96 A2
Montano Antília I . . .106 A2
Montans F . . .77 C4
Montargil P . . .92 B2
Montargis F . . .58 C3
Montastruc-la-Conseillère F . . .77 C4
Montauban F . . .77 B4
Montauban-de-Bretagne F . . .57 B3
Montbard F . . .69 A4
Montbarrey F . . .69 A5
Montbazens F . . .77 B5
Montbazon F . . .67 A5
Montbéliard F . . .70 A1
Montbenoît F . . .69 B6
Montbeugny F . . .68 B3
Montblanc E . . .91 B4
Montbozon F . . .69 A6
Montbron F . . .67 C5
Montbrun-les-Bains F . . .79 B4
Montceau-les-Mines F . . .69 B4
Montcenis F . . .69 B4
Montchanin F . . .69 B4
Montcornet F . . .59 A5
Montcuq F . . .77 B4
Montdardier F . . .78 C2
Mont-de-Marsan F . . .76 C2
Montdidier F . . .58 A3
Monteagudo E . . .101 A4
Monteagudo de las Vicarías E . . .89 C4
Montealegre E . . .88 C2
Montealegre del Castillo E . . .101 A4
Montebello Iónico I . . .109 B4
Montebello Vicentino I . . .71 C6
Montebelluna I . . .72 C2
Montebourg F . . .57 A4
Montecarotto I . . .82 C2
Montecassiano I . . .82 C2
Montecastrilli I . . .102 A5
Montécchio I . . .82 C1
Montécchio Emilia I . . .81 B4
Montécchio Maggiore I . . .71 C6
Montech F . . .77 C4
Montechiaro d'Asti I . . .80 A2
Monte Clara P . . .92 B3
Monte Clérigo P . . .98 B2
Montecórice I . . .103 C7
Montecorvino Rovella I . . .103 C8
Monte da Pedra P . . .92 B3
Monte de Goula P . . .92 B3
Montederramo E . . .87 B3
Montedoro I . . .108 B2
Monte do Trigo P . . .92 C3
Montefalcone di Val Fortore I . . .103 B8

Montefalcone nel Sánnio I . . .103 B7
Montefano I . . .82 C2
Montefiascone I . . .102 A5
Montefiorino I . . .81 B4
Montefortino I . . .82 D2
Montefranco I . . .102 A5
Montefrio E . . .100 B2
Montegiordano Marina I . . .106 A3
Montegiório I . . .82 C2
Monte Gordo P . . .98 B3
Montegranaro I . . .82 C2
Montehermoso E . . .93 A4
Montejicar E . . .100 B2
Montejo de la Sierra E . . .95 A3
Montejo de Tiermes E . . .89 C3
Montel-de-Gelat F . . .68 C2
Monteleone di Púglia I . . .103 B8
Montelepre I . . .108 A2
Montelíbretti I . . .102 A5
Montelier F . . .79 B4
Montella I . . .103 C8
Montellano E . . .99 B5
Montelupo Fiorentino I . . .81 C5
Montemaggiore Belsito I . . .108 B2
Montemagno I . . .80 B2
Montemayor E . . .100 B1
Montemayor de Pinilla E . . .88 C2
Montemésola I . . .104 C3
Montemilletto I . . .103 B7
Montemílone I . . .104 B1
Montemónaco I . . .82 D2
Montemor-o-Novo P . . .92 C2
Montemor-o-Velho P . . .92 A2
Montemurro I . . .104 C1
Montendre F . . .67 C4
Montenegro de Cameros E . . .89 B4
Montenero di Bisáccia I . . .103 B7
Monteneuf F . . .57 C3
Montepaone I . . .106 C3
Montepescali I . . .81 D5
Montepiano I . . .81 B5
Monte Porzio I . . .82 C2
Montepulciano I . . .81 C5
Monte Real P . . .92 B2
Montereale I . . .103 A6
Montereale Valcellina I . . .72 B2
Montereau-Faut-Yonne F . . .59 B3
Monte Redondo P . . .92 B2
Monterénzio I . . .81 B5
Monte Romano I . . .102 A4
Monteroni d'Árbia I . . .81 C5
Monteroni di Lecce I . . .105 C4
Monterosso al Mare I . . .80 B3
Monterosso Almo I . . .109 B3
Monterosso Grana I . . .79 B6
Monterotondo I . . .102 A5
Monterotondo Maríttimo I . . .81 C4
Monterrey E . . .87 C3
Monterroso E . . .86 B3
Monterrubio de la Serena E . . .93 C5
Monterubbiano I . . .82 C2
Montesa E . . .96 C2
Montesalgueiro E . . .86 A2
Monte San Giovanni Campano I . . .103 B6
Montesano sulla Marcellana I . . .104 C1
Monte San Savino I . . .81 C5
Monte Sant'Angelo I . . .104 B1
Montescaglioso I . . .104 C2
Montesclaros E . . .94 B2
Montesilvano I . . .103 A7
Montesquieu-Volvestre F . . .77 C4
Montesquiou F . . .77 C3
Montestruc-sur-Gers F . . .77 C3
Montes Velhos P . . .98 B2
Montevarchi I . . .81 C5
Monteux F . . .79 C4
Monte Vilar P . . .92 B1
Montfaucon F . . .66 A3
Montfaucon-d'Argonne F . . .59 A6
Montfaucon-en-Velay F . . .69 C4
Montferrat
  Isère F . . .69 C5
  Var F . . .79 C5
Montfort-en-Chalosse F . . .76 C2
Montfort-l'Amaury F . . .58 B2
Montfort-le-Gesnois F . . .58 B1
Montfort-sur-Meu F . . .57 B4
Montfort-sur-Risle F . . .58 A1
Montgai E . . .90 B3
Montgaillard F . . .77 C3
Montgenèvre F . . .79 B5
Montgiscard F . . .77 C4
Montgomery GB . . .26 C2
Montguyon F . . .67 C4
Monthermé F . . .59 A5
Monthey CH . . .70 B1
Monthois F . . .59 A5
Monthureux-sur-Saône F . . .60 B1
Monti I . . .110 B2
Monticelli d'Ongina I . . .81 A3
Montichiari I . . .71 C5
Montiel E . . .100 A3
Montier-en-Der F . . .59 B5
Montieri I . . .81 C5
Montiglio I . . .80 A2
Montignac F . . .77 B3
Montigny-le-Roi F . . .60 C1
Montigny-lès-Metz F . . .60 A2
Montigny-sur-Aube F . . .59 C5
Montijo
  E . . .93 C4
  P . . .92 C2
Montilla E . . .100 B1
Montillana E . . .100 B2
Montilly F . . .68 B3
Montivilliers F . . .57 A6
Montjean-sur-Loire F . . .66 A4
Montlhéry F . . .58 B3
Montlieu-la-Garde F . . .67 C4
Mont-Louis F . . .91 A5
Montlouis-sur-Loire F . . .67 A5
Montluçon F . . .68 B2
Montluel F . . .69 C5
Montmarault F . . .68 B2
Montmartin-sur-Mer F . . .57 B4
Montmédy F . . .59 A6
Montmeyan F . . .79 C5
Montmélian F . . .69 C6
Montmirail
  Marne F . . .59 B4
  Sarthe F . . .58 B1
Montmiral F . . .79 A4
Montmirat F . . .78 C3
Montmirey-le-Château F . . .69 A5

Montmoreau-St Cybard
F 67 C5
Montmorency F 58 B3
Montmorillon F 67 B5
Montmort-Lucy F 59 B4
Montoir-de-Bretagne
F 66 A2
Montoire-sur-le-Loir
F 58 C1
Montoito P 92 C3
Montolieu F 77 C5
Montório al Vomano
I 103 A6
Montoro E 100 A1
Montpellier F 78 C2
Montpezat-de-Quercy
F 77 B4
Montpezat-sous-Bouzon
F 78 B3
Montpon-Ménestérol
F 76 A3
Montpont-en-Bresse
F 69 B5
Montréal
Aude F 77 C5
Gers F 76 C3
Montredon-Labessonnié
F 77 C5
Montréjeau F 77 C3
Montrésor F 67 A6
Montresta I 110 B1
Montret F 69 B5
Montreuil
Pas de Calais F 48 C2
Seine St Denis F 58 B3
Montreuil-aux-Lions
F 59 A4
Montreuil-Bellay F 67 A4
Montreux CH 70 B1
Montrevault F 66 A3
Montrevel-en-Bresse
F 69 B5
Montrichard F 67 A6
Montricoux F 77 B4
Mont-roig del Camp E 90 B3
Montrond-les-Bains F 69 C4
Montrose GB 25 B5
Montroy E 96 B2
Montsalvy F 77 B5
Montsauche-les-Settons
F 68 A4
Montseny E 91 B5
Montsoreau F 67 A5
Mont-sous-Vaudrey F 69 B5
Monts-sur-Guesnes F 67 B5
Mont-St Aignan F 58 A2
Mont-St Vincent F 69 B4
Montsûrs F 57 B5
Montuenga E 94 A2
Montuïri E 97 B3
Monturque E 100 B1
Monza I 71 C4
Monzón E 90 B3
Monzón de Campos
E 88 B2
Moorbad Lobenstein
D 52 C1
Moordorf D 43 B4
Moorslede B 49 C4
Moos D 61 C4
Moosburg D 62 B2
Moosburg im Kärnten
A 73 B4
Mór H 74 A3
Mora E 94 C3
Mora P 92 C2
Mora S 36 A1
Moraby S 36 B2
Móra d'Ebre E 90 B3
Mora de Rubielos E 96 A2
Moradillo de Roa E 88 C3
Morag PL 47 B5
Mórahalom H 75 B4
Moraime E 86 A1
Morais P 87 C4
Mòra la Nova E 90 B3
Moral de Calatrava
E 100 A2
Moraleda de Zafayona
E 100 B2
Moraleja E 93 A4
Moraleja del Vino E 88 C1
Morales del Vino E 88 C1
Morales de Toro E 88 C1
Morales de Valverde
E 88 C1
Moralina E 87 C4
Morano Cálabro I 106 B3
Mörarp S 41 C2
Morasverdes E 93 A4
Morata de Jalón E 89 C5
Morata de Jiloca E 89 C5
Morata de Tajuña E 95 B3
Moratalla E 101 A4
Moravče SLO 73 B4
Moravec CZ 64 A2
Moraviţa RO 75 C6
Morávka CZ 65 A4
Moravská Třebová
CZ 64 A2
Moravské Budějovice
CZ 64 A1
Moravské Lieskové
SK 64 B3
Moravske Toplice
SLO 73 B6
Moravský-Beroun CZ 64 A3
Moravský Krumlov
CZ 64 A2
Moravský Svätý Ján
SK 64 B3
Morawica PL 55 C5
Morawin PL 54 B3
Morbach D 60 A3
Morbegno I 71 B4
Morbier F 69 B6
Mörbisch am See A 64 C2
Mörbylånga S 41 C6
Morcenx F 76 B2
Morciano di Romagna
I 82 C1
Morcone I 103 B7
Morcuera E 89 C3
Mordelles F 57 B4
Mordoğan TR 119 D1
Moréac F 56 C3
Morebattle GB 25 C5
Morecambe GB 26 A3
Moreda
Granada E 100 B2
Oviedo E 88 A1
Morée F 58 C2
Moreles de Rey E 88 B1
Morella E 90 C2
Moreruela de los
Infanzones E 88 C1
Morés E 89 C5
Móres I 110 B1
Morestel F 69 C5
Moretonhampstead
GB 28 C4
Moreton-in-Marsh GB 29 B6
Moret-sur-Loing F 58 B3
Moretta I 80 B1
Moreuil F 58 A3
Morez F 69 B6
Mörfelden D 51 D4
Morgat F 56 B1
Morges CH 69 B6
Morgex I 70 C2
Morgongåva S 36 C3
Morhange F 60 B2
Morhet B 49 D6
Mori I 71 C5
Morialmé B 49 C5
Morianes P 98 B3
Moriani Plage F 102 A2
Mórichida H 74 A2
Moriles E 100 B1
Morille E 94 B1
Moringen D 51 B5
Morjärv S 3 C25
Morkarla S 36 B4
Mørke DK 39 C3
Mørkøv DK 39 D4
Morkovice-Slížany
CZ 64 A3
Morlaàs F 76 C2
Morlaix F 56 B2
Morley F 59 B6
Mörlunda S 40 B5
Mormanno I 106 B2
Mormant F 59 B3
Mornant F 69 C4
Mornay-Berry F 68 A2
Morokovo MNE 85 D4
Morón de Almazán E 89 C4
Morón de la Frontera
E 99 B5
Morović SRB 85 A4
Morozzo I 80 B1
Morpeth GB 25 C6
Morphou CY 120 A1
Mörrum S 41 C4
Morsbach D 50 C3
Mörsch D 61 B4
Mörsil S 115 D10
Morsum D 39 E1
Mørsvikbotn N 112 E4
Mortagne-au-Perche
F 58 B1
Mortagne-sur-Gironde
F 66 C4
Mortagne-sur-Sèvre
F 66 B4
Mortágua P 92 A2
Mortain F 57 B5
Mortara I 70 C3
Morteau F 69 A6
Mortegliano I 72 C3
Mortelle I 109 A4
Mortemart F 67 B5
Mortimer's Cross GB 29 A5
Mortrée F 57 B6
Mörtschach A 72 B2
Mortsel B 49 B5
Morud DK 39 D3
Morwenstow GB 28 C3
Moryń PL 45 C6
Morzeszczyn PL 47 B4
Morzewo PL 47 B5
Morzine F 70 B1
Mosalsk RUS 7 D13
Mosbach D 61 A5
Mosbjerg DK 38 B3
Mosby N 33 D4
Mosca P 87 C4
Moscavide P 92 C1
Moščenica HR 73 C6
Mošćenice HR 73 C4
Moščenicka Draga
HR 73 C4
Mosciano Sant'Angelo
I 82 D2
Mościsko PL 54 C1
Moscow = Moskva
RUS 7 D14
Mosina PL 54 A1
Mosjøen N 115 B10
Moskog N 32 A3
Moskorzew PL 55 C4
Moskosel S 115 B16
Moskuvarra FIN 113 E15
Moskva = Moscow
RUS 7 D14
Moslavina Podravska
HR 74 C2
Moşniţa Nouă RO 75 C6
Moso in Passíria I 71 B6
Mosonmagyaróvár H 64 C3
Mošorin SRB 75 C5
Mošovce SK 65 B4
Mosqueruela E 90 C2
Moss N 35 C2
Mossfellsbær IS 111 C4
Mössingen D 61 B5
Mosstrand N 32 C5
Most CZ 52 C3
Mosta M 107 C5
Mostar BIH 84 C2
Mosterhamn N 33 C2
Mostki PL 53 A5
Most na Soči SLO 72 B3
Móstoles E 94 B3
Mostová SK 64 B3
Mostowo PL 46 A2
Mostuéjouls F 78 B2
Mosty PL 45 B6
Mostys'ka UA 11 B7
Mosvik N 114 D7
Mota del Cuervo E 95 C4
Mota del Marqués E 88 C1
Motala S 37 D2
Motherwell GB 25 C4
Möthlow D 45 C4
Motilla del Palancar E 95 C5
Motnik SLO 73 B4
Motovun HR 72 C3
Motril E 100 C2
Motta I 71 C6
Motta di Livenza I 72 C2
Motta Montecorvino
I 103 B8
Motta Visconti I 70 C3
Mottisfont GB 31 C2
Móttola I 104 C3
Mou DK 38 C3
Mouchard F 69 B5
Moudon CH 70 B1
Moudros GR 116 C7
Mougins F 79 C5
Mouilleron en-Pareds
F 66 B4
Mouliherne F 67 A5
Moulinet F 80 C1
Moulins F 68 B3
Moulins-Engilbert F 68 B3
Moulins-la-Marche F 58 B1
Moulismes F 67 B5
Moult F 57 A5
Mountain Ash GB 29 B4
Mountbellew IRL 20 A3
Mountfield GB 19 B4
Mountmellick IRL 21 A4
Mountrath IRL 21 A4
Mountsorrel GB 30 B2
Moura P 98 A3
Mourão P 92 C3
Mourenx F 76 C2
Mouriés F 78 C3
Mourmelon-le-Grand
F 59 A5
Mouronho P 92 A2
Mouscron B 49 C4
Mousehole GB 28 C2
Moussac F 78 C3
Moussey F 60 B2
Mousteru F 56 B2
Moustey F 76 B2
Moustiers-Ste Marie
F 79 C5
Mouthe F 69 B6
Mouthier-Haute-Pierre
F 69 A6
Mouthoumet F 77 D5
Moutier CH 70 A2
Moûtiers F 69 C6
Moutiers-les-Mauxfaits
F 66 B3
Mouy F 58 A3
Mouzaki GR 116 C3
Mouzon F 59 A6
Møvik N 32 B2
Moville IRL 19 A4
Moy
Highland GB 23 D4
Tyrone GB 19 B5
Moycullen IRL 20 A2
Moyenmoutier F 60 B2
Moyenvic F 60 B2
Moylough IRL 18 C3
Mózar E 88 C1
Mozhaysk RUS 7 D14
Mozirje SLO 73 B4
Mözs H 74 B3
Mozzanica I 71 C4
Mramorak SRB 85 B5
Mrčajevci SRB 85 C5
Mrkonjić Grad BIH 84 B2
Mrkopalj HR 73 C4
Mrmoš SRB 85 C6
Mrocza PL 46 B3
Mroczeń PL 54 B2
Mroczno PL 47 B5
Mrozy PL 55 A6
Mrzezyno PL 45 A7
Mšec CZ 53 C3
Mšeno CZ 53 C4
Mstów PL 55 C4
Mstsislaw BY 7 D11
Mszana Dolna PL 65 A6
Mszczonów PL 55 B5
Mtsensk RUS 7 E14
Muć HR 83 C5
Múccia I 82 C2
Much D 50 C3
Mücheln D 52 B1
Much Marcle GB 29 B5
Muchów PL 53 B6
Much Wenlock GB 26 C3
Mucientes E 88 C2
Muckross IRL 20 B2
Mucur TR 16 B7
Muda P 98 B2
Mudanya TR 118 B3
Mudau D 61 A5
Müden D 44 C2
Mudersbach D 50 C3
Mudurnu TR 118 B6
Muel E 90 B1
Muelas del Pan E 88 C1
Muess D 44 B3
Muff IRL 19 A4
Mugardos E 86 A2
Muge P 92 B2
Mügeln
Sachsen D 52 B3
Sachsen-Anhalt D 52 B3
Múggia I 72 C3
Mugnano I 82 C1
Mugron F 76 C2
Mugueimes E 87 C3
Muhi H 65 C6
Mühlacker D 61 B4
Mühlbach am Hochkönig
A 72 A3
Mühlberg
Brandenburg D 52 B3
Thüringen D 51 C6
Mühldorf
A 72 B3
D 62 B3
Muhleberg CH 70 B2
Mühleim D 61 B4
Muhlen-Eichsen D 44 B3
Mühlhausen
Bayern D 62 A1
Thüringen D 51 B6
Mühltroff D 52 C1
Muhos FIN 3 D27
Muhr A 72 A3
Muine Bheag IRL 21 B5
Muirkirk GB 24 C3
Muir of Ord GB 23 D4
Muirteira P 92 B1
Mukacheve UA 11 B7
Muker GB 26 A3
Mula E 101 A4
Muğla TR 119 E3
Mulben GB 23 D5
Mulegns CH 71 B4
Mules I 71 B6
Mülheim D 50 B2
Mulhouse F 60 C3
Muljava SLO 73 C4
Mullanys Cross IRL 18 B3
Müllheim D 60 C3
Mullhyttan S 37 C1
Mullinavat IRL 21 B4
Mullingar IRL 21 A4
Mullion GB 28 C2
Müllrose D 53 A4
Mullsjö S 40 B3
Mulseryd S 40 B3
Munaðarnes IS 111 A4
Munana E 94 B1
Muñás E 86 A4
Münchberg D 52 C1
Müncheberg D 45 C6
München = Munich D 62 B2
Munchen-Gladbach =
Mönchengladbach
D 50 B2
Münchhausen D 51 C4
Mundaka E 89 A4
Münden D 51 B5
Munderfing A 63 B4
Munderkingen D 61 B5
Mundesley GB 30 B5
Munera E 95 C4
Mungia E 89 A4
Munich = München D 62 B2
Muñico E 94 B1
Muniesa E 90 B2
Munka-Ljungby S 41 C2
Munkebo DK 39 D3
Munkedal S 35 D3
Munkflohögen S 115 D11
Munkfors S 34 C5
Munktorp S 37 C3
Münnerstadt D 51 C6
Muñopepe E 94 B2
Muñotello E 94 B1
Münsingen
CH 70 B2
D 61 B5
Munsö S 37 C4
Münster
CH 70 B3
Hessen D 61 A4
Munster D 44 C2
Münster D 50 B3
Munster F 60 B3
Muntibar E 89 A4
Münzkirchen A 63 B4
Muodoslompolo S 113 E12
Muonio FIN 113 E12
Muotathal CH 70 B3
Muradiye TR 118 D2
Murakeresztúr H 74 B1
Murán SK 65 B6
Murano I 72 C2
Muras E 86 A3
Murat F 78 A1
Muratlı TR 118 A2
Murato F 102 A2
Murat-sur-Vèbre F 78 C1
Murau A 73 A4
Muravera I 110 C2
Murazzano I 80 B2
Murça P 87 C3
Murchante E 89 B5
Murchin D 45 B5
Murcia E 101 B4
Murczyn PL 46 C3
Mur-de-Barrez F 77 B5
Mur-de-Bretagne F 56 B2
Mur-de-Sologne F 67 A6
Mureck A 73 B5
Mürefte TR 118 B2
Muret F 77 C4
Murg CH 71 A4
Murguia E 89 B4
Muri CH 70 A3
Murias de Paredes E 86 B4
Muriedas E 88 A3
Muriel Viejo E 89 C4
Murillo de Rio Leza E 89 B4
Murillo el Fruto E 89 B5
Murino MNE 85 D4
Müritz D 105 A5
Murlaggan GB 22 E3
Murmansk RUS 3 B30
Murmashi RUS 3 B30
Murnau D 62 C2
Muro
E 97 B3
F 102 A1
Muro de Alcoy E 96 C2
Murol F 68 C2
Muro Lucano I 103 C8
Muron F 66 B4
Muros E 86 B1
Muros de Nalón E 86 A4
Murowana Goślina
PL 46 C3
Mürren CH 70 B2
Murrhardt D 61 B5
Murska Sobota SLO 73 B6
Mursko Središće HR 73 B6
Murtas E 100 C2
Murten CH 70 B2
Murter HR 83 C4
Murtiçi TR 119 F6
Murtosa P 87 D2
Murvica HR 83 B4
Murviel-lès-Béziers F 78 C2
Mürzsteg A 63 C6
Murzynowo PL 46 C1
Mürzzuschlag A 63 C6
Musculdy F 76 C2
Mushqeta AL 105 B5
Muskö S 37 C5
Mušov CZ 64 B2
Musselburgh GB 25 C4
Musselkanaal NL 43 C4
Mussidan F 77 A3
Mussomeli I 108 B2
Musson B 60 A1
Mussy-sur-Seine F 59 C5
Mustafakemalpaşa
TR 118 B3
Muszaki PL 47 B6
Muszyna PL 65 A6
Mut TR 16 C6
Muta SLO 73 B5
Muthill GB 25 B4
Mutné SK 65 A5
Mutriku E 89 A4
Muttalip TR 118 C5
Mutterbergalm A 71 A6
Muxía E 86 A1
Muxilka-Ugarte E 89 A4
Muzillac F 66 A2
Mužla SK 65 C4
Muzzano del Turgnano
I 72 C3
Mybster GB 23 C5
Myckelgensjö S 115 D14
Myennes F 68 A2
Myjava SK 64 B3
Myking N 32 B2
Myklebust N 114 E2
Mykolayiv = Nikolayev
UA 11 C12
Myra N 33 D6
Myrdal N 32 B4
Myre
Nordland N 112 C4
Nordland N 112 D4
Myresjö S 40 B4
Myrhorod UA 11 B12
Myri IS 111 B8
Myrtou CY 120 A2
Mysen N 35 C3
Mysłakowice PL 53 C5
Myślenice PL 65 A5
Myślibórz PL 45 C6
Mysłowice PL 55 C4
Myszków PL 55 C4
Mytishchi RUS 7 D14
Mýtna SK 65 B5
Mýtne Ludany SK 65 B4
Mýto CZ 63 A4

N

Nå N 32 B3
Naaldwijk NL 49 B5
Naantali FIN 6 A6
Naas IRL 21 A5
Nabais P 92 A3
Nabbelund S 41 B7
Nabburg D 62 A3
Načeradec CZ 63 A5
Náchod CZ 53 C6
Nacław PL 46 A2
Nadarzyce PL 46 B2
Nadarzyn PL 55 A5
Nádasd H 74 B1
Nădlac RO 75 B5
Nádudvar H 75 A6
Nadvirna UA 11 B8
Næfels CH 70 A4
Nafpaktos GR 116 D3
Nafplio GR 117 E4
Nagel D 52 D1
Nagele NL 42 C2
Naggen S 115 E13
Nagłowice PL 55 C5
Nagold D 61 B4
Nagore E 76 D1
Nagyatád H 74 B2
Nagybajom H 74 B2
Nagybaracska H 74 B3
Nagybátony H 65 C5
Nagyberény H 74 B3
Nagybörzsöny H 65 C4
Nagycenk H 64 C2
Nagydorog H 74 B3
Nagyfüged H 65 C6
Nagyhersány H 74 C3
Nagyigmánd H 64 C4
Nagyiván H 75 A5
Nagykanizsa H 74 B1
Nagykáta H 75 A4
Nagykonyi H 74 B3
Nagykörös H 75 A4
Nagykörü H 75 A5
Nagylóc H 65 B5
Nagymágocs H 75 B5
Nagymányok H 74 B3
Nagymaros H 65 C4
Nagyoroszi H 65 B5
Nagyrábé H 75 A6
Nagyréde H 65 C5
Nagyszékely H 74 B3
Nagyszénás H 75 B5
Nagyszokoly H 74 B3
Nagytöke H 75 B5
Nagyvázsony H 74 B2
Nagyvenyim H 74 B3
Naharros E 95 B4
Nahe D 44 B2
Naidăş RO 85 B6
Naila D 52 C1
Nailloux F 77 C4
Nailsworth GB 29 B5
Naintré F 67 B5
Nairn GB 23 D5
Najac F 77 B4
Nájera E 89 B4
Nak H 74 B3
Nakksjø N 33 C6
Nakło nad Notecią
PL 46 B3
Nakskov DK 39 E4
Nalda E 89 B4
Nälden S 115 D11
Nálepkovo SK 65 B6
Nalliers F 66 B3
Nallıhan TR 118 B6
Nalzen F 77 D4
Nalžouské Hory CZ 63 A4
Namdalseid N 114 C8
Náměšť nad Oslavou
CZ 64 A2
Námestovo SK 65 A5
Namnå N 34 B4
Namsos N 114 C8
Namsskogan N 115 C10
Namur B 49 C5
Namysłów PL 54 B2
Nançay F 68 A2
Nanclares de la Oca
E 89 B4
Nancy F 60 B2
Nangis F 59 B4
Nannestad N 34 B3
Nant F 78 B2
Nanterre F 58 B3
Nantes F 66 A3
Nanteuil-le-Haudouin
F 58 A3
Nantiat F 67 B6
Nantua F 69 B5
Nantwich GB 26 B3
Naoussa
Cyclades GR 117 E7
Imathia GR 116 B4
Napajedla CZ 64 A3
Napiwoda PL 47 B6
Naples = Nápoli I 103 C7
Nápoli = Naples I 103 C7
Nar S 37 E5
Nara N 32 A1
Naraval E 86 A4
Narberth GB 28 B3
Nærbø N 33 D2
Narbonne F 78 C1
Narbonne-Plage F 78 C2
Narbuvollen N 114 E8
Narcao I 110 C1
Nardò I 107 A5
Narken S 113 F11
Narmo N 34 B3
Narni I 102 A5
Naro I 108 B2
Naro Fominsk RUS 7 D14
Narón E 86 A2
Narros del Castillo E 94 B1
Narta HR 74 C1
Naruszewo PL 47 C6
Narva EST 7 B10
Narvik N 112 D6
Narzole I 80 B1
Näs FIN 36 B7
Nås S 36 B1
Näs S 37 E5
Näsåker S 115 D13
Năsăud RO 11 C8
Nasavrky CZ 64 A1
Nasbinals F 78 B2
Næsbjerg DK 39 D1
Näshull S 40 B5
Našice HR 74 C3
Nasielsk PL 47 C6
Naso I 109 A3
Nassau D 50 C3
Nassenfels D 62 B2
Nassenheide D 45 C5
Nassereith A 71 A5
Nässjö S 40 B4
Nastätten D 50 C3
Næstved DK 39 D4
Näsum S 41 C4
Näsviken S 115 D12
Natalinci SRB 85 B5
Naters CH 70 B3
Nater-Stetten D 62 B2
Nattavaara S 112 F9
Natters A 71 A6
Nattheim D 61 B6
Nättraby S 41 C5
Naturno I 71 B5
Naucelle F 77 B5
Nauders A 71 B5
Nauen D 45 C4
Naul IRL 19 C5
Naumburg D 52 B1
Naundorf D 52 C3
Naunhof D 52 B2
Naustdal N 32 A2
Nautijaur S 112 F8
Nautsi RUS 113 D18
Nava E 88 A1
Navacerrada E 94 B2
Navaconcejo E 93 A5
Nava de Arévalo E 94 B2
Nava de la Asunción
E 94 A2
Nava del Rey E 88 C1
Navafriá E 94 A3
Navahermosa E 94 C2
Navahrudak BY 7 E8
Naval E 90 A3
Navalacruz E 94 B2
Navalcán E 94 B2
Navalcarnero E 94 B2
Navaleno E 89 C3
Navalmanzano E 94 A2
Navalmoral E 94 B2
Navalmoral de la Mata
E 93 B5
Naválón E 96 C2
Navalonguilla E 93 A5
Navalperal de Pinares
E 94 B2
Navalpino E 94 C2
Navaltalgordo E 94 B2
Navaltoril E 94 C2
Navaluenga E 94 B2
Navalvillar de Pela E 93 B5
Navan IRL 19 C5
Navaperal de Tormes
E 93 A5
Navapolatsk BY 7 D10
Navarclés E 91 B4
Navarredonda de Gredos
E 93 A5
Navarrenx F 76 C2
Navarrés E 96 B2
Navarrete E 89 B4
Navarrevisca E 94 B2
Navás E 91 B4
Navascués E 76 D1
Navas del Madroño E 93 B4
Navas del Rey E 94 B2
Navas de Oro E 94 A2
Navas de San Juan
E 100 A2
Navasfrias E 93 A4
Nave I 71 C5
Nave de Haver P 93 A4
Nävekvarn S 37 D3
Navelli I 103 A6
Navenby GB 27 B5
Näverkärret S 37 C2
Naverstad S 35 D3
Navés E 91 B4
Navezuelas E 93 B5
Navia E 86 A4
Navia de Suarna E 86 B4
Navilly F 69 B5
Navlya RUS 7 E13
Năvodari RO 11 D10
Naxos GR 117 E7
Nay F 76 C2
Nazaré P 92 B1
Nazarje SLO 73 B4
Nazilli TR 119 E3
Nazza D 51 B6
Ndroq AL 105 B5
Nea Anchialos GR 116 C4
Nea Epidavros GR 117 E5
Nea Flippias GR 116 C2
Nea Kalikratia GR 116 B5
Nea Makri GR 117 D5
Nea Moudania GR 116 B5
Neap GB 22 A7
Nea Peramos GR 116 B6
Neapoli
Kozani GR 116 B3
Kriti GR 117 G7
Lakonia GR 117 F5
Nea Stira GR 117 D6
Neath GB 28 B4
Nea Visa GR 118 A1
Nea Zichni GR 116 A5
Nebljusi HR 83 B4
Neblo SLO 72 B3
Nebolchy RUS 7 B12
Nebra D 52 B1
Nebreda E 88 C3
Nechanice CZ 53 C5
Neckargemünd D 61 A4
Neckarsulm D 61 A5
Neda E 86 A2
Neded SK 64 B3
Nedelišće HR 73 B6
Nederweert NL 50 B1
Nedreberg N 34 B3
Nedre Gärdsjö S 36 B2
Nedre Soppero S 113 D10
Nedstrand N 33 C2
Nedvědice CZ 64 A2
Nędza PL 54 C3
Neede NL 50 A2
Needham Market GB 30 B5
Needingworth GB 30 B3
Neermoor D 43 B4
Neeroeteren B 50 B1
Neerpelt B 49 B6
Neesen D 51 A4
Neetze D 44 B2
Nefyn GB 26 C1
Negbina SRB 85 C4
Negotin SRB 11 D7
Negotino MK 116 A4
Negrar I 71 C5
Negredo E 95 A4
Negreira E 86 B2
Nègrepelisse F 77 B4
Negru Vodă RO 11 E10
Negueira de Muñiz E 86 A4
Neheim D 50 B3
Neila E 89 B4
Néive I 80 B2
Nejdek CZ 52 C2
Nekla PL 46 C3
Neksø DK 41 D5
Nelas P 92 A3
Nelaug N 33 D5
Nelidovo RUS 7 C12
Nelim FIN 113 D17
Nellingen D 61 B5
Nelson GB 26 B3
Neman RUS 6 D7
Nemea GR 117 E4
Nemesgörzsöny H 74 A2
Nemeskér H 74 A1
Nemesnádudvar H 75 B4
Nemesszalók H 74 A2
Németkér H 74 B3
Nemours F 58 B3
Nemška Loka SLO 73 C5
Nemšová SK 64 B4
Nenagh IRL 20 B3
Nenince SK 65 B5
Nenita GR 117 D8
Nenzing A 71 A4
Neochori GR 116 C3
Neo Chori GR 116 D3
Neon Petritsi GR 116 A5
Nepi I 102 A5
Nepomuk CZ 63 A4
Nérac F 77 B3
Neratovice CZ 53 C4
Nerchau D 52 B2
Néré F 67 C4
Neresheim D 61 B6
Nereto I 82 D2
Nerezine HR 82 B3
Nerežišća HR 83 C5
Neringa LT 6 D6
Néris-les Bains F 68 B2
Nerito I 103 A6
Nerja E 100 C2
Néronde F 69 C4
Nérondes F 68 B2
Nerpio E 101 A3
Nersingen D 61 B6
Nerva E 99 B4
Nervesa della Battáglia
I 72 C2
Nervi I 80 B3
Nes
N 114 D6
Buskerud N 34 B1
Hedmark N 34 B2
NL 42 B2
Nesbyen N 32 B6
Neset N 114 F7
Nesflaten N 33 C3
Nesjahverfi IS 111 C10
Neskaupstaður IS 111 B12
Nesland N 33 C4
Neslandsvatn N 33 D6
Nesle F 59 A3
Nesna N 115 A10
Nesoddtangen N 34 C2
Nesovice CZ 64 A3
Nesselwang D 61 C6
Nesslau CH 71 A4
Nessmersiel D 43 B4
Nesso I 71 C4
Nesterov UA 11 A7
Nestorio GR 116 B3
Nesttun N 32 B2
Nesvady SK 64 C4
Nesvatnstemmen N 33 D5
Nether Stowey GB 29 B4
Netland N 33 D3
Netolice CZ 63 A5
Netphen D 50 C4
Netstal CH 70 A4
Nettancourt F 59 B5
Nettetal D 50 B2
Nettlingen D 51 A6
Nettuno I 102 B5
Neualbenreuth D 52 D2
Neubeckum D 50 B4
Neubrandenburg D 45 B5
Neubruchhausen D 43 C5
Neubukow D 44 A3
Neuburg D 62 B2
Neuchâtel CH 70 B1
Neu Darchau D 44 B2
Neudau A 73 A6
Neudietendorf D 51 C6
Neudorf D 61 A4
Neuenbürg D 61 B4
Neuenburg D 43 B4
Neuendorf D 45 A5
Neuenhagen D 45 C5
Neuenhaus D 42 C3
Neuenkirchen
Niedersachsen D 43 B6
Niedersachsen D 43 C5
Nordrhein-Westfalen
D 50 A3
Nordrhein-Westfalen
D 50 C3
Neuenrade D 50 B3
Neuenwalde D 43 B5
Neuerburg D 50 C2
Neufahrn
Bayern D 62 B2
Bayern D 62 B3
Neuf-Brisach F 60 B3
Neufchâteau
B 60 A1
F 60 B1
Neufchâtel-en-Bray F 58 A2
Neufchâtel-sur-Aisne
F 59 A5
Neuflize F 59 A5
Neugersdorf D 53 C4
Neuhardenberg D 45 C6
Neuharlingersiel D 43 B4
Neuhaus
Bayern D 62 A2
Bayern D 63 B4
Niedersachsen D 43 B6
Niedersachsen D 44 B2
Niedersachsen D 51 B5
Neuhaus a Rennweg
D 52 C1
Neuhausen
CH 61 C4
D 52 C3
Neuhausen ob Eck D 61 C4
Neuhof
Bayern D 62 A1
Hessen D 51 C5
Neuhofen an der Krems
A 63 B5
Neuillé-Pont-Pierre F 67 A5
Neuilly-en-Thelle F 58 A3
Neuilly-le-Réal F 68 B3
Neuilly-l'Évêque F 60 C1
Neuilly-St Front F 59 A4
Neu-Isenburg D 51 C4
Neukalen D 45 B4
Neu Kaliss D 44 B3
Neukirch D 53 B4
Neukirchen
A 62 B4
Hessen D 51 C5
Schleswig-Holstein D 39 E1
Neukirchen am
Grossvenediger A 72 A2
Neukirchen bei Heiligen
Blut D 62 A3
Neukloster D 44 B3
Neulengbach A 64 B1
Neulise F 68 C4
Neu Lübbenau D 53 A3
Neum BIH 84 D2
Neumagen D 60 A2
Neumarkt D 62 A2
Neumarkt am Wallersee
A 63 C4
Neumarkt im
Hausruckkreis A 63 B4
Neumarkt im Mühlkreis
A 63 B5
Neumarkt im Steiermark
A 73 A4
Neumarkt Sankt Veit
D 62 B3
Neumünster D 44 A1
Neunburg vorm Wald
D 62 A3
Neung-sur-Beuvron F 68 A1
Neunkirch
Luzern CH 70 A3
Schaffhausen CH 61 C4
Neunkirchen
A 64 C2
Nordrhein-Westfalen
D 50 C3
Saarland D 60 A3
Neunkirchen am Brand
D 62 A2
Neuötting D 62 B3
Neupetershain D 53 B4
Neuravensburg D 61 C5
Neureut D 61 A4
Neuruppin D 45 C4
Neusäss D 62 B1
Neusiedl A 64 C2
Neuss D 50 B2
Neussargues-Moissac
F 68 C2
Neustadt
Bayern D 62 A1
Bayern D 62 A3
Bayern D 62 B2
Brandenburg D 44 C4
Hessen D 51 C5
Niedersachsen D 43 C6
Rheinland-Pfalz D 61 A4
Sachsen D 53 B4
Schleswig-Holstein D 44 A2
Thüringen D 52 C1
Thüringen D 52 C1
Neustadt-Glewe D 44 B3
Neustift im Stubaital
A 71 A6
Neustrelitz D 45 B5
Neutal A 73 A6
Neutrebbin D 45 C6
Neu-Ulm D 61 B6
Neuves-Maisons F 60 B2
Neuvic
Corrèze F 68 C2
Dordogne F 77 A3
Neuville-aux-Bois F 58 B3
Neuville-de-Poitou F 67 B5
Neuville-les-Dames F 69 B5
Neuville-sur-Saône F 69 C4
Neuvy-le-Roi F 58 C1
Neuvy-Santour F 59 B4
Neuvy-St Sépulchre
F 68 B1
Neuvy-sur-Barangeon
F 68 A2
Neuwied D 50 C3
Neuzelle D 53 A4
Névache F 79 A5
Nevel RUS 7 D10
Neverfjord N 113 B12
Nevers F 68 B3
Nevesinje BIH 84 C3
Névez F 56 C2
Nevlunghavn N 35 D1
Nevşehir TR 16 B7
New Abbey GB 25 D4
New Aberdour GB 23 D6
New Alresford GB 31 C2
Newark-on-Trent GB 27 B5
Newbiggin-by-the-Sea
GB 25 C6
Newbliss IRL 19 B4
Newborough GB 26 B1
Newbridge IRL 21 A5
Newbridge on Wye
GB 29 A4
Newburgh
Aberdeenshire GB 23 D6
Fife GB 25 B4
Newbury GB 31 C2
Newby Bridge GB 26 A3
Newcastle GB 19 B6
Newcastle Emlyn GB 28 A3
Newcastleton GB 25 C5
Newcastle-under-Lyme
GB 26 B3
Newcastle upon Tyne
GB 25 D6
Newcastle West IRL 20 B2
Newchurch GB 29 A4
New Costessey GB 30 B5
New Cumnock GB 24 C3
Newent GB 29 B5
New Galloway GB 24 C3
Newham GB 31 C4
Newhaven GB 31 D4
Newington GB 31 C5
Newinn IRL 21 B4
Newlyn GB 28 C2
Newmachar GB 23 D6
Newmarket
Suffolk GB 30 B4
Western Isles GB 22 C2
IRL 20 B3
Newmarket-on-Fergus
IRL 20 B3
New Mills GB 27 B4
New Milton GB 31 D2
New Pitsligo GB 23 D6
Newport
Isle of Wight GB 31 D2
Newport GB 29 B5
Pembrokeshire GB 28 A3
Telford & Wrekin GB 26 C3
Mayo IRL 18 C2
Tipperary IRL 20 B3
Newport-on-Tay GB 25 B5
Newport Pagnell GB 30 B3
Newquay GB 28 C2
New Quay GB 28 A3
New Radnor GB 29 A4
New Romney GB 31 D4
New Ross IRL 21 B5
Newry GB 19 B5
New Scone GB 25 B4
Newton Abbot GB 29 C4
Newton Arlosh GB 25 D4
Newton Aycliffe GB 27 A4
Newton Ferrers GB 28 C3
Newtonhill GB 23 D6
Newtonmore GB 23 D4
Newton Stewart GB 24 D3
Newtown
Herefordshire GB 29 A5
Powys GB 26 C2
Newtownabbey GB 19 B6
Newtownards GB 19 B6
Newtownbutler GB 19 B4
Newtown Cunningham
IRL 19 B4
Newtownhamilton GB 19 B5
Newtownmountkennedy
IRL 21 A5
Newtown St Boswells
GB 25 C5
Newtown Sands IRL 20 B2
Newtownshandrum
IRL 20 B3
Newtownstewart GB 19 B4
Nexon F 67 C6
Neyland GB 28 B3
Nibbiano I 80 B3
Nibe DK 38 C2
Nicaj-Shalë AL 105 A5
Nicastro I 106 C3
Niccone I 82 C1
Nice F 80 C1
Nickelsdorf A 64 C3
Nicolosi I 109 B4
Nicosia
CY 120 A2
I 109 B3
Nícotera I 106 C2
Nidda D 51 C5
Niğde TR 16 C7
Nidzica PL 47 B6
Niebla E 99 B4
Nieborów PL 55 A5
Niebüll D 39 E1
Niechanowo PL 46 C3
Niechorze PL 45 A7
Niedalino PL 46 A2
Niederaula D 51 C5
Niederbipp CH 70 A2
Niederbronn-les-Bains
F 60 B3
Niederfischbach D 50 C3
Niedergörsdorf D 52 B2
Niederkrüchten D 50 B2
Niederndorf A 62 C3
Nieder-Olm D 61 A4
Niedersachswerfen D 51 B6
Niederstetten D 61 A5
Niederurnen CH 70 A4
Niederwölz A 73 A4
Niedoradz PL 53 B5
Niedzica PL 65 A6
Niegosławice PL 53 B5
Nieheim D 51 B5
Niemcza PL 54 C1
Niemegk D 52 A2
Niemodlin PL 54 C2
Nienburg
Niedersachsen D 43 C6
Sachsen-Anhalt D 52 B1
Niepołomice PL 55 C5
Nierstein D 61 A4
Niesky D 53 B4
Niestronno PL 46 C3
Nieświń PL 55 B5
Nieszawa PL 47 C4
Nieul-le-Dolent F 66 B3
Nieul-sur-Mer F 66 B3
Nieuw-Amsterdam
NL 42 C3
Nieuw-Buinen NL 42 C3
Nieuwegein NL 49 A6
Nieuwe Niedorp NL 42 C1
Nieuwe-Pekela NL 42 B3
Nieuwerkerken B 49 C6
Nieuwe-schans NL 43 B4
Nieuwolda NL 42 B3
Nieuwpoort B 48 B3
Nieuw-Weerdinge NL 42 C3
Nigrita GR 116 B5
Nigüelas E 100 C2
Nijar E 101 C3
Nijemci HR 75 C4
Nijkerk NL 49 A6
Nijlen B 49 B5
Nijmegen NL 50 B1
Nijverdal NL 42 C3
Nikel RUS 113 C19
Nikinci SRB 85 B4
Nikiti GR 116 B5
Nikitsch A 74 A1
Nikkaluokta S 112 E8
Nikla H 74 B2
Niklasdorf A 73 A5
Nikolayev = Mykolayiv
UA 11 C12
Nikšić MNE 84 D3
Nilivaara S 113 E10
Nîmes F 78 C3
Nimis I 72 B3
Nimtofte DK 39 C3
Nin HR 83 B4
Nindorf D 43 A6
Ninemilehouse IRL 21 B4
Ninove B 49 C5
Niort F 67 B4
Niš SRB 10 E6
Nisa P 92 B3
Niscemi I 109 B3
Nissafors S 40 B3
Nissan-lez-Ensérune
F 78 C2
Nissedal N 33 C5
Nissumby DK 38 C1
Nisterud N 33 C6
Niton GB 31 D2
Nitra SK 64 B4
Nitrianske-Pravno SK 65 B4
Nitrianske Rudno SK 65 B4
Nitry F 59 C4
Nittedal N 34 B2
Nittenau D 62 A3
Nittendorf D 62 A2
Nivala FIN 3 E26
Nivelles B 49 C5
Nivenskoye RUS 47 A6
Nivnice CZ 64 B3
Nižná SK 65 A5
Nižná Boca SK 65 B5
Niżne Repaše SK 65 A6
Nizza Monferrato I 80 B2
Njarðvík IS 111 D3
Njegůsevo SRB 75 C4
Njivice HR 83 A3
Njurundabommen
S 115 E14
Njutånger S 115 F14
Noailles F 58 A3
Noain E 76 D1
Noale I 72 C2
Noalejo E 100 B2
Noblejas E 95 C3
Noceda E 86 B4
Nocera Inferiore I 103 C7
Nocera Terinese I 106 B3
Nocera Umbra I 82 C1
Noceto I 81 B4
Noci I 104 C3
Nociglia I 107 A5
Nodeland N 33 D4
Nödinge S 38 B5
Nods F 69 A6
Noé F 77 C4
Noépoli I 106 A3
Noeux-les-Mines F 48 C3
Noez E 94 C2
Nogales E 93 C4
Nogara I 71 C6
Nogarejas E 87 B4
Nogaro F 76 C2
Nogent F 59 B6
Nogent l'Artaud F 59 B4
Nogent-le-Roi F 58 B2
Nogent-le-Rotrou F 58 B1
Nogent-sur-Seine F 59 B4
Nogent-sur-Vernisson
F 58 C3
Nogersund S 41 C4
Noguera E 95 B5
Noguerones E 100 B1

Nohfelden D 60 A3
Nohn D. 50 C2
Noia E 86 B2
Noicâttaro I 104 B2
Noiretable F 68 C3
Noirmoutier-en-l'Île F 66 A2
Noja E 89 A3
Nojewo PL 46 C2
Nokia FIN 3 F25
Nol S 38 B5
Nola I 103 C7
Nolay F 69 B4
Noli I 80 B2
Nolnyra S 36 B4
Nombela E 94 B2
Nomeny F 60 B2
Nomexy F 60 B2
Nonancourt F 58 B2
Nonant-le-Pin F 57 B6
Nonántola I 81 B5
Nonaspe E 90 B3
None I 80 B1
Nontron F 67 C5
Nonza F 102 A2
Noordhorn NL 42 B3
Noordwijk N 49 A5
Noordwijkerhout NL . . .49 A5
Noordwolde NL 42 C3
Noppikoski S 36 A4
Nora S 37 C2
Nørager DK 38 C2
Norberg S 36 B2
Norboda S 36 B5
Norcia I 82 D2
Nordagutu N 33 C6
Nordanås S 115 C15
Nordausques F 48 C3
Nordborg DK 39 D2
Nordby
  Aarhus Amt. DK. 39 D3
  Ribe Amt. DK. 39 D1
Norddeich D 43 B4
Norddorf D 43 A5
Norden D 43 B4
Nordenham D 43 B5
Norderhov N 34 B2
Norderney D 43 B4
Norderstapel D 43 A6
Norderstedt D 44 B2
Nordfjord N 113 B19
Nordfjordeid N 114 F2
Nordfold N 112 E4
Nordhalben D 52 C1
Nordhausen D 51 B6
Nordheim vor der Rhön
  D. 51 C6
Nordholz D 43 B5
Nordhorn D 43 C4
Nordingrå S 115 E15
Nordkjosbotn N 112 C8
Nordli N 115 C10
Nördlingen D 61 B6
Nordmaling S 115 D16
Nordmark S 34 C6
Nordmela N 112 C4
Nord-Odal N 34 B3
Nordre Osen N 34 A3
Nordsinni N 34 B1
Nørdstedalsseter N . .114 F4
Nordvågen N 113 B15
Nordwalde D 50 A3
Noreña E 88 A1
Noresund N 34 B1
Norg NL 42 B3
Norheimsund N 32 B3
Norie S 41 C4
Norma I 102 B5
Nornäs S 34 A5
Norrahammar S 40 B4
Norråker S 115 C12
Norrala S 36 A3
Norrbäck S 115 B16
Nørre Aaby DK 39 D2
Nørre Alslev DK 39 E4
Nørre Lyndelse DK 39 D3
Nørre Nebel DK 39 D1
Nørre Snede DK 39 D2
Nørre Vorupør DK 38 B2
Nørre Vorupør DK 38 C1
Norrhult Klavreström
  S 40 B5
Norrköping S 37 D3
Norrskedika S 36 B5
Norrsundet S 36 B4
Norrtälje S 36 C5
Nors DK 38 B1
Norsbron S 35 C5
Norsholm S 37 D2
Norsjö S 115 C16
Nörten-Hardenberg D 51 B5
Northallerton GB 27 A4
Northampton GB 30 B3
North Berwick GB 25 B5
North Charlton GB 25 C6
Northeim D 51 B6
Northfleet GB 31 C4
North Frodingham
  GB. 27 B5
North Kessock GB 23 D4
Northleach GB 29 B6
North Molton GB 28 B4
North Petherton GB 29 B4
Northpunds GB 22 B7
North Somercotes
  GB. 27 B6
North Tawton GB 28 C4
North Thoresby GB 27 B5
North Walsham GB 30 B5
Northwich GB 26 B3
Norton GB 27 A5
Nortorf D 44 A1
Nort-sur-Erdre F 66 A3
Nörvenich D 50 C2
Norwich GB 30 B5
Norwick GB 22 A8
Nøsen N 32 B5
Nosivka UA 11 A11
Nossa Senhora do Cabo
  P. 92 C1
Nossebro S 35 D4
Nössemark S 35 C3
Nossen D 52 B3
Notaresco I 103 A6
Noto I 109 C4
Notodden N 33 C6
Nottingham GB 27 C4
Nottuln D 50 B3
Nouan-le-Fuzelier F . . .68 A2
Nouans-les-Fontaines
  F. 67 A6
Nougaroulet F 77 C3
Nouvion F 48 C2
Nouzonville F 59 A5
Nova H 74 B1
Nová Baňa SK 65 B4
Nová Bystrica SK 65 A5
Nová Bystřice CZ 63 A6
Nova Crnja SRB 75 C5
Novafeltria I 82 C1
Nova Gorica SLO 72 C3
Nova Gradiška HR 74 C2
Nováky SK 65 B4
Novalaise F 69 C5
Novales E 90 A2
Nova Levante I 71 B6
Novalja HR 83 B3
Nova Odesa UA 11 C11
Nová Paka CZ 53 C5
Nova Pazova SRB 85 B5
Nová Pec CZ 63 B4
Novara I 70 C3
Novara di Sicília I 109 A4
Nova Siri I 106 A3
Nové Mezzola I 71 B4
Nova Topola BIH 84 A2
Nova Varoš SRB 85 C4
Novaya Ladoga RUS . . .7 A12

Nova Zagora BG 11 E8
Nové Hrady CZ 63 B5
Novelda E 101 A5
Novellara I 81 B4
Nové Město SK 64 B3
Nové Město nad Metují
  CZ. 53 C6
Nové Město na Moravě
  CZ. 64 A2
Nové Město pod Smrkem
  CZ. 53 C5
Nové Mitrovice CZ 63 A4
Noventa di Piave I 72 C2
Noventa Vicentina I 71 C6
Noves F 78 C3
Nové Sady SK 64 B3
Nové de Segre E 91 A4
Nové Strašeci CZ 53 C3
Nové Zámky SK 64 C4
Novgorod RUS 7 B11
Novhorod-Siverskyy
  UA 7 F12
Novi
  Bg 11 E9
  SRB 85 C5
Novi Bečej SRB 75 C5
Novi di Módena I 81 B4
Novigrad
  Istarska HR 72 C3
  Zadarsko-Kninska
  HR. 83 B4
Novigrad Podravski
  HR. 74 B1
Novi Knežavac SRB . . .75 B5
Novi Ligure I 80 B2
Noville B 50 C1
Novi Marof HR 73 B6
Novion-Porcien F 59 A5
Novi Pazar
  Bg 11 E9
  SRB 85 C5
Novi Sad SRB 75 C4
Novi Slankamen SRB . .75 C5
Novi Travnik BIH 84 B2
Novi Vinodolski HR 83 A3
Novo Brdo KOS 85 D6
Novohrad-Volynskyy
  UA. 11 A9
Novo Mesto SLO 73 C5
Novo Miloševo SRB . . .75 C5
Novomirgorod UA 11 B11
Novorzhev RUS. 7 C10
Novoselë AL. 105 C5
Novo Selo
  BIH 84 A2
  KOS 85 D5
  SRB 85 C5
Novoselytsya UA. 11 B9
Novosil RUS 7 E14
Novosokolniki RUS 7 C10
Novoukrayinka UA 11 B11
Novoveská Huta SK . . .65 B6
Novovolynsk UA 11 A8
Novozybkov RUS 7 E11
Nový Bor CZ 53 C4
Nový Bydžov CZ 53 C5
Novy-Chevrières F 59 A5
Nový Dwór Mazowiecki
  PL. 47 C6
Nový-Hrozenkov CZ . . .64 A4
Nový Jičín CZ 64 A4
Nový Knín CZ 63 A5
Novyy Buh UA 11 C12
Nowa Cerekwia PL 54 C2
Nowa Karczma PL 47 A4
Nowa Kościoł PL 53 B5
Nowa Ruda PL 54 C1
Nowa Słupia PL 55 C6
Nowa Sól PL 53 B5
Nowa Wieś PL. 47 B5
Nowa-Wieś Wielka
  PL. 47 C4
Nowe PL 47 B4
Nowe Brzesko PL 55 C5
Nowe Grudze PL 55 A4
Nowe Miasteczko PL . . .53 B5
Nowe Miasto
  Mazowieckie PL 47 C6
  Mazowieckie PL 55 B5
Nowe Miasto Lubawskie
  PL. 47 B5
Nowe Miasto nad Warta
  PL. 54 B2
Nowe Skalmierzyce
  PL. 54 B3
Nowe Warpno PL 45 B6
Nowica PL 47 A5
Nowogard PL 45 B7
Nowogrodziec Bobrzanski
  PL. 53 B5
Nowogrodziec PL 53 B5
Nowosolna PL 55 B4
Nowy Dwór Gdański
  PL. 47 A5
Nowy Korczyn PL 55 C5
Nowy Sącz PL 65 A6
Nowy Staw PL 47 A5
Nowy Targ PL 65 A6
Nowy Tomyśl PL 46 C2
Nowy Wiśnicz PL 65 A6
Noyalo F 56 C3
Noyal-Pontivy F 56 B3
Noyant F 67 A5
Noyelles-sur-Mer F 48 C2
Noyen-sur-Sarthe F . . .57 C5
Noyers F 59 C4
Noyers-sur-Cher F 67 A6
Noyers-sur-Jabron F . . .79 B4
Noyon F 59 A3
Nozay F 66 A3
Nuaillé F 66 A4
Nuaillé-d'Aunis F 66 B4
Nuars F 68 A3
Nubledo E 88 A1
Nuéno E 90 A2
Nuestra Señora Sa Verge
  des Pilar E 96 C2
Nueva E 88 A2
Nueva Carteya E 100 B1
Nuevalos E 95 A5
Nuits F 59 C5
Nuits-St Georges F 69 A4
Nule I 110 B2
Nules E 96 B2
Nulvi I 110 B1
Numana I 82 C2
Numansdorp NL 49 B5
Nümbrecht D 50 C3
Nunchritz D 52 B3
Nuneaton GB 30 B2
Nunnanen FIN 113 D13
N Unnaryd S 40 B3
Nunspeet NL 42 C2
Nuoro I 110 B2
Núoro I 110 B2
Nurallao I 110 C2
Nuremberg = Nürnberg
  D. 62 A2
Nurmes FIN 3 E28
Nürnberg = Nuremberg
  D. 62 A2
Nurri I 110 C2
Nürtingen D 61 B5
Nus I 70 C2
Nusnäs S 36 B1
Nusplingen D 61 B4
Nuštar HR 74 C3
Nyåker S 115 D16
Nyáregyháza H 75 A4
Nyarma BY 7 E9
Nyasvizh BY 7 E9
Nybble S 35 C6
Nybøl DK 39 E2
Nyborg DK 39 D3
Nybro S 40 C5
Nybster GB 23 C5
Nyby DK 39 E5
Nydri GR 116 C2
Nyékládháza H 65 C6
Nyergesújfalu H 65 C4
Nyhammar S 36 B1

Nyhyttan S 37 C1
Nyírád H 74 A2
Nyírbátor H 11 C7
Nyíregyháza H 11 C7
Nyker DK 41 D4
Nykil S 37 D2
Nykirke N 34 B2
Nykøbing
  Falster DK 39 E4
  Vestsjællands Amt.
  DK. 39 D4
Nykøbing Mors DK 38 C1
Nyköping S 37 D4
Nykroppa S 35 C6
Nykvarn S 37 C4
Nyland S 115 D14
Nylars DK 41 D4
Nymburk CZ 53 C5
Nynäshamn S 37 D4
Nyon CH 69 B6
Nyons F 79 B4
Nýřany CZ 63 A4
Nýrsko CZ 62 A4
Nyrud N 113 C18
Nysa PL 54 C2
Nysäter S 35 C4
Nyseter N 114 E5
Nyskoga S 34 B4
Nysted DK 44 A3
Nystrand N 35 C1
Nyúl H 64 C3
Nyvoll N 113 B12

O

Oadby GB 30 B2
Oakengates GB 26 C3
Oakham GB 30 B3
Oanes N 33 D3
Obalj BIH 84 C3
Oban GB 24 B2
O Barco E 86 B4
Obdach A 73 A4
Obejo E 100 A1
Oberammergau D 62 C2
Oberasbach D 62 A1
Oberau D 62 C2
Oberaudorf D 62 C3
Oberbruck F 60 C3
Oberdiessbach CH 70 B2
Oberdorf CH 70 A2
Oberdrauburg A 72 B2
Oberelsbach D 51 C6
Obere Stanz A 73 A5
Ober Grafendorf A 63 B6
Obergünzburg D 61 C6
Obergurgl A 71 B6
Oberhausen D 50 B2
Oberhof D 51 C6
Oberkirch D 61 B4
Oberkirchen D 51 B4
Oberkochen D 61 B6
Obermassfeld-
  Grimmenthal D 51 C6
Ober-Morlen D 51 C4
Obermünchen D 62 B2
Obernai F 60 B3
Obernberg A 63 B4
Obernburg D 61 A5
Oberndorf D 61 B4
Oberndorf bei Salzburg
  A. 62 C3
Obernkirchen D 51 A5
Oberort A 73 A5
Oberpullendorf A 74 A1
Oberriet CH 71 A4
Oberröblingen D 52 B1
Oberrot D 61 A5
Oberstaufen D 61 C6
Oberstdorf D 71 A5
Obertauern A 72 A3
Obertilliach A 72 B2
Obertraubling D 62 A3
Obertraun A 72 A3
Obertrubach D 62 A2
Obertrum A 62 C4
Oberursel D 51 C4
Obervellach A 72 B3
Oberviechtach D 62 A3
Oberwart A 73 A6
Oberwesel D 50 C3
Oberwinter D 50 C3
Oberwölzstadt A 73 A4
Oberzell D 63 B4
Obice PL 55 C5
Obing D 62 C3
Objat F 67 C6
Öbjazda PL 46 A3
Oblarn A 73 A4
Obninsk RUS. 7 D14
O Bolo E 87 B3
Oborniki PL 46 C2
Oborniki Śląskie PL 54 B1
Obornjača SRB 75 C4
Oboyan RUS 7 F14
Obrenovac SRB 85 B5
Óbrež
  Srbija SRB 85 C6
  Vojvodina SRB 85 B4
Obrigheim D 61 A5
Obrov SLO 73 C4
Obrovac
  HR. 83 B4
  SRB 75 C4
Obrovac Sinjski HR 83 C5
Obruk TR 16 B6
Obrzycko PL 46 C2
Obudovac BIH 84 B3
Ocaña E 95 C3
O Carballiño E 86 B2
Occhiobello I 81 B5
Occimiano I 80 A2
Očevlja BIH 84 B3
Ochagavía E 76 D1
Ochakiv UA 11 C11
Ochla PL 53 B5
Ochsenfurt D 61 A6
Ochsenhausen D 61 B5
Ochtendung D 50 C3
Ochtrup D 50 A3
Ocieka PL 55 C6
Ockelbo S 36 B3
Öckerö S 38 B4
Ocnița MD 11 B9
O Corgo E 86 B3
Očová SK 65 B5
Ócsa H 75 A4
Ocseny H 74 B3
Öcsöd H 75 B5
Octeville F 57 A4
Ocypel PL 47 B4
Ödåkra S 41 C2
Odda N 32 B3
Ödeborg S 35 D3
Odeceixe P 98 B2
Odeenów PL 55 B6
Ödeleite P 98 B3
Odemira P 98 B2
Ödemiş TR 119 D2
Odensbacken S 37 C2
Odense DK 39 D3
Odensjö
  Jönköping S 40 B4
  Kronoberg S 40 C3
Oderberg D 45 C6
Oderzo I 72 C2
Odesa = Odessa UA .11 C11
Odeshög S 37 D1
Ödestugu S 40 B4
Odie GB 23 B6
Odiham GB 31 C3
Odintsovo RUS 7 D14

Odivelas P 98 A2
Odolanów PL 54 B2
Odón E 95 B5
Odorheiu Secuiesc
  RO 11 C8
Odoyevo RUS 7 E14
Odrowaz PL 55 B5
Odry CZ 64 A3
Odrzywół PL 55 B5
Ödsbäck S 39 D2
Ödsbyn S 36 A3
Odzak BIH 84 A3
Oebisfelde D 44 C2
Oederan D 52 C3
Oeding D 50 B2
Oegstgeest NL 49 A5
Oelde D 50 B4
Oelsnitz D 52 C2
Oer-Erkenschwick D . . .50 B3
Oerlinghausen D 51 B4
Oettingen D 62 B1
Oetz A 71 A5
Oeventrop D 50 B4
Offanengo I 71 C4
Offenbach D 51 C4
Offenburg D 60 B3
Offida I 82 D2
Offingen D 61 B6
Offranville F 58 A2
Ofte N 33 C5
Ofterschwang D 71 A5
Oggiano I 71 C4
Ogihares E 100 B2
Ogliastro Cilento I 103 C8
Ogliastro Marina I 103 C7
Ogmore-by-Sea GB 29 B4
Ogna N 33 D2
Ogre LV 6 C8
Ogrodzieniec PL 55 C4
Ogulin HR 73 C5
Ögur IS. 111 A3
Ohanes E 101 B3
Ohey B 49 C6
Ohlstadt D 62 C2
Ohrdruf D 51 C6
Ohrid MK 117 G3
Öhringen D 61 A5
Oia E 87 B2
Oiã P 92 A2
Oiartzun E 76 C1
Oilgate IRL 21 B5
Oimbra E 87 C3
Oiselay-et-Grachoux
  F. 69 A5
Oisemont F 48 D2
Oisterwijk NL 49 B6
Öja S 37 E5
Öje S 34 B5
Ojén E 100 C1
Ojrzeń PL 47 C6
Ojuelos Altos E 99 A5
Okalewo PL 47 B5
Okány H 75 B6
Okehampton GB 28 C3
Okhtyrka UA 7 F13
Økneshamn N 112 D4
Okoč SK 64 C3
Okoličné SK 65 A5
Okonek PL 46 B2
Okonin PL 47 B4
Okřisky CZ 64 A1
Oksa PL 55 C5
Oksbøl DK 39 D1
Oksby DK 39 D1
Øksfjord N 113 B11
Øksna N 34 B3
Okučani HR 74 C2
Okulovka RUS 7 B12
Ólafsfjörður IS. 111 A7
Ólafsvík IS 111 C2
Ólagnö S 37 C5
Olague F 76 D1
Oland N 33 D5
Olargues F 78 C1
Oława PL 54 C2
Olazagutía E 89 B4
Olbernhau D 52 C3
Ólbia I 110 B2
Olching D. 62 B2
Oldbury GB 29 B5
Oldcastle IRL. 19 C4
Old Deer GB 23 D6
Oldebroek NL 42 C2
Olden N 114 F3
Oldenbrok D 43 B5
Oldenburg
  Niedersachsen D . . .43 B5
  Schleswig-Holstein D 44 A2
Oldenzaal NL. 50 A2
Olderdalen N 112 C9
Olderfjord N 113 B14
Oldersum D 43 B4
Oldervik N 112 C8
Oldham GB 26 B3
Oldisleben D 52 B1
Oldmeldrum GB 23 D6
Olea E 88 B2
Oleby S 34 B5
Olechów PL 55 B6
Oledo P 92 B3
Oléggio I 70 C3
Oleiros
  Coruña E 86 A2
  Coruña E 86 B1
  P 92 B3
Oleksandriya
  Kirovohrad UA 11 B12
  Rivne UA 11 A9
Oleksandrovka UA . .11 B12
Olen B 49 B5
Olenegorsk RUS 3 B30
Olenino RUS 7 C12
Olesa de Montserrat
  E. 91 B4
Oleśnica CilentoI 100 A2
Olešnice CZ. 64 A2
Olesno PL 54 C3
Oletta F 102 A2
Olette F 91 A5
Olevsk UA 11 A9
Olfen D 50 B3
Olgiate Comasco I 70 C3
Olginate I 71 C4
Ølgod DK 39 D1
Olgrinmore GB 23 C5
Olhão P 98 B3
Olhava FIN 3 D26
Oliana E 91 A4
Olías del Rey E 94 C3
Oliena I 110 B2
Oliete E 90 C2
Olimbos GR 119 G2
Olite E 89 B5
Oliva E 96 C2
Oliva de la Frontera E . .99 A4
Oliva de Mérida E 93 C4
Oliva de Plasencia E . . .93 A4
Olivadi I 106 C3
Olival P 92 B2
Olivar E 100 C2
Olivares E 99 B4
Olivares de Duero E . . .88 C2
Olivares de Júcar E 95 C4
Oliveira de Azeméis
  P 87 D2
Oliveira de Frades P . . .87 D2
Oliveira do Conde P . . .92 A3
Oliveira do Douro P 87 C2
Oliveira do Hospital P . .92 A3
Olivenza E 93 C3
Olivet F 58 C2
Olivone CH 70 B3
Öljehult S 41 C5
Olkusz PL 55 C4
Ollerton GB 27 B4
Ollerup DK 39 D3
Ollierques F 68 C3
Ólmbrotorp S 37 C2

Ölme S 35 C5
Olmedilla de Alarcón
  E. 95 C4
Olmedilla de Roa E 88 C3
Olmedo
  E 88 C2
  I 110 B1
Olmeto F 102 B1
Olmillos de Castro E . . .87 C4
Olmos de Ojeda E 88 B2
Olney GB 30 B3
Olobok PL 54 B3
Olocau del Rey E 90 C2
Olofström S 41 C4
Olomouc CZ 64 A3
Olonets RUS 3 F30
Olonne-sur-Mer F 66 B3
Olonzac F 78 C1
Oloron-Ste Marie F 76 C2
Olost E 91 B5
Olot E 91 A5
Olovo BIH 84 B3
Olpe D 50 B3
Olsberg D 51 B4
Olsene B 49 C4
Olshammar S 37 D1
Olshanka UA 11 B11
Olszana PL 53 B5
Olsztyn
  Śląskie PL 55 C4
  Warmińsko-Mazurskie
  PL. 47 B6
Olsztynek PL 47 B6
Olszyna PL 53 B5
Oltedal N 33 D3
Olten CH 70 A2
Olula del Rio E 101 B3
Ølve N 32 B2
Olvega E 89 C5
Olvera E 99 C5
Olympia GR 117 E3
Olzai I 110 B2
Omagh GB 19 B4
Omalos GR 117 G5
Omegna I 70 C3
Omiš HR 83 C5
Omišalj HR 73 C4
Ommen NL 42 C3
Omodhos CY 120 B1
Omoljica SRB 85 B5
On B 49 C6
Oña E 89 B3
Onano I 81 D5
O Näsberg S 34 B5
Oñati E 89 A4
Onda E 96 B2
Ondara E 96 C3
Ondarroa E 89 A4
Onesse-et-Laharie F . . .76 B1
Oneşti RO 11 C9
Onhaye B 49 C5
Onich GB 24 B2
Onil E 96 C2
Onis E 88 A2
Önnestad S 41 C4
Onsala S 38 B5
Ontinyent E 96 C2
Ontur E 101 A4
Onzain F 67 A6
Onzonilla E 88 B1
Oostburg NL 49 B4
Oostende B 48 B3
Oosterend NL 42 B2
Oosterhout NL 49 B5
Oosterwolde NL 42 C3
Oosterzele B 49 C4
Oosthuizen NL. 42 C2
Oostkamp B 49 B4
Oostmalle B 49 B5
Oost-Vlieland NL 42 B2
Oostvoorne NL 49 B5
Ootmarsum NL 42 C3
Opalenica PL 54 A1
O Páramo E 86 B3
Opařany CZ 63 A5
Opatija HR 73 C4
Opatów
  Śląskie PL 54 B3
  Świętokrzyskie PL . .55 C6
  Wielkopolskie PL . . .54 B3
Opatówek PL 54 B3
Opatowiec PL 55 C5
Opava CZ 64 A3
Opeinde NL 42 B3
Oper Thalkirchdorf D . . .61 C6
Opglabbeerk B 49 B6
Opicina I 72 C3
O Pino E 86 B2
Oplotnica SLO 73 B5
Opmeer NL 42 C1
Opochka RUS 7 C10
Opočno CZ 53 C6
Opoczno PL 55 B5
Opole PL 54 C3
Oporów PL 55 A4
O Porriño E 87 B2
Opovo SRB 85 B5
Oppach D 53 B4
Oppdal N 114 E6
Oppeby
  Östergötland S 40 A5
  Södermanland S 37 D3
Oppedal N 32 A2
Oppegård N 34 C2
Oppenau D 61 B4
Oppenberg A 73 A4
Oppenheim D 61 A4
Óppido Lucano I 104 C1
Óppido Mamertina I . . .106 C2
Opponitz A 63 C5
Oppstad N 34 B3
Oprtalj HR 72 C3
Opsaheden S 34 B5
Opusztaszer H 75 B5
Opuzen HR 84 C2
Ora
  CY 120 B2
  I 71 B6
Orada P 92 C3
Oradea RO 11 C7
Oradour-sur-Glane F . . .67 C6
Oradour-sur-Vayres
  F. 67 C5
Oragonja SLO 72 C3
Orah BIH 84 D3
Orahova BIH 84 B2
Orahovica HR 74 C2
Orahovo BIH 84 A2
Oraison F 79 C4
Orajärvi FIN 113 F13
Orange F 78 B3
Orani I 110 B2
Oranienbaum D 52 B2
Oranienburg D 45 C5
Oranmore IRL 20 A3
Orašac BIH 83 B5
Orašje BIH 84 A3
Oravská Lesná SK 65 A5
Oravská Polhora SK . . .65 A5
Oravské Veselé SK 65 A5
Oravský-Podzámok
  SK. 65 A5
Orba E 96 C2
Orbacém P 87 C2
Ørbæk DK 39 D3
Orbais F 59 B4
Orbassano I 80 A1
Orbe CH 69 B6
Orbec F 57 A6
Orbetello I 102 A4
Orbetello Scalo I 102 A4
Orbigny F 67 A6
Ørby DK 39 D3
Orbyhus S 36 B4
Orce E 101 B3
Orcera E 101 A3
Orchamps-Vennes F . . .69 A6
Orches F 67 B5

Orchete E 96 C2
Orchies F 49 C4
Orchowo PL 47 C4
Orciéres F 79 B5
Ordes E 86 A2
Ordhead GB. 23 D6
Ordino AND 91 A4
Ordizia E 89 A4
Orea E 95 B5
Orebić HR 84 D2
Örebro S 37 C2
Öregcsertő H 75 B4
Öregrund S 36 B5
Orehoved DK 39 E4
Orel RUS 7 E14
Orellana de la Sierra
  E. 93 B5
Orellana E 93 B5
Orencik TR 118 C4
Orestiada GR 118 A1
Organyà E 91 A4
Orgaz E 94 C3
Orgelet F 69 B5
Órgenvika N 34 B1
Orgères-en-Beauce F . .58 B2
Orgibet F 77 D3
Orgnac-l'Aven F 78 B3
Orgon F 79 C4
Orgósolo I 110 B2
Orhalı TR 118 C3
Orhangazi TR 118 B4
Orhei MD 11 C10
Orhomenos GR 116 D4
Oria
  E 101 B3
  I 104 C3
Oria I 104 C3
Origny-Ste Benoite F . .59 A4
Orihuela E 101 A5
Orihuela del Tremedal
  E. 95 B5
Orikum AL 105 C5
Oriola E 92 C3
Oriolo I 106 A3
Oriovac HR 74 C2
Orissaare EST 6 B7
Oristano I 110 C1
Orizzonápfer h 73 B6
Ørje N 35 C3
Orjiva E 100 C2
Orkanger N 114 D6
Örkelljunga S 41 C3
Örkény H 75 A4
Orlamünde D 52 C1
Orlane KOS 85 D6
Orléans F 58 C2
Orlová CZ 65 A4
Orlovat SRB 75 C5
Ormea I 80 B1
Ormelet N 35 C2
Ormemyr N 33 C6
Órmilia GR 116 B5
Ormos GR 117 E6
Ormož SLO 73 B6
Ormskirk GB 26 B3
Ornans F 69 A6
Ornäs S 36 B2
Ørnes N 112 F2
Orneta PL 47 A6
Ørnhøj DK 39 C1
Ørnö S 37 C5
Örnsköldsvik S 115 D15
Orolik HR 75 C4
Orom SRB 75 C5
Oron-la-Ville CH 70 B1
Oronsko PL 55 B5
Oropa I 70 C2
Oropesa
  Castellón de la Plana
  E. 96 A3
  Toledo E 93 B5
O Rosal E 87 C2
Orosei I 110 B2
Oroslavje HR 73 C5
Oroszlány H 74 A3
Oroszló H 74 B3
Orotelli I 110 B2
Orozko E 89 A4
Orphir GB 23 C5
Orpington GB 31 C4
Orreaga-Roncesvalles
  E. 76 C1
Orrefors S 40 C5
Orrviken S 115 D11
Orsa S 36 A1
Orsara di Púglia I 103 B8
Orscholz D 60 A2
Orsennes F 67 B6
Orserum S 40 A4
Orsha BY 7 D11
Orsières CH 70 B2
Örsjö S 40 C5
Ørslev DK 39 D4
Örslösa S 35 D4
Orsogna I 103 A7
Orsomarso I 106 B2
Orşova RO 11 D7
Ørsta N 114 E3
Ørsted DK 38 C3
Örsundsbro S 37 C4
Ortaca TR 119 F3
Ortakent TR 119 E2
Ortaklar TR 119 E2
Ortaköy TR 16 B7
Orta Nova I 104 B1
Orte I 102 A5
Ortenburg D 63 B4
Orth A 64 B2
Orthez F 76 C2
Ortigueira E 86 A3
Ortilla E 90 A2
Ortisei I 72 B1
Ortnevik N 32 A3
Orton GB 26 A3
Ortona I 103 A7
Ortrand D 53 B3
Orubica HR 74 C2
Ørum DK 38 C2
Orune I 110 B2
Orusco E 95 B3
Orvalho P 92 A3
Orvault F 66 A3
Ørvella N 33 C6
Orvieto I 102 A5
Orvínio I 102 A5
Oryahovo BG 11 E7
Orzesze PL 54 C3
Orzinuovi I 71 C4
Orzivécchi I 71 C4
Os
  Hedmark N 34 B3
  Hedmark N 114 E8
Osann-Monzel D 60 A2
Osaonica SRB 85 C5
Osby S 40 C4
Oščadnica SK 65 A4
Oschatz D 52 B3
Oschersleben D 52 A1
Óschiri I 110 B2
Ościsłowo PL 47 C4
Osdorf D 44 A2
Osečina SRB 85 B4
Osečná CZ 53 C4
Osek CZ 52 C3
Osen N 114 C7
Osera de Ebro E 90 B2
Osidda I 110 B2
Osie PL 47 B4
Osieck PL 55 B6
Osieczna
  Pomorskie PL 47 B4
  Wielkopolskie PL . . .54 B1
Osiecznica PL 46 B1

Osiek
  Kujawsko-Pomorskie
  PL 47 B5
  Kujawsko-Pomorskie
  PL 47 C4
  Pomorskie PL 47 B4
  Świętokrzyskie PL . .55 C6
Osiek nad Notecią PL . .46 B3
Osielsko PL 47 B4
Osijek HR 74 C3
Osilnica SLO 73 C4
Ósilo I 110 B1
Ósimo I 82 C2
Osinja BIH 84 B2
Osintorf BY 7 D11
Osipaonica SRB 85 B6
Osjaków PL 54 B3
Oskamull GB 24 B1
Oskarshamn S 40 B6
Oskarström S 40 C2
Öskü H 74 A3
Osladić SRB 85 C4
Oslany SK 65 B4
Oslavany CZ 64 A2
Ošlje HR 84 D2
Osló N 34 C2
Osloß D 44 C2
Osma E 89 C3
Osmancık TR 16 A7
Osmaneli TR 118 B4
Ósmo S 37 C4
Osmolin PL 55 A4
Osnabrück D 50 A4
Ośno Lubuskie PL 45 C6
Osobłaha CZ 54 C2
Osor HR 83 B3
Osorno E 88 B2
Øsoyra N 32 A2
Øsoyro N 32 B2
Óspakseyri IS 111 B4
Os Peares E 86 B3
Ospedaletti I 80 C1
Ospitaletto I 71 C5
Oss NL 49 B6
Ossa de Montiel E 95 C4
Ossi I 110 B1
Óssjøen N 32 B5
Ossun F 76 C2
Ostanå S 41 C4
Ostanvik S 36 A2
Ostashkov RUS. 7 C12
Ostavall S 115 E12
Østbirk DK 39 D2
Østborg N 115 C10
Østby N 34 A4
Osted DK 39 D4
Ostenfeld D 43 A6
Oster UA 11 A11
Øster Assels DK 38 C1
Øster Bjerregrav DK . . .38 C2
Øster Hornum DK 38 C2
Øster Hurup DK 38 C3
Østerild DK 38 B1
Øster Jølby DK 38 C1
Österlövsta S 36 B4
Øster-marie DK 41 D5
Osterburg D 44 C3
Osterburken D 61 A5
Østerbybruk S 36 B4
Österbymo S 40 B5
Østerbyhavn DK 38 B4
Ostercappeln D 43 C5
Österfärnebo S 36 B3
Osterfeld D 52 B1
Osterforse S 115 D14
Osterhever D 43 A5
Osterhofen D 62 B4
Osterholz-Scharmbeck
  D. 43 B5
Øster Hornum DK 38 C2
Øster Hurup DK 38 C3
Østerild DK 38 B1
Øster Jølby DK 38 C1
Østermiething A 62 C3
Osterode am Harz D . . .51 B6
Ostersiel D 43 A5
Östersund S 115 D11
Øster Tørslev DK 38 C3
Östervåla S 36 B4
Östervallskog S 35 C3
Östervik S 38 B3
Osterwieck D 51 B6
Osterzell D 62 C1
Østfyassonyfa H 77 A6
Ostfora S 36 C4
Östhammar S 36 B5
Ostheim D 60 B3
Ostheim vor der Rhön
  D. 51 C6
Osthofen D 61 A4
Ostiano I 71 C5
Ostíglia I 81 A5
Ostiz E 76 D1
Ostmark S 34 B4
Östnor S 36 A1
Ostojiċevo SRB 75 C5
Ostra I 82 C2
Östra Amtervik S 35 C5
Oxford GB 31 C2
Östraby S 41 D3
Ostrach D 61 C5
Östra Husby S 37 D3
Östra Ljungby S 41 C3
Östra Ryd S 37 D3
Ostrau D 52 B3
Ostrava CZ 64 A4
Østre Halsen N 35 C2
Ostrhauderfehn D 43 B4
Ostritz D 53 B4
Ostróda PL 47 B6
Ostroh UA 11 A9
Ostrołęka PL 47 B6
Ostropole PL 46 B2
Ostroróg PL 46 C2
Ostrošovac MNE 105 A5
Ostrov
  CZ. 52 C2
  RUS 7 C10
Ostrov nad Oslavou
  CZ. 64 A1
Ostrówek PL 54 B3
Ostrowiec PL 46 A2
Ostrowiec-Świętokrzyski
  PL. 55 C6
Ostrowite PL 47 B5
Ostrów Mazowiecka
  PL. 47 C6
Ostrowo PL 47 C4
Ostrów Wielkopolski
  PL 54 B2
Ostroż eki PL 54 C2
Ostrzeszów PL 54 B2
Ostseebad Kühlungsborn
  D. 44 A3
Ostuni I 104 C3
Osuna E 99 B5
Osvětimany CZ 64 A3
Oswestry GB 26 C2
Święcim PL 55 C4
Oszkó H 74 B1
Oszmana H 74 B2
Otelec RO 75 C5
Oteo E 89 A3
Oterbekk N 35 C2
Otero de Herreros E . . .94 B2
Otero de O Bodas E . . .87 C4
Othem S 37 E5
Othery GB 29 B5
Otışi BIH 84 C3
Otočac HR 83 B4
Otok
  Splitsko-Dalmatinska
  HR. 83 C5
  Vukovarsko-Srijemska
  HR. 74 C3
Otoka BIH 83 B5
Otranto I 107 A5
Otrić HR 83 B5
Otrokovice CZ 64 A3
Otta N 114 F6
Ottana I 110 B2
Ottaviano I 103 C7
Ottenby S 41 C6
Ottendorf-Okrilla D 53 B3
Ottenhöfen D 61 B4
Ottenschlag A 63 B6
Ottensheim A 63 B5
Otterbach D 60 A3
Otterbäcken S 35 D6

Otterberg D 60 A3
Otterburn GB. 25 C5
Otter Ferry GB 24 B2
Otterndorf D 43 B5
Ottersweier D 61 B4
Otterup DK 39 D3
Ottery St Mary GB 29 C4
Ottignies B 49 C5
Ottmarsheim F 60 C3
Ottobeuren D 61 C6
Ottómös H 75 B4
Ottone I 80 B3
Ottsjö S 115 D10
Ottweiler D 60 A3
Ötvöskónyi H 74 B2
Otwock PL 55 A6
Ouanne F 59 C4
Ouarville F 58 B2
Oucques F 58 C2
Oud-Beijerland NL 49 B5
Ouddorp NL 49 B4
Oudemirdum NL 42 C2
Oudenaarde B 49 C4
Oudenbosch NL 49 B5
Oudenburg B 48 B3
Oude-Pekela NL 43 B4
Oude-Tonge NL 49 B5
Oudewater NL 49 A5
Oud Gastel NL 49 B5
Oude P 92 C2
Oue DK. 38 C2
Oughterard IRL 20 A2
Ouguela P 93 B3
Ouistreham F 57 A5
Oulainen FIN 3 D26
Oulchy-le-Château F . . .59 A4
Oullins F 69 C4
Oulmes F 66 B4
Oulton GB 30 B5
Oulton Broad GB. 30 B5
Oulu FIN. 3 D26
Oulx F 79 A5
Oundle GB 30 B3
Ouranópoli GR 116 B6
Ourém P 92 B2
Ourense E 87 B3
Ouriçue P 98 B2
Ourol E 86 A3
Ouroux-en-Morvan F . .68 A3
Ousdale GB 23 C5
Oust F 77 D4
Outakoski FIN 113 C15
Outeiro P 92 A2
Outeiro de Rei E 86 A3
Outes E 86 B2
Outokumpu FIN. 3 E28
Outreau F 48 C2
Outwell GB 30 B4
Ouzouer-le-Marché F . .58 C2
Ouzouer-sur-Loire F . . .58 C3
Ovada I 80 B2
Ovar P 87 D2
Ovelgönne D 43 B5
Overath D 50 C3
Overbister GB 23 B6
Överbygd N 112 D8
Overdinkel NL 50 A3
Överhörnäs S 37 C4
Overhalla N 114 C8
Overijse B 49 C5
Over-jerstal DK 39 D2
Överkalix S 113 C12
Overlade DK 38 B2
Överlida S 40 B2
Överö FIN 36 B7
Overpelt B 49 B6
Overton GB 26 C3
Övertorneå S 3 C25
Överum S 40 B6
Ovidiopol UA 11 C11
Oviedo E 88 A1
Oviglio I 80 B2
Ovindoli I 103 A6
Ovodda I 110 B2
Øvre Ardal N 32 A4
Øvrebygd N 33 D3
Øvre Rendal N 114 F8
Øvre Sirdal N 33 D3
Ovruch UA 7 F10
Ovtrup DK 39 D1
Owińska PL 46 C2
Oxaback S 40 B2
Oxberg S 34 A6
Oxelösund S 37 D4
Oxenholme GB 26 A3
Oxford GB 31 C2
Oxie S 41 D3
Oxílithos GR 116 D6
Oxted GB 31 C4
Oyaca TR 118 C7
Øye N 32 A5
Øyenkilen N 35 C2
Øyer N 34 A2
Øyeren N 34 B4
Øyfjell N 33 C5
Øygärdslia N 33 D5
Øykel Bridge GB 22 D4
Øymark N 35 C3
Oyonnax F 69 B5
Øystese N 32 B3
Oyten D 43 B6
Øyuvsbu N 33 C4
Ozaeta E 89 B4
Ozalj HR 73 C5
Ožarów Maz PL 55 A5
Ozd H 65 B6
Ožd'any SK 65 B5
Ozieri I 110 B2
Ozimek PL 54 C3
Ozimica BIH 84 B3
Ozora H 74 B3
Ozorków PL 55 B4
Ozzano Monferrato I . . .80 A2

P

Paal B 49 B6
Pabianice PL 55 B4
Pacanów PL 55 C6
Paceco I 108 B1
Pachino I 109 C4
Paḉõs de Ferreira P . . .87 C2
Pacov CZ 63 A6
Pacsa H 74 B2
Pacy-sur-Eure F 58 A2
Paczków PL 54 C2
Padany RUS 3 E30
Padej SRB 75 C5
Padene HR 83 B5
Paderborn D 51 B4
Paderne P 98 B2
Padiham GB 26 B3
Padina SRB 75 C5
Padornelo P 87 C3
Padova I 72 C1
Padragkút H 74 A2
Padrón E 86 B2
Padru I 110 B2
Padstow GB 28 C3
Padul E 100 B2
Padula I 104 C1
Paduli I 103 B7
Paese I 72 C2
Pag HR 83 B4
Pagani I 103 C7
Pagánica I 103 A6
Pagánico I 81 D5
Pagny-sur-Moselle F . .60 B2

Páhi H . . . 75 B4
Pahkakumpu FIN . . . 113 F17
Pahl D . . . 62 C2
Paide EST . . . 7 B8
Paignton GB . . . 29 C4
Pailhès F . . . 77 C4
Paimboeuf F . . . 66 A2
Paimpol F . . . 56 B2
Paimpont F . . . 57 B3
Painswick GB . . . 29 B5
Painten D . . . 62 B2
Paisley GB . . . 24 C3
Pajala S . . . 113 E12
Pajares E . . . 88 A1
Pajares de los Oteros E . . . 88 B1
Pajęczno PL . . . 54 B3
Páka H . . . 74 B1
Pakość PL . . . 47 C4
Pakosławice PL . . . 54 C2
Pakoštane HR . . . 83 C4
Pakrac HR . . . 74 C2
Paks H . . . 74 B3
Palacios de la Sierra E . . . 89 C3
Palaciòs de la Valduerna E . . . 88 B1
Palacios del Sil E . . . 86 B4
Palacios de Sanabria E . . . 87 B4
Palaciosrubios E . . . 94 A1
Palafrugell E . . . 91 B6
Palagiano I . . . 104 C3
Palagonia I . . . 109 B3
Palaía I . . . 81 C4
Palaiseau F . . . 58 B3
Palaj AL . . . 105 A5
Palamas GR . . . 116 C4
Palamòs E . . . 91 B6
Palanga LT . . . 6 D6
Palanzano I . . . 81 B4
Palárikovo SK . . . 64 B4
Palas de Rei E . . . 86 B3
Palata I . . . 103 B7
Palatna KOS . . . 85 C6
Palau I . . . 110 A2
Palavas-les-Flots F . . . 78 C2
Palazuelos de la Sierra E . . . 89 B3
Palazzo Adriano I . . . 108 B2
Palazzo del Pero I . . . 81 C5
Palazzolo Acréide I . . . 109 B3
Palazzolo sull Oglio I . . . 71 C4
Palazzuolo sul Senio I . . . 104 C1
Paldiski EST . . . 6 B8
Pale BIH . . . 84 C3
Palekastro GR . . . 117 G8
Palena I . . . 103 B7
Palencia E . . . 88 B2
Palenciana E . . . 100 B1
Paleochora GR . . . 117 G6
Paleometokho CY . . . 120 A2
Palermo I . . . 108 A2
Paleros GR . . . 116 D2
Palestrina I . . . 102 B5
Pálfa H . . . 74 B3
Palfau A . . . 63 C5
Palhaça P . . . 92 A2
Palheiros da Tocha P . . . 92 A2
Palheiros de Quiaios P . . . 92 A2
Paliaopoli GR . . . 117 E6
Palić SRB . . . 75 B4
Palidoro I . . . 102 B5
Palinuro I . . . 106 A2
Paliouri GR . . . 116 C5
Paliseul B . . . 59 A6
Pallanza I . . . 70 C3
Pallares E . . . 99 A4
Pal.laruelo de Monegros E . . . 90 B2
Pallas Green IRL . . . 20 B3
Pallerols E . . . 91 A4
Palling D . . . 62 B3
Palluau F . . . 66 B3
Palma P . . . 92 C2
Palma Campánia I . . . 103 C7
Palma del Río E . . . 99 B5
Palma de Mallorca E . . . 97 B2
Palma di Montechiaro I . . . 108 B2
Palmádula I . . . 110 B1
Palmanova I . . . 72 C3
Palma Nova E . . . 97 B2
Palmela P . . . 92 C2
Palmi I . . . 106 C2
Pälmonostora H . . . 75 B4
Palo del Colle I . . . 104 B2
Palojärvi FIN . . . 113 D12
Palojoensuu FIN . . . 113 D12
Palomares E . . . 101 B4
Palomares del Campo E . . . 95 C4
Palomas E . . . 93 C4
Palombara Sabina I . . . 102 A5
Palos de la Frontera E . . . 99 B4
Palotás H . . . 65 C5
Pålsboda S . . . 37 C2
Paluzza I . . . 72 B3
Pamhagen A . . . 64 C2
Pamiers F . . . 77 C4
Pamiętowo PL . . . 46 B3
Pampaneira E . . . 100 C2
Pamparato I . . . 80 B1
Pampilhosa
   Aveiro P . . . 92 A2
   Coimbra P . . . 92 A3
Pampliega E . . . 88 B3
Pamplona E . . . 76 D1
Pampow D . . . 44 B3
Pamukçu TR . . . 118 C2
Pamukkale TR . . . 119 E4
Pamukova TR . . . 118 B5
Panagyurishte BG. . . 11 E8
Pancalieri I . . . 80 B1
Pančevo SRB . . . 85 B5
Pancey F . . . 59 B6
Pancorvo E . . . 89 B3
Pancrudo E . . . 90 C1
Pandino I . . . 71 C4
Panenský-Tynec CZ . . . 53 C3
Panes E . . . 88 A2
Panevéžys LT . . . 6 D8
Pangbourne GB . . . 31 C2
Panissières F . . . 69 C4
Panki PL . . . 54 C3
Panes F . . . 58 B3
Panningen NL . . . 50 B1
Pano Lefkara CY . . . 120 B2
Pano Panayia CY . . . 120 B1
Panormos GR . . . 117 E7
Panschwitz-Kuckau D . . . 53 B4
Pansdorf D . . . 44 B2
Pantano de Cíjara E . . . 94 C2
Pantelleria I . . . 108 C1
Panticosa E . . . 76 D2
Pantin F . . . 86 A2
Pantoja E . . . 94 B3
Pantón E . . . 86 B3
Panxon E . . . 87 B2
Pápa H . . . 74 A2
Papasídero I . . . 106 B2
Pápateszér H . . . 74 A2
Papenburg D . . . 43 B4
Paphos CY . . . 120 B1
Papilé LT . . . 6 D7
Papowo PL . . . 47 B4
Pappenheim D . . . 62 B1
Paprotnia PL . . . 47 C6
Parábita I . . . 107 A5
Paraćin SRB . . . 85 C6
Parád H . . . 65 C6

Parada
   Bragança P . . . 87 C4
   Viseu P . . . 92 A2
Paradas E . . . 99 B5
Paradela E . . . 86 B3
Parades de Rubiales E . . . 94 A1
Paradinas de San Juan E . . . 94 B1
Paradiso di Cevadale I . . . 71 B5
Paradyż PL . . . 55 B5
Parainen FIN . . . 6 A7
Parakhino Paddubye RUS . . . 7 B12
Parakka S . . . 113 E10
Paralimni CY . . . 120 A2
Parallo Astros GR . . . 117 E4
Paramé F . . . 57 B4
Paramithia GR . . . 116 C2
Páramo del Sil E . . . 86 B4
Páramo E . . . 86 A4
Parandaça P . . . 87 C3
Paravadella E . . . 86 A3
Paray-le-Monial F . . . 68 B4
Parceiros P . . . 92 B2
Parcey F . . . 69 A5
Parchim D . . . 44 B3
Parcice PL . . . 54 B3
Pardilla E . . . 88 C3
Pardubice CZ . . . 53 C5
Paredes
   E . . . 95 B4
   P . . . 87 C2
Paredes de Coura P . . . 87 C2
Paredes de Nava E . . . 88 B2
Paredes de Siguenza E . . . 95 A4
Pareja E . . . 95 B4
Parennes F . . . 57 B5
Parenti I . . . 106 B3
Parentis-en-Born F . . . 76 B1
Párga GR . . . 116 C2
Pargny-sur-Saulx F . . . 59 B5
Pari-Gagné F . . . 69 B4
Parigné-l'Évêque F . . . 58 C1
Parikkala FIN . . . 3 F28
Paris F . . . 58 B3
Parisot F . . . 77 B4
Parkalompolo S . . . 113 E11
Parkano FIN . . . 3 E25
Parknasilla IRL . . . 20 C2
Parla E . . . 94 B3
Parlavá E . . . 91 A6
Parma I . . . 81 B4
Parndorf A . . . 64 C2
Párnica SK . . . 65 A5
Parnu EST . . . 6 B8
Parolis E . . . 101 A3
Paros GR . . . 117 E7
Parrillas E . . . 94 B1
Parsberg D . . . 62 A2
Parstein D . . . 45 C6
Partakko FIN . . . 113 C16
Partanna I . . . 108 B1
Parthenay F . . . 67 B4
Partinico I . . . 108 A2
Partizani SRB . . . 85 B5
Partizánske SK . . . 65 B4
Partney GB . . . 27 B6
Páryd S . . . 40 C5
Parysów PL . . . 55 B6
Parzymiechy PL . . . 54 B3
Pașcani RO . . . 11 C9
Pasewalk D . . . 45 B5
Pašina Voda MNE . . . 85 C4
Påskallavik S . . . 40 B6
Pasłęk PL . . . 47 A5
Pašman HR . . . 83 C4
Passage East IRL . . . 21 B5
Passage West IRL . . . 20 C3
Passail A . . . 73 A5
Passais F . . . 57 B5
Passau D . . . 63 B4
Passegueiro P . . . 92 A2
Passignano sul Trasimeno I . . . 82 C1
Passo di Tréia I . . . 82 C2
Passopisciaro I . . . 109 B4
Passow D . . . 45 B6
Pastavy BY . . . 7 D9
Pástena I . . . 103 B7
Pastrana E . . . 95 B4
Pastrengo I . . . 71 C5
Pasym PL . . . 47 B6
Pászto H . . . 65 C5
Pata SK . . . 64 B3
Patay F . . . 58 B2
Pateley Bridge GB . . . 27 A4
Paterek PL . . . 46 B3
Paterna E . . . 96 B2
Paterna del Campo E . . . 99 B4
Paterna del Madera E . . . 90 C2
Paterna de Rivera E . . . 99 C5
Paternion A . . . 72 B3
Paternó I . . . 109 B3
Paternópoli I . . . 103 C8
Patersdorf D . . . 62 A3
Paterswolde NL . . . 42 B3
Patitiri GR . . . 116 C5
Patmos GR . . . 119 E1
Patna GB . . . 24 C3
Patnow PL . . . 54 A3
Patoniva FIN . . . 113 C16
Patopirtti FIN . . . 113 E18
Patos AL . . . 105 C5
Patra = Patras GR . . . 117 D3
Patras = Patra GR . . . 117 D3
Patreksfjördur IS . . . 111 B2
Patrickswell IRL . . . 20 B3
Patrimonio F . . . 102 A2
Patrington GB . . . 27 B5
Pattada I . . . 110 B2
Pattensen
   Niedersachsen D . . . 44 B2
   Niedersachsen D . . . 51 A5
Patterdale GB . . . 26 A3
Patti I . . . 109 A3
Pau F . . . 76 C2
Pauillac F . . . 66 C4
Paularo I . . . 72 B3
Paulhaguet F . . . 68 C3
Paulhan F . . . 78 C2
Paulilátino I . . . 110 B1
Paullo I . . . 71 C4
Paulstown IRL . . . 21 B4
Pausa D . . . 52 C2
Pautrásk S . . . 115 C14
Pavia
   I . . . 71 C4
   P . . . 92 C2
Pavias E . . . 96 B2
Pavilly F . . . 58 A1
Påvilosta LV . . . 6 C6
Pavullo nel Frignano I . . . 81 B4
Pawlowice PL . . . 54 B2
Pawlowice PL . . . 54 C3
Paxi GR . . . 116 C2
Payallar TR . . . 119 F6
Payerne CH . . . 70 B1
Paymogo E . . . 98 B3
Payrac F . . . 77 B4
Pazardzhik BG. . . 11 E8
Pazaryeri TR . . . 118 B4
Pazin HR . . . 72 C3
Paziols F . . . 78 D1
Pčelić HR . . . 74 C2
Peal de Becerro E . . . 100 B2
Peasmarsh GB . . . 31 D4
Peć KOS . . . 85 D5
Péccioli I . . . 81 C4
Pecel H . . . 75 A4
Pechao P . . . 98 B3
Pechenga RUS . . . 3 B29

Pechenizhyn UA . . . 11 B8
Pecica RO . . . 75 B6
Pećinci SRB . . . 85 B4
Pecka SRB . . . 85 B4
Peckelsheim D . . . 51 B5
Pečory RUS . . . 7 C9
Pécs H . . . 74 B3
Pécsvárad H . . . 74 B3
Pečurice MNE . . . 105 A5
Peczniew PL . . . 54 B3
Pedaso I . . . 82 C2
Pedavena I . . . 72 B1
Pedérobba I . . . 72 C1
Pedersker DK . . . 41 D4
Pedescala I . . . 71 C6
Pedoulas CY . . . 120 B1
Pedrafita E . . . 86 B3
Pedrajas de San Esteban E . . . 88 C2
Pedralba E . . . 96 B2
Pedralba de la Praderia E . . . 87 B4
Pedras Salgadas P . . . 87 C3
Pedraza E . . . 94 A3
Pedreguer E . . . 96 C3
Pedrera E . . . 100 B1
Pedro Abad E . . . 100 B1
Pedro Bernardo E . . . 94 B2
Pedroche E . . . 100 A1
Pedrógão P . . . 98 A3
Pedrógão P . . . 92 A2
Pedrógão Grande P . . . 92 B2
Pedrola E . . . 90 B1
Pedro-Martínez E . . . 100 B2
Pedro Muñoz E . . . 95 C4
Pedrosa del Rey E . . . 88 B1
Pedrosa del Rio Urbel E . . . 88 B3
Pedrosa de Tobalina E . . . 89 B3
Pedrosillo de los Aires E . . . 94 B1
Pedrosillo el Ralo E . . . 94 A1
Pedzewo PL . . . 47 B4
Peebles GB . . . 25 C4
Peel GB . . . 26 A1
Peenemünde D . . . 45 A5
Peer B . . . 49 B6
Pega P . . . 93 A3
Pegalajar E . . . 100 B2
Pegau D . . . 52 B2
Peggau A . . . 73 A5
Pegli I . . . 80 B2
Pegnitz D . . . 62 A2
Pego E . . . 96 C2
Pegões-Estação P . . . 92 C2
Pegões Velhos P . . . 92 C2
Pegow PL . . . 54 B1
Pehlivanköy TR . . . 118 A1
Peine D . . . 51 A6
Peisey-Nancroix F . . . 70 C1
Peissenberg D . . . 62 C2
Peiting D . . . 62 C1
Peitz D . . . 53 B4
Péjo I . . . 71 B5
Pelagićevo BIH . . . 84 B3
Pelahustán E . . . 94 B2
Pełczyce PL . . . 46 B1
Pelhřimov CZ . . . 63 A6
Pélissanne F . . . 79 C4
Pelkosenniemi FIN . . . 113 E16
Pella I . . . 70 C3
Pellegrino Parmense I . . . 81 B3
Pellegrue F . . . 76 B3
Pellérd F . . . 74 B3
Pellestrina I . . . 72 C2
Pellevoisin F . . . 67 B6
Pellizzano I . . . 71 B5
Pello
   FIN . . . 113 F13
   S . . . 113 F12
Peloche E . . . 93 B5
Pelplin PL . . . 47 B4
Pelussin F . . . 69 C4
Pély H . . . 75 A5
Pembroke GB . . . 28 B3
Pembroke Dock GB . . . 28 B3
Peñacerrada E . . . 89 B4
Penacova P . . . 92 A2
Peña de Cabra E . . . 94 B1
Peñafiel E . . . 88 C2
Penafiel P . . . 87 C2
Peñaflor E . . . 99 B5
Peñalba de Santiago E . . . 86 B4
Peñalsordo E . . . 93 C5
Penalva do Castelo P . . . 92 A3
Penamacor P . . . 93 A3
Peñaranda de Bracamonte E . . . 94 B1
Peñaranda de Duero E . . . 89 C3
Peñarroya de Tastavins E . . . 90 C3
Peñarroya-Pueblonuevo E . . . 99 A5
Peñarrubia E . . . 100 B1
Penarth GB . . . 29 B4
Peñascosa E . . . 101 A3
Peñas de San Pedro E . . . 101 A4
Peñausende E . . . 88 C1
Penc H . . . 65 C5
Pencoed GB . . . 29 B4
Pendalofos GR . . . 116 B3
Pendeen GB . . . 28 C2
Pendine GB . . . 28 B3
Pendueles E . . . 88 A2
Penedono P . . . 87 D3
Penela P . . . 92 A2
Pénestin F . . . 57 C3
Penhas Juntas P . . . 87 C3
Peniche P . . . 92 B1
Penicuik GB . . . 25 C4
Penig D . . . 52 C2
Penilhos P . . . 98 B3
Peñíscola E . . . 90 C3
Penistone GB . . . 27 B4
Penkridge GB . . . 26 C3
Penkun D . . . 45 B6
Penmarch F . . . 56 C1
Pennabilli I . . . 82 C1
Penne I . . . 103 A6
Penne-d'Agenais F . . . 77 B3
Pennes I . . . 71 B6
Pennyghael GB . . . 24 B1
Peno RUS . . . 7 C12
Penpont GB . . . 25 C4
Penrhyndeudraeth GB . . . 26 C1
Penrith GB . . . 26 A3
Penryn GB . . . 28 C2
Pentraeth GB . . . 26 B1
Penybontfawr GB . . . 26 C2
Penygroes
   Carmarthenshire GB. . . 28 B3
   Gwynedd GB . . . 26 B1
Penzance GB . . . 28 C2
Penzberg D . . . 62 C2
Penzlin D . . . 45 B5
Pepelow D . . . 44 A3
Peqin AL . . . 105 B5
Pér H . . . 74 A2
Pera Boa P . . . 92 A3
Perachora GR . . . 117 D4
Perafita P . . . 87 C2
Peraleda de la Mata E . . . 93 B5
Peraleda del Zaucejo E . . . 93 C5
Peraleda de San Román E . . . 93 B5
Perales de Alfambra E . . . 90 C1
Perales del Puerto E . . . 93 B4
Perales de Tajuña E . . . 95 B3
Peralta E . . . 89 B5
Peralta de la Sal E . . . 90 B3
Peralva P . . . 98 B3

Peralveche E . . . 95 B4
Perama GR . . . 117 G6
Perast MNE . . . 105 A4
Perbál H . . . 65 C4
Percy F . . . 7 C9
Perdasdefogu I . . . 110 C2
Perdiguera E . . . 90 B2
Peredo P . . . 87 C4
Peregu Mare RO . . . 75 B5
Pereiro
   Faro P . . . 98 B3
   Guarda P . . . 87 D3
   Santarém P . . . 92 B2
Pereiro de Aguiar E . . . 87 B3
Perelada E . . . 91 A6
Perelejos de las Truchas E . . . 95 B5
Pereña E . . . 87 C4
Pereruela E . . . 88 C1
Pereyaslav-Khmelnytskyy UA . . . 11 A11
Pérfugas I . . . 110 B1
Perg A . . . 63 B6
Pérgine Valsugana I . . . 71 B6
Pérgola I . . . 82 C1
Pergusa I . . . 109 B3
Periam RO . . . 75 B5
Periana E . . . 100 C1
Périers F . . . 57 A4
Périgueux F . . . 67 C5
Perino I . . . 80 B3
Perjasica HR . . . 73 C5
Perković HR . . . 83 C5
Perleberg D . . . 44 B3
Perlez SRB . . . 75 C5
Pérmet AL . . . 116 B2
Pernarec CZ . . . 62 A4
Pernek SK . . . 64 B3
Pernes P . . . 92 B2
Pernes-les-Fontaines F . . . 79 C4
Pernik BG . . . 11 E7
Pernink CZ . . . 52 C2
Pernitz A . . . 64 C1
Peroguarda P . . . 98 A2
Pérols F . . . 78 C2
Péronne F . . . 59 A3
Péronnas F . . . 69 B5
Perorrúbio E . . . 94 A3
Perosa Argentina I . . . 79 B6
Perozinho P . . . 87 C2
Perpignan F . . . 91 A5
Perranporth GB . . . 28 C2
Perranzabuloe GB . . . 28 C2
Perrecy-les-Forges F . . . 69 B4
Perrero I . . . 79 B6
Perrignier F . . . 69 B6
Perros-Guirec F . . . 56 B2
Persan F . . . 58 A3
Persberg S . . . 34 C6
Persenbeug A . . . 63 B6
Pershore GB . . . 29 A5
Perstorp S . . . 41 C3
Perth GB . . . 25 B4
Pertisau A . . . 72 A1
Pertoča SLO . . . 73 B6
Pertuis F . . . 79 C4
Perúcac SRB . . . 85 C4
Perúgia I . . . 82 C1
Perušić HR . . . 83 B4
Péruwelz B . . . 49 C4
Pervomaysk UA . . . 11 B11
Perwez B . . . 49 C5
Pesadas de Burgos E . . . 89 B3
Pesaguero E . . . 88 A2
Pésaro I . . . 82 C1
Pescantina I . . . 71 C5
Pescara I . . . 103 A7
Pescasséroli I . . . 103 B6
Peschici I . . . 104 B2
Peschiera del Garda I . . . 71 C5
Péscia I . . . 81 C4
Pescina I . . . 103 A6
Pescocostanzo I . . . 103 B7
Pescopagano I . . . 103 C8
Pesco Sannita I . . . 103 B7
Peshkopi AL . . . 116 A2
Pesmes F . . . 69 A5
Pesnica SLO . . . 73 B5
Peso da Régua P . . . 87 C3
Pesquera de Duero E . . . 88 C2
Pessac F . . . 76 B2
Pestovo RUS . . . 7 B13
Petalidi GR . . . 117 F3
Pétange L . . . 60 A1
Peteranec HR . . . 74 B1
Peterborough GB . . . 30 B3
Peterculter GB . . . 23 D7
Peterhead GB . . . 23 D7
Peterlee GB . . . 25 D6
Petersfield GB . . . 31 C3
Petershagen
   Brandenburg D . . . 45 C5
   Brandenburg D . . . 45 C6
   Nordrhein-Westfalen D . . . 43 C6
Petershausen D . . . 62 B2
Peterswell IRL . . . 20 A3
Pétervására H . . . 65 B6
Petília Policastro I . . . 107 B3
Petín E . . . 87 B3
Petkus D . . . 52 B3
Petlovac HR . . . 74 C3
Petlovača SRB . . . 85 B4
Petöfiszállás H . . . 75 B4
Petra E . . . 97 B3
Petralia Soprana I . . . 109 B3
Petralia Sottana I . . . 109 B3
Petrčane HR . . . 83 B4
Petrella Tifernina I . . . 103 B7
Petrer E . . . 101 A5
Petreto-Bicchisano F . . . 102 B1
Petrich BG . . . 116 A5
Petrijevci HR . . . 74 C3
Petrinja HR . . . 73 C6
Petrodvorets RUS . . . 7 B10
Petronà I . . . 107 B3
Petronell A . . . 64 B2
Petroşani RO . . . 11 D7
Petrovac
   MNE . . . 105 A4
   SRB . . . 85 B6
Petrovaradin SRB . . . 85 A4
Petrovice
   BIH . . . 84 B3
   CZ . . . 63 A5
Pettenbach A . . . 63 C5
Pettigo IRL . . . 19 B4
Petworth GB . . . 31 D3
Peuerbach A . . . 63 B4
Peuntenansa E . . . 88 A2
Peurasuvanto FIN . . . 113 E15
Pevensey Bay GB . . . 31 D4
Peveragno I . . . 80 B1
Pewsey GB . . . 29 B6
Pewsum D . . . 43 B4
Peyrat-le-Château F . . . 68 C1
Peyrehorade F . . . 76 C1
Peyriac-Minervois F . . . 77 C5
Peyrins F . . . 79 A4
Peyrissac F . . . 67 C6
Peyrolles-en-Provence F . . . 79 C4
Peyruis F . . . 79 B4
Pézarches F . . . 59 B3
Pézenas F . . . 78 C2
Pezinok SK . . . 64 B3
Pezuls F . . . 77 B3
Pfaffenhausen D . . . 61 B6
Pfaffenhofen
   Bayern D . . . 62 B2
   Bayern D . . . 62 B2
Pfaffenhoffen F . . . 60 B3
Pfäffikon CH . . . 70 A3
Pfarrkirchen D . . . 62 B3

Pfeffenhausen D . . . 62 B2
Pfetterhouse F . . . 70 A2
Pforzheim D . . . 61 B4
Pfreimd D . . . 62 A3
Pfronten D . . . 61 C6
Pfullendorf D . . . 61 C5
Pfullingen D . . . 61 B5
Pfunds A . . . 71 B5
Pfungstadt D . . . 61 A4
Pfyn CH . . . 61 C4
Phalsbourg F . . . 60 B3
Philippeville B . . . 49 C5
Philippsreut D . . . 63 B4
Philippsthal D . . . 51 C5
Piacenza I . . . 81 A3
Piacenza d'Adige I . . . 72 C1
Piádena I . . . 71 C5
Piana F . . . 102 A1
Piana Crixia I . . . 80 B2
Piana degli Albanesi I . . . 108 B2
Piana di Monte Verna I . . . 103 B7
Piancastagnáio I . . . 81 D5
Piandelagotti I . . . 81 B4
Pianella
   Abruzzi I . . . 103 A7
   Toscana I . . . 81 C5
Pianello Val Tidone I . . . 80 B3
Pianoro I . . . 81 B5
Pians A . . . 71 A5
Pías E . . . 87 B4
Pias P . . . 98 A3
Piaseczno PL . . . 55 A6
Piasek PL . . . 45 C6
Piaski PL . . . 47 A5
Piástow PL . . . 55 A5
Piaszczyna PL . . . 46 A3
Piątek PL . . . 55 A4
Piatra Neamţ RO . . . 11 C9
Piazza al Sérchio I . . . 81 B4
Piazza Armerina I . . . 109 B3
Piazza Brembana I . . . 71 C4
Piazze I . . . 81 D5
Piazzola sul Brenta I . . . 72 C1
Picassent E . . . 96 B2
Piccione I . . . 82 C1
Picerno I . . . 104 C1
Picher D . . . 44 B3
Pickering GB . . . 27 A5
Pico I . . . 103 B6
Picón E . . . 94 C2
Picquigny F . . . 58 A3
Piechowice PL . . . 53 C5
Piecnik PL . . . 46 B2
Piedicavallo I . . . 70 C2
Piedicroce F . . . 102 A2
Piedimonte Etneo I . . . 109 B4
Piedimonte Matese I . . . 103 B7
Piedimulera I . . . 70 B3
Piedipaterno I . . . 82 D1
Piedrabuena E . . . 94 C2
Piedraescrita E . . . 94 C2
Piedrafita E . . . 88 A1
Piedrahita E . . . 93 A5
Piedralaves E . . . 94 B2
Piedras Albas E . . . 93 B4
Piedras Blancas E . . . 88 A1
Piegaro I . . . 82 C1
Piekary Śl. PL . . . 54 C3
Piekoszów PL . . . 55 C5
Pieksämäki FIN . . . 3 E27
Pielenhofen D . . . 62 A2
Pielgrzymka PL . . . 53 B5
Pienięzno PL . . . 47 A6
Piensk PL . . . 53 B5
Pienza I . . . 81 C5
Piera E . . . 91 B4
Pieranie PL . . . 47 C4
Pierowall GB . . . 23 B6
Pierre-Buffière F . . . 67 C6
Pierrecourt F . . . 60 C1
Pierre-de-Bresse F . . . 69 B5
Pierrefeu-du-Var F . . . 79 C5
Pierrefitte-Nestalas F . . . 76 D2
Pierrefitte-sur-Aire F . . . 59 B6
Pierrefonds F . . . 59 A3
Pierrefontaine-les-Varans F . . . 69 A6
Pierrefort F . . . 78 B1
Pierrelatte F . . . 78 B3
Pierrepont
   Aisne F . . . 59 A4
   Meurthe-et-Moselle F . . . 60 A1
Piesendorf A . . . 72 A2
Pieštany SK . . . 64 B3
Pieszkowo PL . . . 47 A6
Pieszyce PL . . . 54 C1
Pietarsaari FIN . . . 3 E25
Pietragalla I . . . 104 C1
Pietra Ligure I . . . 80 B2
Pietralunga I . . . 82 C1
Pietramelara I . . . 103 B7
Pietraperzia I . . . 109 B3
Pietrasanta I . . . 81 C4
Pietravairano I . . . 103 B7
Pieve del Cáiro I . . . 80 A2
Pieve di Bono I . . . 71 C5
Pieve di Cadore I . . . 72 B2
Pieve di Cento I . . . 81 B5
Pieve di Soligo I . . . 72 C2
Pieve di Teco I . . . 80 B1
Pievepélago I . . . 81 B4
Pieve Santo Stéfano I . . . 82 C1
Pieve Torina I . . . 82 C2
Piges GR . . . 116 C3
Pigna I . . . 80 C1
Pignan F . . . 78 C2
Pignataro Maggiore I . . . 103 B7
Piikkiö FIN . . . 6 A7
Piittisjärvi FIN . . . 113 F15
Pijnacker NL . . . 49 A5
Pikalevo RUS . . . 7 B13
Pilar de la Horadada E . . . 101 B5
Pilas E . . . 99 B4
Pilastri I . . . 81 B5
Pilawa PL . . . 55 B6
Piława Górna PL . . . 54 C1
Piławki PL . . . 47 B5
Pilchowice PL . . . 54 C3
Pilica PL . . . 55 C4
Pilis H . . . 75 A4
Piliscaba H . . . 65 C4
Pilisszántó H . . . 65 C4
Pilisvörösvár H . . . 65 C4
Pilos GR . . . 117 F3
Pilsting D . . . 62 B3
Pilszcz PL . . . 54 C2
Pilterud N . . . 34 C2
Pilu RO . . . 75 B6
Pilzno PL . . . 55 D6
Pina de Ebro E . . . 90 B2
Pinarbaşı TR . . . 118 C1
Pınarhisar TR . . . 118 A2
Pinas F . . . 77 C3
Pincehely H . . . 74 B3
Pinchbeck GB . . . 30 B3
Pińczów PL . . . 55 C5
Pineda de la Sierra E . . . 89 B3
Pineda de Mar E . . . 91 B5
Pinerella I . . . 82 B1
Pinerolo I . . . 79 B6
Pineta Grande I . . . 103 B6
Pineto I . . . 103 A7
Piney F . . . 59 B5
Pinggau A . . . 73 A6
Pinhal Novo P . . . 92 C2
Pinhão P . . . 87 C3
Pinheiro
   Aveiro P . . . 87 C2
   Aveiro P . . . 87 D2
Pinheiro Grande P . . . 92 B2
Pinhel P . . . 93 A3
Pinhoe GB . . . 29 C4

Pinilla E . . . 101 A4
Pinilla de Toro E . . . 88 C1
Pinkafeld A . . . 73 A6
Pinneberg D . . . 44 B1
Pinnow D . . . 53 A3
Pino F . . . 102 A2
Pino del Rio E . . . 88 B2
Pino de Val E . . . 86 B2
Pinofranqueado E . . . 93 A4
Pinols F . . . 78 A2
Piñor E . . . 87 B2
Pinos del Valle E . . . 100 C2
Pinoso E . . . 101 A4
Pinos Puente E . . . 100 B2
Pinsk BY . . . 7 E9
Pinto E . . . 94 B3
Pinzano al Tagliamento I . . . 72 B2
Pinzio P . . . 93 A3
Pinzolo I . . . 71 B5
Pióbbico I . . . 82 C1
Piombino I . . . 81 D4
Pionki PL . . . 55 B6
Pionsat F . . . 68 B2
Pióraco I . . . 82 C1
Piornal E . . . 93 A5
Piotrkowice PL . . . 55 C5
Piotrków-Kujawski PL . . . 47 C4
Piotrków Trybunalski PL . . . 55 B4
Piotrowice PL . . . 55 A6
Piotrowo PL . . . 46 C2
Piove di Sacco I . . . 72 C2
Piovene I . . . 71 C6
Piperskärr S . . . 40 B6
Pipriac F . . . 57 C4
Piraeus = Pireas GR . . . 117 E5
Pireas = Piraeus GR . . . 117 E5
Piré-sur-Seiche F . . . 57 B4
Pirgi GR . . . 117 D7
Pirgos
   Ilia GR . . . 117 E3
   Kriti GR . . . 117 G7
Piriac-sur-Mer F . . . 66 A2
Piringsdorf A . . . 73 A6
Pirmasens D . . . 60 A3
Pirna D . . . 53 C3
Pirnmill GB . . . 24 C2
Pirot SRB . . . 11 E7
Pirovac HR . . . 83 C4
Pirttikoski FIN . . . 3 D24
Pirttivuopio S . . . 112 E8
Pisa I . . . 81 C4
Pisany F . . . 66 C4
Pisarovina HR . . . 73 C5
Pischelsdorf in der Steiermark A . . . 73 A5
Pişchia RO . . . 75 C6
Pisciotta I . . . 106 A2
Písek CZ . . . 63 A5
Pisogne I . . . 71 C5
Pissos F . . . 76 B2
Pissouri CY . . . 120 B1
Pisticci I . . . 104 C2
Pistóia I . . . 81 C5
Piteå S . . . 3 D24
Piteşti RO . . . 11 D8
Pithiviers F . . . 58 B3
Pitigliano I . . . 102 A4
Pitkyaranta RUS . . . 3 F29
Pitlochry GB . . . 25 B4
Pitomača HR . . . 74 C2
Pitres E . . . 100 C2
Pittentrail GB . . . 23 D5
Pitvaros H . . . 75 B5
Pivka SLO . . . 73 C4
Pivnice SRB . . . 75 C4
Piwniczna PL . . . 65 A6
Pizarra E . . . 100 C1
Pizzano I . . . 71 B5
Pizzighettone I . . . 71 C4
Pizzo I . . . 106 C3
Pizzolungo I . . . 108 A1
Pjätteryd S . . . 40 C4
Plabennec F . . . 56 B1
Placencia E . . . 89 A4
Plaffeien CH . . . 70 B2
Plaisance
   Gers F . . . 76 C3
   Haute-Garonne F . . . 77 C4
   Tarn F . . . 77 C5
Plaka GR . . . 116 C7
Plan E . . . 90 A3
Planá CZ . . . 62 A3
Planá nad Lužnicí CZ . . . 63 A5
Plaňany CZ . . . 53 C4
Planchez F . . . 68 A4
Plancios I . . . 72 B1
Plancoët F . . . 57 B3
Plancy-l'Abbaye F . . . 59 B4
Plan-de-Baix F . . . 79 B4
Plandište SRB . . . 75 C5
Plan-d'Orgon F . . . 78 C3
Plánice CZ . . . 63 A4
Planina
   SLO . . . 73 B5
   SLO . . . 73 C4
Plankenfels D . . . 62 A2
Plasencia E . . . 93 A4
Plasenzuela E . . . 93 B4
Plaški HR . . . 83 A4
Plassen
   Buskerud N . . . 32 B4
   Hedmark N . . . 34 A4
Plášťovce SK . . . 65 B4
Plasy CZ . . . 63 A4
Platamona Lido I . . . 110 B1
Platania I . . . 106 B3
Platanos GR . . . 117 G5
Platí I . . . 106 C3
Platičevo SRB . . . 85 B4
Platja d'Aro E . . . 91 B6
Plattling D . . . 62 B3
Plau D . . . 44 B4
Plaue
   Brandenburg D . . . 44 C4
   Thüringen D . . . 51 C6
Plauen D . . . 52 C2
Plav MNE . . . 85 D5
Plavecký Mikuláš SK . . . 64 B3
Plavinas LV . . . 7 C8
Plavna SRB . . . 85 B6
Plavno HR . . . 83 B5
Plavsk RUS . . . 7 E14
Pléaux F . . . 68 C2
Pleine-Fougères F . . . 57 B4
Pleinfeld D . . . 62 A1
Pleinting D . . . 62 B3
Plélan-le-Grand F . . . 57 B3
Plémet F . . . 56 B3
Plénée-Jugon F . . . 57 B3
Plentzia E . . . 89 A4
Plérin F . . . 56 B3
Plešin SK . . . 65 A5
Plessa D . . . 52 B3
Plessé F . . . 66 A3
Plestin-les-Grèves F . . . 56 B2
Pleszew PL . . . 54 B2
Pleternica HR . . . 74 C2
Plettenberg D . . . 50 B3
Pleubian F . . . 56 B2
Pleumartin F . . . 67 B5
Pleumeur-Bodou F . . . 56 B2
Pleurs F . . . 59 B4
Pleven BG . . . 11 E8
Plevlja MNE . . . 85 C4
Plevnik-Drienové SK . . . 65 A4
Pleyben F . . . 56 B2
Pleyber-Christ F . . . 56 B2
Pliego E . . . 101 B4
Pliešovce SK . . . 65 B5
Plitvička Jezera HR . . . 83 B4
Ploaghe I . . . 110 B1
Ploče HR . . . 84 C2
Plochingen D . . . 61 B5
Płock PL . . . 47 C5
Ploemeur F . . . 56 C2

Ploërmel F . . . 56 C3
Ploeuc-sur-Lie F . . . 56 B3
Plogastel St Germain F . . . 56 B1
Plogoff F . . . 56 B1
Ploiesti RO . . . 11 D9
Plomari GR . . . 118 D1
Plombières-les-Bains F . . . 60 C2
Plomin HR . . . 82 A3
Plön D . . . 44 A2
Plonéour-Lanvern F . . . 56 C1
Plonia PL . . . 45 B6
Płońsk PL . . . 47 C6
Płoskinia PL . . . 47 A5
Plössberg D . . . 62 A3
Ploty PL . . . 45 B7
Plouagat F . . . 56 B2
Plouaret F . . . 56 B2
Plouarzel F . . . 56 B1
Plouay F . . . 56 C2
Ploubalay F . . . 57 B3
Ploubazlanec F . . . 56 B2
Ploudalmézeau F . . . 56 B1
Ploudiry F . . . 56 B1
Plouénan F . . . 56 B1
Plouescat F . . . 56 B1
Plouézec F . . . 56 B2
Plougasnou F . . . 56 B2
Plougastel-Daoulas F . . . 56 B1
Plougonven F . . . 56 B2
Plougonnec F . . . 56 B2
Plougrescant F . . . 56 B2
Plouguenast F . . . 56 B3
Plouguerneau F . . . 56 B1
Plouha F . . . 56 B3
Plouharnel F . . . 56 C2
Plouhinec F . . . 56 B1
Plouigneau F . . . 56 B2
Ploumanach F . . . 56 B2
Plounévez-Quintin F . . . 56 B2
Plouray F . . . 56 B2
Plouzévédé F . . . 56 B1
Plovdiv BG . . . 11 E8
Plozévet F . . . 56 C1
Plumbridge GB . . . 19 B4
Pluméliau F . . . 56 C3
Plumlov CZ . . . 64 A3
Plungė LT . . . 6 D6
Pluty PL . . . 47 A6
Pluvigner F . . . 56 C3
Plužine
   BIH . . . 84 C3
Pluznica PL . . . 47 B4
Plymouth GB . . . 28 C3
Plymstock GB . . . 28 C3
Plzeň CZ . . . 63 A4
Pniewy PL . . . 46 C2
Pobędziska PL . . . 46 C3
Pobiedziska PL . . . 46 C3
Pobierowo PL . . . 45 A6
Pobla de Segur E . . . 90 A3
Pobladura del Valle E . . . 88 B1
Pobla-Tornesa E . . . 96 A3
Pobra de Trives E . . . 87 B3
Pobra do Brollón E . . . 86 B3
Pobra do Caramiñal E . . . 86 B2
Počátky CZ . . . 63 A6
Poceirão P . . . 92 C2
Pochep RUS . . . 7 E12
Pöchlarn A . . . 63 B6
Pocinovice CZ . . . 62 A4
Pockau D . . . 52 C3
Pocking D . . . 62 B4
Pocklington GB . . . 27 B5
Podbořany CZ . . . 52 C3
Podbrdo SLO . . . 72 B3
Podbrezová SK . . . 65 B5
Podčetrtek SLO . . . 73 B5
Podebłocie PL . . . 55 B6
Poděbrady CZ . . . 53 C5
Podence P . . . 87 C4
Podensac F . . . 76 B2
Podenzano I . . . 81 B3
Podersdorf am See A . . . 64 C2
Podgaje PL . . . 46 B2
Podgora HR . . . 84 C2
Podgóra PL . . . 55 B6
Podgorač HR . . . 74 C3
Podgorica MNE . . . 105 A5
Podgrad SLO . . . 73 C4
Podhájska SK . . . 64 B4
Podkova BG . . . 116 A7
Podlapača HR . . . 83 B4
Podnovlje BIH . . . 84 B3
Podolie SK . . . 64 B3
Podolínec SK . . . 65 A6
Podolsk RUS . . . 7 D14
Podromanija BIH . . . 84 C3
Podturen HR . . . 74 B1
Podujevo KOS . . . 85 C6
Podvín CZ . . . 64 B2
Podwilk PL . . . 65 A5
Poetto I . . . 110 C2
Poggendorf D . . . 45 A5
Poggiardo I . . . 107 A5
Poggibonsi I . . . 81 C5
Póggio a Caiano I . . . 81 C5
Poggio Imperiale I . . . 103 B8
Póggio Mirteto I . . . 102 A5
Póggio Moiano I . . . 102 A5
Póggio Renatico I . . . 81 B5
Póggio Rusco I . . . 81 B5
Pöggstall A . . . 63 B6
Pogny F . . . 59 B5
Pogorzela PL . . . 54 B2
Pogorzelice PL . . . 46 A3
Pogradec AL . . . 116 B2
Pogrodzie PL . . . 47 A5
Pohorelá SK . . . 65 B6
Pohořelice CZ . . . 64 B2
Pohronská Polhora SK . . . 65 B5
Poiana Mare RO . . . 11 E7
Poianella I . . . 72 C1
Poiares P . . . 92 A2
Poio E . . . 86 B2
Poirino I . . . 80 B1
Poisson F . . . 69 B4
Poissons F . . . 59 B6
Poissy F . . . 58 B3
Poitiers F . . . 67 B5
Poix-de-Picardie F . . . 58 A2
Poix-Terron F . . . 59 A5
Pokka FIN . . . 113 D14
Pokój PL . . . 54 C2
Pokupsko HR . . . 73 C5
Pol E . . . 86 A3
Pola RUS . . . 7 C11
Pola de Allande E . . . 86 A4
Pola de Laviana E . . . 88 A1
Pola de Lena E . . . 88 A1
Pola de Siero E . . . 88 A1
Pola de Somiedo E . . . 86 A4
Polaincourt-et-Clairefontaine F . . . 60 C2
Polán E . . . 94 C2
Polanco E . . . 88 A2
Połaniec PL . . . 55 C6
Polanica-Zdrój PL . . . 54 C1
Polánka nad Odrou CZ . . . 64 A4
Polány H . . . 74 B2
Polath TR . . . 118 C7
Polatsk BY . . . 7 D10
Polch D . . . 50 C3
Polcirkeln S . . . 113 F10
Pólczno PL . . . 46 A3
Połczyn-Zdrój PL . . . 46 B2
Polegate GB . . . 31 D4
Poleñino E . . . 90 B2
Polesella I . . . 81 B5
Polessk RUS . . . 6 D6
Polgár H . . . 65 C6
Polgárdi H . . . 74 A3
Polhov Gradec SLO . . . 73 B4
Police PL . . . 45 B6

Police nad Metují CZ . . . 53 C6
Polichnitos GR . . . 116 C8
Polička CZ . . . 53 D6
Poličnik HR . . . 83 B4
Policoro I . . . 106 A3
Policzna PL . . . 55 B6
Poligiros GR . . . 116 B5
Polignano a Mare I . . . 104 C3
Poligny F . . . 69 B5
Polis CY . . . 120 A1
Polistena I . . . 106 C3
Polizzi Generosa I . . . 109 B3
Poljana SRB . . . 85 B6
Poljanak HR . . . 83 B4
Poljčane SLO . . . 73 B5
Polje BIH . . . 84 B2
Police
   BIH . . . 83 B5
   BIH . . . 84 B3
Poljna SRB . . . 85 C6
Polkowice PL . . . 53 B6
Polla I . . . 104 C1
Pollas E . . . 88 C1
Pöllau A . . . 73 A5
Pollença E . . . 97 B3
Pollenfeld D . . . 62 B2
Pollfoss N . . . 114 F4
Póllica I . . . 106 A2
Polminhac F . . . 77 B5
Polná CZ . . . 63 A6
Polna RUS . . . 7 B10
Polomka SK . . . 65 B5
Polonne UA . . . 11 A9
Polperro GB . . . 28 C3
Polruan GB . . . 28 C3
Pöls A . . . 73 A4
Polska Cerekiew PL . . . 54 C3
Poltár SK . . . 65 B5
Põltsamaa EST . . . 7 B8
Põlva EST . . . 7 B9
Polyarnyye Zori RUS . . . 3 C30
Polzela SLO . . . 73 B5
Pomarance I . . . 81 C4
Pomarez F . . . 76 C2
Pomárico I . . . 104 C2
Pomáz H . . . 65 C5
Pombal P . . . 92 B2
Pomeroy GB . . . 19 B5
Pomézia I . . . 102 B5
Pomichna UA . . . 11 B11
Pommard F . . . 69 A4
Pommelsbrunn D . . . 62 A2
Pomonte I . . . 81 D4
Pomorie BG . . . 11 E9
Pomos CY . . . 120 A1
Pompei I . . . 103 C7
Pompey F . . . 60 B2
Pomposa I . . . 82 B1
Poncin F . . . 69 B5
Pondorf D . . . 62 B2
Ponferrada E . . . 86 B4
Poniec PL . . . 54 B1
Ponikva SLO . . . 73 B5
Poniky SK . . . 65 B5
Pons F . . . 67 C4
Ponsacco I . . . 81 C4
Pont F . . . 70 C2
Pont-a-Celles B . . . 49 C5
Pontacq F . . . 76 C2
Pontailler-sur-Saône F . . . 69 A5
Pontão P . . . 92 B2
Pontardawe GB . . . 28 B4
Pontarddulais GB . . . 28 B3
Pontarion F . . . 68 C1
Pontarlier F . . . 69 B6
Pontassieve I . . . 81 C5
Pontaubault F . . . 57 B4
Pont-Audemer F . . . 58 A1
Pontaumur F . . . 68 C2
Pont-Aven F . . . 56 C2
Pont Canavese I . . . 70 C2
Pontcharra F . . . 69 C6
Pontcharra-sur-Turdine F . . . 69 C4
Pontchâteau F . . . 66 A2
Pont-Croix F . . . 56 B1
Pont d'Ain F . . . 69 B5
Pont-de-Beauvoisin F . . . 69 C5
Pont-de-Buis-lès-Quimerch F . . . 56 B1
Pont-de-Chéruy F . . . 69 C5
Pont de Dore F . . . 68 C3
Pont-de-Labeaume F . . . 78 B3
Pont-de-l'Arche F . . . 58 A2
Pont-de-Molins E . . . 91 A5
Pont-de-Roide F . . . 70 A1
Pont-de-Salars F . . . 78 B1
Pont-d'Espagne F . . . 76 D2
Pont-de-Suert E . . . 90 A3
Pont-de-Vaux F . . . 69 B4
Pont-de-Veyle F . . . 69 B5
Pont-d'Ouilly F . . . 57 B5
Pont-du-Château F . . . 68 C3
Pont-du-Navoy F . . . 69 B5
Ponte a Moriano I . . . 81 C4
Ponte Arche I . . . 71 B5
Ponte da Barca P . . . 87 C2
Pontebba I . . . 72 B3
Ponte Cáffaro I . . . 71 C5
Ponte-Caldelas E . . . 87 B2
Ponteceso E . . . 86 A2
Pontecesures E . . . 86 B2
Pontecorvo I . . . 103 B6
Ponte de Lima P . . . 87 C2
Ponte dell'Ólio I . . . 80 B3
Pontedera I . . . 81 C4
Ponte de Sor P . . . 92 B2
Pontedeume E . . . 86 A2
Ponte di Barbarano I . . . 72 C1
Ponte di Legno I . . . 71 B5
Ponte di Piave I . . . 72 C2
Ponte Felcino I . . . 82 C1
Ponte Gardena I . . . 71 B6
Pontelagoscuro I . . . 81 B5
Ponte-Leccia F . . . 102 A2
Pontelandolfo I . . . 103 B7
Ponte nelle Alpi I . . . 72 B2
Pont-en-Royans F . . . 79 A4
Pontevedra E . . . 86 B2
Pontevico I . . . 71 C5
Pont Farcy F . . . 57 B4
Pontfaverger-Moronvillers F . . . 59 A5
Pontgibaud F . . . 68 C2
Ponticino I . . . 81 C5
Pontínia I . . . 103 B6
Pontinvrea I . . . 80 B2
Pontivy F . . . 56 B3
Pont-l'Abbé F . . . 56 C1
Pont-l'Évêque F . . . 57 A6
Pontlevoy F . . . 67 A6
Pontoise F . . . 58 A3
Pontones E . . . 101 A3
Pontonx-sur-l'Adour F . . . 76 C2
Pontoon IRL . . . 18 C2
Pontorson F . . . 57 B4

Pontrémoli I ... 81 B3
Pont-Remy F ... 48 C2
Pontresina CH ... 71 B4
Pontrhydfendigaid GB ... 28 A4
Pontrieux F ... 56 B2
Ponts E ... 91 B4
Ponts-aux-Dames F ... 59 B3
Pont Scorff F ... 56 C2
Pöntsö FIN ... 113 E13
Pont-Ste Maxence F ... 58 A3
Pont-St Esprit F ... 78 B3
Pont-St Mamet F ... 77 B3
Pont-St Martin
  F ... 66 A3
  F ... 70 C2
Pont-St Vincent F ... 60 B2
Pont-sur-Yonne F ... 59 B4
Pontvallain F ... 57 C6
Pontypool GB ... 29 B4
Pontypridd GB ... 29 B4
Ponza I ... 102 C5
Poo E ... 88 A2
Poole GB ... 29 C6
Poolewe GB ... 22 D3
Poperinge B ... 48 C3
Pópoli I ... 103 A6
Popovac SRB ... 85 C6
Popovača HR ... 74 C1
Popow PL ... 55 A4
Poppel B ... 49 B6
Poppenhausen
  Bayern D ... 51 C6
  Hessen D ... 51 C5
Poppi I ... 81 C5
Poprad SK ... 65 A6
Popučke SRB ... 87 C3
Pópulo P ... 87 C3
Populónia I ... 81 D4
Pörböly H ... 74 B3
Porcuna E ... 100 B1
Pordenone I ... 72 C2
Pordic F ... 56 B3
Poręba PL ... 55 C4
Poreč HR ... 72 C3
Pori FIN ... 3 F24
Porjus S ... 112 F8
Porkhov RUS ... 7 C10
Porlezza I ... 71 B4
Porlock GB ... 29 B4
Pörnbach D ... 62 B2
Pornic F ... 66 A2
Pornichet F ... 66 A2
Porodin SRB ... 85 B6
Poronin PL ... 65 A5
Poros
  Attiki GR ... 117 E5
  Kefalonia GR ... 117 D2
Poroszló H ... 65 C6
Porozina HR ... 82 A3
Porquerolles F ... 79 D5
Porrentruy CH ... 70 A2
Porreres E ... 97 B3
Porretta Terme I ... 81 B4
Porsgrunn N ... 35 C1
Porspoder F ... 56 B1
Port-a-Binson F ... 59 A4
Portacloy IRL ... 18 B2
Portadown GB ... 19 B5
Portaferry GB ... 19 B6
Portaje E ... 93 B4
Portalegre P ... 92 B3
Portarlington IRL ... 21 A4
Portavadie GB ... 24 C2
Portavogie GB ... 24 C2
Portbail F ... 57 A4
Port Bannatyne GB ... 24 C2
Port-Barcarès F ... 78 D2
Portbou E ... 91 A6
Port-Camargue F ... 78 C3
Port Charlotte GB ... 24 C1
Port d'Andratx E ... 97 B2
Port-de-Bouc F ... 78 C3
Port-de-Lanne F ... 76 C1
Port de Pollença E ... 97 B3
Port-des-Barques F ... 66 C3
Port de Sóller E ... 97 B2
Portegrandi I ... 72 C2
Portel P ... 92 C3
Portela P ... 92 A2
Port Ellen GB ... 24 C1
Portelo P ... 87 C4
Portemouro E ... 86 B2
Port-en-Bessin F ... 57 A5
Port'Ercole I ... 102 A4
Port Erin GB ... 26 A1
Portes-lès-Valence F ... 78 B3
Portets F ... 76 B2
Port Eynon GB ... 28 B3
Portezuelo E ... 93 B4
Port Glasgow GB ... 24 C3
Portglenone GB ... 19 B5
Porthcawl GB ... 28 B4
Port Henderson GB ... 22 D3
Porthleven GB ... 28 C2
Porthmadog GB ... 26 C1
Porticcio F ... 102 B1
Portici I ... 103 C7
Pórtico di Romagna I ... 81 B5
Portilla de la Reina E ... 88 A2
Portillo E ... 88 C2
Portimao P ... 98 B2
Portinatx E ... 97 B1
Portinho da Arrabida P ... 92 C1
Port Isaac GB ... 28 C3
Portishead GB ... 29 B5
Port-Joinville F ... 66 B2
Portknockie GB ... 23 D6
Port-la-Nouvelle F ... 78 C2
Portlaoise IRL ... 21 A4
Portlethen GB ... 23 D6
Port Logan GB ... 24 D3
Port Louis F ... 56 C2
Portmagee IRL ... 20 C1
Portmahomack GB ... 23 D5
Portman E ... 101 B5
Portnacroish GB ... 24 B2
Portnahaven GB ... 24 C1
Port Nan Giuran GB ... 22 C2
Port-Navalo F ... 66 A2
Port Nis GB ... 22 C2
Porto
  F ... 102 A1
  P ... 87 C2
Porto-Alto P ... 92 C2
Porto Azzurro I ... 81 D4
Portocannone I ... 103 B8
Pozzuoli I ... 103 C7
Porto Cerésio I ... 70 C3
Porto Cervo I ... 110 A2
Porto Cesáreo I ... 107 A4
Porto Colom E ... 97 B3
Porto Cristo E ... 97 B3
Porto d'Áscoli I ... 82 C2
Porto de Lagos P ... 98 B2
Porto de Mos P ... 92 B2
Porto de Rei P ... 92 C2
Porto do Son E ... 86 B2
Porto Empédocle I ... 108 B2
Portoferráio I ... 81 D4
Portofino I ... 80 B3
Porto Garibaldi I ... 82 B1
Portokhelion GR ... 117 E5
Portomaggiore I ... 81 B5
Portomarin E ... 86 B3
Porton GB ... 29 B6
Portopalo di Capo
  Passero I ... 109 C4
Porto Petro E ... 97 B3
Porto Pino I ... 110 D1
Porto Potenza Picena I ... 82 C2
Porter N ... 33 D6
Porto Recanati I ... 82 C2

Porto San Giórgio I ... 82 C2
Porto Sant'Elpídio I ... 82 C2
Porto Santo Stéfano
  I ... 102 A4
Portoscuso I ... 110 C1
Porto Tolle I ... 82 B1
Porto Tórres I ... 110 B1
Porto-Vecchio F ... 102 B2
Portovénere I ... 81 B3
Portpatrick GB ... 24 D2
Portreath GB ... 28 C2
Portree GB ... 22 D2
Portroe IRL ... 20 B3
Portrush GB ... 19 A5
Port St Mary GB ... 26 A1
Portsall F ... 56 B1
Portsmouth GB ... 31 D2
Portsoy GB ... 23 D6
Port-Ste Marie F ... 77 B3
Portstewart GB ... 19 A5
Port-St-Louis-du-Rhône
  F ... 78 C3
Port-sur-Saône F ... 60 C1
Portumna IRL ... 20 A3
Port-Vendres F ... 91 A6
Port William GB ... 24 D3
Porvoo FIN ... 7 A8
Porzuna E ... 94 C2
Posada
  Oviedo E ... 88 A1
  Oviedo E ... 88 A2
  I ... 110 B2
Posada de Valdeón E ... 88 A2
Posadas E ... 99 B5
Poschiavo CH ... 71 B5
Posedarje HR ... 83 B4
Positano I ... 103 C7
Possagno I ... 72 C1
Posseck D ... 52 C2
Possesse F ... 59 B5
Pössneck D ... 52 C1
Posta I ... 102 A6
Posta Piana I ... 104 B1
Postbauer-Heng D ... 62 A2
Posterholt NL ... 50 B2
Postioma I ... 72 C2
Postira HR ... 83 C5
Postojna SLO ... 73 C4
Postoloprty CZ ... 53 C3
Postomino PL ... 46 A2
Posušje BIH ... 84 C2
Potamos
  Attiki GR ... 117 F4
  Attiki GR ... 117 G5
Potegowo PL ... 46 A3
Potenza I ... 104 C1
Potenza Picena I ... 82 C2
Potes E ... 88 A2
Potigny F ... 57 B5
Potkrajci MNE ... 85 C4
Potočari BIH ... 85 B4
Potoci
  BIH ... 83 B5
  BIH ... 84 C2
Potony H ... 74 C2
Potries E ... 96 C2
Potsdam D ... 45 C5
Potštát CZ ... 64 A3
Potštejn CZ ... 53 C6
Pottenbrunn A ... 63 B6
Pottendorf A ... 64 C2
Pottenstein
  D ... 64 C2
  D ... 62 A2
Pöttmes D ... 62 B2
Pöttsching A ... 64 C2
Potworów PL ... 55 B5
Pouancé F ... 57 C4
Pougues-les-Eaux F ... 68 A3
Pouilly-en-Auxois F ... 69 A4
Pouilly-sous-Charlieu F ... 68 B4
Pouilly-sur-Loire F ... 68 A2
Poujol-sur-Orb F ... 78 C2
Poullaouen F ... 56 B2
Poulton-le-Fylde GB ... 26 B3
Poundstock GB ... 28 C3
Pourcy F ... 59 A4
Pourrain F ... 59 C4
Pouy-de-Touges F ... 77 C4
Pouzauges F ... 66 B4
Pova de Santa Iria P ... 92 C1
Považská Bystrica SK ... 65 A4
Povedilla E ... 101 A3
Povlja HR ... 84 C1
Povljana HR ... 83 B4
Póvoa
  Beja P ... 98 A3
  Santarém P ... 92 B2
Póvoa de Lanhoso P ... 87 C2
Póvoa de Varzim P ... 87 C2
Póvoa e Meadas P ... 92 B3
Powidz PL ... 46 C3
Poyales del Hoyo E ... 93 A5
Poynton GB ... 26 B3
Poyntz Pass GB ... 19 B5
Poysdorf A ... 64 B2
Poza de la Sal E ... 89 B3
Pozaldez E ... 88 C2
Pozán de Vero E ... 90 A3
Požarevac SRB ... 85 B6
Požega
  HR ... 74 C2
  SRB ... 85 C5
Poznań PL ... 46 C2
Pozo Alcón E ... 100 B3
Pozoantiguo E ... 88 C1
Pozoblanco E ... 100 A1
Pozo Cañada E ... 101 A4
Pozo de Guadalajara E ... 95 B3
Pozo de la Serna E ... 100 A3
Pozohondo E ... 101 A4
Pozondón E ... 95 B5
Poźrzadło Wielkie PL ... 46 B1
Pozuelo E ... 101 A4
Pozuelo de Alarcón E ... 94 B3
Pozuelo de Calatrava E ... 100 A2
Pozuelo del Páramo E ... 88 B1
Pozuelo de Zarzón E ... 93 A4
Pozzallo I ... 109 C3
Pozzomaggiore I ... 110 B1
Pozzo San Nicola I ... 110 B1
Pozzuoli I ... 103 C7
Pozzuolo I ... 81 C5
Prabuty PL ... 47 B5
Prača BIH ... 84 C3
Prachatice CZ ... 63 A4
Prada E ... 87 B3
Pradelle F ... 79 B4
Pradelles F ... 78 B2
Prades
  E ... 90 B3
  F ... 91 A5
Pradła PL ... 55 C4
Prado
  E ... 88 A1
  P ... 87 C2
Prado del Rey E ... 99 C5
Pradoluengo E ... 89 B3
Pragelato I ... 79 A5
Prägraten A ... 72 B2
Prague = Praha CZ ... 53 C4
Prahecq F ... 67 B4
Praia a Mare I ... 106 B2
Praia da Rocha P ... 98 B2
Praia da Tocha P ... 92 A2
Praia de Mira P ... 92 A2
Praiano I ... 103 C7

Pralboino I ... 71 C5
Pralognan-la-Vanoise
  F ... 70 C1
Pramanda GR ... 116 C3
Pranjani SRB ... 85 B5
Prapatnica HR ... 83 C5
Præstø DK ... 39 D5
Praszka PL ... 54 B3
Prat F ... 77 C3
Prata I ... 81 C4
Prata di Pordenone I ... 72 C2
Pratau D ... 52 B2
Pratella I ... 103 B7
Prato I ... 81 C5
Prátola Peligna I ... 103 A6
Prátola Serra I ... 103 C7
Prats-de-Mollo-la-Preste
  F ... 91 A5
Prauthoy F ... 59 C6
Pravia E ... 88 A1
Praxmar A ... 71 A6
Prayssac F ... 77 B4
Prazzo I ... 79 B6
Prebold SLO ... 73 B5
Préchac F ... 76 B2
Précy-sur-Thil F ... 69 A4
Predáppio I ... 81 B5
Predazzo I ... 72 B1
Predeal RO ... 11 D8
Predejane SLO ... 73 C4
Predel SLO ... 72 B3
Predești RO ...
Predjame SLO ... 73 C4
Predlitz A ... 72 A3
Predmeja SLO ... 72 A3
Predoi I ... 72 B2
Pré-en-Pail F ... 57 B5
Prees GB ... 26 C3
Preetz D ... 44 A2
Préfailles F ... 66 A2
Pregarten A ... 63 B5
Pregrada HR ... 73 B5
Preignan F ... 77 C3
Preili LV ... 7 C9
Preitenegg A ... 73 B4
Prekaja BIH ... 83 B5
Preko HR ... 83 B4
Preljina SRB ... 85 C5
Prelog HR ... 74 B1
Prelošćica HR ... 74 C1
Přelouč CZ ... 53 C5
Prem SLO ... 73 C4
Premantura HR ... 82 B2
Prémery F ... 68 A3
Premià de Mar E ... 91 B5
Premnitz D ... 44 C4
Prémont F ... 49 C4
Prenzlau D ... 45 B5
Preodac BIH ... 83 B5
Přerov CZ ... 64 A3
Prerow D ... 44 A4
Presencio E ... 88 B3
Presicce I ... 107 B5
Presly F ... 68 A2
Pressac F ... 67 B5
Pressath D ... 62 A2
Pressbaum A ... 64 B2
Prestatyn GB ... 26 B2
Prestebakke N ... 35 D3
Presteigne GB ... 29 A4
Přeštice CZ ... 63 A4
Preston
  Lancashire GB ... 26 B3
  Scottish Borders GB ... 25 C5
Prestonpans GB ... 25 C5
Prestwick GB ... 24 C3
Prettin D ... 52 B2
Pretoro I ... 103 A6
Pretzchendorf D ... 52 C3
Pretzier D ... 44 C3
Pretzsch D ... 52 B2
Preuilly-sur-Claise F ... 67 B5
Prevalje SLO ... 73 B4
Prevenchères F ... 78 B2
Préveranges F ... 68 B2
Preveza GR ... 116 D2
Prevršac HR ... 73 C6
Prezid HR ... 73 C4
Priaranza del Bierzo
  E ... 86 B4
Priay F ... 69 B5
Pribeta SK ... 64 C4
Priboj
  BIH ... 84 B3
  SRB ... 85 C4
Příbor CZ ... 64 A4
Příbram CZ ... 63 A5
Pribylina SK ... 65 A5
Přibyslav CZ ... 63 A6
Pričević SRB ... 85 B4
Pridjel BIH ... 84 B3
Priego E ... 95 B4
Priego de Córdoba
  E ... 100 B1
Priekule LV ... 6 C6
Prien D ... 62 C3
Prienai LT ... 6 D7
Prievidza SK ... 65 B4
Prigradica HR ... 84 D1
Prigrevica SRB ... 75 C4
Prijeboj HR ... 83 B4
Prijedor BIH ... 83 B5
Prijepolje SRB ... 85 C4
Prilep MK ... 116 A3
Priluka BIH ... 84 C1
Primda CZ ... 62 A3
Primel-Trégastel F ... 56 B2
Primišlje HR ... 73 C5
Primorsk
  Kaliningrad RUS ... 47 A6
  Severo-Zapadnyy
  RUS ... 7 A10
Primošten HR ... 83 C4
Primstal D ... 60 A2
Princes Risborough
  GB ... 31 C3
Princetown GB ... 28 C3
Principina a Mare I ... 81 D5
Priolo Gargallo I ... 109 B4
Prioro E ... 88 B2
Priozersk RUS ... 113 F29
Prirechnyy RUS ... 113 C19
Prisoje BIH ... 84 C2
Priston RUS ... 7 F14
Priština KOS ... 85 D6
Pritzerbe D ... 44 C4
Pritzier D ... 44 B3
Pritzwalk D ... 44 B4
Privas F ... 78 B3
Priverno I ... 102 B6
Privlaka
  Vukovarsko-Srijemska
  HR ... 74 C3
  Zadarska HR ... 83 B4
Prizna HR ... 83 B3
Prizren KOS ... 10 E6
Prizzi I ... 108 B2
Prnjavor
  BIH ... 84 B2
  HR ... 73 C6
  SRB ... 85 B4
Proaza E ... 86 A4
Probstzella D ... 52 C1
Probus GB ... 28 C3
Prócchio I ... 81 D4
Prochowice PL ... 53 B6
Prócida I ... 103 C7
Prodhromos CY ... 120 B1
Prodo I ... 82 D1
Proença-a-Nova P ... 92 B3
Proença-a-Velha P ... 92 A3
Profondeville B ... 49 C5
Prokuplje SRB ... 10 E6
Propriano F ... 102 B1
Prosec CZ ... 64 A2
Prösen D ... 52 B3
Prossedi I ... 102 B6
Prossotsáni GR ... 116 A5
Prostějov CZ ... 64 A3
Prószków PL ... 54 C2

Proszowice PL ... 55 C5
Protić BIH ... 84 B1
Protivanov CZ ... 64 A2
Protivín CZ ... 63 A5
Prötzel D ... 45 C5
Provins F ... 59 B4
Prozor BIH ... 84 C2
Prrenjas AL ... 116 A2
Prudhoe GB ... 25 D6
Prudnik PL ... 54 C2
Pruggern A ... 72 A3
Prüm D ... 50 C2
Pruna E ... 99 C5
Prunelli-di-Fiumorbo
  F ... 102 A2
Prunetta I ... 81 B4
Pruniers F ... 68 B2
Prusice PL ... 54 B1
Pruské SK ... 64 A4
Pruszce PL ... 47 B4
Pruszcz Gdański PL ... 47 A4
Pruszków PL ... 55 A5
Prutz A ... 71 A5
Prüzen D ... 44 B4
Pruzhany BY ... 6 E8
Pružina SK ... 65 A4
Pryluky UA ... 11 A12
Pryzleg PL ... 46 C1
Przechlewo PL ... 46 B3
Przecław PL ... 55 C6
Przedbórz PL ... 55 B4
Przedecz PL ... 54 A3
Przejęslav PL ... 53 B5
Przemków PL ... 53 B5
Przemocze PL ... 45 B6
Przemyśl PL ... 11 B7
Przerąb PL ... 55 B4
Przewodnik PL ... 47 B4
Przewóz PL ... 53 B4
Przezmark PL ... 47 B5
Przodkowo PL ... 47 A4
Przybiernów PL ... 45 B6
Przyborowice PL ... 47 C6
Przybyszew PL ... 55 B5
Przybyszów PL ... 55 B4
Przylęg PL ... 46 C1
Przysucha PL ... 55 B5
Przytoczna PL ... 46 C1
Przytyk PL ... 55 B5
Przywidz PL ... 47 A4
Psachna GR ... 116 D5
Psara GR ... 116 D7
Psary PL ... 54 B3
Pskov RUS ... 7 C10
Pszczew PL ... 46 C1
Pszczółki PL ... 47 A4
Pszczyna PL ... 54 D3
Pszów PL ... 54 C3
Pteleos GR ... 116 C4
Ptolemaida GR ... 116 B3
Ptuj SLO ... 73 B5
Ptusza PL ... 46 B2
Puch A ... 62 C4
Puchberg am Schneeberg
  A ... 64 C1
Puchevillers F ... 48 C3
Puchheim D ... 62 B2
Púchov SK ... 64 A4
Pučišća HR ... 83 C5
Puck PL ... 47 A4
Puçol E ... 96 B2
Puconci SLO ... 73 B6
Pudasjärvi FIN ... 3 D27
Puderbach D ... 50 C3
Puebla de Albortón E ... 90 B2
Puebla de Alcocer E ... 93 C5
Puebla de Beleña E ... 95 B3
Puebla de Don Fadrique
  E ... 101 B4
Puebla de Don Rodrigo
  E ... 94 C2
Puebla de Guzmán E ... 98 B3
Puebla de la Calzada
  E ... 93 C4
Puebla de la Reina E ... 93 C4
Puebla de Lillo E ... 88 A1
Puebla del Maestre E ... 99 A4
Puebla del Principe
  E ... 100 A3
Puebla de Obando E ... 93 B4
Puebla de Sanabria E ... 87 B4
Puebla de Sancho Pérez
  E ... 93 C4
Puente Almuhey E ... 88 B2
Puente de Domingo
  Flórez E ... 86 B4
Puente de Génave E ... 101 A3
Puente del Congosto
  E ... 93 A5
Puente de Montañana
  E ... 90 A3
Puente Duero E ... 88 C2
Puente-Genil E ... 100 B1
Puente la Reina E ... 89 B5
Puente la Reina de Jaca
  E ... 90 A2
Puentelarra E ... 89 B3
Puente Mayorga E ... 99 C5
Puente Viesgo E ... 88 A3
Puertas
  Asturias E ... 88 A2
  Salamanca E ... 87 C4
Puerto de Mazarrón
  E ... 101 B4
Puerto de Santa Cruz
  E ... 93 B5
Puerto de San Vicente
  E ... 94 C1
Puerto-Lápice E ... 95 C3
Puertollano E ... 100 A1
Puerto Lumbreras E ... 101 B4
Puerto Moral E ... 99 B4
Puerto Real E ... 99 C4
Puerto Rey E ... 94 C1
Puerto Seguro E ... 87 D4
Puerto Serrano E ... 99 C5
Puget-sur-Argens F ... 79 C5
Puget-Théniers F ... 79 C5
Puget-ville F ... 79 C5
Pugnochiuso I ... 104 B2
Puigcerdà E ... 91 A4
Puigpunyent E ... 97 B2
Puig Reig E ... 91 B4
Puillon F ... 76 C2
Puimichel F ... 79 C5
Puimoisson F ... 79 C5
Puiseaux F ... 58 B3
Puisieux F ... 48 C3
Puisserguier F ... 78 C2
Puivert F ... 77 D5
Pujols F ... 76 B2
Pukanec SK ... 65 B4
Pukavik S ... 41 C4
Pukë AL ... 105 A5
Pula
  HR ... 82 B2
  I ... 110 D1
Puławy PL ... 10 A6
Pulborough GB ... 31 D3
Pulfero I ... 72 B3
Pulgar E ... 94 C2
Pulheim D ... 50 B2
Pulkau A ... 64 B1
Pulpi E ... 101 B4
Pulsano I ... 104 C3
Pulsnitz D ... 53 B4
Pułtusk PL ... 6 E6
Pumpsaint GB ... 28 A4
Punat HR ... 83 A3
Punta Marina I ... 82 B1
Punta Prima E ... 97 B4
Punta Sabbioni I ... 72 C2
Puntas de Calnegre
  E ... 101 B4
Punta Umbria E ... 99 B4
Puolanka FIN ... 3 D27
Puoltikasvaara S ... 112 E9
Puoltsa S ... 112 E8
Puračić BIH ... 84 B3
Purbach am Neusiedler
  See A ... 64 C2
Purchena E ... 101 B3

Purfleet GB ... 31 C4
Purgstall A ... 63 B6
Purkersdorf A ... 64 B2
Purmerend NL ... 42 C1
Purullena E ... 100 B2
Pushkin RUS ... 7 B11
Pushkino RUS ... 7 C14
Püspökladány H ... 75 A6
Pusté Ulany SK ... 64 B3
Pustoshka RUS ... 7 C10
Puszcza Mariańska
  PL ... 55 A5
Puszczykowo PL ... 54 A1
Pusztamagyaród H ... 74 B1
Pusztamonostor H ... 75 A4
Pusztaszabolcs H ... 74 A3
Pusztavám H ... 74 A3
Putanges-Pont-Ecrepin
  F ... 57 B5
Putbus D ... 45 A5
Putignano I ... 104 C3
Putlitz D ... 44 B4
Putnok H ... 65 B6
Putte B ... 49 B5
Puttelange-aux-Lacs
  F ... 60 A2
Puttgarden D ... 44 A3
Püttlingen D ... 60 A2
Putzu Idu I ... 110 B1
Puy-Guillaume F ... 68 C3
Puylaroque F ... 77 B4
Puylaurens F ... 77 C5
Puy-l'Évêque F ... 77 B4
Puymirol F ... 77 B4
Puyôo F ... 76 C2
Puyrolland F ... 67 B4
Pwllheli GB ... 26 C1
Pyatykhatky UA ... 11 B12
Pyetrikaw BY ... 7 E10
Pyhäjärvi FIN ... 3 E26
Pyla CY ... 120 B2
Pyla-sur-Mer F ... 76 B1
Pyrryatyn UA ... 11 A12
Pyrzyce PL ... 45 B6
Pysely CZ ... 63 A5
Pyskowice PL ... 54 C3
Pytalovo RUS ... 7 C9
Pyzdry PL ... 54 A2

Q

Quakenbrück D ... 43 C4
Quargnento I ... 80 B2
Quarré-les-Tombes F ... 68 A3
Quarteira P ... 98 B2
Quartu Sant'Élena I ... 110 C2
Quatre-Champs F ... 59 A5
Quedlinburg D ... 52 B1
Queensferry
  Edinburgh GB ... 25 C4
  Flintshire GB ... 26 B2
Queige F ... 69 C6
Queipo E ... 99 B4
Queixans E ... 91 A4
Quel E ... 89 B4
Quelaines-St-Gault F ... 57 C5
Quelgada P ... 87 C2
Quemada E ... 89 C3
Queralbs E ... 91 A5
Quercianella I ... 81 C4
Querfurt D ... 52 B1
Quérigut F ... 77 D5
Quero
  E ... 95 C3
  I ... 72 C1
Querqueville F ... 57 A4
Quesada E ... 100 B2
Questembert F ... 56 C3
Quettehou F ... 57 A4
Quevauvillers F ... 58 A3
Quevy B ... 49 C5
Quiaios P ... 92 A2
Quiberon F ... 66 A1
Quiberville F ... 58 A1
Quickborn D ... 44 B1
Quiévrain B ... 49 C4
Quillan F ... 77 D5
Quillebeuf F ... 58 A1
Quimper F ... 56 B1
Quimperlé F ... 56 C2
Quincampoix F ... 58 A2
Quincoces de Yuso E ... 89 B3
Quincy F ... 68 A2
Quinéville F ... 57 A4
Quingey F ... 69 A5
Quinson F ... 79 C4
Quinssaines F ... 68 B2
Quinta-Grande P ... 92 C2
Quintana de la Serena
  E ... 93 C5
Quintana del Castillo
  E ... 86 B4
Quintana del Marco E ... 88 B1
Quintana del Puente E ... 88 B2
Quintana-Martín Galíndez
  E ... 89 B3
Quintanaortuño E ... 88 B3
Quintanapalla E ... 89 B3
Quintanar de la Orden
  E ... 95 C3
Quintanar de la Sierra
  E ... 89 C3
Quintanar del Rey E ... 95 C5
Quintana Redonda E ... 89 C4
Quintanilla de la Mata
  E ... 88 C3
Quintanilla del Coco E ... 89 C3
Quintanilla de Onésimo
  E ... 88 C2
Quintanilla de Somoza
  E ... 87 B4
Quintas de Valdelucio
  E ... 88 B2
Quintela P ... 87 D3
Quintin F ... 56 B3
Quinto E ... 90 B2
Quinzano d'Oglio I ... 71 C5
Quiroga E ... 87 B3
Quismondo E ... 94 B2
Quissac F ... 78 C2
Quistello I ... 81 A4

R

Raab A ... 63 B4
Raabs an der Thaya
  A ... 63 B6
Raahe FIN ... 3 D26
Rääkkylä FIN ... 115 F15
Raalte NL ... 42 C3
Raamsdonksveer NL ... 49 B5
Raanujarvi FIN ... 113 F13
Raattama FIN ... 113 D13
Rab HR ... 83 B3
Rabac HR ... 82 A3
Rábade E ... 86 A3
Rábafüzes H ... 73 B6
Rábahidvég H ... 74 A1
Rabanales E ... 87 C4
Rábapatona H ... 64 C3
Rabapordány H ... 64 C3
Rabastens F ... 77 C4
Rabastens-de-Bigorre
  F ... 76 C3
Rabat = Victoria M ... 107 C5
Rabat M ... 107 D5
Rabča SK ... 65 A5
Rabe SRB ... 75 B5
Rabi CZ ... 63 A4
Rabino PL ... 46 B1
Rabka PL ... 65 A5
Rabrovo SRB ... 85 B6
Rača
  Srbija SRB ... 85 B6
  Srbija SRB ... 85 B5
Ráccale I ... 107 A5
Rácalmás H ... 75 A3

Racalmuto I ... 108 B2
Racconigi I ... 80 B1
Rače SLO ... 73 B5
Rachecourt-sur-Marne
  F ... 59 B6
Raciąż PL ... 47 C6
Racibórz PL ... 54 C3
Račinovci HR ... 84 B3
Ráckeve H ... 75 A3
Racławice PL ... 55 C5
Racławice Śląskie
  PL ... 54 C2
Racot PL ... 54 A1
Rada
  Skaraborg S ... 35 D5
  Värmland S ... 34 B5
Radalj SRB ... 85 B4
Radda in Chianti I ... 81 C5
Raddusa I ... 109 B3
Radeberg D ... 53 B3
Radebeul D ... 53 B3
Radeburg D ... 53 B3
Radeče SLO ... 73 B5
Radekhiv UA ... 11 A8
Radenci SLO ... 73 B6
Radenthein A ... 72 B3
Radevormwald D ... 50 B3
Radicófani I ... 81 D5
Radicóndoli I ... 81 C5
Radišići BIH ... 84 C2
Radizel SLO ... 73 B5
Radków PL ... 53 C6
Radlje ob Dravi SLO ... 73 B5
Radłów PL ... 55 C5
Radmer an der Stube
  A ... 73 A4
Radnejaur S ... 115 B15
Radnice CZ ... 63 A4
Radohova BIH ... 84 B2
Radojevo SRB ... 75 C5
Radolfzell D ... 61 C4
Radom PL ... 55 B6
Radomice PL ... 47 C5
Radomin PL ... 47 B5
Radomsko PL ... 55 B4
Radomyshl UA ... 11 A10
Radomyśl Wielki PL ... 55 C6
Radošina SK ... 64 B3
Radošovce SK ... 64 B3
Radoszewice PL ... 54 B3
Radoszyce PL ... 55 B5
Radoviš MK ... 116 A4
Radovljica SLO ... 73 B4
Radowo Wielkie PL ... 46 B1
Radstadt A ... 72 A3
Radstock GB ... 29 B5
Raduc HR ... 83 B4
Radučić HR ... 83 B4
Raduša MK ... 116 A3
Radviliškis LT ... 6 D7
Radzanów
  Mazowieckie PL ... 47 C6
  Mazowieckie PL ... 55 B5
Radziejów PL ... 47 C4
Radziejowice PL ... 55 A5
Radzovce SK ... 65 B5
Radzyń Chełmiński
  PL ... 47 B4
Raeren B ... 50 C2
Raesfeld D ... 50 B2
Raffadali I ... 108 B2
Rafina GR ... 117 D5
Rafsbotn N ... 113 B12
Ragachow BY ... 7 E11
Ragály H ... 65 B6
Rägelin D ... 44 C4
Raglan GB ... 29 B5
Ragnitz A ... 73 B5
Rahden D ... 43 C5
Råholt N ... 34 B3
Raiano I ... 103 A6
Raigada E ... 87 B3
Rain D ... 62 B2
Rainbach im Mühlkreis
  A ... 63 B5
Rainham GB ... 31 C4
Rairiz de Veiga E ... 87 B3
Raisdorf D ... 44 A2
Raisio FIN ... 7 A7
Raiva
  Aveiro P ... 87 C2
  Coimbra P ... 92 A2
Raja-Joosseppi FIN ... 113 D17
Rajala FIN ... 113 E15
Rajcza PL ... 65 A5
Rajec SK ... 65 A4
Rájec-Jestřebí CZ ... 64 A2
Rajecké Teplice SK ... 65 A4
Rajevo Selo HR ... 84 B3
Rajhrad CZ ... 64 A2
Rajić HR ... 74 C2
Rajka H ... 64 C3
Rakaca H ... 65 B6
Rakek SLO ... 73 C4
Rakhiv UA ... 11 B8
Rakitna SLO ... 73 C4
Rakkestad N ... 35 C3
Rakoniewice PL ... 53 A6
Rakoszyce PL ... 54 B1
Raková SK ... 65 A4
Rakovac BIH ... 84 A2
Rakovica HR ... 83 B4
Rakovník CZ ... 63 A4
Raków PL ... 55 C6
Rakvere EST ... 7 B9
Ralja SRB ... 85 B5
Rälla S ... 40 C6
Ramacastañas E ... 94 B1
Ramacca I ... 109 B3
Ramales de la Victoria
  E ... 89 A3
Ramberg N ... 112 D2
Rambervillers F ... 60 B2
Rambouillet F ... 58 B2
Rambucourt F ... 60 B1
Ramdala S ... 41 C5
Ramerupt F ... 59 B5
Ramingstein A ... 72 A3
Ramirás E ... 87 B2
Ramiswil CH ... 70 A2
Ramkvilla S ... 40 B4
Ramme DK ... 38 C1
Rämmen S ... 34 C6
Rämnäs S ... 36 C3
Râmnicu Vâlcea RO ... 11 D8
Ramonville-St Agne
  F ... 77 C4
Rampside GB ... 26 A2
Ramsau D ... 62 C3
Ramsbeck D ... 51 B4
Ramsberg S ... 36 C2
Ramsele S ... 115 D13
Ramsey
  Cambridgeshire GB ... 30 B3
  Isle of Man GB ... 26 A1
Ramseycleuch GB ... 25 C4
Ramsgate GB ... 31 C5
Ramsjö S ... 115 E12
Ramstein-Meisenbach
  D ... 60 A3
Ramsund N ... 112 D6
Ramvik S ... 115 E14
Ranalt A ... 71 A6
Rånäs S ... 36 C4
Rånåsfoss N ... 34 B3
Rance B ... 49 C5
Ránchio I ... 82 C1
Randaberg N ... 33 C2
Randalstown GB ... 19 B5
Randan F ... 68 B3
Randazzo I ... 109 B3
Randegg A ... 63 B5
Randers DK ... 38 C3
Randijaur S ... 112 F8

Randin E ... 87 C3
Randsverk N ... 114 F6
Rânes F ... 57 B5
Rångedala S ... 40 B3
Ranis D ... 52 C1
Rankweil A ... 71 A4
Rännelanda S ... 35 D3
Rännäväg S ... 40 B3
Rannoch Station GB ... 24 B3
Ranovac SRB ... 85 B6
Ransäter S ... 34 C5
Ransbach-Baumbach
  D ... 50 C3
Ransta S ... 36 C3
Ranttila FIN ... 113 C14
Ranua FIN ... 3 D27
Rapallo I ... 80 B3
Rapla EST ... 6 B8
Rapness GB ... 23 B6
Rapolano Terme I ... 81 C5
Rapolla I ... 104 C1
Raposa P ... 92 B2
Rapperswil CH ... 70 A3
Raša HR ... 82 A3
Rasal E ... 90 A2
Rascafría E ... 94 B3
Rasdorf D ... 51 C5
Raseiniai LT ... 6 D7
Rašica SLO ... 73 C4
Rasines E ... 89 A3
Raška SRB ... 85 C5
Rasquera E ... 90 B3
Rássina I ... 81 C5
Rastatt D ... 61 B4
Rastede D ... 43 B5
Rastenberg D ... 52 B1
Rastošnica BIH ... 84 B3
Rastovac MNE ... 84 D3
Rasueros E ... 94 A1
Rasy PL ... 55 B4
Raszków PL ... 54 B2
Rátaje SRB ... 85 C6
Rätan S ... 115 E11
Rateče SLO ... 72 B3
Ratekau D ... 44 B2
Ratež SLO ... 73 C5
Rathangan IRL ... 21 A5
Rathcoole IRL ... 21 A5
Rathcormack IRL ... 20 B3
Rathdrum IRL ... 21 B5
Rathebur D ... 45 B5
Rathenow D ... 44 C4
Rathfriland GB ... 19 B5
Rathkeale IRL ... 20 B3
Rath Luirc IRL ... 20 B3
Rathmelton IRL ... 19 A4
Rathmolyon IRL ... 21 A5
Rathmore IRL ... 20 B2
Rathmullan IRL ... 19 A4
Rathnew IRL ... 21 B5
Rathvilly IRL ... 21 B5
Ratibořské Hory CZ ... 63 A5
Ratingen D ... 50 B2
Ratková SK ... 65 B6
Ratkovo SRB ... 75 C4
Ratne UA ... 11 A8
Ratoath IRL ... 21 A5
Rattelsdorf D ... 51 C6
Ratten A ... 73 A5
Rattosjärvi FIN ... 113 F13
Rattray GB ... 25 B4
Rättvik S ... 36 B2
Ratzeburg D ... 44 B2
Rätzlingen D ... 44 C3
Raucourt-et-Flaba F ... 59 A5
Raudeberg N ... 114 F2
Raufarhöfn IS ... 111 A10
Raufoss N ... 34 B2
Rauhala FIN ... 113 E13
Rauland N ... 33 C5
Rauma FIN ... 3 F24
Raundal N ... 32 B3
Raunds GB ... 30 B3
Rauris A ... 72 A2
Rautas S ... 112 E8
Rautavaara FIN ... 3 E28
Rauville-la-Bigot F ... 57 A4
Rauzan F ... 76 B2
Ravanusa I ... 108 B2
Ravča HR ... 84 C2
Ravels B ... 49 B5
Rävemåla S ... 40 C5
Ravenglass GB ... 26 A2
Ravenna I ... 82 B1
Ravensburg D ... 61 C5
Rävlanda S ... 40 B2
Ravna Gora HR ... 73 C4
Ravne na Koroškem
  SLO ... 73 B4
Ravnište SRB ... 85 C6
Ravnje SRB ... 85 B4
Ravno BIH ... 84 D2
Ravno Selo SRB ... 75 C4
Rawa Mazowiecka PL ... 55 B5
Rawicz PL ... 54 B1
Rawtenstall GB ... 26 B3
Rayleigh GB ... 31 C4
Ražana SRB ... 85 B4
Ražanac HR ... 83 B4
Razboj BIH ... 84 A2
Razes F ... 67 B6
Razkrižje SLO ... 73 B6
Razo E ... 86 A2
Reading GB ... 31 C3
Réalmont F ... 77 C5
Rebais F ... 59 B4
Reboly RUS ... 3 E29
Rebordelo P ... 87 C3
Recanati I ... 82 C2
Recas E ... 94 B3
Recco I ... 80 B3
Recess IRL ... 18 C2
Recey-sur-Ource F ... 59 C5
Recezinhos P ... 87 C2
Rechnitz A ... 73 A6
Rechytsa BY ... 7 E11
Recke D ... 43 C4
Recklinghausen D ... 50 B3
Recoaro Terme I ... 71 C6
Recogne B ... 59 A6

Réggio di Calábria I ... 109 A4
Réggiolo I ... 81 B4
Réggio nell'Emília I ... 81 B4
Reghin RO ... 11 C8
Régil E ... 89 A4
Regna S ... 37 D2
Regniéville F ... 60 B1
Regny F ... 69 C4
Rego da Leirosa P ... 92 A2
Regöly H ... 74 B3
Regueiro E ... 86 B2
Reguengo
  Portalegre P ... 92 B3
  Santarém P ... 92 B2
Reguengos de Monsaraz
  P ... 92 C3
Rehau D ... 52 C2
Rehburg D ... 43 C6
Rehden D ... 43 C5
Rehna D ... 44 B3
Reichelsheim D ... 61 A4
Reichelshofen D ... 61 A6
Reichenau D ... 64 C1
Reichenbach
  Sachsen D ... 52 C2
  Sachsen D ... 53 B4
Reichenfels A ... 73 A4
Reichenschwand D ... 51 B6
Reichertshofen D ... 62 B2
Reichshoffen F ... 60 B3
Reiden CH ... 70 A2
Reigada
  E ... 86 A4
  P ... 87 D4
Reigate GB ... 31 C3
Reillanne F ... 79 C4
Reillo E ... 95 C5
Reims F ... 59 A5
Reinach CH ... 70 A3
Reinbek D ... 44 B2
Reinberg D ... 45 A5
Reine N ... 112 E2
Reinfeld D ... 44 B2
Reinheim D ... 61 A4
Reinli N ... 32 B6
Reinosa E ... 88 A2
Reinstorf D ... 44 B3
Reinsvoll N ... 34 B3
Reisach A ... 72 B3
Reiss GB ... 23 C5
Reitan N ... 114 E8
Reit im Winkl D ... 62 C3
Reitmyre S ... 37 C3
Rekavice BIH ... 84 B2
Rekovac SRB ... 85 C6
Relleu E ... 96 C2
Rém H ... 75 B4
Rémalard F ... 58 B1
Rembercourt-aux-Pots
  F ... 59 B6
Remedios P ... 92 B1
Remels D ... 43 B4
Remetea Mare RO ... 75 C6
Remich L ... 60 A2
Rémilly F ... 60 A2
Remiremont F ... 60 C2
Remolinos E ... 90 B1
Remoulins F ... 78 C3
Remscheid D ... 50 B3
Remungol F ... 56 C3
Rémuzat F ... 79 B4
Rena N ... 34 A3
Renaison F ... 68 B3
Renazé F ... 57 C4
Renchen D ... 61 B4
Rencurel F ... 79 A4
Rende I ... 106 B3
Rendina GR ... 116 C4
Rendsburg D ... 43 A6
Renedo E ... 88 C2
Renens CH ... 69 B6
Renfrew GB ... 24 C3
Rengsjö S ... 36 A3
Reni UA ... 11 D10
Rennebu N ... 114 E6
Rennerod D ... 50 C4
Rennertshofen D ... 62 B2
Rennes F ... 57 B4
Rennes-les-Bains F ... 77 D5
Rennweg A ... 72 A3
Rens DK ... 39 E2
Rensjön S ... 112 D8
Rentería E ... 76 C1
Rentjärn S ... 115 B15
Renwez F ... 59 A5
Répcelak H ... 74 A2
Repojoki FIN ... 113 D14
Repvåg N ... 113 B14
Requena E ... 96 B1
Réquista F ... 77 B5
Rerik D ... 44 A3
Resana I ... 72 C1
Resarö S ... 37 C5
Reschen = Résia I ... 71 B5
Resen MK ... 116 A3
Resende P ... 87 C3
Résia = Reschen I ... 71 B5
Reşiţa RO ... 10 D6
Resko PL ... 46 B1
Resnik SRB ... 85 B5
Ressons-sur-Matz F ... 58 A3
Restábal E ... 100 C2
Resuttano I ... 109 B3
Retamal E ... 93 C4
Retascón E ... 90 C1
Retford GB ... 27 B5
Retortillo E ... 93 A4
Retortillo de Soria E ... 89 C4
Retournac F ... 78 A3
Rétság H ... 65 C5
Rettenegg A ... 73 A5
Retuerta del Bullaque
  E ... 94 C2

Revel F ... 77 C5
Revello I ... 80 B1
Revenga E ... 94 B2
Revest-du-Bion F ... 79 B4
Révfülöp H ... 74 B2
Revigny-sur-Ornain F ... 59 B5
Revin F ... 59 A5
Řevničov CZ ... 53 C3
Revo I ... 71 B6
Revsnes N ... 32 A4
Revúca SK ... 65 B6
Rewa PL ... 47 A4
Rewal PL ... 45 A7
Rexbo S ... 36 B2
Reyðarfjörður IS ... 111 B11
Reyero E ... 88 B1
Reykhólar IS ... 111 B3
Reykholt
  Árnessýsla IS ... 111 C5
  Borgarfjarðarsýsla
  IS ... 111 C4
Reykjahlið IS ... 111 B9
Reykjavík IS ... 111 C4
Rezé F ... 66 A3
Rēzekne LV ... 7 C9
Rezzato I ... 71 C5
Rezzoáglio I ... 80 B3
Rhade D ... 43 B6
Rhaunen D ... 60 A3
Rhayader GB ... 29 A4
Rheda-Wiedenbrück
  D ... 50 B4

Rhede
Niedersachsen D 43 B4
Nordrhein-Westfalen D 50 B2
Rheinau D 60 B3
Rheinbach D 50 C2
Rheinberg D 50 B2
Rheine D 50 A3
Rheinfelden D 70 A2
Rheinsberg D 45 B4
Rhêmes-Notre-Dame I 70 C2
Rhenen NL 49 B6
Rhens D 50 C3
Rheydt D 50 B2
Rhiconich GB 22 C4
Rhinow D 44 C4
Rhiw GB 26 C1
Rho I 70 C4
Rhodes GR 119 F3
Rhondda GB 29 B4
Rhosllanerchrugog GB 26 B2
Rhosneigr GB 26 B1
Rhossili GB 28 B3
Rhubodach GB 24 C2
Rhuddlan GB 26 B2
Rhyl GB 26 B2
Rhynie GB 23 D6
Riala S 37 C5
Riallé F 66 A3
Riaño E 88 B1
Riano I 102 A5
Rians F 79 C4
Rianxo E 86 B2
Riaza E 89 C3
Riba E 89 A3
Ribadavia E 87 B2
Ribadeo E 86 A3
Riba de Saelices E 95 B4
Ribadesella E 88 A1
Ribaflecha E 89 B4
Ribaforada E 89 C5
Ribare SRB 85 B6
Ribariće SRB 85 D5
Riba-roja d'Ebre E 90 B3
Riba-Roja de Turia E 96 B2
Ribe DK 39 D1
Ribeauvillé F 60 B3
Ribécourt-Dreslincourt F 59 A3
Ribeira da Pena P 87 C3
Ribeira de Piquín E 86 A3
Ribemont F 59 A4
Ribera I 108 B2
Ribérac F 67 C5
Ribera de Cardós E 91 A4
Ribera del Fresno E 93 C4
Ribesalbes E 96 A2
Ribes de Freser E 91 A5
Ribiers F 79 B4
Ribnica
BIH 84 B3
SLO 73 C4
SRB 85 C5
Ribnica na Potorju SLO 73 B5
Ribnik HR 73 C5
Rîbnița MD 11 C10
Ribnitz-Damgarten D 44 A4
Ribolla I 81 D5
Řicany CZ 64 A2
Říčany CZ 53 D4
Riccia I 103 B7
Riccione I 82 B1
Ricco Del Golfo I 81 B3
Richebourg F 59 B6
Richelieu F 67 A5
Richisau CH 70 A3
Richmond
Greater London GB 31 C3
North Yorkshire GB 27 A4
Richtenberg D 45 A4
Richterswil CH 70 A3
Rickling D 44 A2
Rickmansworth GB 31 C3
Ricla E 89 C5
Riddarhyttan S 36 C2
Ridderkerk NL 49 B5
Riddes CH 70 B2
Ridjica SRB 75 C4
Riec-sur-Bélon F 56 C2
Ried A 63 B4
Riedenburg D 62 B2
Ried im Oberinntal A 71 A5
Riedlingen D 61 B5
Riedstadt D 61 A4
Riegersburg A 73 B5
Riego de la Vega E 88 B1
Riego del Camino E 88 C1
Riello E 88 B1
Riemst B 49 C6
Rienne B 49 D5
Riénsena E 88 A2
Riesa D 52 B3
Riese Pio X I 72 C1
Riesi I 109 B3
Riestedt D 52 B1
Rietberg D 51 B4
Rieti I 102 A5
Rietschen D 53 B4
Rieumes F 77 C4
Rieupeyroux F 77 B5
Rieux-Volvestre F 77 C4
Riez F 79 C5
Rīga LV 6 C8
Riggisberg CH 70 B2
Rignac F 77 B5
Rignano Gargánico I 104 B1
Rigolato I 72 B2
Rigside GB 25 C4
Rigutino I 81 C5
Riihimäki FIN 3 F26
Rijeka HR 73 C4
Rijeka Crnojeviča MNE 105 A5
Rijen NL 49 B5
Rijkevorsel B 49 B5
Rijssen NL 50 A2
Rilić BIH 84 C2
Rilievo I 108 B1
Rillé F 67 A5
Rillo de Gallo E 95 B5
Rimavská Baňa SK 65 B5
Rimavská Seč SK 65 B6
Rimavská Sobota SK 65 B6
Rimbo S 36 C5
Rimforsa S 37 D2
Rímini I 82 B1
Rîmnicu Sărat RO 11 D9
Rimogne F 59 A5
Rimpar D 61 A5
Rimske Toplice SLO 73 B5
Rincón de la Victoria E 100 C1
Rincón de Soto E 89 B5
Rindal N 114 D6
Rinde N 32 A3
Ringarum S 37 D3
Ringaskiddy IRL 20 C3
Ringe DK 39 D3
Ringebu N 34 A2
Ringkøbing DK 39 C1
Ringsaker N 34 B2
Ringsted DK 39 D4
Ringwood GB 29 C6
Rinkaby S 41 D4
Rinkabyholm S 40 C6
Rinlo E 86 A3
Rinn A 71 A6
Rinteln D 51 A5
Rio E 86 B3
Riobo E 86 B2
Riodeva E 96 A1
Rio do Coures P 92 B2
Rio Douro P 87 C3
Riofrio E 94 B2
Rio Frio P 92 C2
Riofrio de Aliste E 87 C4
Rio frio de Riaza E 95 A3
Riogordo E 100 C1
Rioja E 101 C3
Riola I 81 B5
Riola Sardo I 110 C1
Riolobos E 93 B4
Riom F 68 C3
Riomaggiore I 81 B3
Rio Maior P 92 B2
Rio Marina I 81 D4
Riom-ès-Montagnes F 68 C2
Rion-des-Landes F 76 C2
Rionegro del Puente E 87 B4
Rionero in Vúlture I 104 C1
Riopar E 101 A3
Riós E 87 C3
Rioseco E 88 A1
Rioseco de Tapia E 88 B1
Rio Tinto P 87 C2
Riotord F 69 C4
Riotorto E 86 A3
Rioz F 69 A6
Ripač BIH 83 B4
Ripacándida I 104 C1
Ripanj SRB 85 B5
Ripatransone I 82 D2
Ripley GB 27 B4
Ripoll E 91 A5
Ripon GB 27 A4
Riposto I 109 B4
Ripsa S 37 D3
Risan MNE 105 A4
Risbäck S 115 C12
Risca GB 29 B4
Rischenau D 51 B5
Riscle F 76 C2
Risebo S 40 A6
Risnes N 32 A2
Rišňovce SK 64 B3
Risør N 33 D6
Risøyhamn N 112 D4
Rissna S 115 D12
Ritsem S 112 E6
Ritterhude D 43 B5
Riutula FIN 113 D15
Riva del Garda I 71 C5
Riva Ligure I 80 C1
Rivanazzano I 80 B3
Rivarolo Canavese I 70 C2
Rivarolo Mantovano I 81 A4
Rive-de-Gier F 69 C4
Rivedoux-Plage F 66 B3
Rivello I 106 A2
Rivergaro I 80 B3
Rives F 69 C5
Rivesaltes F 78 D1
Rivignano I 72 C3
Rivne UA 11 A9
Rívoli I 80 A1
Rivolta d'Adda I 71 C4
Rixheim F 60 C3
Rixo S 35 D3
Riza GR 116 B5
Rizokarpaso CY 120 A3
Rjukan N 32 C5
Rø DK 41 D4
Rö S 37 C5
Roa
E 88 C3
N 34 B2
Roade GB 30 B3
Roager DK 39 D1
Roaldkvam N 33 C3
Roanne F 68 B4
Robakowo PL 47 B4
Róbbio I 70 C3
Röbel D 45 B4
Roberton GB 25 C5
Robertville B 50 C2
Robin Hood's Bay GB 27 A5
Robleda E 93 A4
Robledillo de Trujillo E 93 B5
Robledo
Albacete E 101 A3
Orense E 86 B4
Robledo de Chavela E 94 B2
Robledo del Buey E 94 C2
Robledo del Mazo E 94 C2
Robledollano E 93 B5
Robles de la Valcueva E 88 B1
Robliza de Cojos E 87 D5
Robres E 90 B2
Robres del Castillo E 89 B4
Rocafort de Queralt E 91 B4
Rocamadour F 77 B4
Roccabernarda I 107 B3
Roccabianca I 81 A4
Roccadáspide I 103 C8
Rocca di Mezzo I 103 A6
Rocca di Papa I 102 B5
Roccagorga I 102 B6
Rocca Imperiale I 106 A3
Roccalbegna I 81 D5
Roccalumera I 109 B4
Roccamena I 108 B2
Roccamonfina I 103 B6
Roccanova I 106 A3
Roccapalumba I 108 B2
Roccapassa I 103 A6
Rocca Priora I 82 C2
Roccaraso I 103 B7
Rocca San Casciano I 81 B5
Roccasecca I 103 B6
Rocca Sinibalda I 102 A5
Roccastrada I 81 C5
Roccatederighi I 81 C5
Roccella Iónica I 106 C3
Rocchetta Sant'António I 103 B8
Rocester GB 27 C4
Rochdale GB 26 B3
Rochechouart F 67 C5
Rochefort
B 49 C6
F 66 C4
Rochefort-en-Terre F 56 C3
Rochefort-Montagne F 68 C2
Rochefort-sur-Nenon F 69 A5
Roche-lez-Beaupré F 69 A6
Rochemaure F 78 B3
Rocheservière F 66 B3
Rochester
Medway GB 31 C4
Northumberland GB 25 C5
Rochlitz D 52 B2
Rociana del Condado E 99 B4
Rockenhausen D 60 A3
Rockhammar S 37 C2
Rockneby S 40 C6
Ročko Polje HR 73 C4
Ročov CZ 53 C3
Rocroi F 59 A5
Rodach D 51 C6
Roda de Bara E 91 B4
Roda de Ter E 91 B5
Rodalben D 60 A3
Rødberg N 32 B5
Rødby DK 44 A3
Rødbyhavn DK 44 A3
Rødding
Sonderjyllands Amt. DK 39 D2
Viborg Amt. DK 38 C1
Rödeby S 41 C5
Rodeiro E 86 B3
Rødekro DK 39 D2
Roden NL 42 B3
Ródenas E 95 B5
Rodenkirchen D 43 B5
Rödental D 52 C1
Rödermark D 51 D4
Rodewisch D 52 C2
Rodez F 77 B5
Rodi Gargánico I 104 B1
Roding D 62 A3
Rödjebro S 36 B4
Rødkærsbro DK 39 C2
Rodolivas GR 116 B5
Rodoñá E 91 B4
Rødvig DK 41 D2
Roermond NL 50 B1
Roesbrugge B 48 C3
Roeschwoog F 61 B4
Roeselare B 49 C4
Roetgen D 50 C2
Roffiac F 78 A2
Röfors S 37 D1
Rofrano I 106 A2
Rogač HR 83 C5
Rogačica SRB 85 B4
Rogalinek PL 54 A1
Rogaška Slatina SLO 73 B5
Rogatec SLO 73 B5
Rogatica BIH 84 C4
Rogatyn UA 11 B8
Rogätz D 52 A1
Roggendorf D 44 B3
Roggiano Gravina I 106 B3
Roghadal GB 22 D2
Rogliano
F 102 A2
I 106 B3
Rognan N 112 E4
Rogne N 32 A6
Rognes F 79 C4
Rogny-les-7-Ecluses F 59 C3
Rogowo PL 46 C3
Rogóz PL 47 A6
Rogoznica HR 83 C4
Rogoźnica PL 53 B6
Rogoźno PL 46 C2
Rohan F 56 B3
Röhlingen D 61 B6
Rohožnik SK 64 B3
Rohr D 51 C6
Rohrbach A 63 B4
Rohrbach-lès-Bitche F 60 A3
Rohrberg D 44 C3
Rohr im Gebirge A 63 C6
Röhrnbach D 63 B4
Roisel F 59 A4
Roja LV 6 C7
Rojales E 96 C2
Röjeråsen S 36 B1
Rojewo PL 47 C4
Rokiciny PL 55 B4
Rokietnica PL 46 C2
Rokiškis LT 7 D8
Rokitki PL 53 B5
Rokitno RUS 7 F13
Rokycany CZ 63 A4
Rolampont F 59 C6
Rold DK 38 C2
Røldal N 32 C3
Rolde NL 42 C3
Rollag N 32 B6
Rollán E 94 B1
Rolle CH 69 B6
Roma = Rome I 102 B5
Roma S 37 E5
Romagnano Sésia I 70 C3
Romagné F 57 B4
Romakloster S 37 E5
Roman RO 11 C9
Romana I 110 B1
Romanèche-Thorins F 69 B4
Romano di Lombardia I 71 C4
Romanshorn CH 71 A4
Romans-sur-Isère F 79 A4
Rombas F 60 A2
Rome = Roma I 102 B5
Romeán E 86 B3
Romenay F 69 B5
Romeral E 95 C3
Römerstein D 61 B5
Rometta I 109 A4
Romford GB 31 C4
Romhány H 65 C5
Römhild D 51 C6
Romilly-sur-Seine F 59 B4
Romny UA 11 A12
Romodan UA 11 B12
Romont CH 70 B1
Romorantin-Lanthenay F 68 A1
Romrod D 51 C5
Romsey GB 31 D2
Rømskog N 35 C3
Rønbjerg DK 38 C1
Roncal E 76 D2
Ronce-les-Bains F 66 C3
Ronchamp F 60 C2
Ronchi dei Legionari I 72 C3
Ronciglione I 102 A5
Ronco Canavese I 70 C2
Ronco Scrivia I 80 B2
Ronda E 99 C5
Rønde DK 39 C3
Rone S 37 E5
Ronehamn S 37 E5
Rong N 32 B1
Rönnäng S 38 B4
Rønne DK 41 D4
Ronneburg D 52 C2
Ronneby S 41 C5
Rönneshytta S 37 D2
Rönninge S 37 C4
Rönnöfors S 115 D10
Rönö S 37 D3
Ronov nad Doubravou CZ 63 A6
Ronse B 49 C4
Roosendaal NL 49 B5
Roosky IRL 19 C4
Ropczyce PL 55 C6
Ropeid N 33 C3
Ropinsalmi FIN 113 D10
Ropuerelos del Páramo E 88 B1
Roquebillière F 79 B6
Roquebrun F 78 C2
Roquecourbe F 77 C5
Roquefort F 76 B2
Roquemaure F 78 B3
Roquesteron F 79 C6
Roquetas de Mar E 101 C3
Roquetes E 90 C3
Roquevaire F 79 C4
Røra N 114 D8
Rörbäcksnäs S 34 A4
Rørbæk DK 38 C2
Rore BIH 83 B5
Röro S 38 B4
Røros N 114 E8
Rorschach CH 71 A4
Rørvig DK 39 D4
Rørvik N 114 C8
Rörvik S 40 B4
Rosà I 72 C1
Rosal de la Frontera E 98 B3
Rosalina Mare I 72 C2
Rosa Marina I 104 C3
Rosans F 79 B4
Rosário P 98 B2
Rosarno I 106 C2
Rosbach D 50 C3
Rosche D 44 C2
Rościszewo PL 47 C5
Roscoff F 56 B2
Roscommon IRL 18 C3
Roscrea IRL 21 B4
Rosdorf D 51 B5
Rose I 106 B3
Rosegg A 73 B4
Rosehall GB 22 D4
Rosehearty GB 23 D6
Rosel GB 57 A3
Rosell E 90 C3
Roselló E 90 B3
Rosendal N 32 C3
Rosenfeld D 61 B4
Rosenfors S 40 B5
Rosenheim D 62 C3
Rosenow D 45 B5
Rosenthal D 51 B4
Rosersberg S 37 C4
Roses E 91 A6
Roseto degli Abruzzi I 103 A7
Roseto Valfortore I 103 B8
Rosheim F 60 B3
Rosia I 81 C5
Rosice CZ 64 A2
Rosières-en-Santerre F 58 A3
Rosignano Maríttimo I 81 C4
Rosignano Solvay I 81 C4
Roșiori-de-Vede RO 11 D8
Roskhill GB 22 D2
Roskilde DK 39 D5
Roskovec AL 105 C5
Röslau D 52 C1
Roslavl RUS 7 E12
Roslev DK 38 C1
Rosmaninhal P 93 B3
Rosmult IRL 21 B4
Rosnowo PL 46 A2
Rosolini I 109 C3
Rosova MNE 85 C4
Rosoy F 59 B4
Rosporden F 56 C2
Rosquete P 92 B2
Rosrath D 50 C3
Rossa CH 71 B4
Rossano I 106 B3
Rossas
Aveiro P 87 D2
Braga P 87 C2
Rossdorf D 51 C6
Rossett GB 26 B3
Rosshaupten D 62 C1
Rossiglione I 80 B2
Rossignol B 60 A1
Rossla D 52 B1
Rosslare IRL 21 B5
Rosslare Harbour IRL 21 B5
Rosslau D 52 B2
Rosslea GB 19 B4
Rossleben D 52 B1
Rossön S 115 D13
Ross-on-Wye GB 29 B5
Rossoszyca PL 54 B3
Rosswein D 52 B3
Röstånga S 41 C3
Roštár SK 65 B6
Rostock D 44 A4
Rostrenen F 56 B2
Røsvik N 112 E4
Rosyth GB 25 B4
Röszke H 75 B5
Rot S 34 A6
Rota E 99 C4
Rota Greca I 106 B3
Rot am See D 61 A6
Rotberget N 34 B4
Rotella I 82 D2
Rotenburg
Hessen D 51 C5
Niedersachsen D 43 B6
Roth
Bayern D 62 A2
Rheinland-Pfalz D 50 C3
Rothbury GB 25 C6
Rothemühl D 45 B5
Röthenbach D 62 A2
Rothenburg D 53 B4
Rothenburg ob der Tauber D 61 A6
Rothéneuf F 57 B4
Rothenklempenow D 45 B6
Rothenstein D 62 B2
Rotherham GB 27 B4
Rothes GB 23 D5
Rothesay GB 24 C2
Rothwell GB 30 B3
Rotnes N 34 B2
Rotonda I 106 B3
Rotondella I 106 A3
Rotova E 96 C2
Rott
Bayern D 62 C1
Bayern D 62 C3
Rottach-Egern D 62 C2
Röttenbach D 62 A2
Rottenbuch D 62 C1
Rottenburg
Baden-Württemberg D 61 B4
Bayern D 62 B3
Rottenmann A 73 A4
Rotterdam NL 49 B5
Rotthalmünster D 63 B4
Rottingdean GB 31 D3
Röttingen D 61 A5
Rottleberode D 51 B6
Rottne S 40 B4
Rottneros S 34 C5
Rottofreno I 80 A3
Rottweil D 61 B4
Rötz D 62 A3
Roubaix F 49 C4
Roudnice nad Labem CZ 53 C4
Roudouallec F 56 B2
Rouen F 58 A2
Rouffach F 60 C3
Rougé F 57 C4
Rougemont F 69 A6
Rougemont le-Château F 60 C2
Rouillac F 67 C4
Rouillé F 67 B5
Roujan F 78 C2
Roulans F 69 A6
Roundwood IRL 21 A5
Rousinov CZ 64 A2
Roussac F 67 B6
Roussennac F 77 B5
Rousses F 78 B2
Roussillon F 69 C4
Rouvroy-sur-Audry F 59 A5
Rouy F 68 A3
Rovaniemen maalaiskunta FIN 113 F14
Rovaniemi FIN 113 F14
Rovato I 71 C4
Rovensko pod Troskami CZ 53 C5
Roverbella I 71 C5
Rovereto I 71 C6
Rövershagen D 44 A4
Roverud N 34 B4
Rovigo I 81 A5
Rovinj HR 82 A2
Rovišće HR 74 C1
Rów PL 45 C6
Rowy PL 46 A3
Royal Leamington Spa GB 30 B2
Royal Tunbridge Wells GB 31 C4
Royan F 66 C3
Royat F 68 C3
Roybon F 69 C5
Roybridge GB 24 B3
Roye F 58 A3
Royère-de-Vassivière F 68 C1
Røykenvik N 34 B2
Royos E 101 B3
Røyrvik N 115 C10
Royston GB 30 B3
Rozadas E 86 A4
Rožaj MNE 85 D5
Rozalén del Monte E 95 C4
Różańsko PL 45 C6
Rožanstvo SRB 85 C4
Rozay-en-Brie F 59 B3
Roždalovice CZ 53 C5
Rozdilna UA 11 C11
Rozental PL 47 B5
Rozhyshche UA 11 A8
Rožmitál pod Třemšínem CZ 63 A4
Rožňava SK 65 B6
Rožnov pod Radhoštěm CZ 64 A4
Rozoy-sur-Serre F 59 A5
Rozprza PL 55 B4
Roztoky CZ 53 C4
Rozvadov CZ 62 A3
Rozzano I 71 C4
Rranxë AL 105 B5
Rrëshen AL 105 B5
Rrogozhine AL 105 B5
Ruanes E 93 B5
Rubbestadnesset N 32 C2
Rubi E 91 B5
Rubiá E 86 B4
Rubiacedo de Abajo E 89 B3
Rubielos Bajos E 95 C4
Rubielos de Mora E 96 A2
Rubiera I 81 B4
Rubik AL 105 B5
Rucandio E 89 B3
Rud
Akershus N 34 B3
Buskerud N 34 B2
Ruda
PL 54 B3
S 40 B6
Rudabánya H 65 B6
Ruda Maleniecka PL 55 B5
Ruda Pilczycka PL 55 B5
Ruda Śl. PL 54 C3
Ruddervorde B 49 B4
Ruden A 73 B4
Rudersberg D 61 B5
Rudersdorf A 73 A6
Rüdersdorf D 45 C5
Ruderting D 63 B4
Rüdesheim D 50 D3
Rudkøbing DK 39 E3
Rudmanns A 63 B6
Rudna
CZ 53 C4
PL 53 B6
Rudnik
KOS 85 D5
SRB 85 B5
Rudniki
Opolskie PL 54 B3
Śląskie PL 55 C4
Rudno
Dolnośląskie PL 54 B1
Pomorskie PL 47 B4
Rudnya RUS 7 D11
Rudo BIH 85 C4
Rudolstadt D 52 C1
Rudowica PL 53 B5
Rudozem BG 116 A6
Rudskoga S 35 C6
Rudston GB 27 A5
Ruds Vedby DK 39 D4
Rudy PL 54 C3
Rue F 48 C2
Rueda E 88 C2
Rueda de Jalón E 90 B1
Ruelle-sur-Touvre F 67 C5
Ruerrero E 88 B3
Ruffano I 107 B5
Ruffec F 67 B5
Rufina I 81 C5
Rugby GB 30 B2
Rugeley GB 27 C4
Ruggstrop S 40 C6
Rugles F 58 B1
Rugozero RUS 3 D30
Rühen D 44 C2
Ruhla D 51 C6
Ruhland D 53 B3
Ruhle D 43 C4
Ruhpolding D 62 C3
Ruhstorf D 63 B4
Ruidera E 95 D4
Ruillé-sur-le-Loir F 58 C1
Ruinen NL 42 C3
Ruiselede B 49 B4
Rulles B 60 A1
Rülzheim D 61 A4
Rum H 74 A1
Ruma SRB 85 A4
Rumboci BIH 84 C2
Rumburk CZ 53 C4
Rumenka SRB 75 C4
Rumia PL 47 A4
Rumigny F 59 A5
Rumilly F 69 C5
Rumma S 37 D3
Rumney GB 29 B4
Rumont F 59 B6
Rumy PL 47 B6
Runa P 92 B1
Runcorn GB 26 B3
Rundmoen N 115 A11
Rungsted DK 41 D2
Runhällen S 36 B3
Runowo PL 47 A6
Runtuna S 37 D4
Ruokojärvi FIN 113 E13
Ruokolahti FIN 3 F28
Ruokto S 112 E8
Ruoms F 78 B3
Ruoti I 104 C1
Rupa HR 73 C4
Ruppichteroth D 50 C3
Rupt-sur-Moselle F 60 C2
Rus E 100 A2
Ruse BG 11 E9
Ruše SLO 73 B5
Ruselе S 115 C15
Ruševo HR 74 C3
Rush IRL 21 A5
Rushden GB 30 B3
Rusiec PL 54 B3
Rusinowo
Zachodnio-Pomorskie PL 46 B1
Zachodnio-Pomorskie PL 46 B2
Ruskele S 115 C15
Ruski Krstur SRB 75 C4
Ruskington GB 27 B5
Rusovce SK 64 B3
Rüsselsheim D 51 D4
Russelv N 112 C9
Russi I 81 B6
Rust A 64 C2
Rustefjelbma N 113 B17
Rustrel F 79 C4
Ruszki PL 55 A5
Ruszów PL 53 B5
Rute E 100 B1
Rüthen D 51 B4
Rutherglen GB 24 C3
Ruthin GB 26 B2
Ruthven GB 23 D4
Ruthwell GB 25 D4
Rüti CH 70 A3
Rutigliano I 104 B3
Rutledal N 32 A2
Rutoši SRB 85 C4
Ruurlo NL 50 A2
Ruuvaoja FIN 113 E17
Ruvo del Monte I 104 C1
Ruvo di Púglia I 104 B2
Ruynes-en-Margeride F 78 B2
Ružic HR 83 C5
Ružomberok SK 65 A5
Ruzsa H 75 B4
Ry DK 39 C2
Rybany SK 64 B4
Rybina PL 47 A5
Rybinsk RUS 7 B15
Rybnik PL 54 C3
Rychliki PL 47 B5
Rychlocice PL 54 B3
Rychnov nad Kněžnou CZ 53 C6
Rychnowo PL 47 B6
Rychtal PL 54 B2
Rychwał PL 54 A3
Ryczywół PL 55 B6
Ryczywól PL 46 C2
Ryd S 40 C4
Rydaholm S 40 C4
Rydal S 40 B2
Rydbo S 37 C5
Rydboholm S 40 B2
Ryde GB 31 D2
Rydöbruk S 40 C3
Rydsgård S 41 D3
Rydsnäs S 40 B5
Rydultowy PL 54 C3
Rydzyna PL 54 B1
Rye GB 31 D4
Rygge N 35 C2
Ryjewo PL 47 B4
Rykene N 33 D5
Rylsk RUS 7 F13
Rymań PL 46 B1
Rýmařov CZ 64 A3
Rynarzewo PL 46 B3
Ryomgård DK 39 C3
Rypefjord N 113 B12
Rypin PL 47 B5
Rysjedalsvika N 32 A2
Ryssby S 40 C4
Rytel PL 46 B3
Rytro PL 65 A6
Rywociny PL 47 B6
Rzeczenica PL 46 B3
Rzeczniów PL 55 B6
Rzeczyca PL 55 B5
Rzęgnowo PL 47 B6
Rzejowice PL 55 B4
Rzemień PL 55 C6
Rzepin PL 45 C6
Rzesznikowo PL 46 B1
Rzeszów PL 10 A6
Rzgów PL 55 B4
Rzhev RUS 7 C13

S

Saal
Bayern D 51 C6
Bayern D 62 B2
Saalbach A 72 A2
Saalburg D 52 C1
Saales F 60 B3
Saalfeld D 52 C1
Saalfelden am Steinernen Meer A 72 A2
Saanen CH 70 B2
Saarbrücken D 60 A2
Saarburg D 60 A2
Saarijärvi FIN 3 E26
Saarlouis D 60 A2
Saas-Fee CH 70 B2
Šabac SRB 85 B4
Sabadell E 91 B5
Sabáudia I 102 B6
Sabbioneta I 81 B4
Sabero E 88 B1
Sabiñánigo E 90 A2
Sabiote E 100 A2
Sables-d'Or-les-Pins F 56 B3
Sablé-sur-Sarthe F 57 C5
Sabóia P 98 B2
Saborsko HR 83 A4
Sæbøvik N 32 C2
Sabres F 76 B2
Sabrosa P 87 C3
Sabugal P 93 A3
Sabuncu TR 118 C5
Sæby DK 38 B3
Săcălaz RO 75 C6
Sacecorbo E 95 B4
Saceda del Rio E 95 B4
Sacedón E 95 B4
Săcele RO 11 D8
Saceruela E 94 D2
Sachsenburg A 72 B3
Sachsenhagen D 43 C6
Sacile I 72 C2
Sacramenia E 88 C3
Sada E 86 A2
Sádaba E 90 A1
Saddell GB 24 C2
Sadernes E 91 A5
Sadki PL 46 B3
Sadkowice PL 55 B5
Sadlinki PL 47 B4
Sadów PL 53 A4
Sadská CZ 53 C4
Saelices E 95 C4
Saelices de Mayorga E 88 B1
Saerbeck D 50 A3
Saeul L 60 A1
Safaalan TR 118 A3
Safara P 98 A3
Säffle S 35 C4
Saffron Walden GB 31 B4
Safonovo RUS 7 D12
Safranbolu TR 16 A6
Säfsnäs S 36 B1
Şag RO 75 C6
Sagard D 45 A5
S'Agaro E 91 B6
Sågmyra S 36 B2
Sagone F 102 A1
Sagres P 98 C2
Ságújfalu H 65 B5
Sagunt E 96 B2
Sagvåg N 32 C2
Ságvár H 74 B3
Sagy F 69 B5
Sahagún E 88 B1
Šahy SK 65 B4
Saignelégier CH 70 A1
Saignes F 68 C2
Saija FIN 113 E17
Saillagouse F 91 A5
Saillans F 79 B4
Sains Richaumont F 59 A4
St Abb's GB 25 C5
St Affrique F 78 C1
St Agnan F 68 B3
St Agnant F 66 C4
St Agnes GB 28 C2
St Agrève F 78 A3
St Aignan F 67 A6
St Aignan-sur-Roë F 57 C4
St Albans GB 31 C3
St Alban-sur-Limagnole F 78 B2
St Amand-en-Puisaye F 68 A3
St Amand-les-Eaux F 49 C4
St Amand-Longpré F 58 C2
St Amand-Montrond F 68 B2
St Amans F 78 B2
St Amans-Soult F 77 C5
St Amant-Roche-Savine F 68 C3
St Amarin F 60 C2
St Ambroix F 78 B3
St Amé F 60 B2
St Amour F 69 B5
St André-de-Corcy F 69 C4
St André-de-Cubzac F 76 B2
St André-de-l'Eure F 58 B2
St André-de-Roquepertuis F 78 B3
St André-de-Sangonis F 78 C2
St Andre-de-Valborgne F 78 B2
St André-les-Alpes F 79 C5
St Andrews GB 25 B5
St Angel F 68 C2
St Anthème F 68 C3
St Antoine F 102 A2
St Antoine-de-Ficalba F 77 B3
St Antönien CH 71 B4
St Antonin-Noble-Val F 77 B4
St Août F 68 B1
St Armant-Tallende F 68 C3
St Arnoult F 58 B2
St Asaph GB 26 B2
St Astier F 67 C5
St Athan GB 29 B4
St Auban F 79 C5
St Aubin
CH 70 B1
F 69 A5
GB 57 A3
St Aubin-d'Aubigné F 57 B4
St Aubin-du-Cormier F 57 B4
St Aubin-sur-Aire F 60 B1
St Aubin-sur-Mer F 57 A5
St Aulaye F 67 C5
St Austell GB 28 C3
St Avit F 68 C2
St Avold F 60 A2
St Aygulf F 79 C5
St Bauzille-de-Putois F 78 C2
St Béat F 77 D3
St Beauzély F 78 B1
St Bees GB 26 A2
St Benim-d'Azy F 68 B3
St Benoît-du-Sault F 67 B6
St Benoit-en-Woëvre F 60 B1
St Berthevin F 57 B5
St Blaise-la-Roche F 60 B3
St Blazey GB 28 C3
St Blin F 59 B6
St Bonnet F 79 B5
St Bonnet Briance F 67 C6
St Bonnet-de-Joux F 69 B4
St Bonnet-le-Château F 68 C4
St Bonnet-le-Froid F 69 C4
St Brévin-les-Pins F 66 A2
St Briac-sur-Mer F 57 B3
St Brice-en-Coglès F 57 B4
St Brieuc F 56 B3
St Bris-le-Vineux F 59 C4
St Broladre F 57 B4
St Calais F 58 C1
St Cannat F 79 C4
St Cast-le-Guildo F 57 B3
St Céré F 77 B4
St Cergue CH 69 B6
St Cergues F 69 B6
St Cernin F 77 A5
St Chamant F 68 C1
St Chamas F 79 C4
St Chamond F 69 C4
St Chély-d'Apcher F 78 B2
St Chély-d'Aubrac F 78 B1
St Chinian F 78 C1
St Christol F 79 B4
St Christol-lès-Alès F 78 B3
St Christoly-Médoc F 66 C4
St Christophe-du-Ligneron F 66 B3
St Christophe-en-Brionnais F 69 B4
St Ciers-sur-Gironde F 67 C4
St Clair-sur-Epte F 58 A2
St Clar F 77 C3
St Claud F 67 C5
St Claude F 69 B5
St Clears GB 28 B3
St Columb Major GB 28 C3
St Come-d'Olt F 78 B1
St Cosme-en-Vairais F 58 B1
St Cyprien
Dordogne F 77 B4
Pyrenées-Orientales F 91 A6
St Cyr-sur-Loire F 67 A5
St Cyr-sur-Mer F 79 C4
St Cyr-sur-Methon F 69 B4
St David's GB 28 B2
St Denis F 58 B3
St Denis-d'Oléron F 66 B3
St Denis d'Orques F 57 B5
St Didier F 69 B4
St Didier-en-Velay F 69 C4
St Dié F 60 B2
St Dier-d'Auvergne F 68 C3
St Dizier F 59 B5
St Dizier-Leyrenne F 68 B1
St Dogmaels GB 28 A3
Ste Adresse F 57 A6
Ste Anne F 58 B1
Ste Anne-d'Auray F 56 C3
Ste Croix CH 69 B6
Ste Croix-Volvestre F 77 C4
Ste Engrâce F 76 C2
Ste Enimie F 78 B2
St Efflam F 56 B2
Ste Foy-de-Peyrolières F 77 C4
Ste Foy-la-Grande F 76 B3
Ste Foy l'Argentiere F 69 C4
Ste Gauburge-Ste Colombe F 58 B1
Ste Gemme la Plaine F 66 B3
Ste Geneviève F 58 A3
St Égrève F 69 C5
Ste Hélène F 76 B2
Ste Hélène-sur-Isère F 69 C6
Ste Hermine F 66 B3
Ste Jalle F 79 B4
Ste Livrade-sur-Lot F 77 B3
St Eloy-les-Mines F 68 B2
Ste Marie-aux-Mines F 60 B3
Ste Marie-du-Mont F 57 A4
Ste Maure-de-Touraine F 67 A5
Ste Maxime F 79 C5
Ste Ménéhould F 59 A5
Ste Mère-Église F 57 A4
St Emiland F 69 B4
St Émilion F 76 B2
St Enoder GB 28 C3
Sainteny F 57 A4
Ste Ode B 49 C6
Saintes F 67 C4
Ste Savine F 59 B5
Ste Sévère-sur-Indre F 68 B2
Ste Sigolène F 69 C4
St Esteben F 76 C1
St Estèphe F 66 C4
Ste Suzanne F 57 B5
St Étienne F 69 C4
St Étienne-de-Baigorry F 76 C1
St Étienne-de-Cuines F 69 C6
St Étienne-de-Fursac F 67 B6
St Étienne-de-Montluc F 66 A3
St Étienne-de-St Geoirs F 69 C5
St Étienne-de-Tinée F 79 B5
St Étienne-du-Bois F 69 B5
St Étienne-du-Rouvray F 58 A2
St Étienne-les-Orgues F 79 B4
Ste Tulle F 79 C4
St Fargeau F 59 C4
St Félicien F 78 A3
St Felix-de-Sorgues F 78 C1
St Félix-Lauragais F 77 C4
Saintfield GB 19 B6
St Fillans GB 24 B3
St Firmin F 79 B5
St Florent F 102 A2
St Florentin F 59 C4
St Florent-le-Vieil F 66 A3
St Florent-sur-Cher F 68 B2
St Flour F 78 A2
St Flovier F 67 B6
St Fort-sur-le-Né F 67 C4
St Fulgent F 66 B3
St Galmier F 69 C4
St Gaudens F 77 C3
St Gaultier F 67 B6
St Gély-du-Fesc F 78 C2
St Genest-Malifaux F 69 C4
St Gengoux-le-National F 69 B4
St Geniez F 79 B5
St Geniez-d'Olt F 78 B1
St Genis-de-Saintonge F 67 C4
St Genis-Pouilly F 69 B6
St Genix-sur-Guiers F 69 C5
St Georges Buttavent F 57 B5
St Georges-d'Aurac F 68 C3
St Georges-de-Commiers F 79 A4
St Georges-de-Didonne F 66 C4
St Georges-de-Luzençon F 78 B1
St Georges-de Mons F 68 C2
St Georges-de-Reneins F 69 B4
St Georges d'Oléron F 66 C3
St Georges-en-Couzan F 68 C3
St Georges-lès-Baillargeaux F 67 B5
St Georges-sur-Loire F 66 A4
St Georges-sur-Meuse B 49 C6
St Geours-de-Maremne F 76 C1
St Gérand-de-Vaux F 68 B3
St Gérand-le-Puy F 68 B3
St Germain F 60 C2
St Germain-Chassenay F 68 B3
St Germain-de-Calberte F 78 B2
St Germain-de-Confolens F 67 B5
St Germain-de-Joux F 69 B5
St Germain-des-Fossés F 68 B3
St Germain-du-Bois F 69 B5
St Germain-du-Plain F 69 B4
St Germain-du Puy F 68 A2
St Germain-en-Laye F 58 B3
St Germain-Laval F 68 C4
St Germain-Lembron F 68 C3
St Germain-les-Belles F 67 C6
St Germain-Lespinasse F 68 B3
St Germain-l'Herm F 68 C3
St Gervais-d'Auvergne F 68 B2
St Gervais-les-Bains F 70 C1
St Gervais-sur-Mare F 78 C2
St Gildas-de-Rhuys F 66 A2
St Gildas-des-Bois F 66 A2
St Gilles
Gard F 78 C3
Ille-et-Vilaine F 57 B4
St Gilles-Croix-de-Vie F 66 B3
St Gingolph F 70 B1
St Girons
Ariège F 77 D4
Landes F 76 C1
St Girons-Plage F 76 C1
St Gobain F 59 A4
St Gorgon-Main F 69 A6
St Guénolé F 56 C1
St Harmon GB 29 A4
St Helens GB 26 B3
St Helier GB 57 A3
St Herblain F 66 A3
St Hilaire
Allier F 68 B3
Aude F 77 C5
St Hilaire-de-Riez F 66 B3
St Hilaire-des-Loges F 67 B4
St Hilaire-de-Villefranche F 67 C4
St Hilaire-du-Harcouët F 57 B4
St Hilaire-du-Rosier F 79 A4
St Hippolyte
Aveyron F 77 B5
Doubs F 70 A1
St Hippolyte-du-Fort F 78 C2
St Honoré-les-Bains F 68 B3
St Hubert B 49 C6
St Imier CH 70 A2
St Issey GB 28 C3
St Ives
Cambridgeshire GB 30 B3
Cornwall GB 28 C2
St Izaire F 78 C1
St Jacques-de-la-Lande F 57 B4
St Jacut-de-la-Mer F 57 B3
St James F 57 B4
St Jaume d'Enveja E 90 C3
St Jean-Brévelay F 56 C3
St Jean-d'Angély F 67 C4
St Jean-de-Belleville F 69 C6
St Jean-de-Bournay F 69 C5
St Jean-de-Braye F 58 C2
St Jean-de-Côle F 67 C5
St Jean-de-Daye F 57 A4
St Jean de Losne F 69 A5
St Jean-de-Luz F 76 C1
St Jean-de-Maurienne F 69 C6
St Jean-de-Monts F 66 B2
St Jean-d'Illac F 76 B2
St Jean-du-Bruel F 78 B2
St Jean-du-Gard F 78 B2
St Jean-en-Royans F 79 A4
St Jean-la-Riviere F 79 C6
St Jean-Pied-de-Port F 76 C1
St Jean-Poutge F 77 C3
St Jeoire F 69 B6
St Joachim F 66 A2
St Johnstown IRL 19 B4
St Jorioz F 69 C6
St Joris Winge B 49 C5
St Jouin-de-Marnes F 67 B4
St Juéry F 77 C5
St Julien F 69 B5
St Julien-Chapteuil F 78 A3
St Julien-de-Vouvantes F 57 C4
St Julien-du-Sault F 59 B4
St Julien-du-Verdon F 79 C5
St Julien-en-Born F 76 B1
St Julien-en-Genevois F 69 B6
St Julien-l'Ars F 67 B5
St Julien la-Vêtre F 68 C3
St Julien-Mont-Denis F 69 C6
St Julien-sur-Reyssouze F 69 B5
St Junien F 67 C5

St Just
F 78 B3
GB 28 C2
St Just-en-Chaussée F 58 A3
St Just-en-Chevalet F 68 C3
St Justin F 76 C2
St Just-St Rambert F 69 C4
St Keverne GB 28 C2
St Lary-Soulan F 77 D3
St Laurent-d'Aigouze F 78 C3
St Laurent-de-Chamousset F 69 C4
St Laurent-de-Condel F 57 A5
St Laurent-de-la-Cabrerisse F 78 C1
St Laurent-de-la-Salanque F 78 D1
St Laurent-des-Autels F 66 A3
St Laurent-du-Pont F 69 C5
St Laurent-en-Caux F 58 A1
St Laurent-en-Grandvaux F 69 B5
St Laurent-Médoc F 76 A2
St Laurent-sur-Gorre F 67 C5
St Laurent-sur-Mer F 57 A5
St Laurent-sur-Sèvre F 66 B4
St Leger B 60 A1
St Léger-de-Vignes F 68 B3
St Léger-sous-Beuvray F 68 B4
St Léger-sur-Dheune F 69 B4
St Léonard-de-Noblat F 67 C6
St Leonards GB 31 D4
St Lô F 57 A4
St Lon-les-Mines F 76 C1
St Louis F 60 C3
St Loup F 68 B3
St Loup-de-la-Salle F 69 B4
St Loup-sur-Semouse F 60 C2
St Lunaire F 57 B3
St Lupicin F 69 B5
St Lyphard F 66 A2
St Lys F 77 C4
St Macaire F 76 B2
St Maclou F 58 A1
St Maixent-l'École F 67 B4
St Malo F 57 B3
St Mamet-la-Salvetat F 77 B5
St Mandrier-sur-Mer F 79 C4
St Marcel
Drôme F 78 B3
Saône-et-Loire F 69 B4
St Marcellin F 69 C5
St Marcellin sur Loire F 68 C4
St Marcet F 77 C3
St Mards-en-Othe F 59 B4
St Margaret's-at-Cliffe GB 31 C5
St Margaret's Hope GB 23 C6
St Mars-la-Jaille F 66 A3
St Martin-d'Ablois F 59 B4
St Martin-d'Auxigny F 68 A2
St Martin-de-Belleville F 69 C6
St Martin-de-Bossenay F 59 B4
St Martin-de-Crau F 78 C3
St Martin-de-Londres F 78 C2
St Martin-d'Entraunes F 79 B5
St Martin-de-Queyrières F 79 B5
St Martin-de-Ré F 66 B3
St Martin des Besaces F 57 A5
St Martin-d'Estreaux F 68 B3
St Martin-de-Valamas F 78 B3
St Martin-d'Hères F 69 C5
St Martin-du-Frêne F 69 B5
St Martin-en-Bresse F 69 B5
St Martin-en-Haut F 69 C4
St Martin-la-Méanne F 68 C1
St Martin-sur-Ouanne F 59 C4
St Martin-Valmeroux F 77 A5
St Martin-Vésubie F 79 B6
St Martory F 77 C3
St Mary's GB 23 C6
St Mathieu F 67 C5
St Mathieu-de-Tréviers F 78 C2
St Maurice CH 70 B1
St Maurice-Navacelles F 78 C2
St Maurice-sur-Moselle F 60 C2
St Mawes GB 28 C2
St Maximin-la-Ste Baume F 79 C4
St Méard-de-Gurçon F 76 B3
St Médard-de-Guizières F 76 A2
St Médard-en-Jalles F 76 B2
St Méen-le-Grand F 57 B3
St Menges F 59 A5
St Merløse DK 39 D4
St Město CZ 54 C1
St M'Hervé F 57 B4
St Michel
Aisne F 59 A5
Gers F 77 C3
St Michel-Chef-Chef F 66 A2
St Michel-de-Castelnau F 76 B2
St Michel-de-Maurienne F 69 C6
St Michel-en-Grève F 56 B2
St Michel-enl'Herm F 66 B3
St Michel-Mont-Mercure F 66 B4
St Mihiel F 60 B1
St Monance GB 25 B5
St Montant F 78 B3
St Moritz CH 71 B4
St Nazaire F 66 A2
St Nazaire-en-Royans F 79 A4
St Nazaire-le-Désert F 79 B4
St Nectaire F 68 C2
St Neots GB 30 B3
St Nicolas-de-Port F 60 B2
St Nicolas-de-Redon F 57 C3
St Nicolas-du-Pélem F 56 B2
St Niklaas B 49 B5
St Omer F 48 C3
St Pair-sur-Mer F 57 B4
St Palais F 76 C1
St Palais-sur-Mer F 66 C3
St Pardoux-la-Rivière F 67 C5
St Paul-Cap-de-Joux F 77 C4
St Paul-de-Fenouillet F 77 D5
St Paul-de-Varax F 69 B5
St Paulien F 68 C3
St Paul-le-Jeune F 78 B3
St Paul-lès-Dax F 76 C1
St Paul-Trois-Châteaux F 78 B3
St Pé-de-Bigorre F 76 C2
St Pée-sur-Nivelle F 76 C1
St Péravy-la-Colombe F 58 C2
St Péray F 78 B3
St Père-en-Retz F 66 A2
St Peter Port GB 56 A3
St Petersburg = Sankt-Peterburg RUS 7 B11
St Philbert-de-Grand-Lieu F 66 A3
St Pierre F 78 C1
St Pierre-d'Albigny F 69 C6
St Pierre-d'Allevard F 69 C6
St Pierre-de-Chartreuse F 69 C5
St Pierre-de-Chignac F 77 A3
St Pierre-de-la-Fage F 78 C2
St Pierre-d'Entremont F 69 C5
St Pierre-d'Oléron F 66 C3
St Pierre-Eglise F 57 A4
St Pierre-en-Port F 58 A1
St Pierre-le-Moûtier F 68 B3
St Pierre Montlimart F 66 A3
St Pierre-Quiberon F 66 A1
St Pierre-sur-Dives F 57 A5
St Pierreville F 78 B3
St Pieters-Leeuw B 49 C5
St Plancard F 77 C3
St Poix F 57 C4
St Pol-de-Léon F 56 B2
St Polgues F 68 C3
St Pol-sur-Ternoise F 48 C3
St Pons-de-Thomières F 78 C1
St Porchaire F 66 C4
St Pourçain-sur-Sioule F 68 B3
St Priest F 69 C4
St Privat F 68 C2
St Quay-Portrieux F 56 B3
St Quentin F 59 A4
St Quentin-la-Poterie F 78 B3
St Quentin-les-Anges F 57 C5
St Rambert-d'Albon F 69 C4
St Rambert-en-Bugey F 69 C5
St Raphaël F 79 C5
St Rémy-de-Provence F 78 C3
St Rémy-du-Val F 57 B6
St Remy-en-Bouzemont F 59 B5
St Renan F 56 B1
St Révérien F 68 A3
St Riquier F 48 C2
St Romain-de-Colbosc F 58 A1
St Rome-de-Cernon F 78 B1
St Rome-de-Tarn F 78 B1
St Sadurní-d'Anoia E 91 B4
St Saëns F 58 A2
St Sampson GB 56 A3
St Samson-la-Poterie F 58 A2
St Saturnin-de-Lenne F 78 B2
St Saturnin-lès-Apt F 79 C4
St Sauflieu F 58 A3
St Saulge F 68 A3
St Sauveur
Finistère F 56 B2
Haute-Saône F 60 C2
St Sauveur-de-Montagut F 78 B3
St Sauveur-en-Puisaye F 59 C4
St Sauveur-en-Rue F 69 C4
St Sauveur-Lendelin F 57 A4
St Sauveur-le-Vicomte F 57 A4
St Sauveur-sur-Tinée F 79 B6
St Savin
Gironde F 76 A2
Vienne F 67 B5
St Savinien F 67 C4
St Savournin F 79 C4
St Seine-l'Abbaye F 69 A4
St Sernin-sur-Rance F 77 C5
St Sevan-sur-Mer F 57 B3
St Sever F 76 C2
St Sever-Calvados F 57 B4
St Sorlin-d'Arves F 69 C6
St Soupplets F 58 A3
St Sulpice F 77 C4
St Sulpice-Laurière F 67 B6
St Sulpice-les-Feuilles F 67 B6
St Symphorien F 76 B2
St Symphorien-de-Lay F 69 C4
St Symphorien d'Ozon F 69 C4
St Symphoriensur-Coise F 69 C4
St Teath GB 28 C3
St Thégonnec F 56 B2
St Thiébault F 60 B1
St Trivier-de-Courtes F 69 B5
St Trivier sur-Moignans F 69 B4
St Trojan-les-Bains F 66 C3
St Tropez F 79 C5
St Truiden B 49 C6
St Vaast-la-Hougue F 57 A4
St Valérien F 59 B4
St Valery-en-Caux F 58 A1
St Valéry-sur-Somme F 48 C2
St Vallier
Drôme F 69 C4
Saône-et-Loire F 69 B4
St Vallier-de-Thiey F 79 C5
St Varent F 67 B4
St Vaury F 68 B1
St Venant F 48 C3
St Véran F 79 B5
St Vincent I 70 C2
St Vincent-de-Tyrosse F 76 C1
St Vit F 69 A5
St Vith B 50 C2
St Vivien-de-Médoc F 66 C3
St Yan F 68 B4
St Ybars F 77 C4
St Yorre F 68 B3
St Yrieix-la-Perche F 67 C6
Saissac F 77 C5
Saja E 88 A2
Šajan SRB 75 C5
Šajkaš SRB 75 C5
Sajókaza H 65 B6
Sajószentpéter H 65 B6
Sajóvámos H 65 B6
Şakarya TR 118 B5
Šakiai LT 6 D7
Sakskøbing DK 39 E4
Sakule SRB 75 C5
Sala S 36 C3
Šal'a SK 64 B3
Sala Baganza I 81 B4
Sala Consilina I 104 C1
Salakovac SRB 85 B6
Salamanca E 94 B1
Salamina GR 117 E5
Salandra I 104 C2
Salaparuta I 108 B1
Salar E 100 B1
Salardú E 90 A3
Salas E 86 A4
Salas de los Infantes E 89 B3
Salau F 77 D4
Salavaux CH 70 B2
Salbertrand I 79 A5
Salbohed S 36 C3
Salbris F 68 A2
Salbu N 32 A2
Salce E 86 B4
Salching D 62 B3
Salcombe GB 28 C4
Saldaña E 88 B2
Saldus LV 6 C7
Sale I 80 B2
Saleby S 35 D5
Salem D 61 C5
Salemi I 108 B1
Salen
Argyll & Bute GB 24 B2
Highland GB 24 B2
N 114 C8
Sälen S 34 A5
Salernes F 79 C5
Salerno I 103 C7
Salers F 68 C2
Salford GB 26 B3
Salgótarján H 65 B5
Salgueiro P 92 B3
Salhus N 32 B2
Sali HR 83 C4
Sálice Salentino I 105 C3
Salientes E 86 B4
Salies-de-Béarn F 76 C2
Salies-du-Salat F 77 C3
Salignac-Eyvigues F 77 B4
Saligney-sur-Roudon F 68 B3
Salihli TR 119 D3
Salihorsk BY 7 E9
Salinas
Alicante E 101 A5
Huesca E 90 A3
Salinas de Medinaceli E 95 A4
Salinas de Pisuerga E 88 B2
Salindres F 78 B3
Saline di Volterra I 81 C4
Salins-les-Bains F 69 B5
Salir P 98 B2
Salisbury GB 29 B6
Salla
A 73 A4
FIN 113 F17
Sallachy GB 23 C4
Sallanches F 70 C1
Sallent E 91 B4
Sallent de Gállego E 76 D2
Salles F 76 B2
Salles-Curan F 78 B1
Salles-sur-l'Hers F 77 C4
Sallins IRL 21 A5
Sällsjö S 115 D10
Salmerón E 95 B4
Salmiech F 77 B5
Salmivaara FIN 113 F17
Salmoral E 94 B1
Salo FIN 6 A7
Salò I 71 C5
Salobreña E 100 C2
Salon-de-Provence F 79 C4
Salonica = Thessaloniki GR 116 B4
Salonta RO 10 C6
Salorino E 93 B3
Salornay-sur-Guye F 69 B4
Salorno I 71 B6
Salou E 91 B4
Šalovci SLO 73 B6
Salsbruket N 114 C8
Salses-le-Château F 78 D1
Salsomaggiore Terme I 81 B3
Salt E 91 B5
Saltaire GB 27 B4
Saltara I 82 C1
Saltash GB 28 C3
Saltburn-by-the-Sea GB 27 A5
Saltcoats GB 24 C3
Saltfleet GB 27 B6
Salto P 87 C3
Saltrød N 33 D5
Saltsjöbaden S 37 C5
Saltvik
FIN 36 B7
S 40 B6
Saludécio I 82 C1
Salussola I 70 C3
Saluzzo I 80 B1
Salvacañete E 95 B5
Salvada P 98 B3
Salvagnac F 77 C4
Salvaleon E 93 C4
Salvaterra de Magos P 92 B2
Salvaterra do Extremo P 93 B4
Salvatierra
Avila E 89 B4
Badajoz E 93 C4
Salvatierra de Santiago E 93 B4
Salviac F 77 B4
Salzburg A 62 C4
Salzgitter D 51 A6
Salzgitter Bad D 51 A6
Salzhausen D 44 B2
Salzhemmendorf D 51 A5
Salzkotten D 51 B4
Salzmünde D 52 B1
Salzwedel D 44 C3
Samadet F 76 C2
Samandıra TR 118 B4
Samassi I 110 C1
Samatan F 77 C3
Sambiase I 106 C3
Sambir UA 11 B7
Samborowo PL 47 B5
Sambuca di Sicilia I 108 B2
Samedan CH 71 B4
Samer F 48 C2
Sami GR 117 D2
Şamlı TR 118 C2
Sammichele di Bari I 104 C2
Samnaun CH 71 B5
Samobor HR 73 C5
Samoëns F 70 B1
Samogneux F 59 A6
Samokov BG 11 E7
Samora Correia P 92 C2
Šamorín SK 64 B3
Samos
E 86 B3
GR 119 E1
Samoš SRB 75 C5
Samothraki GR 116 B7
Samper de Calanda E 90 B2
Sampéyre I 79 B6
Sampieri I 109 C3
Sampigny F 60 B1
Samplawa PL 47 B5
Samproniano I 81 D5
Samtens D 45 A5
Samugheo I 110 C1
San Adrián E 89 B5
San Agustín E 101 C3
San Agustin de Guadalix E 94 B3
Sanaigmore GB 24 C1
San Alberto I 82 B1
San Amaro E 87 B2
Sânandrei RO 75 C6
San Andrês del Rabanedo E 88 B1
San Antanio di Santadi I 110 C1
San Antolín de Ibias E 86 A4
San Arcángelo I 104 C2
Sanary-sur-Mer F 79 C4
San Asensio E 89 B4
San Bartoloméde las Abiertas E 94 C2
San Bartoloméde la Torre E 99 B3
San Bartoloméde Pinares E 94 B2
San Bartolomeo in Galdo I 103 B8
San Benedetto del Tronto I 82 D2
San Benedetto in Alpe I 81 C5
San Benedetto Po I 81 A4
San Benito E 100 A1
San Benito de la Contienda E 93 C3
San Biágio Plátani I 108 B2
San Biágio Saracinisco I 103 B6
San Bonifacio I 71 C6
San Calixto E 99 B5
San Cándido I 72 B2
San Carlo
CH 70 B3
I 108 B2
San Carlos del Valle E 100 A2
San Casciano dei Bagni I 81 D5
San Casciano in Val di Pesa I 81 C5
San Cataldo
Puglia I 105 C4
Sicilia I 108 B2
San Cebrián de Castro E 88 C1
Sancergues F 68 A2
Sancerre F 68 A2
San Cesário di Lecce I 105 C4
Sancey-le-Long F 69 A6
Sanchiorian E 94 B2
San Chírico Raparo I 106 A3
Sanchonuño E 88 C2
San Cibrao das Viñas E 87 B3
San Cipirello I 108 B2
San Ciprián E 86 A3
San Clemente E 95 C4
San Clodio E 86 B3
Sancoins F 68 B2
San Colombano al Lambro I 71 C4
San Costanzo I 82 C2
San Crisóbal de Entreviñas E 88 B1
San Cristóbal de la Polantera E 88 B1
San Cristóbal de la Vega E 94 A2
San Cristovo E 87 C3
Sancti-Petri E 99 C4
Sancti-Spiritus E 87 D4
Sand
Hedmark N 34 B3
Rogaland N 33 C3
Sanda S 37 E5
San Damiano d'Asti I 80 B2
San Damiano Macra I 79 B6
Sandane N 114 F3
San Daniele del Friuli I 72 B3
Sandanski BG 116 A5
Sandared S 40 B2
Sandarne S 36 A4
Sandau D 44 C4
Sandbach
D 63 B4
GB 26 B3
Sandbank GB 24 C3
Sandbanks GB 29 C6
Sandbukt N 112 C10
Sandby DK 39 E4
Sande
D 43 B5
Sogn og Fjordane N 32 A2
Vestfold N 35 C2
Sandefjord N 35 C2
Sandeid N 33 C2
San Demétrio Corone I 106 B3
San Demétrio né Vestini I 103 A6
Sandersleben D 52 B1
Sanderstølen N 32 B6
Sandes N 33 D4
Sandesneben D 44 B2
Sandhead GB 24 D3
Sandhem S 40 B3
Sandhorst D 43 B4
Sandhurst GB 31 C3
Sandıklı TR 119 D5
Sandillon F 58 C3
Sandl A 63 B5
Sandnes N 33 D2
Sandness GB 22 A7
Sandnessjøen N 115 A9
Sando E 87 D4
Sandomierz PL 55 C6
San Dónaci I 105 C3
San Donà di Piave I 72 C2
San Donato Val di Comino I 103 B6
Sándorfalva H 75 B5
Sandown GB 31 D2
Sandøysund N 35 C2
Sandrigo I 72 C1
Sandsele S 115 B14
Sandset N 112 D3
Sandsjöfors S 40 B4
Sandstad N 114 D6
Sandvatn N 33 D3
Sandvig-Allinge DK 41 D4
Sandvika
Akershus N 34 C2
Hedmark N 34 B3
Nord-Trøndelag N 114 D9
Sandviken S 36 B3
Sandvikvåy N 32 C2
Sandwich GB 31 C5
Sandy GB 30 B3
San Emiliano E 86 B5
San Enrique E 99 C5
San Esteban E 86 A4
San Esteban de Gormaz E 89 C3
San Esteban de la Sierra E 93 A5
San Esteban de Litera E 90 B3
San Esteban del Molar E 88 C1
San Esteban del Valle E 94 B2
San Esteban de Valdueza E 86 B4
San Fele I 104 C1
San Felice Circeo I 102 B6
San Felices E 88 B3
San Felices de los Gallégos E 87 D4
San Felice sul Panaro I 81 B5
San Ferdinando di Púglia I 104 B2
San Fernando E 99 C4
San Fernando de Henares E 95 B3
San Fili I 106 B3
San Foca I 105 C4
San Fratello I 109 B3
Sangatte F 48 C2
San Gavino Monreale I 110 C1
San Gémini Fonte I 102 A5
Sangerhausen D 52 B1
San Germano Vercellese I 70 C3
San Giácomo
Trentino Alto Adige I 72 B1
Umbria I 82 D1
San Gimignano I 81 C5
San Ginésio I 82 C2
Sangineto Lido I 106 B2
San Giórgio a Liri I 103 B6
San Giorgio della Richinvelda I 72 B2
San Giórgio del Sánnio I 103 B7
San Giórgio di Lomellina I 70 C3
San Giórgio di Nogaro I 72 C3
San Giorgio di Piano I 81 B5
San Giórgio Iónico I 104 C3
San Giovanni a Piro I 106 A2
San Giovanni Bianco I 71 C4
San Giovanni di Sinis I 110 C1
San Giovanni in Croce I 81 A4
San Giovanni in Fiore I 106 B3
San Giovanni in Persiceto I 81 B5
San Giovanni Reatino I 102 A5
San Giovanni Rotondo I 104 B1
San Giovanni Suérgiu I 110 C1
San Giovanni Valdarno I 81 C5
San Giuliano Terme I 81 C4
San Giustino I 82 C1
San Godenzo I 81 C5
Sangonera la Verde E 101 B4
San Gregorio Magno I 103 C8
Sangüesa E 90 A1
Sanguinet F 76 B1
San Guiseppe Jato I 108 B2
Sanica BIH 83 B5
Sanitz D 44 A4
San Javier E 101 B5
San Jorge P 92 B2
San José E 101 C3
San Juan E 89 B3
San Juan de Alicante E 96 C2
San Juan de la Nava E 94 B2
San Justo de la Vega E 86 B4
Sankt Aegyd am Neuwalde A 63 C6
Sankt Andrä A 73 B4
Sankt Andreasberg D 51 B6
Sankt Anna S 37 D3
Sankt Anna am Aigen A 73 B5
Sankt Anton am Arlberg A 71 A5
Sankt Anton an der Jessnitz A 63 C6
Sankt Augustin D 50 C3
Sankt Blasien D 61 C4
Sankt Englmar D 62 A3
Sankt Gallen
A 63 C5
CH 71 A4
Sankt Gallenkirch A 71 A4
Sankt Georgen
A 63 B5
D 61 B4
Sankt Georgen am Reith A 63 C5
Sankt Georgen ob Judenburg A 73 A4
Sankt Georgen ob Murau A 73 A4
Sankt Gilgen A 63 C4
Sankt Goar D 50 C3
Sankt Goarshausen D 50 C3
Sankt Ingbert D 60 A3
Sankt Jacob A 73 B4
Sankt Jakob in Defereggen A 72 B2
Sankt Johann am Tauern A 73 A4
Sankt Johann am Wesen A 63 B4
Sankt Johann im Pongau A 72 A3
Sankt Johann in Tirol A 72 A2
Sankt Katharein an der Laming A 73 A5
Sankt Kathrein am Hauenstein A 73 A5
Sankt Lambrecht A 73 A4
Sankt Leonhard am Forst A 63 B6
Sankt Leonhard im Pitztal A 71 A5
Sankt Lorenzen A 72 B2
Sankt Marein
Steiermark A 73 A5
Steiermark A 73 A5
Sankt Margarethen im Lavanttal A 73 B4
Sankt Margrethen CH 71 A4
Sankt Michael A 73 A5
Sankt Michael im Burgenland A 73 A6
Sankt Michael im Lungau A 72 A3
Sankt Michaelisdonn D 43 B6
Sankt Niklaus CH 70 B2
Sankt Nikolai im Sölktal A 73 A4
Sankt Olof S 41 D4
Sankt Oswald D 63 B4
Sankt Paul
A 73 B4
F 79 B5
Sankt Peter D 61 B4
Sankt Peter am Kammersberg A 73 A4
Sankt-Peterburg = St Petersburg RUS 7 B11
Sankt Peter-Ording D 43 A5
Sankt Pölten A 63 B6
Sankt Radegund A 73 A5
Sankt Ruprecht an der Raab A 73 A5
Sankt Salvator A 73 B4
Sankt Stefan A 73 B4
Sankt Stefan an der Gail A 72 B3
Sankt Stefan im Rosental A 73 B5
Sankt Valentin A 63 B5
Sankt Veit an der Glan A 73 B4
Sankt Veit an der Gölsen A 63 B6
Sankt Veit in Defereggen A 72 B2
Sankt Wendel D 60 A3
Sankt Wolfgang
A 63 C4
D 62 B3
San Lazzaro di Sávena I 81 B5
San Leo I 82 C1
San Leonardo de Yagüe E 89 C3
San Leonardo in Passiria I 71 B6
San Lorenzo al Mare I 80 C1
San Lorenzo a Merse I 81 C5
San Lorenzo Bellizzi I 106 B3
San Lorenzo de Calatrava E 100 A2
San Lorenzo de El Escorial E 94 B2
San Lorenzo de la Parrilla E 95 C4
San Lorenzo di Sebato I 72 B1
San Lorenzo in Campo I 82 C1
San Lorenzo Nuovo I 81 D5
San Lourenco P 98 A2
San Luca I 106 C3
Sanlúcar de Barrameda E 99 C4
Sanlúcar de Guadiana E 98 B3
Sanlúcar la Mayor E 99 B4
San Lúcido I 106 B3
Sanluri I 110 C1
San Marcello I 82 C2
San Marcello Pistoiese I 81 B4
San Marcial E 88 C1
San Marco I 103 C7
San Marco Argentano I 106 B3
San Marco dei Cavoti I 103 B7
San Marco in Lámis I 104 B1
San Marino RSM 82 C1
San Martín de Castañeda E 87 B4
San Martín de la Vega E 95 B3
San Martin de la Vega del Alberche E 93 A5
San Martín del Tesorillo E 99 C5
San Martin de Luiña E 86 A4
San Martin de Montalbán E 94 C2
San Martin de Oscos E 86 A4
San Martin de Pusa E 94 C2
San Martin de Unx E 89 B5
San Martín de Valdeiglesias E 94 B2
San Martino di Campagna I 72 B2
San Martino di Castrozza I 72 B1
San-Martino-di-Lota F 102 A2
San Martino in Pensilis I 103 B8
San Mateo de Gallego E 90 B2
San Máuro Forte I 104 C2
San Michele all'Adige I 71 B6
San Michele di Ganzaria I 109 B3
San Michele Mondov ì I 80 B1
San Miguel de Aguayo E 88 A2
San Miguel de Bernuy E 88 C3
San Miguel del Arroyo E 88 C2
San Miguel de Salinas E 101 B5
Sânmihaiu Roman RO 75 C6
San Millán de la Cogolla E 89 B4
San Miniato I 81 C4
San Muñoz E 87 D4
Sänna S 37 D1
Sannazzaro de'Burgondi I 80 A2
Sanne D 44 C3
Sannicandro di Bari I 104 B2
Sannicandro Gargánico I 104 B1
San Nicola del'Alto I 107 B3
San Nicolás del Puerto E 99 B5
Sânnicolau Mare RO 75 B5
San Nicolò I 81 B5
San Nicolò Gerrei I 110 C2
Sannidal N 33 D6
Sanniki PL 47 C5
Sanok PL 11 B7
San Pablo de los Montes E 94 C2
San Pancrázio Salentino I 105 C3
San Pantaleo I 110 A2
San Páolo di Civitate I 103 B8
San Pawl il-Bahar M 107 C5
San Pedro
Albacete E 101 A3
Oviedo E 86 A4
San Pedro de Alcántara E 100 C1
San Pedro de Ceque E 87 B4
San Pedro del Arroyo E 94 B2
San Pedro de Latarce E 88 C1
San Pedro del Pinatar E 101 B5
San Pedro del Romeral E 88 A3
San Pedro de Merida E 93 C4
San Pedro de Valderaduey E 88 B2
San Pedro Manrique E 89 B4
San Pellegrino Terme I 71 C4
San Piero a Sieve I 81 C5
San Piero in Bagno I 81 C5
San Piero Patti I 109 A3
San Pietro I 109 B3
San Pietro in Casale I 81 B5
San Pietro in Gu I 72 C1
San Pietro in Palazzi I 81 C4
San Pietro in Volta I 72 C2
San Pietro Vara I 80 B3
San Pietro Vernótico I 105 C3
San Polo d'Enza I 81 B4
Sanquhar GB 25 C4
San Quírico d'Órcia I 81 C5
San Rafael del Río E 90 C3
San Remo I 80 C1
San Román de Cameros E 89 B4
San Roman de Hernija E 88 C1
San Román de la Cuba E 88 B2
San Roman de los Montes E 94 B2
San Romao P 92 C3
San Roque E 99 C5
San Roque de Riomera E 88 A3
San Rufo I 104 C1
San Sebastián de los Ballesteros E 100 B1
San Salvador de Cantamuda E 88 B2
San Salvo I 103 A7
San Salvo Marina I 103 A7
San Sebastián de los Reyes E 94 B3
San Sebastiano Curone I 80 B3
San Secondo Parmense I 81 B4
Sansepolcro I 82 C1
San Severino Marche I 82 C2
San Severino Lucano I 106 A3
San Severo I 103 B8
San Silvestre de Guzmán E 98 B3
Sanski Most BIH 83 B5
San Sosti I 106 B3
San Stéfano di Cadore I 72 B2
San Stino di Livenza I 72 C2
Santa Agnès E 97 B1
Santa Amalia E 93 B4
Santa Ana
Cáceres E 93 B5
Jaén E 100 B2
Santa Ana de Pusa E 94 C2
Santa Barbara E 90 C3
Santa Bárbara P 98 B2
Santa Barbara de Casa E 98 B3
Santa Bárbara de Padrões P 98 B3
Santacara E 89 B5
Santa Catarina P 98 B3
Santa Caterina di Pittinuri I 110 B1
Santa Caterina Villarmosa I 109 B3
Santa Cesárea Terme I 107 A5
Santa Clara-a-Nova P 98 B2
Santa Clara-a-Velha P 98 B2
Santa Clara de Louredo P 98 B3
Santa Coloma de Farners E 91 B5
Santa Coloma de Gramenet E 91 B5
Santa Coloma de Queralt E 91 B4
Santa Colomba de Curueño E 88 B1
Santa Colomba de Somoza E 86 B4
Santa Comba E 86 A2
Santa Comba Dáo P 92 A2
Santa Comba de Rossas P 87 C4
Santa Cristina I 71 C4
Santa Cristina de la Polvorosa E 88 B1
Santa Croce Camerina I 109 C3
Santa Croce di Magliano I 103 B7
Santa Cruz
E 86 A2
P 92 B1
Santa Cruz de Alhama E 100 B2
Santa Cruz de Campezo E 89 B4
Santa Cruz de Grio E 89 C5
Santa Cruz de la Salceda E 89 C3
Santa Cruz de la Sierra E 93 B5
Santa Cruz de la Zarza E 95 C3
Santa Cruz del Retamar E 94 B2
Santa Cruz del Valle E 94 B1
Santa Cruz de Moya E 96 B1
Santa Cruz de Mudela E 100 A2
Santa Cruz de Paniagua E 93 A4
Santadi I 110 C1
Santa Doménica Talao I 106 B2
Santa Doménica Vittória I 109 B3
Santa Elena E 100 A2
Santa Elena de Jamuz E 88 B1
Santaella E 100 B1
Santa Eufemia E 100 A1
Santa Eufémia d'Aspromonte I 106 C2
Santa Eulalia E 95 B5
Santa Eulália P 92 C3
Santa Eulalia de Oscos E 86 A3
Santa Eulàlia des Riu E 97 C1
Santa Fe E 100 B2
Santa Fiora I 81 D5
Sant'Ágata dei Goti I 103 B7
Sant'Ágata di Ésaro I 106 B2
Sant'Ágata di Puglia I 103 B8
Sant'Agata Feltria I 82 C1
Sant'Ágata Militello I 109 A3
Santa Gertrude I 71 B5
Santa Giustina I 72 B2
Sant Agust ide Lluçanès E 91 A5
Santa Iria P 98 B3
Santa Leocadia P 87 C2
Santa Lucia del Mela I 109 A4
Santa Lucia-de-Porto-Vecchio F 102 B2
Santa Luzia P 98 B2
Santa Maddalena Vallalta I 72 B2
Santa Magdalena de Polpis E 90 C3
Santa Margalida E 97 B3
Santa Margarida P 92 B2
Santa Margarida do Sado P 98 A2
Santa Margaridao de Montbui E 91 B4
Santa Margherita I 110 D1
Santa Margherita di Belice I 108 B2
Santa Margherita Ligure I 80 B3
Santa Maria
CH 71 B5
E 90 A2
Santa Maria al Bagno I 107 A4
Santa Maria Cápua Vétere I 103 B7
Santa Maria da Feira P 87 D2
Santa Maria de Cayón E 88 A3
Santa Maria de Corco E 91 A5
Santa Maria de Huerta E 95 A4
Santa Maria de la Alameda E 94 B2
Santa Maria de las Hoyas E 89 C3
Santa Maria del Camí E 97 B2
Santa Maria del Campo E 88 B3
Santa Maria del Campo Rus E 95 C4
Santa Maria della Versa I 80 B3
Santa Maria del Páramo E 88 B1
Santa Maria del Taro I 80 B3
Santa Maria de Mercadillo E 89 C3
Santa Maria de Nieva E 101 B4
Santa Maria de Trassierra E 100 B1
Santa Maria di Licodia I 109 B3
Santa Maria-di-Rispéscia I 81 D5
Santa Maria la Palma I 110 B1
Santa María la Real de Nieva E 94 A2
Santa Maria Maggiore I 70 B3
Santa Maria Ribarredonda E 89 B3
Santa Marina del Rey E 88 B1
Santa Marinella I 102 A4
Santa Marta
Albacete E 95 C4
Badajoz E 93 C4
Santa Marta de Magasca E 93 B4
Santa Marta de Penaguião P 87 C3
Santa Marta de Tormes E 94 B1
Santana
Évora P 92 C2
Setúbal P 92 C1
Santana da Serra P 98 B2
Sant'Ana de Cambas P 98 B3
Santana do Mato P 92 C2
Sant'Anastasia I 103 C7
Santander E 88 A3
Sant'Andrea Frius I 110 C2
Sant'Ángelo dei Lombardi I 103 C8
Sant'Angelo in Vado I 82 C1
Sant'Angelo Lodigiano I 71 C4
Santa Ninfa I 108 B1
Sant'Antíoco I 110 C1
Sant Antoni de Calonge E 91 B6
Sant Antoni de Portmany E 97 C1
Sant'Antonio-di-Gallura I 110 B2
Santanyí E 97 B3
Santa Olalla
Huelva E 99 B4
Toledo E 94 B2
Santa Pau E 91 A5
Santa Pola E 96 C2
Santa Ponça E 97 B2
Santarcángelo di Romagna I 82 B1
Santarém P 92 B2
Santa Severa
F 102 A2
I 102 A4
Santa Severina I 107 B3
Santas Martas E 88 B1
Santa Sofia I 81 C5
Santa Susana P 92 C2
Santa Suzana P 92 C3
Santa Teresa di Riva I 109 B4
Santa Teresa Gallura I 110 A2
Santa Uxía E 86 B2
Santa Valburga I 71 B5
Santa Vittória in Matenano I 82 C2
Sant Boi de Llobregat E 91 B5
Sant Carles de la Ràpita E 90 C3
Sant Carlos E 97 B1
Sant'Caterina I 81 D5
Sant Celoni E 91 B5
Sant Climent E 97 B4
Santed E 95 A5
Sant'Egídio alla Vibrata I 82 D2
Sant'Elia a Pianisi I 103 B7
Sant'Elia Fiumerapido I 103 B6
Santelices E 88 A3
San Telmo E 99 B4
Sant'Elpídio a Mare I 82 C2
Santéramo in Colle I 104 C2
Santervas de la Vega E 88 B2
Sant' Eufemia Lamezia I 106 C3
Sant Felíu E 91 B5
Sant Feliu de Codines E 91 B5
Sant Feliu de Guíxols E 91 B6
Sant Feliu Sasserra E 91 B5
Sant Ferran E 97 C1
Sant Francesc de Formentera E 97 C1
Sant Francesc de ses Salines E 97 C1
Santhià I 70 C3
Sant Hilari Sacalm E 91 B5
Sant Hipòlit de Voltregà E 91 A5
Santiago de Alcántara E 92 B3
Santiago de Calatrava E 100 B1
Santiago de Compostela E 86 B2
Santiago de la Espade E 101 A3
Santiago de la Puebla E 94 B1
Santiago de la Ribera E 101 B5
Santiago del Campo E 93 B4
Santiago de Litem P 92 B2
Santiago do Cacém P 98 B2
Santiago do Escoural P 92 C2
Santiago Maior P 92 C3
Santibáñez de Béjar E 93 A5
Santibáñez de la Peña E 88 B2
Santibáñez de Murias E 88 A1
Santibáñez de Vidriales E 87 B4
Santibáñez el Alto E 93 A4
Santibáñez el Bajo E 93 A4
Santillana E 88 A2
Santiponce E 99 B4
San Tirso de Abres E 86 A3
Santisteban del Puerto E 100 A2
Santiuste de San Juan Bautiste E 94 A2
Santiz E 94 A1
Sant Jaume dels Domenys E 91 B4
Sant Joan Baptista E 97 B1
Sant Joan de les Abadesses E 91 A5
Sant Jordi E 90 C3
Sant Josep de sa Talaia E 97 C1
Sant Juliàde Loria AND 91 A4
Sant'Ilario d'Enza I 81 B4
Sant Llorençde Morunys E 91 A4
Sant Llorençdes Carctassar E 97 B3
Sant Llorenç Savall E 91 B5
Sant Luis E 97 B4
Sant Mart ide Llemaná E 91 A5
Sant Marti de Maldá E 91 B4

Sant Marti Sarroca E .91 B4
Sant Mateu E 90 C3
Sant Miquel E 97 B1
Santo Aleixo P. 98 A3
Santo Amado E 98 A3
Santo Amaro P 92 C3
Santo André P 98 A2
Santo Domingo E 93 C3
Santo Domingo de la
Calzada E 89 B4
Santo Domingo de Silos
E 89 C3
Santo Estêvão
Faro P 98 B3
Santarém P 92 C2
Santok PL 46 C1
Santomera E 101 A4
Santoña E 89 A3
Santovenia
Burgos E 89 B3
Zamora E 88 C1
Sant Pau de Seguries
E 91 A5
Santpedor E 91 B4
Sant Pere de Riudebitlles
E 91 B4
Sant Pere Pescador
E 91 A6
Sant Quirze de Besora
E 91 A5
Sant Rafel E 97 C1
Sant Ramon E 91 B4
Santu Lussurgiu I . . .110 B1
Santutzi E 89 A3
Sant Vincençde Castellet
E 91 B4
San Valentino alla Muta
. . . . .71 B5
San Venanzo I 82 D1
San Vicente de Alcántara
E 93 B3
San Vicente de Arana
E 89 B4
San Vicente de la
Barquera E 88 A2
San Vicente de la
Sonsierra E 89 B4
San Vietro E 87 C4
San Vigilio I 72 B1
San Vincente del Raspeig
E 96 C2
San Vincenzo I 81 C4
San Vito I 104 C1
San Vito al Tagliamento
I 72 C2
San Vito Chietino I . .103 A7
San Vito dei Normanni
I 104 C3
San Vito di Cadore I . .72 B2
San Vito lo Capo I . . .108 A1
San Vito Romano I . . .102 B5
Sanxenxo E 86 B2
Sanza I 104 C1
São Aleixo P 92 C3
São Barnabé P 98 B2
São Bartoloméda Serra
P 98 A2
São Bartolomeu de
Messines P 98 B2
São Bento P 87 C2
São Bras P 98 B3
São Brás de Alportel
P 98 B3
São Braz do Reguedoura
P 92 C2
São Cristóvão P 92 C2
São Domingos P 98 B2
São Geraldo P 92 C2
São Jacinto P 92 A2
São João da Madeira
P 87 D2
São João da Pesqueira
P 87 C3
São João da Ribeira
P 92 B2
São João da Serra P .87 D2
São João da Venda
P 98 B3
São João dos
Caldeireiros P 98 B3
São Julião P 92 B3
São Leonardo P 92 C3
São Luis P 98 B2
São Manços P 92 C3
São Marcos da Ataboeira
P 98 B3
Saõ Marcos da Serra
P 98 B2
São Marcos de Campo
P 92 C3
São Martinho da Cortiça
P 92 A2
São Martinho das
Amoreiras P 98 B2
São Martinho do Porto
P 92 B1
São Matias
Beja P 98 A3
Évora P 92 C3
São Miguel d'Acha P .92 A3
São Miguel de Machede
P 92 C3
São Pedro da Torre
P 87 C2
São Pedro de Cadeira
P 92 B1
São Pedro de Moel P .92 B1
São Pedro de Solis P .98 B3
São Pedro do Sul P . .87 D2
Saorge F 80 C1
São Romão P 92 C2
São Sebastião dos
Carros P 98 B3
São Teotónio P 98 B2
São Torcato P 87 C2
Sapataria P 92 C1
Sapes GR 116 A7
Sapião P 87 C3
Sa Pobla E 97 B3
Sappada I 72 B2
Sappen N 112 C10
Sapri I 106 A2
Sarajevo BIH 84 C3
Saramon F 77 C3
Sarandë AL 116 C2
Saranovo SRB 85 B5
Saranzá SRB 85 B5
Sa Rapita E 97 B3
Saray TR 118 A2
Saraycık TR 118 C4
Saraylar TR 118 B2
Sarayönü TR 119 D7
Sarbia PL 46 C2
Sarbinowo
Zachodnio-Pomorskie
PL 45 C6
Zachodnio-Pomorskie
PL 46 A1
Sárbogárd H 74 B3
Sarcelles F 58 A3
Sarche I 71 B5
Sardara I 110 C1

Sardoal P 92 B2
Sardón de Duero E . . .88 C2
Sare F 76 C1
S'Arenal E 97 B2
Sarengrad HR 75 C4
Sarentino I 71 B6
Sarezzo I 71 C5
Sargans CH 71 A4
Sárí H 75 A4
Sandeyler TR 118 C2
Saricakaya TR 118 B5
Sari-d'Orcino F 102 A1
Sargól TR 119 D3
Sarıkaya TR 16 B7
Sarıköy TR 118 B2
Sarilhos Grandes P . . .92 C2
Sariñena E 90 B2
Sarkad H 75 B6
Sárkeresztes H 74 A3
Sárkeresztúr H 74 A3
Sármellék H 74 B2
Särna S 115 F10
Sarnadas P 92 B3
Sarnano I 82 C2
Sarnen CH 70 B3
Sarnesfield GB 29 A5
Sárnico I 71 C4
Sarno I 103 C7
Sarnow D 45 B5
Sarny UA 11 A9
Sáró S 38 B4
Saronno I 71 C4
Sárošd H 74 A3
Šarovce SK 65 B4
Sarpoil F 68 C3
Sarpsborg N 35 C3
Sarracin E 88 B3
Sarral E 91 B4
Sarralbe F 60 A3
Sarrancolin F 77 D3
Sarras F 69 C4
Sarre I 70 C2
Sarreaus E 87 B3
Sarrebourg F 60 B3
Sarreguemines F 60 A3
Sárrétudvari H 75 A6
Sarria E 86 B3
Sarrià de Ter E 91 A6
Sarrión E 96 A2
Sarroca de Lleida E . .90 B3
Sarroch I 110 C2
Sarron F 76 C2
Sársina I 82 C1
Særslev DK 39 D3
Sarstedt D 51 A5
Sárszentlőrinc H 74 B3
Sárszentmihaly H 74 A3
Sárszentmiklós H 74 B3
Sarteano I 81 D5
Sartène F 102 B1
Sartilly F 57 B4
Sartirana Lomellina I . .80 A2
Saruhanlı TR 118 D2
Särvar H 74 A1
Sarvisvaara S 113 F10
Sarzana I 81 B3
Sarzeau F 66 A2
Sarzedas P 92 B3
Sasalli TR 119 D1
Sasamón E 88 B2
Sa Savina E 97 C1
Sásd H 74 B3
Sasino PL 46 A3
Sássari I 110 B1
Sassello I 80 B2
Sassenberg D 50 B4
Sassetta I 81 C4
Sassnitz D 45 A5
Sassocorvaro I 82 C1
Sasso d'Ombrone I . . .81 D5
Sassoferrato I 82 C1
Sassoleone I 81 B5
Sasso Marconi I 81 B4
Sassuolo I 81 B4
Šástago E 90 B2
Šaštinske Stráže SK . .64 B3
Sas van Gent NL 49 B4
Sátáhangan N 114 E7
Sátáo P 87 D3
Sätenäs S 35 D4
Säter S 36 B2
Sätila S 40 B2
Satnica Đakovačka
HR 74 C3
Sátoraljaújhely H 10 B6
Satow D 44 B3
Sätra-brunn S 36 C3
Sætre N 35 C2
Satrup D 43 A6
Satteins A 71 A4
Satu Mare RO 11 C7
Saturnia I 102 A4
Saucats F 76 B2
Saucelle E 87 C4
Sauda N 33 C3
Sauðárkrókur IS 111 B6
Saudasjøen N 33 C3
Sauerlach D 62 C2
Saugues F 78 B2
Sauherad N 33 C6
Saujon F 66 C4
Sauland N 33 C5
Saulces Monclin F 59 A5
Saulgau D 61 B5
Saulgrub D 62 C2
Saulieu F 69 A4
Saulnot F 60 C2
Sault F 79 B4
Sault-Brénaz F 69 C5
Sault-de-Navailles F . .76 C2
Saulx F 60 C2
Saulxures-sur-Moselotte
F 60 C2
Saulzais-le-Potier F . . .68 B2
Saumos F 76 B1
Saumur F 67 A4
Saunavaara FIN 113 E16
Saundersfoot GB 28 B3
Saurat F 77 D4
Saurbær
Borgarfjarðarsýsla
IS. 111 C4
Dalasýsla IS 111 B4
Eyjafjarðarsýsla IS . .111 B7
Sáuris I 72 B2
Sausset-les-Pins F . . .79 C4
Sauteyrargues F 78 C2
Sauvagnat F 68 C2
Sauve F 78 C2
Sauveterre-de-Béarn
F 76 C2
Sauveterre-de-Guyenne
F 76 B2
Sauviat-sur-Vige F . . .67 C6
Sauxillanges F 68 C3
Sauzet
Drôme F 78 B3
Lot F 77 B4
Sauzé-Vaussais F 67 B5
Sauzon F 66 A1
Sava I 104 C3
Sævareid N 32 B2
Savarsin RO 11 C7
Savaștepe TR 118 C2
Savci SLO 73 B6
Säve S 38 B4
Savelletri I 104 C3
Savelli I 107 B3
Savenay F 66 A3
Saverdun F 77 C4
Saverne F 60 B3

Savières F 59 B4
Savigliano I 80 B1
Savignac-les-Eglises
F 67 C5
Savignano Irpino I . . .103 B8
Savignano sul Rubicone
I 82 B1
Savigny-sur-Braye F . .58 C1
Savináñ E 89 C5
Savino Selo SRB 75 C4
Savio I 82 B1
Šávja S 36 C4
Šavnik MNE 85 D4
Savognin CH 71 B4
Savona I 80 B2
Savonlinna FIN 9 B6
Savournon F 79 B4
Sævråsvåg N 32 B2
Sävsjö S 40 B4
Savsjön S 36 C1
Sävsjöström S 40 B5
Savudrija HR 72 C3
Savukoski FIN 113 E17
Sawbridgeworth GB . . .31 C4
Sawtry GB 30 B3
Sax E 101 A5
Saxdalen S 36 B1
Saxilby GB 27 B5
Saxmundham GB 30 B5
Saxnäs S 115 C12
Saxthorpe GB 30 B5
Sayalonga E 100 C1
Sayatón E 95 B4
Sayda D 52 C3
Säytsjärvi FIN 113 C16
Šázava CZ 64 A1
Šázava CZ 63 A5
Scaër F 56 B2
Scafa I 103 A7
Scalasaig GB 24 B1
Scalby GB 27 A5
Scalea I 106 B2
Scaletta Zanclea I . . .109 A4
Scalloway GB 22 A7
Scamblesby GB 27 B5
Scandale I 107 B3
Scandicci I 81 B5
Scandolara Ravara I . .81 A4
Scanno I 103 B6
Scansano I 81 D5
Scanzano Jónico I . . .104 C2
Scarborough GB 27 A5
Scardoy GB 22 D4
Scarinish GB 24 B1
Scarperia I 81 C5
Scarriff IRL 20 B3
Scey-sur-Saône et St
Albin F 60 C1
Schachendorf A 73 A6
Schaffhausen CH 61 C4
Schafstädt D 52 B1
Schafstedt D 43 A6
Schaftlarn D 62 C2
Schagen NL 42 C1
Schalkau D 51 C7
Schangnau CH 70 B2
Schapbach D 61 B4
Scharding A 63 B4
Scharnitz A 71 A6
Scharrel D 43 B4
Schattendorf A 64 C2
Scheemda NL 42 B3
Scheessel D 43 B6
Schéggia I 82 C1
Scheibbs A 63 B6
Scheibenberg D 52 C2
Scheidegg D 61 C5
Scheifling A 73 A4
Scheinfeld D 61 A6
Schelklingen D 61 B5
Schenefeld
Schleswig-Holstein
D 43 A6
Schleswig-Holstein D . .44 B1
Schenklengsfeld D . . .51 C5
Scherfede D 51 B5
Schermbeck D 50 B2
Schernberg D 51 B6
Schesslitz D 52 D1
Scheveningen NL 49 A5
Schiedam NL 49 B5
Schierling D 62 B3
Schiers CH 71 B4
Schildau D 52 B2
Schillingen D 60 A2
Schillingsfürst D 61 A6
Schilpário I 71 B5
Schiltach D 61 B4
Schiltigheim F 60 B3
Schio I 71 C6
Schirmeck F 60 B3
Schirnding D 52 C2
Schkeuditz D 52 B2
Schkölen D 52 B1
Schlabendorf D 53 B3
Schladen D 51 A6
Schladming A 72 A3
Schlangen D 51 B4
Schleiden D 50 C2
Schleiz D 52 C1
Schleswig D 43 A6
Schleusingen D 51 C6
Schlieben D 52 B3
Schliengen D 60 C2
Schliersee D 62 C2
Schlitz D 51 C5
Schloss Neuhans D . .51 B4
Schlossvippach D 52 B1
Schlotheim D 51 B6
Schluchsee D 61 C4
Schlüchtern D 51 C5
Schmallenberg D 50 B4
Schmelz D 60 A2
Schmidmühlen D 62 A2
Schmiedeberg D 52 C3
Schmiedefeld D 51 C6
Schmirn A 72 A1
Schmölln
Brandenburg D 45 B6
Sachsen D 52 C2
Schnaittach D 62 A2
Schneeberg D 52 C2
Schneizlreuth D 62 C3
Schneverdingen D 44 B1
Schöder A 73 A4
Schoenburg B 50 C2
Schollene D 44 C4
Schöllkrippen D 51 C5
Schomberg D 61 B4
Schönach D 62 B3
Schönau
Baden-Württemberg
D 60 C3
Bayern D 62 B3
Schönbeck D 45 B5
Schönberg
Bayern D 63 B4
Mecklenburg-
Vorpommern D . . .44 B2
Schleswig-Holstein D . .44 A2
Schönebeck D 52 A1
Schöneck D 52 C2
Schönecken-D 50 C2
Schönermark D 45 B5
Schönewalde D 52 B3
Schongau D 62 C1
Schöngrabern A 64 B2
Schönhagen D 51 B5
Schönhausen D 44 C4
Schöningen D 51 A6
Schönkirchen D 44 A2
Schönsee D 62 A3
Schöntal D 61 A5
Schönthal D 62 B3
Schonungen D 51 C6
Schönwalde D 44 A2

Schoondijke NL 49 B4
Schoonebeek NL 42 C3
Schoonhoven NL 49 B5
Schopfheim D 60 C3
Schöppenstedt D 51 A6
Schörfling A 63 C4
Schorndorf D 61 B5
Schortens D 43 B4
Schotten D 51 C5
Schramberg D 61 B4
Schraplau D 52 B1
Schrattenberg A 64 B2
Schrems A 63 B6
Schrobenhausen D . . .62 B2
Schröcken A 71 A5
Schrozberg D 61 A5
Schruns A 71 A4
Schüpfheim CH 70 B3
Schüttorf D 50 A3
Schwaan D 44 B4
Schwabach D 62 A2
Schwäbisch Gmünd
D 61 B5
Schwäbisch Hall D . . .61 A5
Schwabmünchen D . . .62 B1
Schwadorf A 64 B2
Schwagstorf D 43 C4
Schwaigern D 61 A5
Schwalmstadt D 51 C5
Schwanberg A 73 B5
Schwanden CH 70 B4
Schwandorf D 62 A3
Schwanebeck D 52 B1
Schwanenstadt A 63 B4
Schwanewede D 43 B5
Schwanfeld D 61 A6
Schwangau D 62 C1
Schwarmstedt D 43 C6
Schwarza D 51 C6
Schwarzach im Pongau
A 72 A3
Schwarzau im Gebirge
A 63 C6
Schwarzenau A 63 B6
Schwarzenbach D 52 C1
Schwarzenbach am Wald
D 52 C1
Schwarzenberg D 52 C2
Schwarzenburg CH . . .70 B2
Schwarzenfeld D 62 A3
Schwarz-heide D 53 B3
Schwaz A 72 A1
Schwechat A 64 B2
Schwedt D 45 B6
Schwei D 43 B5
Schweich D 60 A2
Schweighausen D 60 B3
Schweinfurt D 51 C6
Schweinitz D 52 B3
Schweinrich D 45 B4
Schwelm D 50 B3
Schwemsal D 52 B2
Schwenningen D 61 B4
Schwepnitz D 53 B3
Schwerin D 44 B3
Schwerte D 50 B3
Schweskau D 44 B3
Schwetzingen D 61 A4
Schwyz CH 70 A3
Sciacca I 108 B2
Scicli I 109 C3
Sciechów PL 46 C3
Scigliano I 106 B3
Scilla I 109 A4
Scinawa PL 54 B1
Scionzier F 69 B6
Scoglitti I 109 C3
Scole GB 30 B5
Sconser GB 22 D2
Scopello
Piemonte I 70 C3
Sicília I 108 A1
Scordia I 109 B3
Scorzè I 72 C2
Scotch Corner GB 27 A4
Scotter GB 27 B5
Scourie GB 22 C3
Scousburgh GB 22 B7
Scrabster GB 23 C5
Screeb IRL 20 A2
Scremerston GB 25 C6
Scritto I 82 C1
Scuol CH 71 B5
Scúrcola Marsicana
I 103 A6
Seaford GB 31 D4
Seaham GB 25 D6
Seahouses GB 25 C6
Seascale GB 26 A2
Seaton GB 29 C7
Sebazac-Concourès
F 77 B5
Sebečevo SRB 85 C5
Seben TR 118 B6
Sebersdorf A 73 A5
Sebezh RUS 7 C10
Sebnitz D 53 C4
Seborga I 80 C1
Seby S 41 C6
Seč
Vychodočeský CZ . .63 A6
Západočeský CZ . . .62 A4
Sečanj SRB 75 C5
Secemin PL 55 C4
Séchault F 59 A5
Seckau A 73 A5
Seclin F 49 C4
Secondigny F 67 B4
Seda P 92 B3
Sedan F 59 A5
Sedano E 88 B3
Sedbergh GB 26 A3
Sedella E 100 C1
Séderon F 79 B4
Sedgefield GB 27 A4
Sedella I 72 B1
Sédilo I 110 B1
Sédini I 110 B1
Sedlarica HR 74 C2
Sedlčany CZ 63 A5
Sedlec-Prčice CZ 63 A5
Sedlice CZ 63 A4
Sédlo I 110 D1
Sedziejowice PL 55 B4
Sedziszów PL 55 C5
Sedziszów Małopolski
PL 55 C6
Seebach D 60 B3
Seeboden A 72 B3
Seefeld
Brandenburg D 45 C5
Niedersachsen D . . .43 B5
Seefeld in Tirol A 71 A6
Seeg D 62 C1
Seehausen
Sachsen-Anhalt D . .44 C3
Sachsen-Anhalt D . .52 A1
Seeheim-Jugenheim
D 61 A4
Seelbach D 60 B3
Seelow D 45 C6
Seelze D 43 C6
Seerhausen D 52 B3
Sées F 57 B6
Seesen D 51 B6
Seeshaupt D 62 C2
Seewalchen A 63 C4
Seferihisar TR 119 D1
Sefkerin SRB 85 A5
Segård N 35 B2
Segerstad S 35 C5
Segesd H 74 B2
Seglinge FIN 36 B7
Segmon S 35 C5
Segonzac F 67 C4
Segorbe E 96 B2
Segovia E 94 B2
Segré F 57 C5

Segura
E 89 B4
P 93 B3
Segura de León E 99 A4
Segura de los Baños
E 90 C2
Serifos GR 117 E6
Sehnde D 51 A5
Seia P 92 A3
Seiches-sur-le-Loir F . .67 A4
Seifhennersdorf D 53 C4
Seignelay F 59 C4
Seijo E 87 C2
Seilhac F 68 C1
Seilles B 49 C6
Seim N 32 B2
Seinäjoki FIN 3 E25
Seissan F 77 C3
Seitenstetten Markt A .63 B5
Seixal P 92 C1
Seiz A 73 A4
Seizthal A 73 A4
Sejerslev DK 38 C1
Seksna RUS 7 B15
Selargius E 110 C2
Selb D 52 C2
Selby GB 27 B4
Selca HR 84 C1
Selce AL 105 A5
Selce HR 73 C4
Selçuk TR 119 E2
Selde DK 38 C2
Selekta SRB 75 C4
Selendi
Manisa TR 118 D2
Manisa TR 118 D3
Selenicë AL 105 C5
Sélestat F 60 B3
Seleuš SRB 75 C5
Selevac SRB 85 B5
Selfoss IS 111 D5
Selgua E 90 B3
Selice SK 64 B3
Seligenstadt D 51 C4
Seligenthal D 51 C6
Selimiye TR 119 E2
Selizharovo RUS 7 C12
Selja S 36 A1
Seljelvnes N 112 C8
Seljord N 33 C5
Selkirk GB 25 C5
Sellano I 82 D1
Selles-St Denis F 68 A1
Selles-sur-Cher F 67 A6
Sellières F 69 B5
Sellin D 45 A5
Sellye H 74 C2
Selm D 50 B3
Selnica ob Dravi SLO .73 B5
Selongey F 59 C6
Selonnet F 79 B5
Selow D 44 B3
Selsey GB 31 D3
Seltjarnanes IS 111 C4
Seltso RUS 7 E13
Seltz F 61 B4
Selva E 97 B2
Selva di Cadore I 72 B2
Selva di Val Gardena
I 72 B1
Selvik
Sogn og Fjordane
N 32 A2
Vestfold N 35 C2
Selvino I 71 C4
Selyatyn UA 11 C8
Sem N 35 C2
Semeljci HR 74 C3
Semenovka
Chernihiv UA 7 D11
Kremenchuk UA . . .11 B12
Semič SLO 73 C5
Semide
F 59 A5
P 92 A2
Semily CZ 53 C5
Seminara I 106 C2
Semlac RO 75 B5
Semmen-stedt D 51 A6
Šempeter SLO 73 B5
Semriach A 73 A5
Semur-en-Auxois F . . .69 A4
Sena E 90 B2
Sena de Luna E 88 B1
Senarpont F 58 A2
Sénas F 79 C4
Senćanski Trešnjevac
SRB 75 C4
Sencelles E 97 B2
Senčur SLO 73 B5
Senden
Bayern D 61 B6
Nordrhein-Westfalen
D 50 B3
Sendenhorst D 50 B3
Sendim P 87 C4
Senec SK 64 B3
Seneffe B 49 C5
Séneghe I 110 B1
Senés E 101 B3
Senftenberg D 53 B3
Sengouagnet F 77 D3
Sengwarden D 43 B5
Senica SK 64 B3
Senice na Hané CZ . . .64 A3
Senigállia I 82 C2
Senirkent TR 119 D5
Senis I 110 C1
Senise I 106 A3
Senj HR 83 B3
Senje SRB 85 C6
Senjehopen N 112 C6
Senjski Rudnik SRB . .85 C6
Senlis F 58 A3
Sennan S 40 C2
Sennecey-le-Grand F .69 B4
Sennen GB 28 C2
Senno BY 7 D10
Sénnori I 110 B1
Sennwald CH 71 A4
Sennybridge GB 29 B4
Senohrad SK 65 B5
Senonches F 58 B2
Senones F 60 B2
Senorbì I 110 C2
Senovo SLO 73 B5
Senožeče SLO 73 C4
Senožeti SLO 73 B4
Sens F 59 B4
Sens-de-Bretagne F . .57 B4
Senta SRB 75 C5
Senterada E 90 A3
Sentjernej SLO 73 C5
Šentjur SLO 73 B5
Senumstad N 33 D5
Seoane E 86 B3
Seon CH 70 A3
Sépeaux F 59 C4
Sépey CH 70 B2
Sepino I 103 B7
Sępólno Krajeńskie
PL 46 B3
Seppois F 70 A2
Septeuil F 58 B2
Sepúlveda E 88 C3
Sequals I 72 B2
Sequeros E 93 A4
Seraincourt F 59 A5
Seraing B 49 C6
Seravezza I 81 C4
Sered' SK 64 B3
Seredka RUS 7 B10
Şereflikoçhisar TR . . .16 B7
Seregélyes H 74 A3
Seregno I 71 C4

Sérent F 56 C3
Serfaus A 71 A5
Sergiyev Posad RUS . .7 C15
Seriate I 71 C4
Sérifontaine F 58 A2
Serifos GR 117 E6
Sérignan F 78 C2
Serik TR 119 F6
Serina I 71 C4
Serinhisar TR 119 E4
Sermaises F 58 B3
Sermaize-les-Bains F .59 B5
Sérmide I 81 B5
Sermoneta I 102 B5
Sernache de Bonjardim
P 92 B2
Sernancelhe P 87 D3
Seròn E 101 B3
Serón de Najima E . . .89 C4
Seroosskerke NL 49 B4
Serós E 90 B3
Serpa P 98 B3
Serpukhov RUS 7 D14
Serracapriola I 103 B8
Serrada E 88 C2
Serra de Outes E 86 B2
Serradifalco I 108 B2
Serradilla E 93 B4
Serradilla del Arroyo
E 93 A4
Serramanna I 110 C1
Serramazzoni I 81 B4
Serranillos E 94 B2
Serrapetrona I 82 C2
Serra San Bruno I . . .106 C3
Serrastretta I 106 B3
Serravalle
Piemonte I 70 C3
Umbria I 82 D2
Serravalle di Chienti I .82 C1
Serravalle Scrivia I . . .80 B2
Serre I 103 C8
Serrejón E 93 B5
Serres
F 79 B4
GR 116 A5
Serrières F 69 C4
Serrières-de-Briord F .69 C5
Sersale I 106 B3
Sertã P 92 B2
Sertig Dörfli CH 71 B4
Servance F 60 C2
Serverette F 78 B2
Servia GR 116 B4
Servian F 78 C2
Serviers F 78 B3
Servigliano I 82 C2
Sérvos GR 117 E4
Serzedelo P 87 C2
Seseña Nuevo E 95 B3
Sesimbra P 92 C1
Seskinore GB 19 B4
Sesma E 89 B4
Sessa Aurunca I 103 B6
Sesta Godano I 80 B3
Šestanovac HR 84 C1
Sestao E 89 A4
Sestino I 82 C1
Sesto I 72 B2
Sesto Calende I 70 C3
Sesto Fiorentino I 81 C5
Séstola I 81 B4
Sesto San Giovanni I .71 C4
Sestriere I 79 B5
Sestri Levante I 80 B3
Sestroretsk RUS 7 A11
Sestu I 110 C2
Sesvete HR 73 C6
Setcases E 91 A5
Sète F 78 C2
Setenil E 99 C5
Setermoen N 112 D7
Šetonje SRB 85 B6
Setskog N 34 C3
Settalsjølia N 114 E7
Séttimo Torinese I 70 C2
Settimo Vittone I 70 C2
Settle GB 26 A3
Setúbal P 92 C2
Seubersdorf D 62 A2
Seúil F 110 C2
Seúlo I 110 C2
Seurre F 69 B5
Sevastel AL 105 C5
Sevel DK 38 C1
Sevenoaks GB 31 C4
Sevel N 90 B2
Sevenoaks GB 31 C4
Sévérac-le-Château
F 78 B2
Sever do Vouga P 87 D2
Severin D 44 B3
Severomorsk RUS 3 B30
Séveso I 71 C4
Ševětin CZ 63 A5
Sevettijärvi FIN 113 C17
Sévigny F 59 A5
Sevilla = Seville E 99 B5
Sevilla la Nueva E 94 B2
Seville = Sevilla E 99 B5
Sevilleja de la Jara E .94 C2
Sevlievo BG 11 E8
Sevnica SLO 73 B5
Sevojno SRB 85 C4
Sevrier F 69 C6
Sexdrega S 40 B3
Seyches F 77 B3
Seyda D 52 B2
Seydişehir TR 119 E6
Seydisfjörður IS 111 B12
Seyitgazi TR 118 C5
Seyitömer TR 118 C4
Seymen TR 118 A2
Seyne F 79 B5
Seynes F 78 B3
Seyssel F 69 C5
Sežana SLO 72 C3
Sézanne F 59 B4
Sezulfe P 87 C3
Sezze I 102 B6
Sfântu Gheorghe RO .11 D8
Sforzacosta I 82 C2
Sgarasta Mhor GB . . .22 D1
Shaftesbury GB 29 B5
Shaldon GB 29 C4
Shanagolden IRL 20 B2
Shanklin GB 31 D2
Shannon IRL 20 B3
Shap GB 26 A3
Sharpness GB 29 B5
Shawbury GB 26 C3
Shchekino RUS 7 D14
Shchors UA 7 E11
's-Heerenberg NL 50 B2
Sheerness GB 31 C4
Sheffield GB 27 B4
Shefford GB 31 B3
Shenfield GB 31 C4
Shëngjergj AL 116 A2
Shepetivka UA 11 A9
Shepshed GB 27 C4
Shepton Mallet GB . . .29 B5
Sherborne GB 29 C5
Shercock IRL 19 C5
Sheringham GB 30 B5
's-Hertogenbosch NL .49 B6
Shiel Bridge GB 22 D3
Shijak AL 105 B5
Shilbottle GB 25 C6
Shillelagh IRL 21 B5
Shimsk RUS 7 B11
Shipston-on-Stour
GB 29 A4
Shirgjan AL 105 B6
Shklow BY 7 D11

Shkodër AL 105 A5
Shoeburyness GB 31 C4
Shoreham-by-Sea GB .31 D3
Shoshka UA 7 F12
Shotley Gate GB 31 C5
Shpola UA 11 B11
Shrewsbury GB 26 C3
Shugozero RUS 7 B13
Shumen BG 11 E9
Siabost GB 22 C2
Siamanna I 110 C1
Sianow PL 46 A2
Siatista GR 116 B3
Siauges-St Romain F .78 A2
Šiauliai LT 6 D7
Sibari I 106 B3
Sibbhult S 41 C4
Šibenik HR 83 C4
Siberar E 101 B3
Sibinj HR 74 C2
Sibiu RO 11 D8
Sibnica SRB 85 B5
Sibsey GB 27 B6
Šiculiana I 108 B2
Sid SRB 85 A4
Sidari GR 116 C1
Siddeburen NL 42 B3
Sidensjö S 115 D15
Siderno I 106 C3
Sidirokastro GR 116 A5
Sidmouth GB 29 C4
Sidzina PL 65 A5
Siebe N 113 D12
Siebenlehn D 52 B3
Siedlce PL 6 E7
Siedlice PL 46 B1
Siedlinghausen D 51 B4
Siedlisko PL 46 C2
Siegburg D 50 C3
Siegen D 50 C4
Siegenburg D 62 B2
Sieghartskirchen A . . .64 B2
Siegsdorf D 62 C3
Siekierki PL 45 C6
Sielpia PL 55 B5
Siemiany PL 47 B5
Siena I 81 C5
Sieniawka PL 53 C4
Siennica PL 55 A6
Sienno PL 55 B6
Sieppijärvi FIN 113 E13
Sieradz PL 54 B3
Sierakow
Śląskie PL 54 C3
Wielkopolskie PL . . .46 C2
Sierakowice PL 46 A3
Sierck-les-Bains F 60 A2
Sierentz F 60 C3
Sierning A 63 B5
Sierpc PL 47 C5
Sierra de Fuentes E . .93 B4
Sierra de Luna E 90 A2
Sierra de Yeguas E . .100 B1
Sierre CH 70 B2
Siestrzeń PL 55 A5
Sietamo E 90 A2
Siewierz PL 55 C4
Sigdal N 34 B1
Sigean F 78 C1
Sigerfjord N 112 D4
Sighetu-Marmatiei
RO 11 C7
Sighișoara RO 11 C8
Sigillo I 82 C1
Siglufjörður IS 111 A7
Sigmaringen D 61 B5
Signa I 81 C5
Signes F 79 C4
Signy-l'Abbaye F 59 A5
Signy-le-Petit F 59 A5
Sigogne F 67 C4
Sigri GR 116 C7
Sigtuna S 37 C4
Sigüenza E 95 A4
Sigueró E 94 A3
Sigües E 90 A1
Siguldá LV 6 C8
Siilinjärvi FIN 3 E27
Sikenica SK 65 B4
Sikia GR 116 B5
Sikinos GR 117 F7
Sikkilsdalseter N 32 A6
Siklós H 74 C3
Sikórz PL 47 C5
Sikselet N 115 A14
Silandro I 71 B5
Silánus I 110 B1
Silbaš SRB 75 C4
Sile TR 118 A4
Siles E 101 A3
Silgueiros P 87 D3
Silifke TR 16 C6
Siliqua I 110 C1
Silistra BG 11 D9
Silivri TR 118 A3
Siljan N 33 C6
Siljansnäs S 36 B1
Silkeborg DK 39 C2
Silla E 96 B2
Sillamäe EST 7 B9
Silleda E 86 B2
Sillé-le-Guillaume F . .57 B5
Sillenstede D 43 B4
Sillerud S 35 C4
Sillian A 72 B2
Silloth GB 25 D4
Silno PL 46 B3
Silo HR 73 C4
Sils E 91 B5
Silsand N 112 C6
Silte S 37 E5
Silute LT 6 D6
Silvalen N 114 B9
Silvaplana CH 71 B4
Silvares P 92 A3
Silverdalen S 40 B5
Silvermines IRL 20 B3
Silverstone GB 30 B2
Silverton GB 29 C4
Silves P 98 B2
Silvi Marina I 103 A7
Simandre F 69 B5
Šimanovci SRB 85 B5
Simard F 69 B5
Simat de Valldigna E . .96 B2
Simav TR 118 C3
Simbach
Bayern D 62 B3
Bayern D 62 B4
Simbário I 106 C3
Simeria RO 11 D7
Simi GR 119 F2
Simicevo SRB 85 B6
Simitli BG 116 A5
Simlångsdalen S 40 C3
Simmerath D 50 C2
Simmerberg D 61 C5
Simmern D 50 D3
Simo FIN 3 D26
Simonovci SRB 85 B5
Simonsbath GB 28 B4
Simonstorp S 37 D3
Simontornya H 74 B3
Simplon CH 70 B3
Simrishamn S 41 D4
Sinaia RO 11 D8
Sinalunga I 81 C5
Sinanaj AL 105 C5
Sinarcas E 96 B1
Sincan TR 118 C6
Sincanli TR 118 D5
Sindal DK 38 B3
Sindelfingen D 61 B5
Sindia I 110 B1
Sindirği TR 118 C3
Sinekçi TR 118 B2
Sines P 98 B2
Sinetta FIN 113 F14
Sineu E 97 B3
Singen D 61 C4

Singsås N 114 E7
Siniscóla I 110 B2
Sinj HR 83 C5
Sinlabajos E 94 A2
Sinn D 50 C4
Sinnai I 110 C2
Sinnes N 33 D3
Sinop TR 16 A7
Sins CH 70 A3
Sinsheim D 61 A4
Sint Annaland NL 49 B5
Sint Annaparochie
NL 42 B2
Sint Athonis NL 50 B1
Sint Nicolaasga NL . . .42 C2
Sint Oedenrode NL . . .49 B6
Sintra P 92 C1
Sinzheim D 61 B4
Sinzig D 50 C3
Siófok H 74 B3
Sion CH 70 B2
Sion Mills GB 19 B4
Siorac-en-Périgord F .77 B3
Šipanska Luka HR 84 D2
Šípovo BIH 84 B2
Sira N 33 D3
Siracusa I 109 B4
Siret RO 11 C9
Sirevåg N 33 D2
Sirig SRB 75 C4
Sirkka FIN 113 E13
Sirmione I 71 C5
Sirok H 65 C6
Siroka SK 65 B6
Široki Brijeg BIH 84 C2
Sirolo I 82 C2
Siruela E 94 D1
Sisak HR 73 C6
Sisante E 95 C4
Šišljavić HR 73 C5
Sissach CH 70 A2
Sissonne F 59 A4
Sistelo P 87 C2
Sisteron F 79 B4
Sistiana I 72 C3
Sistranda N 114 D5
S 112 E6
Sitges E 91 B4
Sitia GR 117 G8
Sittard NL 50 C1
Sittensen D 43 B6
Sittingbourne GB 31 C4
Sitzenroda D 52 B2
Sivac SRB 75 C4
Sivaslı TR 119 D4
Siverić HR 83 C5
Sivrihisar TR 118 C6
Sixt-Fer-à-Cheval F . . .70 B1
Siziano I 71 C4
Sizun F 56 B1
Sjenica SRB 85 C5
Sjoa N 114 F6
Sjøåsen N 114 C8
Sjöbo S 41 D3
Spenden
Hedmark N 34 A3
Hedmark N 34 B3
Sjøholt N 114 E3
Søli N 34 A3
Søli N 114 C9
Sjölunda S 37 C2
Sjömarken S 40 B2
Sjørring DK 38 C1
Sjötofta S 40 B3
Sjötorp S 35 D5
Sjoutnäset S 115 C11
Sjøvegan N 112 D6
Sjuntorp S 35 D4
Skåbu N 32 A6
Skadovsk UA 11 C12
Skælskør DK 39 D4
Skærbæk DK 39 D1
Skærup DK 39 D2
Skævinge DK 39 D4
Skafós N 33 A5
Skagaströnd IS 111 B5
Skagen DK 38 B3
Skagersvik S 35 D6
Skaiå N 33 D4
Skaidi N 113 B13
Skalkdalseter N 32 A6
Skala PL 55 C4
Skała PL 55 C4
Skaland N 112 D6
Skala Oropou GR . . .117 D5
Skała-Podlaska UA . . .11 A8
Skalat UA 11 B8
Skalbmierz PL 55 C5
Skålevik N 33 D5
Skalica SK 64 B3
Skalité SK 65 A4
Skällinge S 40 B2
Skalná CZ 52 C2
Skalstugan S 114 D9
Skanderborg DK 39 C2
Skåne-Fagerhult S . . .41 C3
Skåne-Tranås S 41 D3
Skänevik N 33 C2
Skänninge S 37 D2
. . . . .41 D2
Skåpafors S 35 C4
Skåpe PL 53 A5
Skäran S 115 D15
Skärblacka S 37 D2
Skarð IS 111 B3
Skare N 33 C3
Skåre S 35 C5
Skärhamn S 38 B4
Skarnes N 34 B3
Skärplinge S 36 B4
Skarp Salling DK 38 C2
Skarrild DK 39 D1
Skarstad N 112 D5
Skärstad S 40 B4
Skarsvåg N 113 A14
Skarszewy PL 47 A4
Skårup DK 39 D3
Skärvången S 115 D11
Skärvsjöby S 115 C14
Skarżysko-Kamienna
PL 55 B5
Skarżysko Ksiazece
PL 55 B5
Skatøy N 33 D6
Skattkärr S 35 C5
Skattungbyn S 36 A1
Skatval N 114 D7
Skaulo S 112 E10
Skave DK 39 C1
Skawina PL 55 D4
Skebobruk S 36 C5
Skebokvarn S 37 C3
Skee S 35 D3
Skegness GB 27 B6
Skei N 114 F2
Skela SRB 85 B5
Skelani BIH 85 C4
Skellefteå S 3 D24
Skelleftehamn S 3 D24
Skelmersdale GB 26 B3
Skelmorlie GB 24 C3
Skels N 34 C3
Skender Vakuf BIH . . .84 B2
Skender N 40 B2
Skene S 40 B2
Skepe PL 47 C5
Skępe PL 47 C5
Skeppshult S 40 B3
Skerries IRL 19 C5
Ski N 35 C2
Skibbereen IRL 20 C2
Skibotn N 112 C9

Skidra GR ... 116 B4
Skien N ... 35 C1
Skierniewice PL ... 55 B5
Skillingaryd S ... 40 B4
Skillinge S ... 41 D4
Skillingmark S ... 34 C4
Skilloura CY ... 120 A2
Skinnardai S ... 37 C5
Skinnskatteberg S ... 36 C2
Skipmannvik N ... 112 E4
Skipness GB ... 24 C2
Skipsea GB ... 27 B5
Skipton GB ... 26 B3
Skiptvet N ... 35 C3
Skiros GR ... 116 D6
Skivarp S ... 41 D3
Skive DK ... 38 C2
Skjanes N ... 113 B17
Skjærhalden N ... 35 C3
Skjeberg N ... 35 C3
Skjeggedal N ... 32 B3
Skjeljavik N ... 32 B1
Skjeljavik N ... 32 C2
Skjern DK ... 39 D1
Skjervøy N ... 112 B9
Skjold
  Rogaland N ... 33 C2
  Troms N ... 112 C8
Skjoldastraumen N ... 33 C2
Skjolden N ... 32 A4
Skjønhaug N ... 35 C3
Skjøtningsberg N ... 113 A16
Škocjan SLO ... 73 C5
Skoczów PL ... 65 A4
Skodborg DK ... 39 D2
Škofja Loka SLO ... 73 B4
Škofjica SLO ... 73 C4
Skog S ... 36 A3
Skoganvarre N ... 113 C14
Skogen S ... 35 C4
Skogfoss N ... 113 C18
Skoghall S ... 35 C5
Skogly N ... 113 C18
Skogn N ... 114 D8
Skognes N ... 112 C8
Skogstorp
  Halland S ... 40 C2
  Södermanland S ... 37 C3
Skoki PL ... 46 C3
Skokloster S ... 37 C4
Sköldinge S ... 37 C3
Skole UA ... 11 B7
Skollenborg N ... 35 C1
Sköllersta S ... 37 C2
Skomlin PL ... 54 B3
Skonseng N ... 115 A11
Skopelos GR ... 116 C5
Skopje MK ... 10 E6
Skoppum N ... 35 C2
Skórcz PL ... 47 B4
Skoroszczcz PL ... 54 C2
Skoroszów PL ... 54 B2
Skorovatn N ... 115 C10
Skorped S ... 115 D14
Skørping DK ... 38 C2
Skotfoss N ... 33 C6
Skotniki PL ... 55 B4
Skotselv N ... 34 C1
Skotterud N ... 34 C4
Skottorp S ... 40 C2
Skovby DK ... 39 E2
Skövde S ... 35 D5
Skovsgård DK ... 38 B2
Skradin HR ... 83 C4
Skradnik HR ... 73 C5
Skråmestø N ... 32 B1
Škrdlovice CZ ... 64 A1
Skrea S ... 40 C2
Skreia N ... 34 B2
Skrolsvik N ... 112 C6
Skruv S ... 40 C5
Skrwilno PL ... 47 B5
Skrydstrup DK ... 39 D2
Skucani BIH ... 84 C1
Skudeneshavn N ... 33 C2
Skui N ... 34 C2
Skulsk PL ... 47 C4
Skultorp S ... 35 D5
Skultuna S ... 37 C3
Skuodas LT ... 6 C6
Skurup S ... 41 D3
Skute N ... 34 B2
Skuteč CZ ... 64 A1
Skutskär S ... 36 B4
Skutvik N ... 112 D4
Skvyra UA ... 11 B10
Skwierzyna PL ... 46 C1
Skýcov SK ... 65 B4
Skýdra S ... 37 D1
Skyttmon S ... 115 D12
Skyttorp S ... 36 B4
Sládkovičovo SK ... 64 B3
Slagelse DK ... 39 D4
Slagharen NL ... 42 C3
Slagnäs S ... 115 B15
Slaidburn GB ... 26 B3
Slane IRL ... 19 C5
Slangerup DK ... 41 D2
Slano HR ... 84 D2
Slantsy RUS ... 7 B10
Slaný CZ ... 53 C4
Šlap SLO ... 72 B3
Slapanice CZ ... 64 A2
Slåstad N ... 34 B3
Slatina
  BIH ... 84 C2
  HR ... 74 C2
  RO ... 11 D8
  SRB ... 85 C5
Slatiňany CZ ... 64 A1
Slatinice CZ ... 64 A3
Slättberg S ... 36 A1
Slattum N ... 34 C2
Slavičin CZ ... 64 A3
Slavkov CZ ... 64 B3
Slavkovica SRB ... 85 B5
Slavkov u Brna CZ ... 64 B2
Slavonice CZ ... 63 B6
Slavonski Brod HR ... 74 C3
Slavonski Kobas HR ... 84 A2
Slavošovce SK ... 65 B6
Slavskoye RUS ... 47 A6
Slavuta UA ... 11 A9
Sława
  Lubuskie PL ... 53 B6
  Zachodnio-Pomorskie PL ... 46 B1
Sławharad BY ... 7 E11
Sławków PL ... 55 C4
Sławno
  Wielkopolskie PL ... 46 C3
  Zachodnio-Pomorskie PL ... 46 A2
Sławoborze PL ... 46 B1
Sl'ažany SK ... 65 B4
Sleaford GB ... 27 B5
Sledmere GB ... 27 A5
Śleðerðdur IS ... 111 B11
Sleights GB ... 27 A5
Slemmestad N ... 34 C2
Ślesin PL ... 47 C4
Sliač SK ... 65 B5
Sliema M ... 107 C6
Sligo IRL ... 18 B3
Slite S ... 37 E5
Slitu N ... 35 C3
Sliven BG ... 11 E9
Śliwice PL ... 47 B4
Slobozia RO ... 11 D9
Slochteren NL ... 42 B3
Slöinge S ... 40 C2
Słomniki PL ... 55 C5
Slonim BY ... 7 E8
Słońsk PL ... 45 C6
Sloten NL ... 42 C2
Slough GB ... 31 C3

Slovenj Gradec SLO ... 73 B5
Slovenska Bistrica SLO ... 73 B5
Slovenská L'upča SK ... 65 B5
Slovenská-Ves SK ... 65 A6
Slovenské Darmoty SK ... 65 B5
Slovenske Konjice SLO ... 73 B5
Słubice PL ... 45 C6
Sluderno I ... 71 B5
Śluis NL ... 49 B4
Šluknov CZ ... 53 B4
Slunj HR ... 83 A4
Słupca PL ... 54 B2
Słupia PL ... 54 B2
Słupiec PL ... 54 C1
Słupsk PL ... 46 A3
Slutsk BY ... 7 E9
Smålandsstenar S ... 40 B3
Smalåsen N ... 115 B10
Smarden BY ... 7 D9
Smarhon BY ... 7 D9
Šmarje SLO ... 73 B5
Šmarjeta SLO ... 73 C5
Šmartno SLO ... 73 B4
Smečno CZ ... 53 C4
Smedby S ... 40 C6
Smědec CZ ... 63 B5
Smederevo SRB ... 85 B5
Smederevska Palanka SRB ... 85 B5
Smedjebacken S ... 36 B2
Smęgorzów PL ... 55 C6
Smeland N ... 33 D5
Šmidary CZ ... 53 C5
Śmigiel PL ... 54 A1
Smila UA ... 11 B11
Smilde NL ... 42 C3
Smilčic CZ ... 53 C5
Smithfield GB ... 25 D5
Śmitowo PL ... 46 B2
Smögen S ... 35 D3
Smogulec PL ... 46 B3
Smołdzino PL ... 46 A3
Smolenice SK ... 64 B3
Smolensk RUS ... 7 D12
Smolník SK ... 65 B6
Smolyan BG ... 116 A6
Smuka SLO ... 73 C4
Smygehamn S ... 41 D3
Smykow PL ... 55 B5
Snainton GB ... 27 A5
Snaith GB ... 39 D3
Snaptun DK ... 39 D3
Snarby N ... 112 C8
Snarum N ... 34 B1
Snåsa N ... 115 C9
Snedsted DK ... 38 C1
Sneek NL ... 42 B2
Sneem IRL ... 20 C2
Sniatyn UA ... 11 B8
Snillfjord N ... 114 D6
Šnjegotina BIH ... 84 B2
Snøde DK ... 39 D3
Snøfjord N ... 113 B13
Snogebaek DK ... 41 D5
Snyatyn UA ... 11 B8
Soave I ... 71 C6
Sober E ... 86 B3
Sobernheim D ... 60 A3
Sobeslav CZ ... 63 A5
Sobienie Jeziory PL ... 55 B6
Sobota
  Dolnośląskie PL ... 53 B5
  Łódzkie PL ... 55 A4
Sobotište SK ... 64 B3
Sobótka
  Dolnośląskie PL ... 54 C1
  Wielkopolskie PL ... 54 B2
Sobra HR ... 84 D2
Sobrado
  Coruña E ... 86 A2
  Lugo E ... 86 B3
Sobral da Adiça P ... 98 A3
Sobral de Monte Agraço P ... 92 C1
Sobreira Formosa P ... 92 B3
Søby DK ... 39 E3
Soca SLO ... 72 B3
Sočanica KOS ... 85 C5
Sochaczew PL ... 55 A5
Sochos GR ... 116 B5
Socodor RO ... 75 B6
Socol RO ... 85 B6
Socovos E ... 101 A4
Socuéllamos E ... 95 C4
Sodankylä FIN ... 113 E15
Söderåkra S ... 40 C6
Söderala S ... 36 A3
Söderås S ... 36 B2
Söderbärke S ... 36 C2
Söderfors S ... 36 B4
Söderhamn S ... 36 A4
Söderköping S ... 37 D3
Söderö S ... 40 A5
Södertälje S ... 37 C4
Södingberg A ... 73 A5
Södra Finnö S ... 37 D3
Södra Ny S ... 35 C5
Södra Råda S ... 35 C5
Södra Sandby S ... 41 D3
Södra Vi S ... 40 B5
Sodražica SLO ... 73 C4
Sodupe E ... 89 A3
Soengas P ... 87 C2
Soest
  D ... 50 B4
  NL ... 49 A6
Sofades GR ... 116 C4
Sofia BG ... 11 E7
Sofikon GR ... 117 E5
Şofronea RO ... 75 B6
Sögel D ... 43 C4
Sogliano al Rubicone I ... 82 B1
Sogndalsfjøra N ... 32 A4
Søgne N ... 33 D4
Söğütköy TR ... 119 F3
Soham GB ... 30 B4
Sohland D ... 53 B4
Sohren D ... 60 A3
Soignies B ... 49 C5
Soissons F ... 59 A4
Söjtör H ... 74 B1
Sokal' UA ... 11 A8
Söke TR ... 119 E2
Sokna N ... 34 B1
Sokndal N ... 33 D3
Soknedal N ... 114 E7
Soko Banja SRB ... 85 C6
Sokolac BIH ... 84 C3
Sokółka PL ... 6 E7
Sokolov CZ ... 52 C2
Sokołowo PL ... 54 A3
Sokołów Podlaski PL ... 6 E7
Sola N ... 33 D2
Solana de los Barros E ... 93 C4
Solana del Pino E ... 100 A1
Solánas I ... 110 C2
Solares E ... 89 A3
Solarino I ... 109 B4
Solarussa I ... 110 C1
Solás GB ... 22 D1
Solberg S ... 115 D14
Solberga S ... 40 B4
Solbjørg N ... 32 B2
Solčany SK ... 64 B4
Solčava SLO ... 73 B4
Solda I ... 71 B5
Sölden A ... 71 B6
Solec Kujawski PL ... 47 B4
Solec nad Wisłą PL ... 55 B6
Soleils F ... 79 C5
Solenzara F ... 102 B2
Solera E ... 100 B2
Solesmes F ... 49 C4

Soleto I ... 107 A5
Solgne F ... 60 B2
Solheim N ... 32 B2
Solheimsvik N ... 33 C3
Solignac F ... 67 C6
Solihull GB ... 27 C4
Solin HR ... 83 C5
Solingen D ... 50 B3
Solivella E ... 91 B4
Solkan SLO ... 72 C3
Söll A ... 72 A2
Sollana E ... 96 B2
Sollebrunn S ... 35 D4
Sollefteå S ... 115 D14
Sollenau A ... 64 C2
Sollen-tuna S ... 37 C4
Søller E ... 97 B2
Sollerön S ... 36 B1
Sollested DK ... 39 E4
Solliès-Pont F ... 79 C5
Sollihøgda N ... 34 C2
Solnechnogorsk RUS ... 7 C14
Solnice CZ ... 53 C6
Solofra I ... 103 C7
Solomiac F ... 77 C3
Solopaca I ... 103 B7
Solórzano E ... 89 A3
Solothurn CH ... 70 A2
Solre-le-Château F ... 49 C5
Solsona E ... 91 B4
Solsvik N ... 32 B1
Solt H ... 75 B4
Soltau D ... 44 C1
Soltszentimre H ... 75 B4
Soltvadkert H ... 75 B4
Solumsmoen N ... 34 C1
Solund N ... 32 A1
Solva GB ... 28 B2
Sölvesborg S ... 41 C4
Solymár H ... 65 C4
Soma TR ... 118 C2
Somain F ... 49 C4
Somberek H ... 74 B3
Sombernon F ... 69 A4
Sombor SRB ... 75 C4
Sombreffe B ... 49 C5
Someren NL ... 50 B1
Somero FIN ... 6 A7
Somersham GB ... 30 B3
Somerton GB ... 29 B5
Sominy PL ... 46 A3
Somma Lombardo I ... 70 C3
Sommariva del Bosco I ... 80 B1
Sommarøy N ... 112 C7
Sommarset N ... 112 E4
Sommatino I ... 109 B3
Sommeilles F ... 59 B5
Sommen S ... 37 D1
Sommepy-Tahure F ... 59 A5
Sömmerda D ... 52 B1
Sommerfeld D ... 45 C5
Sommersted DK ... 39 D2
Sommesous F ... 59 B5
Somme-Tourbe F ... 59 A5
Sommières F ... 78 C3
Sommières-du-Clain F ... 67 B5
Somo E ... 88 A3
Somogyfajsz H ... 74 B2
Somogyjád H ... 74 B2
Somogysámson H ... 74 B2
Somogysárd H ... 74 B2
Somogyszil H ... 74 B3
Somogyszob H ... 74 B2
Somogyvár H ... 74 B2
Sompolno PL ... 47 C4
Sompuis F ... 59 B5
Son N ... 35 C2
Son Bou E ... 97 B4
Soncoboz CH ... 70 A2
Soncillo E ... 88 B3
Soncino I ... 71 C4
Sóndalo I ... 71 B5
Søndeled N ... 33 D6
Sønder Bjert N ... 39 D2
Sønderborg DK ... 39 E2
Sønderby DK ... 39 E2
Sønder Felding DK ... 39 D1
Sønder Hygum DK ... 39 D1
Sønder Omme DK ... 39 D1
Sondershausen D ... 51 B6
Søndersø DK ... 39 D3
Søndervig DK ... 39 D1
Søndre Enningdal Kappel N ... 35 D3
Sóndrio I ... 71 B4
Soneja E ... 96 B2
Son en Breugel NL ... 49 B6
Songe N ... 33 D6
Songeons F ... 58 A2
Sonkamuotka FIN ... 113 D12
Sonkovo RUS ... 7 C14
Sönnarslöv S ... 41 D4
Sonneberg D ... 52 C1
Sonnefeld D ... 52 C1
Sonnewalde D ... 52 B3
Sonnino I ... 102 B6
Sonogno CH ... 70 B3
Sonsbeck D ... 50 B2
Sonseca E ... 94 C3
Son Servera E ... 97 B3
Sonstorp S ... 37 D2
Sonta SRB ... 75 C4
Sontheim D ... 61 B6
Sonthofen D ... 71 A5
Sontra D ... 51 B5
Sopelana E ... 89 A4
Sopje HR ... 74 C2
Sopot
  PL ... 47 A4
  SRB ... 85 B5
Sopotnica MK ... 116 A3
Sopron H ... 64 C2
Šor SRB ... 85 B4
Sora I ... 103 B6
Soragna I ... 81 B4
Söråker S ... 115 E14
Sorano I ... 81 D5
Sorbas E ... 101 B3
Sörbygden S ... 115 E13
Sordal N ... 33 D4
Sore F ... 76 B2
Sörenberg CH ... 70 B3
Soresina I ... 71 C4
Sörfjord N ... 112 D5
Sörfold N ... 112 E4
Sörfors S ... 115 E14

Sortino I ... 109 B4
Sortland N ... 112 D4
Sørum N ... 34 B2
Sørumsand N ... 34 C3
Sorunda S ... 37 C4
Sörup D ... 44 A1
Sørvågen N ... 112 E1
Sørvær N ... 113 B11
Sorvik S ... 36 B2
Sørvika N ... 114 E8
Sos F ... 76 B3
Sösdala S ... 41 C3
Sos del Rey Católico E ... 90 A1
Sošice HR ... 73 C5
Sośnica PL ... 46 B2
Sośnicowice PL ... 54 C2
Sośno PL ... 46 B3
Sosnovyy Bor RUS ... 7 B10
Sosnowiec PL ... 55 C4
Sospel F ... 80 B1
Sostanj SLO ... 73 B5
Sotaseter N ... 114 F4
Sotillo de Adrada E ... 94 B2
Sotillo de la Ribera E ... 88 C3
Sotin HR ... 75 C4
Sotkamo FIN ... 3 D28
Sotobañado y Priorato E ... 88 B2
Soto de la Marina E ... 88 A3
Soto del Barco E ... 86 A4
Soto de los Infantes E ... 86 A4
Soto de Real E ... 94 B3
Soto de Ribera E ... 88 A1
Sotoserrano E ... 93 A4
Soto y Amío E ... 88 B1
Sotresgudo E ... 88 B2
Sotrondío E ... 88 A1
Sotta F ... 102 B2
Sottomarina I ... 72 C2
Sottrum D ... 43 B6
Sottunga FIN ... 36 B7
Sotuelamos E ... 95 C4
Souain F ... 59 A5
Soual F ... 77 C5
Soucy F ... 59 B4
Souda GR ... 117 G6
Soudron F ... 59 B5
Souesmes F ... 68 A2
Soufflenheim F ... 60 B3
Souffli GR ... 116 A8
Souillac F ... 77 B4
Souilly F ... 59 A6
Soulac-sur-Mer F ... 66 C3
Soulaines-Dhuys F ... 59 B5
Soulatgé F ... 77 D5
Soultz-Haut-Rhin F ... 60 C3
Soultz-sous-Forêts F ... 60 B3
Soumagne B ... 50 C1
Soumoulou F ... 76 C2
Souppes-sur-Loing F ... 58 B3
Souprosse F ... 76 C2
Sourdeval F ... 57 B5
Soure P ... 92 A2
Sournia F ... 77 D5
Souro Pires P ... 87 D3
Sourpi GR ... 116 C4
Sours F ... 58 B2
Sousceyrac F ... 77 B5
Sousel P ... 92 C3
Soustons F ... 76 C1
Söğüt
  Bilecik TR ... 118 B5
  Burdur TR ... 119 E4
Soutelo de Montes E ... 86 B2
Southam GB ... 30 B2
Southampton GB ... 31 D2
Southborough GB ... 31 C4
South Brent GB ... 28 C4
South Cave GB ... 27 B5
Southend GB ... 24 C2
Southend-on-Sea GB ... 31 C4
South Hayling GB ... 31 D3
South Molton GB ... 28 B4
South Ockendon GB ... 31 C4
South Petherton GB ... 29 C5
Southport GB ... 26 B2
South Shields GB ... 25 D6
South Tawton GB ... 28 C4
Southwell GB ... 27 B5
South Woodham Ferrers GB ... 31 C4
Söğütlü TR ... 118 B5
Souto P ... 92 A3
Soutochao E ... 87 C3
Souto da Carpalhosa P ... 92 B2
Souvigny F ... 68 B3
Souzay-Champigny F ... 67 A4
Soverato I ... 106 C3
Soveria Mannelli I ... 106 B3
Sövestad S ... 41 D3
Sovetsk RUS ... 6 D6
Sovići BIH ... 84 C2
Sovicille I ... 81 C5
Søvik N ... 114 E3
Sowerby GB ... 27 A4
Soyaux F ... 67 C5
Sozopol BG ... 11 E9
Spa B ... 50 C1
Spadafora I ... 109 A4
Spaichingen D ... 61 B4
Spakenburg NL ... 49 A6
Spalding GB ... 30 B3
Spálené Poříčí CZ ... 63 A4
Spalt D ... 62 A1
Spangenberg D ... 51 B5
Spangereid N ... 33 D4
Spantekow D ... 45 B5
Sparanise I ... 103 B7
Sparbu N ... 114 D8
Sparkær DK ... 38 C2
Sparkford GB ... 29 B5
Sparreholm S ... 37 C3
Sparta = Sparti GR ... 117 E4
Spárti I ... 109 A4
Sparti = Sparta GR ... 117 E4
Spas-Demensk RUS ... 7 D13
Spean Bridge GB ... 24 B3
Speicher D ... 60 A2
Speichersdorf D ... 52 C1
Speke GB ... 26 B3
Spello I ... 82 D1
Spennymoor GB ... 25 D6
Spentrup DK ... 38 C3
Sperenberg D ... 52 A3
Sperlinga I ... 109 B3
Sperlonga I ... 103 B6
Spetalen N ... 35 C2
Spetses GR ... 117 E5
Speyer D ... 61 A4
Spézet F ... 56 B2
Spezzano Albanese I ... 106 B3
Spezzano della Sila I ... 106 B3
Spiddal IRL ... 20 A2
Spiegelau D ... 63 B4
Spiekeroog D ... 43 B4
Spiez CH ... 70 B2
Spigno Monferrato I ... 80 B2
Spijk NL ... 42 B3
Spijkenisse NL ... 49 B5
Spilamberto I ... 81 B5
Spili GR ... 117 G6
Spilimbergo I ... 72 B2
Spilsby GB ... 27 B6
Spinazzola I ... 104 C1
Spincourt F ... 60 A1
Spind N ... 33 D3
Spindleruv-Mlyn CZ ... 53 C5
Spinoso I ... 104 C1
Špišić Bukovica HR ... 74 C2
Spišská Belá SK ... 65 A6
Spišská Nová Ves SK ... 65 B6
Spisská Stará Ves SK ... 65 A6

Spišské-Hanušovce SK ... 65 A6
Spišské Podhradie SK ... 65 B6
Spišské Vlachy SK ... 65 B6
Spišský-Štvrtok SK ... 65 B6
Spital A ... 63 C5
Spital am Semmering A ... 63 C6
Spittal an der Drau A ... 72 B3
Spittle of Glenshee GB ... 25 B4
Spjald DK ... 39 C1
Spjærøy N ... 35 C2
Spjelkavik N ... 114 E3
Spjutsbygd S ... 41 C5
Split HR ... 83 C5
Splügen CH ... 71 B4
Spodsbjerg DK ... 39 E3
Spofforth GB ... 27 B4
Spohle D ... 43 B5
Spoleto I ... 82 D1
Spoltore I ... 103 A7
Spondigna I ... 71 B5
Sponvika N ... 35 C3
Spornitz D ... 44 B3
Sporotno I ... 80 B2
Spraitbach D ... 61 B5
Sprakensehl D ... 44 C2
Spręcowo PL ... 47 B6
Spremberg D ... 53 B4
Spresiano I ... 72 C2
Sprimont B ... 49 C6
Springe D ... 51 A5
Sproatley GB ... 27 B5
Spuz MNE ... 105 A5
Spychowo PL ... 47 B6
Spytkowice PL ... 55 D4
Squillace I ... 106 C3
Squinzano I ... 105 C4
Sračinec HR ... 73 B6
Srbac BIH ... 84 A2
Srbica KOS ... 85 D5
Srbobran SRB ... 75 C4
Srebrenica BIH ... 85 B4
Srebrenik BIH ... 84 B3
Sredets BG ... 11 E9
Središče SLO ... 73 B6
Srem PL ... 54 A2
Sremska Mitrovica SRB ... 85 B4
Sremski Karlovci SRB ... 75 C4
Srni CZ ... 63 A4
Srnice Gornje BIH ... 84 B3
Šrock PL ... 55 B4
Staatz A ... 64 B2
Stabbursnes N ... 113 B13
Staberdorf D ... 44 A3
Stabroek B ... 49 B5
Stachy CZ ... 63 A4
Stadarfell IS ... 111 B3
Stade D ... 43 B6
Staden B ... 49 C4
Stadl an der Mur A ... 72 A3
Stadskanaal NL ... 42 C3
Stadtallendorf D ... 51 C5
Stadthagen D ... 51 A5
Stadtilm D ... 52 C1
Stadtkyll D ... 50 C2
Stadtlauringen D ... 51 C6
Stadtlengsfeld D ... 51 C5
Stadtlohn D ... 50 B2
Stadtoldendorf D ... 51 B5
Stadtroda D ... 52 C1
Stadtsteinach D ... 52 C1
Stäfa CH ... 70 A3
Staffanstorp S ... 41 D3
Staffelstein D ... 51 C6
Staffin GB ... 22 D2
Stafford GB ... 26 C3
Stainach A ... 73 A4
Staindrop GB ... 27 A4
Staines-upon-Thames GB ... 31 C3
Stainville F ... 59 B6
Stainz A ... 73 B5
Staithes GB ... 27 A5
Staiti I ... 106 D3
Stäket S ... 37 C4
Stakroge DK ... 39 D1
Stalač SRB ... 85 C6
Stalden CH ... 70 B2
Stalham GB ... 30 B5
Stalheim N ... 32 B3
Stallarholmen S ... 37 C4
Ställberg S ... 36 C1
Ställdalen S ... 36 C1
Stallhofen A ... 73 A5
Stalon S ... 115 C12
Stalowa Wola PL ... 6 F7
Stamford GB ... 30 B3
Stamford Bridge GB ... 27 B5
Stamnes N ... 32 B2
Stams A ... 71 A5
Stamsried D ... 62 A3
Stamsund N ... 112 D3
Stanford le Hope GB ... 31 C4
Stånga S ... 37 E5
Stange N ... 34 B3
Stanghella I ... 72 C1
Stanhope GB ... 25 D5
Staniśić SRB ... 75 C4
Stanisławów PL ... 55 A6
Staňkov CZ ... 62 A4
Stankovci HR ... 83 C4
Stanley GB ... 25 D6
Stans CH ... 70 B3
Stansted Mountfitchet GB ... 31 C4
Stanzach A ... 71 A5
Stapar SRB ... 75 C4
Staphorst NL ... 42 C3
Staplehurst GB ... 31 C4
Stąporków PL ... 55 B5
Stara Baška HR ... 83 B3
Starachowice PL ... 55 B6
Stara Fužina SLO ... 72 B3
Stara Kamienica PL ... 53 C5
Stara Kiszewa PL ... 47 B4
Stará L'ubovňa SK ... 65 A6
Stara Moravica SRB ... 75 C4
Stara Novalja HR ... 83 B3
Stara Pazova SRB ... 85 B5
Stará Tura SK ... 64 B3
Staraya Russa RUS ... 7 C11
Stara Zagora BG ... 11 E8
Stärbsnäs S ... 36 C6
Starčevo SRB ... 85 B5
Staré Jablonki PL ... 47 B6
Stare Miasto PL ... 54 A3
Stare Pole PL ... 47 A5
Stare Strącze PL ... 53 B6
Stargard Szczeciński PL ... 45 B7
Stårheim N ... 114 F2
Stari Banovci SRB ... 85 B5
Stari Bar MNE ... 105 A5
Stari Gradac HR ... 74 C2
Starigrad-Paklenica
  Ličko-Senjska HR ... 83 B4
  Splitsko-Dalmatinska HR ... 83 B5
Stari Majdan BIH ... 83 B5
Stari-Mikanovci HR ... 74 C3
Stari Raušić KOS ... 85 D5
Staritsa RUS ... 7 C13
Starkenbach A ... 71 A5

Starnberg D ... 62 C2
Starodub RUS ... 7 E12
Starogard PL ... 46 A3
Starogard Gdański PL ... 47 B4
Starokonstantyniv UA ... 11 B9
Staro Petrovo Selo HR ... 74 C2
Staro Selo
  HR ... 73 C5
  SRB ... 85 B6
Stary Dzierzgoń PL ... 47 B5
Stary Hrozenkov CZ ... 64 B3
Stary Jaroslaw PL ... 46 A2
Stary Plzenec CZ ... 63 A4
Stary Sącz PL ... 65 A6
Stary Smokovec SK ... 65 A6
Staryy Chartoriysk UA ... 11 A8
Staškov SK ... 65 A4
Stassfurt D ... 52 B1
Staszów PL ... 55 C6
Stathelle N ... 35 C1
Staufen D ... 60 C3
Staunton GB ... 29 B5
Stavang N ... 32 A2
Stavanger N ... 33 D2
Stavåsnäs S ... 34 B4
Stavby S ... 36 B5
Staveley GB ... 27 B4
Stavelot B ... 50 C1
Stavenisse NL ... 49 B5
Stavern N ... 35 C2
Stavišče UA ... 11 B11
Stavne N ... 33 C5
Stavreviken S ... 115 E14
Stavros
  CY ... 120 A1
  GR ... 116 B5
Stavroupoli GR ... 116 A6
Stavseng N ... 32 A6
Stavsjø N ... 34 B2
Stavsnäs S ... 37 C5
Stavtrup DK ... 39 C3
Stawiski PL ... 6 E7
Stawiszyn PL ... 54 B3
Steane N ... 33 C5
Steblevë AL ... 116 A2
Štechelberg CH ... 70 B2
Štěchovice CZ ... 63 A5
Stechow D ... 44 C4
Steckborn CH ... 61 C4
Stede Broek NL ... 42 C2
Steeg A ... 71 A5
Steenbergen NL ... 49 B5
Steenvoorde F ... 48 C3
Steenwijk NL ... 42 C3
Stefaniná GR ... 116 B5
Steffeln D ... 50 C2
Steffisburg CH ... 70 B2
Štefanje HR ... 74 C1
Stegaurach D ... 62 A1
Stege DK ... 39 E5
Stegelitz D ... 45 B5
Stegersbach A ... 73 A6
Stegna PL ... 47 A5
Steimbke D ... 43 C6
Stein GB ... 22 D2
Steinach
  A ... 71 A6
  Baden-Württemberg D ... 61 B4
  Bayern D ... 51 C6
  Thüringen D ... 52 C1
Stein an Rhein CH ... 61 C4
Steinau
  Bayern D ... 51 C5
  Niedersachsen D ... 43 B5
Steinbeck D ... 44 B2
Steinberg am Rofan A ... 72 A1
Steindorf A ... 73 B4
Steine N ... 112 D3
Steinen D ... 60 C3
Steinfeld
  A ... 72 B3
  Bayern D ... 61 B6
  Nordrhein-Westfalen D ... 43 C5
Steinfurt D ... 50 A3
Steingaden D ... 62 C1
Steinhagen D ... 51 A4
Steinheid D ... 52 C1
Steinheim
  Bayern D ... 61 B6
  Nordrhein-Westfalen D ... 51 B5
Steinhöfel D ... 45 C6
Steinhorst D ... 44 C2
Steinigtwolmsdorf D ... 53 B4
Steinkjer N ... 114 C8
Steinsholt N ... 35 C1
Stekene B ... 49 B5
Stelle D ... 44 B2
Stellendam NL ... 49 B5
Stenasa S ... 41 C6
Stenay F ... 59 A6
Stenberga S ... 40 B5
Stendal D ... 44 C3
Stenhammar S ... 37 D5
Stengårdshult S ... 40 B3
Stenhamra S ... 37 C4
Stenhousemuir GB ... 25 B4
Stenlose DK ... 41 D2
Stensätra S ... 36 B3
Stensele S ... 115 B14
Stensjön S ... 40 B5
Stenstorp S ... 35 D5
Stenstrup DK ... 39 D3
Stenudden S ... 112 F6
Stenungsund S ... 38 A4
Štěpánov CZ ... 64 A3
Stephanskirchen D ... 62 C3
Stepnica PL ... 45 B6
Stepojevac SRB ... 85 B5
Stepping DK ... 39 D2
Sterbfritz D ... 51 C5
Sternberg D ... 44 B3
Šternberk CZ ... 64 A3
Sterup D ... 44 A1
Stes Maries-de-la-Mer F ... 78 C3
Stęszew PL ... 54 A1
Štěti CZ ... 53 C4
Stevenage GB ... 31 C3
Stevenston GB ... 24 C3
Stewarton GB ... 24 C3
Steyerburg D ... 43 C6
Steyning GB ... 31 D3
Steyr A ... 63 B5
Stężyca PL ... 47 A4
Stezzano I ... 71 C4
Stia I ... 81 C5
Stibb Cross GB ... 28 C3
Sticciano Scalo I ... 81 D5
Stidsvig S ... 41 C3
Stiens NL ... 42 B2
Stige DK ... 39 D3
Stigen S ... 35 D4
Stigliano I ... 104 C2
Stigtomta S ... 37 D3
Stilida GR ... 116 D4
Stillington GB ... 27 A4
Stilo I ... 106 C3
Stintino I ... 110 B1
Stio I ... 103 C8
Štip MK ... 116 A4
Stira GR ... 116 D6
Stirling GB ... 25 B4
Štítník SK ... 65 B6
Štíty CZ ... 54 C1
Stjärnhov S ... 37 C4
Stjärnsund S ... 36 B3
Stjørdalshalsen N ... 114 D8
St-Martin-Osmonville F ... 58 A2

Stocksbridge GB ... 27 B4
Stockton-on-Tees GB ... 27 A4
Stod CZ ... 63 A4
Stöde S ... 115 E13
Stodi N ... 112 F4
Stöðvarfjörður IS ... 111 C12
Stoer GB ... 22 C3
Stoholm DK ... 38 C2
Stoke Ferry GB ... 30 B4
Stoke Fleming GB ... 29 C4
Stoke Mandeville GB ... 31 C3
Stoke-on-Trent GB ... 26 B3
Stokesley GB ... 27 A4
Stokke N ... 35 C2
Stokkemarke DK ... 39 E4
Stokken N ... 33 D5
Stokkseyri IS ... 111 D4
Stokkvågen N ... 115 A10
Stokmarknes N ... 112 D3
Stoky CZ ... 63 A6
Stolac BIH ... 84 C2
Stølaholmen N ... 32 A3
Stolberg D ... 50 C2
Stolin BY ... 7 F9
Stollberg D ... 52 C2
Stöllet S ... 34 B5
Stollhamm D ... 43 B5
Stolno PL ... 47 B4
Stolpen D ... 53 B4
Stolzenau D ... 43 C6
Stompetoren NL ... 42 C1
Ston HR ... 84 D2
Stonařov CZ ... 63 A6
Stone GB ... 26 C3
Stonehaven GB ... 25 B5
Stonehouse GB ... 26 B3
Stongfjorden N ... 32 A2
Stonndalen N ... 32 A6
Stony Stratford GB ... 30 B3
Stopanja SRB ... 85 C6
Stopnica PL ... 55 C5
Storå S ... 37 C2
Storås N ... 114 D6
Storby FIN ... 36 B6
Storebø N ... 32 B2
Storebro S ... 40 B5
Store Damme DK ... 41 D2
Store Heddinge DK ... 41 D2
Store Herrestad S ... 41 D3
Store Levene S ... 35 D4
Store Molvik N ... 113 B16
Store Skedvi S ... 36 B2
Storelv N ... 113 B13
Storfjord N ... 112 C8
Storfjorden N ... 114 E2
Storfors S ... 35 C6
Storforshei N ... 115 A10
Storhøjliseter N ... 32 A6
Storjord N ... 112 F4
Storkow
  Brandenburg D ... 53 A3
  Mecklenburg-Vorpommern D ... 45 B6
Storli N ... 114 E6
Storlien S ... 114 D9
Stornara I ... 104 B1
Stornoway GB ... 22 C2
Storo I ... 71 C5
Storožynets UA ... 11 B8
Storrington GB ... 31 D3
Storseleby S ... 115 C13
Storsjön S ... 36 A3
Storslett N ... 112 C10
Storsteinnes N ... 112 C8
Storuman S ... 115 B14
Störvattnet S ... 115 E9
Storvik
  N ... 112 F2
  S ... 36 B3
Stouby DK ... 39 D2
Stourbridge GB ... 26 C3
Stourport-on-Severn GB ... 29 A5
Støvring DK ... 38 C2
Stow GB ... 25 C5
Stowbtsy BY ... 7 E9
Stowmarket GB ... 30 B5
Stow-on-the-Wold GB ... 29 B6
Strabane GB ... 19 B4
Strachan GB ... 25 B5
Strachur GB ... 24 B2
Strackholt D ... 43 B4
Stradbally IRL ... 21 B4
Stradella I ... 80 A3
Straelen D ... 50 B2
Stragari SRB ... 85 B5
Strakonice CZ ... 63 A4
Stralsund D ... 45 A5
Stranda N ... 114 E4
Strandby DK ... 38 B3
Strandebarm N ... 32 B3
Strandhill IRL ... 18 B3
Strandlykkja N ... 34 B3
Strandvik N ... 32 B2
Strangford GB ... 19 B6
Strängnäs S ... 37 C4
Strångsjö S ... 37 D3
Stráni CZ ... 64 B3
Stranice SLO ... 73 B5
Stranorlar IRL ... 19 B4
Stranraer GB ... 24 D2
Strasatti I ... 108 B1
Strasbourg F ... 60 B3
Strasburg D ... 45 B5
Strašice CZ ... 63 A4
Stråssa S ... 37 C2
Strassburg A ... 73 B4
Strass im Steiermark A ... 73 A5
Strasskirchen D ... 62 B3
Strasswalchen A ... 63 C4
Stratford-upon-Avon GB ... 29 A6
Strathaven GB ... 24 C3
Strathdon GB ... 23 D5
Strathkanaird GB ... 22 D3
Strathpeffer GB ... 23 D4
Strathy GB ... 23 C5
Strathyre GB ... 24 B3
Stratinska BIH ... 84 B2
Stratton GB ... 28 C3
Straubing D ... 62 B3
Straulas I ... 110 B2
Straume N ... 112 D5
Straumen
  Nordland N ... 112 E4
  Nord-Trøndelag N ... 114 C8
Straumsjøen N ... 112 D3
Straumsnes N ... 112 D4
Straupitz D ... 53 B4
Strausberg D ... 45 C5
Straußfurt D ... 51 B7
Strawczyn PL ... 55 C5
Straža
  SRB ... 85 B6
  SLO ... 73 C5
Stráž nad Nežárkou CZ ... 63 A5
Strážnice CZ ... 64 B3
Strážný CZ ... 63 B4
Strážské SK ... 11 B7
Štrba SK ... 65 A5
Štrbské Pleso SK ... 65 A5
Strečno SK ... 65 A4
Street GB ... 29 B5

Strehla D ... 52 B3
Strekov SK ... 65 C4
Strem A ... 73 A6
Stremska-Rača SRB ... 85 B4
Strengberg A ... 63 B5
Strengelvåg N ... 112 D4
Strengen
  A ... 71 A5
  N ... 33 C6
Streoci KOS ... 85 D5
Stresa I ... 70 C3
Streufdorf D ... 51 C6
Strib DK ... 39 D2
Striberg S ... 37 C1
Stříbro CZ ... 62 A3
Strichen GB ... 23 D6
Strigno I ... 71 B6
Strigova HR ... 73 B6
Strijen NL ... 49 B5
Strizivojna HR ... 74 C3
Strmica HR ... 83 B5
Strmilov CZ ... 63 A6
Strobl A ... 63 C4
Ströhen D ... 43 C5
Strokestown IRL ... 18 C3
Stromberg
  Nordrhein-Westfalen D ... 50 B4
  Rheinland-Pfalz D ... 60 A3
Stromeferry GB ... 22 D3
Stromness GB ... 23 C5
Strömsberg S ... 36 B4
Strömsbruk S ... 115 F14
Strömsfors S ... 37 D3
Strömsnäsbruk S ... 40 C4
Strömstad S ... 35 D3
Strömsund
  Jämtland S ... 115 D12
  Västerbotten S ... 115 B13
Stronachlachar GB ... 24 B3
Stróngoli I ... 107 B4
Stronie Śląskie PL ... 54 C1
Strontian GB ... 24 B2
Stroppiana I ... 70 C3
Stroud GB ... 29 B5
Stroumbi CY ... 120 B1
Stróża PL ... 65 A5
Strücklingen D ... 43 B4
Struer DK ... 38 C1
Struga MK ... 116 A2
Strugi Krasnyye RUS ... 7 B10
Strumica MK ... 116 A4
Strumien PL ... 65 A4
Struy GB ... 23 D4
Stružec HR ... 74 C1
Stryków PL ... 55 B4
Stryn N ... 114 F3
Stryy UA ... 11 B7
Strzałkowo PL ... 54 A2
Strzegocin PL ... 47 C6
Strzegom PL ... 54 C1
Strzegowo PL ... 47 C6
Strzelce Krajeńskie PL ... 46 C1
Strzelce Kurowo PL ... 46 C1
Strzelce Opolskie PL ... 54 C3
Strzelin PL ... 54 C2
Strzelno PL ... 47 C4
Strzepcz PL ... 47 A4
Strzybnica PL ... 54 C3
Strzygi PL ... 47 B5
Stubal SRB ... 85 C6
Stubbekøbing DK ... 39 E5
Stuben A ... 71 A5
Stubenberg A ... 73 A5
Stubline SRB ... 85 B5
Studená CZ ... 63 A6
Studenci HR ... 84 C1
Studenica SRB ... 85 C5
Studenka CZ ... 64 A4
Studenzen A ... 73 A5
Studienka SK ... 64 B3
Studland GB ... 29 C6
Studley GB ... 29 A6
Stugudal N ... 114 E8
Stugun S ... 115 D12
Stuhr D ... 43 B5
Stukenbrock D ... 51 B4
Stülpe D ... 52 A3
Stupava SK ... 64 B3
Stupnik HR ... 73 C5
Stupsk PL ... 47 B6
Sturkö S ... 41 C5
Sturminster Newton GB ... 29 C5
Sturno I ... 103 B8
Štúrovo SK ... 65 C4
Sturton GB ... 27 B5
Stuttgart D ... 61 B5
Stykkishólmur IS ... 111 B3
Styri S ... 36 C3
Styrsö S ... 38 B4
Suances E ... 88 A2
Subiaco I ... 102 B6
Subotica SRB ... 75 B4
Subotište SRB ... 85 B4
Sučany SK ... 65 A4
Suceava RO ... 11 C9
Sucha-Beskidzka PL ... 65 A5
Suchacz PL ... 47 A5
Suchań PL ... 46 B1
Suchdol nad Lužnice CZ ... 63 B5
Suchedniów PL ... 55 B5
Suchorze PL ... 46 A3
Suchteln D ... 50 B2
Sucina E ... 101 B5
Suckow D ... 44 B3
Sućuraj HR ... 84 C2
Súðavík IS ... 111 A3
Sudbury GB ... 30 B4
Suddesjaur S ... 115 B16
Süderlügum D ... 39 E1
Sudomeřice u Bechyně CZ ... 63 A5
Sudovec HR ... 73 B6
Suðureyri IS ... 111 A2
Sudzha RUS ... 7 F13
Sueca E ... 96 B2
Suelli I ... 110 C2
Sugères F ... 68 C3
Sugny B ... 59 A5
Suhl D ... 51 C6
Suhlendorf D ... 44 C2
Suhopolje HR ... 74 C2
Suho Polje BIH ... 85 B4
Şuhut TR ... 119 D5
Suica BIH ... 84 C2
Suippes F ... 59 A5
Sukošan HR ... 83 B4
Sükösd H ... 75 B3
Suków PL ... 55 C5
Suldalsosen N ... 33 C3
Suldrup DK ... 38 C2
Sulechów PL ... 53 A5
Sulęcin PL ... 45 C7
Sulęczyno PL ... 46 A3
Sulejów PL ... 55 B4
Sulejówek PL ... 55 A6
Sülfeld D ... 44 B2
Sulgen CH ... 71 A4
Sulików PL ... 53 B5
Sulina RO ... 11 D10
Sulingen D ... 43 C5
Suliszewo PL ... 46 B1
Sulitjelma N ... 112 E5
Süller TR ... 119 D4
Sully-sur-Loire F ... 58 C3
Sulmierzyce
  Łódzkie PL ... 55 B4
  Wielkopolskie PL ... 54 B2
Sulmona I ... 103 A6
Süloğlu TR ... 118 A1
Sułów PL ... 54 B2
Sułoszowa PL ... 55 C4

Column 1

Sulów PL 54 B2
Sulsdorf D 44 A3
Sultandağı TR 119 D6
Sülüklü TR 118 D7
Suluova TR 16 A7
Sulvik S 35 C4
Sülysáp H 75 A4
Sülz D 61 B4
Sulzbach
  Baden-Württemberg
  D 61 A5
  Baden-Württemberg
  D 61 B5
  Bayern D 61 A5
  Saarland D 60 A3
Sulzbach-Rosenberg
  D 62 A2
Sülze D 44 C2
Sulzfeld D 51 C6
Sumartin HR 84 C1
Sumburgh GB 22 B7
Šumeg H 74 B2
Sumiswald CH 70 A2
Šumná CZ 64 B1
Šumperk CZ 54 D1
Šumvald CZ 64 A3
Sumy UA 7 F13
Sunbilla E 76 C1
Sünching D 62 B3
Sund
  FIN 36 B7
  S 35 C3
Sundborn S 36 B2
Sundby DK 38 C1
Sunde bru N 33 D6
Sunde bru N 33 D6
Sunderland GB 25 D6
Sundern D 50 B4
Sundhultsbrunn S . . .40 B4
Sundnäs S 115 A14
Sundö DK 39 C2
Sundsfjord N 112 F3
Sundsvall S 115 E14
Sungurlu TR 16 A7
Suni I 110 B1
Sunja HR 74 C1
Sunnansjö S 36 B1
Sunnaryd S 40 B3
Sunndalsøra N 114 E5
Sunne S 34 C5
Sunnemo S 34 C5
Sunnersberg S 35 D5
Suolovuopmio N . . .113 C12
Suomussalmi FIN . . .3 D28
Suoyarvi RUS 3 E30
Super Sauze F 79 B5
Supetar HR 83 C5
Supetarska Draga HR .83 B3
Supino I 102 B6
Šuplja Stijena MNE . .84 C4
Surahammar S 37 C3
Šurany SK 64 B4
Surazh
  BY 7 D11
  RUS 7 E12
Surbo I 105 C4
Surčin SRB 85 B5
Surgères F 66 B4
Surhuisterveen NL . .42 B3
Súria E 91 B4
Surin F 67 B5
Surka N 34 B2
Surnadalsøra N 114 E5
Sursee CH 70 A3
Surte S 38 B5
Surwold D 43 C4
Sury-le-Comtal F 69 C4
Susa I 70 C2
Šušara SRB 85 B6
Susch CH 71 B5
Susegana I 72 C2
Süsel D 44 A2
Sušice CZ 63 A4
Sušnjevica HR 73 C4
Sussen D 61 B5
Susurluk TR 118 C3
Susz PL 47 B5
Sütçüler TR 119 E5
Sutivan HR 83 C5
Sutjeska SRB 75 C5
Sutomore MNE 105 A5
Sutri I 102 A5
Sutton GB 31 C3
Sutton Coldfield GB . .27 C4
Sutton-in-Ashfield
  GB 27 B4
Sutton-on-Sea GB . .27 B6
Sutton-on-Trent GB . .27 B5
Sutton Scotney GB . .31 C2
Sutton Valence GB . .31 C4
Suvaja BIH 83 B5
Suvereto I 81 C4
Suvorov RUS 7 D14
Suwałki PL 6 D7
Suze-la-Rousse F . . .78 B3
Suzzara I 81 B4
Svabensverk S 36 A2
Svalbard IS 111 A10
Svalöv S 41 D3
Svanabyn S 115 C13
Svanberga S 36 C5
Svaneke DK 41 D5
Svanesund S 35 D3
Svängsta S 41 C4
Svannäs S 115 A15
Svanskog S 35 C4
Svanstein S 113 F12
Svappavaara S 112 E10
Svärdsjö S 36 B2
Svarstad N 35 C1
Svärta S 37 C4
Svarta S 34 C5
Svärtinge S 37 D3
Svartnäs S 36 B3
Svartnes N 112 E4
Svarttjärn S 115 B13
Svatsum S 34 A1
Svätý Jur SK 64 B3
Svätý Peter SK 64 C4
Svedala S 41 D3
Sveg S 115 E11
Sveindal N 33 D4
Sveio N 33 C2
Svejbæk DK 39 C2
Svelgen N 114 F2
Svelvik N 35 C2
Svendborg DK 39 D3
Svene N 32 C6
Svenljunga S 40 B3
Svennevad S 37 C2
Svenstavik S 115 E11
Svenstrup DK 38 C2
Švermov CZ 53 C4
Světlá nad Sázavou
  CZ 63 A6
Svetlyy RUS 47 A6
Švetvinčenat HR 82 A2
Švica HR 83 B4
Svidník SK 10 B6
Svihov CZ 63 A4
Svilajnac SRB 85 B6
Svilengrad BG 11 F9
Svindal N 35 C3
Svinhult S 40 B5
Svinna SK 64 B4
Svinninge
  DK 39 D4
  S 37 C5
Sviritsa RUS 7 A12
Svislach BY 6 E8
Svit SK 65 A6
Svitavy CZ 64 A2
Svitlovodsk UA 11 B12
Svodin SK 65 C4
Svolvær N 112 D3

Column 2

Svortemyr N 32 A2
Svortland N 32 C2
Svratka CZ 64 A2
Svrcinovec SK 65 A4
Svullrya N 34 B4
Svyetlahorsk BY 7 E10
Swadlincote GB 27 C4
Swaffham GB 30 B4
Swanage GB 29 C6
Swanley GB 31 C4
Swanlinbar IRL 19 B4
Swansea GB 28 B4
Swarzędz PL 46 C3
Swatragh GB 19 B5
Świątki PL 47 B6
Świdnica
  Dolnośląskie PL . .54 C1
  Lubuskie PL 53 B5
Świdnik PL 11 A7
Świdwin PL 46 B1
Świebodzice PL 53 C6
Świebodzin PL 53 A5
Świecie PL 47 B4
Świedziebnia PL 47 B5
Świerki PL 54 C1
Świerzawa PL 53 B5
Świerzno PL 45 B6
Świeta PL 45 B6
Święta Anna PL 55 C4
Świętno PL 53 A6
Swiftterbant NL 42 C2
Swindon GB 29 B6
Swineshead GB 30 B3
Swinford IRL 18 C3
Świnoujście PL 45 B6
Swinton GB 25 C5
Swobnica PL 45 B6
Swords IRL 21 A5
Swornegacie PL 46 B3
Sya S 37 D2
Syasstroy RUS 7 A12
Sycewice PL 46 A2
Sychevka RUS 7 D13
Syców PL 54 B2
Sycowice PL 53 A5
Sydnes N 33 C2
Syfteland N 32 B2
Syke D 43 C5
Sykkylven N 114 E3
Sylling N 34 C2
Sylte N 114 E4
Symbister GB 22 A7
Symington GB 25 C4
Symonds Yat GB 29 B5
Sypniewo
  Kujawsko-Pomorskie
  PL 46 B3
  Wielkopolskie PL . .46 B2
Syserum S 40 B6
Sysslebäck S 34 B4
Syväjärvi FIN 113 E14
Szabadbattyán H 74 A3
Szabadegyháza H . . .74 A3
Szabadszállás H 75 B4
Szadek PL 54 B3
Szajol H 75 A5
Szakály H 74 B3
Szakcs H 74 B3
Szakmár H 75 B4
Szalánta H 74 C3
Szालonna H 65 B6
Szamocin PL 46 B3
Szamotuły PL 46 C2
Szany H 74 A2
Szarvas H 75 B5
Szászvár H 74 B3
Százhalombatta H . . .74 A3
Szczawa PL 65 A6
Szczawnica PL 65 A6
Szczawno-Zdrój PL . .53 C6
Szczecin PL 45 B6
Szczecinek PL 46 B2
Szczekociny PL 55 C4
Szczerców PL 55 C6
Szczucin PL 55 C6
Szczuczarz PL 46 B2
Szczurowa PL 55 C5
Szczyrk PL 65 A5
Szczytna PL 54 C1
Szczytno PL 6 E6
Szécsény H 65 B5
Szederkény H 74 C3
Szedres H 74 B3
Szeged H 75 B5
Szeghalom H 75 A6
Szegvár H 75 B5
Székesfehérvár H . . .74 A3
Székkutas H 75 B5
Szekszárd H 74 B3
Szemplino Czarne PL .47 B6
Szemud PL 47 A4
Szendehely H 65 C5
Szendrő H 65 B6
Szentendre H 65 C5
Szentes H 75 B5
Szentgotthárd H 73 B6
Szentlászló H 74 B2
Szentlőrinc H 74 B2
Szentmártonkáta H . .75 A4
Szenyér H 74 B2
Szerencs H 10 C6
Szerep H 75 A6
Szigetszentmiklós H . .75 A4
Szigetvár H 74 B2
Szikáncs H 75 B5
Szikszó H 65 B6
Szil H 74 A2
Szilvásvárad H 65 B6
Szklarska Poreba PL . .53 C5
Szlichtyngowa PL . . .53 B6
Szob H 65 C4
Szolnok H 75 A5
Szombathely H 74 A1
Szorosad H 74 B3
Szprotawa PL 53 B5
Szreńsk PL 47 B6
Sztum PL 47 B5
Sztutowo PL 47 A5
Szubin PL 46 B3
Szücsi H 65 C5
Szulmierz PL 47 C6
Szulok H 74 B2
Szumanie PL 47 C5
Szwecja PL 46 B2
Szydłów
  Łódzkie PL 55 B4
  Świętokrzyskie PL . .55 C6
Szydłowiec PL 55 B5
Szydłowo PL 46 B2
Szydłowo PL 47 C6
Szymankowo PL 47 A5
Szymbark PL 65 A6
Szynkielów PL 54 B3
Szynwałd PL 55 D6

Column 3 — T

Taastrup DK 41 D2
Tab H 74 B3
Tabanera la Luenga E .88 B1
Tabaqueros E 96 B1
Tábara E 88 C1
Tabenera de Cerrato
  E 88 B2
Taberg S 40 B4
Tabernas E 101 B3
Taberno E 101 B4
Tábiano Bagni I 81 B4
Taboada E 86 B3
Taboadela E 87 B3
Tábor CZ 63 A5
Táborfalva H 75 A4
Tábua P 92 A2
Tabuaco P 87 C3
Tabuenca E 89 C5
Tabuyo del Monte E . .87 B4

Column 4

Tâby S 37 C5
Tác H 74 A3
Tachov CZ 62 A3
Tadcaster GB 27 B4
Tadley GB 31 C2
Tafalla E 89 B5
Taganheira P 98 B2
Tågarp S 41 D2
Tággia I 80 C1
Tagliacozzo I 102 A6
Táglio di Po I 82 A1
Tagnon F 59 A5
Tahal E 101 B3
Tahitótfalu H 65 C5
Tahtaköprü TR 118 C4
Tailfingen D 61 B5
Taillis F 57 B4
Tain GB 23 D4
Tain-l'Hermitage F . . .78 A3
Taipadas P 92 C2
Taivalkoski FIN 3 D28
Takene S 35 C5
Takovo SRB 85 B5
Taksony H 75 A4
Tal E 86 B2
Talachyn BY 7 D10
Talamello I 82 C1
Talamone I 102 A4
Talant F 69 A4
Talarrubias E 93 B5
Talaván E 93 B4
Talavera de la Reina
  E 94 C2
Talavera la Real E . . .93 C4
Talayuela E 93 B5
Talayuelas E 96 B1
Talgarth GB 29 B4
Talgje N 33 C2
Talhadas P 92 A2
Táliga E 93 C3
Talizat F 78 A2
Tálknafjörður IS 111 B2
Talla I 81 C5
Talladale GB 22 D3
Tallaght IRL 21 A5
Tallard F 79 B5
Tällberg S 36 B1
Tallinn EST 6 B8
Talloires F 69 C6
Tallow IRL 21 B4
Tallsjö S 115 C15
Talmay F 69 A5
Talmont-St Hilaire F . .66 B3
Talmont-sur-Gironde
  F 66 C4
Talne UA 11 B11
Talsano I 104 C3
Talsi LV 6 C7
Talvik N 113 B11
Tal-Y-Llyn GB 26 C2
Tamajón E 95 B3
Tamame E 88 C1
Tamames E 93 A4
Tamarit de Mar E . . .91 B4
Tamarite de Litera E . .90 B3
Tamariu E 91 B6
Tamási H 74 B3
Tambach-Dietharz D . .51 C6
Tameza E 86 A4
Tammisaari FIN 6 A7
Tampere FIN 3 F25
Tamsweg A 72 A3
Tamurejo E 94 D2
Tamworth GB 27 C4
Tana bru N 113 B17
Tañabueyes E 89 B3
Tanakajd H 74 A1
Tananger N 33 D2
Tananuella I 110 B2
Tánaset N 34 A3
Tåndsjöborg S 115 F11
Tånga S 41 C2
Tangelic H 74 B3
Tangen N 34 B3
Tangerhütte D 44 C3
Tangermünde D 44 C3
Tanhua FIN 113 E16
Taninges F 69 B6
Tankavaara FIN 113 D16
Tann D 51 C6
Tanna D 52 C1
Tannadice GB 25 B5
Tännäker S 40 C3
Tännäs S 115 E9
Tannay
  Ardennes F 59 A5
  Nièvre F 68 A3
Tannenbergsthal D . .52 C2
Tännesberg D 62 A3
Tannheim A 71 A5
Tanowo PL 45 B6
Tanum S 35 D3
Tanumshede S 35 D3
Tanus F 77 B5
Tanvald CZ 53 C5
Taormina I 109 B4
Tapa EST 7 B8
Tapfheim D 62 B1
Tapia de Casariego E .86 A4
Tapio F 77 C4
Tápióbicske H 75 A4
Tápiógyörgye H 75 A4
Tápióság H 75 A4
Tápiószecső H 75 A4
Tápiószele H 75 A4
Tápiószentmárton H . .75 A4
Tapolca H 74 B2
Tapolcafő H 74 A2
Tar HR 72 C3
Tarabo S 40 B2
Taradell E 91 B5
Taraklı TR 118 B5
Taranco E 89 B3
Táranto I 104 C3
Tarare F 69 C4
Tarascon F 78 C3
Tarascon-sur-Ariège
  F 77 D4
Tarashcha UA 11 B11
Tarazona E 89 C5
Tarazona de la Mancha
  E 95 C5
Tarbena E 96 C2
Tarbert
  GB 24 C2
  IRL 20 B2
Tarbes F 76 C3
Tarbet GB 24 B3
Tarbolton GB 24 C3
Tarcento I 72 B3
Tarčin BIH 84 C3
Tarczyn PL 55 B5
Tardajos E 88 B3
Tardelcuende E 89 C4
Tardets-Sorholus F . .76 C2
Tardienta E 90 B2
Tärendö S 113 E11
Targon F 76 B2
Tárgoviste BG 11 E9
Târgoviste
  RO 11 D8
Targovishte BG 11 E9
Târgu-Jiu RO 11 D7
Târgu Mures RO 11 C8
Târgu Ocna RO 11 C9
Târgu Secuiesc RO . .11 D9
Tarifa E 99 C5
Tariquejas E 98 B3
Tarján H 65 C4
Tárkány H 64 C4
Tarland GB 23 D6
Tarłów PL 55 B6
Tarm DK 39 D1
Tarmstedt D 43 B6
Tärnaby S 115 B12
Tarnalelesz H 65 B6
Tarnaörs H 65 C6
Târnăveni RO 11 C8
Tårnet N 113 C19
Tarnobrzeg PL 55 C6

Column 5

Tarnos F 76 C1
Tarnów
  Lubuskie PL 45 C6
  Małopolskie PL . . .55 C5
Tarnów Podgórne
  PL 46 C2
Tarnowskie Góry PL . .54 C3
Tärnsjö S 36 B3
Tärnvik N 112 E4
Tarouca P 87 C3
Tarp D 43 A6
Tarquinia I 102 A4
Tarquinia Lido I 102 A4
Tarragona E 91 B4
Tàrrega E 91 B4
Tarpan AL 105 C6
Tarpa E 89 B4
Tarracina I 102 B6
Terrak N 115 B9
Terralba I 110 C1
Terranova di Pollino
  I 106 B3
Terranova di Sibari I .106 B3
Terras do Bouro P . . .87 C2
Terrasini I 108 A2
Terrassa E 91 B5
Terrazos-Lavilledieu
  F 77 A4
Terriente E 95 B5
Terrugem P 92 C3
Tertenia I 110 C2
Teruel E 90 C1
Tervola FIN 3 C26
Tervuren B 49 C5
Terzaga E 95 B5
Tešanj BIH 84 B2
Tešáske-Mlyňany SK . .65 B4
Teslić BIH 84 B2
Tessin D 44 A4
Tessy-sur-Vire F 57 B4
Tét H 74 A2
Tetbury GB 29 B5
Teterchen F 60 A2
Teterow D 45 B4
Teteven BG 11 E8
Tetiyev UA 11 B10
Tetovo MK 10 E6
Tettau D 52 C1
Tettnang D 61 C5
Teublitz D 62 A3
Teuchern D 52 B2
Teulada
  E 96 C3
  I 110 D1
Teupitz D 52 A3
Teurajärvi S 113 F11
Teutschenthal D 52 B1
Tevel H 74 B3
Tevioyhead GB 25 C5
Tewkesbury GB 29 B5
Thale D 51 B6
Thalfang D 60 A2
Thalgau A 63 C4
Thalkirch CH 71 B4
Thalmässing D 62 A2
Thalwil CH 70 A3
Thann F 60 C3
Thannhausen D 61 B6
Thaon-les-Vosges F . .60 B2
Tharandt D 52 C3
Tharsis E 99 B3
Thasos GR 116 B6
Thatcham GB 31 C2
Thaxted GB 31 C4
Thayngen CH 61 C4
Theale GB 31 C2
The Barony GB 23 B5
Thebes = Thiva GR . .117 D5
Theding-hausen D . . .43 C6
Theessen D 52 A1
The Hague = 's-
  Gravenhage NL . . .49 A5
Themar D 51 C6
Thénezay F 67 B4
Thenon F 67 C6
Therouanne F 48 C3
Thessaloniki = Salonica
  GR 116 B4
Thetford GB 30 B4
Theth AL 105 A5
Theux B 50 C1
Thézar-les-Corbières
  F 78 C1
Thèze F 76 C2
Thiberville F 58 A1
Thibie F 59 B5
Thiéblemont-Farémont
  F 59 B5
Thiendorf D 53 B3
Thiene I 71 C6
Thierrens CH 70 B1
Thiers F 68 C3
Thiesi I 110 B1
Thiessow D 45 A5
Thiezac F 77 B5
Þingeyri IS 111 B2
Þingvellir IS 111 C4
Thionville F 60 A2
Thira GR 117 F7
Thiron-Gardais F 58 B1
Thirsk GB 27 A4
Thisted DK 38 C1
Thiva = Thebes GR . .117 D5
Thivars F 58 B2
Thiviers F 67 C5
Thizy F 69 B4
Tholen NL 49 B5
Tholey D 60 A3
Thomas Street IRL . . .20 A3
Thomastown IRL 21 B4
Þónes F 69 C6
Thonnance-les-Joinville
  F 59 B6
Thonon-les-Bains F . .69 B6
Thorame-Basse F . . .79 B5
Thorame-Haute F . . .79 B5
Thorens-Glières F . . .69 C6
Thorigny-sur-Oreuse
  F 59 B4
Þórl A 111 A7
Þorlákshöfn IS 111 D4
Thornaby on Tees GB .27 A4
Thornbury GB 29 B5
Thorne GB 27 B5
Thornhill
  Dumfries & Galloway
  GB 25 C4
  Stirling GB 24 B3
Thornthwaite GB 26 A2
Thornton-le-Dale GB . .27 A5
Þórshöfn IS 111 A10
Thouarcé F 67 A4
Thouars F 67 B4
Thrapston GB 30 B3
Threlkeld GB 26 A2
Thrumster GB 23 C5
Thueyts F 78 B3
Thuin B 49 C5
Thuir F 91 A5
Thumau D 52 C1
Thun CH 70 B2
Thuret F 68 C3
Thurey F 69 B5
Thüringen A 71 A4
Thürkow D 45 B4
Thurles IRL 21 B4
Thurmaston GB 30 B2
Thurø By DK 39 D3
Thursby GB 26 A2
Thurso GB 23 C5
Thury-Harcourt F 57 B5
Thusis CH 71 B4
Þykkvibær IS 111 D5
Thyregod DK 39 D2
Tibi E 96 C2
Tibro S 35 D6
Tidaholm S 35 D5
Tidan S 35 D6

Column 6

Terme di Súio I 103 B6
Terme di Valdieri I . . .79 B6
Termens E 90 B3
Termes F 78 B2
Términi Imerese I . . .108 B2
Terminillo I 102 A5
Térmoli I 103 B8
Termonfeckin IRL 19 C5
Ternberg A 63 C5
Terndrup DK 38 C3
Terneuzen NL 49 B4
Terni I 102 A5
Ternitz A 64 C2
Ternopil UA 11 B8
Terpan AL 105 C6
Terpni GR 116 B5
Terracina I 102 B6
Terrak N 115 B9
Terralba I 110 C1
Tersley S 35 C4

Column 7 — Tidersrum

Tidersrum S 40 B5
Tiedra E 88 C1
Tiefenbach D 62 A3
Tiefencastel CH 71 B4
Tiefenort D 51 C6
Tiefensee D 45 C5
Tiel NL 49 B6
Tielmes E 95 B3
Tielt B 49 C4
Tienen B 49 C5
Tiengen D 61 C4
Tiénot P 57 C7
Tierga E 89 C5
Tiermas E 90 A1
Tierp S 36 B4
Tierrantona E 90 A3
Tighina MD 11 C10
Tighnabruaich GB . . .24 C2
Tignes F 70 C1
Tigy F 58 C3
Tihany H 74 B2
Tijnje NL 42 B2
Tijola E 101 B3
Tikhvin RUS 7 B12
Tilburg NL 49 B6
Til Châtel F 69 A5
Tillac F 76 C3
Tillberga S 37 C3
Tille F 58 A3
Tillicoultry GB 25 B4
Tilloy Bellay F 59 A5
Tilly-sur-Seulles F . . .57 A5
Tim DK 39 C1
Timahoe IRL 21 B4
Timau I 72 B3
Timbaki GR 117 G6
Timboon AUS . . . . . . — —
Timi CY 120 B1
Timişoara RO 75 C6
Timmele S 40 B3
Timmendorfer Strand
  D 44 B2
Timmernabben S 40 C6
Timmersdala S 35 D5
Timoleague IRL 20 C3
Timolin IRL 21 B5
Timrå S 115 E14
Timsfors S 40 C3
Timsgearraidh GB . . .22 C1
Tinajas E 95 B4
Tinalhas P 92 B3
Tinchebray F 57 B5
Tincques F 48 C3
Tineo E 86 A4
Tinglev DK 39 E2
Tingsryd S 40 C5
Tingstäde S 37 E5
Tingvoll N 114 E5
Tinlot B 49 C6
Tinnoset N 33 C6
Tinos GR 117 E7
Tintagel GB 28 C3
Tinténiac F 57 B4
Tintern GB 29 B5
Tintigny B 60 A1
Tione di Trento I 71 B5
Tipperary IRL 20 B3
Tiptree GB 31 C4
Tirana = Tiranë AL . .105 B5
Tiranë = Tirana AL . .105 B5
Tirano I 71 B5
Tiraspol MD 11 C10
Tire TR 119 D2
Tires I 71 B6
Tiriez E 95 C4
Tîrig E 90 C3
Tiriolo I 106 C3
Tirnavos GR 116 C4
Tírrénia I 81 C4
Tirschenreuth D 62 A3
Tirstrup DK 39 C3
Tirteafuera E 94 D2
Tisno HR 83 C4
Tišňov CZ 64 A2
Tisovec SK 65 B5
Tistedal N 35 C3
Tistrup DK 39 D1
Tisvildeleje DK 39 C5
Tiszabúj P 75 B4
Tiszaadorogma H . . .65 C6
Tiszafed I 75 C6
Tiszaföldvár H 75 B5
Tiszafüred H 65 C6
Tiszajenő H 75 B5
Tiszakécske H 75 B5
Tiszakürt H 75 B5
Tiszanána H 75 A5
Tiszaörs H 75 A5
Tiszaroff H 75 A5
Tiszasüly H 75 A5
Tiszasziget H 75 B5
Tiszaszőlős H 75 A5
Titaguas E 96 B1
Titel SRB 75 C5
Titisee-Neustadt D . .61 B4
Tito I 104 C1
Titova Korenica HR . .83 B4
Titran N 114 D5
Tittling D 63 B4
Tittmoning D 62 B3
Tiurajärvi FIN 113 E13
Tived S 37 D1
Tiverton GB 29 C4
Tivisa E 90 B3
Tívoli I 102 B5
Tjällmo S 37 D2
Tjåmotis S 112 F9
Tjäreborg DK 39 D1
Tjautjas S 112 E9
Tjøme N 35 C2
Tjong N 112 F2
Tjonnefoss N 33 D5
Tjörn S 112 C4
Tjörnarp S 41 D3
Tjøtta N 115 B9
Tkon HR 83 C4
Tleń PL 47 B4
Tlmače SK 65 B4
Tluchowo PL 47 C5
Tlumačov CZ 64 A3
Tóalmás H 75 A4
Toano I 81 B4
Toba D 51 B7
Tobarra E 101 A4
Tobelbad A 73 A5
Tobermore GB 19 B5
Tobermory GB 24 B1
Toberonochy GB 24 B2
Tobha Mor GB 22 D1
Tobo S 36 B4
Tocane-St Apre F 67 C5
Tocha P 92 A2
Tocina E 99 B5
Töcksfors S 35 C3
Tocón E 100 B2
Todal N 114 E5
Todi I 102 A5
Todmorden GB 26 B3
Todorici BIH 84 B2
Todtmoos D 61 C4
Toén E 87 B3
Tofta
  Gotland S 37 E5
  Skaraborg S 35 D5
Toftbyn S 36 B2
Tofte N 35 C2
Töftedal S 35 D3
Tofterup DK 39 D1
Toftlund DK 39 D2
Tohmo FIN 3 F16
Tohmajärvi FIN 113 F16
Tokarnia PL 55 C5
Tokary PL 54 B3
Tököl H 75 A3
Tolastadh bho Thuath
  GB 22 C2
Toledo E 94 C2

Column 8

Tolentino I 82 C2
Tolfa I 102 A4
Tolg S 40 B4
Tolga N 114 E8
Tolkmicko PL 47 A5
Tolko PL 47 A6
Tollarp S 41 D3
Tølløse DK 39 D4
Tolmachevo RUS 7 B10
Tolmezzo I 72 B3
Tolmin SLO 72 B3
Tolna H 74 B3
Tolnanémedi H 74 B3
Tolob GB 22 B7
Tolosa
  E 89 A4
  P 92 B3
Tolox E 100 C1
Tolpuddle GB 29 C5
Tolva E 90 A3
Tolve I 104 C2
Tomar P 92 B2
Tomarza TR 16 B7
Tomašević SRB 75 C5
Tomašica BIH 83 B5
Tomášikovo SK 64 B3
Tomašouri P 87 D2
Tomášouka BY 6 F7
Tomaszów Mazowiecki
  PL 55 B5
Tomatin GB 23 D5
Tombeboeuf F 77 B3
Tomdoun GB 22 D3
Tomelilla S 41 D3
Tomellosa E 95 B4
Tomelloso E 95 C4
Tomiño E 87 C2
Tomintoul GB 23 D5
Tomislavgrad BIH . . .84 C2
Tomisław PL 53 B5
Tomisławice PL 47 C4
Tomnavoulin GB 23 D5
Tompa H 75 B4
Tompaládony H 74 A1
Tomra N 114 E3
Tomter N 35 C2
Tona E 91 B5
Tonara I 110 B2
Tonbridge GB 31 C4
Tondela P 92 A2
Tønder DK 39 E1
Tongeren B 49 C6
Tongue GB 23 C4
Tönisvorst D 50 B2
Tønjum N 32 A4
Tonkopuro FIN 113 F17
Tonnay-Boutonne F . .67 C4
Tonnay-Charente F . .66 C4
Tonneins F 77 B3
Tonnerre F 59 C4
Tönning D 43 A5
Tonsåsen S 32 B6
Tønsberg N 35 C2
Tonstad N 33 D3
Toomyvara IRL 20 B3
Toormore IRL 20 C2
Topares E 101 B3
Topas E 94 A1
Topała RO 11 C8
Topli Dol SRB 11 E7
Toplița RO 11 C8
Topola SRB 85 B5
Topolčani MK 116 A3
Topol'čany SK 64 B4
Topol'čianky SK 65 B4
Topolje HR 73 C6
Topólka PL 47 C4
Topol'niky SK 64 C3
Toporów PL 53 A5
Topsham GB 29 C4
Topusko HR 73 C5
Toqué S 36 B3
Torá E 91 B4
Toral de los Guzmanes
  E 88 B1
Toral de los Vados E .86 B4
Torås N 114 E3
Torbalı TR 119 D2
Torbjörntorp S 35 D5
Torbole I 71 C5
Torchiarolo I 105 C4
Torcross GB 29 C4
Torcy-le-Petit F 58 A2
Torda SRB 75 C5
Tørdal N 33 D5
Tordehumos E 88 C1
Tordera E 91 B5
Tordesillas E 88 C1
Tordesilos E 95 B5
Töre S 3 D25
Töreboda S 35 D6
Toreby DK 39 E4
Torekov S 41 C2
Torella dei Lombardi
  I 103 C8
Torelló E 91 A5
Toreno E 86 B4
Torfou F 66 A3
Torgau D 52 B3
Torgelow D 45 B6
Torgueda P 87 C3
Torhamn S 41 C5
Torhout B 49 B4
Torigni-sur-Vire F . . .57 A5
Torija E 95 B3
Toril E 95 B5
Torino = Turin I 80 A1
Toritto I 104 C2
Torkovichi RUS 7 B11
Tormánen FIN 113 C16
Tormestorp S 41 C3
Tórmini I 71 C5
Tornada P 92 B1
Tornal'a SK 65 B6
Tornavacas E 93 A5
Tornby DK 38 B2
Tornesch D 43 B6
Torness GB 22 D4
Torniella I 81 C5
Torninparte I 103 A6
Tórning DK 39 C2
Tornió FIN 3 D25
Tornjoš SRB 75 C4
Tornos E 90 C1
Toro E 88 C1
Törökszentmiklós H . .75 A5
Toropets RUS 7 C11
Torpa S 40 B2
Torpè I 110 B2
Torphins GB 23 D6
Torpo N 32 B5
Torpoint GB 28 C3
Torpsbruk S 40 C4
Torquay GB 29 C4
Torquemada E 88 B2
Torralba de Calatrava
  E 94 C3
Torrão P 98 A2
Torre Annunziata I . .103 C7
Torre Beretti I 80 A3
Torreblanca E 90 C3
Torreblascopedro E . .100 A2
Torrecaballeros E . . .94 B2
Torrecampo E 100 A1
Torre Cannone I 104 C3
Torre Cardela E 100 B2
Torrecilla E 95 B4
Torrecilla de la Jara
  E 94 C2
Torrecilla de la Orden
  E 94 A1
Torrecilla del Pinar E .88 C2
Torrecilla en Cameros
  E 89 B4
Torrecillas de la Tiesa
  E 93 B5
Torre das Vargens P . .92 B3
Torre de Coelheiros
  P 92 C3

Column 9

Torre de Dom Chama
  P 87 C3
Torre de Juan Abad
  E 100 A2
Torre de la Higuera E .99 B4
Torre del Bierzo E . . .86 B4
Torre del Burgo E . . .95 B3
Torre del Campo E . .100 B2
Torre del Greco I . . .103 C7
Torre del Lago Puccini
  I 81 C4
Torre dell'Orso I . . .105 C4
Torre del Mar E 100 C1
Torredembarra E 91 B4
Torre de Miguel Sesmero
  E 93 C4
Torre de Moncorvo P .87 C3
Torre de Santa Maria
  E 93 B4
Torredonjimeno E . . .100 B2
Torre do Terranho P . .87 D3
Torre Faro I 109 A4
Torregrosa E 90 B3
Torreira P 87 D2
Torrejón de Ardoz E . .95 B3
Torrejón de la Calzada
  E 94 B3
Torrejón del Rey E . . .95 B3
Torrejón el Rubio E . .93 B4
Torrelaguna E 95 B3
Torrelapaja E 89 C5
Torre la Ribera E 90 A3
Torrelavega E 88 A2
Torrelobatón E 88 C1
Torrelodones E 94 B3
Torre los Negros E . .90 C1
Torremaggiore I 103 B8
Torremanzanas E . . .96 C2
Torremayor E 93 C4
Torremezzo di Falconara
  I 106 B3
Torremocha E 93 B4
Torremolinos E 100 C1
Torrenieri I 81 C5
Torrenostra E 90 C3
Torrenova I 102 B5
Torreorgaz E 93 B4
Torre Orsáia I 106 A2
Torre-Pacheco E . . .101 B5
Torre Péllice I 79 B6
Torreperogil E 100 A2
Torres E 100 B2
Torresandino E 88 C3
Torre Santa Susanna
  I 105 C3
Torres-Cabrera E . . .100 B1
Torres de la Alameda
  E 95 B3
Torres Novas P 92 B2
Torres Vedras P 92 B1
Torrevieja E 96 C2
Torricella I 104 C3
Torri del Benaco I . . .71 C5
Torridon GB 22 D3
Torriglia I 80 B3
Torrijas E 96 A2
Torrijo E 90 C1
Torrijos E 94 C2
Tørring DK 39 D2
Torrita di Siena I 81 C5
Torroal P 92 C2
Torroella de Montgrì
  E 91 A6
Torrox E 100 C2
Torrskog S 35 C4
Torsåker S 36 B3
Torsang S 36 B2
Torsås S 41 C6
Torsby S 34 B4
Torsetra N 34 B2
Torshälla S 37 C3
Tórshavn FO 2 E10
Torslanda S 38 B4
Torsminde DK 39 C1
Torsnes N 32 B3
Törtel H 75 A4
Tórtoles E 94 B1
Tórtoles de Esgueva
  E 88 C2
Tortol I 110 C2
Tortona I 80 B3
Tórtora I 106 B2
Tortoreto Lido I 103 A7
Tortorici I 109 A3
Tortosa E 90 C3
Tortosendo P 92 A3
Tortuera E 95 B5
Tortuero E 95 B3
Torup S 40 C3
Tor Vaiánica I 102 B5
Torver GB 26 A2
Tørvikbygde N 32 B3
Torviscón E 100 C2
Torvizcón E 100 C2
Torzhok RUS 7 C13
Torzym PL 53 A5
Tosbotn N 115 B10
Toscolano-Maderno I .71 C5
Tosno RUS 7 B11
Tossa de Mar E 91 B5
Tossåsen S 115 E10

Column 10

. . . . .87 C3
Torre . . . .
P 87 C3
E 100 A2
E 93 C4
. . . . .92 B3
E 93 C4
E 95 B3
E 94 B3
E 89 A4
P 92 B3
Torredonjimeno E . . .100 B2
E 94 A1
Ciudad Real E . . .100 A2
Granada E 100 C2
. . . . .93 B4
P 87 C3
E 95 B3
E 93 B4
E 95 B3
E 88 A2
E 88 A2
E 88 C1
E 94 B3
E 90 C1
. . . . .106 B3
. . . . .93 B4
. . . . .100 C1
I 103 B8
E 96 C2
E 93 C4
. . . . .106 B3
. . . . .93 B4
. . . . .81 C5
. . . . .90 C3
. . . . .102 B5
. . . . .93 B4
. . . . .106 A2
. . . . .101 B5
. . . . .79 B6
. . . . .100 A2
. . . . .100 B2
. . . . .105 C3
E 88 C3
. . . . .100 B1
. . . . .95 B3
P 92 B2
P 92 B1
E 96 C2
. . . . .104 C3
. . . . .71 C5
. . . . .22 D3
. . . . .80 B3
E 96 A2
E 90 C1
E 94 C2
. . . . .39 D2
. . . . .81 C5
P 92 C2
E 91 A6
E 100 C2
S 35 C4
S 36 B3
S 36 B2
S 41 C6
S 34 B4
S 34 B2
S 37 C3
FO 2 E10
S 38 B4
DK 39 C1
N 32 B3
H 75 A4
E 94 B1
E 88 C2
I 110 C2
I 80 B3
I 106 B2
I 103 A7
I 109 A3
E 90 C3
P 92 A3
E 95 B5
E 95 B3
S 40 C3
I 102 B5
GB 26 A2
N 32 B3
E 100 C2
RUS 7 C13
PL 53 A5
N 115 B10
I 71 C5
RUS 7 B11
E 91 B5
S 115 E10
Tosse F 76 C1
Tösse S 35 D4
Tostedt D 43 B6
Tosya TR 16 A7
Tószeg H 75 A5
Tószentmárton H 74 B2
Totana E 101 B4
Töteborn N 33 D4
Tôtes F 58 A2
Tótkomlós H 75 B5
Totland N 114 F2
Tøtlandsvik N 33 C3
Totnes GB 29 C4
Tótszerdahely H 74 B1
Tøttdal N 114 C8
Totton GB 31 D2
Touça P 87 C3
Toucy F 59 C4
Toueffreville F 58 A1
Toul F 60 B1
Toulon F 79 C4
Toulon-sur-Allier F . . .68 B3
Toulon-sur-Arroux F . .69 B4
Toulouse F 77 C4
Tourcoing F 49 C4
Tour de la Parata F . .102 B1
Tourlaville F 57 A4
Tournai B 49 C4
Tournan-en-Brie F . . .58 B3
Tournay F 76 C3
Tournon-d'Agenais F . .77 B3
Tournon-St Martin F . .67 B5
Tournus F 69 B4
Touro
  E 86 B2
  P 87 C3
Tourouvre F 58 B1
Tourriers F 67 C5
Tours F 67 A5
Tourteron F 59 A5
Tourves F 79 C4
Toury F 58 B2
Touvedo P 87 C2
Touvois F 66 B3
Toužim CZ 52 C2
Tovačov CZ 64 A3
Tovariševo SRB 75 C4
Tovarnik HR 75 C4
Tovdal N 33 D5
Töverud S 35 C4
Towcester GB 30 B3
Town Yetholm GB . . .25 C5

Tråastølen N....32 B4
Trabada E....86 A3
Trabadelo E....86 B4
Trabanca E....87 C4
Trabazos E....87 C4
Traben-Trarbach D....50 D3
Trabia I....108 B2
Tradate I....70 C3
Trädet S....40 B3
Trafaria P....92 C1
Tragacete E....95 B5
Tragwein A....63 B5
Traiguera E....90 C3
Trainel F....59 B4
Traisen A....63 B6
Traismauer A....64 B1
Traitsching D....62 A3
Trákhonas CY....120 A2
Tralee IRL....20 B2
Tramacastilla de Tena
E....76 D2
Tramagal P....92 B2
Tramariglio I....110 B1
Tramatza I....110 B1
Tramelan CH....70 A2
Tramonti di Sopra I....72 B2
Tramore IRL....21 B4
Trampot F....60 B1
Trillo E....95 B4
Tranås S....40 A1
Tranbjerg DK....39 C3
Tranby N....34 C2
Trancoso P....87 D3
Tranebjerg DK....39 D3
Tranekær DK....39 E3
Tranemo S....40 B3
Tranent GB....25 C5
Tranevåg N....33 D3
Trängslet S....34 A5
Tranhult S....40 B3
Trani I....104 B2
Trans-en-Provence F....79 C5
Transtrand S....34 A5
Tranum DK....38 B2
Tranvik S....37 C5
Trápani I....108 A1
Trappes F....58 B3
Traryd S....40 C3
Trasacco I....103 B6
Trasierra E....99 A4
Träslövsläge S....40 B2
Trasmiras E....87 C3
Traspinedo E....88 C2
Trate SLO....73 B5
Trauchgau D....62 C1
Traun A....63 B5
Traunreut D....62 C3
Traunstein D....62 C3
Traunwalchen D....62 C3
Trávad S....35 D5
Travemünde D....44 B2
Traversétolo I....81 B4
Travnik
 BIH....84 B2
 SLO....73 C4
Travo
 F....102 B2
 I....80 B3
Trawsfynydd GB....26 C2
Trbovlje SLO....73 B5
Trbušani SRB....85 C5
Treban F....68 B3
Třebařov CZ....64 A2
Trebatsch D....53 A4
Trebbin D....52 A3
Trebechovice pod
 Orebem CZ....53 C5
Trebel D....44 C3
Třebenice CZ....53 C3
Trébeurden F....56 B2
Třebíč CZ....64 A1
Trebinje BIH....84 D3
Trebisacce I....106 B3
Trebitz D....52 B2
Třeboň CZ....63 A5
Třebovice CZ....64 A2
Trebsen D....52 B2
Trebujena E....99 C4
Trecastagni I....109 B4
Trecate I....70 C3
Trecenta I....81 A5
Tredegar GB....29 B4
Tredózio I....81 B5
Treffen A....72 B3
Treffort F....69 B5
Treffurt D....51 B6
Trefnant GB....26 B2
Tregaron GB....28 A4
Trégastel-Plage F....56 B2
Tregnago I....71 C6
Tregony GB....28 C3
Tréguier F....56 B2
Trégunc F....56 C2
Treharris GB....29 B4
Trehörningsjö S....115 D15
Treia
 I....82 C2
 D....51 A6
Treignac F....68 C1
Treignat F....68 B1
Treignes B....49 C5
Treis-Karden D....50 C3
Trekanten S....40 C6
Trélazé F....67 A4
Trelech GB....28 B3
Trélissac F....67 C5
Trelleborg S....41 D3
Trélon F....49 C4
Trélou-sur-Marne F....59 A4
Tremblay-le-Vicomte
 F....58 B2
Tremés P....92 B2
Tremezzo I....71 C4
Třemošná CZ....63 A4
Tremp E....90 A3
Trenčianska Stankovce
 SK....64 B3
Trenčianska Turná
 SK....64 B3
Trenčianske Teplá
 SK....64 B3
Trenčianske Teplice
 SK....64 B3
Trenčín SK....64 B4
Trendelburg D....51 B5
Trengereid N....32 B2
Trensacq F....76 B2
Trent D....45 A5
Trento I....71 B6
Treorchy GB....29 B4
Trepča KOS....85 D5
Trept F....69 C5
Trepuzzi I....105 C4
Trescore Balneário I....71 C4
Tresenda I....71 B5
Tresfjord N....114 E4
Tresigallo I....81 B5
Trešnjevica SRB....85 C6
Tresnurághes I....110 B1
Trespaderne E....89 B3
Třešt CZ....63 A6
Trestina I....82 C1
Tretower GB....29 B4
Trets F....79 C4
Tretten N....34 A2
Treuchtlingen D....62 B1
Treuen D....52 C2
Treuenbrietzen D....52 A2
Treungen N....33 C5
Trevelez E....100 C2
Trevi I....82 D1
Treviana E....89 B3
Treviglio I....71 C4
Trevignano Romano
 I....102 A5
Trevi nel Lázio I....102 B6
Treviso I....72 C2
Trévoux F....69 C4
Treysa D....51 C5
Trézelles F....68 B3

Trezzo sull'Adda I....71 C4
Trhová Kamenice CZ....64 A1
Trhové Sviny CZ....63 B5
Triacastela E....86 B3
Triaize F....66 B3
Trianda GR....119 F3
Tribanj Krušćica HR....83 B4
Triberg D....61 B4
Tribsees D....45 A4
Tříblice SLO....73 C5
Tricárico I....104 C2
Tricase I....107 B5
Tricésimo I....72 B3
Trieben A....73 A4
Triebes D....52 C2
Triepkendorf D....45 B5
Trier D....60 A2
Trieste I....72 C3
Trie-sur-Baïse F....77 C3
Triggiano I....104 B2
Triglitz D....44 B4
Trignac F....66 A2
Trigueros E....99 B4
Trigueros del Valle E....88 C2
Trikala GR....116 C3
Trikeri GR....116 C5
Trikomo CY....120 A2
Trilj HR....83 C5
Trillo E....95 B4
Trilport F....59 B3
Trim IRL....21 A5
Trimdon GB....25 D6
Trindade
 Beja P....98 B3
 Bragança P....87 C3
Třinec CZ....65 A4
Trinità d'Agultu I....110 B1
Trinitápoli I....104 B2
Trino I....70 C3
Trinta P....92 A3
Triora I....80 C1
Tripoli GR....117 E4
Triponzo I....82 D1
Triptis D....52 C1
Trieste E....90 A2
Trittau D....44 B2
Trivento I....103 B7
Trivero I....70 C3
Trivigno I....104 C1
Trn BIH....84 B2
Trnava
 HR....74 C3
 SK....64 B3
Trnovec SK....64 B3
Trnovo BIH....84 C3
Trnovska vas SLO....73 B5
Troarn F....57 A5
Trochtelfingen D....61 B5
Tródje S....36 B4
Troense DK....39 D3
Trofa P....87 C2
Trofaiach A....73 A5
Trofors N....115 B10
Trogir HR....83 C5
Trøgstad N....35 C3
Tróia I....103 B8
Troia I....92 C2
Troina I....109 B3
Troisdorf D....50 C3
Trois-Ponts B....50 C1
Troisvierges L....50 C2
Trojane SLO....73 B4
Trojanów PL....55 B6
Troldhede DK....39 D1
Trollhättan S....35 D4
Trolog BIH....84 C1
Tromello I....70 C3
Tromøy N....33 D5
Tromsø N....112 C8
Trondheim N....114 D7
Tronget F....68 B3
Trönninge S....40 C2
Trönningeby S....40 B2
Trönö S....36 A3
Tronzano-Vercellese
 I....70 C3
Troon GB....24 C3
Tropea I....106 C2
Tropojë AL....105 A5
Tropy Sztumskie PL....47 B5
Trosa S....37 D4
Trösken S....36 B3
Trossingen D....61 B4
Trostberg D....62 B3
Trostyanets UA....7 F13
Trouville-sur-Mer F....57 A6
Trowbridge GB....29 B5
Troyes F....59 B5
Trpanj HR....84 C2
Trpezi MNE....85 D5
Trpinja HR....74 C3
Tršće HR....73 C4
Tršice SK....64 A3
Trstená SK....65 A5
Trstenci BIH....84 A2
Trstenik
 KOS....85 D5
 SRB....85 C6
Trsteno HR....84 D2
Trstin SK....64 B3
Trubchevsk RUS....7 E12
Trubia E....88 A1
Trubjela MNE....84 D3
Truchas E....87 B4
Trujillanos E....93 C4
Trujillo E....93 B5
Trumieje PL....47 B5
Trun
 CH....70 B3
 F....57 B6
Truro GB....28 C2
Trusetal D....51 C6
Truskavets' UA....11 B7
Trustrup DK....39 C3
Trutnov CZ....53 C5
Tryserum S....37 D3
Trysil N....34 A4
Tryszczyn PL....46 B3
Trzcianka PL....46 B2
Trzciel PL....46 C1
Trzcińsko Zdrój PL....45 A7
Trzebiatów PL....45 A7
Trzebiel PL....53 B4
Trzebielino PL....46 A3
Trzebień PL....53 B5
Trzebień PL....55 C4
Trzebnica PL....54 B2
Trzebnice PL....53 B6
Trzeciewiec PL....46 B3
Trzemeszno PL....46 C3
Trzemeszno-Lubuskie
 PL....46 C1
Trzetrzewina PL....65 A6
Tržič SLO....73 B4
Tsamandas GR....116 C2
Tschagguns A....71 A4
Tschernitz D....53 B4
Tsebrykove UA....11 C11
Tsvetkovo UA....7 E8
Tua P....87 C3
Tuam IRL....20 A3
Tubbercurry IRL....18 B3
Tubbergen NL....42 C3
Tubilla del Lago E....89 C3
Tubize B....49 C5
Tučapy CZ....63 A5
Tučepi HR....84 C2
Tüchen D....44 B4
Tuchan F....78 D1
Tüchern D....52 B1
Tuchola PL....46 B3
Tuchomie PL....46 A3
Tuchów PL....65 A6

Tuczno PL....46 B2
Tuddal N....32 C5
Tudela E....89 B5
Tudela de Duero E....88 C2
Tudweiliog GB....26 C1
Tuejar E....96 B1
Tuffé F....58 B1
Tufsingdalen N....114 E8
Tuhaň CZ....53 C4
Tui E....87 B2
Tukums LV....6 C7
Tula
 RUS....7 D14
 I....110 B1
Tulcea RO....11 D10
Tul'chyn UA....11 B10
Tulette F....78 B3
Tuliszków PL....54 A3
Tulla IRL....20 B3
Tullamore IRL....21 A4
Tulle F....69 C5
Tullins F....69 C5
Tulln A....64 B2
Tullow IRL....21 B5
Tułowice PL....54 C2
Tulppio FIN....113 E18
Tulsk IRL....18 C3
Tumba S....37 C4
Tummel Bridge GB....24 B3
Tun S....35 D4
Tuna
 Kalmar S....40 B6
 Uppsala S....36 B5
Tuna Hästberg S....36 B2
Tunçbilek TR....118 C4
Tunes P....98 B2
Tungelsta S....37 C5
Tunje AL....105 C6
Tunnerstad S....40 A4
Tunnhovd N....32 B5
Tunstall GB....30 B5
Tuohikotti FIN....3 F27
Tuoro sul Trasimeno
 I....82 C1
Tupadly PL....47 C4
Tupanari BIH....84 B3
Tupik RUS....7 D12
Tuplice PL....53 B4
Tura H....65 C5
Turany SK....65 A5
Turbe BIH....84 B2
Turbenthal CH....70 A3
Turcia E....88 B1
Turčianske Teplice
 SK....65 B4
Turcifal P....92 B1
Turckheim F....60 B3
Turda RO....11 C7
Turégano E....94 A3
Turek PL....54 A3
Turgutlu TR....119 D2
Turgutreis TR....119 E2
Turi I....104 C3
Turin = Torino I....80 A1
Türje H....74 B2
Turka UA....11 B7
Türkeve H....75 A5
Türkheim D....75 B5
Türkmenli TR....118 C1
Turku FIN....6 A7
Turleque E....94 C3
Turňa nad Bodvou SK....65 B6
Turnberry GB....24 C3
Turnhout B....49 B5
Türnitz A....63 C6
Turnov CZ....53 C5
Turnu RO....75 B6
Turnu Măgurele RO....11 E8
Turón E....100 C2
Turoszów PL....53 C4
Turowo PL....47 B6
Turquel P....92 B1
Turri I....110 C1
Turries F....79 B5
Turriff GB....23 D6
Tursi I....104 C2
Turtmann CH....70 B2
Turtola FIN....113 F12
Turza PL....54 B2
Turzovka SK....65 A4
Tusa I....109 B3
Tuscánia I....102 A4
Tuse DK....39 D4
Tušilovic HR....73 C5
Tuszyn PL....55 B4
Tutow D....45 B5
Tutrakan BG....11 E9
Tuttlingen D....61 C4
Tutzing D....62 C2
Tuzi MNE....105 A5
Tuzla
 BIH....84 B3
 TR....16 B7
Tuzlukçu TR....119 D6
Tvååker S....40 B2
Tvärålund S....115 C16
Tvärskog S....40 C6
Tvedestrand N....33 D5
Tveit
 Hordaland N....32 B4
 Rogaland N....33 C3
Tver RUS....7 C13
Tverrelvmo N....112 D8
Tversted DK....38 B3
Tvørøyri FO....4 A3
Tvrdošin SK....65 A5
Tvrdošovce SK....64 B4
Twardogóra PL....54 B2
Twatt GB....23 B5
Twello NL....50 A2
Twimberg A....73 B4
Twist D....43 C4
Twistringen D....43 C5
Tworóg PL....54 C3
Twyford
 Hampshire GB....31 C2
 Wokingham GB....31 C3
Tyachiv UA....11 B7
Tychówka PL....46 B2
Tychowo PL....46 B2
Tychy PL....54 C3
Tydal N....114 D8
Týec nad Labem CZ....53 C5
Tyfors S....34 B6
Tygelsjö S....41 D2
Tylldal N....114 E7
Tylstrup DK....38 B2
Tymbark PL....65 A6
Tymowa PL....65 A6
Tyndrum GB....24 B3
Týec nad Sázavou
 CZ....63 A5
Tynemouth GB....25 C6
Tyngsjö S....34 B5
Týn nad Vltavou CZ....63 A5
Tynset N....114 E7
Tyresö S....37 C5
Tyringe S....41 C3
Tyristrand N....34 B2
Tyrislöt S....37 D3
Tysnes N....32 B2
Tysse N....32 B2
Tyssebotnn N....32 B2
Tyssedal N....32 B3
Tystberga S....37 D4
Tysvær N....33 C2
Tywyn GB....26 C1
Tzermiádo GR....117 G7
Tzummarum NL....42 B2

U
Ub SRB....85 B5
Úbby DK....39 D4
Úbeda E....100 A2
Überlingen D....61 C5

Ubidea E....89 A4
Ubli
 HR....84 D1
 MNE....105 A5
Ubrique E....99 C5
Ucero E....89 C3
Uchaud F....78 C3
Uchte D....43 C5
Uckerath D....50 C3
Uckfield GB....31 D4
Ucklum S....38 A4
Uclés E....95 C4
Ucria I....109 A3
Udbina HR....83 B4
Udbyhøj DK....38 C3
Uddebo S....40 B3
Uddeholm S....34 B5
Uddevalla S....35 D3
Uddheden S....34 C4
Uden NL....49 B6
Uder D....51 B6
Údiča SK....64 A4
Udine I....72 B3
Udvar H....74 C3
Ueckermünde D....45 B6
Uelsen D....42 C2
Uelzen D....44 C2
Uetendorf CH....70 B2
Uetersen D....43 B6
Uetze D....44 C2
Uffculme GB....29 C4
Uffenheim D....61 A6
Ugarana E....89 A4
Ugento I....107 B5
Ugerløse DK....39 D4
Uggdorf DK....38 B3
Uggerslev DK....39 D3
Uggiano la Chiesa I....107 A5
Ugíjar E....100 C2
Ugine F....69 C6
Uglejevik BIH....84 B4
Uglenes N....32 B2
Ugljane HR....84 C1
Ugod H....74 A2
Uherské Hradiště CZ....64 A3
Uherský Brod CZ....64 A3
Uherský Ostroh CZ....64 B3
Uhingen D....61 B5
Uhlířské-Janovice
 CZ....63 A6
Uhřiněves CZ....53 C4
Uhyst D....53 B4
Uig GB....22 D2
Uitgeest NL....42 C1
Uithoorn NL....49 A5
Uithuizen NL....42 B3
Uithuizermeeden NL....42 B3
Uivar RO....75 C5
Ujazd
 Łódzkie PL....55 B4
 Opolskie PL....54 C3
Ujezd u Brna CZ....64 A2
Ujhartyán H....75 A4
Újkígyós H....75 B6
Ujpetre H....74 C3
Ujście PL....46 B2
Ujsolt H....75 B4
Újszász H....75 A5
Ujué E....89 B5
Ukanc SLO....72 B3
Ukmergė LT....6 D8
Ukna S....40 A6
Ula TR....119 E3
Ul'anka SK....65 B5
Ulaş TR....118 A2
Ulássai I....110 C2
Ulbjerg DK....38 C2
Ulbster GB....23 C5
Ulceby GB....27 B5
Ulcinj MNE....105 B5
Uldum DK....39 D2
Ulefoss N....33 C6
Uleila del Campo E....101 B3
Ulëz AL....105 B5
Ulfborg DK....39 C1
Uljma SRB....85 B6
Ulm D....61 B5
Ulme P....92 B2
Ulmen D....50 C2
Ulog BIH....84 C3
Ulricehamn S....40 B3
Ulrichstein D....51 C5
Ulrika S....37 D2
Ulriksfors S....115 D12
Ulrum NL....42 B3
Ulsberg N....114 E6
Ulsta GB....22 A7
Ulsted DK....38 B3
Ulstein N....114 E2
Ulstrup
 Vestsjællands Amt.
  DK....39 D3
 Viborg Amt. DK....38 C2
Ulsvåg N....112 D4
Ulubey TR....119 D4
Uluborlu TR....119 D5
Ulukışla TR....16 C7
Ulverston GB....26 A2
Ulvik N....32 B3
Umag HR....72 C2
Uman UA....11 B11
Umba RUS....3 C31
Umbertide I....82 C1
Umbriático I....107 B3
Umčari SRB....85 B5
Umeå S....3 E24
Umgransele S....115 C15
Umhausen A....71 A5
Umka SRB....85 B5
Umljanovic HR....83 C5
Ummendorf D....61 B5
Ummerstadt D....51 C6
Umnäs S....115 B13
Umurbey TR....118 B1
Unaðsdalur IS....111 A3
Unapool GB....22 C3
Unari FIN....113 E14
Uncastillo E....90 A1
Undenäs S....37 D1
Undersaker S....115 D10
Undredal N....32 B4
Unecha RUS....7 E12
Unešić HR....83 C5
Úněšov CZ....62 A4
Ungheni MD....11 C9
Unhais da Serra P....92 A3
Unhošt CZ....53 C3
Unichowo PL....46 A3
Unidad PL....54 C3
Uničov CZ....64 A3
Uniejów PL....54 A3
Unisław PL....47 B4
Unkel D....50 C3
Unken A....62 C3
Unna D....50 B3
Unnaryd S....40 C3
Unterach A....63 C4
Unteraegeri CH....70 A3
Unterammergau D....62 C2
Unterhaching D....62 B2
Unteriberg CH....70 A3
Unterkochen D....61 B6
Unter-Langkampen A....72 A2
Unterlaussa A....63 C5
Untermünkheim D....61 A5
Unterschächen CH....70 B3
Unterschleißheim D....62 B2
Unterschwaningen D....62 A1
Untersiemau D....51 C6
Unter-steinbach D....61 A6
Unterweissenbach A....63 B5

Unterzell D....62 A3
Upavon GB....29 B6
Úpice CZ....53 C6
Upiłka PL....46 B3
Uplengen D....43 B4
Uppingham GB....30 B3
Upplands-Väsby S....37 C4
Uppsala S....36 B4
Uppsjøhytta N....34 A1
Upton-upon-Severn
 GB....29 A5
Ur F....91 A4
Ura e Shtrenjtē AL....105 B5
Uras I....110 C1
Ura-Vajgurorë AL....105 C5
Uraz PL....54 B1
Urbánia I....82 C1
Urbino I....82 C1
Urçay F....68 B2
Urda E....94 C3
Urdax E....76 C1
Urdilde E....86 B2
Urdos F....76 D2
Urk NL....42 C2
Úrkút H....74 A2
Urla TR....119 D1
Urlingford IRL....21 B4
Urnäsch CH....71 A4
Uroševac KOS....10 E6
Uroševici BIH....84 D2
Urraccal E....101 B3
Urries E....90 A1
Urroz E....76 D1
Ursensollen D....62 A2
Urshult S....40 C4
Uršna Sela SLO....73 C5
Urszulewo PL....47 C5
Ury F....58 B3
Urziceni RO....11 D9
Urzulei I....110 B2
Usagre E....93 C4
Uşak TR....118 A4
Ušče SRB....85 C5
Usedom D....45 B5
Useldange L....60 A1
Usellus I....110 C1
Ushakovo RUS....47 A6
Usingen D....51 C4
Usini I....110 B1
Usk GB....29 B5
Úskedal N....32 C2
Üsküdar TR....118 A4
Uslar D....51 B5
Úsov CZ....64 A3
Usquert NL....42 B3
Ussássai I....110 C2
Ussé F....67 A5
Usséglio I....70 C2
Ussel
 Cantal F....78 A1
 Corrèze F....68 C2
Usson-du-Poitou F....67 B5
Usson-en-Forez F....68 C3
Usson-les-Bains F....77 D5
Ustaoset N....32 B5
Ustaritz F....76 C1
Uštěk CZ....53 C4
Úster CH....70 A3
Ústi CZ....64 A3
Ustibar BIH....85 C4
Ustikolina BIH....84 C3
Ústí nad Labem CZ....53 C4
Ústí nad Orlicí CZ....64 A2
Ustiprača BIH....84 C4
Ustka PL....46 A2
Ust Luga RUS....7 B10
Ustroné Morskie PL....46 A1
Ustyuzhna RUS....7 B14
Uszód H....74 B3
Utåker N....32 C2
Utansjö S....115 E14
Utebo E....90 B2
Utena LT....7 D8
Utery CZ....62 A3
Uthaug N....114 D6
Utiel E....96 B1
Utne N....32 B3
Utö S....37 D5
Utrecht NL....49 A6
Utrera E....99 B5
Utrillas E....90 C2
Utsjoki FIN....113 C16
Utstein kloster N....33 C2
Uttendorf A....72 A2
Uttenweiler D....61 B5
Utterslev DK....39 E4
Uttoxeter GB....27 C4
Utvålinge S....41 C2
Utvorda N....114 C7
Uusikaarlepyy FIN....3 E25
Uusikaupunki FIN....3 F21
Uvac BIH....85 C4
Uvaly CZ....53 C4
Uvdal N....32 B5
Uza F....76 B1
Uzdin SRB....75 C5
Uzdowo PL....47 B6
Uzel F....56 B3
Uzerche F....68 C1
Uzès F....78 B3
Uzhhorod UA....11 B7
Uzhok UA....11 B7
Užice SRB....85 C4
Uznach CH....70 A3
Üzümlü
 Konya TR....119 E6
 Muğla TR....119 F4
Uzunköprü TR....118 A1

V
Vaalajärvi FIN....113 E15
Vaas F....58 C1
Vaasa FIN....3 E24
Vabre F....77 C5
Vác H....65 C5
Vacha D....51 C6
Vachartyán H....65 C5
Väckelsång S....40 C4
Vacqueyras F....78 B3
Vad I....81 C4
Väddö S....36 B5
Väderstad S....37 D1
Vadheim N....32 A2
Vadillo de la Sierra E....93 B5
Vadillos E....95 B4
Vadla N....33 C3
Vado I....81 B5
Vado Ligure I....80 B2
Vadsø N....113 B18
Vadstena S....37 D1
Vaduz FL....71 A4
Våg N....114 B7
Vågåmo N....114 F6
Væggerløse DK....44 A3
Vaggeryd S....40 B4
Vaghia GR....117 D5
Vagney F....60 B2
Vagnhärad S....37 D4
Vagos P....92 A2
Vai GR....117 G8
Vaiano I....81 C5
Vaiges F....57 B5
Vaihingen D....61 B4
Vaillant F....59 C6
Vailly-sur-Aisne F....59 A4
Vailly-sur-Sauldre F....68 A2
Vairano Scalo I....103 B7
Vaison-la-Romaine F....79 B4
Vaïte F....60 C1
Väja S....115 E14
Vajkijärv FIN....3 E24
Vajszló H....74 C2
Vál H....74 A3
Valaam RUS....3 F29
Valada P....92 B1
Vålådalen S....115 D10
Valadares P....87 C2
Valado P....92 B1
Valalta RUS....112 D9
Valandovo MK....116 A4
Valašská Belá SK....65 B4
Valašská Dubová SK....65 A5
Valašská Polanka CZ....64 A3
Valašské Klobouky
 CZ....64 A4
Valašské Meziříčí CZ....64 A3
Valberg F....79 B5
Vålberg S....35 C5
Valbo S....36 B4
Valbom P....87 C2
Valbondione I....71 B5
Valbonë AL....105 A5
Valbonnais F....79 B4
Valbuena de Duero E....88 C2
Vălcani RO....75 B5
Valdagno I....71 C6
Valdaj RUS....7 C12
Valdealgorfa E....90 C2
Valdecaballeros E....93 B5
Valdecabras E....95 B4
Valdecarros E....94 B1
Valdeconcha E....95 B4
Valdeflores E....99 B4
Valdefresno E....88 B1
Valdeganga E....95 C5
Valdelacasa E....94 B1
Valdelacasa de Tajo
 E....93 B5
Valdelarco E....99 B4
Valdelosa E....94 A1
Valdeltormo E....90 C3
Valdemanco de Esteras
 E....94 D2
Valdemarsvik S....37 D3
Valdemorillo E....94 B2
Valdemoro E....94 B3
Valdemoro Sierra E....95 B5
Valdenoceda E....89 B3
Valdeobispo E....93 A4
Valdeolivas E....95 B4
Valdepeñas E....100 A2
Valdepeñas de Jaén
 E....100 B2
Valdepiélago E....88 B1
Valdepolo E....88 B1
Valderas E....88 B1
Valderice I....108 A1
Valderrobres E....90 C3
Valderrueda E....88 B1
Valdestillas E....88 C2
Valdetorres E....93 C4
Valdetorres de Jarama
 E....95 B3
Valdeverdeja E....93 B5
Valdevimbre E....88 B1
Valdieri I....80 B1
Valdilecha E....95 B3
Val-d'Isère F....70 C1
Valdobbiádene I....72 C1
Valdocondes E....89 C3
Valdovino E....86 A2
Valea lui Mihai RO....11 C7
Vale de Açor
 Beja P....98 B3
 Portalegre P....92 B3
Vale de Cambra P....87 D2
Vale de Lobo P....98 C2
Vale de Prazeres P....92 A3
Vale de Reis P....92 C2
Vale de Rosa P....98 B3
Vale de Santarém P....92 B2
Vale de Vargo P....98 B3
Vale do Peso P....92 B3
Valega P....92 A2
Valéggio sul Mincio I....71 C5
Valeiro P....92 C2
Valença P....87 B2
Valençay F....67 A6
Valence
 Charente F....67 C5
 Drôme F....79 B3
Valence d'Agen F....77 B3
Valence-d'Albigeois
 F....77 B5
Valence-sur-Baïse F....77 C3
Valencia E....96 B2
Valencia de Alcántara
 E....92 B3
Valencia de Don Juan
 E....88 B1
Valencia de las Torres
 E....93 C4
Valencia del Ventoso
 E....99 A4
Valencia de Mombuey
 E....99 A3
Valenciennes F....49 C4
Valensole F....79 C4
Valentano I....102 A4
Valentigney F....70 A1
Valentine F....77 C3
Valenza I....80 A2
Valenzuela E....100 B1
Valenzuela de Calatrava
 E....100 A2
Våler
 Hedmark N....34 B3
 Østfold N....35 C2
Valera de Abajo E....95 C4
Valeria E....95 C4
Valestrand N....33 C2
Valestrandfossen N....32 B2
Valevåg N....33 C2
Valfabbrica I....82 C1
Valflaunes F....78 C2
Valga EST....7 C9
Valgorge F....78 B3
Valgrisenche I....70 C2
Valguarnera Caropepe
 I....109 B3
Valhelhas P....92 A3
Valjala EST....6 C7
Valka LV....7 C8
Valkeakoski FIN....3 F26
Valkenburg NL....50 C1
Valkenswaard NL....49 B6
Valkó H....75 A5
Valla S....37 C3
Valladolid E....88 C2
Vallada E....96 B2
Vallata I....103 B8
Vallberga S....40 C3
Vall d'Alba E....96 A2
Valldemossa E....97 B2
Valle
 I....81 C4
 N....33 D4
Valle Castellana I....82 D2
Valle de Abdalajis E....100 C1
Valle de Cabuérniga
 E....88 A2
Valle de la Serena E....93 C5
Valle de Matamoros
 E....93 C4
Valle de Santa Ana E....93 C4
Valledolmo I....108 B2
Valle Mosso I....70 C3
Vallendar D....50 C3
Vallentuna S....37 C5
Valleraugue F....78 B2
Vallermosa I....110 C1
Vallet F....66 A3
Valletta M....107 C5
Valley GB....26 B1
Vallfogona de Riucorb
 E....91 B4
Valli del Pasúbio I....71 C6
Vallo della Lucánia I....103 C8
Valloire F....69 C6
Vallombrosa I....81 C5
Vallon-Pont-d'Arc F....78 B3
Vallorbe CH....69 B6
Vallouise F....79 B5
Valls E....91 B4
Vallset N....34 B3
Vallsta S....36 A3
Vallstena S....37 E5
Valmadrid E....90 B2
Valmiera LV....7 C8
Valmojado E....94 B2
Valmont F....58 A1
Valmontone I....102 B5
Valö S....36 B5
Valognes F....57 A4
Valonga P....92 A2
Valongo P....87 C2
Válor E....100 C2
Valoria la Buena E....88 C2
Valøy N....114 C7
Valozhyn BY....7 D9
Valpaços P....87 C3
Valpelline I....70 C2
Valpiana I....81 C4
Valpovo HR....74 C3
Valras-Plage F....78 C2
Valréas F....78 B3
Vals CH....71 B4
Valsavarenche I....70 C2
Vålse DK....39 E4
Valsequillo E....93 C5
Valsjöbyn S....115 C11
Vals-les-Bains F....78 B3
Valsonne F....69 C4
Valstagna I....72 C1
Val-Suzon F....69 A4
Valtablado del Rio E....95 B4
Valþjófsstaður IS....111 B11
Val Thorens F....69 C6
Valtice CZ....64 B2
Valtiendas E....88 C3
Valtierra E....89 B5
Valtopina I....82 C1
Valtorta I....71 C4
Valtournenche I....70 C2
Valverde E....89 C5
Valverde de Burguillos
 E....93 C4
Valverde de Júcar E....95 C4
Valverde de la Vera E....93 A5
Valverde de la Virgen
 E....88 B1
Valverde del Camino
 E....99 B4
Valverde del Fresno
 E....93 A4
Valverde de Mérida E....93 C4
Vamberk CZ....53 C6
Vamdrup DK....39 D2
Våmhus S....34 A6
Vamlingbo S....37 F5
Vammala FIN....3 F25
Vamos GR....117 G6
Vámosmikola H....65 C4
Vámosszabadi H....64 C3
Vanault-les-Dames F....59 B5
Vandel DK....39 D2
Vandenesse F....68 B3
Vandenesse-en-Auxois
 F....69 A4
Vandóies I....72 B1
Väne-Åsaka S....35 D4
Vänersborg S....35 D4
Vang N....32 A5
Vänge S....36 B4
Vangsnes N....32 A3
Vänjaurbäck S....115 C15
Vännacka S....35 C4
Vannareid N....112 B8
Vännäs S....115 D16
Vannes F....56 C3
Vannsätter S....36 A3
Vannvåg N....112 B8
Vansbro S....34 B6
Vanse N....33 D3
Vantaa FIN....3 F26
Vanttauskoski FIN....113 F15
Vanyarc H....65 C5
Vaour F....77 B4
Vápenná CZ....65 A4
Vaprio d'Adda I....71 C4
Vaqueiros P....98 B3
Vara S....35 D4
Varacieux F....69 C5
Varades F....66 A3
Varages F....79 C4
Varaldsøy N....32 B2
Varallo I....70 C3
Varangerbotn N....113 B17
Varano de'Melegari I....81 B4
Varaždin HR....73 B6
Varaždinske Toplice
 HR....73 B6
Varazze I....80 B2
Varberg S....40 B2
Vardal N....34 B2
Varde DK....39 D1
Vårdö FIN....36 B7
Vardø N....113 B19
Vardomb H....74 B3
Varèl D....43 B5
Varena LT....6 D8
Vårenes N....33 C2
Varengeville-sur-Mer
 F....58 A1
Varenna I....71 B4
Varennes-en-Argonne
 F....59 A6
Varennes-le-Grand F....69 B4
Varennes-St Sauveur
 F....69 B5
Varennes-sur-Allier F....68 B3
Varennes-sur-Amance
 F....60 C1
Vareš BIH....84 B3
Varese I....70 C3
Varese Ligure I....81 B3
Vârfurile RO....11 C7
Vårgårda S....40 A2
Vargas
 E....88 A3
 P....92 B1
Vargön S....35 D4
Varhaug N....33 D2
Variaşu Mic RO....75 B5
Varilhes F....77 C4
Varín SK....65 A4
Väring S....35 D5
Váriz P....87 C4
Varkaus FIN....3 E27
Varmahlíð IS....111 B6
Varmdal N....33 C2
Värmlands Bro S....35 C5
Varmo I....72 C3
Varna
 BG....11 E9
 SRB....85 B4
Värnamo S....40 B4
Varnhem S....35 D5
Varnsdorf CZ....53 C4
Varoška Rijeka BIH....83 A5
Városlőd H....74 A2
Várpalota H....74 A3
Varreddes F....59 B3
Vars F....79 B5
Varsi I....81 B4
Varsseveld NL....50 B2
Vårsta S....37 C4
Vartdal N....114 E3
Vartofta S....40 A3
Varvarin SRB....85 C6
Várvölgy H....74 B2
Varzi I....80 B3
Varzjelas P....92 A2
Varzo I....70 B3
Varzy F....68 A3
Vasad H....75 A4
Väse S....35 C5
Vásárosbéc H....85 A4
Vasilevichi BY....7 E10
Väskinde S....37 E5
Vaskút H....75 B3
Vassbotn N....33 D5
Vassenden N....114 F2
Vassieux-en-Vercors
 F....79 B4
Vassmolösa S....40 C6
Vassy F....57 B5
Västanå S....115 D12
Västanvik S....36 B1
Västerås S....37 C3
Västerby S....36 B3
Västerfärnebo S....36 C3
Västerhaninge S....37 C5
Västervik S....40 B6
Vasto I....103 A7
Västra Ämtervik S....35 C5
Västra-Bodarne S....40 B2
Västra Karup S....41 C2
Vasvár H....74 A1
Vasylkiv UA....11 A11
Vát H....74 A1
Vatan F....68 A1
Väte S....37 E5
Vathia GR....117 F4
Vatican City = Cittádel
 Vaticano I....102 B5
Vatili CY....120 A2
Vatin SRB....75 C6
Vatland N....33 D4
Vatnar N....33 C6
Vatnås N....32 B6
Vatne N....33 D4
Vatnestrøm N....33 D5
Vätö S....36 B5
Vätra-Dornei RO....11 C8
Vatry F....59 B5
Vattholma S....36 B4
Vättis CH....71 B4
Vauchamps F....59 B4
Vauchassis F....59 B4
Vaucouleurs F....60 B1
Vaudoy-en-Brie F....59 B4
Vaulen N....33 D2
Vaulruz CH....70 B1
Vaulx Vraucourt F....48 C3
Vaumas F....68 B3
Vausseroux F....67 B4
Vauvenargues F....79 C4
Vauvert F....78 C3
Vauvillers F....60 C2
Vaux-sur-Sure B....60 A1
Vawkavysk BY....6 E8
Vaxholm S....37 C5
Växjö S....40 C4
Våxtorp S....41 C3
Vayrac F....77 B4
Važec SK....65 A5
Veberöd S....41 D3
Vechelde D....51 A6
Vechta D....43 C5
Vecinos E....94 B1
Veckholm S....37 C4
Vecsés H....75 A4
Vedavågen N....33 C2
Veddige S....40 B2
Vedersø DK....39 C1
Vedeseta I....71 C4
Vedevåg S....37 C2
Vedra E....86 B2
Vedum S....35 D4
Veendam NL....42 B3
Veenendaal NL....49 A6
Vega
 Asturias E....88 A1
 Asturias E....88 A1
Vegadeo E....86 A3
Vega de Espinareda
 E....86 B4
Vega de Infanzones E....88 B1
Vegas del Condado E....88 B1
Vega de Pas E....88 A3
Vega de Valdetronco
 E....88 C1
Vegby S....40 B3
Vegger DK....38 C2
Veggli N....32 B6
Veghel NL....49 B6
Veglast D....45 A4
Véglie I....105 C3
Vegusdal N....33 D5
Veidholmen N....114 D4
Veidnes N....113 B15
Veikåker N....34 B1
Veinge S....40 C3
Vejbystrand S....41 C2
Vejen DK....39 D2
Vejer de la Frontera E....99 C5
Vejle DK....39 D2
Vejprty CZ....52 C3
Vela Luka HR....84 D1
Velada E....94 B2
Velagići BIH....83 B5
Velayos E....94 B2
Velbert D....50 B3
Velburg D....62 A2
Velden
 Bayern D....62 A2
 Bayern D....62 B3
Velden am Worther See
 A....73 B4
Veldhoven NL....49 B6
Velefique E....101 B3
Velen D....50 B2
Velenje SLO....73 B5
Veles MK....116 A3
Velešin CZ....63 B5
Velestino GR....116 C4
Vélez Blanco E....101 B3
Vélez de Benaudalla
 E....100 C2
Vélez-Málaga E....100 C1
Vélez Rubio E....101 B3
Velika
 HR....74 C2
 MNE....85 D4
Velika Drenova SRB....85 C6
Velika Gorica HR....73 C6
Velika Grdevac HR....74 C2
Velika Greda SRB....75 C5
Velika Ilova BIH....84 B2
Velika Kladuša BIH....83 A5
Velika Krsna SRB....85 B5
Velika Obarska BIH....85 B4
Velika Pisanica HR....74 C2
Velika Plana
 Srbija SRB....85 B6
 Srbija SRB....85 C6
Velike Lašče SLO....73 C4
Veliki Gaj SRB....75 C5
Veliki Popovici SRB....85 B6
Veliki Šiljegovac SRB....85 C6
Velikiye Luki RUS....7 C11
Veliko Gradište SRB....85 B6
Veliko Orašje SRB....85 B6
Veliko Selo SRB....85 B6
Veliko Tarnovo BG....11 E8
Velilla del Río Carrió
 E....88 B2

Velilla de San Antonio
E 95 B3
Veli Lošinj HR 83 B3
Velipojë AL 105 B5
Velizh RUS 7 D11
Veljun HR 73 C5
Velká Bíteš CZ 64 A2
Velka Hled'scbe CZ 52 D2
Velká Lomnica SK 65 A6
Velkánad Veličkou
CZ 64 B3
Velké Bystřice CZ 64 A3
Velké Heraltice CZ 54 D2
Velké Karlovice CZ 64 A4
Vel'ke'Kostol'any SK 64 B3
Vel'ké Leváre SK 64 B3
Velké Losiny CZ 54 C2
Velké Meziříčí CZ 64 A2
Velké Pavlovice CZ 64 B2
Vel'ké Rovné SK 65 A4
Vel'ké Uherce SK 65 B4
Vel'ké Zálužie SK 64 B3
Vel'ký Blahovo SK 65 B6
Velky Bor CZ 63 A4
Vel'ký Cetin SK 64 B4
Vel'ký Krtíš SK 65 B5
Vel'ký Meder SK 64 C3
Velky Ujezd CZ 64 A3
Vellahn D 44 B2
Vellberg D 61 A5
Velles F 67 B6
Velletri I 102 B5
Vellinge S 41 D3
Vellisca E 95 B4
Velliza E 88 C2
Vellmar D 51 B5
Velp NL 50 A1
Velten D 45 C5
Velvary CZ 53 C4
Velvendos GR 116 B4
Vemb DK 39 C1
Vemdalen S 115 E10
Veme N 34 B2
Véménd H 74 B3
Vemmedrup DK 39 D5
Vena S 40 B5
Venaco F 102 A2
Venafro I 103 B7
Venarey-les-Laumes
F 69 A4
Venaría I 70 C2
Venasca I 80 B1
Venčane SRB 85 B5
Vence F 79 C6
Venda Nova
Coimbra P 92 A2
Leiria P 92 B2
Vendas Novas P 92 C2
Vendays-Montalivet F 66 C3
Vendel S 36 B4
Vendelso S 37 C5
Vendeuil F 59 A4
Vendeuvre-sur-Barse
F 59 B5
Vendoeuvres F 67 B6
Vendôme F 58 C2
Venelles F 79 C4
Veness GB 23 B6
Venézia = Venice I 72 C2
Venialbo E 88 C1
Venice = Venézia I 72 C2
Vénissieux F 69 C4
Venjan S 34 B5
Venlo NL 50 B2
Vennesla N 33 D4
Vennesund N 114 B9
Vennezey F 60 B2
Venn Green GB 28 C3
Venosa I 104 C1
Venray NL 50 B1
Vent A 71 B5
Venta de Baños E 88 C2
Venta del Moro E 96 B1
Venta de los Santos
E 100 A2
Venta las Ranas E 88 A1
Ventanueva E 86 A4
Ventas de Huelma E 100 B2
Ventas de Zafarraya
E 100 C1
Ventavon F 79 B4
Ventimíglia I 80 C1
Ventnor GB 31 D2
Ventosa de la Sierra
E 89 C4
Ventosilla E 89 C4
Ventspils LV 6 C6
Venturina I 81 C4
Venzolasca F 102 A2
Venzone I 72 B3
Vép H 74 A1
Vera
E 101 B4
N 115 D9
Vera Cruz P 98 A3
Vera de Bidasoa E 76 C1
Vera de Moncayo E 89 C5
Verbánia I 70 C3
Verberie F 58 A3
Verbicaro I 106 B2
Verbier CH 70 B2
Vercelli I 70 C3
Vercel-Villedieu-le-Camp
F 69 A6
Verchen D 45 B4
Vercheny F 79 B4
Verclause F 79 B4
Verdalsøra N 114 D8
Verden D 43 C6
Verdens Ende N 35 C2
Verdikoussa GR 116 C3
Verdille F 67 C4
Verdú E 91 B4
Verdun F 59 A6
Verdun-sur-Garonne
F 77 C4
Verdun-sur-le-Doubs
F 69 B5
Veresegyház H 65 C5
Verfeil F 77 C4
Vergato I 81 B5
Vergel E 96 C3
Vergeletto CH 70 B3
Verges E 91 A6
Vergiate I 70 C3
Vergt F 77 A3
Veria GR 116 B4
Verín E 87 C3
Veringenstadt D 61 B5
Verkhovye RUS 7 E14
Verl D 51 B4
Verma N 114 E5
Vermand F 59 A4
Vermelha P 92 B1
Vermenton F 59 C4
Vermosh AL 85 D4
Vernago I 71 B5
Vernante I 80 B1
Vernantes F 67 A5
Vernár SK 65 B6
Vernasca I 81 B3
Vernayaz CH 70 B2
Vernazza I 81 B3
Vern-d'Anjou F 57 C5
Verneřice CZ 53 C4
Vernet F 77 C4
Vernet-les-Bains F 91 A5
Verneuil F 59 A4
Verneuil-sur-Avre F 58 B1
Vernier CH 69 B6
Vérnio I 81 B5
Vérnole I 105 C4
Vernon F 58 A2
Vernoux-en-Vivarais
F 78 B3
Veróce H 65 C5
Verolanuova I 71 C5
Véroli I 103 B6
Verona I 71 C6
Verpelét H 65 C6
Verrabotn N 114 D7
Verrès I 70 C2
Verrey-sous-Salmaise
F 69 A4
Verrières F 67 B5
Versailles F 58 B3
Versam CH 71 B4
Verseg H 65 C5
Versmold D 50 A4
Versoix CH 69 B6
Verteillac F 67 C5
Vértesacsa H 74 A3
Vertou F 66 A3
Vertus F 59 B4
Verviers B 50 C1
Vervins F 59 A4
Verwood GB 29 C6
Veryan GB 28 C3
Veržej SLO 73 B6
Verzuolo I 80 B1
Verzy F 59 A5
Vescovato F 102 A2
Vése H 74 B2
Veselie BG 11 E9
Veselínad Lužnicí CZ 63 A5
Veselínad Moravou
CZ 64 B3
Vésime I 80 B2
Veskoniemi FIN 113 D16
Vesoul F 60 C2
Vespolate I 70 C3
Vessigebro S 40 C2
Vestbygd N 33 D3
Vestenanova I 71 C6
Vester Husby S 37 D3
Vester Nebel DK 39 D2
Vesterøhavn DK 38 B3
Vester Torup DK 38 B2
Vester Vedsted DK 39 D1
Vestervig DK 38 C1
Vestfossen N 35 C1
Vestmannaeyjar IS 111 D5
Vestmarka N 34 C3
Vestnes N 114 E4
Vestone I 71 C5
Vestre Gausdal N 34 A2
Vestre Jakobselv N 113 B18
Vestre Slidre N 32 A5
Vesyegonsk RUS 7 B14
Veszprém H 74 A2
Veszprémvarsány H 74 A2
Vésztö H 75 B6
Vetlanda S 40 B5
Vetovo HR 74 C2
Vetralla I 102 A5
Větrný Jeníkov CZ 63 A6
Vétroz CH 70 B2
Vetschau D 53 B4
Vettasjärvi S 113 E10
Vetto I 81 B4
Vetulónia I 81 D4
Veules-les-Roses F 58 A1
Veulettes-sur-Mer F 58 A1
Veum N 33 C5
Veurne B 48 B3
Veverská Bítýška CZ 64 A2
Vevey CH 70 B1
Vevi GR 116 B3
Vevring N 32 A2
Vex CH 70 B2
Veynes F 79 B4
Veyre-Monton F 68 C3
Veyrier F 69 C6
Vézelay F 68 A3
Vézelise F 60 B2
Vézenobres F 78 B3
Vezins F 67 A4
Vézins-de-Lévézou F 78 B1
Vezirhan TR 118 B5
Vezirköprü TR 16 A7
Vezza di Óglio I 71 B5
Vezzani F 102 A2
Vezzano I 71 B6
Vezzano sul Cróstolo
I 81 B4
Vi S 115 E14
Viadana I 81 B4
Via Gloria P 98 B3
Viana E 89 B4
Viana do Alentejo P 92 C2
Viana do Bolo E 87 B3
Viana do Castelo P 87 C2
Vianden L 60 A2
Viannos GR 117 G7
Viaréggio I 81 C4
Viator E 101 C3
Vibble S 37 E5
Viborg DK 38 C2
Vibo Valéntia I 106 C3
Vibraye F 58 B1
Vic E 91 B5
Vícar E 101 C3
Vicarello I 81 C4
Vicari I 108 B2
Vicchio I 81 C5
Vicdesses F 77 D4
Vic-en-Bigorre F 76 C3
Vicenza I 71 C6
Vic-Fézensac F 76 C3
Vichy F 68 B3
Vickan S 38 B5
Vickerstown GB 26 A2
Vic-le-Comte F 68 C3
Vico F 102 A1
Vico del Gargano I 104 B1
Vico Equense I 103 C7
Vicopisano I 81 C4
Vicosoprano CH 71 B4
Vicovaro I 102 A5
Vic-sur-Aisne F 59 A4
Vic-sur-Cère F 77 B5
Victoria = Rabat M 107 C5
Vidago P 87 C3
Vidauban F 79 C5
Vide P 92 A3
Videbæk DK 39 C1
Videm SLO 73 C4
Videseter N 114 F4
Vidigueira P 98 A3
Vidin BG 11 E7
Vidlin GB 22 A7
Vidzy BY 7 D9
Viechtach D 62 A3
Vieille-Brioude F 68 C3
Vieira P 92 B2
Vieira do Minho P 87 C2
Vieiros P 92 C3
Vielha E 90 A3
Vielle-Aure F 77 D3
Viellespesse F 68 C3
Viellevigne F 66 B3
Vielmur-sur-Agout F 77 C5
Vielsalm B 50 C1
Viels Maison F 59 B4
Vienenburg D 51 B6
Vienna = Wien A 64 B2
Vienne F 69 C4
Vieritz D 44 C4
Viernheim D 61 A4
Vierraden D 45 B6
Viersen D 50 B2
Vierville-sur-Mer F 57 A5
Vierzon F 68 A2
Vieselbach D 52 C1
Vieste I 104 B2
Vietas S 112 E7
Vieteren B 48 C3
Vietri di Potenza I 104 C1
Vietri sul Mare I 103 C7
Vieux-Boucau-les-Bains
F 76 C1
Vif F 79 A4
Vig DK 39 D4
Vigásio I 71 C5
Vigaun A 63 C4
Vigeland N 33 D4
Vigeois F 67 C6
Vigévano I 70 C3
Viggianello I 106 B3
Viggiano I 104 C1
Vigliano I 102 A6
Vigmostad N 33 D4
Vignale I 80 A2
Vignanello I 102 A5
Vigneulles-lès-Hattonchâtel F 60 B1
Vignevieille F 77 D5
Vignola I 81 B5
Vignory F 59 B6
Vignoux-sur Barangeon
F 68 A2
Vigo E 87 B2
Vigo di Fassa I 72 B1
Vigone I 80 B1
Vigrestad N 33 D2
Vihiers F 67 A4
Viitasaari FIN 3 E26
Vík IS 111 D6
Vik
Nordland N 114 B9
Rogaland N 33 D2
Sogn og Fjordane N 32 A3
S 41 D4
Vika S 36 B2
Vikajärvi FIN 113 F15
Vikane N 35 C2
Vikarbyn S 36 B2
Vike N 32 B2
Vikedal N 33 C2
Vikeland N 33 D4
Viken
Jämtland S 115 C10
Skåne S 41 C2
Viker N 34 B2
Vikersund N 34 C1
Vikeså N 33 D3
Vikevåg N 33 C2
Vikingstad S 37 D2
Vikmanshyttan S 36 B2
Vikna N 114 C7
Vikøy N 32 B3
Vikran
Troms N 112 C7
Troms N 112 D5
Viksjö S 115 E14
Viksøyri N 32 A3
Viksta S 36 B4
Vila Boim P 92 C3
Vila Chãde Ourique P 92 B2
Viladamat E 91 A6
Vila de Cruces E 86 B2
Vila de Rei P 92 B2
Vila do Bispo P 98 B2
Vila do Conde P 87 C2
Viladrau E 91 B5
Vila Flor P 87 C3
Vila Franca das Navas
P 87 D3
Vilafranca del Maestrat
E 90 C2
Vilafranca del Penedès
E 91 B4
Vila Franca de Xira P 92 C1
Vila Fresca P 92 C1
Vilagarcía de Arousa
E 86 B2
Vilajuiga E 91 A6
Vilamarin E 86 B3
Vilamartín de Valdeorras
E 86 B3
Vila Nogueira P 92 C1
Vila Nova da Baronia
P 98 A2
Vilanova de Castelló
E 96 B2
Vila Nova de Cerveira
P 87 C2
Vila Nova de Famalicão
P 87 C2
Vila Nova de Foz Côa
P 87 C3
Vila Nova de Gaia P 87 C2
Vila Nova de Milfontes
P 98 B2
Vila Nova de Paiva P 87 D3
Vila Nova de São Bento
P 98 B3
Vilanova de Sau E 91 B5
Vilanova i la Geltrú E 91 B4
Vilapedre E 86 A3
Vila Pouca de Aguiar
P 87 C3
Vila Praja de Ancora
P 87 C2
Vilarandelo P 87 C3
Vilar de Santos E 87 B3
Vilardevós E 87 C3
Vila Real P 87 C3
Vila-real de los Infantes
E 96 B2
Vila Real de Santo António P 98 B3
Vilar Formosa P 93 A4
Vila-Rodona E 91 B4
Vila Ruiva P 98 A3
Vilasantar E 86 A2
Vilaseca E 91 B4
Vila Seca P 92 A2
Vilassar de Mar E 91 B5
Vilasund S 115 A11
Vila Velha de Ródão
P 92 B3
Vila Verde
Braga P 87 C2
Lisboa P 92 B1
Vila Verde de Filcalho
P 98 B3
Vila Viçosa P 92 C3
Vilches E 100 A2
Vildbjerg DK 39 C1
Vilémov CZ 63 A6
Vileyka BY 7 D9
Vilhelmina S 115 C13
Vilia GR 117 D5
Viljandi EST 7 B8
Villabáñez E 88 C2
Villablanca E 98 B3
Villablino E 86 B4
Villabona E 89 A4
Villabragima E 88 C1
Villabuena del Puente
E 88 C1
Villacadima E 95 A3
Villacañas E 95 C3
Villacarriedo E 88 A3
Villacarrillo E 100 A2
Villa Castelli I 104 C3
Villacastín E 94 B2
Villach A 72 B3
Villacidro I 110 C1
Villaconejos E 95 B3
Villaconejos de Trabaque
E 95 B4
Villa Cova de Lixa P 87 C2
Villada E 88 B2
Villadangos del Páramo
E 88 B1
Villadecanes E 86 B4
Villa del Prado E 94 B2
Villa del Rio E 100 B1
Villadepera E 87 C4
Villa de Peralonso E 87 C4
Villa di Chiavenna I 71 B4
Villadiego E 88 B2
Villadompardo E 100 B1
Villadóssola I 70 B3
Villaeles de Valdavia
E 88 B2
Villaescusa de Haro
E 95 C4
Villafáfila E 88 C1
Villafeliche E 95 A5
Villaflores E 94 A1
Villafrades de Campos
E 88 B2
Villafranca
Avila E 93 A5
Navarra E 89 B5
Villafranca de Córdoba
E 100 B1
Villafranca del Bierzo
E 86 B4
Villafranca de los Barros
E 93 C4
Villafranca de los Caballeros E 95 C3
Villafranca di Verona
I 71 C5
Villafranca in Lunigiana
I 81 B3
Villafranca-Montes de Oca
E 89 B3
Villafranca Tirrena I 109 A4
Villafranco del Campo
E 95 B5
Villafranco del Guadalquivir E 99 B4
Villafrati I 108 B2
Villafrechós E 88 C1
Villafruela E 88 C3
Villagarcia de las Torres
E 93 C4
Villaggio Mancuso I 106 B3
Villagonzalo E 93 C4
Villagotón E 86 B4
Villagrains F 76 B2
Villaharta E 100 A1
Villahermosa E 100 A3
Villaherreros E 88 B2
Villahoz E 88 B3
Villaines-la-Juhel F 57 B5
Villajoyosa E 96 C2
Villalago I 103 B6
Villalba
E 86 A3
I 108 B2
Villalba de Calatrava
E 100 A2
Villalba de Guardo E 88 B2
Villalba del Alcor E 99 B4
Villalba de la Sierra E 95 B4
Villalba de los Alcores
E 88 C2
Villalba de los Barros
E 93 C4
Villalba del Rey E 95 B4
Villalcampo E 87 C4
Villalcázar de Sirga E 88 B2
Villalengua E 89 C5
Villalgordo del Júcar
E 95 C4
Villalgordo del Marquesado E 95 C4
Villalmóndar E 89 B3
Villalón de Campos E 88 B1
Villalonga E 96 C2
Villalonso E 88 C1
Villalpando E 88 C1
Villaluenga E 94 B3
Villalumbroso E 88 B2
Villálvaro E 89 C3
Villamalea E 95 C5
Villamanán E 88 B1
Villamanín E 88 B1
Villamanrique E 100 A3
Villamanrique de la Condesa E 99 B4
Villamanta E 94 B2
Villamantilla E 94 B2
Villamar I 110 C1
Villamartín E 99 C5
Villamartin de Campos
E 88 B2
Villamartin de Don Sancho E 88 B1
Villamassárgia I 110 C1
Villamayor E 88 A1
Villamayor de Calatrava
E 100 A1
Villamayor de Campos
E 88 C1
Villamayor de Santiago
E 95 C4
Villamblard F 77 A3
Villamejil E 86 B4
Villamesias E 93 B5
Villaminaya E 94 C3
Villa Minozzo I 81 B4
Villamor de los Escuderos
E 88 C1
Villamoronta E 88 B2
Villamuelas E 94 C3
Villamuriel de Cerrato
E 88 C2
Villandraut F 76 B2
Villanova I 104 C3
Villanova d'Asti I 80 B1
Villanova del Battista
I 103 B8
Villanova Mondov ì I 80 B1
Villanova Monteleone
I 110 B1
Villante E 88 B3
Villantério I 71 C4
Villanubla E 88 C2
Villanueva de Alcardete
E 95 C3
Villanueva de Alcorón
E 95 B4
Villanueva de Algaidas
E 100 B1
Villanueva de Argaña
E 88 B3
Villanueva de Bogas
E 95 C3
Villanueva de Córdoba
E 100 A1
Villanueva de Gállego
E 90 B2
Villanueva del Aceral
E 94 A2
Villanueva de la Concepcion E 100 C1
Villanueva de la Fuente
E 101 A3
Villanueva de la Jara
E 95 C5
Villanueva de la Reina
E 100 A2
Villanueva del Arzobispo
E 100 A3
Villanueva de la Serena
E 93 C5
Villanueva de la Sierra
E 93 A4
Villanueva de las Manzanas E 88 B1
Villanueva de las Peras
E 88 C1
Villanueva de las Torres
E 100 B2
Villanueva de la Vera
E 93 A5
Villanueva del Campo
E 88 C1
Villanueva del Duque
E 100 A1
Villanueva del Fresno
E 93 C3
Villanueva del Huerva
E 90 B1
Villanueva de los Castillejos E 98 B3
Villanueva de los Infantes
E 100 A3
Villanueva del Rey E 99 A5
Villanueva del Rio E 99 B5
Villanueva del Río y Minas
E 99 B5
Villanueva del Rosario
E 100 C1
Villanueva del Trabuco
E 100 B1
Villanueva de Mesia
E 100 B2
Villanueva de Nía E 88 B2
Villanueva de Oscos
E 86 A4
Villanueva de San Carlos
E 100 A2
Villanueva de San Juan
E 99 B5
Villanueva de Tapia
E 100 B1
Villanueva de Valdegovia
E 89 B3
Villány H 74 C3
Villaputzu I 110 C2
Villaquejida E 88 B1
Villaquilambre E 88 B1
Villaquiran de los Infantes
E 88 B2
Villaralto E 100 A1
Villarcayo E 89 B3
Villard-de-Lans F 79 A4
Villar de Barrio E 87 B3
Villar de Cañas E 95 C4
Villar de Chinchilla E 96 C1
Villar de Ciervo E 87 D4
Villardeciervos E 87 C4
Villar de Domingo Garcia
E 95 B4
Villardefrades E 88 C1
Villar del Arzobispo E 96 B2
Villar del Buey E 87 C4
Villar del Cobo E 95 B5
Villar del Humo E 95 C5
Villar de los Navarros
E 90 B1
Villar del Pedroso E 93 B5
Villar del Rey E 93 B4
Villar del Rio E 89 B4
Villar del Saz de Navalón
E 95 B4
Villar de Rena E 93 B5
Villarejo E 95 A3
Villarejo de Fuentes
E 95 C4
Villarejo de Orbigo E 88 B1
Villarejo de Salvanes
E 95 B3
Villarejo-Periesteban
E 95 C4
Villares del Saz E 95 C4
Villaretto I 79 A6
Villargordo del Cabriel
E 96 B1
Villarino E 87 C4
Villarino de Conso E 87 B3
Villarluengo E 90 C2
Villarobe E 89 B3
Villarosa I 109 B3
Villar Perosa I 79 B6
Villarramiel E 88 B2
Villarrasa E 99 B4
Villarreal de San Carlos
E 93 B4
Villarrin de Campos
E 88 C1
Villarrobledo E 95 C4
Villarroya de la Sierra
E 89 C5
Villarroya de los Pinares
E 90 C2
Villarrubia de los Ojos
E 95 C3
Villarrubia de Santiago
E 95 C3
Villarrubio E 95 C4
Villars-les-Dombes F 69 B5
Villarta E 95 C5
Villarta de los Montes
E 94 C2
Villarta de San Juan
E 95 C3
Villasana de Mena E 89 A3
Villasandino E 88 B2
Villa San Giovanni I 109 A4
Villa Santa Maria I 103 B7
Villasante E 89 A3
Villa Santina I 72 B2
Villasarracino E 88 B2
Villasayas E 89 C4
Villasdardo E 87 C4
Villaseca de Henares
E 95 B4
Villaseca de Laciana
E 86 B4
Villaseca de la Sagra
E 94 C3
Villaseco de los Gamitos
E 87 C4
Villaseco de los Reyes
E 87 C4
Villasequilla de Yepes
E 94 C3
Villasimíus I 110 C2
Villasmundo I 109 B4
Villasor I 110 C1
Villastar E 90 C1
Villastellone I 80 B1
Villatobas E 95 C3
Villatorp E 93 A5
Villatoya E 96 B1
Villavaliente E 96 B1
Villavelayo E 89 B4
Villavella E 87 B3
Villaver de de Guadalimar
E 101 A3
Villaverde del Rio E 99 B5
Villaviciosa E 88 A1
Villaviciosa de Córdoba
E 99 A6
Villaviciosa de Odón
E 94 B3
Villavieja de Yeltes E 87 D4
Villayón E 86 A4
Villé F 60 B3
Villebois-Lavalette F 67 C5
Villecerf F 59 B3
Villecomtal F 77 B5
Villedieu-les-Poêles
F 57 B4
Villedieu-sur-Indre F 67 B6
Ville-di-Pietrabugno
F 102 A2
Villedômain F 67 A6
Villefagnan F 67 B5
Villefontaine F 69 C5
Villefort F 78 B2
Villefranche-d'Albigeois
F 77 C5
Villefranche-d'Allier F 68 B2
Villefranche-de-Lauragais
F 77 C4
Villefranche-de-Lonchat
F 76 B3
Villefranche-de-Panat
F 78 B1
Villefranche-de-Rouergue
F 77 B5
Villefranche-du-Périgord
F 77 B4
Villefranche-sur-Cher
F 68 A1
Villefranche-sur-Mer
F 80 C1
Villefranche-sur-Saône
F 69 B4
Villegenon F 68 A2
Villel E 96 A1
Villemaur-sur-Vanne
F 59 B4
Villemontais F 68 C3
Villemur-sur-Tarn F 77 C4
Villena E 101 A5
Villenauxe-la-Grande
F 59 B4
Villenave-d'Ornon F 76 B2
Villeneuve
CH 70 B1
F 77 B5
Villeneuve-d'Ascq F 49 C4
Villeneuve-de-Berg F 78 B3
Villeneuve-de-Marsan
F 76 C2
Villeneuve-de-Rivière
F 77 C3
Villeneuve-la-Guyard
F 59 B4
Villeneuve-l'Archevêque
F 59 B4
Villeneuve-le-Comte
F 58 B3
Villeneuve-lès-Avignon
F 78 C3
Villeneuve-les-Corbières
F 78 D1
Villeneuve-St Georges
F 58 B3
Villeneuve-sur-Allier
F 68 B3
Villeneuve-sur-Lot F 77 B3
Villeneuve-sur-Yonne
F 59 B4
Villeréal F 77 B3
Villerias E 88 C2
Villeromain F 58 C2
Villers-Bocage
Calvados F 57 A5
Somme F 48 D3
Villers-Bretonneux F 58 A3
Villers-Carbonnel F 59 A3
Villers-Cotterêts F 59 A4
Villersexel F 60 C2
Villers-Farlay F 69 B5
Villers-le-Gambon B 49 C5
Villers-le-Lac F 70 A1
Villers-sur-Mer F 57 A6
Villerupt F 60 A1
Villerville F 57 A6
Villeseneux F 59 B5
Ville-sous-la-Ferté F 59 B5
Ville-sur-Illon F 60 B2
Ville-sur-Tourbe F 59 A5
Villetrun F 58 C2
Villetta Barrea I 103 B6
Villeurbanne F 69 C4
Villeveyrac F 78 C2
Villevocance F 69 C4
Villiers-St Benoit F 59 C4
Villiers-St Georges F 59 B4
Villingen D 61 B4
Villmar D 50 C4
Villoldo E 88 B2
Villon F 59 C5
Villoria E 94 B1
Vilnes N 32 A1
Vilnius LT 7 D8
Vils
A 62 C1
DK 38 C1
Vilsbiburg D 62 B3
Vilseck D 62 A2
Vilshofen D 63 B4
Vilshult S 41 C4
Vilusi MNE 84 D3
Vilvestre E 87 C4
Vilvoorde B 49 C5
Vimeiro P 92 B1
Vimercate I 71 C4
Vimianzo E 86 A1
Vimieiro P 92 C3
Vimioso P 87 C4
Vimmerby S 40 B5
Vimoutiers F 57 B6
Vimperk CZ 63 A4
Vimy F 48 C3
Vinadi CH 71 B5
Vinadio I 79 B6
Vinaixa E 90 B3
Vinarós E 90 C3
Vinäs S 36 B1
Vinay F 69 C5
Vinberg S 40 C2
Vinca F 91 A5
Vinča SRB 85 B5
Vinchiaturo I 103 B7
Vinci I 81 C4
Vindeby DK 39 D3
Vindelgransele S 115 B15
Vindeln S 115 C16
Vinderup DK 38 C1
Vindsvik N 33 C3
Vinets F 59 B5
Vineuil F 58 C2
Vinga RO 75 B6
Vingåker S 37 C2
Vingnes N 34 A2
Vingrau F 78 D1
Vingrom N 34 A2
Vinhais P 87 C4
Vinica
HR 73 B6
SK 65 B5
SLO 73 C5
Vinicka MNE 85 D4
Viniegra de Arriba E 89 B4
Vinje
Hordaland N 32 B3
Sør-Trøndelag N 114 D6
Telemark N 33 C4
Vinkovci HR 74 C3
Vinliden S 115 C14
Vinninga S 35 D5
Vinnytsya UA 11 B10
Vinon F 68 A2
Vinon-sur-Verdon F 79 C4
Vinslöv S 41 C3
Vintjärn S 36 B3
Vintrosa S 37 C1
Viñuela E 100 C1
Viñuela de Sayago E 87 C5
Viñuelas E 95 B3
Vinuesa E 89 C4
Vinzelberg D 44 C3
Viöl D 43 A6
Viola I 80 B1
Violay F 69 C4
Vipava SLO 72 C3
Vipiteno I 71 B6
Vipperow D 45 B4
Vir
BIH 84 C2
HR 83 B4
Vira CH 70 B3
Vire F 57 B5
Vireda S 40 B4
Vireux F 49 C5
Virgen A 72 A2
Virgen de la Cabeza
E 100 A1
Virginia IRL 19 C4
Virieu F 69 C5
Virieu-le-Grand F 69 C5
Virje HR 74 B1
Virklund DK 39 C2
Virovitica HR 74 C2
Virpazar MNE 105 A5
Virsbo S 36 C3
Virserum S 40 B5
Virtaniemi FIN 113 D17
Virton B 60 A1
Virtsu EST 6 B7
Viry F 69 B6
Vis HR 83 C5
Visbek D 43 C5
Visby
DK 39 D1
S 37 E5
Visé B 50 C1
Višegrad BIH 85 C4
Viserba I 82 B1
Viseu P 92 A3
Visiedo E 90 C1
Viskafors S 40 B2
Visland N 33 D3
Vislanda S 40 C4
Visnes N 33 C2
Višnja Gora SLO 73 C4
Višnjan HR 72 C3
Višnové CZ 64 B2
Visnums-Kil S 35 C6
Viso del Marqués E 100 A2
Visoko
BIH 84 C3
SLO 73 B4
Visone I 80 B2
Visp CH 70 B2
Vissefjärda S 40 C5
Visselhövede D 43 C6
Vissenbjerg DK 39 D3
Visso I 82 D2
Vistabella del Maestrat
E 96 A2
Vita I 108 B1
Vitanje SLO 73 B5
Vitanovac SRB 85 C5
Vitebsk = Vitsyebsk
BY 7 D11
Viterbo I 102 A5
Vitez BIH 84 B2
Vithkuq AL 116 B2
Vitigudino E 87 C4
Vitina
BIH 84 C2
GR 117 E4
Vitis A 63 B6
Vítkov CZ 64 A3
Vitkovac SRB 85 C5
Vitomirica KOS 85 D5
Vitoria-Gasteiz E 89 B4
Vitré F 57 B4
Vitrey-sur-Mance F 60 C1
Vitry-en-Artois F 48 C3
Vitry-le-François F 59 B5
Vitry-sur-Seine F 58 B3
Vitsand S 34 B4
Vitsyebsk = Vitebsk
BY 7 D11
Vittangi S 113 E10
Vittaryd S 40 C3
Vitteaux F 69 A4
Vittel F 60 B1
Vittinge S 36 C4
Vittória I 109 C3
Vittório Véneto I 72 C2
Vittsjö S 41 C3
Viù I 70 C2
Viul N 34 B2
Vivario F 102 A2
Viveiro E 86 A3
Vivel del Rio Martin E 90 C2
Viver E 96 B2
Viverols F 68 C3
Viveros E 101 A3
Viviers F 78 B3
Vivonne F 67 B5
Vivy F 67 A4
Vize TR 118 A2
Vizille F 79 A4
Viziňada HR 72 C3
Viziru RO 11 D9
Vizovice CZ 64 A3
Vizvár H 74 B2
Vizzavona F 102 A2
Vizzini I 109 B3
Vlachiotis GR 117 F4
Vlachovice CZ 64 A3
Vlachovo SK 65 B6
Vláchovo Březi CZ 63 A4
Vladimirci SRB 85 B4
Vladimirovac SRB 85 A5
Vladislav CZ 64 A1
Vlagtwedde NL 43 B4
Vlajkovac SRB 85 A6
Vlasenica BIH 84 B3
Vlašim CZ 63 A5
Vlatkovići BIH 84 B2
Vledder NL 42 C3
Vlissingen NL 49 B4
Vlkolínec SK 65 A5
Vlorë AL 105 C5
Vlotho D 51 A4
Vnanje Gorice SLO 73 C4
Vobarno I 71 C5
Voćin HR 74 C2
Vöcklabruck A 63 B4
Vöcklamarkt A 63 C4
Vodanj SRB 85 B5
Voderady SK 64 B3
Vodice
Istarska HR 73 C4
Šibenska HR 83 C4
SLO 73 B4
Vodňany CZ 63 A5
Vodnjan HR 82 B2
Vodskov DK 38 B3
Voe GB 22 A7
Voerså DK 38 B3
Voghera I 80 B3
Vogogna I 70 B3
Vogošća BIH 84 C3
Vogué F 78 B3
Vohburg D 62 B2
Vohenstrauss D 62 A3
Vöhl D 51 B4
Vöhrenbach D 61 B4
Vöhringen D 61 B6
Void-Vacon F 60 B1
Voiron F 69 C5
Voise F 58 B2
Voisey F 60 C1
Voiteg RO 75 C6
Voiteur F 69 B5
Voitsberg A 73 A5
Vojens DK 39 D2
Vojka SRB 85 B5
Vojlovica SRB 85 B5
Vojnić HR 73 C5
Vojnice SK 65 C4
Vojnik SLO 73 B5
Vojvoda Stepa SRB 75 C5
Volada GR 119 G2
Volargne I 71 C5
Volary CZ 63 B4
Volče SLO 72 B3
Volda N 114 E3
Volendam NL 42 C2
Volga RUS 7 B15
Volimes GR 117 E2
Volissos GR 116 D7
Volkach D 61 A6
Völkermarkt A 73 B4
Volkhov RUS 7 B12
Völklingen D 60 A2
Volkmarsen D 51 B5
Voll N 114 E4
Vollenhove NL 42 C2
Vollore-Montagne F 68 C3
Vollsjö S 41 D3
Volodymyr-Volyns'kyy
UA 11 A8
Volokolamsk RUS 7 C13
Volos GR 116 C4
Volosovo RUS 7 B10
Volovets UA 11 B7
Voltággio I 80 B2
Volta Mantovana I 71 C5
Volterra I 81 C4
Voltri I 80 B2
Volturara Áppula I 103 B8
Volturara Irpina I 103 C7
Volvic F 68 C3
Volx F 79 C4
Volyně CZ 63 A4
Vonitsa GR 116 D2
Vönöck H 74 A2
Vonsild DK 39 D2
Voorschoten NL 49 A5
Vopnafjörður IS 111 B11
Vorau A 73 A5
Vorbasse DK 39 D2
Vorchdorf A 63 C4
Vorden
D 43 C5
NL 50 A2
Vordernberg A 73 A4
Vordingborg DK 39 D4
Vorë AL 105 B5
Voreppe F 69 C5
Vorey F 68 C3
Vorgod DK 39 C1
Vormsund N 34 B3
Voronezh UA 7 F12
Võru EST 7 C9
Voskopojë AL 116 B2
Voss N 32 B3
Votice CZ 63 A5
Voué F 59 B5
Vouillé F 67 B5
Voulx F 59 B3
Voussac F 68 B3
Vouvray F 67 A5
Vouvry CH 70 B1
Vouzela P 87 D2
Vouziers F 59 A5
Voves F 58 B2
Voxna S 36 A2
Voy GB 23 B5
Voynitsa RUS 3 D29
Voznesensk UA 11 C11
Voznesenye RUS 7 A13
Vrå
DK 38 B2
S 40 C3
Vráble SK 64 B4
Vračenovići MNE 84 D3
Vračev Gaj SRB 85 B6
Vraćevsnica SRB 85 B5
Vrådal N 33 C5
Vrakneika GR 117 D3
Vrana HR 83 B3
Vranduk BIH 84 B2
Vrångö S 38 B4
Vrani RO 85 A6
Vranić SRB 85 B5
Vraniči BIH 84 C3
Vranja HR 73 C4
Vranjak BIH 84 B3
Vranje SRB 10 E6
Vranovice CZ 64 B2
Vranov nad Dyje CZ 64 B1
Vransko SLO 73 B4
Vrapčići BIH 84 C2
Vratimov CZ 64 A4
Vratsa BG 11 E7
Vrbanja HR 84 B3
Vrbanjci BIH 84 B2
Vrbas SRB 75 C4
Vrbaška BIH 84 A2
Vrbnik
Primorsko-Goranska
HR 83 A3
Zadarsko-Kninska
HR 83 B5
Vrbno pod Pradědem
CZ 54 C2
Vrboska HR 83 C5
Vrbov SK 65 A6
Vrbovce SK 64 B3
Vrbové SK 64 B3
Vrbovec HR 73 C6
Vrbovski SRB 85 B5
Vrbovsko HR 73 C5
Vrchlabí CZ 53 C5
Vrčin SRB 85 B5
Vrdy CZ 63 A6
Vrebac HR 83 B4
Vreden D 50 A2
Vrela KOS 85 D5
Vreoci SRB 85 B5
Vretstorp S 37 C1
Vrginmost HR 73 C5
Vrgorac HR 84 C2
Vrhnika SLO 73 C4
Vrhovine HR 83 B4
Vrhpolie SRB 85 B4
Vriezenveen NL 42 C3
Vrigne-aux-Bois F 59 A5
Vrigstad S 40 B4
Vrlika HR 83 C5
Vrmbaje SRB 85 C5
Vrnjačka Banja SRB 85 C5
Vrnograč BIH 73 C5
Vron F 48 C2
Vroomshoop NL 42 C3
Vroutek CZ 52 C3
Vrpolje HR 74 C3
Vršac SRB 85 A6
Vrsar HR 82 A2
Vrsi HR 83 B4
Vrtoče BIH 83 B5
Vrútky SK 65 A4
Všeruby CZ 62 A3
Všestary CZ 53 C5
Vsetín CZ 64 A3
Vuča MNE 85 D5
Vučitrn KOS 85 D5
Vučkovica SRB 85 C5
Vught NL 49 B6
Vuillafans F 69 A6
Vukovar HR 75 C4
Vuku N 114 D8
Vulcan RO 11 D7
Vulcăneşti MD 11 D10
Vuoggatjålme S 112 F5
Vuojärvi FIN 113 E15
Vuolijoki FIN 3 D27
Vuotso FIN 113 D16
Vuzenica SLO 73 B5
Vyartsilya RUS 3 E29
Vyazma RUS 7 D13
Vyborg RUS 3 F28
Výčapy CZ 64 A1
Výčapy-Opatovce SK 64 B4
Východna SK 65 A5
Vydrany SK 64 B3
Vyerkhnyadzvinsk BY 7 D9
Vyhne SK 65 B4
Vy-lès Lure F 60 C2
Vylkove UA 11 D10
Vynohradiv UA 11 B7
Vyshniy Volochek
RUS 7 C13
Vyškov CZ 64 A3
Vysokánad Kysucou
SK 65 A4
Vysoké Mýto CZ 53 D6
Vysokovsk RUS 7 C14
Vyšší Brod CZ 63 B5
Vytegra RUS 7 A14

W

Waabs D 44 A1
Waalwijk NL 49 B6
Waarschoot B 49 B4
Wabern D 51 B5
Wąbrzeźno PL 47 B4
Wąchock PL 55 B6
Wachow D 45 C4
Wachów PL 54 C3
Wächtersbach D 51 C5
Wackersdorf D 62 A3
Waddington GB 27 B5
Wadebridge GB 28 C3
Wadelsdorf D 53 B4
Wädenswil CH 70 A3
Wadern D 60 A2
Wadersloh D 50 B4
Wadlew PL 55 B4
Wadowice PL 65 A5
Wagenfeld D 43 C5
Wageningen NL 49 B6
Waghäusel D 61 A4
Waging D 62 C3
Wagrain A 72 A3
Wagrowiec PL 46 C3
Wahlsdorf D 52 B3
Wahlstedt D 44 B2
Wahrenholz D 44 C2
Waiblingen D 61 B5
Waidhaus D 62 A3
Waidhofen an der Thaya
A 63 B6
Waidhofen an der Ybbs
A 63 C5
Waimes B 50 C2
Wainfleet All Saints
GB 27 B6
Waizenkirchen A 63 B4
Wakefield GB 27 B4
Wałbrzych PL 53 C6
Walchensee D 62 C2
Walchsee A 62 C3
Wałcz PL 46 B2
Wald CH 70 A3
Waldaschaff D 51 D5
Waldbach A 73 A5
Waldböckelheim D 60 A3
Waldbröl D 50 C3
Waldeck D 51 B5
Waldenburg D 52 C2
Waldfischbach-Burgalben
D 60 A3
Waldheim D 52 B3
Waldkappel D 51 B5
Waldkirch D 60 B3
Waldkirchen D 63 B4

Waldkirchen am Wesen
A 63 B4
Waldkraiburg D 62 B3
Wald-Michelbach D . . 61 A4
Waldmohr D 60 A3
Waldmünchen D 62 A3
Waldring A 62 C3
Waldshut D 61 C4
Waldstatt CH 71 A4
Waldwisse F 60 A2
Walenstadt CH 71 A4
Walentynów PL 55 B6
Walichnowy PL 54 B3
Walincourt F 49 C4
Walkenried D 51 B6
Walkeringham GB . . . 27 B5
Wallasey GB 26 B2
Walldürn D 61 A5
Wallenfells D 52 C1
Wallenhorst D 43 C5
Wallers F 49 C4
Wallersdorf D 62 B3
Wallerstein D 61 B6
Wallingford GB 31 C2
Wallitz D 45 B4
Walls GB 22 A7
Wallsbüll D 39 E2
Walmer GB 31 C5
Walsall GB 27 C4
Walshoutem B 49 C6
Walsrode D 43 C6
Waltenhofen D 61 C6
Waltershausen D 51 C6
Waltham Abbey GB . . 31 C4
Waltham on the Wolds
GB 30 B3
Walton-on-Thames
GB 31 C3
Walton-on-the-Naze
GB 31 C5
Wamba E 88 C2
Wanderup D 43 A6
Wandlitz D 45 C5
Wanfried D 51 B6
Wangen im Allgäu D . 61 C5
Wangerooge D 43 B4
Wangersen D 43 B6
Wängi CH 70 A3
Wanna D 43 B5
Wansford D 30 B3
Wantage GB 31 C2
Wanzleben D 52 A1
Waplewo PL 47 B6
Wapnica PL 46 B1
Wapno PL 46 C3
Warburg D 51 B5
Wardenburg D 43 B5
Ware GB 31 C3
Waregem B 49 C4
Wareham GB 29 C5
Waremme B 49 C6
Waren D 45 B4
Warendorf D 50 B3
Warga NL 42 B2
Warin D 44 B3
Wark GB 25 C5
Warka PL 55 B6
Warkworth GB 25 C6
Warlubie PL 47 B4
Warminster GB 29 B5
Warnemünde D 44 A4
Warnow D 44 B3
Warnsveld NL 50 A2
Warrenpoint GB 19 B5
Warrington GB 26 B3
Warsaw = Warszawa
PL 55 A6
Warsingsfehn D 43 B4
Warsow D 44 B3
Warstein D 51 B4
Warszawa = Warsaw
PL 55 A6
Warta PL 54 B3
Wartberg A 63 C5
Warth A 71 A5
Warwick GB 30 B2
Warza D 51 C6
Wasbister GB 23 B5
Washington GB 25 D6
Wasosz PL 54 B1
Wasselonne F 60 B3
Wassen CH 70 B3
Wassenaar NL 49 A5
Wasserauen CH 71 A4
Wasserburg D 62 B3
Wassertrüdingen D . . 62 A1
Wassy F 59 B5
Wasungen D 51 C6
Watchet GB 29 B4
Waterford IRL 21 B4
Watergrasshill IRL . . 20 B3
Waterloo B 49 C5
Waterville IRL 20 C1
Watford GB 31 C3
Wathlingen D 44 C2
Watten
F 48 C3
GB 23 C5
Wattens A 72 A1
Watton GB 30 B4
Wattwil CH 71 A4
Waunfawr GB 26 B1
Wavignies F 58 A3
Wavre B 49 C5
Wearhead GB 25 D5
Wechadłow PL 55 C5
Wedel D 43 B6
Wedemark D 43 C6
Weedon Bec GB 30 B2
Weener D 43 B4
Weert NL 50 B1
Weesp NL 49 A6
Weeze D 50 B2
Weferlingen D 52 A1
Wegeleben D 52 B1
Weggis CH 70 A3
Węgierska-Górka PL . 65 A5
Wegorzyno PL 46 B1
Węgrzynice PL 53 A5
Wegscheid D 63 B4
Wehdel D 43 B5
Wehr
Baden-Württemberg
D 61 C4
Rheinland-Pfalz D . . 50 C3
Weibersbrunn D 61 A5
Weichering D 62 B2
Weida D 52 C2
Weiden D 62 A3
Weidenberg D 52 D1
Weidenhain D 52 B2
Weidenstetten D 61 B5
Weierbach D 60 A3
Weikersheim D 61 A5
Weil D 62 B1
Weil am Rhein D 60 C3
Weilburg D 50 C4
Weil der Stadt D 61 B4
Weilerswist D 50 C2
Weilheim
Baden-Württemberg
D 61 B5
Bayern D 62 C2
Weilmünster D 51 C4
Weiltensfeld A 73 B4
Weimar D 52 C1
Weinberg D 61 A6

Weinfelden CH 71 A4
Weingarten
Baden-Württemberg
D 61 B4
Baden-Württemberg
D 61 C5
Weinheim D 61 A4
Weinstadt D 61 B5
Weismain D 52 C1
Weissbriach A 72 B3
Weissenbach A 71 A5
Weissenberg D 53 B4
Weissenbrunn D 52 C1
Weissenburg D 62 A1
Weissenfels D 52 B1
Weissenhorn D 61 B6
Weissenkirchen A . . . 63 B6
Weissensee D 52 B1
Weissenstadt D 52 C1
Weisskirchen im
Steiermark A 73 A4
Weisstannen CH 71 B4
Weisswasser D 53 B4
Weitendorf D 44 B4
Weitersfeld A 64 B1
Weitersfelden A 63 B5
Weitnau D 61 C6
Wéitra A 63 B5
Weiz A 73 A5
Wejherowo PL 47 A4
Wekerom NL 50 C1
Welbourn GB 30 B2
Welburg D 49 C6
Wellin B 49 C6
Wielgie
Kujawsko-Pomorskie
PL 47 C5
Łódzkie PL 54 B3
Mazowieckie PL . . . 55 B6
Wielgomłyny PL 55 A4
Wielichowo PL 54 A1
Wieliczka PL 55 D5
Wielka Łąka PL 47 B4
Wielowieś PL 54 C3
Wieluń PL 54 B3
Wien = Vienna A 64 B2
Wiener Neustadt A . . 64 C2
Wierbka PL 55 C4
Wierden NL 42 C3
Wieren D 44 C2
Wieruszów PL 54 B3
Wierzbica PL 55 B6
Wierzbięcin PL 45 B7
Wierzbno PL 55 A6
Wierzchowo PL 46 B2
Wierzchucino PL 47 A4
Wies A 73 B5
Wiesau D 62 A3
Wiesbaden D 50 C4
Wieselburg A 63 B6
Wiesen CH 71 B4
Wiesenburg D 52 A2
Wiesenfelden D 62 A3
Wiesensteig D 61 B5
Wiesentheid D 61 A6
Wiesloch D 61 A4
Wiesmath A 64 C2
Wiesmoor D 43 B4
Wietmarschen D 43 C4
Wietze D 43 C6
Wigan GB 26 B3
Wiggen CH 70 B2
Wigston GB 30 B2
Wigton GB 25 D4
Wigtown GB 24 D3
Wijhe NL 42 C3
Wijk bij Duurstede NL 49 B6
Wil CH 70 A4
Wilamowice PL 65 A4
Wilczęta PL 47 A5
Wilczkowice PL 55 A4
Wilczyn PL 47 C4
Wildalpen A 63 C5
Wildbad D 61 B4
Wildberg
Baden-Württemberg
D 61 B4
Brandenburg D 45 C4
Wildegg CH 70 A3
Wildendürnbach A . . . 64 B2
Wildeshausen D 43 C5
Wildon A 73 B5
Wilfersdorf A 64 B2
Wilga PL 55 B6
Wilhelmsburg
A 63 B6
Wilhelmsdorf D 61 C5
Wilhelmshaven D . . . 43 B5
Wilhermsdorf D 62 A1
Willebadessen D 51 B5
Willebroek B 49 B5
Willgottheim F 60 B3
Willich D 50 B2
Willingen D 51 B4
Willington GB 25 D6
Willisau CH 70 A3
Wilmslow GB 26 B3
Wilsdruff D 52 B3
Wilster D 43 B6
Wilsum D 42 C3
Wilton GB 29 B6
Wiltz L 50 D1
Wimborne Minster
GB 29 C6
Wimereux F 48 C2
Wimmis CH 70 B2
Wincanton GB 29 B5
Winchcombe GB 29 B6
Winchelsea GB 31 D4
Winchester GB 31 C2
Windermere GB 26 A3
Windischeschenbach
D 62 A3
Windischgarsten A . . 63 C5
Windorf D 63 B4
Windsbach D 62 A1
Windsor GB 31 C3
Windygates GB 25 B4
Wingene B 49 B4
Wingham GB 31 C5
Winkleigh GB 28 C4
Winklern A 72 B2
Winnenden D 61 B5
Winnigstedt D 51 A6
Winnica PL 47 C6
Winnweiler D 60 A3
Winschoten NL 43 B4
Winsen
Niedersachsen D . . 44 B2
Niedersachsen D . . 44 C1
Winsford GB 26 B3
Wińsko PL 54 B1
Winslow GB 31 C3
Winsum
Friesland NL 42 B2
Groningen NL 42 B3
Winterberg D 51 B4
Winterfeld D 44 C3
Winterswijk NL 50 B2
Winterthur CH 70 A3
Winterton GB 27 B5
Wintzenheim F 60 B3
Winzer D 62 B4
Wipperdorf D 51 B6
Wipperfürth D 50 B3

Whitegate IRL 20 C3
Whitehaven GB 26 A2
Whitehead GB 19 B6
Whithorn GB 24 D3
Whitley Bay GB 25 C6
Whitstable GB 31 C5
Whittington GB 26 C3
Whittlesey GB 30 B3
Wiązów PL 54 C2
Wiązowna PL 55 A6
Wick GB 23 C5
Wickede D 50 B3
Wickford GB 31 C4
Wickham Market GB . 30 B5
Wicklow IRL 21 B5
Wicko PL 46 A3
Widawa PL 54 B3
Widdrington GB 25 C6
Widecombe in the Moor
GB 28 C4
Widemouth GB 28 C3
Widnes GB 26 B3
Widuchowo PL 45 B6
Więcbork PL 46 B3
Wiefelstede D 43 B5
Wiehe D 52 B1
Wiehl D 50 C3
Wiek D 45 A5
Więckowice PL 54 C2
Wiele PL 46 B3
Wieleń PL 46 C2

Wirksworth GB 27 B4
Wisbech GB 30 B4
Wischhafen D 43 B6
Wishaw GB 25 C4
Wisła Wielka PL 54 D3
Wislica PL 55 C5
Wismar D 44 B3
Wiśniewo PL 47 B6
Wiśniowa PL 65 A6
Wissant F 48 C2
Wissembourg F 60 A3
Wissen D 50 C3
Witanowice PL 65 A5
Witham GB 31 C4
Withern GB 27 B6
Withernsea GB 27 B6
Witkowo PL 46 C3
Witmarsum NL 42 B2
Witney GB 31 C2
Witnica PL 45 C6
Witry-les-Reims F . . . 59 A5
Wittdün D 43 A5
Wittelsheim F 60 C3
Witten D 50 B3
Wittenberge D 44 B3
Wittenburg D 44 B3
Wittenheim F 60 C3
Wittichenau D 53 B4
Wittighausen D 61 A5
Wittingen D 44 C2
Wittislingen D 61 B6
Wittlich D 50 D2
Wittmannsdorf A 73 B5
Wittmund D 43 B4
Wittorf D 44 B2
Wittstock D 44 B4
Witzenhausen D 51 B5
Wiveliscombe GB . . . 29 B4
Wivenhoe GB 31 C4
Władysławowo PL . . . 47 A4
Wleń PL 53 B5
Włocławek PL 47 C5
Włodawa PL 6 F7
Włodzimierzów PL . . . 55 B4
Włosień PL 53 B5
Włostów PL 55 C6
Włoszakowice PL . . . 54 B1
Włoszczowa PL 55 C4
Wöbbelin D 44 B3
Woburn GB 31 C3
Wodzisław PL 55 C5
Wodzisław Śląski PL . 54 C3
Woerden NL 49 A5
Woerth F 60 B3
Wohlen CH 70 A3
Woippy F 60 A2
Wojciechy PL 47 A6
Wojcieszow PL 53 C5
Wojkowice Kościelne
PL 55 C4
Wojnicz PL 55 C5
Woking GB 31 C3
Wokingham GB 31 C3
Wola Jachowa PL . . . 55 C5
Wola Niechcicka PL . 55 B4
Wolbórz PL 55 B4
Wolbrom PL 55 C4
Wołczyn PL 54 B3
Woldegk D 45 B5
Wolfach D 61 B4
Wolfegg D 61 C5
Wolfen D 52 B2
Wolfenbüttel D 51 A6
Wolfersheim D 51 C4
Wolfhagen D 51 B5
Wolfratshausen D . . . 62 C2
Wolfsberg A 73 B4
Wolfsburg D 44 C2
Wolf's Castle GB 28 B3
Wolfshagen D 45 B5
Wolfstein D 60 A3
Wolfurt A 71 A4
Wolgast D 45 A5
Wolhusen CH 70 A3
Wolin PL 45 B6
Wolka PL 55 B5
Wolkenstein D 52 C3
Wolkersdorf A 64 B2
Wöllersdorf A 64 C2
Wollin D 52 A2
Wöllstadt D 51 C4
Wolmirstedt D 52 A1
Wolnzach D 62 B2
Wolomin PL 55 A6
Wołów PL 54 B1
Wolsztyn PL 53 A6
Wolvega NL 42 C2
Wolverhampton GB . . 26 C3
Wolverton GB 31 B3
Wombwell GB 27 B4
Woodbridge GB 30 B5
Woodhall Spa GB . . . 27 B5
Woodstock GB 31 C2
Wookey Hole GB 29 B5
Wool GB 29 C5
Woolacombe GB 28 B3
Wooler GB 25 C5
Woolwich GB 31 C4
Wooperton GB 25 C6
Worb CH 70 B2
Worbis D 51 B6
Worcester GB 29 A5
Wörgl A 64 B2
Workington GB 26 A2
Worksop GB 27 B4
Workum NL 42 C2
Wörlitz D 52 B2
Wormer NL 42 C1
Wormhout F 48 C3
Worms D 61 A4
Worpswede D 43 B5
Wörrstadt D 61 A4
Wörschach A 73 A4
Worsley GB 26 B3
Wörth
Bayern D 61 A5
Bayern D 62 A3
Bayern D 62 B3
Rheinland-Pfalz D . . 61 A4
Worthing GB 31 D3
York GB 27 B4
Youghal IRL 21 C4
Yoğuntaş TR 118 A2
Yozgat TR 16 B7
Yport F 57 A1
Ypres = Ieper B 48 C3
Yssingeaux F 68 C4
Ystad S 41 D3
Ystalyfera GB 28 B4
Ystebrød N 33 D2
Ystradgynlais GB . . . 28 B4
Ytre Enebakk N 35 C3
Ytre Rendal N 114 F8
Ytteran S 115 D11
Ytterhogdal S 115 E11
Yttermalung S 34 B5
Yukhnov RUS 7 D13
Yumurtalık TR 16 C7
Yuncos E 94 B3
Yunquera E 100 C1
Yunquera de Henares
E 95 B3
Yushkozero RUS 3 D30

Wulkau D 44 C4
Wünnenberg D 51 B4
Wünsdorf D 52 A3
Wunsiedel D 52 C2
Wunstorf D 43 C6
Wuppertal D 50 B3
Wurmannsquick D . . 62 B3
Würselen D 50 C2
Wurzbach D 52 C1
Würzburg D 61 A5
Wurzen D 52 B2
Wust D 44 C4
Wusterhausen D 44 C4
Wusterwitz D 44 C4
Wustrau-Altfriesack
D 45 C4
Wustrow D 44 A3
Wuustwezel B 49 B5
Wye GB 31 C4
Wygiełzów PL 55 B6
Wyk D 43 A5
Wykroty PL 53 B5
Wylye GB 29 B6
Wymiarki PL 53 B5
Wymondham GB 30 B5
Wyrzysk PL 46 B3
Wyśmierzyce PL 55 B5
Wysoka
Dolnośląskie PL . . . 53 B5
Wielkopolskie PL . . 46 B3
Wyszanów PL 54 B3
Wyszogród PL 47 C6

X

Xanten D 50 B2
Xanthi GR 116 A6
Xarrë AL 116 C2
Xàtiva E 96 C2
Xeraco E 96 B2
Xert E 90 C3
Xerta E 90 C3
Xertigny F 60 B2
Xilagani GR 116 B7
Xilokastro GR 117 D4
Xinzo de Limia E 87 B3
Xixón = Gijón E 88 A1
Xove E 86 A3
Xubia E 86 A2
Xunqueira de Ambia
E 87 B3
Xunqueira de
Espadañedo E 87 B3
Xylophagou CY 120 B2

Y

Yablanitsa BG 11 E8
Yağcılar TR 118 C4
Yahotyn UA 11 A11
Yahyalı TR 16 B7
Yalova TR 118 B4
Yalvaç TR 119 D6
Yambol BG 11 E9
Yampil UA 11 B10
Yaniskoski RUS 113 D17
Yarbasan TR 118 D3
Yarcombe GB 29 C4
Yaremcha UA 11 B8
Yarm GB 27 A4
Yarmouth GB 31 D2
Yarrow GB 25 C4
Yartsevo RUS 7 D12
Yasinya UA 11 B8
Yatağan TR 119 E3
Yate GB 29 B5
Yatton GB 29 B5
Yavoriv UA 11 B7
Yaxley GB 30 B3
Yazıca TR 118 B6
Yazıköy TR 119 F2
Ybbs A 63 B6
Ybbsitz A 63 C5
Ydby DK 38 C1
Yddal N 32 B2
Ydes F 68 C2
Yealmpton GB 28 C4
Yebra de Basa E 90 A2
Yecla E 101 A4
Yecla de Yeltes E . . . 87 D4
Yelnya RUS 7 D12
Yelsk BY 7 E10
Yelverton GB 28 C3
Yenice
Ankara TR 16 B6
Aydın TR 119 E3
Çanakkale TR 118 C2
Edirne TR 118 B6
Yenifoça TR 118 D1
Yeniköy TR 118 D4
Yeniköy Plaji TR 118 C4
Yenipazar TR 119 E3
Yenisarbademli TR . . 119 E6
Yenişehir TR 118 B4
Yenne F 69 C5
Yeovil GB 29 C5
Yepes E 95 C3
Yerköy TR 16 B7
Yerólakkos CY 120 A2
Yeroskipos CY 120 B1
Yersekë NL 49 B5
Yerville F 58 A1
Yeşildağ TR 119 E6
Yeşilhisar TR 16 B7
Yeşilova TR 119 E4
Yeşilyurt TR 119 D3
Yesnogorsk RUS . . . 7 D14
Yeste E 101 A3
Yezeryshche BY 7 D10
Y Felinheli GB 26 B1
Ygos-St Saturnin F . . 76 C2
Ygrande F 68 B2
Yialousa CY 120 A3
Yığılca TR 118 B6
Yli-Muonio FIN 113 D12
Ylitornio FIN 3 C25
Ylivieska FIN 3 D26
Yllästunturi FIN 113 D13
Ymonville F 58 B2
Yngsjö S 41 D4

Yverdon-les-Bains
CH 70 B1
Yvetot F 58 A1
Yvignac F 57 B3
Yvoir B 49 C5
Yvonand CH 70 B1
Yxnerum S 37 D3
Yzeure F 68 B3

Z

Zaamslag NL 49 B4
Zaanstad NL 42 C1
Žabalj SRB 75 C5
Zabar H 65 B6
Žabari SRB 85 B6
Žabiče SLO 73 C4
Zabierzów PL 55 C4
Żabki PL 55 A6
Ząbkowice Śląskie
PL 54 C1
Zablaće HR 83 C4
Žabljak MNE 85 C4
Żabno PL 55 C5
Zabok HR 73 B5
Zabor PL 53 B5
Zábřeh CZ 64 A3
Zabrowo PL 46 B1
Zabrze PL 54 C3
Zabrzeź PL 65 A6
Zachara GR 117 E3
Zadar HR 83 B4
Zadzim PL 54 B3
Zafarraya E 100 C1
Zafferana Etnea I . . . 109 B4
Zafra E 93 C4
Žaga SLO 72 B3
Zagajica SRB 85 B6
Żagań PL 53 B5
Zaglav HR 83 C4
Zaglavak SRB 85 C4
Zagnansk PL 55 C5
Zagora GR 116 C5
Zagorc SLO 73 B5
Zagorcani BIH 84 C2
Zagórów PL 54 A2
Zagradje SRB 85 B5
Zagreb HR 73 C5
Zagrilla E 100 B1
Zagvozd HR 84 C2
Zagwiździe PL 54 C2
Zagyvarékas H 75 A5
Zagyvaróna H 65 B5
Zahara E 99 C5
Zahara de los Atunes
E 99 C5
Zahinos E 93 C4
Zahna D 52 B2
Záhoří CZ 63 A5
Zahrádka CZ 63 A6
Zahrensdorf D 44 B2
Zaidín E 90 B3
Zaječar SRB 11 E7
Zákamenné SK 65 A5
Zákány H 74 B1
Zákányszék H 75 B4
Zakliczyn PL 65 A6
Zakopane PL 65 A5
Zakroczym PL 47 C6
Zakrzew PL 55 B6
Zakrzewo PL 47 C4
Zakupy CZ 53 C4
Zakynthos GR 117 E2
Zalaapáti H 74 B2
Zalabaksa H 74 B1
Zalaegerszeg H 74 B1
Zalakomár H 74 B2
Zalakoppány H 74 B2
Zalalövö H 74 B1
Zalamea de la Serena
E 93 C5
Zalamea la Real E . . . 99 B4
Zalaszentgrót H 74 B2
Zalaszentiván H 74 B1
Zalău RO 11 C7
Zalavár H 74 B2
Zaldibar E 89 A4
Žalec SLO 73 B5
Zalesie PL 47 B6
Zalewo PL 47 B5
Zalishchyky UA 11 B8
Zalla E 89 A3
Zaltbommel NL 49 B6
Zámárdi H 74 B2
Zamárka CZ 64 A2
Zambrana E 89 B4
Zambra E 100 B1
Zambugueira do Mar
P 98 B2
Zámoly H 74 A3
Zamora E 88 C1
Zamość PL 11 A7
Zams A 71 A5
Zandhoven B 49 B5
Zandov CZ 53 C4
Zandvoort NL 42 C1
Zangliveri GR 116 B5
Zánka H 74 B2
Zaorejas E 95 B4
Zaovine SRB 85 C4
Zapadnaya Dvina
RUS 7 D12
Zapfend D 51 C6
Zapole PL 54 B3
Zapolyarnyy RUS . . . 3 B29
Zapponeta I 104 B1
Zaprešić HR 73 C5
Zaragoza E 90 B2
Zarań PL 55 B6
Zarasai LT 7 D9
Zarautz E 89 A4
Zarcilla de Ramos E . 101 B4
Żarki PL 55 C4
Zarko GR 116 C4
Zárkˇov PL 54 B3
Žarnovica SK 65 B4
Zarnowiec PL 47 A4
Zarńsk PL 46 B2
Žarošice CZ 64 A2
Zarów PL 54 C1
Żary PL 53 B5
Zarren B 48 B3
Zarrentin D 44 B2
Zarza Capilla E 93 C5
Zarza de Alange E . . . 93 C4
Zarza de Granadilla E 93 A4
Zarza de Tajo E 95 B3
Zarzadilla de Totana
E 101 B4
Zarza la Mayor E 93 B4
Zarzuela del Monte E 94 B2
Zarzuela del Pinar E . 88 C2
Zas E 86 A2
Zasavica SRB 85 B4
Zasieki PL 53 B4
Zasów PL 55 C6
Zastražišče HR 84 C1
Zaton HR 84 D3
Zatonie PL 53 B5
Zator PL 55 D4
Zauchwitz D 52 A3
Zavala BIH 84 D2

Zavalje BIH 83 B4
Zavattarello I 80 B3
Zavidovići BIH 84 B3
Zavlaka SRB 85 B4
Zawady PL 55 B5
Zawadzkie PL 54 C3
Zawdy PL 54 B3
Zawidów PL 53 B5
Zawidz PL 47 C5
Zawiercie PL 55 C4
Zawoja PL 65 A5
Zawonia PL 54 B2
Žažina HR 73 C6
Zázrivá SK 65 A5
Zbarazh UA 11 B8
Zbąszyń PL 53 A5
Zbąszynek PL 53 A5
Zbehy SK 64 B3
Zbiersk PL 54 B3
Zbiroh CZ 63 A4
Zblewo PL 47 B4
Zbójno PL 47 B5
Zbrachlin PL 47 B4
Zbraslav CZ 63 A4
Zbraslavice CZ 63 A6
Ždala HR 74 B2
Ždánice CZ 64 A3
Žďár nad Sázavou
CZ 64 A1
Ždbice PL 46 B2
Ždenci HR 74 C2
Ždiar SK 65 A6
Ždice CZ 63 A4
Zdirec nad Doubravou
CZ 64 A1
Zdolbuniv UA 11 A9
Zdounky CZ 64 A3
Zdravinje SRB 85 C6
Ždrelo SRB 85 B6
Zduńska Wola PL . . . 54 B3
Zduny
Łódzkie PL 55 A4
Wielkopolskie PL . . 54 B2
Zdziechowice
Opolskie PL 54 B3
Wielkopolskie PL . . 54 A2
Zdziszowice PL 54 C3
Zeberio E 89 A4
Žebrák CZ 63 A4
Zebreira P 93 B3
Zebrzydowa PL 53 B5
Zechlin D 45 B4
Zechlinerhütte D 45 B4
Zederhaus A 72 A3
Żednik SRB 75 C4
Zeebrugge B 49 B4
Zehdenick D 45 C5
Zehren D 52 B3
Zeil D 51 C6
Zeilarn D 62 B3
Zeist NL 49 A6
Zeithain D 52 B3
Zeitz D 52 B2
Želatava CZ 63 A6
Želazno PL 46 A3
Zele B 49 B5
Zelenoborskiy RUS . 3 C30
Zelenogorsk RUS . . . 7 A10
Zelenograd RUS 7 C14
Zelenogradsk RUS . . 6 D6
Železná Ruda CZ . . . 63 A4
Železnice CZ 53 C5
Železnik SRB 85 B5
Železný Brod CZ 53 C5
Zelhem NL 50 A2
Żelichów PL 55 C5
Żelikowo PL 46 A3
Zell
CH 70 A2
Baden-Württemberg
D 60 C3
Baden-Württemberg
D 61 C4
Rheinland-Pfalz D . . 50 C3
Zella-Mehlis D 51 C6
Zell am See A 72 A2
Zell am Ziller A 72 A1
Zell an der Pram A . . 63 B4
Zell bei Zellhof A 63 B5
Zellerndorf A 64 B1
Zellingen D 61 A5
Želovce SK 65 B5
Zelów PL 55 B4
Zeltweg A 73 A4
Zelzate B 49 B4
Zemberovce SK 65 B4
Zembrzyce PL 65 A5
Zemianske-Kostol'any
SK 65 B4
Zemitz D 45 B5
Zemné SK 64 C3
Zemst B 49 C5
Zemun SRB 85 B5
Zemunik Donji HR . . . 83 B4
Zenica BIH 84 B2
Zennor GB 28 C2
Žepa BIH 85 C4
Žepče BIH 84 B3
Zeppenami I 102 A5
Zerbst D 52 B2
Zerf D 60 A2
Żerków PL 54 A2
Zermatt CH 70 B2
Zernez CH 71 B5
Zerpen-schleuse D . . 45 C5
Zestoa E 89 A4
Zetel D 43 B4
Zeulenroda D 52 C1
Zeven D 43 B6
Zevenaar NL 50 B2
Zevenbergen NL 49 B5
Zévio I 71 C6
Zeytinbaği TR 118 B3
Zeytindağ TR 118 D2
Zgorzelec PL 53 B5
Zgošča BIH 84 B3
Zhabinka BY 6 E8
Zharkovskiy RUS . . . 7 D11
Zhashkiv UA 11 B11
Zheleznogorsk RUS . 7 E13
Zhizdra RUS 7 E13
Zhlobin BY 7 E11
Zhmerynka UA 11 B10
Zhodzina BY 7 D10
Zhovti Vody UA 11 B12
Zhovtneve UA 11 C12
Zhukovka RUS 7 E12
Zhytomyr UA 11 A10
Žiar nad Hronom SK . 65 B4
Zicavo F 102 B2
Zidani Most SLO 73 B5
Ziddorf D 44 B4
Židlochovice CZ 64 A2
Ziębice PL 54 C2
Ziegendorf D 44 B4
Ziegenrück D 52 C1
Zielenice
Dolnośląskie PL . . . 54 C1
Zachodnio-Pomorskie
PL 46 B1
Zielona PL 46 B1
Zielona Góra PL 53 B5
Zielonka PL 55 A6
Zieluń-Osada PL 47 B5
Ziemetshausen D . . . 61 B6

Zierenberg D 51 B5
Zierikzee NL 49 B4
Ziersdorf A 64 B1
Zierzow D 44 B3
Ziesar D 52 A2
Ziesendorf D 44 B4
Ziethen D 45 C5
Žihle CZ 52 C3
Žilina SK 65 A4
Ziltendorf D 53 A4
Zimandu Nou RO . . . 75 B6
Zimna Woda PL 47 B6
Zimnicea RO 11 E8
Zinal CH 70 B2
Zinasco I 70 C4
Zingst D 45 A4
Zinkgruvan S . . . . 37 . . .
Zinnowitz D 45 A5
Zirc H . . . .
Žiri SLO . . . .
Zirl A 71 A6
Zirndorf D 62 A1
Zirovnica SRB 85 B6
Žirovnice CZ 63 A6
Zisterdorf A 64 B2
Žitište SRB 75 C5
Zitsa GR 116 C2
Zittau D 53 C4
Živaja HR 74 C1
Živinice BIH 84 B3
Zlatar HR 73 B6
Zlatar Bistrica HR . . . 73 B6
Zlate Klasy SK 64 B3
Zlaté Moravce SK . . . 65 B4
Zlatná Ostrove SK . . 64 C3
Zlatniky SK 64 B3
Zlatograd BG 116 A7
Zlebic SLO 73 C4
Zlin CZ 64 A3
Zločeniec PL 46 B2
Złoczew PL 54 B3
Zlonice CZ 53 C4
Złotniki Kujawskie
PL 47 C4
Zlotoryja PL 53 B5
Złotów PL 46 B3
Zloty Stok PL 54 C1
Zlutice CZ 52 C3
Zmajevac BIH 83 B5
Zmajevo SRB 75 C4
Žmigród PL 54 B1
Žminj HR 82 A3
Znamyanka UA 11 B12
Żnin PL 46 C3
Znojmo CZ 64 B2
Zöblitz D 52 C3
Zocca I 81 B4
Zoetermeer NL 49 A5
Zofingen CH 70 A2
Zogno I 71 C4
Zohor SK 64 B3
Zolling D 62 B2
Zolochiv UA 11 B8
Zolotonosha UA 11 B12
Zomba H 74 B3
Zomergem B 49 B4
Zoñán E 86 A3
Zonguldak TR 118 A6
Zonhoven B 49 C6
Zonza F 102 B2
Zörbig D 52 B2
Zorita E 93 B5
Zory PL 54 C3
Zossen D 52 A3
Zottegem B 49 C4
Zoutkamp NL 42 B3
Zovi Do BIH 84 C3
Zreče SLO 73 B5
Zrenjanin SRB 75 C5
Žrnovica HR 83 C5
Zručnad Sazavou CZ 63 A6
Zsámbék H 65 C4
Zsámbok H 75 A4
Zsana H 75 B4
Zschopau D 52 C3
Zuberec SK 65 A5
Zubieta E 76 C1
Zubin Potok KOS . . . 85 D5
Zubiri E 76 D1
Zubtsov RUS 7 C13
Zucaina E 96 A2
Zudar D 45 A5
Zuera E 90 B2
Zufre E 99 B4
Zug CH 70 A3
Zuheros E 100 B1
Zuidhorn NL 42 B3
Zuidlaren NL 42 B3
Zuidwolde NL 42 C3
Zújar E 101 B3
Żukowo PL 47 A4
Žuljana HR 84 D2
Žulová CZ 54 C2
Zundert NL 49 B5
Županja HR 84 A3
Zurgena E 101 B3
Zürich CH 70 A3
Żuromin PL 47 B5
Zurzach CH 70 A3
Zusmarshausen D . . . 62 B1
Zusow D 44 B3
Żużemberk SLO 73 C4
Zvečan KOS 85 D5
Zvenyhorodka UA . . . 11 B11
Zvikovske Podhradi
CZ 63 A5
Zvolen SK 65 B5
Zvolenská Slatina SK 65 B5
Zvornik BIH 85 B4
Zwartsluis NL 42 C3
Zweibrücken D 60 A3
Zweisimmen CH 70 B2
Zwettl A 63 B6
Zwettl an der Rodl A . 63 B5
Zwickau D 52 C2
Zwiefalten D 61 B5
Zwieryn PL 46 C1
Zwierzno PL 47 A5
Zwiesel D 63 A4
Zwieselstein A 71 B6
Zwoleń PL 55 B6
Zwolle NL 42 C3
Zwönitz D 52 C2
Zydowo
Wielkopolskie PL . . 46 C3
Zachodnio-Pomorskie
PL 46 A2
Żyrardów PL 55 A5
Żytno PL 55 B4
Żywiec PL 65 A5
Zyyi CY 120 B2